# Land Use and Zoning Law

# Land Use and Zoning Law

## Planning for Accessible Communities

### SECOND EDITION

**Robin Paul Malloy**

E.I. White Chair and Distinguished Professor of Law
Kauffman Professor of Entrepreneurship and Innovation
College of Law, Syracuse University

**Dylan Oliver Malagrinò**
Professor of Law
Charleston School of Law

Carolina Academic Press
Durham, North Carolina

LCCN:  2021950977
ISBN      978-1-5310-2018-7
e-ISBN  978-1-5310-2019-4

Carolina Academic Press
700 Kent Street
Durham, North Carolina 27701
(919) 489-7486
www.cap-press.com

Printed in the United States of America

*For*

*Gina, Andrew, Cormick, Macklin, McKinley,
Giovanni, Whendy*

*Robin Paul Malloy*


*For*

*My Colleagues, Friends, Family, and, of course,
My Students*

*Dylan Oliver Malagrinò*

# Contents

# Preface

Our casebook is one that focuses on the key elements of the law of zoning, planning, and property development as needed for practice. We cover the cases and concepts that are most critical to the actual practice of zoning law. As part of our coverage, we include cases and materials on accessibility. This means that we integrate coverage of disability law and accessibility into every chapter of the book. Disability rights are becoming critical in the process of developing safe and sustainable communities that are accessible to everyone, and that are capable of supporting people as they age in place. This is an important element of planning and zoning as America has a rapidly aging population and because some 25% of Americans have a disability of one type or another. Disability law has a significant impact on how we practice zoning and planning law.

Our book is both traditional and unique. It is traditional in that it covers all of the basic elements of zoning and planning law. At the same time, our book is unique in that it includes cases on accessibility. We integrate zoning cases that include a disability law element in each chapter. These cases are mixed in with the standard and classic cases that are typical of a casebook in this area. This gives our casebook a contemporary relevance for understanding the requirements for making our communities accessible to a diverse population. In addition, our book offers other important features that enhance discussion of the materials in each chapter.

The five key features of each chapter in this book include:

1) **Cases that integrate Zoning Law with Disability Law.** While limited in number, these cases allow students to see issues of accessibility as a normal part of a zoning and land use practice. The cases enhance understanding of basic zoning and land use law while introducing important elements of our disability laws.

2) **Questions for Consideration.** These questions follow each case in the book. For the most part, these questions are designed to assist students in focusing on key aspects of the case that they are reading. This will improve their understanding of the case and prepare them to participate in class.

3) **Takeaways.** After each case we provide a section identified as Takeaway. Here we set out some key points that every student should understand after having read the case.

4) **Discussion Problems.** Within each chapter, we include Discussion Problems that set up hypothetical fact patterns that can be used in class. These problems facilitate class discussion and assist students in integrating concepts from

different parts of a chapter. These questions may be discussed orally in class or combined with having students draft answers in addition to the discussion. This provides multiple assessment opportunities.

5) **Practice Problems.** These Practice Problems get students to think about the kind of issues that come up in practice, and many of them require students to use a local zoning code to develop their answers. These practice problems provide an opportunity for students to develop important practice skills and serve as excellent tools for assessment and feedback.

Our book is designed to be a straightforward and easy to use casebook. As to our integration of materials on accessibility, the book is designed to be readily usable by people with little or no expertise in disability law. The primary aim of our inclusion of cases and materials on disability law in every chapter is to make students aware of the need to think about the accessibility of our built environment. To have sustainable cities and livable communities, we must plan for making them accessible to people of all abilities and all ages.

The key elements of disability law are addressed in the text, in the cases, and in an **Appendix** provided in the back of the casebook. The Appendix provides a clear and readily understandable overview of the key elements of disability law. The key provisions are set out along with definitions. Referring to the Appendix when reading relevant cases will make disability law understandable while informing students about the relevance of disability law to their zoning and planning law practice. In general, disability law addresses design issues that make the built environment more accessible, and it addresses land uses to ensure that everyone enjoys an equal opportunity to live in a neighborhood, and to enjoy the lawful use of their property in ways that are similar to that of people without disabilities.

The sections of disability law that are most important in land use and zoning are very limited in number. For the most part, they deal with matters of discrimination, and these discrimination issues are similar to claims raised in other courses in law school. In addition, disability law makes it a matter of discrimination to deny a person with a disability a reasonable accommodation or a reasonable modification. In particular, disability law requires providing a reasonable accommodation and modification to *programs, services, and activities* of local governments. This means that the disability laws apply directly to all planning and zoning functions, because courts have held that planning and zoning are *programs, services, and activities* of state and local governments. Knowing when an accommodation is required is important to a zoning and planning practice. We make this easy. There are three basic criteria to review when addressing a request for a reasonable accommodation and reasonable modification, and we cover all of them very clearly in our materials.

More generally, the overarching structure of the book is focused on land use and zoning law as an exercise of governmental police power. The book considers problems related to externalities, spillover effects, and the difficulties of self-coordination of land uses in an increasingly complex world. Chapter one provides an overview on issues related to the process of zoning and gives an introduction to accessibility and the Americans with Disabilities Act (ADA). This chapter provides a clear context for the remaining materials in the book. Beginning with chapter two and continuing into chapter three, the materials focus on the exercise of the police power and its limitations. The traditional limits to the exercise of the police power discussed in chapter three include: due process, equal protection, and the Takings Clause. Chapter four covers the relationship between comprehensive planning and zoning. In chapter five, the material expands on our understanding of the limits of the exercise of the police power. The focus in chapter five is on limitations imposed by tensions with other fundamental rights, such as those related to free speech, freedom of association, freedom of religion, and the rights of people with disabilities. Chapter six addresses a variety of standard concepts central to a land use and zoning law practice. It also includes discussion of fair housing, discrimination, and the imposition of exactions. Takings law is discussed in several chapters rather than as a "stand alone" topic. In instances where a limited number of cases are used to illustrate a point, we have selected well-known classic cases and cases that discuss other key cases within their opinions. This permits greater coverage of important concepts with the use of fewer total cases.

The entire book should be able to be covered in a one semester course.

# Learning Outcomes

We have designed our casebook to achieve certain learning outcomes.

1. Students will learn the rules, standards, and requirements of American zoning, planning, and development law.

2. Students will learn the requirements of American disability law and how these laws apply to a zoning, planning, and development law practice.

3. Students will sharpen their skills at parsing a case and analyzing a case opinion.

4. Students will learn the relationship among local, state, and federal law in dealing with zoning, planning, and development issues. This is particularly important given that local activities often have implications that extend beyond the boundaries of local government jurisdictions.

5. Students will learn the difficulty of dealing with negative externalities and spillover effects between and among various property owners.

6. Students will learn basic administrative law and standards of review in dealing with decisions of a zoning board of appeal.

7. By focusing on the *Questions for Consideration* after each case, students will improve their analytical skills.

8. By considering the *Takeaway* after each case, students will be able to assess their ability to extract key legal and practice pointers from a case.

9. By preparing and engaging in the *Discussion Problems*, students will improve their ability to synthesize materials from several cases.

10. By preparing and engaging in the work for our *Practice Problems* at the end of each chapter, students will learn to use a zoning code, a zoning map, and a comprehensive plan, and students will improve their ability to evaluate a situation and provide possible resolutions.

11. In responding to our various opportunities for answering *Questions for Consideration*, *Discussion Problems*, and *Practice Problems*, students will develop an improved ability to analyze, synthesize, and evaluate complex legal problems. Likewise, in preparing oral or written responses to these questions, students will improve their ability to effectively communicate with colleagues, clients, and others.

In preparing these materials for the second edition, we have benefited from the research assistance of several students. Robin wishes to thank Michael Anthony Annesi, Robert M. Baurley, Christopher G. Doak, Justin Fowler, and Dominique Kelly; and, Dylan wishes to thank Thomas P. Krahe, Forrest W. Lewis, AshleyAnn Sander, and Amy M. Saukas.

ROBIN PAUL MALLOY
E.I. White Chair and Distinguished
 Professor of Law
Kauffman Professor of Entrepreneurship
 and Innovation
College of Law, Syracuse University
Syracuse, NY

DYLAN OLIVER MALAGRINÒ
Professor of Law
Charleston School of Law
Charleston, SC

# Acknowledgments

We gratefully acknowledge the permission granted to reproduce the following materials:

As indicated herein, excerpts drawn from: ROBIN PAUL MALLOY, LAND USE LAW AND DISABILITY: PLANNING AND ZONING FOR ACCESSIBLE COMMUNITIES © Robin Paul Malloy 2015, published by Cambridge University Press, reproduced with permission.

Also, an excerpt drawn from: D.O. Malagrinò, *Among Justice Stevens's Landmark Legacies:* Tahoe-Sierra Preservation Council, Inc. v. Tahoe Regional Planning Agency, 53 CREIGHTON L. REV. 77 (2019), reproduced with permission.

For the Appendix much of the material is drawn from: Malloy, *A Primer on Disability for Land Use and Zoning Law*, 4 JOURNAL OF LAW, PROPERTY, AND SOCIETY 1 (2018).

# Table of Cases

# Land Use and Zoning Law

# Chapter 1

# Introduction to Planning and Zoning for Accessible Communities

## A. Setting the Stage

### Zoning: An Introduction to the History, Purpose, and Nature of Legislative Land Use Controls

Zoning is a way to control private land use through the public, legislative process. Zoning laws are specific governmental land use regulations adopted by legislative bodies for the management and coordination of land uses. Zoning is traditionally done at the local level. Today, however, there is an increasing tendency toward more regional, state, and federal coordination of land uses. In a very real sense, a community's zoning laws define the relationships between a landowner and the general public concerning activities on private land. Zoning laws are varied, and these laws may be directed at regulating general land uses, the height and location of improvements on land, population density, and other land development efforts.

Zoning laws are of relatively modern origin.[1] They began in the United States in the late 1800s and early 1900s.[2] In 1916, New York City adopted the first comprehensive,

---

1. Vill. of Euclid, Ohio v. Ambler Realty Co., 272 U.S. 365, 386–87 (1926).

2. *Id.* In 1885, the city of San Francisco banned public laundries in most areas, cloaked as safety measures, but overtly targeting Chinese businesses in the city. In 1886, the U.S. Supreme Court invalidated the application of the S.F. ordinance in *Yick Wo v. Hopkins*, 118 U.S. 356 (1886) on Equal Protection grounds. However, in invalidating the S.F. ordinance, the Court upheld San Francisco's right to impose restrictions against the operation of laundries on the grounds that they were a clear fire risk and public nuisance. The Court said:

> By section 11 of article 11 of the constitution of California it is provided that "any county, city, town, or township may make and enforce within its limits all such local, police, sanitary, and other regulations as are not in conflict with general laws." By section 74 of the act of April 19, 1856, usually known as the "Consolidation Act," the board of supervisors is empowered, among other things, "to provide by regulation for the prevention and summary removal of nuisances to public health, the prevention of contagious diseases; * * * to prohibit the erection of wooden buildings within any fixed limits where the streets shall have been established and graded; * * * to regulate the sale, storage, and use of gunpowder, or other explosive or combustible materials and substances, and make all needful regulations for protection against fire; to make such regulations concerning the erection and use of buildings as may be necessary for the safety of the inhabitants."

Yick Wo v. Hopkins, 118 U.S. 356, 359–60 (1886). And, in 1915, in *Hadacheck v. Sebastian*, 239 U.S. 394 (1915), the U.S. Supreme Court upheld the ban on brickyards in Los Angeles. In 1885, the N.Y.

general municipal zoning ordinance, which remained in effect until 1961. Prior to rapid industrialization during the 1900s, urban life was comparatively simple. But, with rapid industrial growth, population increases, and higher population densities, problems developed. Communities became crowded and noisy, and the proximity of conflicting land uses often raised safety concerns. This was the case, for example, of locating a school or a playground across from a busy factory. Moreover, streets became increasingly congested with the rapid rise in the production and demand for automobiles. Pollution from a variety of sources was also on the rise but seen as a natural and acceptable by-product of economic development. Today, we understand many of these issues as ones of negative externalities and spillover effects. We also understand the difficulties of overcoming transactions costs and coordination problems when private property owners attempt to solve all of these land use issues themselves. Thus, public land regulation through zoning now supplements traditional private efforts to control land uses. In this way, communities work to manage and coordinate land uses to protect the public health, safety, welfare, and morals.

All private land is held subject to some land use controls, either imposed by the common law or by the state, through legislation exercising either the power of eminent domain or the police power, including zoning. Zoning is a classic example of an exercise of the police power of the state. By police power, we refer to the inherent powers of the sovereign to regulate and act to protect the public health, safety, welfare, and morals. In the United States, the police power is traditionally vested in the individual states rather than in the federal government. The federal government has other grounds for implementing regulations. The states in their own constitutions and statutes may delegate police powers to local jurisdictions and municipalities. It is through a delegation of state police power that local planning and zoning officials are empowered to regulate land uses.

Zoning laws developed to address the problems of community growth that the common law did not otherwise effectively regulate. Consider that the basic common laws for controlling land use are the law of nuisance, which prohibits the landowner from committing nuisances, whether public or private, and the law of servitudes, which are restrictions such as easements, licenses, profits, and covenants (both real covenants running with the land or equitable servitudes) that individuals voluntarily impose on themselves and reciprocally impose on each other. Although useful, the common law has some limitations. For example, nuisance law requires a showing of both substantial harm and an unreasonable interference with the use

---

State legislature passed a bill restricting the height of all residential buildings to be built in Manhattan to a maximum of 70 feet on narrower streets, and 80 feet on wider streets, Michael R. Montgomery, *Keeping the Tenants Down: Height Restrictions and Manhattan's Tenement House System, 1885–1930*, 22 Cato Journal 495, 503 (2003), *citing* Ford, J., Slums and Housing (with Special Reference to New York City): History, Conditions, Policy, 2 vols. (Cambridge, Mass.: Harvard University Press. 1936) (in 1898, Massachusetts restricted buildings around Copley Square in Boston to 90 feet, and in 1903, Massachusetts enacted other height restrictions in Boston, which in *Welch v. Swasey*, 214 U.S. 919 (1919), the U.S. Supreme Court upheld the height restrictions).

or enjoyment of land, to prevail in an action claiming a nuisance has occurred or is occurring. Servitudes largely require an underlying agreement between landowners that creates mutually enforceable restrictions among them.[3] The evidentiary problems in the case of a nuisance claim, and the transactions costs and coordination problems with private land restrictions, make these common law tools of limited value. Nonetheless, they are still important. For example, many residential housing subdivisions have land regulations imposed by private covenants and restrictions that run with the land. A land developer typically imposes these types of restrictions at the time when the developer owns the entire parcel of land to be developed prior to the subdivision. In this way, there are no coordination or transactions costs problems with getting lot buyers to agree to the restrictions. The developer just imposes the blanket restrictions on the land and the buyers take subject to them. In addition to private land restrictions, landowners may want to establish a plan for protecting the character of the broader community by imposing some public land use controls to manage and coordinate land uses by regulating height restrictions on buildings, maintaining areas between structures, and by separating residential, commercial, industrial, and agricultural uses, for example. These goals may be accomplished by zoning laws, enacted when the state exercises its "police power" to regulate land use.

In 1926, in *Village of Euclid v. Ambler Realty*, 272 U.S. 365 (1926), the Court held that comprehensive zoning laws are a constitutional exercise of a state's police power.[4] A state government's police power is its constitutional authority to pass laws, which among other purposes may be to regulate land use. The police power is a rather flexible concept that can encompass such things as promoting aesthetics and architectural order, as well as regulating the traditional subjects of health, safety, and morals. Municipalities, such as towns, cities, and counties, are subdivisions of a state and may only exercise police power when the state has expressly delegated such power to them. These express delegations of power to regulate land use are found in the state's zoning enabling act. Every state has a zoning enabling act authorizing local jurisdictions and municipalities to pass land use regulations.[5] Such regulations

---

3. *See generally* George W. Kuney, *Further Misinterpretation of Bankruptcy Code Section 363(f): Elevating In Rem Interests and Promoting the Use of Property Law to Bankruptcy-Proof Real Estate Developments*, 76 Am. Bankr. L.J. 289, 298 (explaining "An equitable servitude is similar to a covenant although privity of estate between the covenantor and the covenantee is not necessary. As a result, an equitable servitude is enforceable only against those with actual knowledge of it as it fails to meet one or more of the formalities required for enforcement as a real covenant.").

4. *Vill. of Euclid v. Ambler Realty Co.*, 272 U.S. 365, 397 (1926) (holding "This process applies with peculiar force to the solution of questions arising under the due process clause of the Constitution as applied to the exercise of the flexible powers of police, with which we are here concerned.").

5. *See* 6 Patrick J. Rohan, Zoning and Land Use Controls § 37.03 (2020) (explaining "With a legislative process, or a quasi-judicial one with few statutory guidelines, the principle legal and practical context for re-zonings is the comprehensive plan. The Standard Zoning Enabling Act, in use at one time in every state and still the basis of most state enabling acts, required that zoning actions be "consistent with a comprehensive plan.").

are legitimate to the extent they fall within the scope of the powers as delegated to them in the zoning enabling act.

Historically, most land use regulations and zoning laws have been left, primarily, to local governments regulating land use through legislative action, or by administrative actions executing those laws by granting, denying, or modifying permits for specific land uses, or by judicial action interpreting those laws in disputes between the government and a landowner over the validity of a land use regulation or "as applied" to a particular parcel of land.[6] Local, municipal zoning ordinances form the core of most land use regulations.[7] Such regulations are accompanied by subdivision controls, and are also sometimes constrained by regional or state planning controls or growth management schemes.

Both the zoning law itself and particular decisions made by administrative bodies enforcing the zoning law must comply with the procedural and substantive criteria set out in the zoning enabling act. Property owners sometimes challenge local regulations as *ultra vires* or beyond the powers of the municipality to regulate. Any regulation that exceeds the scope of the powers granted to the municipality by the zoning enabling act may be challenged by a landowner as unlawful.

State and federal regulations further restrict private land use for a variety of reasons, including to protect the environment and historic landmarks.[8] Other laws regulate land use by prohibiting invidious discrimination, such as the Fair Housing Act,[9] which prohibits discrimination on the basis of race, sex, national origin, religion, familial status, or disability, with respect to dwellings,[10] or the Americans with Disabilities Act,[11] which prohibits discrimination against people with disabilities

---

6. A regulatory measure or zoning ordinance may be perfectly valid as it is drawn. It may be valid in its application to one set of conditions because it brings about reasonable results. But the same ordinance may be quite invalid as applied to another set of conditions because it brings about arbitrary and unreasonable results. The great bulk of litigation concerning zoning ordinances has involved the application of the ordinances, rather than their facial constitutionality.

7. *See* 6 PATRICK J. ROHAN, ZONING AND LAND USE CONTROLS § 37.03 (2020) (explaining, "Today the concept of consistency is changing and there is a much greater expectation that local governments will follow their own plans in making zoning decisions.").

8. *Cty. Bd. of Arlington Cty. v. Richards*, 434 U.S. 5 (1977) (holding the zoning ordinance did not offend the Fourteenth Amendment because the ordinance rationally promoted the state's objectives of reducing air pollution, and of enhancing the quality of life in the surrounding neighborhoods).

9. *See* Civil Rights Act of 1968; Fair Housing Act, 90 P.L. 284, 82 Stat. 73.

10. *See* 42 U.S.C. § 3604(a) ("It shall be unlawful . . . To refuse to sell or rent after the making of a bona fide offer, or to refuse to negotiate for the sale or rental of, or otherwise make unavailable or deny, a dwelling to any person because of race, color, religion, sex, familial status, or national origin.").

11. *See* 42 U.S.C. § 12112 (stipulating, "No covered entity shall discriminate against a qualified individual with a disability because of the disability of such individual in regard to job application procedures, the hiring, advancement, or discharge of employees, employee compensation, job training, and other terms, conditions, and privileges of employment.").

with respect to employment, state and local governmental services, public accommodation, and telecommunications.[12]

However, the governmental power to enact zoning laws that regulate the property rights of a landowner by restricting uses is not unlimited. State statutes or city ordinances still must conform to police power standards. Zoning laws attempting to exercise police power must be reasonable and not arbitrary; otherwise they either take property without due process of law or deny equal protection of the law under the Fourteenth Amendment to the U.S. Constitution.[13] In addition, zoning ordinances must meet the requirements of other provisions of federal and state constitutions — that is, for example, they may not violate the free speech or associational rights of landowners or occupiers. Hence, such an ordinance is invalid if it is: unreasonable and arbitrary (no rational bases for the classification); or discriminatory (there is no reasonable basis for the classification); or confiscatory (the property cannot be used for any purpose for which it is reasonably suited).

Furthermore, state statutes or city ordinances cannot impose restrictions if they do not bear "a substantial relation to the public health, safety, morals, or general welfare."[14] But great deference is afforded public officers to regulate land use by enacting zoning laws. If the validity of a state statute or ordinance is "fairly debatable,"[15] then generally the legislative judgment will control and the enactment is constitutional — that is, there is a presumption of constitutionality. A court will not set aside the determination of public officers unless it is clear that a regulation has "no foundation in reason and is a mere arbitrary or irrational exercise of power having no substantial relation to the public health, the public morals, the public safety or the public welfare in its proper sense."[16]

Yet, a state's police power is not confined to the elimination and prevention of nuisances such as filth, stench, and unhealthy places. Sure, many zoning laws do aim to prevent problems caused by the "pig in the parlor instead of the barnyard"[17] scenario; but, the police power also includes the authority to lay out zones or

---

12. *Id.*

13. If a land use regulation is reasonable yet still causes damage to the landowner it is *damnum absque injuria*, "a loss without injury," and the landowner suffers the loss without compensation because the law provides no means for recovery. As a result, the exercise of zoning power is often constitutional notwithstanding that it causes serious injury to a property owner.

14. Nectow v. Cty. of Cambridge, 277 U.S. 183, 188 (1928), *referring to* Vill. of Euclid, Ohio v. Ambler Realty Co., 272 U.S. 365, 395 (1926); Cty. of Eastlake v. Forest City Enterprises, Inc., 426 U.S. 668, 676 (1976) *citing* Vill. of Euclid, Ohio v. Ambler Realty Co., 272 U.S. 365, 395 (1926). Under *Euclid*, a landowner can challenge a zoning law if the restriction is "clearly arbitrary and unreasonable, having no substantial relation to the public health, safety, morals, or general welfare." *Id.*

15. Village of Euclid v. Ambler Realty Co., 272 U.S. 365, 388 (1926) ("If the validity of the legislative classification for zoning purposes be fairly debatable, the legislative judgment must be allowed to control.").

16. Nectow v. Cty. of Cambridge, 277 U.S. 183, 187–88 (1928), *citing* Vill. of Euclid, Ohio v. Ambler Realty Co., 272 U.S. 365, 395 (1926).

17. Vill. of Euclid v. Ambler Realty Co., 272 U.S. 365, 388 (1926).

districts wherein family values, youth values, and the blessings of quiet seclusion and clean air make the area a sanctuary for its people.[18] Zoning laws generally designate "districts in which only compatible uses are allowed and incompatible uses are excluded."[19] As such, these restrictions typically categorize uses and zone such districts as single-family residential, multiple-family residential, commercial, agricultural, or industrial. For example, reserving land for single-family residences preserves the character of neighborhoods, securing "zones where family values, youth values, and the blessings of quiet seclusion and clean air make the area a sanctuary for people"[20] free from conflicting uses.

Additionally, the power to pass land use regulations is limited by the basic constitutional protections for property owners and potential property owners. The Fifth Amendment to the U.S. Constitution states, in part: "nor shall private property be taken for public use, without just compensation."[21] In a very real sense, every restriction to land use imposed in the exercise of police power deprives the landowner of some property right enjoyed, and is, in that sense, a state action abridging property rights without providing just compensation. However, restrictions imposed to protect the public health, safety, morals, or general welfare from real dangers threatened is not an unconstitutional taking without just compensation, instead, it is lawful zoning.[22] In this sense, the extent of landowners' property rights are on a spectrum. Property rights are not absolute, and a state actor may lawfully regulate land use to a certain extent in exercising its police power. The general rule provides a threshold on that spectrum wherein if the state statute or a city ordinance goes *too far* in regulating a landowner's property rights, it will be recognized as a taking and, thusly, unconstitutional absent just compensation.[23]

These are just some of the basic issues and tensions involved in the law of land use planning and zoning. In exploring these issues, this book covers land use and zoning law by examining foundational cases and statutes interpreting the authority and scope of a state's power to enact laws regulating land uses. This book also gives attention to a variety of contemporary issues in land development, involving free speech, rights of association, affordable housing, inclusionary zoning, and prevention of discrimination. In addition, this book provides a unique focus on matters of accessibility by integrating cases and materials on the Americans with Disabilities Act (ADA), the Fair Housing Act (FHA), and the Rehabilitation Act (RHA). This integrated approach to matters of accessibility is important. Accessibility affects

---

18. *Id.*; Vill. of Belle Terre v. Boraas, 416 U.S. 1, 9 (1974).

19. DANIEL R. MANDELKER, LAND USE LAW § 4.16, pp. 113–14 (3d ed. 1993).

20. Cty. of Edmonds v. Oxford House, Inc., 514 U.S. 725, 732–33 (1995), *citing* Vill. of Belle Terre v. Boraas, 416 U.S. 1, 9 (1974); *see also* Moore v. East Cleveland, 431 U.S. 494, 521 (1977) (Burger, C.J., dissenting) (purpose of East Cleveland's single-family zoning ordinance "is the traditional one of preserving certain areas as family residential communities.").

21. U.S. Const. amend. V.

22. *Pennsylvania Coal Co. v. Mahon*, 260 U.S. 393, 417 (1922).

23. *Pennsylvania Coal Co. v. Mahon*, 260 U.S. 393, 415 (1922).

many people and is important to the livability of our communities. In fact, 20–25% of Americans have a disability of some kind, the incidence of disability increases with age, and America has an aging population. Moreover, when we think about the need to safely and easily navigate the built environment, we find that approximately 20% or more of American families have a family member with a mobility impairment. Making communities accessible requires attention to design, planning, and zoning. We not only need to remove physical barriers to access, we need to address the coordination of permissible uses, including the location of such uses as group homes, senior housing, drug rehabilitation centers, and access to counseling and specialized health care services. These uses often raise conflicts with current property owners. With this in mind, the book integrates materials on accessibility and aging in place in every chapter.

To begin our study of land use and zoning, we start with an excerpt from a book on Land Use Law and Disability.

## Robin Paul Malloy, Land Use Law and Disability: Planning and Zoning for Accessible Communities (Cambridge University Press, 2015)

(from Chapter 1 of the book, most footnotes omitted and renumbered)

### Thinking beyond a civil rights paradigm

### Pauli: Age 28

Pauli was a passenger in an automobile being driven by his mother when they were hit by a drunk driver.[24] The accident left Pauli unable to walk, paralyzed from the waist down. That was 11 years ago. Today, at age 28, Pauli has just been promoted to junior partner of a local management consulting firm.

While he finishes his work for the day, Pauli looks forward to attending a celebratory party for all the newly promoted people in the firm. The party is being held later this night at the home of the firm's senior partner. Pauli organizes his desk, makes a call to request a wheelchair-accessible bus, freshens up in the men's room, and then rolls himself down the hallway to the elevator. He makes his way out the front door of his building and rolls his wheelchair down the sidewalk to the curb cut, where he crosses the street to wait for the wheelchair-accessible bus that will take him to his home. Two regular city buses that cover his route come and go while Pauli waits the 40 minutes that will be required on this day for the accessible bus to arrive with one other passenger already on it. As Pauli waits for his bus, he thinks about the way his life has changed since that accident 11 years ago. In his wheelchair, life is so much different from the time when he played football, ran track, and danced with his high school sweetheart at the junior prom. Although those memories are cherished,

---

24. The opening vignettes also appear in Robin Paul Malloy, *Inclusion by Design: Accessible Housing and Mobility Impairment*, 60 HASTINGS L.J. 699 (2009).

he has since adjusted to a new life and reflects positively on the many changes that have recently improved his quality of life, such as curb cuts, accessible buses, roll-in entrances to buildings, bathrooms with lower sinks and light switches, and new building designs with doorways and facilities that provide adequate space for moving and manipulating his wheelchair. He knows that such changes have come slowly and that there is a need for additional design changes, but he also appreciates the increasing community awareness of the need for greater accessibility. While acknowledging that much work needs to be done, Pauli feels lucky because his office is in a new building with many inclusive design features, which was not the case in his prior job location, nor is it the case in many of the office buildings downtown, some of which were built 40 or more years ago and have done a poor job of updating. Pauli also feels fortunate because the city, after threats of litigation, recently purchased two new wheelchair-accessible buses, and he now enjoys being able to take advantage of one of the few bus routes served by such a bus, even if service is often slower than that provided by the regular city bus service. The city still has not looked at demographic trends and the need for future bus routes, but at least Pauli can see improvements in transportation and building designs that are beneficial to many people with low functional mobility, not just people in wheelchairs. Within a few minutes, the bus arrives, and Pauli, aware of all the hard work that has gone into becoming a junior partner, rolls onto the bus and is headed home.

After arriving at home, Pauli changes for the party and, together with his wife, drives to the home of the senior partner. The senior partner lives in a newly developed suburban neighborhood to which Pauli has never been before. By the time they locate the partner's home, there are already a number of cars parked along the street. From their car, they can hear the music of laughter and joyful conversation spilling out into the neighborhood. They park the car and head toward the front of the house. There are no sidewalks in the neighborhood, and Pauli's wheelchair does not work well in the soft grass, so they make their way down the center of the street and past the wall of parked cars. Pauli's sense of excitement dissipates, and his gut wrenches as he looks out at a tiered three-level stone sidewalk terracing up the front lawn to a porch with a two-step entry to a relatively narrow front door. Disheartened, but with a well-practiced smile on her face, Pauli's wife goes to the front door to inquire about another, more suitable entrance to the house.

As she waits at the door, she cannot help but notice the way in which the warm glow of the party inside contrasts with the sullen lines of distress on Pauli's face. The senior partner comes to the door and offers her regrets for not thinking about the issue of Pauli's access to her home. She pauses and thinks for a minute about the entrance from the garage, but that too has steps — three steps up from the garage to the main living room — and the doorway is too narrow. Finally, she suggests that Pauli roll around the side of the house, past the line of garbage cans, and come in through the rear mud room. "This," she says, "is the door we use to let the dogs in and out. I am sure that they won't mind." She goes on to explain that there is only one step at this entrance and that she will send several guests back to help lift Pauli through the doorway — the only doorway in her home wide enough to accommodate a wheelchair. Pauli makes his way past the trash cans thinking of all the family gatherings and all the college and Super Bowl parties hosted at homes in which the same old issue arises. He wonders to himself if people anguish as much over "having" to invite him to their homes as he does over being invited.

### Ann: Age 15

Sally and Jim have a 15-year-old daughter, Ann, born with a mobility-impairing condition necessitating the use of a wheelchair or scooter. Ann attends the public school, which provides an inclusive and open environment. Ann is a good student, and with the aid of her motorized scooter, she is able to get around the school and participate in some school activities, such as helping to manage the school track team and playing an instrument in the band. Ann has many friends and is well liked by her classmates. All of this is good, but there is a problem: Ann never gets invited to anyone's home for a play date or a sleepover, or for general socializing, not because of personal discrimination but because of exclusion by design in the homes of her classmates and friends. Although her home is a model of accessibility, there are no sidewalks in her neighborhood, and her school friends and extended family members do not have homes able to easily and safely accommodate her use of a wheelchair. Thus, Ann lives in a partitioned world of public inclusion at school and social exclusion after school. Ann lives in a space of truncated social relationships, and indirectly, her parents' relationships are also hindered, as they find it increasingly difficult to visit others who occupy exclusionary housing units. The implications of these truncated relationship networks are isolating and stigmatizing for everyone, but perhaps more so for young school-age children and teenagers, because reciprocal social networking is so important to a healthy self-image and to their proper social development.

### Celia: Age 74

Celia, a 74-year-old woman, until recently has been living independently in her own home. Celia had lived in the same home for 50 years, ever since she was married to her now deceased husband. She had six children while living in that house and has many cherished memories of the people and events that filled the home with love and laughter over the years. Now, at age 74, Celia has difficulty living in her home. Celia suffers from arthritis in her joints and occasionally loses feeling in her right foot, causing minor interference with keeping her balance. With her arthritis and her foot problem, she is no longer able to navigate the five concrete steps that lead into and out of her home. Inside of her home, she struggles with the layout of the house, which has all three bedrooms and the only bathroom on the second floor. There is a 12-step stairway between the main floor of the house and the second floor. On flat surfaces, she is fine and does not need, or use, either a walker or a wheelchair. Doctors estimate that Celia has many years ahead of her and that she would be able to live independently in her home for several more years if it were not for the presence of so many stairs. Celia prefers to age in place, but she recently had to sell her home and move 10 miles away to a senior living facility in a nearby town because her town has none. This facility is easier to navigate, but it removes her from a neighborhood populated with families and people of all ages and places her in an environment where everyone is her age and older. As was the case with her private residence, the neighborhood by the nursing home has no sidewalks and no form of public transportation.

She misses looking out her window and watching the neighborhood children play and seeing the new moms and dads proudly pushing carriages with newborn babies along the sidewalk. She misses the joy of participating in front yard neighborhood chatter and of the children coming around on Halloween and singing carols at Christmas. The hardest thing to deal with is the realization that in addition to having to leave her own home after so many years, she is no longer able to visit the homes of her children, grandchildren, nephew, sister, and friends, who all reside nearby but occupy houses that are not readily accessible because of entry steps and internal stairways. Despite her lack of need for a wheelchair or even a walker, Celia finds that almost every home that she used to visit now represents a barrier to the normalcy of her prior pattern of social interaction. Celia misses the opportunity to visit the homes of the people she cares so much about and finds herself prematurely disconnected from many of the important social networks that she had enjoyed over the years.

### Tiffany: Age 65

Tiffany is 65 years old and lives in a small city, on the third floor of a walk-up apartment building. She no longer drives, and she uses a cane when she walks because of an injury to her right leg. In recent years, going up and down the stairway to her third-floor apartment has become increasingly difficult. As life in the city has changed over time, Tiffany has witnessed the increase in broken sidewalks and the closing up of the downtown drug store, grocery store, and two restaurants, which, in her younger days, were all located within a three-block radius of her home. Tiffany finds it to be increasingly difficult to live independently because of where she is located.

The nearest grocery store, drug store, and restaurant are located several miles away in a suburban shopping center. The shopping center features a new store that is fully accessible. Housing costs in the suburb are too high for Tiffany to afford. The public transit system provides service between the neighborhood of her home in the city and the suburban shopping center, but the four-mile trip takes two hours and requires two transfers. Once in the suburb, there are no sidewalks in the town because property owners do not want to pay for them, and they worry about having to keep them free of snow during the four months when snow is typically on the ground. Across a six-lane highway from the shopping center is a hair salon and a movie theater, but Tiffany has never had the courage to cross the busy road that slices through the town on the way into the city. The grocery store, although fully accessible and having won awards for its inclusive design, is still very difficult for Tiffany to access and enjoy because it is poorly integrated into the surroundings that she must navigate to get there in the first place. Similar difficulties arise when

Tiffany attempts to visit the city-based senior citizen's center and when she wishes to visit her local church; sidewalks are in disrepair, and crossing streets is difficult because of traffic and because few intersections have safe crosswalks. Even getting in and out of her home is difficult, because it is an apartment in an older building that still has a difficult stairway to climb. The problem is magnified during winter months, when very few of the sidewalks are properly cleared of snow. Tiffany has found that neither city nor suburban living is necessarily ideal for a person with low functional mobility and living without an automobile.

———————

Unfortunately, the experiences of Pauli, Ann, Celia, and Tiffany are not unique. Their experiences are shared each day by millions of people representing almost 20 percent of American families, and their particular situations simply illustrate the broader set of problems arising from the fact that functional mobility levels vary among people. They also illustrate the fact that many communities are doing a less than ideal job of planning for inclusive design. As indicated in these narratives, we see examples of communities failing to provide adequate planning for accessible bus routes, neglecting the building and repairing of sidewalks, making inadequate provision for senior housing, and failing to make streets safe for easy crossing. In short, poor planning is leaving many of our communities inaccessible even as we declare more and more rights to access.

Without good land use planning, people using walkers, wheelchairs, and crutches, for example, or people dealing with debilitating arthritis as well as hip and knee conditions, may have difficulty navigating a home, a neighborhood, or a community. Lack of sidewalks, barriers to entranceways, narrow hallways, the presence of steps, and busy streets can all make mobility more difficult and less safe. A key to making our communities safer and more inclusive is in recognizing that mobility issues relate not only to the functional ability of individuals, but also to the design of the natural and built environments in which they live. Good planning and zoning require careful evaluation of demographic trends and available resources to address the needs of residents with declining functional mobility and a desire to age in place. This calls for comprehensive planning that looks at patterns of property development, changes in local and regional demographics, and the connectivity of people and places across the entire community. As such, functional mobility issues are ones that inherently involve choices regarding property development and land use regulation. This means that accessibility is a land use issue as well as a civil rights matter.

A problem confronting many communities, however, is that there is little attention directed at planning for accessibility and aging in place. This is because mobility impairment and inclusive design are not typically thought of as planning and zoning issues. Instead, they are treated as a matter of civil and constitutional rights. Although civil and constitutional rights are involved in protecting people with disabilities from unlawful discrimination, there is also a need to understand accessibility and aging in place as planning and land use issues. Unfortunately, the disability rights literature is almost exclusively framed by the concerns of civil rights law and the desire to eliminate discrimination on the basis of disability, in ways analogous to matters of race. This approach has facilitated a design process heavily driven by remedial regulation of detailed construction guidelines, and a case-by-case exercise in "planning by litigation." For example, regulations are passed requiring sidewalks to have curb cuts, and lawsuits are brought to make communities provide those cuts, but little planning may go into determining the best locations for sidewalk development as the community grows and changes over time. Likewise, lawsuits are brought to establish the rights to an accessible sidewalk and an accessible public bus system, but these rights to access may be of little value to a resident living in a community with no plans for any sidewalks or public buses.

Planning for the dynamic and changing needs of our communities is important. This includes planning for the needs of people with mobility impairment and for those who desire to age in place. Planning should be by design and with intention, not simply in response to litigation. Therefore, this book seeks to explain the issues of mobility impairment and of aging in place in terms of the way they might look through the lens of a property development and zoning professional. In this regard, the undertaking is one of reclaiming an active role for local and regional governments in the coordination of land uses by making a case for intentional planning and zoning to address issues of mobility impairment and aging in place. This is done by addressing these issues in terms of a proper exercise of the police powers in advancing and protecting the public health, safety, welfare, and morals. This is the traditional legal foundation for local zoning and planning, and when properly exercised, it can enhance the civil rights of people with disabilities because it produces a more thoughtful, coherent, and inclusive approach to property development and land use. Reclaiming a strong role for local and regional government regulation under the police powers adds to our ability to successfully build inclusive design communities; it does not subtract from a civil rights agenda for people with disabilities.

A corollary to the need for more active and intentional planning is a need to evaluate the coordination of land uses with reference to the public health, safety, welfare, and morals. This traditionally means looking at *use* and not at how a property is owned (e.g., public vs. private ownership or individual vs. corporate ownership), and not considering the particular identity or characteristics of the user. Thus, the race and religion of a property user are not material, nor is the question of if the property is owned by an individual, a partnership, a corporation, or a not-for-profit organization. Moreover, it is important in the planning process to distinguish the coordination of land use from the development of guidelines for inclusive design. These are two different functions; inclusive design guidelines may be more appropriately and effectively handled at a national level, while coordination of land use and approval of property development may best be handled at the state and local levels. Design guidelines are more akin to building codes than to land use regulation, and in this book, references to local government authority to control land use include the traditional concerns for regulating not only use but lot area, height, bulk, density, appearance, and other matters typically covered by the police power. Consequently, planning for more accessible communities involves a careful consideration of both design and land use.

When we look at community planning from this perspective, the lack of inclusive design in our residential neighborhoods becomes apparent. Many single-family residential properties have barriers to safe and easy access and navigation. This is problematic because residential uses make up a significant portion of land uses in many communities. A reason for this lack of accessibility is that federal disability law, while pervasive in its guidelines for public buildings, places of public accommodation, and multifamily housing, has little to say about private, single-family residential homes. The lack of strong inclusive design standards for all residential properties perpetuates problems of low accessibility for many residents and weakens the sustainability of our neighborhoods because it hinders the opportunities for social interaction and participation.

One problem to address in planning with respect to residential uses is that the legal system frames the discourse of accessibility to residential housing in terms of a dichotomy between the private and public spheres, with the home understood as private space — a space of intimate relationships, a space easily hidden from public view, and a space carrying high expectations of privacy. The concern for protecting privacy in the home, however, is not a sound basis for treating privately funded housing as devoid of a legitimate public interest. Although the home may be understood as a private space, where the occupants enjoy the legal expectations of privacy, a right to exclude, and a right of association, the housing structure itself, as a physical place, is in some respects a quasi-public place because it is an integrated part of the broader built environment and imposes itself on the community in ways that are physical, environmental, and aesthetic. Therefore, it is important not to conflate the two ideas (house and home), because they are not one and the same, and failure to keep this in mind hinders one's ability to understand the difference between a concern for privacy in the home and accessibility of the house.

Distinguishing private, single-family residential homes from other properties in terms of requirements for accessible design is not based on a concern for the public health, safety, welfare, and morals, because such a concern would seemingly seek to make all properties safe and easy to navigate. A distinction based on how a property is owned, as a public building or a place of public accommodation rather than a single-family residence, for instance, has little intrinsic relationship to the question of safety and ease of use in design. As an integrated part of a "complete community," all buildings, including single-family residential homes, should be safe and easy to enter and navigate. The legal distinctions made with respect to regulation of accessibility in single-family residential homes relative to other types of uses are political. They are political distinctions that have something to do with striking a compromise between competing interest groups: disability rights advocates and residential housing interests. Whereas disability rights advocates look to the federal government to impose regulations for greater access on local communities, real estate professionals worry about the impact of added design and construction costs on housing afford-ability and about the potential for local voter pushback if residential homeowners have to spend their own resources to upgrade or retrofit current residential housing to achieve greater levels of accessibility.

Another way of understanding the relative hands-off approach to regulating single-family residential homes is from a market perspective. From this perspective, one might suggest that federal disability law functionally treats single-family resi-dential housing like other private consumption goods, presuming that individuals are empowered by market forces to bargain for socially optimal housing outcomes. This assumption would be consistent with Adam Smith's notion of the "invis-ible hand," which assumes that self-interested individuals will make choices that advance the public interest even though it is no part of their original intention. This means that there is a presumed invariance between public and private marginal costs and marginal benefits. If this is true, we do not need regulatory guidelines for accessible housing because private individuals dealing with private home builders will bargain for the optimal social outcome in housing design. The problem is that we know that this assumption is problematic. We know that such things as transac-tions costs, wealth effects, the tragedy of the commons, asymmetrical information, poorly defined property rights, and cognitive assessment problems create variance between the pursuit of individual self-interest and optimal social outcomes. It is not clear, therefore, that the actual outcome of market bargaining with respect to hous-ing design produces socially optimal results in terms of accessibility and the public health, safety, welfare, and morals.

In addition to being consistent with a market-based presumption about the power of self-interested individuals to effectively coordinate inclusive design stan-dards and land uses on their own, the distinctions that have been made between public and private places in the current law of inclusive design are consistent with a civil rights approach to disability. In civil rights law, we have traditionally focused on access and diversification of public spaces and services as well as on those pri-vate places that serve the public as part of interstate commerce (i.e., locations that amount to being places of public accommodation). We have also tended to treat private places, such as a person's home, and private clubs and organizations as dif-ferent from public places and public organizations. Counterpoints to requiring inte-gration, diversity, and inclusion have been concerns for protecting an individual's right to privacy and to freedom of association. Thus, one may not be legally able to exclude a person of a particular race from entering the public library or a local restaurant, but it may be perfectly legal to exclude that same person from your pri-vate home. Similar logic supports detailed construction design guidelines for public places while exempting private homes. The difference in treatment between public and private places is misplaced, however, because making a physical place safe and easy to navigate for all invited guests is a totally separate matter from the exercise of one's legal right to exclude particular individuals from a private place. The design preferences of homeowners are not equivalent to the rights of exclusion that they enjoy as a consequence of owning an interest in property, and, to the extent that certain design preferences are counter to the public health, safety, welfare, and morals, they can be regulated pursuant to the police power.

A civil rights approach to inclusive design focuses on equality of access; a land use planning approach focuses on protecting the public health, safety, welfare, and morals. The buildings and structures that make up the built environment do not have rights to privacy, association, or exclusion; people have such rights. Although people have legally recognizable rights to exclude and to expectations of privacy and association, safe and inclusive designs in no way affect the right of homeowners to include or exclude people from their homes based on race or any other associational preferences. Consequently, it is important to distinguish the individual rights that we are seeking to protect from the ownership and use of structures, which impact the navigability of the built environment. A more modern and inclusive approach to planning and zoning should allow us to focus on health and safety issues without having to deal with detailed regulatory distinctions for classifying structures as public places, as places of public accommodation, or as private residences. The real focus should be on making the complete and integrated community safe and easy to navigate without regard to the public or private nature of property ownership.

The responsibility of planning for accessible communities ought to rest, to a large extent, with local and regional government rather than with the federal government. Coordinating land uses and promoting the public health, safety, welfare, and morals have long been the province of local government acting pursuant to the police powers. To date, however, many local zoning and planning professionals have failed to fully appreciate the extent to which accessibility relates to their authority to regulate land *uses*. Similarly, many disability rights advocates have failed to understand the positive contribution that property development and land use professionals can offer to the process of making our communities more accessible. Too frequently, issues of inclusion and accessibility are presented to local governments as matters to be addressed by building design guidelines developed pursuant to federal disability law rather than as matters for local government planning. The truth is that effective planning for accessibility and aging in place requires appropriate input from a variety of professionals, including those responsible for local government regulation of property development and land use.

The traditional emphasis on local land use planning and regulation, however, has given way in recent years to a growing trend in favor of regional and national planning. Examples of this trend include federal regulations pursuant to the Clean Water Act, Clean Air Act, and Migratory Birds Act and regulations related to wetlands protection and the management of coastal lands.[25] This trend recognizes that many

---

25. Migratory Bird Treaty Act, 16 U.S.C. §§ 703–712 (2006); Clean Water Act, Pub. L. No. 95-217, 91 Stat. 1566 (1977) (codified as amended at 33 U.S.C. § 1251 et seq. (2006); Clean Air Act, 42 U.S.C.

localized land uses have implications that extend beyond the property line and the jurisdictional boundary of the location of the use. For instance, certain uses can impact traffic, air quality, water quality, and noise levels well beyond the jurisdiction of one local government. In many cases, the justification for a national approach is that the cumulative effects of disaggregated local decision making can lead to extensive spillover effects and to numerous negative externalities across jurisdictional boundaries. Another justification is less focused on the spillover effects and more concerned with advancing a positive economic environment for communities to grow as dynamic "network enterprises," competing for residents and for businesses on the basis of providing a particular "quality of life." When understood as a "network enterprise," national inclusive design standards for accessibility make sense, just as national standards for cell phone protocols do. At the same time, local and state coordination of land use may continue to best reflect important differences among communities in a diverse and democratic system of governance.

The coordination of land uses among communities might occur in several ways and typically focuses on establishing compatibility measures and performance standards that facilitate desirable outcomes across jurisdictional lines. One way of doing this is by requiring *consistency* in planning among different levels of local government. This might include having local planning and zoning legislation reviewed by regional and state authorities for consistency with state objectives and for evaluation of spillover effects that might be detrimental to surrounding properties located within the legal boundaries of other local governments. Another way of achieving compatibility and standardization is by having planning take place at the national level rather than at the local or state level. To a large extent, the Americans with Disabilities Act (ADA) has worked to establish uniform national standards with respect to the protection of people with disabilities, and pursuant thereto, detailed national guidelines on accessible design and construction have been promulgated.[26] Following the lead of the national government, many states have adopted similar approaches to disability legislation.[27]

---

§ 7401 et seq. (2006); 33 C.F.R. § 323.1 et seq. (2013); 40 C.F.R. § 25.1 (2013); 40 C.F.R. § 124.1 et seq. (2005).

26. Americans with Disabilities Act of 1990, Pub. L. No. 101-336, 104 Stat. 327 (codified as amended at 42 U.S.C. § 12131 et seq. (2006)); 28 C.F.R. pt. 35.151 (2011); 28 C.F.R. pts. 36.401-36.406 (2011); 36 C.F.R. Architectural Barriers Act § 1191, *amended by* Accessibility Guidelines; Outdoor Developed Areas, 78 Fed. Reg. 59,476 (Sept. 26, 2013) (to be codified at 36 C.F.R. § 1191). *See also* U.S. Dep't of Housing & Urban Dev. & U.S. Dep't of Justice, Accessibility (Design and Construction) Requirements for Covered Multifamily Dwellings Under the Fair Housing Act (2013); U.S. Dep't of Justice, 2010 ADA Standards for Accessible Design (2010), *available at* www.ada.gov/2010ADAstandards_index.htm; Marcela Abadi Rhoads, The ADA Companion Guide: Understanding the Americans with Disabilities Act Accessibility Guidelines (ADAAG and the Architectural Barriers Act (ABA)) (2010).

27. *See, e.g.,* Ariz. Rev. Stat. Ann. § 41-1401 et seq. (2010); Cal. Code. Regs. tit. 24 § 5-101 et seq. (2011); Md. Code Ann., State Gov't § 20-601 et seq. (West 2013); Md. Code Ann., Health-Gen § 7-101 et seq. (2009); N.Y. Exec. Law § 290 et seq. (McKinney 2013).

Developing these national standards provides people with an expectation that they will receive similar treatment in every state, and it can facilitate interstate activity based on providing a set of predictable, compatible, and standardized guidelines for building design. This eliminates competition on the cost of accessible construction because all developers face the same guidelines, and it enhances mobility because people can more freely relocate to new communities knowing that accessibility design standards are the same in all states.

Even with national standards for prevention of discrimination and for regulating details of building design, it is still important for local government to *coordinate* property development and land *uses* pursuant to the police power, because local governments are closest to the land and the community in question. Local governments understand the local geography and circumstances, and they are more likely to be aware of the concerns of local residents. Local land use regulation can also generate local stakeholder support for the values and goals underlying particular efforts at coordinating land use, such as efforts directed at advancing inclusive and accessible design to address the needs of people aging in place as well as the needs of people with mobility impairment. At the same time, the federal government has no inherent expertise and enjoys no significant economies of scale in planning for the best locations for particular land uses within a local community, even if it has such advantages in establishing civil rights guidelines and in setting uniform national design standards for such construction features as doorways and bathrooms.

Modern communities have many planning needs, and it is important to think in terms of planning for mobility in the broader context of addressing a wide range of other needs, such as those related to housing affordability, poverty, sustainability, education, transportation, health care, and financial stability. In this context, there must be an understanding of local and regional input into the planning and zoning process under state law as well as an appreciation of a federal role in advancing the rights of people with disabilities.

Modern property development and land use regulations should be comprehensive in nature and informed by investigation, fact finding, and a combination of expert and community-based input. This means that planning must be done for "complete communities" and that a silo mentality of building inclusive design structures without regard to the connectivity of these structures to the broader community is insufficient. Making an individual house safe and easy to navigate for a person of low functional mobility, for example, does little to improve her quality of life in the community when barriers to safe and easy navigation exist everywhere outside of her home and if she lacks easy access to health care or other goods and services. Understanding this fact and planning for the proper integration of land uses and services across the built environment are traditional functions of local land use and zoning professionals, even if construction design guidelines are standardized at a national level. Moreover, setting detailed guidelines for building construction is not the same thing as planning for the needs of a community and coordinating its land uses to achieve desired outcomes.

A first step in developing better planning for accessibility and aging in place involves thinking of mobility impairment and inclusive design as land use issues. Thinking of ADA accessibility requirements in terms of local zoning and land use regulation should not be difficult. The ADA and related legislation already divide property into different categories of "use," and these categories in turn trigger different requirements and standards for accessibility. For example, under these federal regulations, there are properties identified as public places, places of public accommodation, multifamily residential and single-family residential.[28] Each of these categories is defined not only in terms of the purpose of a structure that might be located on a property but also in terms of how the place and space are used. It is the "use" of the property as a public place, or as a place of public accommodation, that is important in determining the construction design guidelines for accessibility. This focus on use is central to land use planning and zoning, and the coordination of uses within a community is traditionally a function of local government.

Local governments have long regulated property development based on different types of use categories, such as residential, retail, light industrial, industrial, and recreational.[29] Consequently, local governments are fully equipped to effectively understand the use categories of federal disabilities law. Furthermore, inasmuch as accessibility and aging in place are facilitated by good coordination of land uses, it is important to develop an understanding of the role of local government in advancing inclusive design as part of protecting the public health, safety, welfare, and morals. The current literature on disability law and policy, however, provides very little focus on issues of zoning and land use regulation. Instead, the literature is dominated by civil rights and constitutional law concerns. Although this literature and focus are important, they do not fully address the issues that must be confronted by property developers and land use regulators concerned with inclusion and accessibility. In part, the lack of a land use focus in the disability law literature might be attributed to the fact that contemporary approaches to disability law and policy are strategically framed with reference to race discrimination. This framing avoids a direct consideration of the land use issues involved in developing inclusive design communities. In fact, the current approach to disability law obscures the inherent link between accessibility, zoning, and land use planning. Perhaps this has been an oversight in the literature, or perhaps it reflects a desire to require mandated design requirements outside of a consideration of the police powers of local governments

---

28. Properties identified as public places, places of public accommodation, multifamily residential, and single-family residential. "Places of Public Accommodation," Americans with Disabilities Act of 1990, 42 U.S.C. § 12181(7) (2006).

29. Standard State Zoning Enabling Act (SZEA), U.S. Dep't of Commerce (1926); *Euclid*, 272 U.S. at 365; Julian C. Juergensmeyer & Thomas E. Roberts, Land Use Planning and Development Regulation Law §§ 4:1–4:2 (3d ed. 2013). *See generally* J. Berry Cullingworth, The Political Culture of Planning: American Land Use Planning in Comparative Perspective, Chapter 2 (1993); Zoning and the American Dream: Promises Still to Keep (Charles M. Haar & Jarold S. Kayden eds., 1989); Mandelker, Land Use Law, *supra* note 19, at §§ 5.01–5.86.

and to avoid potential challenges from property rights advocates opposing overly aggressive and potentially expensive regulation.

As to property rights advocates, they have been fairly aggressive about trying to limit the extent to which government can regulate land use, and they may interpret the extensive regulatory requirements for accessibility as overreaching, and in some cases as unnecessarily costly to property owners. For example, when the law requires buildings to have a zero-step entryway, wheelchair-accessible bathrooms, wider hallways, and elevators to accommodate a person with low functional mobility, it imposes costs on property owners and limits their development and design choices. Property rights advocates may assert that government lacks, or ought to lack, the authority to regulate land use in such a way or to such an extent. Such assertions are unlikely to be deemed legally meritorious by anyone who has an informed understanding of the law relevant to land use regulation. Just the same, the strength of the claims to accessibility and inclusion are made stronger by addressing underlying land use questions rather than avoiding them — and the opportunity for good zoning and planning is enhanced when local governments are involved in the process. This is because local land use regulation offers a process for considering a variety of present and future community needs in the context of comprehensive planning, and comprehensive planning can account for the integrated nature of communities while addressing the strategic deployment of scarce resources.

As this introduction indicates, mobility impairment and aging in place are complex issues confronting many communities. They are issues that raise concerns at the interface of disability law and land use regulation. They are shaped by physical, medical, and cultural factors, and they put competing values in tension. Developing successful responses to the challenges raised by mobility impairment and aging in place will require local zoning and land use professionals to be active participants in shaping policy and in developing appropriate regulations. These challenges, although great, are not beyond the ability and expertise of local zoning and planning professionals; local zoning and land use professionals have been addressing similar challenges for years. They have confronted similar challenges in dealing with the tension between a number of deeply held and competing values. For example, the First Amendment protects such things as the right to operate adult entertainment venues, but planners can regulate the location as well as the intensity and density of such operations. Similarly, the First Amendment protects the freedom of religion, but local land use regulators can set site development guidelines and control certain types of auxiliary activities connected with the primary religious use. Local planning and zoning regulations frequently deal with freedom of expression by controlling signs and aesthetics, and the rights of association frequently create tension with efforts to zone certain properties for single-family use. The fact that we have a number of deeply held values that frequently come into tension, and that the world is dynamic and ever changing, is exactly why we need planning. We need to plan for change — for demographic, social, political, economic, and cultural change — so that our communities remain vibrant and sustainable over time. Defining, clarifying, and articulating rights is one thing; planning and zoning to effectuate those rights in the design of the built environment is another. Thinking about planning, zoning, and the way in which we effectuate inclusion by design is important.

This book challenges us to rethink the legal frame used to address the issue of inclusion in the way that we develop property and regulate land use. Building better and more inclusive communities is going to require cooperation among local land use regulators and advocates for disability rights, and effective cooperation is more likely when efforts are made to address and reconcile the concerns of inclusive design with the underlying law of zoning and land use regulation.

From a zoning and planning perspective, we need to have places that are safe and healthy for all of the people living in our community, even as we acknowledge that functional mobility varies across a given population. This requires that our communities be safe and easy to navigate as people age in place, and this means that our communities must be designed to meet multiple intergenerational mobility needs to make them sustainable in terms of supporting a lifelong and meaningful opportunity for participation in community life by all residents. Residents should not need to prematurely or involuntarily relocate to another community simply as a result of the normal aging process or as a consequence of declining mobility. Our communities should be planned to provide meaningful pathways and networks to navigability for as many people as possible.

In examining the planning implications of mobility impairment, and its relationship to the aging process, it must be understood that low functional mobility is a physical condition, the meaning and consequences of which are shaped and influenced by the natural and built environments. As to the natural environment, it is easy to appreciate the differences in functional mobility among people. Some people can easily cross rocky paths, climb mountains, wade across river rapids, and traverse rough and varied terrain; others cannot. The built environment, unlike the natural environment, expresses the power of humans to shape their surroundings. This power is not unlimited, however, as buildings, highways, and other human interventions all must correspond in one way or another to the natural geography, topography, and weather conditions of the area. For example, many homes built in the city of New Orleans must be elevated from the ground because much of the city is below sea level. Local conditions drive building requirements, and the building requirements make it more difficult to design appropriately ramped entranceways to some structures. Thinking about the influence of local conditions on the accessibility of the built environment takes planning, and planning involves something more than identifying a civil right to access. Similarly, constraints imposed by technology and other scarce resources limit our ability to fully free ourselves from some of the mobility-based advantages and disadvantages that nature imposes. Nonetheless, good zoning and planning can facilitate design and construction that enhance the safety and ease of navigation for many people in a given community.

As we think about the need to ensure a safe and inclusive environment for people to live, work, and play, it is also important to recognize that functional mobility can vary over a lifetime and that diminishing levels of mobility impact people of all ages, races, religions, and ethnicities. Fortunately, many issues of functional mobility can be addressed through technology and design; functional mobility is not an immutable characteristic, and the goal of good zoning and planning ought to be to advance the public health, safety, welfare, and morals. This includes working for inclusive design standards in property development.

To put the problem of mobility into perspective, consider that the traditional view on mobility impairment is that it affects about 1 percent of the population of the United States. This 1 percent figure relates to the percentage of people using wheelchairs and to the fact that the wheelchair is the universal symbol for signifying accessibility to people with low functional mobility. The symbolic translation for many people is that they do not see many people in wheelchairs, so low functional mobility must be a rather minor issue. Contrary to the perception, however, the reality is that almost 17 percent or more of American families have a family member with some form of mobility impairment and that the rate of low functional mobility in the population increases dramatically as a population ages.[30] As of 2006, 23 percent of the population of the United States was aged 55 years and older,[31] and it is anticipated that within the next 10 to 15 years, 25 percent of the population in the United States will be age 65 years or older (this is up from 12.4 percent in the year 2000).[32] People in these age groups have much higher rates of low functional mobility than the general population, with as many as 40 to 50 percent of people over age 65 years having some type of limited mobility.[33] This means that as the general population ages over the next few years (absorbing the baby boomers into the ranks of those 55 years of age and older), we could likely have more than 20 percent of American families dealing with issues of mobility impairment. These changing demographics raise an important set of issues for community developers and planners.

An aging population is not the only factor to consider when planning for needs related to low functioning mobility. There are, of course, always going to be people who experience short-term or long-term declines in mobility without regard to age. People will be born with conditions that cause lowered functional mobility, or they may experience declining mobility as a result of illness, injury, accident, or some other cause. In addition to concerns generated by an aging population, declining functional mobility is likely to increase as a result of other factors. For example, rising rates of obesity and the increasing number of people losing limbs to diabetes and other causes also adds to the number of people with low-level

---

30. Qi Wang, U.S. Dep't of Com., Report No. CENSR-23, Disability and American Families: 2000, at 4 (2005), *available at* http://www.census.gov/prod/2005pubs/censr-23.pdf. *See also* Linda L. Nussbaumer, Inclusive Design: A Universal Need 4–6 (2012).

31. Cheryl Russell, Demographics of the U.S.: Trends and Projections 361 (3d ed. 2007).

32. *Id.* at 362.

33. Nat'l Inst. on Aging, *The Health and Retirement Study: Growing Older in America* 36–37 (Mar. 2007).

mobility. [34] Likewise, as we deal with modern forms of warfare and the ability to save life on the battlefield, we are now confronted with many thousands of surviving combat troops who have returned home from active duty with a need to adjust to decreased levels of mobility resulting from serious injury to or loss of a limb. [35] As a consequence, it is becoming increasingly important for us to rethink the design and navigability of the built environment. We need to expand on the use of inclusive design and develop what I refer to as inclusive design communities (IDCs): communities that take an integrated approach to property development and planning and that enable people to remain active and lifelong participants in community life. Inclusive design communities bring the two worlds of land use regulation and disability rights together to inspire planning and zoning that are inclusive and open to all residents over their entire lifetimes.

In addition to issues of inclusive design, planning and zoning officials must also consider questions related to the location of uses such as senior housing, drug rehabilitation centers, medical marijuana dispensaries, and group homes.

. . . .

## B. Basic Federal Law Addressing Accessibility

In integrating issues of disability and land use law, this book covers a lot of ground. The cases included in this casebook cover key issues in both zoning and disability law. The Appendix provides a summary overview of the primary regulations of applicable federal disability law for planning and zoning that one should be aware of (excerpted from Chapter 3 of Robin Paul Malloy, LAND USE LAW AND DISABILITY (Cambridge University Press, 2015)). As the regulations in the Appendix indicate, federal disability law has broad applicability. It is important to understand that these regulations address more than design. They also address land use. In this casebook, we are primarily concerned with matters of land use. In practice, the elements of disability law that are most significant for land use planning and zoning law are narrowly focused.

---

34. *See* Ctr. for Disease Control, *Long-Term Trends in Diagnosed Diabetes*, U.S. DEP'T OF HEALTH AND HUMAN SERVS. (2011), www.cdc.gov/diabetes/statistics/slides/long_term_trends.pdf; Ctr. for Disease Control, *National Diabetes Fact Sheet*, U.S. DEP'T OF HEALTH AND HUMAN SERVS. (2011), http://www.cdc.gov/diabetes/pubs/pdf/ndfs_2011.pdf; Ctr. for Disease Control, *Crude and Age-Adjusted Percentage of Adults with Diagnosed Diabetes Reporting Any Mobility Limitation, United States, 1997–2011*, U.S. DEP'T OF HEALTH AND HUMAN SERVS., https://www.cdc.gov/diabetes /statistics/meduse/fig3.htm (last visited Oct. 1, 2013).

35. David Wood, *U.S. Wounded in Iraq, Afghanistan Includes More Than 1,500 Amputees*, THE HUFFINGTON POST (Nov. 7, 2012, 5:38 PM EST), www.huffingtonpost.com/2012/11/07/iraq -afghanistan-am_n_2089911.html.

## Discussion Problem 1.1

Read the Appendix to this book and consider the various elements of our disability laws. In general, American law focuses on preventing discrimination against people with disabilities rather than on granting affirmative rights. Likewise, the prohibitions on discrimination often times come with requirements for taking actions that are limited by qualifying terms that invoke economic considerations. You will notice that, within the various provisions, we find references to compliance standards qualified by such language as, *reasonable* accommodations, *reasonable* modifications, *readily* achievable barrier removal, unless imposing an *undue financial or administrative burden*, and to the extent that accommodations do not *fundamentally alter* a program, service, or activity. The qualifying language generally imposes a requirement for some type of cost conscious balancing of competing interests when determining what must be done in the way of providing for accessibility. In contrast to this American approach, the United Nations Convention on the Rights of People with Disabilities (UN-CRPD) generally takes a position in favor of providing positive rights for people with disabilities. Positive rights are not generally qualified by a need to balance cost conscious considerations. The United States has not signed on to the UN-CRPD.

A) Why do you think American disability law takes the form that is does? Should the rights of people with disabilities be contingent upon a favorable cost and benefit analysis?

B) Under a positive rights approach such as that taken by the UN-CRPD, how many scarce resources should be devoted to pursuing incremental increases in accessibility?

C) In making a decision about a reasonable accommodation or modification, a readily achievable elimination of a barrier to accessibility, or the extent to which something is a financial or administrative burden, who should decide? For example, should a person with a disability be able to determine the particular accommodation that should be deemed reasonable, or should someone else decide what is reasonable in a given case by making a rational determination based on weighing the appropriate legal criteria; even if it results in a different accommodation from that requested or no accommodation at all?

## City of Edmonds v. Oxford House, Inc.

Supreme Court of the United States
514 U.S. 725 (1995)

Ginsburg, Justice. The Fair Housing Act (FHA or Act) prohibits discrimination in housing against, *inter alios*, persons with handicaps. Section 807(b)(1) of the Act entirely exempts from the FHA's compass "any reasonable local, State, or Federal restrictions regarding the maximum number of occupants permitted to occupy a dwelling." 42 U.S.C. § 3607(b)(1). This case presents the question whether a provision in petitioner City of Edmonds' zoning code qualifies for § 3607(b)(1)'s complete exemption from FHA scrutiny. The provision, governing areas zoned for single-family dwelling units, defines "family" as "persons [without regard to number] related by genetics, adoption, or marriage, or a group of five or fewer [unrelated] persons." Edmonds Community Development Code (ECDC) § 21.30.010 (1991).

The defining provision at issue describes who may compose a family unit; it does not prescribe "the maximum number of occupants" a dwelling unit may house. We hold that § 3607(b)(1) does not exempt prescriptions of the family-defining kind, i.e., provisions designed to foster the family character of a neighborhood. Instead, § 3607(b)(1)'s absolute exemption removes from the FHA's scope only total occupancy limits, i.e., numerical ceilings that serve to prevent overcrowding in living quarters.

## I

In the summer of 1990, respondent Oxford House opened a group home in the City of Edmonds, Washington (City), for 10 to 12 adults recovering from alcoholism and drug addiction. The group home, called Oxford House-Edmonds, is located in a neighborhood zoned for single-family residences. Upon learning that Oxford House had leased and was operating a home in Edmonds, the City issued criminal citations to the owner and a resident of the house. The citations charged violation of the zoning code rule that defines who may live in single-family dwelling units. The occupants of such units must compose a "family," and family, under the City's defining rule, "means an individual or two or more persons related by genetics, adoption, or marriage, or a group of five or fewer persons who are not related by genetics, adoption, or marriage." ECDC § 21.30.010. Oxford House-Edmonds houses more than five unrelated persons, and therefore does not conform to the code.

Oxford House asserted reliance on the Fair Housing Act, 102 Stat. 1619, 42 U.S.C. § 3601 *et seq.*, which declares it unlawful "[t]o discriminate in the sale or rental, or to otherwise make unavailable or deny, a dwelling to any buyer or renter because of a handicap of . . . that buyer or renter." § 3604(f)(1)(A). The parties have stipulated, for purposes of this litigation, that the residents of Oxford House-Edmonds "are recovering alcoholics and drug addicts and are handicapped persons within the meaning" of the Act. . . .

Discrimination covered by the FHA includes "a refusal to make reasonable accommodations in rules, policies, practices, or services, when such accommodations may be necessary to afford [handicapped] person[s] equal opportunity to use and enjoy a dwelling." § 3604(f)(3)(B). Oxford House asked Edmonds to make a "reasonable accommodation" by allowing it to remain in the single-family dwelling it had leased. Group homes for recovering substance abusers, Oxford urged, need 8 to 12 residents to be financially and therapeutically viable. Edmonds declined to permit Oxford House to stay in a single-family residential zone, but passed an ordinance listing group homes as permitted uses in multifamily and general commercial zones.

Edmonds sued Oxford House in the United States District Court for the Western District of Washington, seeking a declaration that the FHA does not constrain the City's zoning code family definition rule. Oxford House counterclaimed under the

FHA, charging the City with failure to make a "reasonable accommodation" permitting maintenance of the group home in a single-family zone. The United States filed a separate action on the same FHA "reasonable accommodation" ground, and the two cases were consolidated. Edmonds suspended its criminal enforcement actions pending resolution of the federal litigation.

On cross-motions for summary judgment, the District Court held that ECDC § 21.30.010, defining "family," is exempt from the FHA under § 3607(b)(1) as a "reasonable . . . restriction[n] regarding the maximum number of occupants permitted to occupy a dwelling." . . . The United States Court of Appeals for the Ninth Circuit reversed; holding § 3607(b)(1)'s absolute exemption inapplicable, the Court of Appeals remanded the cases for further consideration of the claims asserted by Oxford House and the United States. *Edmonds v. Washington State Building Code Council*, 18 F.3d 802 (1994).

The Ninth Circuit's decision conflicts with an Eleventh Circuit decision declaring exempt under § 3607(b)(1) a family definition provision similar to the Edmonds prescription. See *Elliott v. Athens*, 960 F.2d 975 (1992). . . . We granted certiorari to resolve the conflict, . . . , and we now affirm the Ninth Circuit's judgment. . . .

## II

The sole question before the Court is whether Edmonds' family composition rule qualifies as a "restrictio[n] regarding the maximum number of occupants permitted to occupy a dwelling" within the meaning of the FHA's absolute exemption. 42 U.S.C. § 3607(b)(1). . . . In answering this question, we are mindful of the Act's stated policy. "to provide, within constitutional limitations, for fair housing throughout the United States." § 3601. We also note precedent recognizing the FHA's "broad and inclusive" compass, and therefore according a "generous construction" to the Act's complaint-filing provision. *Trafficante v. Metropolitan Life Ins. Co.*, 409 U.S. 205, 209, 212 (1972). Accordingly, we regard this case as an instance in which an exception to "a general statement of policy" is sensibly read "narrowly in order to preserve the primary operation of the [policy]." *Commissioner v. Clark*, 489 U.S. 726, 739 (1989). . . .

## A

Congress enacted § 3607(b)(1) against the backdrop of an evident distinction between municipal land-use restrictions and maximum occupancy restrictions.

Land-use restrictions designate "districts in which only compatible uses are allowed and incompatible uses are excluded." D. Mandelker, Land Use Law § 4.16, pp. 113–114 (3d ed.1993) (hereinafter Mandelker). These restrictions typically categorize uses as single-family residential, multiple-family residential, commercial, or industrial. See, *e.g.*, 1 E. Ziegler, Jr., Rathkopf's The Law of Zoning and Planning § 8.01, pp. 8–2 to 8–3 (4th ed. 1995); Mandelker § 1.03, p. 4; 1 E. Yokley, Zoning Law and Practice § 7–2, p. 252 (4th ed. 1978).

Land-use restrictions aim to prevent problems caused by the "pig in the parlor instead of the barnyard." *Village of Euclid v. Ambler Realty Co.*, 272 U.S. 365, 388

(1926). In particular, reserving land for single-family residences preserves the character of neighborhoods, securing "zones where family values, youth values, and the blessings of quiet seclusion and clean air make the area a sanctuary for people." *Village of Belle Terre v. Boraas*, 416 U.S. 1, 9 (1974); see also *Moore v. East Cleveland*, 431 U.S. 494 (1977) (Burger, C.J., dissenting) (purpose of East Cleveland's single-family zoning ordinance "is the traditional one of preserving certain areas as family residential communities"). To limit land use to single-family residences, a municipality must define the term "family"; thus family composition rules are an essential component of single-family residential use restrictions.

Maximum occupancy restrictions, in contradistinction, cap the number of occupants per dwelling, typically in relation to available floor space or the number and type of rooms. See, *e.g.*, International Conference of Building Officials, Uniform Housing Code § 503(b) (1988); Building Officials and Code Administrators International, Inc., BOCA National Property Maintenance Code §§ PM-405.3, PM-405.5 (1993) (hereinafter BOCA Code); Southern Building Code Congress, International, Inc., Standard Housing Code §§ 306.1, 306.2 (1991); E. Mood, APHA-CDC Recommended Minimum Housing Standards § 9.02, p. 37 (1986) (hereinafter APHA-CDC Standards).... These restrictions ordinarily apply uniformly to *all* residents of *all* dwelling units. Their purpose is to protect health and safety by preventing dwelling overcrowding. See, *e.g.*, BOCA Code §§ PM-101.3, PM-405.3, PM-405.5 and commentary; Abbott, Housing Policy, Housing Codes and Tenant Remedies, 56 B. U. L. Rev. 1, 41–45 (1976).

We recognized this distinction between maximum occupancy restrictions and land-use restrictions in *Moore v. East Cleveland*, 431 U.S. 494 (1977). In *Moore*, the Court held unconstitutional the constricted definition of "family" contained in East Cleveland's housing ordinance. East Cleveland's ordinance "select[ed] certain categories of relatives who may live together and declare[d] that others may not"; in particular, East Cleveland's definition of "family" made "a crime of a grandmother's choice to live with her grandson." *Id.*, at 498–499 (plurality opinion). In response to East Cleveland's argument that its aim was to prevent overcrowded dwellings, streets, and schools, we observed that the municipality's restrictive definition of family served the asserted, and undeniably legitimate, goals "marginally, at best." *Id.*, at 500 (footnote omitted). Another East Cleveland ordinance, we noted, "specifically addressed ... the problem of overcrowding"; that ordinance tied "the maximum permissible occupancy of a dwelling to the habitable floor area." *Id.*, at 500, n. 7; accord, *id.*, at 520, n. 16, (Stevens, J., concurring in judgment). Justice Stewart, in dissent, also distinguished restrictions designed to "preserv[e] the character of a residential area," from prescription of "a minimum habitable floor area per person," *id.*, at 539, n. 9, in the interest of community health and safety....

Section 3607(b)(1)'s language — "restrictions regarding the maximum number of occupants permitted to occupy a dwelling" — surely encompasses maximum occupancy restrictions. But the formulation does not fit family composition rules typically tied to land-use restrictions. In sum, rules that cap the total number of occupants in order to prevent overcrowding of a dwelling "plainly and unmistakably," see *A.H. Phillips, Inc. v. Walling*, 324 U.S. 490 (1945), fall within §3607(b)(1)'s absolute exemption from the FHA's governance; rules designed to preserve the family character of a neighborhood, fastening on the composition of households rather than on the total number of occupants living quarters can contain, do not. . . .

B

Turning specifically to the City's Community Development Code, we note that the provisions Edmonds invoked against Oxford House, ECDC §§16.20.010 and 21.30.010, are classic examples of a use restriction and complementing family composition rule. These provisions do not cap the number of people who may live in a dwelling. In plain terms, they direct that dwellings be used only to house families. Captioned "USES," ECDC §16.20.010 provides that the sole "Permitted Primary Us[e]" in a single-family residential zone is "[s]ingle-family dwelling units." Edmonds itself recognizes that this provision simply "defines those uses permitted in a single family residential zone." . . .

A separate provision caps the number of occupants a dwelling may house, based on floor area:

> "Floor Area. Every dwelling unit shall have at least one room which shall have not less than 120 square feet of floor area. Other habitable rooms, except kitchens, shall have an area of not less than 70 square feet. Where more than two persons occupy a room used for sleeping purposes, the required floor area shall be increased at the rate of 50 square feet for each occupant in excess of two." ECDC §19.10.000 (adopting Uniform Housing Code §503(b) (1988)). . . .

This space and occupancy standard is a prototypical maximum occupancy restriction.

Edmonds nevertheless argues that its family composition rule, ECDC §21.30.010, falls within §3607(b)(1), the FHA exemption for maximum occupancy restrictions, because the rule caps at five the number of unrelated persons allowed to occupy a single-family dwelling. But Edmonds' family composition rule surely does not answer the question: "What is the maximum number of occupants permitted to occupy a house?" So long as they are related "by genetics, adoption, or marriage," any number of people can live in a house. Ten siblings, their parents and grandparents, for example, could dwell in a house in Edmonds' single-family residential zone without offending Edmonds' family composition rule.

Family living, not living space per occupant, is what ECDC §21.30.010 describes. Defining family primarily by biological and legal relationships, the provision also accommodates another group association: Five or fewer unrelated people are allowed to live together as though they were family. This accommodation is the peg on which Edmonds rests its plea for §3607(b)(1) exemption. Had the City defined a family solely by biological and legal links, §3607(b)(1) would not have been the ground on which Edmonds staked its case. . . . It is curious reasoning indeed that converts a family values preserver into a maximum occupancy restriction once a town adds to a related persons prescription "and also two unrelated persons." . . .

Edmonds additionally contends that subjecting single-family zoning to FHA scrutiny will "overturn Euclidian zoning" and "destroy the effectiveness and purpose of single-family zoning." . . . This contention both ignores the limited scope of the issue before us and exaggerates the force of the FHA's antidiscrimination provisions. We address only whether Edmonds' family composition rule qualifies for § 3607(b)(1) exemption. Moreover, the FHA antidiscrimination provisions, when applicable, require only "reasonable" accommodations to afford persons with handicaps "equal opportunity to use and enjoy" housing. §§ 3604(f)(1)(A) and (f)(3)(B).

The parties have presented, and we have decided, only a threshold question: Edmonds' zoning code provision describing who may compose a "family" is not a maximum occupancy restriction exempt from the FHA under § 3607(b)(1). It remains for the lower courts to decide whether Edmonds' actions against Oxford House violate the FHA's prohibitions against discrimination set out in §§ 3604(f)(1)(A) and (f)(3)(B). For the reasons stated, the judgment of the United States Court of Appeals for the Ninth Circuit is

*Affirmed.*

THOMAS, JUSTICE. (dissenting). Congress has exempted from the requirements of the Fair Housing Act (FHA) "*any* reasonable local, State, or Federal restrictions regarding the maximum number of occupants permitted to occupy a dwelling." 42 U.S.C. § 3607(b)(1) (emphasis added). In today's decision, the Court concludes that the challenged provisions of petitioner's zoning code do not qualify for this exemption, even though they establish a specific number — five — as the maximum number of unrelated persons permitted to occupy a dwelling in the single-family neighborhoods of Edmonds, Washington. Because the Court's conclusion fails to give effect to the plain language of the statute, I respectfully dissent.

I

Petitioner's zoning code reserves certain neighborhoods primarily for "[s]ingle-family dwelling units." Edmonds Community Development Code (ECDC) § 16.20.010(A)(1) (1991) . . . . To live together in such a dwelling, a group must constitute a "family," which may be either a traditional kind of family, comprising "two or more persons related by genetics, adoption, or marriage," or a nontraditional one, comprising "a group of five or fewer persons who are not [so] related." § 21.30.010 . . . . As respondent United States conceded at oral argument, the effect of these provisions is to establish a rule that "no house in [a single-family] area of the city shall have more than five occupants unless it is a [traditional kind of] family." . . . In other words, petitioner's zoning code establishes for certain dwellings "a five-occupant limit, [with] an exception for [traditional] families." . . .

To my mind, the rule that "no house . . . shall have more than five occupants" (a "five-occupant limit") readily qualifies as a "restriction[n] regarding the maximum number of occupants permitted to occupy a dwelling." In plain fashion, it "restrict[s]" — to five — "the maximum number of occupants permitted to occupy a dwelling." To be sure, as the majority observes, the restriction imposed by petitioner's zoning code is not an absolute one, because it does not apply to related persons. . . . But § 3607(b)(1) does not set forth a narrow exemption only for "absolute" or "unqualified" restrictions regarding the maximum number of occupants. Instead, it sweeps broadly to exempt any restrictions regarding such maximum number. It is difficult to imagine what broader terms Congress could have used to signify the categories or kinds of relevant governmental restrictions that are exempt from the FHA. . . .

Consider a real estate agent who is assigned responsibility for the city of Edmonds. Desiring to learn all he can about his new territory, the agent inquires: "Does the city have any restrictions regarding the maximum number of occupants permitted to occupy a dwelling?" The accurate answer must surely be in the affirmative — yes, the maximum number of unrelated persons permitted to occupy a dwelling in a single-family neighborhood is five. Or consider a different example. Assume that the Federal Republic of Germany imposes no restrictions on the speed of "cars" that drive on the Autobahn but does cap the speed of "trucks" (which are defined as all other vehicles). If a conscientious visitor to Germany asks whether there are "any restrictions regarding the maximum speed of motor vehicles permitted to drive on the Autobahn," the accurate answer again is surely the affirmative one — yes, there is a restriction regarding the maximum speed of trucks on the Autobahn.

The majority does not ask whether petitioner's zoning code imposes any restrictions regarding the maximum number of occupants permitted to occupy a dwelling. Instead, observing that pursuant to ECDC § 21.30.010, "any number of people can live in a house," so long as they are "related 'by genetics, adoption, or marriage,'" the majority concludes that § 21.30.010 does not qualify for § 3607(b)(1)'s exemption because it "surely does not answer the question: 'What is the maximum number of occupants permitted to occupy a house?'" . . . The majority's question, however, does not accord with the text of the statute. To take advantage of the exemption, a local, state, or federal law need not impose a restriction establishing an absolute maximum number of occupants; under § 3607(b)(1), it is necessary only that such law impose a restriction "regarding" the maximum number of occupants. Surely, a restriction can "regar[d]" — or "concern," "relate to," or "bear on" — the maximum number of occupants without establishing an absolute maximum number in all cases. . . .

I would apply § 3607(b)(1) as it is written. Because petitioner's zoning code imposes a qualified "restriction[n] regarding the maximum number of occupants permitted to occupy a dwelling," and because the statute exempts from the FHA "any" such restrictions, I would reverse the Ninth Circuit's holding that the exemption does not apply in this case.

## II

The majority's failure to ask the right question about petitioner's zoning code results from a more fundamental error in focusing on "maximum occupancy restrictions" and "family composition rules." . . . These two terms—and the two categories of zoning rules they describe—are simply irrelevant to this case. . . .

## A

As an initial matter, I do not agree with the majority's interpretive premise that "this case [is] an instance in which an exception to 'a general statement of policy' is sensibly read 'narrowly in order to preserve the primary operation of the [policy].'" . . . (quoting *Commissioner v. Clark*, 489 U.S. 726 (1989)). Why *this* case? Surely, it is not because the FHA has a "policy"; every statute has that. Nor could the reason be that a narrow reading of 42 U.S.C. § 3607(b)(1) is necessary to preserve the primary operation of the FHA's stated policy "to provide . . . for fair housing throughout the United States." § 3601. Congress, the body responsible for deciding how specifically to achieve the objective of fair housing, obviously believed that § 3607(b)(1)'s exemption for "any . . . restrictions regarding the maximum number of occupants permitted to occupy a dwelling" is consistent with the FHA's general statement of policy. We do Congress no service—indeed, we *negate* the "primary operation" of § 3607(b)(1)—by giving that congressional enactment an artificially narrow reading. See *Rodriguez v. United States*, 480 U.S. 522 (*per curiam*) ("[I]t frustrates rather than effectuates legislative intent simplistically to assume that whatever furthers the statute's primary objective must be law"); *Board of Governors, FRS v. Dimension Financial Corp.*, 474 U.S. 361, 374 (1986) ("Invocation of the 'plain purpose' of legislation at the expense of the terms of the statute itself . . . , in the end, prevents the effectuation of congressional intent"). . . .

## B

I turn now to the substance of the majority's analysis, the focus of which is "maximum occupancy restrictions" and "family composition rules." The first of these two terms has the sole function of serving as a label for a category of zoning rules simply invented by the majority: rules that "cap the number of occupants per dwelling, typically in relation to available floor space or the number and type of rooms," that "ordinarily apply uniformly to *all* residents of *all* dwelling units," and that have the "purpose . . . to protect health and safety by preventing dwelling overcrowding." . . . The majority's term does bear a familial resemblance to the statutory term "restrictions regarding the maximum number of occupants permitted to occupy a dwelling," but it should be readily apparent that the category of zoning rules the majority labels "maximum occupancy restrictions" does not exhaust the category of restrictions exempted from the FHA by § 3607(b)(1). The plain words of the statute do not refer to "available floor space or the number and type of rooms"; they embrace no requirement that the exempted restrictions "apply uniformly to all residents of all dwelling units"; and they give no indication that such restrictions must have the "purpose . . . to protect health and safety by preventing dwelling overcrowding." . . .

Of course, the majority does not contend that the language of §3607(b)(1) precisely describes the category of zoning rules it has labeled "maximum occupancy restrictions." Rather, the majority makes the far more narrow claim that the statutory language "surely encompasses" that category. . . . I readily concede this point. . . . But the obvious conclusion that §3607(b)(1) encompasses "maximum occupancy restrictions" tells us nothing about whether the statute also encompasses ECDC §21.30.010, the zoning rule at issue here. In other words, although the majority's discussion will no doubt provide guidance in future cases, it is completely irrelevant to the question presented in *this* case.

The majority fares no better in its treatment of "family composition rules," a term employed by the majority to describe yet another invented category of zoning restrictions. Although today's decision seems to hinge on the majority's judgment that ECDC §21.30.010 is a "classic exampl[e] of a . . . family composition rule," . . . the majority says virtually nothing about this crucial category. Thus, it briefly alludes to the derivation of "family composition rules" and provides a single example of them. . . . Apart from these two references, however, the majority's analysis consists *solely* of announcing its conclusion that "the formulation [of §3607(b)(1)] does not fit family composition rules." . . . This is not reasoning; it is *ipse dixit*. Indeed, it is not until after this conclusion has been announced that the majority (in the course of summing up) even defines "family composition rules" at all . . . (referring to "rules designed to preserve the family character of a neighborhood, fastening on the composition of households rather than on the total number of occupants living quarters can contain").

Although the majority does not say so explicitly, one might infer from its belated definition of "family composition rules" that §3607(b)(1) does not encompass zoning rules that have one particular purpose ("to preserve the family character of a neighborhood") or those that refer to the qualitative as well as the quantitative character of a dwelling (by "fastening on the composition of households rather than on the total number of occupants living quarters can contain"). . . . Yet terms like "family character," "composition of households," "total [that is, absolute] number of occupants," and "living quarters" are noticeably absent from the text of the statute. Section 3607(b)(1) limits neither the permissible purposes of a qualifying zoning restriction nor the ways in which such a restriction may accomplish its purposes. Rather, the exemption encompasses "any" zoning restriction — whatever its purpose and by whatever means it accomplishes that purpose — so long as the restriction "regard[s]" the maximum number of occupants. . . . As I have explained, petitioner's zoning code does precisely that. . . .

In sum, it does not matter that ECDC §21.30.010 describes "[f]amily living, not living space per occupant," . . . because it is immaterial under §3607(b)(1) whether §21.30.010 constitutes a "family composition rule" but not a "maximum occupancy restriction." The sole relevant question is whether petitioner's zoning code imposes "any . . . restrictions regarding the maximum number of occupants permitted to occupy a dwelling." Because I believe it does, I respectfully dissent.

## *Questions for Consideration*

1) *Should* the City of Edmonds's family-definition rule qualify for exemption from the requirements of the FHAA?

2) Why does the FHA exempt from its restrictions municipal code or zoning rules that constitute reasonable restrictions on the maximum number of people permitted to occupy a dwelling?

3) In *City of Edmonds*, the Court rules that a cap on the total number of occupants per dwelling would fall within the FHA exemption, but rules designed to protect the family character of the neighborhoods do not; what was the City of Edmonds trying to achieve by providing an exception from the cap to relatives?

## *Takeaway*

- In *City of Edmonds*, the housing policy was a limit on the number of unrelated persons who can live together. Both the FHA and the ADA prohibit governmental entities from implementing or enforcing housing policies in a discriminatory manner against persons with disabilities.

- Discrimination under the FHA includes a refusal to make "reasonable accommodation" for handicapped persons.

- The FHA protections apply to city zoning codes.

## Discussion Problem 1.2

Helpful Hearts, Inc., a private, nonprofit corporation, purchases a house in the City of Easterly, within a neighborhood zoned for single-family, residential use. Easterly's cap on the maximum number of residents in a house of this size is five. Helpful Hearts purchased the house intending to provide a group home to four people with HIV or AIDS. People with HIV or AIDS are protected from discrimination under the ADA and the FHA. The four residents in this house would be unrelated. Opposition to the group home develops in the neighborhood. Easterly, seemingly in response to neighborhood pressure, amends its zoning ordinance to require that all dwellings wherein more than two unrelated persons reside together must have one off-street parking space for every two residents in the dwelling. Easterly justifies the ordinance as a means for addressing traffic congestion within the city, and notes that unrelated persons are less likely to share a vehicle, and so are likely to have more cars. Also, Easterly is an old city, largely fully developed, and most houses within the city limits, just like the house purchased by Helpful Hearts, do not have off-street parking. The effect of this ordinance is that it is financially impossible to operate a group home in Easterly. Helpful Hearts sues Easterly, arguing that the new ordinance violates the Fair Housing Act. Who should prevail in this dispute?

# Tennessee v. Lane

Supreme Court of the United States
541 U.S. 509 (2004)

STEVENS, JUSTICE. Title II of the Americans with Disabilities Act of 1990 (ADA or Act), 104 Stat. 337, 42 U.S.C. §§ 12131–12165, provides that "no qualified individual with a disability shall, by reason of such disability, be excluded from participation in or be denied the benefits of the services, programs or activities of a public entity, or be subjected to discrimination by any such entity." § 12132. The question presented in this case is whether Title II exceeds Congress' power under § 5 of the Fourteenth Amendment.

## I

In August 1998, respondents George Lane and Beverly Jones filed this action against the State of Tennessee and a number of Tennessee counties, alleging past and ongoing violations of Title II. Respondents, both of whom are paraplegics who use wheelchairs for mobility, claimed that they were denied access to, and the services of, the state court system by reason of their disabilities. Lane alleged that he was compelled to appear to answer a set of criminal charges on the second floor of a county courthouse that had no elevator. At his first appearance, Lane crawled up two flights of stairs to get to the courtroom. When Lane returned to the courthouse for a hearing, he refused to crawl again or to be carried by officers to the courtroom; he consequently was arrested and jailed for failure to appear. Jones, a certified court reporter, alleged that she has not been able to gain access to a number of county courthouses, and, as a result, has lost both work and an opportunity to participate in the judicial process. Respondents sought damages and equitable relief.

The State moved to dismiss the suit on the ground that it was barred by the Eleventh Amendment. The District Court denied the motion without opinion, and the State appealed. . . . The United States intervened to defend Title II's abrogation of the States' Eleventh Amendment immunity. On April 28, 2000, after the appeal had been briefed and argued, the Court of Appeals for the Sixth Circuit entered an order holding the case in abeyance pending our decision in *Board of Trustees of Univ. of Ala. v. Garrett*, 531 U.S. 356 (2001).

In *Garrett*, we concluded that the Eleventh Amendment bars private suits seeking money damages for state violations of Title I of the ADA. We left open, however, the question whether the Eleventh Amendment permits suits for money damages under Title II. *Id.*, at 360, n. 1. Following the *Garrett* decision, the Court of Appeals, sitting en banc, heard argument in a Title II suit brought by a hearing-impaired litigant who sought money damages for the State's failure to accommodate his disability in a child custody proceeding. *Popovich v. Cuyahoga County Court*, 276 F.3d 808 (CA6 2002). A divided court permitted the suit to proceed despite the State's assertion of Eleventh Amendment immunity. The majority interpreted *Garrett* to bar private ADA suits against States based on equal protection principles, but not those that rely on due process principles. 276 F.3d, at 811–816. The minority concluded that

Congress had not validly abrogated the States' Eleventh Amendment immunity for any Title II claims, *id.*, at 821, while the concurring opinion concluded that Title II validly abrogated state sovereign immunity with respect to both equal protection and due process claims, *id.*, at 818.

Following the en banc decision in *Popovich*, a panel of the Court of Appeals entered an order affirming the District Court's denial of the State's motion to dismiss in this case. . . . The order explained that respondents' claims were not barred because they were based on due process principles. In response to a petition for rehearing arguing that *Popovich* was not controlling because the complaint did not allege due process violations, the panel filed an amended opinion. It explained that the Due Process Clause protects the right of access to the courts, and that the evidence before Congress when it enacted Title II "established that physical barriers in government buildings, including courthouses and in the courtrooms themselves, have had the effect of denying disabled people the opportunity to access vital services and to exercise fundamental rights guaranteed by the Due Process Clause." 315 F.3d 680, 682 (2003). Moreover, that "record demonstrated that public entities' failure to accommodate the needs of qualified persons with disabilities may result directly from unconstitutional animus and impermissible stereotypes." *Id.*, at 683. The panel did not, however, categorically reject the State's submission. It instead noted that the case presented difficult questions that "cannot be clarified absent a factual record," and remanded for further proceedings. . . . We granted certiorari, . . . and now affirm.

## II

The ADA was passed by large majorities in both Houses of Congress after decades of deliberation and investigation into the need for comprehensive legislation to address discrimination against persons with disabilities. In the years immediately preceding the ADA's enactment, Congress held 13 hearings and created a special task force that gathered evidence from every State in the Union. The conclusions Congress drew from this evidence are set forth in the task force and Committee Reports. . . . Central among these conclusions was Congress' finding that

> "individuals with disabilities are a discrete and insular minority who have been faced with restrictions and limitations, subjected to a history of purposeful unequal treatment, and relegated to a position of political powerlessness in our society, based on characteristics that are beyond the control of such individuals and resulting from stereotypic assumptions not truly indicative of the individual ability of such individuals to participate in, and contribute to, society." 42 U.S.C. § 12101(a)(7).

Invoking "the sweep of congressional authority, including the power to enforce the fourteenth amendment and to regulate commerce," the ADA is designed "to provide a clear and comprehensive national mandate for the elimination of discrimination against individuals with disabilities." §§ 12101(b)(1), (b)(4). It forbids discrimination against persons with disabilities in three major areas of public life:

employment, which is covered by Title I of the statute; public services, programs, and activities, which are the subject of Title II; and public accommodations, which are covered by Title III.

Title II, §§ 12131–12134, prohibits any public entity from discriminating against "qualified" persons with disabilities in the provision or operation of public services, programs, or activities. The Act defines the term "public entity" to include state and local governments, as well as their agencies and instrumentalities. § 12131(1). Persons with disabilities are "qualified" if they, "with or without reasonable modifications to rules, policies, or practices, the removal of architectural, communication, or transportation barriers, or the provision of auxiliary aids and services, mee[t] the essential eligibility requirements for the receipt of services or the participation in programs or activities provided by a public entity." § 12131(2). Title II's enforcement provision incorporates by reference § 505 of the Rehabilitation Act of 1973, 92 Stat. 2982, as added, 29 U.S.C. § 794a, which authorizes private citizens to bring suits for money damages. 42 U.S.C. § 12133.

### III

The Eleventh Amendment renders the States immune from "any suit in law or equity, commenced or prosecuted . . . by Citizens of another State, or by Citizens or Subjects of any Foreign State." Even though the Amendment "by its terms . . . applies only to suits against a State by citizens of another State," our cases have repeatedly held that this immunity also applies to unconsented suits brought by a State's own citizens. *Garrett*, 531 U.S., at 363; *Kimel v. Florida Bd. of Regents*, 528 U.S. 62, 72–73 (2000). Our cases have also held that Congress may abrogate the State's Eleventh Amendment immunity. To determine whether it has done so in any given case, we "must resolve two predicate questions: first, whether Congress unequivocally expressed its intent to abrogate that immunity; and second, if it did, whether Congress acted pursuant to a valid grant of constitutional authority." *Id.*, at 73.

The first question is easily answered in this case. The Act specifically provides: "A State shall not be immune under the eleventh amendment to the Constitution of the United States from an action in Federal or State court of competent jurisdiction for a violation of this chapter." 42 U.S.C. § 12202. As in *Garrett*, see 531 U.S., at 363–364, no party disputes the adequacy of that expression of Congress' intent to abrogate the States' Eleventh Amendment immunity. The question, then, is whether Congress had the power to give effect to its intent.

In *Fitzpatrick v. Bitzer*, 427 U.S. 445 (1976), we held that Congress can abrogate a State's sovereign immunity when it does so pursuant to a valid exercise of its power under § 5 of the Fourteenth Amendment to enforce the substantive guarantees of that Amendment. *Id.*, at 456. This enforcement power, as we have often acknowledged, is a "broad power indeed." *Mississippi Univ. for Women v. Hogan*, 458 U.S. 718, 732 (1982), citing *Ex parte Virginia*, 100 U.S. 339, 346 (1880). . . . It includes "the authority both to remedy and to deter violation of rights guaranteed [by the Fourteenth Amendment] by prohibiting a somewhat broader swath of conduct, including that which is not itself forbidden by the Amendment's text." *Kimel*, 528 U.S., at 81. We have thus repeatedly affirmed that "Congress may enact so-called prophylactic legislation that proscribes facially constitutional conduct, in order to prevent and deter unconstitutional conduct." *Nevada Dept. of Human Resources v. Hibbs*, 538 U.S. 721, 727–728 (2003). See also *City of Boerne v. Flores*, 521 U.S. 507, 518 (1997). . . . The most recent affirmation of the breadth of Congress' § 5 power came in *Hibbs*, in which we considered whether a male state employee could recover money damages against the State for its failure to comply with the family-care leave provision of the Family and Medical Leave Act of 1993 (FMLA), 107 Stat. 6, 29 U.S.C. § 2601 *et seq*. We upheld the FMLA as a valid exercise of Congress' § 5 power to combat unconstitutional sex discrimination, even though there was no suggestion that the State's leave policy was adopted or applied with a discriminatory purpose that would render it unconstitutional under the rule of *Personnel Administrator of Mass. v. Feeney*, 442 U.S. 256 (1979). When Congress seeks to remedy or prevent unconstitutional discrimination, § 5 authorizes it to enact prophylactic legislation proscribing practices that are discriminatory in effect, if not in intent, to carry out the basic objectives of the Equal Protection Clause.

Congress' § 5 power is not, however, unlimited. While Congress must have a wide berth in devising appropriate remedial and preventative measures for unconstitutional actions, those measures may not work a "substantive change in the governing law." *Boerne*, 521 U.S., at 519. In *Boerne*, we recognized that the line between remedial legislation and substantive redefinition is "not easy to discern," and that "Congress must have wide latitude in determining where it lies." *Id.*, at 519–520. But we also confirmed that "the distinction exists and must be observed," and set forth a test for so observing it: Section 5 legislation is valid if it exhibits "a congruence and proportionality between the injury to be prevented or remedied and the means adopted to that end." *Id.*, at 520.

In *Boerne*, we held that Congress had exceeded its § 5 authority when it enacted the Religious Freedom Restoration Act of 1993 (RFRA), 107 Stat. 1488, 42 U.S.C. § 2000bb *et seq*. We began by noting that Congress enacted RFRA "in direct response" to our decision in *Employment Div., Dept. of Human Resources of Ore. v. Smith*, 494 U.S. 872 (1990), for the stated purpose of "restor[ing]" a constitutional rule that *Smith* had rejected. 521 U.S., at 512, 515 (internal quotation marks omitted). Though the respondent attempted to defend the statute as a reasonable means of enforcing the Free Exercise Clause as interpreted in *Smith*, we concluded that RFRA was "so out of proportion" to that objective that it could be understood only as an attempt to work a "substantive change in constitutional protections." 521 U.S., at 529, 532. Indeed, that was the very purpose of the law.

This Court further defined the contours of *Boerne*'s "congruence and proportionality" test in *Florida Prepaid Postsecondary Ed. Expense Bd. v. College Savings Bank*, 527 U.S. 627 (1999). At issue in that case was the validity of the Patent and Plant Variety Protection Remedy Clarification Act (hereinafter Patent Remedy Act), a statutory amendment Congress enacted in the wake of our decision in *Atascadero*

*State Hospital v. Scanlon*, 473 U.S. 234 (1985), to clarify its intent to abrogate state sovereign immunity from patent infringement suits. *Florida Prepaid*, 527 U.S., at 631–632. Noting the virtually complete absence of a history of unconstitutional patent infringement on the part of the States, as well as the Act's expansive coverage, the Court concluded that the Patent Remedy Act's apparent aim was to serve the Article I concerns of "provid[ing] a uniform remedy for patent infringement and . . . plac[ing] States on the same footing as private parties under that regime," and not to enforce the guarantees of the Fourteenth Amendment. *Id.*, at 647–648. See also *Kimel*, 528 U.S. 62 (finding that the Age Discrimination in Employment Act exceeded Congress' §5 powers under *Boerne*); *United States v. Morrison*, 529 U.S. 598, (2000) (Violence Against Women Act).

Applying the *Boerne* test in *Garrett*, we concluded that Title I of the ADA was not a valid exercise of Congress' §5 power to enforce the Fourteenth Amendment's prohibition on unconstitutional disability discrimination in public employment. As in *Florida Prepaid*, we concluded Congress' exercise of its prophylactic §5 power was unsupported by a relevant history and pattern of constitutional violations. 531 U.S., at 368, 374. Although the dissent pointed out that Congress had before it a great deal of evidence of discrimination by the States against persons with disabilities, *id.*, at 379 (opinion of BREYER, J.), the Court's opinion noted that the "overwhelming majority" of that evidence related to "the provision of public services and public accommodations, which areas are addressed in Titles II and III," rather than Title I, *id.*, at 371, n. 7. We also noted that neither the ADA's legislative findings nor its legislative history reflected a concern that the States had been engaging in a pattern of unconstitutional employment discrimination. We emphasized that the House and Senate Committee Reports on the ADA focused on "'[d]iscrimination [in] . . . *employment in the private sector*,'" and made no mention of discrimination in public employment. *Id.*, at 371–372 (quoting S. Rep. No. 101–116, p. 6 (1989), and H. R. Rep. No. 101–485, pt. 2, p. 28 (1990) (emphasis in *Garrett*)). Finally, we concluded that Title I's broad remedial scheme was insufficiently targeted to remedy or prevent unconstitutional discrimination in public employment. Taken together, the historical record and the broad sweep of the statute suggested that Title I's true aim was not so much to enforce the Fourteenth Amendment's prohibitions against disability discrimination in public employment as it was to "rewrite" this Court's Fourteenth Amendment jurisprudence. 531 U.S., at 372–374.

In view of the significant differences between Titles I and II, however, *Garrett* left open the question whether Title II is a valid exercise of Congress' §5 enforcement power. It is to that question that we now turn.

## IV

The first step of the *Boerne* inquiry requires us to identify the constitutional right or rights that Congress sought to enforce when it enacted Title II. *Garrett*, 531 U.S., at 365. In *Garrett* we identified Title I's purpose as enforcement of the Fourteenth Amendment's command that "all persons similarly situated should be treated alike." *Cleburne v. Cleburne Living Center, Inc.*, 473 U.S. 432, 439 (1985). As we observed, classifications based on disability violate that constitutional command if they lack a rational relationship to a legitimate governmental purpose. *Garrett*, 531 U.S., at 366 (citing *Cleburne*, 473 U.S., at 446).

Title II, like Title I, seeks to enforce this prohibition on irrational disability discrimination. But it also seeks to enforce a variety of other basic constitutional guarantees, infringements of which are subject to more searching judicial review. See, *e.g., Dunn v. Blumstein*, 405 U.S. 330, 336–337 (1972); *Shapiro v. Thompson*, 394 U.S. 618, 634 (1969); *Skinner v. Oklahoma ex rel. Williamson*, 316 U.S. 535, 541 (1942). These rights include some, like the right of access to the courts at issue in this case, that are protected by the Due Process Clause of the Fourteenth Amendment. The Due Process Clause and the Confrontation Clause of the Sixth Amendment, as applied to the States via the Fourteenth Amendment, both guarantee to a criminal defendant such as respondent Lane the "right to be present at all stages of the trial where his absence might frustrate the fairness of the proceedings." *Faretta v. California*, 422 U.S. 806, 819, n. 15 (1975). The Due Process Clause also requires the States to afford certain civil litigants a "meaningful opportunity to be heard" by removing obstacles to their full participation in judicial proceedings. *Boddie v. Connecticut*, 401 U.S. 371, 379 (1971); *M.L.B. v. S.L.J.*, 519 U.S. 102 (1996). We have held that the Sixth Amendment guarantees to criminal defendants the right to trial by a jury composed of a fair cross section of the community, noting that the exclusion of "identifiable segments playing major roles in the community cannot be squared with the constitutional concept of jury trial." *Taylor v. Louisiana*, 419 U.S. 522, 530 (1975). And, finally, we have recognized that members of the public have a right of access to criminal proceedings secured by the First Amendment. *Press-Enterprise Co. v. Superior Court of Cal., County of Riverside*, 478 U.S. 1, 8–15 (1986).

Whether Title II validly enforces these constitutional rights is a question that "must be judged with reference to the historical experience which it reflects." *South Carolina v. Katzenbach*, 383 U.S. 301, 308 (1966). See also *Florida Prepaid*, 527 U.S., at 639–640; *Boerne*, 521 U.S., at 530. While § 5 authorizes Congress to enact reasonably prophylactic remedial legislation, the appropriateness of the remedy depends on the gravity of the harm it seeks to prevent. "Difficult and intractable problems often require powerful remedies," *Kimel*, 528 U.S., at 88, but it is also true that "[s]trong measures appropriate to address one harm may be an unwarranted response to another, lesser one," *Boerne*, 521 U.S., at 530.

It is not difficult to perceive the harm that Title II is designed to address. Congress enacted Title II against a backdrop of pervasive unequal treatment in the administration of state services and programs, including systematic deprivations of fundamental rights. For example, "[a]s of 1979, most States ... categorically disqualified 'idiots' from voting, without regard to individual capacity." ... The majority of these laws remain on the books, ... and have been the subject of legal challenge as recently as 2001. ... Similarly, a number of States have prohibited and continue to prohibit persons with disabilities from engaging in activities such as marrying ... and serving as jurors. ... The historical experience that Title II reflects is also documented in this Court's cases, which have identified unconstitutional treatment of disabled persons by state agencies in a variety of settings, including unjustified commitment, *e.g.*, *Jackson v. Indiana*, 406 U.S. 715 (1972); the abuse and neglect of persons committed to state mental health hospitals, *Youngberg v. Romeo*, 457 U.S. 307 (1982); . . . and irrational discrimination in zoning decisions, *Cleburne v. Cleburne Living Center, Inc.*, 473 U.S. 432 (1985). The decisions of other courts, too, document a pattern of unequal treatment in the administration of a wide range of public services, programs, and activities, including the penal system, . . . public education, . . . and voting. Notably, these decisions also demonstrate a pattern of unconstitutional treatment in the administration of justice. . . .

This pattern of disability discrimination persisted despite several federal and state legislative efforts to address it. In the deliberations that led up to the enactment of the ADA, Congress identified important shortcomings in existing laws that rendered them "inadequate to address the pervasive problems of discrimination that people with disabilities are facing." S. Rep. No. 101-116, at 18. See also H. R. Rep. No. 101-485, pt. 2, at 47. . . . It also uncovered further evidence of those shortcomings, in the form of hundreds of examples of unequal treatment of persons with disabilities by States and their political subdivisions. See *Garrett*, 531 U.S., at 379 (BREYER, J., dissenting). See also *id.*, at 391 (App. C to opinion of BREYER, J., dissenting). As the Court's opinion in *Garrett* observed, the "overwhelming majority" of these examples concerned discrimination in the administration of public programs and services. *Id.*, at 371, n. 7 . . . .

With respect to the particular services at issue in this case, Congress learned that many individuals, in many States across the country, were being excluded from courthouses and court proceedings by reason of their disabilities. A report before Congress showed that some 76% of public services and programs housed in state-owned buildings were inaccessible to and unusable by persons with disabilities, even taking into account the possibility that the services and programs might be restructured or relocated to other parts of the buildings. U.S. Commission on Civil Rights, Accommodating the Spectrum of Individual Abilities 39 (1983). Congress itself heard testimony from persons with disabilities who described the physical inaccessibility of local courthouses. Oversight Hearing on H.R. 4498 before the House Subcommittee on Select Education of the Committee on Education and Labor, 100th Cong., 2d Sess., 40–41, 48 (1988). And its appointed task force heard numerous examples of the exclusion of persons with disabilities from state judicial services and programs, including exclusion of persons with visual impairments and hearing impairments from jury service, failure of state and local governments to provide interpretive services for the hearing impaired, failure to permit the testimony of adults with developmental disabilities in abuse cases, and failure to make courtrooms accessible to witnesses with physical disabilities. . . . See also Task Force on the Rights and Empowerment of Americans with Disabilities, From ADA to Empowerment (Oct. 12, 1990). . . .

. . . .

The conclusion that Congress drew from this body of evidence is set forth in the text of the ADA itself: "[D]iscrimination against individuals with disabilities persists in such critical areas as . . . education, transportation, communication, recreation, institutionalization, health services, voting, and *access to public services.*" 42 U.S.C. § 12101(a)(3) (emphasis added). This finding, together with the extensive record of disability discrimination that underlies it, makes clear beyond peradventure that inadequate provision of public services and access to public facilities was an appropriate subject for prophylactic legislation.

V

The only question that remains is whether Title II is an appropriate response to this history and pattern of unequal treatment. At the outset, we must determine the scope of that inquiry. Title II—unlike RFRA, the Patent Remedy Act, and the other statutes we have reviewed for validity under § 5—reaches a wide array of official conduct in an effort to enforce an equally wide array of constitutional guarantees. . . . Whatever might be said about Title II's other applications, the question presented in this case is not whether Congress can validly subject the States to private suits for money damages for failing to provide reasonable access to hockey rinks, or even to voting booths, but whether Congress had the power under § 5 to enforce the constitutional right of access to the courts. Because we find that Title II unquestionably is valid § 5 legislation as it applies to the class of cases implicating the accessibility of judicial services, we need go no further. See *United States v. Raines,* 362 U.S. 17, 26 (1960). . . .

Congress' chosen remedy for the pattern of exclusion and discrimination described above, Title II's requirement of program accessibility, is congruent and proportional to its object of enforcing the right of access to the courts. The unequal treatment of disabled persons in the administration of judicial services has a long history, and has persisted despite several legislative efforts to remedy the problem of disability discrimination. Faced with considerable evidence of the shortcomings of previous legislative responses, Congress was justified in concluding that this "difficult and intractable proble[m]" warranted "added prophylactic measures in response." *Hibbs,* 538 U.S., at 737 (internal quotation marks omitted).

The remedy Congress chose is nevertheless a limited one. Recognizing that failure to accommodate persons with disabilities will often have the same practical effect as outright exclusion, Congress required the States to take reasonable measures to remove architectural and other barriers to accessibility. 42 U.S.C. § 12131(2). But Title II does not require States to employ any and all means to make judicial services accessible to persons with disabilities, and it does not require States to compromise their essential eligibility criteria for public programs. It requires only "reasonable modifications" that would not fundamentally alter the nature of the service provided, and only when the individual seeking modification is otherwise eligible for the service. . . . As Title II's implementing regulations make clear, the reasonable modification requirement can be satisfied in a number of ways. In the case of facilities built or altered after 1992, the regulations require compliance with specific architectural accessibility standards. 28 CFR § 35.151 (2003). But in the case of older facilities, for which structural change is likely to be more difficult, a public entity may comply with Title II by adopting a variety of less costly measures, including relocating services to alternative, accessible sites and assigning aides to assist persons with disabilities in accessing services. § 35.150(b)(1). Only if these measures are ineffective in achieving accessibility is the public entity required to make reasonable structural changes. . . . And in no event is the entity required to undertake measures that would impose an undue financial or administrative burden, threaten historic preservation interests, or effect a fundamental alteration in the nature of the service. §§ 35.150(a)(2), (a)(3).

This duty to accommodate is perfectly consistent with the well-established due process principle that, "within the limits of practicability, a State must afford to all individuals a meaningful opportunity to be heard" in its courts. *Boddie*, 401 U.S., at 379 (internal quotation marks and citation omitted). . . . Our cases have recognized a number of affirmative obligations that flow from this principle: the duty to waive filing fees in certain family-law and criminal cases, . . . the duty to provide transcripts to criminal defendants seeking review of their convictions, . . . and the duty to provide counsel to certain criminal defendants. . . . Each of these cases makes clear that ordinary considerations of cost and convenience alone cannot justify a State's failure to provide individuals with a meaningful right of access to the courts. Judged against this backdrop, Title II's affirmative obligation to accommodate persons with disabilities in the administration of justice cannot be said to be "so out of proportion to a supposed remedial or preventive object that it cannot be understood as responsive to, or designed to prevent, unconstitutional behavior." *Boerne*, 521 U.S., at 532; *Kimel*, 528 U.S., at 86. It is, rather, a reasonable prophylactic measure, reasonably targeted to a legitimate end.

For these reasons, we conclude that Title II, as it applies to the class of cases implicating the fundamental right of access to the courts, constitutes a valid exercise of Congress' § 5 authority to enforce the guarantees of the Fourteenth Amendment. The judgment of the Court of Appeals is therefore affirmed.

It is so ordered.

[Justice Souter filed a concurring opinion, in which Justice Ginsburg joined. In this opinion, Justice Souter writes that the judiciary itself has endorsed the basis for some of the very discrimination subject to congressional remedy under § 5. *Buck v. Bell*, 274 U.S. 200 (1927), was not grudging in sustaining the constitutionality of the once-pervasive practice of involuntarily sterilizing those with mental disabilities. See *id.*, at 207 ("It is better for all the world, if instead of waiting to execute degenerate offspring for crime, or to let them starve for their imbecility, society can prevent those who are manifestly unfit from continuing their kind. . . . Three generations of imbeciles are enough"). Laws compelling sterilization were often accompanied by others indiscriminately requiring institutionalization, and prohibiting certain individuals with disabilities from marrying, from voting, from attending public schools, and even from appearing in public. One administrative action along these lines was judicially sustained in part as a justified precaution against the very sight of a child with cerebral palsy, lest he "produc[e] a depressing and nauseating effect" upon others. *State ex rel. Beattie v. Board of Ed. of Antigo*, 169 Wis. 231, 232 (1919) (approving his exclusion from public school). "In sustaining the application of Title II today, the Court takes a welcome step away from the judiciary's prior endorsement of blunt instruments imposing legal handicaps."]

[Justice Ginsburg filed a concurring opinion, in which Justices Souter and Breyer joined. In this opinion, Justice Ginsburg writes that The Americans with Disabilities Act of 1990 is a measure expected to advance equal-citizenship stature for persons with disabilities by the elimination or reduction of physical and social structures that impede people with some present, past, or perceived impairments from contributing, according to their talents, to our Nation's social, economic, and civic life.]

[Chief Justice Rehnquist filed a dissenting opinion, in which Justices Kennedy and Thomas joined. Justice Scalia and Justice Thomas filed dissenting opinions. These opinions are omitted here.]

## *Questions for Consideration*

1) *Should* Congress have the power to override, the states' immunity from suit and authorize Title II plaintiffs to seek damages from the states?

2) Why treat claims under Title II differently than claims under Title I, as was the claim in *Garrett*?

3) What would have been the effect on Title II of the ADA if the Court had held, instead, that Title II does not validly abrogate the states' sovereign immunity? Would such a holding have rendered Title II ineffective?

## *Takeaway*

- Recognizing congressional power to override the states' sovereign immunity in enacting Title II has had significant implications for people with disabilities. Title II covers essentially all activities of state and local governments — statutes, administrative regulations, and day-to-day decisions by state officials.

- In *Lane*, the Court recognizes that the states have frequently discriminated against people with disabilities by denying access to facilities and excluding people with disabilities from government programs and services.

# C. A State Law Example

In addition to federal laws related to disability, the various states also have statutes and regulations relating to land use issues and disability. As one example, consider the Padavan Law in New York, section 41.34 of the New York Mental Hygiene Law. This law establishes the procedural process and the substantive guidelines for permitting group homes for people with disabilities (up to fourteen people) to be established in communities. Under the statute, notice is given to a municipality of the plan to locate a group home within its jurisdiction. The municipality can accept the site recommended for the group home; can suggest one or more alternative and suitable sites for the location; or object to the establishment of the group home because it would result in an over-concentration of community residential group home facilities in the municipality or in the area. Basically, the case law suggests that it is difficult to prevent a group home from locating in an area. To block a group home from locating at a particular site, one would have to show that its presence would substantially alter the nature and character of the area. This is typically, but not exclusively, demonstrated by showing that the addition of this group home will result in an over-concentration of group homes in the area. To accomplish this, one must also establish the relevant area or neighborhood to be considered.

The purpose behind the Padavan Law is one of dealing with the "Not in My Backyard" or NIMBY attitude of many property owners. Many property owners in single-family residential housing zones do not want group homes located in their neighborhood. This feeling is often intensified when the residents of the group home will be people with disabilities. The Padavan Law seeks to make it easier for group homes to be located in communities by making it more difficult for local property owners to use the local zoning process to exclude group homes. In this way, state law seeks to provide individuals with disabilities a right to live inclusively in regular community settings.

# D. Practice Problems

1.1 Our client, Natural Homes, Inc., is a national homebuilder from out of state. Natural Homes is proposing a new housing project in our city, and this will be its first project in our state. Natural Homes seeks to build residential apartments with a design featuring a single front landing made of concrete that will serve the front entranceways of two apartment units. From the landing, there will be two steps up to the threshold of the doorway to each of the apartments. A sidewalk from the parking lot will connect each landing with the other apartment units in the building. Altogether, there will be six buildings, and each building will have six apartments. In order to keep a traditional two-step design at the front of the building, Natural Homes plans to have sidewalks that extend to the rear of the buildings and will locate wheel chair accessible access in the back of each apartment.

Natural Homes has asked us to answer three questions. First, does our local zoning code include any specific provisions requiring compliance with the ADA, and if so, identify them and explain the requirements. Second, does the ADA apply to a shared landing platform at the entrance to two separate residential apartments? Third, is it okay to have the wheelchair accessible access in the back of the building rather than at the front? As a starting point, see *United States v. Edward Rose & Sons*, 384 F.3d 258 (6th Cir. 2004).

a) Assume you are a summer law clerk in the firm. Prepare a memo to the partner responding to these questions.

b) Assume you are a mid-level associate in the firm and you are the attorney in charge of this client. How might you change or modify the memo from part "a" above, if you are instead writing a letter directly to the client?

1.2 Most communities have a written comprehensive plan describing the goals, objectives, needs, and plans for the community in terms of short-term and long-term goals. As will be addressed later in this book, zoning is done pursuant to a comprehensive plan; thus, the plan is important. Generally, the comprehensive plan as well as the zoning code are available on the local government web pages. Go to the web pages for the local government where you are located or to the web pages of a nearby city and find a copy of the comprehensive plan.

a) Assume you are a summer law clerk. Prepare a memo for the attorney you work for identifying the contents of the local comprehensive plan with respect to the following:

i. Information on the age demographics of the local population, and the provisions for assuring adequate and affordable housing for senior citizens seeking to age in place in their local community.

ii. Elements relating to accessibility of pathways, sidewalks, and buildings for people with disabilities.

iii. Elements related to accessible and affordable public transportation for the elderly and for people with disabilities.

iv. Information on how plans for accessibility and aging in place will be financed.

v. To the extent that these elements are not present in the comprehensive plan, point this out in your memo and provide your thoughts as to the omissions.

1.3 Assume the local government in the community where you are located is unclear about ADA requirements for sidewalks. In particular, as they plan for the addition of a number of new sidewalks and pathways in coming years, they are concerned about compliance with curb cut ramping requirements. Here is the URL address of the United States Access Board with guidelines applicable to this issue: https://www.access-board.gov/guidelines-and-standards/buildings-and-sites/about-the-ada-standards/guide-to-the-ada-standards/chapter-4-ramps-and-curb-ramps.

a) Prepare a PowerPoint presentation for the local government explaining, in simple terms, the requirements for curb cuts and ramping as set out by the United States Access Board.

b) On your own or together with a partner, select an area of your local community and see if you can determine if the curb cuts and ramping comply with the requirements. Feel free to take photographic evidence of what you find. Include your on-the-ground findings in your PowerPoint presentation.

# Chapter 2

# Prelude to Modern Zoning

## A. Introduction

To appreciate modern zoning law, one must have a basic understanding of property. Traditionally, property ownership was said to be *cujus est solum, eius est usque ad coelum et ad inferos*, meaning that property ownership included rights to the center of the earth as well as to the heights of the heavens. Thus, a property owner held subsurface, surface, and air rights for a specifically identified geographic location. These rights, under the common law, could be held in a variety of ways; and ownership of property included: 1) a right to the use and possession of the property; 2) a right to exclude others from the property; 3) a right to transfer the property; and, 4) a right to the profit attributable to ownership of the property (such as equity appreciation of real property). During the 18th and 19th centuries, many Americans held a strong belief in the protection of private property, coupled with a belief that the government generally should not restrict what people may do with their property. Private property was considered an important element of freedom. The Fifth Amendment to the U.S. Constitution affirms the importance of property with the following language:

> *No person shall . . . be deprived of life, liberty, or property, without due process of law; nor shall private property be taken for public use, without just compensation.*

Although the meaning of this language has been a matter of continuous litigation over the years, it expresses the importance of property in our constitutional framework.

Historically, property owners are generally the more wealthy members of society, and no matter how large or small one's property holdings are, it is popular to speak of such ownership in terms of sovereignty. Thus, people might say, "My home is my castle, and I am the king or queen of my castle." Although this is not literally true, it has great power as a metaphor in expressing a common belief about one's rights in property. It expresses a sense of control and of authority over place and space. In a world of competing claims to resources, the castle metaphor functions as an assertion of sovereignty. This same sense of sovereignty is readily observed when we hear parents tell their children that while the children are in the home of the parents, they must obey the parents' rules. This castle mentality raises tension with the idea that one's property is subject to regulation and control by someone else or by the government. The main idea behind the metaphor is that no one, including the government, should be able to tell a person what to do with her own property. Traditionally, this view was coupled with an understanding that one must make a *lawful* use of property — meaning that one's use of property should cause no harm to others.

As one can imagine, the early common law had difficulty determining when a use caused harm to another. Ideas about externalities, spillover effects, and interconnected ecosystems were not well developed, and the scientific tools and technology for demonstrating harm were not what they are today. The primary legal tools available to address harms under the common law were generally limited to nuisance and trespass. This is where we start the study of planning and zoning law.

# B. Nuisance and Trespass

Nuisance law protects a property owner's right to the quiet and peaceful enjoyment of her land. A nuisance disrupts this quiet and peaceful enjoyment, and depending on the nature of the nuisance-based activity and the extent of the disruption it causes, it might be either a private or a public nuisance. Trespass involves an invasion of a person's property. Early cases typically involved some type of physical invasion, but more difficult legal issues arose with efforts to control the invasion of unwanted sounds, lights, and other less obvious types of "invasions." These various "invasions" might also involve a nuisance. Early common law cases often struggled to regulate land uses by trying to manipulate the traditional causes of action in nuisance and trespass.

### Hadacheck v. Sebastian

Supreme Court of the United States
239 U.S. 394 (1915)

MCKENNA, Justice. . . . Plaintiff in error, to whom we shall refer as petitioner, was convicted of a misdemeanor for the violation of an ordinance of the city of Los Angeles which makes it unlawful for any person to establish or operate a brick yard or brick kiln, or any establishment, factory, or place for the manufacture or burning of brick within described limits in the city

. . . .

The petition sets forth . . . that petitioner is the owner of a tract of land within the limits described in the ordinance, upon which tract of land there is a very valuable bed of clay, of great value for the manufacture of brick of a fine quality, worth to him not less than $100,000 per acre, or about $800,000 for the entire tract for brickmaking purposes, and not exceeding $60,000 for residential purposes, or for any purpose other than the manufacture of brick. That he has made excavations of considerable depth and covering a very large area of the property, and that on account thereof the land cannot be utilized for residential purposes or any purpose other than that for which it is now used. That he purchased the land because of such bed of clay and for the purpose of manufacturing brick; that it was, at the time of purchase, outside of the limits of the city, and distant from dwellings and other habitations, and that he did not expect or believe, nor did other owners of property in the vicinity expect or believe, that the territory would be annexed to the city. That he has erected expensive machinery for the manufacture of bricks of fine quality which have been and are being used for building purposes in and about the city.

That if the ordinance be declared valid, he will be compelled to entirely abandon his business and will be deprived of the use of his property.

That the manufacture of brick must necessarily be carried on where suitable clay is found, and the clay cannot be transported to some other location; and, besides, the clay upon his property is particularly fine, and clay of as good quality cannot be found in any other place within the city where the same can be utilized for the manufacture of brick. That within the prohibited district there is one other brickyard besides that of plaintiff in error.

That there is no reason for the prohibition of the business; that its maintenance cannot be and is not in the nature of a nuisance as defined in § 3479 of the Civil Code of the state, and cannot be dangerous or detrimental to health or the morals or safety or peace or welfare or convenience of the people of the district or city.

That the business is so conducted as not to be in any way or degree a nuisance; no noises arise therefrom, and no noxious odors, and that by the use of certain means (which are described) provided and the situation of the brickyard an extremely small amount of smoke is emitted from any kiln, and what is emitted is so dissipated that it is not a nuisance nor in any manner detrimental to health or comfort. That during the seven years which the brickyard has been conducted no complaint has been made of it, and no attempt has ever been made to regulate it.

That the city embraces 107.62 square miles in area and 75 per cent of it is devoted to residential purposes; that the district described in the ordinance includes only about 3 square miles, is sparsely settled, and contains large tracts of unsubdivided and unoccupied land; and that the boundaries of the district were determined for the sole and specific purpose of prohibiting and suppressing the business of petitioner and that of the other brickyard.

That there are and were, at the time of the adoption of the ordinance, in other districts of the city thickly built up with residences brickyards maintained more detrimental to the inhabitants of the city. That a petition was filed, signed by several hundred persons, representing such brickyards to be a nuisance, and no ordinance or regulation was passed in regard to such petition, and the brickyards are operated without hindrance or molestation. That other brickyards are permitted to be maintained without prohibition or regulation.

That no ordinance or regulation of any kind has been passed at any time regulating or attempting to regulate brickyards, or inquiry made whether they could be maintained without being a nuisance or detrimental to health.

That the ordinance does not state a public offense, and is in violation of the Constitution of the state and the 14th Amendment to the Constitution of the United States.

That the business of petitioner is a lawful one, none of the materials used in it are combustible, the machinery is of the most approved pattern, and its conduct will not create a nuisance.

There is an allegation that the ordinance, if enforced, fosters and will foster a monopoly, and protects and will protect other persons engaged in the manufacture of brick in the city, and discriminates and will discriminate against petitioner in favor of such other persons, who are his competitors, and will prevent him from entering into competition with them.

The petition, after almost every paragraph, charges a deprivation of property, the taking of property without compensation, and that the ordinance is in consequence invalid.

We have given this outline of the petition, as it presents petitioner's contentions, with the circumstances (which we deem most material) that give color and emphasis to them.

But there are substantial traverses made by the return to the writ, among others, a denial of the charge that the ordinance was arbitrarily directed against the business of petitioner, and it is alleged that there is another district in which brickyards are prohibited.

There was a denial of the allegations that the brickyard was conducted or could be conducted sanitarily, or was not offensive to health. And there were affidavits supporting the denials. In these it was alleged that the fumes, gases, smoke, soot, steam, and dust arising from petitioner's brickmaking plant have from time to time caused sickness and serious discomfort to those living in the vicinity.

There was no specific denial of the value of the property, or that it contained deposits of clay, or that the latter could not be removed and manufactured into brick elsewhere. There was, however, a general denial that the enforcement of the ordinance would "entirely deprive petitioner of his property and the use thereof."

How the supreme court dealt with the allegations, denials, and affidavits we can gather from its opinion. The court said, through Mr. Justice Sloss, 165 California, p. 416: "The district to which the prohibition was applied contains about 3 square miles. The petitioner is the owner of a tract of land, containing 8 acres, more or less, within the district described in the ordinance. He acquired his land in 1902, before the territory to which the ordinance was directed had been annexed to the city of Los Angeles. His land contains valuable deposits of clay suitable for the manufacture of brick, and he has, during the entire period of his ownership, used the land for brickmaking, and has erected thereon kilns, machinery, and buildings necessary for such manufacture. The land, as he alleges, is far more valuable for brickmaking than for any other purpose."

The court considered the business one which could be regulated, and that regulation was not precluded by the fact "that the value of investments made in the business prior to any legislative action will be greatly diminished," and that no complaint could be based upon the fact that petitioner had been carrying on the trade in that locality for a long period.

And, considering the allegations of the petition, the denials of the return, and the evidence of the affidavits, the court said that the latter tended to show that the district created has become primarily a residential section, and that the occupants of the neighboring dwellings are seriously incommoded by the operations of petitioner; and that such evidence, "when taken in connection with the presumptions in favor of the propriety of the legislative determination, is certainly sufficient to overcome any contention that the prohibition [of the ordinance] was a mere arbitrary invasion of private right, not supported by any tenable belief that the continuance of the business . . . was so detrimental to the interests of others as to require suppression."

The court, on the evidence, rejected the contention that the ordinance was not in good faith enacted as a police measure; and that it was intended to discriminate against petitioner, or that it was actuated by any motive of injuring him as an individual.

The charge of discrimination between localities was not sustained. The court expressed the view that the determination of prohibition was for the legislature, and that the court, without regard to the fact shown in the return that there was another district in which brickmaking was prohibited, could not sustain the claim that the ordinance was not enacted in good faith, but was designed to discriminate against petitioner and the other brickyard within the district. "The facts before us," the court finally said, "would certainly not justify the conclusion that the ordinance here in question was designed, in either its adoption or its enforcement, to be anything but what it purported to be; viz., a legitimate regulation, operating alike upon all who come within its terms."

We think the conclusion of the court is justified by the evidence and makes it unnecessary to review the many cases cited by petitioner in which it is decided that the police power of a state cannot be arbitrarily exercised. The principle is familiar, but in any given case it must plainly appear to apply. It is to be remembered that we are dealing with one of the most essential powers of government, one that is the least limitable. It may, indeed, seem harsh in its exercise, usually is on some individual, but the imperative necessity for its existence precludes any limitation upon it when not exerted arbitrarily. A vested interest cannot be asserted against it because of conditions once obtaining. *Chicago & A.R. Co. v. Tranbarger*, 238 U.S. 67, 78 [(1915)]. To so hold would preclude development and fix a city forever in its primitive conditions. There must be progress, and if in its march private interests are in the way, they must yield to the good of the community. The logical result of petitioner's contention would seem to be that a city could not be formed or enlarged against the resistance of an occupant of the ground, and that if it grows at all it can only grow as the environment of the occupations that are usually banished to the purlieus.

The police power and to what extent it may be exerted we have recently illustrated in *Reinman v. Little Rock*, 237 U.S. 171 [(1915)]. The circumstances of the case were very much like those of the case at bar, and give reply to the contentions of petitioner, especially that which asserts that a necessary and lawful occupation that is not a nuisance *per se* cannot be made so by legislative declaration. There was a like investment in property, encouraged by the then conditions; a like reduction of value and deprivation of property was asserted against the validity of the ordinance there considered; a like assertion of an arbitrary exercise of the power of prohibition. Against all of these contentions, and causing the rejection of them all, was adduced the police power. There was a prohibition of a business, lawful in itself, there as here. It was a livery stable there; a brickyard here. They differ in particulars, but they are alike in that which cause and justify prohibition in defined localities — that is, the effect upon the health and comfort of the community.

The ordinance passed upon prohibited the conduct of the business within a certain defined area in Little Rock, Arkansas. This court said of it: granting that the business was not a nuisance *per se*, it was clearly within the police power of the state to regulate it, "and to that end to declare that in particular circumstances and in particular localities a livery stable shall be deemed a nuisance in fact and in law." And the only limitation upon the power was stated to be that the power could not be exerted arbitrarily or with unjust discrimination. There was a citation of cases. We think the present case is within the ruling thus declared.

There is a distinction between *Reinman v. Little Rock* and the case at bar. There a particular business was prohibited which was not affixed to or dependent upon its locality; it could be conducted elsewhere. Here, it is contended, the latter condition does not exist, and it is alleged that the manufacture of brick must necessarily be carried on where suitable clay is found, and that the clay on petitioner's property cannot be transported to some other locality. This is not urged as a physical impossibility, but only, counsel say, that such transportation and the transportation of the bricks to places where they could be used in construction work would be prohibitive "from a financial standpoint." But upon the evidence the supreme court considered the case, as we understand its opinion, from the standpoint of the offensive effects of the operation of a brickyard, and not from the deprivation of the deposits of clay, and distinguished *Ex parte Kelso*, 147 California, 609 [(1905)], wherein the court declared invalid an ordinance absolutely prohibiting the maintenance or operation of a rock or stone quarry within a certain portion of the city and county of San Francisco. The court there said that the effect of the ordinance was "to absolutely deprive the owners of real property within such limits of a valuable right incident to their ownership, viz., the right to extract therefrom such rock and stone as they may find it to their advantage to dispose of." The court expressed the view that the removal could be regulated, but that "an absolute prohibition of such removal under the circumstances" could not be upheld.

In the present case there is no prohibition of the removal of the brick clay; only a prohibition within the designated locality of its manufacture into bricks. And to this feature of the ordinance our opinion is addressed. Whether other questions would arise if the ordinance were broader, and opinion on such questions, we reserve.

Petitioner invokes the equal protection clause of the Constitution and charges that it is violated in that the ordinance (1) "prohibits him from manufacturing brick upon his property while his competitors are permitted, without regulation of any kind, to manufacture brick upon property situated in all respects similarly to that of plaintiff in error"; and (2) that it "prohibits the conduct of his business while it permits the maintenance within the same district of any other kind of business, no matter how objectionable the same may be, either in its nature or in the manner in which it is conducted."

If we should grant that the first specification shows a violation of classification, that is, a distinction between businesses which was not within the legislative power, petitioner's contention encounters the objection that it depends upon an inquiry of fact which the record does not enable us to determine. It is alleged in the return to the petition that brickmaking is prohibited in one other district, and an ordinance is referred to regulating business in other districts. To this plaintiff in error replied that the ordinance attempts to prohibit the operation of certain businesses having mechanical power, and does not prohibit the maintenance of any business or the operation of any machine that is operated by animal power. In other words, petitioner makes his contention depend upon disputable considerations of classification and upon a comparison of conditions of which there is no means of judicial determination, and upon which, nevertheless, we are expected to reverse legislative action exercised upon matters of which the city has control.

To a certain extent the latter comment may be applied to other contentions; and, besides, there is no allegation or proof of other objectionable businesses being permitted within the district, and a speculation of their establishment or conduct at some future time is too remote.

In his petition and argument something is made of the ordinance as fostering a monopoly and suppressing his competition with other brickmakers. The charge and argument are too illusive. It is part of the charge that the ordinance was directed against him. The charge, we have seen, was rejected by the supreme court, and we find nothing to justify it.

It may be that brickyards in other localities within the city where the same conditions exist are not regulated or prohibited, but it does not follow that they will not be. That petitioner's business was first in time to be prohibited does not make its prohibition unlawful. And it may be, as said by the supreme court of the state, that the conditions justify a distinction. However, the inquiries thus suggested are outside of our province.

There are other and subsidiary contentions which, we think, do not require discussion. They are disposed of by what we have said. It may be that something else than prohibition would have satisfied the conditions. Of this, however, we have no means of determining, and besides, we cannot declare invalid the exertion of a power which the city undoubtedly has because of a charge that it does not exactly accommodate the conditions, or that some other exercise would have been better or less harsh. We must accord good faith to the city in the absence of a clear showing to the contrary and an honest exercise of judgment upon the circumstances which induced its action.

We do not notice the contention that the ordinance is not within the city's charter powers, nor that it is in violation of the state constitution, such contentions raising only local questions which must be deemed to have been decided adversely to petitioner by the supreme court of the state.

*Judgment affirmed.*

## *Questions for Consideration*

1) Although the government may use the police power to control nuisances, why should the government never have to pay just compensation for doing so?

2) In *Spur Industries, Inc. v. Del E. Webb Development Co.*, 494 P.2d 700 (Ariz. 1972), the court enjoined a feedlot from continuing its lawful operations when it became a nuisance only because a developer brought residences into the area, but noted that fairness requires the developer to indemnify the feedlot for losses caused by the injunction. Here, to be fair, *should* the City of Los Angeles have had to "indemnify" Hadacheck for losses as a result of the zoning ordinance making previously lawful operations unlawful?

3) Who defines what is and is not a nuisance? In *Lucas v. South Carolina Coastal Council*, 505 U.S. 1003 (1992), the Court clarified that the nuisance exception to the regulatory takings doctrine is limited to common law nuisances. Do you see why only common law nuisances are exempt?

## *Takeaway*

• The police power is one of the most essential powers of government, not to be limited by the fact that the use sought to be controlled was at one time harmless because it was in an undeveloped area — an area that later became developed.

• Landowners do not have a legally protected right to engage in a nuisance.

• Zoning laws may regulate nuisances — that is, a nuisance exception to regulatory takings doctrine is that there is no regulatory taking when the ordinance restricts uses that amount to nuisance.

• So long as the use controlled by an ordinance can reasonably be regarded as a nuisance — detrimental to the health and comfort of the community — it can be regulated.

## Discussion Problem 2.1

Oscar owns a 38-acre tract within the Town of Westerly on which he had been mining sand and gravel continuously for more than 40 years. During his first year of operations, the excavation reached the water table, leaving a water-filled crater which had since been widened and deepened until it became a 20-acre lake with an average depth of 25 feet, around which Westerly had expanded until, within a radius of 3,500 feet, there were more than 2,200 homes and four public schools with a combined enrollment of 4,500 pupils. Last year, as a safety measure, Westerly amended its ordinance regulating such excavations so as to prohibit any excavating below the water table. Then, Westerly brought an action against Oscar to enjoin further mining on the grounds that he had not complied with the ordinance. Oscar defends that the ordinance is unconstitutional because it was not regulating his business, but instead completely prohibitory, and confiscated his property without compensation because the ordinance prohibits the beneficial use to which Oscar's property had previously been devoted. Who shall prevail in this dispute?

## Bove v. Donner-Hanna Coke Corp.

Supreme Court of New York, Appellate Division, Fourth Department
258 N.Y.S. 229 (N.Y. App. Div. 1932)

EDGCOMB, Judge. The question involved upon this appeal is whether the use to which the defendant has recently put its property constitutes a private nuisance, which a court of equity should abate.

In 1910 plaintiff purchased two vacant lots at the corner of Abby and Baraga streets in the city of Buffalo, and two years later built a house thereon. The front of the building was converted into a grocery store, and plaintiff occupied the rear as a dwelling. She rented the two apartments on the second floor.

Defendant operates a large coke oven on the opposite side of Abby street. The plant runs twenty-four hours in the day, and three hundred and sixty-five days in the year. Of necessity, the operation has to be continuous, because the ovens would be ruined if they were allowed to cool off. The coke is heated to a temperature of around 2,000 degrees F., and is taken out of the ovens and run under a "quencher," where 500 or 600 gallons of water are poured onto it at one time. This is a necessary operation in the manufacture of coke. The result is a tremendous cloud of steam, which rises in a shaft and escapes into the air, carrying with it minute portions of coke, and more or less gas. This steam and the accompanying particles of dirt, as well as the dust which comes from a huge coal pile necessarily kept on the premises, and the gases and odors which emanate from the plant, are carried by the wind in various directions, and frequently find their way onto the plaintiff's premises and into her house and store. According to the plaintiff this results in an unusual amount of dirt and soot accumulating in her house, and prevents her opening the windows on the street side; she also claims that she suffers severe headaches by breathing the impure air occasioned by this dust and these offensive odors, and that her health and that of her family has been impaired, all to her very great discomfort and annoyance; she also asserts that this condition has lessened the rental value of her property, and has made it impossible at times to rent her apartments.

Claiming that such use of its plant by the defendant deprives her of the full enjoyment of her home, invades her property rights, and constitutes a private nuisance, plaintiff brings this action in equity to enjoin the defendant from the further maintenance of said nuisance, and to recover the damages which she asserts she has already sustained.

As a general rule, an owner is at liberty to use his property as he sees fit, without objection or interference from his neighbor, provided such use does not violate an ordinance or statute. There is, however, a limitation to this rule; one made necessary by the intricate, complex and changing life of to-day. The old and familiar maxim that one must so use his property as not to injure that of another (*sic utere tuo ut alienum non loedas*) is deeply imbedded in our law. An owner will not be permitted to make an unreasonable use of his premises to the material annoyance of his neighbor if the latter's enjoyment of life or property is materially lessened thereby. This principle is aptly stated by Andrews, Ch. J., in *Booth v. R., W. & O.T.R.R. Co.* (140 N.Y. 267, 274) as follows: "The general rule that no one has absolute freedom in the use of his property, but is restrained by the co-existence of equal rights in his neighbor to the use of his property, so that each in exercising his right must do no act which causes injury to his neighbor, is so well understood, is so universally recognized, and stands so impregnably in the necessities of the social state, that its vindication by argument would be superfluous. The maxim which embodies it is sometimes loosely interpreted as forbidding all use by one of his own property, which annoys or disturbs his neighbor in the enjoyment of his property. The real meaning of the rule is that one may not use his own property to the injury of any legal right of another."

Such a rule is imperative, or life today in our congested centers would be intolerable and unbearable. If a citizen was given no protection against unjust harassment arising from the use to which the property of his neighbor was put, the comfort and value of his home could easily be destroyed by any one who chose to erect an annoyance nearby, and no one would be safe, unless he was rich enough to buy sufficient land about his home to render such disturbance impossible. When conflicting rights arise, a general rule must be worked out which, so far as possible, will preserve to each party that to which he has a just claim.

While the law will not permit a person to be driven from his home, or to be compelled to live in it in positive distress or discomfort because of the use to which other property nearby has been put, it is not every annoyance connected with business which will be enjoined. Many a loss arises from acts or conditions which do not create a ground for legal redress. *Damnum absque injuria* is a familiar maxim. Factories, stores and mercantile establishments are essential to the prosperity of the nation. They necessarily invade our cities, and interfere more or less with the peace and tranquillity [sic] of the neighborhood in which they are located.

One who chooses to live in the large centers of population cannot expect the quiet of the country. Congested centers are seldom free from smoke, odors and other pollution from houses, shops and factories, and one who moves into such a region cannot hope to find the pure air of the village or outlying district. A person who prefers the advantages of community life must expect to experience some of the resulting inconveniences. Residents of industrial centers must endure without redress a certain amount of annoyance and discomfiture which is incident to life in such a locality. Such inconvenience is of minor importance compared with the general good of the community.

Whether the particular use to which one puts his property constitutes a nuisance or not is generally a question of fact, and depends upon whether such use is reasonable under all the surrounding circumstances. What would distress and annoy one person would have little or no effect upon another; what would be deemed a disturbance and a torment in one locality would be unnoticed in some other place; a condition which would cause little or no vexation in a business, manufacturing or industrial district might be extremely tantalizing [sic] to those living in a restricted and beautiful residential zone; what would be unreasonable under one set of circumstances would be deemed fair and just under another. Each case is unique. No hard and fast rule can be laid down which will apply in all instances.

The inconvenience, if such it be, must not be fanciful, slight or theoretical, but certain and substantial, and must interfere with the physical comfort of the ordinarily reasonable person.

Applying these general rules to the facts before us, it is apparent that defendant's plant is not a nuisance per se, and that the court was amply justified in holding that it had not become one by reason of the manner in which it had been conducted. Any annoyance to plaintiff is due to the nature of the business which the defendant conducts, and not to any defect in the mill, machinery or apparatus. The plant is modern and up to date in every particular. It was built under a contract with the Federal government, the details of which are not important here. The plans were drawn by the Kopperas Construction Company, one of the largest and best known manufacturers of coke plants in the world, and the work was done under the supervision of the War Department. No reasonable change or improvement in the property can be made which will eliminate any of the things complained of. If coke is made, coal must be used. Gas always follows the burning of coal, and steam is occasioned by throwing cold water on red hot coals.

The cases are legion in this and other States where a defendant has been held guilty of maintaining a nuisance because of the annoyance which he has caused his neighbor by reason of noise, smoke, dust, noxious gases and disagreeable smells which have emanated from his property. But smoke and noisome odors do not always constitute a nuisance. I find none of these cases controlling here; they all differ in some particular from the facts in the case at bar.

It is true that the appellant was a resident of this locality for several years before the defendant came on the scene of action, and that, when the plaintiff built her house, the land on which these coke ovens now stand was a hickory grove. But in a growing community changes are inevitable. This region was never fitted for a residential district; for years it has been peculiarly adapted for factory sites. This was apparent when plaintiff bought her lots and when she built her house. The land is low and lies adjacent to the Buffalo river, a navigable stream connecting with Lake Erie. Seven different railroads run through this area. Freight tracks and yards can be seen in every direction. Railroads naturally follow the low levels in passing through a city. Cheap transportation is an attraction which always draws factories and industrial plants to a locality. It is common knowledge that a combination of rail and water terminal facilities will stamp a section as a site suitable for industries of the heavier type, rather than for residential purposes. In 1910 there were at least eight industrial plants, with a total assessed valuation of over a million dollars, within a radius of a mile from plaintiff's house.

With all the dirt, smoke and gas which necessarily come from factory chimneys, trains and boats, and with full knowledge that this region was especially adapted for industrial rather than residential purposes, and that factories would increase in the future, plaintiff selected this locality as the site of her future home. She voluntarily moved into this district, fully aware of the fact that the atmosphere would constantly be contaminated by dirt, gas and foul odors; and that she could not hope to find in this locality the pure air of a strictly residential zone. She evidently saw certain advantages in living in this congested center. This is not the case of an industry, with its attendant noise and dirt, invading a quiet, residential district. It is just the opposite. Here a residence is built in an area naturally adapted for industrial purposes and already dedicated to that use. Plaintiff can hardly be heard to complain at this late date that her peace and comfort have been disturbed by a situation which existed, to some extent at least, at the very time she bought her property, and which condition she must have known would grow worse rather than better as the years went by.

Today there are twenty industrial plants within a radius of less than a mile and three-quarters from appellant's house, with more than sixty-five smokestacks rising in the air, and belching forth clouds of smoke; every day there are 148 passenger trains, and 225 freight trains, to say nothing of switch engines, passing over these various railroad tracks near to the plaintiff's property; over 10,000 boats, a large portion of which burn soft coal, pass up and down the Buffalo river every season. Across the street, and within 300 feet from plaintiff's house, is a large tank of the Iroquois Gas Company which is used for the storage of gas.

The utter abandonment of this locality for residential purposes, and its universal use as an industrial center, becomes manifest when one considers that in 1929 the assessed valuation of the twenty industrial plants above referred to aggregated over $20,000,000, and that the city in 1925 passed a zoning ordinance putting this area in the third industrial district, a zone in which stockyards, glue factories, coke ovens, steel furnaces, rolling mills and other similar enterprises were permitted to be located.

One has only to mention these facts to visualize the condition of the atmosphere in this locality. It is quite easy to imagine that many of the things of which the plaintiff complains are due to causes over which the defendant has no control. At any rate, if appellant is immune from the annoyance occasioned by the smoke and odor which must necessarily come from these various sources, it would hardly seem that she could consistently claim that her health has been impaired, and that the use and enjoyment of her home have been seriously interfered with solely because of the dirt, gas and stench which have reached her from defendant's plant.

It is very true that the law is no respecter of persons, and that the most humble citizen in the land is entitled to identically the same protection accorded to the master of the most gorgeous palace. However, the fact that the plaintiff has voluntarily chosen to live in the smoke and turmoil of this industrial zone is some evidence, at least, that any annoyance which she has suffered from the dirt, gas and odor which have emanated from defendant's plant is more imaginary and theoretical than it is real and substantial.

I think that the trial court was amply justified in refusing to interfere with the operation of the defendant's coke ovens. No consideration of public policy or private rights demands any such sacrifice of this industry.

Plaintiff is not entitled to the relief which she seeks for another reason.

Subdivision 25 of section 20 of the General City Law (added by Laws of 1917, chap. 483) gives to the cities of this State authority to regulate the location of industries and to district the city for that purpose. Pursuant to such authority the common council of the city of Buffalo adopted an ordinance setting aside the particular area in which defendant's plant is situated as a zone in which coke ovens might lawfully be located.

After years of study and agitation it has been found that development in conformity with some well-considered and comprehensive plan is necessary to the welfare of any growing municipality. The larger the community the greater becomes the need of such plan. Haphazard city building is ruinous to any city. Certain areas must be given over to industry, without which the country cannot long exist. Other sections must be kept free from the intrusion of trade and the distraction of business, and be set aside for homes, where one may live in a wholesome environment. Property owners, as well as the public, have come to recognize the absolute necessity of reasonable regulations of this character in the interest of public health, safety and general welfare, as well as for the conservation of property values. Such is the purpose of our zoning laws.

After due consideration the common council of Buffalo decreed that an enterprise similar to that carried on by the defendant might properly be located at the site of this particular coke oven. It is not for the court to step in and override such decision, and condemn as a nuisance a business which is being conducted in an approved and expert manner, at the very spot where the council said that it might be located. A court of equity will not ordinarily assume to set itself above officials to whom the law commits a decision, and reverse their discretion and judgment, unless bad faith is involved. No such charge is made here.

Other defenses have been urged by the defendant, which it is unnecessary to discuss, in view of the conclusion which has already been reached.

I see no good reason why the decision of the Special Term should be disturbed. I think that the judgment appealed from should be affirmed.

## *Questions for Consideration*

1) What are the requirements of a nuisance action? Does the *Bove* case involve an action to abate a public or a private nuisance? What is the difference, in terms of enforcement, between a public and a private nuisance?

2) Bove was first in time with respect to her ownership of the property, and the nuisance arose afterwards. How did the court deal with the first-in-time issue? How does being first in time affect a property owner's reasonable expectations?

3) When did the city of Buffalo establish a zoning district permitting the industrial uses complained of by Bove? Should this timing influence the decision in the case?

4) Should property owners be required to anticipate future uses of surrounding land? If so, to what degree?

## *Takeaway*

- Two common ways of dealing with a nuisance include an injunction to abate the use, and the awarding of damages to the affected party for damages while permitting the offending use to continue. When the option to pay damages is selected, it is important to consider the "first in time rule" of general property law. If the nuisance comes to you (you were there first), damages might be sufficient to compensate for a diminution in value. On the other hand, if the complained about use was there first, it can be argued that the price of surrounding property already reflects a discount due to the undesirable aspects of the use. In the *Bove* case, even though Bove was there first, the court takes time to explain that she should have anticipated future growth and industrialization. Since industrialization was obvious, the price of the property would already reflect this use and be discounted from what it might otherwise be worth. In a sense, therefore, Bove was already compensated.

# Amphitheaters, Inc. v. Portland Meadows

Supreme Court of Oregon
198 P.2d 847 (Or. 1948)

BRAND, Justice. At the trial, evidence to the following effect was introduced. During the summer of 1945 the defendant commenced arrangements for the purchase of land and the construction thereon of a one-mile race track. On 25 August, 1945, an option for the purchase of 21 acres of the required land was secured from H.M. Seivert who is one of the promoters of the theater project and is the owner of the land on which the theater is situated. On 15 October, 1945, defendant applied for a license to operate a race meet to be held in May, 1946, and the license was issued. In October and early November, 1945, extensive newspaper publicity was given to the race track project, featuring the fact that the property would be lighted for night racing. On 15 October, 1945, a contractor was employed to plan and construct the race track and the facilities incidental thereto. Grading was commenced in November and the work was continued until the project was completed on 14 September, 1946.

During the fall of 1945 the land on which the plaintiff's theater is located was being prepared and equipped for night auto racing by Northwest Sports, Inc., an activity which, like that of defendant, would have involved the use of flood lights. On 29 November, 1945, a lease agreement was executed between Northwest Sports, Inc. and the promoters of the plaintiff corporation, entitling the lessees and their assignee, Amphitheaters, Inc., to construct and operate a drive-in outdoor motion picture theater upon the property adjoining the race track of defendants. But the lease provided that the operation of the theater must not interfere with the operations of the same property for auto racing. Plans for the construction of the theater were turned over in March, 1946, and construction was commenced in May or June of that year. At least some of the promoters of the theater project knew that the race track was to be lighted for night racing, though they may not have known the volume or extent of the proposed lighting.

The outdoor theater was completed and commenced operating on 31 August, 1946. The race track was completed and the first races held fifteen days later. The plaintiff invested $135,000 in the construction of the outdoor theater and sums greatly in excess of that amount were expended by the defendant in the development of the race track and facilities. The lighting facilities alone involved an investment by the defendant of $100,000. The two tracts operated by plaintiff and defendant respectively are located just north of the city limits of Portland, Oregon. They adjoin and lie between two arterial highways, Denver Avenue and Union Avenue. The defendant's track consists of a mile-long oval extending in a general northerly and southerly direction. The auto race track which encloses the plaintiff's moving picture amphitheater lies between Union Avenue and the Northeast curve of the defendant's oval track. Union Avenue runs in a northwesterly direction along and parallel to the plaintiff's property of which it forms the northeasterly boundary. The theater screen, approximately 40 feet high and 50 feet wide, is backed up against the westerly line of Union Avenue and faces slightly south of west and directly toward the defendant's race track. At the trial a photograph showing the relative positions of the two properties and the nature of the adjacent territory was offered in evidence by the plaintiff and received without objection. It fairly represents the true situation. . . .

In installing outdoor moving picture theaters, it is necessary to protect the premises from outside light interference. For that purpose the plaintiff constructed wing fences for a considerable distance on each side of the screen and along the westerly line of Union Avenue for the purpose of shutting off the light from the cars traveling on that arterial highway. It was also necessary to construct a shadow box extending on both sides and above the screen for the purpose of excluding the light from the moon and stars. The testimony indicates that the construction of the shadow box was necessary if a good picture was to be presented on the screen. The extreme delicacy of plaintiff's operation and the susceptibility of outdoor moving pictures to light in any form was conclusively established by the evidence.

In order to illuminate the defendant's track for night horse racing, approximately 350 1500-watt lights are mounted in clusters on 80-foot poles placed at intervals of approximately 250 feet around the track. The flood lights are in general, directed at the track, but there is substantial evidence to the effect that reflected light "spills" over onto the plaintiff's premises and has a serious effect on the quality of pictures shown on the screen. The nearest cluster of lights on the defendant's track is 832 feet distant from the plaintiff's screen. The light from the defendant's track not only impairs the quality of the pictures exhibited by the plaintiff, but there is also substantial evidence that plaintiffs have suffered financial loss as the result of the illumination of which they complain. On one occasion at least, plaintiffs felt themselves required to refund admission fees to their patrons on account of the poor quality of the picture exhibited. The evidence discloses that the light from the defendant's race track when measured at plaintiff's screen is approximately that of full moonlight.

Upon the opening of the racing season in September, 1946, the plaintiff immediately complained to the defendant concerning the detrimental effect of defendant's lights, and shortly thereafter suit was filed. In the fall of 1946 the defendant, while denying liability, nevertheless made substantial efforts to protect the plaintiff from the effect of defendant's lights. One hundred hoods were installed on the lights, and particular attention was given to those nearest to the plaintiff's property. In 1947, and prior to the spring racing season, which was to last 25 days, thirty louvers were also installed for the purpose of further confining the light to the defendant's property. These efforts materially reduced, but did not eliminate the conditions of which plaintiff complains.

Plaintiff contends that the defendant, by casting light equivalent to that of a full moon upon plaintiff's screen has committed a trespass upon real property and error is assigned by reason of the failure of the court to submit to the jury the question of trespass. While the dividing line between trespass and nuisance is not always a sharp one, we think it clear that the case at bar is governed by the law of nuisance and not by the law of trespass. Under our decisions every unauthorized entry upon land of another, although without damage, constitutes actionable trespass. Restatement of the Law of Torts, Vol. 1, § 158, p. 359. The mere suggestion that the casting of light upon the premises of a plaintiff would render a defendant liable without proof of any actual damage, carries its own refutation. Actions for damages on account of smoke, noxious odors and the like have been universally classified as falling within the law of nuisance. In fact, cases of this type are described in the Restatement of the Law as "non-trespassory" invasions.

Many of the cases on which plaintiff relies in support of its theory of trespass involve the flight of airplanes at low level over plaintiffs' land. The modern law with reference to trespass by airplanes has developed under the influence of ancient rules concerning the nature of property. Ownership of lands, it has been said, "includes, not only the face of the earth, but everything under it or over it, and has in its legal signification an indefinite extent upward and downward, giving rise to the maxim, *Cujus est solum ejus est usque ad coelum*." Harmonizing the ancient rule with the necessities of modern life, the Restatement of the Law declares that one who intentionally and without a privilege enters land, is a trespasser. Restatement of the Law of Torts, Vol. 1, § 158, p. 359. Air travel over a plaintiff's land is still recognized as trespass prima facie imposing liability but the rights of airplane travel are established or recognized by the doctrine of privilege.

In support of its theory of trespass, the plaintiff cites *Swetland v. Curtiss Airports Corporation*, 55 F. (2d) 201, 83 A.L.R. 319; *United States v. Causby*, 328 U.S. 256, 90 L. Ed. 1206, 66 S. Ct. 1062; and *Guith v. Consumers Power Co.*, 36 F. Supp. 21. They are all cases which involve the flight of airplanes and which reflect the influence of the ancient rules of ownership *ad coelum* as modified by the rules of privilege. . . . The historical background of these cases distinguishes them from the non-trespassory cases which are controlled by the law of nuisance. *Portsmouth Harbor Land & Hotel Co. v. United State*s, 260 U.S. 327, 67 L. Ed. 287, 43 S. Ct. 135, was similar in principle to the *Causby* case, *supra*. The case involved a taking by the United States by means of the continuous firing of artillery over the petitioners' land. We need not argue the distinction between a cannon ball and a ray of light. Upon this issue plaintiff also cites *National Refining Co. v. Batte*, 135 Miss. 819, 100 So. 388, 35 A.L.R. 91, and *The Shelburne, Inc. v. Crossan Corporation*, 95 N.J. Eq. 188, 122 Atl. 749, both of which cases involve the shedding of light upon defendant's property, but both were decided upon the theory of nuisance and not of trespass. . . .

As its second assignment, the plaintiff asserts that the trial court erred in failing to submit the case to the jury on the theory of nuisance.

This is a case of first impression. It differs in essential particulars from any case which has received consideration by this court. The nuisance cases appearing in our reports fall into four easily recognizable classes: (1) Cases involving harm to human comfort, safety or health by reason of the maintenance by a defendant upon his land of noxious or dangerous instrumentalities causing damage to the plaintiff in respect to legally protected interests of the plaintiff in his land. (2) Cases involving illegal or immoral practices, most of them being public as distinct from private nuisances. They relate to bawdy houses, gambling, abortions, lotteries, illegal possession of liquor, and acts outraging public decency. (3) Cases involving obstructions to streets, public ways, common rights, access to property and the like. (4) Cases involving damage to the land itself, as by flooding. The cases, with the exception of those falling in the first class, bear no resemblance to the one at bar, and require no further comment.

. . . .

The cases listed in the first class are the only ones which bear any faint resemblance to the case at bar. Examination of those cases will disclose that no Oregon decision has ever held that the casting of light in any quantity or form upon the land of another gives rise to a cause of action upon any legal theory. If the cases involving smoke, noxious odors, flies and disease germs are claimed to be analogous to the case at bar, it must be answered that in every case the activity or thing which has been held to be a nuisance has been something which was, 1, inherently harmful, and 2, an unreasonable and substantial interference with the ordinary use or enjoyment of property. No one can contend that light is inherently harmful to persons in the ordinary enjoyment of property.

Since there is no Oregon precedent to support plaintiff's contention, we must go back to fundamental principles. Plaintiff relies upon the general definition of a nuisance as set forth in *Adams v. City of Toledo*, [163 Or. 185, 96 P.2d 1078,] *supra*, and *State ex rel Rudd v. Ringold*, 102 Or. 401, 202 P. 734. A private nuisance is defined as "anything done to the hurt, annoyance or detriment of the lands or hereditaments of another, and not amounting to a trespass." Definitions in such general terms are of no practical assistance to the court.

. . . .

> "What is a reasonable use and whether a particular use is a nuisance cannot be determined by any fixed general rules, but depend upon the facts of each particular case, such as location, character of the neighborhood, nature of the use, extent and frequency of the injury, the effect upon the enjoyment of life, health, and property, and the like." 39 Am. Jur. 298, § 16.

Notwithstanding the fact that the existence vel non of a nuisance is generally a question of fact, there have arisen several rules of law which guide and sometimes control decision. It is established law that an intentional interference with the use and enjoyment of land is not actionable unless that interference be both substantial and unreasonable. Restatement of the Law of Torts, Vol. 4, § 822, Comment g, and § 826, comment a.

Again it is held that whether a particular annoyance or inconvenience is sufficient to constitute a nuisance depends upon its effect upon an ordinarily reasonable man, that is, a normal person of ordinary habits and sensibilities. . . . The rule announced . . . , "Lex non favet delicatorum votis", was quoted with approval by this court. . . . This doctrine has been applied in many cases involving smoke, dust, noxious odors, vibration and the like, in which the injury was not to the land itself but to the personal comfort of dwellers on the land.

It is highly significant that an identical principle has been applied where the uses to which a plaintiff puts his land are abnormally sensitive to the type of interference caused by the defendant.

> "No action will lie for a nuisance in respect of damage which, even though substantial, is due solely to the fact that the plaintiff is abnormally sensitive to deleterious influences, or uses his land for some purpose which requires exceptional freedom from any such influences.

> "So if I carry on a manufacture or other business which is so sensitive to adverse influences that it suffers damage from smoke, fumes, vibrations, or heat, which would in no way interfere with the ordinary occupation of land, the law of nuisance will not confer upon me any such special and extraordinary protection. . . ."

The same rule has been laid down by another author:

> "It has been shown that the interference with property or personal comfort must be substantial. But even if the interference is substantial, no action will lie where it can be shown that, but for the infirmity of the person or property, there would have been no substantial interference. . . . Nor again can damage to sensitive property be complained of if the act causing the damage would not have harmed more ordinary things. . . ." Pearce and Meston, Ch. 1, p. 19.

. . . .

It follows from the application of this rule that the plaintiff's only basis of complaint is the fact that it is attempting to show upon the screen moving pictures, and that the operation is such a delicate one that it has been necessary for the plaintiff to build high fences to prevent the light of automobiles upon the public highway from invading the property and to build a shadow box over the screen to protect it from the ordinary light of moon and stars, and that it now claims damage because the lights from the defendant's property, which it has not excluded by high fences, shine with the approximate intensity of full moonlight upon the screen and interfere thereby with the showing of the pictures. We think that this is a clear case coming within the doctrine of the English and American cases, and that a man cannot increase the liabilities of his neighbor by applying his own property to special and delicate uses, whether for business or pleasure.

. . . .

The only case which has been brought to our attention, and in which it has been held that light unaccompanied by any other element of an offensive character constitutes a nuisance, is the case of *The Shelburne, Inc. v. Crossan Corporation, supra.* The plaintiff was the owner of a large hotel on the board walk in Atlantic City which had been operated in the same location for many years. Sixty of its bedrooms had a southerly or southwesterly exposure. The defendant corporation was the owner of property immediately to the southwest, upon which was erected an apartment house. On the roof of the apartment house defendants had erected a sign 66 feet in height and 72 feet in length on which there were 1084 15-watt lights and 6 100-watt lights and 28 75-watt lights. The sign was parallel to the wing of the hotel and about 110 feet distant therefrom. The evidence disclosed that the sign "lights up 40 or 45 rooms in the new wing of the hotel", disturbs the guests and lowers the value of the rooms. The court held that light "may become a nuisance if it materially interferes with the ordinary comfort physically of human existence." The trial judge held that the complainant was entitled to a decree restricting the operation of the electric lights during each night *after the hour of 12 o'clock midnight.* The plaintiff's hotel was located on the famous board walk at Atlantic City, where the primary activity appears to be the entertainment of luxury-loving people. We suspect that the court was moved by a comparison of the utility of plaintiff's hotel in that district with the utility of an advertising sign. In any event, the interference was with the normal and ordinary sensibilities of dwellers in the hotel, and with the ordinary use of property.

. . . .

By way of summary, we have found no case in which it has been held that light alone constitutes a nuisance merely because it damaged one who was abnormally sensitive or whose use of his land was of a peculiarly delicate and sensitive character.

It is not our intention to decide the case . . . divorced from reason or public policy. The photographic evidence discloses that the properties of the respective parties are not in a residential district, and in fact are outside the city limits of Portland, and lie adjacent to a considerable amount of unimproved land. Neither party can claim any greater social utility than the other. Both were in the process of construction at the same time, and the case should not be decided upon the basis of the priority of occupation. The case differs fundamentally from other cases . . . in that light is not a noxious, but is, in general, a highly beneficial element. The development of parks and playgrounds equipped for the enjoyment of the working public, whose recreation is necessarily taken after working hours, and frequently after dark, is a significant phenomenon in thousands of urban communities. The court takes judicial knowledge that many lighted parks and fields are located adjacent to residential property and must to some extent interfere with the full enjoyment of darkness (if desired) by the residents.

We do not say that the shedding of light upon another's property may never under any conditions become a nuisance, but we do say that extreme caution must be employed in applying any such legal theory. The conditions of modern city life impose upon the city dweller and his property many burdens more severe than that of light reflected upon him or it.

In this case, the court directed a verdict for the defendant. We recognize the general rule to be that the existence or nonexistence of a private nuisance is ordinarily a question of fact for the jury, but the rule is subject to exceptions. . . .

. . . We limit our decision to the specific facts of this case and hold as a matter of law that the loss sustained by the plaintiff by the spilled light which has been reflected onto the highly sensitized moving picture screen from the defendant's property 832 feet distant, and which light in intensity is approximately that of a full moon, is *damnum abseque injuria.*

The trial court did not err in directing a verdict. The judgment is affirmed.

## Questions for Consideration

1) What is the externality in this case? How is the externality in this case similar or different from the externality in the *Bove* case?

2) What additional elements does this case add to the previously stated rules on nuisance set out in the *Bove* case?

3) What is a "non-trespassory" invasion, and how does it relate to nuisance?

4) What consideration does the court give to the economic value of the activity of the two property owners? How does the consideration of social utility in this case compare to the social utility of development in the *Bove* case? How should social utility affect property rights with respect to coordinating land uses?

5) How might you respond to neighbors who complain about a nearby residential homeowner's newly installed security flood lights? Could the flood lights be subject to removal? Does the intrusion of light on the property of a neighbor amount to a trespass, even if it is not a nuisance?

## Takeaway

- As evidenced in the closing paragraphs of the opinion, the courts will look at the social utility of the competing land uses involved in a nuisance complaint. This involves an evaluation of costs and benefits, as well as an assessment of social utility. Therefore, an attorney in such a case must be prepared to present evidence on these economic points as part of the legal case. Moreover, nuisance cases are fact specific determinations. Rather than having case by case assessments of social utility, it may be better to address the social utility of potentially competing land uses by developing a land use plan and a zoning code.

## Prah v. Maretti

Supreme Court of Wisconsin
321 N.W.2d 182 (Wis. 1982)

ABRAHAMSON, Judge. This appeal from a judgment of the circuit court for Waukesha county, Max Raskin, circuit judge, was certified to this court by the court of appeals as presenting an issue of first impression, namely, whether an owner of a solar-heated residence states a claim upon which relief can be granted when he asserts that his neighbor's proposed construction of a residence (which conforms to existing deed restrictions and local ordinances) interferes with his access to an unobstructed path for sunlight across the neighbor's property. This case thus involves a conflict between one landowner (Glenn Prah, the plaintiff) interested in unobstructed access to sunlight across adjoining property as a natural source of energy and an adjoining landowner (Richard D. Maretti, the defendant) interested in the development of his land.

The circuit court concluded that the plaintiff presented no claim upon which relief could be granted and granted summary judgment for the defendant. We reverse the judgment of the circuit court and remand the cause to the circuit court for further proceedings.

## I.

According to the complaint, the plaintiff is the owner of a residence which was constructed during the years 1978–1979. The complaint alleges that the residence has a solar system which includes collectors on the roof to supply energy for heat and hot water and that after the plaintiff built his solar-heated house, the defendant purchased the lot adjacent to and immediately to the south of the plaintiff's lot and commenced planning construction of a home. The complaint further states that when the plaintiff learned of defendant's plans to build the house he advised the defendant that if the house were built at the proposed location, defendant's house would substantially and adversely affect the integrity of plaintiff's solar system and could cause plaintiff other damage. Nevertheless, the defendant began construction. The complaint further alleges that the plaintiff is entitled to "unrestricted use of the sun and its solar power" and demands judgment for injunctive relief and damages.

After filing his complaint, the plaintiff moved for a temporary injunction to restrain and enjoin construction by the defendant. In ruling on that motion the circuit court heard testimony, received affidavits and viewed the site.

The record made on the motion reveals the following additional facts: Plaintiff's home was the first residence built in the subdivision, and although plaintiff did not build his house in the center of the lot it was built in accordance with applicable restrictions. Plaintiff advised defendant that if the defendant's home were built at the proposed site it would cause a shadowing effect on the solar collectors which would reduce the efficiency of the system and possibly damage the system. To avoid these adverse effects, plaintiff requested defendant to locate his home an additional several feet away from the plaintiff's lot line, the exact number being disputed. Plaintiff and defendant failed to reach an agreement on the location of defendant's home before defendant started construction. The Architectural Control Committee and the Planning Commission of the City of Muskego approved the defendant's plans for his home, including its location on the lot. After such approval, the defendant apparently changed the grade of the property without prior notice to the Architectural Control Committee. The problem with defendant's proposed construction, as far as the plaintiff's interests are concerned, arises from a combination of the grade and the distance of defendant's home from the defendant's lot line.

The circuit court denied plaintiff's motion for injunctive relief, declared it would entertain a motion for summary judgment and thereafter entered judgment in favor of the defendant.

## II.

. . . .

. . . We . . . consider this as an appeal from a judgment entered on a motion for summary judgment.

In deciding a motion for summary judgment the initial question is the same as that on a motion to dismiss the complaint for failure to state a claim upon which relief can be granted, namely, whether the complaint states a claim upon which relief can be granted. If the complaint states a claim and the pleadings show the existence of factual issues, the court then examines the affidavits and other proof and determines whether there are disputed material facts that entitle the non-moving party to a trial. On summary judgment the court does not decide those issues of fact; it merely decides whether genuine issues of fact exist.

In this case there is some ambiguity whether the judgment was based on the complaint or on factual matters outside the pleadings which were presented to the circuit court in connection with the motion for a temporary injunction. Consequently, we shall first test the sufficiency of the complaint and then determine whether the matters outside the pleadings present disputed material facts sufficient to justify a trial.

## III.

In testing the sufficiency of the complaint the facts pleaded by the plaintiff, and all reasonable inferences therefrom, are accepted as true.

The plaintiff presents three legal theories to support his claim that the defendant's continued construction of a home justifies granting him relief: (1) the construction constitutes a common law private nuisance; (2) the construction is prohibited by sec. 844.01, Stats. 1979–80 ["any person owning or claiming an interest in real property may bring an action claiming physical injury to, or interference with, the property or his interest therein. . . ."]; and (3) the construction interferes with the solar easement plaintiff acquired under the doctrine of prior appropriation.

As to the claim of private nuisance the circuit court concluded that the law of private nuisance requires the court to make "a comparative evaluation of the conflicting interests and to weigh the gravity of the harm to the plaintiff against the utility of the defendant's conduct." The circuit court concluded: "A comparative evaluation of the conflicting interests, keeping in mind the omissions and commissions of both Prah and Maretti, indicates that defendant's conduct does not cause the gravity of the harm which the plaintiff himself may well have avoided by proper planning." The circuit court also concluded that sec. 844.01 does not apply to a home constructed in accordance with deed and municipal ordinance requirements. Further, the circuit court rejected the prior appropriation doctrine as "an intrusion of judicial egoism over legislative passivity."

We consider first whether the complaint states a claim for relief based on common law private nuisance. This state has long recognized that an owner of land does not have an absolute or unlimited right to use the land in a way which injures the rights of others. The rights of neighboring landowners are relative; the uses by one must not unreasonably impair the uses or enjoyment of the other. When one landowner's use of his or her property unreasonably interferes with another's enjoyment of his or her property, that use is said to be a private nuisance.

The private nuisance doctrine has traditionally been employed in this state to balance the rights of landowners, and this court has recently adopted the analysis of private nuisance set forth in the Restatement (Second) of Torts. The Restatement defines private nuisance as "a nontrespassory invasion of another's interest in the private use and enjoyment of land." Restatement (Second) of Torts sec. 821D (1977). The phrase "interest in the private use and enjoyment of land" as used in sec. 821D is broadly defined to include any disturbance of the enjoyment of property. The comment in the Restatement describes the landowner's interest protected by private nuisance law as follows:

> "The phrase 'interest in the use and enjoyment of land' is used in this Restatement in a broad sense. It comprehends not only the interests that a person may have in the actual present use of land for residential, agricultural, commercial, industrial and other purposes, but also his interests in having the present use value of the land unimpaired by changes in its physical condition. Thus the destruction of trees on vacant land is as much an invasion of the owner's interest in its use and enjoyment as is the destruction of crops or flowers that he is growing on the land for his present use. 'Interest in use and enjoyment' also comprehends the pleasure, comfort and enjoyment that a person normally derives from the occupancy of land. Freedom from discomfort and annoyance while using land is often as important to a person as freedom from physical interruption with his use or freedom from detrimental change in the physical condition of the land itself." Restatement (Second) of Torts, Sec. 821D, Comment *b*, p. 101 (1977).

Although the defendant's obstruction of the plaintiff's access to sunlight appears to fall within the Restatement's broad concept of a private nuisance as a nontrespassory invasion of another's interest in the private use and enjoyment of land, the defendant asserts that he has a right to develop his property in compliance with statutes, ordinances and private covenants without regard to the effect of such development upon the plaintiff's access to sunlight. In essence, the defendant is asking this court to hold that the private nuisance doctrine is not applicable in the instant case and that his right to develop his land is a right which is *per se* superior to his neighbor's interest in access to sunlight. This position is expressed in the maxim "*cujus est solum, ejus est usque ad coelum et ad infernos,*" that is, the owner of land owns up to the sky and down to the center of the earth. The rights of the surface owner are, however, not unlimited. *U.S. v. Causby*, 328 U.S. 256, 260–1, 66 S. Ct. 1062, 1065, 90 L. Ed. 1206 (1946). *See also* 114.03, Stats. 1979–80.

The defendant is not completely correct in asserting that the common law did not protect a landowner's access to sunlight across adjoining property. At English common law a landowner could acquire a right to receive sunlight across adjoining land by both express agreement and under the judge-made doctrine of "ancient lights." Under the doctrine of ancient lights if the landowner had received sunlight across adjoining property for a specified period of time, the landowner was entitled to continue to receive unobstructed access to sunlight across the adjoining property. Under the doctrine the landowner acquired a negative prescriptive easement and could prevent the adjoining landowner from obstructing access to light.

Although American courts have not been as receptive to protecting a landowner's access to sunlight as the English courts, American courts have afforded some protection to a landowner's interest in access to sunlight. American courts honor express easements to sunlight. American courts initially enforced the English common law doctrine of ancient lights, but later every state which considered the doctrine repudiated it as inconsistent with the needs of a developing country. Indeed, for just that reason this court concluded that an easement to light and air over adjacent property could not be created or acquired by prescription and has been unwilling to recognize such an easement by implication.

Many jurisdictions in this country have protected a landowner from malicious obstruction of access to light (the spite fence cases) under the common law private nuisance doctrine. If an activity is motivated by malice it lacks utility and the harm it causes others outweighs any social values. This court was reluctant to protect a landowner's interest in sunlight even against a spite fence, only to be overruled by the legislature. Shortly after this court upheld a landowner's right to erect a useless and unsightly sixteen-foot spite fence four feet from his neighbor's windows, the legislature enacted a law specifically defining a spite fence as an actionable private nuisance. Thus a landowner's interest in sunlight has been protected in this country by common law private nuisance law at least in the narrow context of the modern American rule invalidating spite fences.

This court's reluctance in the nineteenth and early part of the twentieth century to provide broader protection for a landowner's access to sunlight was premised on three policy considerations. First, the right of landowners to use their property as they wished, as long as they did not cause physical damage to a neighbor, was jealously guarded.

Second, sunlight was valued only for aesthetic enjoyment or as illumination. Since artificial light could be used for illumination, loss of sunlight was at most a personal annoyance which was given little, if any, weight by society.

Third, society had a significant interest in not restricting or impeding land development. This court repeatedly emphasized that in the growth period of the nineteenth and early twentieth centuries change is to be expected and is essential to property and that recognition of a right to sunlight would hinder property development. . . .

Considering these three policies, this court concluded that in the absence of an express agreement granting access to sunlight, a landowner's obstruction of another's access to sunlight was not actionable. These three policies are no longer fully accepted or applicable. They reflect factual circumstances and social priorities that are now obsolete.

First, society has increasingly regulated the use of land by the landowner for the general welfare. *Euclid v. Ambler Realty Co.*, 272 U.S. 365, 47 S. Ct. 114, 71 L. Ed. 303 (1926).

Second, access to sunlight has taken on a new significance in recent years. In this case the plaintiff seeks to protect access to sunlight, not for aesthetic reasons or as a source of illumination but as a source of energy. Access to sunlight as an energy source is of significance both to the landowner who invests in solar collectors and to a society which has an interest in developing alternative sources of energy.

Third, the policy of favoring unhindered private development in an expanding economy is no longer in harmony with the realities of our society. The need for easy and rapid development is not as great today as it once was, while our perception of the value of sunlight as a source of energy has increased significantly.

Courts should not implement obsolete policies that have lost their vigor over the course of the years. The law of private nuisance is better suited to resolve landowners' disputes about property development in the 1980's than is a rigid rule which does not recognize a landowner's interest in access to sunlight. As we said in *Ballstadt v. Pagel*, 202 Wis. 484, 489, 232 N.W. 862 (1930), "What is regarded in law as constituting a nuisance in modern times would no doubt have been tolerated without question in former times." . . .

. . . We recognized . . . that common law rules adapt to changing social values and conditions.

Yet the defendant would have us ignore the flexible private nuisance law as a means of resolving the dispute between the landowners in this case and would have us adopt an approach, already abandoned in *Deetz*, of favoring the unrestricted development of land and of applying a rigid and inflexible rule protecting his right to build on his land and disregarding any interest of the plaintiff in the use and enjoyment of his land. This we refuse to do.

Private nuisance law, the law traditionally used to adjudicate conflicts between private landowners, has the flexibility to protect both a landowner's right of access to sunlight and another landowner's right to develop land. Private nuisance law is better suited to regulate access to sunlight in modern society and is more in harmony with legislative policy and the prior decisions of this court than is an inflexible doctrine of non-recognition of any interest in access to sunlight across adjoining land.

We therefore hold that private nuisance law, that is, the reasonable use doctrine as set forth in the Restatement, is applicable to the instant case. Recognition of a nuisance claim for unreasonable obstruction of access to sunlight will not prevent land development or unduly hinder the use of adjoining land. It will promote the reasonable use and enjoyment of land in a manner suitable to the 1980's. That obstruction of access to light might be found to constitute a nuisance in certain circumstances does not mean that it will be or must be found to constitute a nuisance under all circumstances. The result in each case depends on whether the conduct complained of is unreasonable.

. . . .

## IV.

. . . .

Because the plaintiff has stated a claim of common law private nuisance upon which relief can be granted, the judgment of the circuit court must be reversed. We need not, and do not, reach the question of whether the complaint states a claim under sec. 844.01, Stats. 1979–80, or under the doctrine of prior appropriation.

For the reasons set forth, we reverse the judgment of the circuit court dismissing the complaint and remand the matter to circuit court for further proceedings not inconsistent with this opinion.

The judgment of the circuit court is reversed and the cause remanded for proceedings not inconsistent with this opinion.

Ceci, Judge, not participating.

Callow, Justice. (dissenting). The majority has adopted the Restatement's reasonable use doctrine to grant an owner of a solar heated home a cause of action against his neighbor who, in acting entirely within the applicable ordinances and statutes, seeks to design and build his home in such a location that it may, at various times during the day, shade the plaintiff's solar collector, thereby impeding the efficiency of his heating system during several months of the year. Because I believe the facts of this case clearly reveal that a cause of action for private nuisance will not lie, I dissent.

. . . .

It is a fundamental principle of law that a "landowner owns at least as much of the space above the ground as he can occupy or use in connection with the land." As stated in the frequently cited and followed case of *Fontainebleau Hotel Corp. v. Forty-Five Twenty-Five, Inc.*, 114 So. 2d 357 (Fla. Dist. Ct. App. 1959), *cert. denied*, 117 So. 2d 842 (Fla. 1960):

> "There being, then, no legal right to the free flow of light and air from the adjoining land, it is universally held that where a structure serves a useful and beneficial purpose, it does not give rise to a cause of action, either for damages or for an injunction under the maxim *sic utere tuo ut alienum non*

*laedas*, even though it causes injury to another by cutting off the light and air and interfering with the view that would otherwise be available over adjoining land in its natural state, regardless of the fact that the structure may have been erected partly for spite."

I firmly believe that a landowner's right to use his property within the limits of ordinances, statutes, and restrictions of record where such use is necessary to serve his legitimate needs is a fundamental precept of a free society which this court should strive to uphold.

. . . .

Because I do not believe that the facts of the present case give rise to a cause of action for private nuisance, I dissent.

## *Questions for Consideration*

1) What are a property owner's rights to sunlight, a view, and wind (for wind power)?

2) Should it matter who was the first occupier of the land? Why?

3) Is there a difference between an activity that blocks sunlight and an activity that casts a shadow on adjoining property?

4) This is a case about adapting property rules to new technologies; what is the best way to modify property rules to account for new technologies that raise new legal issues between property owners?

5) Can the problem of new technologies be solved by the private marketplace? Why not require the individual property owners to bargain for and pay for the rights that are in dispute? For example, owners could buy and sell easements for a view or for access to unobstructed sunlight. As between the two property owners in this case, who has the initial property right and who should have to pay to acquire an easement? What if the person with the initial right refuses to sell an easement for sunlight to the other party?

## *Takeaway*

- The court says: "[T]he law of private nuisance requires the court to make 'a comparative evaluation of the conflicting interests and to weigh the gravity of the harm to the plaintiff against the utility of the defendant's conduct.'" As in the *Amphitheaters* case, an economic analysis of the harms and benefits is an important element of the determination. In practice, you will need to think carefully about the quality and quantity of economic evidence that is needed to make your case. Consider the type of economic and financial experts that you might need to use, and the types of calculations and valuation formulas that might be beneficial. There are multiple ways of calculating these values, and therefore, it becomes critical to think of the evidence presented in terms of the applicable standard of review if the initial judgment is appealed. You need enough evidence on the record to support a ruling in your favor, even if there are other potentially good outcomes that might have been selected.

## City of New York v. Smart Apts. LLC

Supreme Court of New York, New York County
959 N.Y.S.2d 890 (N.Y. Sup. Ct. 2013)

ENGORON, Judge. The complaint sets forth causes of action for deceptive trade practices under the consumer protection law and for public nuisance under the common law.

Plaintiff, The City of New York, now moves, pursuant to New York City Admin. Code § 20-703(d), CPLR 6301, and CPLR 6311, to enjoin defendants, essentially, and simply put, (a) from advertising, contracting for, and/or allowing the transient occupancy of New York City Class A Multiple Dwellings, or any other buildings as to which transient occupancy is illegal; (b) to remove any such advertising from all Internet websites and other media, whether or not directly controlled or maintained by defendants; and (c) from disposing or modifying the records maintained and used in the management and operation of such properties. The above-named defendants now cross-move, pursuant to CPLR 3211(a)(7) and the doctrine of selective enforcement, to dismiss.

### Plaintiff's Claims

According to plaintiff, whose factual allegations are exceedingly well-documented and not significantly denied by defendants, "Defendants operate a multi-tiered business, advertising, booking, operating and maintaining transient accommodations for short-term stays of less than 30-days in as many as 50 or more Class A [*i.e.*, non-transient] multiple dwellings in New York City, as well as in other buildings for which the legally permissible occupancy prohibits transient occupancy." The business includes (or, at least included) a website ("smartapartments.com"), world-wide advertisements, online photographs of apartments, reservation and booking records, and even laundry services for the subject apartments. The advertising touts the short stays, but fails to mention the illegality and fire safety hazards (*infra*), much less the numerous fire safety code violation notices. According to plaintiff (and not denied by defendants), defendants Smart Apartments and Toshi nominally run the business, and defendant Chan is a principal of them and is "actively engaged" in their management.

Plaintiff claims that defendants' placement of tourists and other visitors to New York in residential apartments for "transient" stays of less than 30 days is illegal, unsafe, a deceptive business practice, a public nuisance, and annoys the heck out of the non-transient residents of the building. In particular, plaintiff claims that defendants' business practices are illegal because they violate Chapter 225 of the Laws of New York of 2010, codified in Multiple Dwelling Law ("MDL") § 4.a.8(a), New

York City Housing Maintenance Code ("NYCHMC") § 27-2004.a.8.(a), and New York City Building Code ("NYCBC") § 310.1.2; they are unsafe because the transient occupants are denied the fire safety devices and protections, such as fire extinguishers, sprinklers, alarms, evacuation plans, etc. required of transient hotels; they are a deceptive business practice because defendants' customers are not told that their transient occupancy is illegal and unsafe; they constitute a public nuisance because they are depleting the City's stock of affordable, long-term housing and create security risks and quality-of-life problems in the subject buildings; and they bother the non-transient residents of the buildings because the transient occupants host loud, late night parties; vomit, dump garbage, and smoke in the hallways; damage the elevators with all those bulky suitcases; and generally do not conduct themselves in the civilized, genteel manner of the locals.

Plaintiff claims that defendants are violating (1) Chapter 225 of the Laws of New York of 2010, effective May 1, 2011, which amended the MDL, NYCHMC, and the NYCBC to provide that stays of less than 30 days in a residential building are illegal (indeed, a misdemeanor under the MDL); (2) NYC Admin. Code ("NYCAC") § 28-118, which prohibits changing the use of a building, such as from long-term to transient use, even in one apartment in a building, without obtaining a building permit and new certificate of occupancy; and (3) NYCAC § 20-700, which prohibits deceptive trade practices, including (§ 20-701) "any false or misleading statement made in connection with the lease [or] rental of consumer goods or services which has the capacity, tendency or effect of deceiving or misleading consumers." Pursuant to § 20-701(c), "consumer goods or services" are those "which are primarily for personal, household or family purposes." Pursuant to § 20-710(d), a "consumer" is a "purchaser or lessee or prospective purchaser or lessee of consumer goods or services" (which seems rather obvious). Pursuant to § 20-703(d), the Supreme Court may enjoin violations of § 20-700; and, pursuant to § 20-703(e), that is regardless of whether "consumers are being or were actually injured." Furthermore, a transient resident is a consumer of consumer goods and/or services. . . .

### Legal and Safe

Whether or not, in our cynical age, most people would consider engaging in illegal activity as a plus, minus, or neutral, they have the right to know whether it is or is not. . . .

The New York City Fire and Building Codes require transient residences to observe significantly higher fire safety standards than non-transient residences, because, the theory goes the occupants of the former are less familiar than the latter with their surroundings, with fire evacuation procedures, etc. Whether this is justified, as plaintiff and this Court believe, or faintly ridiculous, as defendants argue, it is the law. These higher safety standards include fire extinguishers, sprinklers, alarms, evacuation plans, diagrams, "fire safety directors," fire brigades, command centers, training, the whole nine yards. Plaintiff cogently argues that such procedures and paraphernalia save lives.

## Public Nuisances

New York State takes an extremely broad view of what constitutes a public nuisance:

> It consists of conduct or omissions which offend, interfere with or cause damage to the public in the exercise of rights common to all, in a manner such as to offend public morals, interfere with the use by the public of a public place or endanger or injure the property, health, safety or comfort of a considerable number of persons.

This definition certainly covers placing unwary tourists in fire-traps and subjecting them to the possibility of serious injury or death (tragic hotel fires, not to mention garden-variety apartment house conflagrations, are a staple of front-page news). . . .

Furthermore, municipalities may bring actions to abate public nuisances. . . .

## Defendants' Defenses

According to an old legal adage, with many variations, "If the law is against you, pound the facts; if the facts are against you, pound the law; if they both are against you, pound the table." Here, plaintiff has defendants "dead to rights." In response to plaintiff's overwhelming avalanche of evidence that defendants' acts violate the Consumer Protection Law and constitute a public nuisance, defendants have opted to pound the table (they do not claim that they are not doing what plaintiff alleges, and they do no more than quibble with plaintiff's interpretation of the law). Their main contentions (this Court has considered all the others and found them unavailing) are (1) that some of their operations are actually legal; (2) that they are changing their ways, "laying the groundwork to be the future leader of the 30-day and over New York City apartment rental business"; (3) that plaintiff is using strong-arm, "Police-State," "stop-at-nothing" tactics to "rid" New York City of Smart Apartments; (4) that they are not committing a "public" nuisance; (5) that defendant Robert Chan's acts are shielded by the corporate veil; (6) that only the Commissioner of Consumer Protection can bring an action for a violation of the Consumer Protection Law; and (7) that plaintiff is engaged in "selective enforcement," inasmuch as an enterprise called "Airbnb" (probably denoting "air (travel) bed and breakfast") operates on a much larger scale and heretofore has not been targeted because New York City Mayor Michael Bloomberg owns 88% of Bloomberg LP, which "is a major financial investor in the venture capital fund Andreessen Horowitz, which, in turn, has an investment of approximately one hundred million dollars in Airbnb," and that "while Airbnb markets its vast inventory of illegal short term rentals, the Mayor's Office is using all of its power to try and bully Smart Apartments' occupants and completely eliminate it as a possible competitor."

## Contentions 1–3

Contentions (1) to (3) are simply irrelevant.

## Contention 4

Contention (4), that defendants are not committing a *public* nuisance, is belied by their own formulation of the law: "A public nuisance consists of conduct or omissions which endanger the safety or comfort of a considerable number of persons at one time." The "public" element of plaintiff's nuisance cause of action is satisfied by the fire *safety* hazards to defendants' customers and the loss of *comfort* sustained by the non-transient tenants of buildings used by defendants (both groups numbering well into the thousands). Public nuisances should not be able to hide behind private property. Defendants argue that a public nuisance is "an unreasonable interference with a right common to the general public." In this Court's view, the general public has a right not to be sold housing accommodations that are dangerous and illegal. Although defendants harp on the idea that the apartments at issue are "*private* property" they are available, indeed advertised to, the general public, more like hotel rooms than private apartments.

## Contention 5

Contention (5), that plaintiff cannot pierce the defendants' (or defendant Smart Apartment's, as Toshi appears to be out of business) corporate veils, misses the point. As this Court sees the matter, plaintiff is not seeking to pierce any corporate veil; rather, it is seeking to hold defendant Chan accountable for his own actions. Corporations can only act through their employees; but that does not mean that any act done in furtherance of the corporation's business is shielded by the corporate veil, which limits personal financial liability for a corporation's financial debts. For example, an employee who dumps a corporation's toxic waste is still liable for violating anti-pollution laws. To take an extreme example, an employee who murders the principal of a corporation's competitor, even if only done to further the corporation's business (and not out of personal animosity), is still guilty of murder. Plaintiff alleges, and Chan does not deny, that he [*sic*] is a principal of Smart Apartments and is "actively engaged" in its management. Thus, he is clearly subject to an injunction aimed at preventing Smart Apartments from violating the law and is not entitled to dismissal of the complaint as against him.

## Contention 6

Contention (6) seems to have been abandoned. . . .

## Contention 7

[As to the assertion of selective and discriminatory] enforcement[.] . . .

. . . .

*The burden of proving a claim of discriminatory enforcement is a weighty one. Common sense and public policy dictate that it be so. The presumption is that the enforcement of laws is undertaken in good faith and without discrimination. Moreover, latitude must be accorded authorities charged with making decisions related to legitimate law enforcement interests, at times permitting them to proceed with an unequal hand....* [*Matter of 303 W. 42nd St. Corp. v. Klein*, 46 N.Y.2d 686, 693-96 (1979) (emphasis added).]

. . . .

After careful consideration of the multitudinous facts of this case and the multifarious factors to be considered, this Court finds that defendants have not demonstrated entitlement to a hearing on selective enforcement. . . .

. . . .

### Injunctive Relief

The New York standard for granting a preliminary injunction is well established: a movant must show (1) the likelihood of success on the merits; (2) irreparable injury absent the granting of a preliminary injunction; and (3) a balancing of the equities that favors the movant's position. Plaintiff here satisfies this strict general standard; but the standard in this particular case is much looser. "[I]rreparable injury is presumed from the continuing existence of an unremedied public nuisance." . . .

Again, even using the strict general test, placing unsuspecting tourists in illegal, dangerous accommodations constitutes irreparable injury, especially if there is a tragic fire; and the equities lie in favor of shutting down an illegal, unsafe, deceptive business, rather than in allowing said business to continue to operate (to defendants' presumed financial advantage).

### Conclusion and Disposition

For the reasons set forth herein, . . . defendants and their employees, agents etc. are hereby preliminarily enjoined (a) from advertising, contracting for, and/or allowing the transient occupancy, *i.e.*, less than 30 days, of New York City Class A Multiple Dwellings, or any other buildings as to which transient occupancy is illegal; (b) from advertising such occupancies on any and all Internet websites and other media, and to remove whatever such advertising currently is on those sites, whether or not directly controlled or maintained by defendants; and (c) from disposing or modifying the records maintained and used to manage and operate such transient use; all until the resolution of this case or further court order.

## *Questions for Consideration*

1) What type of a nuisance action is this: private or public?

2) If a person owns a single-family residential home in an area zoned for such a use, why shouldn't she be able to rent it out for a year? Six months? One week? Two nights? What does it mean when an ordinance says that a property must be used for a single-family residential use? How do we interpret the meaning of single-family?

3) If a homeowner can have four of her relatives visit and stay in her home for four weeks, why can't she have a stranger pay to stay in the home for three days?

4) Should it make a difference if the activity is for profit?

## *Takeaway*

- Services such as AirBnB take advantage of advances in technology that enable assets to be easily employed in new ways. In this instance, turning residential properties into short-term rental properties. These changes may affect land use even in communities that have highly developed zoning regulations. When property is used in new ways, the issue arises as to whether the new use is covered by the existing regulations, and if not, whether a community can find other ways of regulating the use.

## MX Group, Inc. v. City of Covington

United States Court of Appeals for the Sixth Circuit
293 F.3d 326 (2002)

CLAY, Circuit Judge. Defendants, the City of Covington, Kentucky, the Covington Board of Adjustment, [et al.], appeal the judgment of the district court, after a bench trial, in favor of Plaintiff pursuant to claims brought under Title II of the Americans with Disabilities Act ("ADA"), 42 U.S.C. § 12131, *et seq.*, and the Rehabilitation Act of 1973 ("Rehabilitation Act"), 29 U.S.C. § 701 et seq. Plaintiff, MX Group, Inc., alleged that Defendants discriminated against it because of Plaintiff's association with its potential clients, who are drug addicted persons, by refusing to issue a zoning permit to Plaintiff so that it could open a methadone clinic in the City of Covington. Plaintiff claims that Defendants further discriminated against it by amending the city's zoning ordinance to completely prohibit the clinic from opening anywhere in the city. The district court found that Plaintiff's clients or potential clients were persons with a disability and that Defendants discriminated against Plaintiff because of Plaintiff's association with its clients/potential clients. For the reasons that follow, we affirm.

### Background

### Procedural History

On January 16, 1998, Plaintiff filed a two-count complaint in the district court, alleging violations of the ADA and the Rehabilitation Act. On July 21, 1998, Plaintiff amended its complaint, adding as a third cause of action denial of substantive due process. According to the district court's opinion, Plaintiff also asserted a constitutional equal protection claim. Defendants filed an answer on August 20, 1998. Defendants moved for summary judgment on August 2, 1999. The district court held a hearing on the motion and denied it on December 17, 1999. . . .

### Facts

The parties agree that the facts are essentially undisputed. Plaintiff, MX Group, is in the business of providing drug treatment through the use of methadone.

In 1997, Plaintiff began the process of locating a site to open a methadone clinic in Covington, Kentucky. The proposed purpose of the clinic was to provide methadone treatment, counseling, medical examinations, and other services for recovering opium addicts.

Melissa Fabian and Edith McNeill, both of whom were then affiliated with Plaintiff, contacted Chuck Eilerman, a realtor, who provided them with a list of properties in Covington that met the needs of the facility. Fabian testified that in searching for a location, affordability was important as was location. She testified that she was not looking in residential areas, but only business or commercial areas. Further, it was important that the location be accessible to clients. After looking at several potential sites, Plaintiff found a suitable location at 200 West Pike Street. The building was divided into office condominiums and used to serve as a train station. Plaintiff entered into a lease agreement with one of the owners of office space in the building, and contacted Covington's Zoning Administrator Ralph Hopper to apply for a zoning permit for that location.

After he was first contacted by Plaintiff regarding the permit but before Plaintiff actually sought a zoning permit for the clinic, Hopper contacted his superiors about the methadone clinic. Although this was not normal procedure, Hopper thought the clinic would be "potentially controversial." Hopper completed the application for the zoning permit and issued the permit on the day Plaintiff applied for it, August 19, 1997.

After the zoning permit was issued, town residents expressed their displeasure regarding the proposed clinic at a City Commission meeting. As a result, on September 8, 1997, the city held a hearing chaired by Assistant City Manager Tom Steidel regarding Plaintiff's application for a zoning permit. Steidel testified at trial that the hearing was informational in nature, and was intended to provide information for and against the establishment of the clinic. Steidel testified that the meeting was intended to provide Plaintiff and concerned Covington citizens an opportunity to air their concerns regarding the clinic. The meeting lasted two to three hours, and was not transcribed or recorded. Steidel also testified that there was a wide range of reaction and emotion at the meeting, ranging from "proper decorum" to anger regarding the proposed clinic.

Another owner of an office in the building where the clinic was to be located appealed Hopper's decision to issue the permit. On December 17, 1997, the Covington Board of Adjustment held a hearing on the matter. Numerous persons testified at the hearing for and against Hopper's decision. Covington Assistant Police Chief William Dorsey testified that from a police officer's perspective, he saw no need for a methadone clinic in Covington. Dorsey testified that based on his research, he found that for-profit methadone clinics spawn criminal activity. He contacted other clinics in other towns and was told about trouble outside of clinics, such as drug use and/or trafficking and drug trade, violence, shootings and death. He testified that there is a large number of burglaries at methadone clinics as a result of people breaking in to steal drugs. He also testified that the town should be concerned about the safety of the neighborhood children inasmuch as there is a school near the proposed site.

Further, he added that "addicts" generally find a way to wean themselves from the drugs and then sell the take-home dosages they are provided. Dorsey did not provide any statistics or other specifics regarding these alleged ill effects. Apparently under the impression that Plaintiff operated a clinic in Greentree, Pennsylvania, as part of Dorsey's research, he contacted the Greentree police department, which told him there had been increased police runs to the clinic. However, the security officer in the building where Plaintiff is located in Greentree told him that he had experienced no problems. Dorsey admitted that he told the Board of Adjustment about the police statements but not about the statements of the security officer. Other residents also testified for, but mostly against, allowing the facility to open.

Sergeant John Burke, commander of the Pharmaceutical Diversion Squad of the Cincinnati Police Division testified that he had experienced problems regarding criminal activity, such as drug dealers preying on those using drugs outside of methadone clinics in his town. . . .

One person who spoke in support of the facility had herself been a heroin addict for ten years, and testified that she would travel to Covington to pick up her drugs. She testified that in April 1996, she entered a clinic located in Indiana, and was stabilized and able to obtain a job in a school. . . . As a result of her methadone treatment, she testified that she was drug free. Plaintiff also put on videotape evidence of Wayne Crabtree, a program director of a methadone clinic in Louisville. Crabtree testified that his clinic had experienced no acts of violence committed against anyone in the community, although he stated that there once had been a problem between two clients. Essentially, he stated that his clinic operated without incident.

The Board of Adjustment voted to overrule Hopper's decision and revoked the zoning permit. . . .

During the spring of 1998, Plaintiff contacted Hopper again about obtaining another location in the city, at 1 West 43rd Street. The site had been a doctor's office, and it was located in a shopping center zone. The site was in front of the City's trash compacting station, bordering an industrial zone, and separated from housing by a four-lane highway. The building was in a location with good public transportation, was affordable and was available. Hopper again thought this use would be a permitted use under the zoning code, and told McNeil so. However, recognizing the controversy concerning the clinic, Hopper also informed the city manager, Greg Jarvis, of Plaintiff's latest request. In response, on March 17, 1998, the city solicitor sent a letter to Hopper, which according to Hopper, basically stated that as the zoning ordinances then stood, a methadone clinic, such as Plaintiff's, was not a permitted use in any zone in the city.

After the Board of Adjustment hearing, the Covington General Affairs Committee and Hopper met, and issued a report entitled "Preventing the Proliferation of Addiction Treatment Facilities in Covington." The report included a proposed amendment to the zoning code, which was adopted by Covington in June 1998. The amendment expanded the definition of "addiction treatment facility" in the zoning code to include any place whose primary function is to care for the chemically dependent. The zoning code previously only used the term to apply to programs that provided overnight or housing accommodations. The ordinance limited the number of all such facilities to one facility for every 20,000 persons in the city. The amendment completely foreclosed Plaintiff's opportunity to locate in the city.

Hopper testified that one residential treatment facility had previously wanted to locate in the city, but at that time the business did not fit into a category as listed in the zoning code. The facility, the Women's Residential Assistance Treatment Program ("WRATP"), requested an amendment and both it and another facility, operated by the same group that operates the WRATP, were allowed to locate in the city as a result of the ordinance amendments. . . .

Fabian testified at trial that the program MX intended to establish would not only provide methadone treatment, but also offer other services, such as counseling. She testified that often a drug addiction affects a person's life in numerous ways, including loss of employment, spouses and children. She testified that the addiction affects a person's ability to hold a job, to engage in parenting, or to function socially. . . .

McNeil testified at trial that [MX's] clinic in Erie, Pennsylvania had experienced none of the problems Dorsey raised at the Board of Adjustment hearing. She testified that she had experienced no trouble with robberies, murders, arrests or diversion at the Erie facility.

At trial, Mark Caverly of the Drug Enforcement Agency also testified. He testified about concern regarding drug diversion at methadone programs, but stated that such concern arises anywhere that drugs are present, such as pharmacies or doctors' offices.

### Discussion

The district court's findings of fact will be set aside only for clear error. "This standard does not entitle a reviewing court to reverse a district court's findings of fact because the reviewing court is convinced it would have decided the case differently." The district court's conclusions of law, however, are reviewed *de novo*.

. . . .

As a preliminary matter, we note that Plaintiff asserts claims under both the ADA and the Rehabilitation Act. The district court analyzed Plaintiff's claims under both acts together, and referred only to the ADA in its analysis, "since the results are the same under both Acts." *MX Group, Inc.*, 106 F. Supp. 2d at 915. We will do the same inasmuch as both acts are interpreted consistently with one another.

. . . .

Title II of the ADA states that "no qualified individual with a disability shall, by reasons of such disability, be excluded from participation in or be denied the benefits of the services, programs or activities of a public entity, or be subjected to discrimination by any such entity." 42 U.S.C. §12132.

. . . .

. . . According to the regulations implementing Title II,

> A public entity shall not exclude or otherwise deny equal services, programs, or activities to an individual or entity because of the known disability of an individual with whom the individual or entity is known to have a relationship or association.

28 C.F.R. § 35.130(g).

. . . .

To determine whether an individual is disabled under [the ADA], the Supreme Court has stated that courts should determine whether an individual has a mental or physical impairment that substantially limits a major life activity. Drug abuse can constitute such an impairment. . . .

In the instant case, Plaintiff presented evidence that its potential clients are recovering drug addicts. . . .

However, merely having an impairment does not make one disabled for purposes of the ADA; a plaintiff must also show the impairment substantially limits a major life activity. Such an inquiry must be made on a case-by-case basis. . . .

Major life activities constitute tasks central to most people's daily lives. According to the regulations implementing Title II, major life activities include such functions as caring for one's self, performing manual tasks, walking, seeing, hearing, speaking, breathing, learning, and working. 28 C.F.R. § 35.104. This list is merely illustrative and not exhaustive. . . .

. . . .

Although the ADA states that the impairment must "substantially" limit the major life activities, the requirement does not mean that Plaintiff must show an utter incapability to work, parent or function socially in every day life, but only that these "significant limitations result from the impairment." . . .

Moreover, by including recovering drug addicts among those to be protected under the ADA, Congress recognized "that many people continue to participate in drug treatment programs long after they have stopped using drugs illegally, *and that such persons should be protected under the Act.*" . . .

. . . .

Defendants further argue, however, that to the extent they discriminated against Plaintiff's potential clients or Plaintiff (because of its association with its potential clients), such discrimination was based on fear of criminal activity. The discrimination, Defendants contend, was not based on a mental or physiological impairment. Defendants essentially contend that a drug addict's "propensity . . . to commit a crime or to attract criminal activity is not a mental or physiological impairment recognized under the ADA."

. . . Defendants here contend that it was the secondary effects of criminality and not a physiological impairment that resulted in the discrimination. . . .

... [T]he district court relied on the Board of Adjustment hearing transcript to support its finding that Defendants regarded Plaintiff's clients or potential clients as disabled. At the hearing, Dorsey testified that in the cases in which he had contacted clinics, he was told the same story. He was informed of altercations outside the clinics, open-air drug markets, and violence and drug thefts. "In near and around, wherever the for-profit clinics are located, there appears to be an increased level of criminal activity which involves violence, guns and drugs." As the district court found, he provided no statistics and gave no specifics.

There was also testimony at the hearing from Sergeant John Burke, commander of the Pharmaceutical Diversion Squad of the Cincinnati Police Division. Burke testified that he had experienced problems regarding criminal activity, such as drug dealers preying on those using drugs outside of clinics. He testified that he had no direct experience with for-profit clinics, except reports from a nearby clinic in Indiana, of which he was familiar.

. . . .

One of the purposes of the ADA is to prevent discrimination against those regarded as being disabled. According to the regulations, "a person who is denied services or benefits by a public entity because of myths, fears, or stereotypes associated with disabilities would be covered under" the regarded as [criterion], "whether or not the persons' physical or mental condition would be considered a disability under the first or second test in the definition." 28 C.F.R., pt. 35, App. A to 28, § 35.104 at 518–19. Defendants apparently contend that because the discrimination Plaintiff encountered was based on the alleged increased crime that drug addicts bring to an area instead of the actual impairment of drug addiction, the ADA was not violated. However, ... where the discrimination results from unfounded fears and stereotypes that merely because Plaintiff's potential clients are recovering drug addicts, they would necessarily attract increased drug activity and violent crime to the city, such discrimination violates the ADA and Rehabilitation Act.

*Based on witness testimony at the Board of Adjustment hearing, we believe that Plaintiff adduced sufficient evidence to show that the reason the city denied Plaintiff the zoning permit was because the city feared that Plaintiff's clients would continue to abuse drugs, continue in their drug activity, and attract more drug activity to the city. In other words, based on fear and stereotypes, residents believed that the drug addiction impairment of Plaintiff's potential clients, at the very least, limited the major life activity of productive social functioning, as their status as recovering drug addicts was consistently equated with criminality.* [emphasis in original] The record also supports the district court's finding that the Board of Adjustment denied Plaintiff's permit primarily for these reasons.

There was ample evidence before the district court, however, that Plaintiff's other clinic in Pennsylvania had operated without incident of criminal activity, and that methadone clinics present no more problems in the way of drug trafficking and diversion than other facilities that deal with lawfully administered drugs, such as hospitals and pharmacies. By way of video, Wayne Crabtree, program director of a methadone clinic in Louisville, explained at the Board of Adjustment hearing that his clinic had experienced no acts of violence committed against anyone in the community, and essentially had operated without incident. Defendants point to no other evidence from any other methadone clinic representatives indicating that such clinics attract increased drug activity or crime. Therefore, we believe that the district court correctly found that the board's decision to deny Plaintiff a zoning permit, and the city's subsequent decision to change the zoning ordinance to ban Plaintiff from operating anywhere in the city, were based on stereotypes and fear and violated the ADA and Rehabilitation Act. [Given that the court resolved the case on the basis of the ADA and the Rehabilitation Act, it did not go into the plaintiff's claims related to violation of due process and equal protection.]

. . . .

### Conclusion

For the foregoing reasons, we affirm the judgment of the district court.

## Questions for Consideration

1) This case was decided under the ADA and the Rehabilitation Act. If the facts were presented to the court prior to the passage of the ADA and the Rehabilitation Act, how would you argue the case in terms of nuisance law?

2) What evidence supports a conclusion of discrimination as the basis for the permit denial?

3) What evidence supports the claim that the permit denial was based on safety issues related to secondary effects?

4) How much input should current residents have in the process of locating and permitting a drug rehabilitation center? How and by what process should that input occur?

5) How important should evidence of loss of value to nearby properties be when considering a permit for a drug rehabilitation center?

6) Assume you live in a quiet and reasonably upscale middle class neighborhood, and only single-family residential homes are permitted. If someone wishes to purchase the house next door to your house and use it for a drug rehabilitation program for four unrelated adults recovering from drug addiction, what can or should you be able to do in an effort to prevent this use?

## Takeaway

- As the above case illustrates, complexity arises in trying to figure out how local, state, and federal law work together in the context of zoning. People with disabilities are protected by a variety of federal laws, and these federal laws may come into conflict with local zoning regulations enacted pursuant to state law.

This means that even in a local land use and zoning practice, one must have a strong understanding of our constitutional framework.

## Discussion Problem 2.2

The Town of Brookside is a small suburban community of about 5,000 residents within the metropolitan area of Lake View, a city of 300,000 residents. Brookside is what many refer to as a bedroom community. Most of Brookside is made up of single and two-family homes. In fact, about 90% of the land space within Brookside is zoned for either single-family or two-family housing. There is a small half-mile stretch of a state road going through Brookside zoned for C-1 Commercial and Office Use. Some of the uses included in the C-1 zone are a gas station, grocery store, a Starbucks, a Taco Bell, a bank, a professional building with several lawyers, a psychiatrist, and a small accounting firm located therein, a Veterans Counseling Clinic, and a small local drop-in wellness center operated as part of a health network of a hospital located in downtown Lake View. In addition, there is another half-mile stretch of road that is on the city line with Lake View that is zoned as X-2 for "Adult uses." Adult uses are separated from uses such as schools, parks, places of worship, family shopping and entertainment venues, and restaurants. This separation by zones is established by the zoning code, and it is directed at managing and containing the spillover and secondary effects of adult entertainment such as strip clubs, adult movies houses, vendors of legally protected pornography and sellers of so called, "sex toys." This zone is also the only location in Brookside that permits property to be used for the retail sale of recently legalized marijuana, and for such uses as a drug rehabilitation and treatment center, or a drug and alcohol recovery and counseling facility. The rationale for this separation of uses is based on a study done of two major urban areas in which the evidence showed that criminal activity was higher within 2,000 feet of an adult use and of a liquor store than it was in other locations and neighborhoods. Brookside had no liquor stores, but alcohol was available in a section of the local grocery store.

The Town of Brookside reasoned that it was important for public health, welfare, and safety to keep certain uses located in one manageable location so that the local Town police could better control crime around the properties used for the regulated purposes. The Town determined that a retail marijuana store was akin to a liquor store, and that drug rehabilitation centers and places for counseling recovering drug and alcohol abusers were of a similar type when it comes to the secondary effects of crime. Furthermore, the Town reasoned that these uses could be readily found within the city limits of Lake View. The property within the X-2 zone is fully developed, and there are seldom sales of existing businesses or spaces within this zone.

Recently, a building of about 4,500 square feet became available for sale in the C-1 zone of Brookside. Two interested parties have expressed an interest in buying the property, or perhaps even partnering to use the building jointly. One interested party is Bud's Pot Shop, and the other is a not-for-profit named Recovering Hope.

Bud's Pot Shop asserts that its business is not like a liquor store and that, in addition to general recreational uses, many customers are going to be people with disabilities seeking the benefits of doctor directed use of marijuana. Recovering Hope focuses exclusively on clients with disabilities by counseling and assisting people recovering from drug and alcohol addiction.

The Town of Brookside requests your legal counsel on the question of whether or not to grant a permit for one or both of these interested parties. Based on what you have learned so far, and on reference to the Appendix in the back of the book, what issues and concerns might you raise in terms of how Brookside should deal with this matter? What questions are likely to be raised? What kind of evidence should be taken at a hearing on the request for a permit? What political reaction and legal challenges might you expect Town officials to deal with in holding public hearings to address these two requests?

# C. Practice Problems

2.1 Pedro is the owner of a single-family home in the community where our law firm is located. Pedro has a four bedroom and three bathroom home. Now that his children are grown and moved away, Pedro would like to earn some extra money by listing his house with AirBnB. Pedro has come to our law office because we have handled matters for him in the past, such as the purchase and financing of the house he lives in. Pedro tells us that he talked to his neighbor about his plan, and his neighbor informed him that short-term rentals and AirBnB are not permitted uses in single-family residential home districts. Furthermore, his neighbor indicated that she would consider such a use to be a nuisance, and that she would work to organize other neighbors to stop Pedro from using his house as he hopes to do. As a new associate in the firm, prepare an opinion letter for the client as to his intended use being sure to address the following two matters.

   a) Examine the local zoning regulations and opine as to whether short-term rentals and AirBnB uses are permitted or regulated.

   b) Opine as to the viability of a nuisance suit independent of any regulations in the local zoning code.

2.2 We have a client interested in opening a medical marijuana dispensary in our community (assume your state either already permits such a use or that your state is considering passing legislation to approve such a use, and our client wishes to be prepared to enter the market). No one in the firm really knows anything about this topic, but one of our paralegals came across a case out of California that might be a good place to start some research. The case is *City of Claremont v. Kruse*, 177 Cal. App. 4th 1153 (Court of Appeal of California, Second Appellate District, Division Two, 2009). Read this case and write up a memorandum that briefs the case with an analysis of the implications of the case from a nuisance and land use perspective.

2.3 In many communities across the country, there is a problem with abandoned homes and buildings. These homes and buildings are frequently in prolonged fore-closure proceedings and vacated by the owners. Such properties are sometimes referred to as *zombie properties*. Often, these properties end up having doors and windows boarded up with sheets of plywood. Some communities think that the use of plywood on these homes and buildings adds to the look of decay in the neighbor-hood and that these zombie properties are a nuisance. One idea being discussed by some local governments is to impose a new requirement on owners and lenders holding mortgages on these properties. The idea is that, in addition to nuisance law, land use and zoning regulations can prevent owners and lenders from using ply-wood to board up abandoned and zombie properties. In lieu of plywood, owners and lenders will be required to use clear polycarbonate windows and doors. By some estimates, the cost of the clear polycarbonate is five to six times more expensive than the cost of plywood sized the same to accomplish the same outcome. Most observ-ers agree that the clear polycarbonate looks much better than plywood, and some people assert that it is stronger and provides great security against unwanted entry.

a) Assume you are a community development consultant with a law degree working at a local not-for-profit entity focused on developing sustainable neighborhoods. Somehow, a major newspaper obtains your name as someone to contact to provide an opinion on the use of land use and zoning law to prevent abandoned properties from being boarded up with plywood. Write a thoughtful opinion piece on this issue in response to the request of the news-paper's editor.

# Chapter 3

# The Police Power and Its Limitations

## A. Introduction to the Police Power

The police power is an inherent power of every sovereign state. This includes the power to regulate for the public health, safety, welfare, and morals (in contemporary practice, "morals" includes aesthetics). In general, the police power under American law is located in the individual states. The federal government exercises police power over the District of Columbia, but generally the federal power to regulate is based on the *Necessary and Proper* Clause of the Constitution.

In the individual states, there will be enabling legislation that delegates state police power to municipalities and local governments. The state can limit the delegation of its police power, thus, it is always important to determine the scope of the power that has been delegated to municipal and local government. When a municipality or local government has police power, it generally has the authority to establish an executive branch (mayor), a legislative branch (city council), and a judicial system (city court). Under the police power, municipalities and local governments may also set up administrative agencies and enact regulations. In terms of land use and zoning law, cities and local governments generally establish planning boards and zoning boards to regulate and control land uses. In the typical situation, the local legislative branch will adopt a zoning and land use code to regulate land in accordance with an overall plan for the community. A planning board will work to facilitate property use and development in accordance with the plan; and, a zoning board of appeal will be in place to address questions regarding the interpretation and application of the code to particular property and to decide requests for variances and exceptions from the strict requirements of the code.

In this chapter, we focus on the exercise of the police power as a way of dealing with land use and its regulation. The police power permits regulation of property that goes beyond the common law actions related to nuisance and trespass. The police power permits the government to regulate the use of property, but in regulating property, the police power is limited. Thus, we have to develop an understanding of the police power and of the ways in which the police power may be limited. In general, we will see that the police power must be exercised to promote the *public* health, safety, welfare, and morals; not to create benefits for private individuals. The exercise of the police power, in limiting a property owner's rights to use her property in a lawful way, is also subject to the requirements of due process, equal protection, the Fifth Amendment Takings Clause, and by other laws protecting other fundamental rights. For example, a land use regulation designed to control the use and placement of signs, flags, and other messages on residential property may conflict with the First Amendment right to free speech and expression. Likewise, land regulations that affect property owned by churches, temples, and mosques may raise conflicts with the First Amendment right to the free exercise of religion.

A significant tension in land use and zoning law involves the conflict between an individual's right to use property in a lawful way, and the government's power to regulate and limit that use under the police power. Historically, the right to property has been important to Americans, thus the regulation and limitation of lawful uses of land has created a great deal of tension between those seeking to regulate the use of property and those who own property subject to regulation. As we will learn in this book, one response to government regulation of private property can result in a claim of *regulatory taking*. That is, a claim asserting the government regulation of property has gone so far that it amounts to a virtual "taking" of the property within the meaning of the Fifth Amendment to the Constitution.

Understanding the exercise of the police power and its limitations is an important part of being a land use and zoning lawyer. In this book, the approach is one of starting from the traditional presumption that when the government was formed under the Constitution, the people held the full bundle of rights to their property and then delegated certain powers to a limited government. Among these powers is the authority of government to exercise the police power to protect and advance the public health, safety, welfare, and morals. The police power, however, is limited. Moreover, since the traditional common law presumption is in favor of being able to use one's property in a lawful way without limitation by the government, the government should have a justification and rationale for limiting a person's use of her property. In chapter two, we saw that the common law actions for nuisance and for trespass were ways of restricting an individual's use of property based on doing things that interfere with the rights of others or that cause harm to others. In this chapter, we will see that the police power goes beyond regulating nuisance and trespass; it extends to regulating a variety of externalities and spillover effects that cause harm to others.

## Thurlow v. Massachusetts

Supreme Court of the United States
46 U.S. 504 (1847)

. . . .

McLean, Justice. It has been said, indeed, that quarantine and health laws are passed by the States, not by virtue of a power to regulate commerce, but by virtue of their police powers, and in order to guard the lives and health of their citizens. . . . [B]ut what are the police powers of a State? They are nothing more or less than the powers of government inherent in every sovereignty to the extent of its dominions. And whether a State passes a quarantine law, or a law to punish offences, or to establish courts of justice, or requiring certain instruments to be recorded, or to regulate commerce within its own limits, in every case it exercises the same power; that is to say, the power of sovereignty, the power to govern men and things within the limits of its dominion. It is by virtue of this power that it legislates; and its authority to make regulations of commerce is as absolute as its power to pass health laws, except in so far as it has been restricted by the constitution of the United States. And when the validity of a State law making regulations of commerce is drawn into question in a judicial tribunal, the authority to pass it cannot be made to depend upon the motives that may be supposed to have influenced the legislature, nor can the court inquire whether it was intended to guard the citizens of the State from pestilence and disease, or to make regulations of commerce for the interests and convenience of trade.

Upon this question the object and motive of the State are of no importance, and cannot influence the decision. It is a question of power.

. . . .

We cannot overrate the importance of police powers to the States. The means of social improvement, the success of all institutions of learning and religion, depend on the preservation of this power. We look to the States for the exercise of their authority in aid of all institutions which tend to improve and elevate the moral and intellectual character of the people.

. . . .

## *Questions for Consideration*

1) Explain the concept of the police power.

2) How does the exercise of the police power relate to complaints about over regulation and the intrusive nature of the so-called "administrative state"?

3) Do you think that the contemporary complaints about over regulation are justified or not?

## *Takeaway*

- When government undertakes to regulate commerce and land use, it exercises the police power. The exercise of this power is given deference by a reviewing court. As we shall see, the courts give the legislature a high degree of deference when exercising the police power to regulate on behalf of the public health, safety, welfare, and morals. When challenging legislation, the general test is that the legislation will be upheld if it is rational using a "fairly debatable" standard of rationality. Under the fairly debatable standard, we do not look at the specific motives of the individual legislators in passing the regulation, but rather, ask if the legislation is supportable under any rational set of facts and circumstances. This is the standard applied in cases where a facial challenge is made to a regulation. We will see this standard applied in the next case in this chapter. In later material we will see that different standards apply in different situations.

- In exercising the police power to regulate land uses, it is important to emphasize that it is the *use* that is regulated; not the person or people using the property. Likewise, the regulation of the use is not based on how the property is owned (by an individual, a corporation, a partnership, etc.).

To develop a sound understanding of the basis for land use regulation, it is important to appreciate some basic concepts regarding externalities and spillover effects. To begin with, we must understand that there has been some form of land regulation in the United States since colonial times. These early regulations covered such things as the layout of roads and the spacing of buildings. As America industrialized and became more urban, cities were often dirty, smelly, and crowded places with few facilities for proper sewage treatment or water purification. Consequently, cities were often unsanitary and possessed conditions favorable to disease. Concerns for the public health prompted a movement toward government regulation. By the year 1924, the Standard State Zoning Enabling Act was approved as a model for state legislatures to adopt in delegating zoning authority to local governments. It was quickly adopted by hundreds of cities. In 1926, the first challenge to local zoning authority reached the U.S. Supreme Court, with the landmark case of *Village of Euclid v. Ambler Realty Co.*, 272 U.S. 365 (1926).

The excerpt below introduces some basic concepts that are important to thinking about how and why we regulate land use for the benefit of the public health, safety, welfare, and morals.

## Robin Paul Malloy, Land Use Law and Disability: Planning and Zoning for Accessible Communities *30–35*

(Cambridge University Press, 2015)
(Footnotes have been omitted)

. . . .

. . . [We begin our discussion] . . . with background information concerning nuisance and the idea of regulating externalities. This discussion serves as a prelude to consideration of the case of *Village of Euclid v. Ambler Realty Co.*, 272 U.S. 365 (1926). . . .

a. Prelude to *Euclid*

In an idealized world, complex property relationships could be easily coordinated by innumerable individuals negotiating among themselves to achieve reasonably and mutually beneficial outcomes. Such an outcome would be consistent with the image that Adam Smith, the founder of modern-day economics, offered in his conception of the *invisible hand*. For Smith, the idea of an invisible hand was that individuals, pursuing their own self-interest, are guided by an invisible hand that leads them to promote the public interest, even though the public interest is no part of their original intention. In other words, people with good information and an ability to negotiate with each other ought to be able to attain desirable outcomes that simultaneously maximize their own individual preferences as well as those of the community more generally. This means that marginal private costs are equal to marginal social costs and that marginal private benefits are equal to marginal public benefits. In such a situation, there is little or no variance between public and private interests and presumably no need for government to be involved in regulating property development and the coordination of land uses.

In practice, Smith understood that the world was more complicated. Coordinating property uses in a highly complex and integrated world is difficult for individuals, and when acting in their own self-interest, they are generally unlikely to achieve perfect unity between private and public interest. There are multiple reasons for this: problems of incomplete information; lack of clearly defined property rights; transactions costs; problems of coordinating collective action with neighbors; difficulty enforcing performance and enforcing remedies when an agreement is achieved; and the problem of wealth effects, which may skew outcomes in favor of higher income property owners. The point is that in an idealized world, we might not need land use regulation, but in the real world we need some mechanism for coordinating land uses — and this mechanism must be able to mediate the tensions arising from the push and pull of competing preferences among self-interested individuals. These tensions are not just economic but also political, social, cultural, and emotional. To achieve beneficial and acceptable results in a very diverse community of individuals, the coordinating mechanism must be deemed fair, accessible, predictable, and rational (not arbitrary, capricious, or completely subjective), and because many people feel that the current distribution of resources is itself unfair, the mechanism cannot simply be driven by a desire to confirm private market arrangements among people of economic means.

For better or for worse, in the absence of a perfect identity between private and public interest, government has taken on the role of mediating the coordination of land uses. Importantly, it should be understood that this role for government is not altogether inconsistent with Adam Smith's idea of the invisible hand, because Smith also suggested a role for an *impartial spectator*, who would constrain and temper the pursuit of individual self-interest. In some ways, therefore, representative government acting pursuant to the rule of law provides the mediating presence required of Smith's impartial spectator. Moreover, appreciating a role for government in the regulation of property development and land use need not be considered an anti-market view; Adam Smith, after all, was himself a government agent working in a customhouse in Scotland, and the idea of representative government functioning as an impartial spectator in certain situations would probably not have struck him as overly problematic.

Given acceptance of the idea that government regulation of land use is important in situations where individuals cannot themselves easily coordinate such uses, let us consider an example that illustrates some of the background issues that shape an understanding of land use regulation. As a starting point, let us begin with an example based on the facts of the well-known case of *Boomer v. Atlantic Cement Co.*, 257 N.E.2d 870 (N.Y. 1970).

The *Boomer* case involved a private nuisance dispute among adjoining property owners. Atlantic Cement owned property on which it operated a facility that discharged pollutants into the ambient air. These discharges affected the property of surrounding landowners and in response, they brought a lawsuit seeking to enjoin further operation of the cement facility. In deciding the case, the court considered the potential for development of new technology to mitigate future discharges but noted that the company was using current technology at the time. The court found that enjoining the operation of the facility would cost Atlantic Cement in excess of $45 million, whereas the negative impact of the operation on surrounding property owners was less than $1 million. In this case, the decision was made to permit Atlantic Cement to continue operating. As an alternative to closing down the facility, the surrounding property owners were compensated for the negative impact on the value of their property. One way of looking at this outcome is that awarding $1 million to correct the problem (making surrounding property owners "whole" by awarding compensation) was much cheaper than enjoining the operation of the facility at a cost to its owner of more than $45 million. In addition, because the company employed a number of people and added value to the local economy, closing the plant would have had negative economic repercussions for the entire community, beyond the $45 million cost to Atlantic Cement.

The action in this case was brought as a private nuisance, meaning that the operation of the facility was a nuisance to a limited number of people and that the operation of such a facility (a cement factory) was not a nuisance to the public in general. Under similar facts, an action might have been brought by a public official to enjoin the activity as a public nuisance if the operation of the facility posed a threat to public health, perhaps because it could be shown that the discharging of dust and dirt into the ambient air is a triggering factor in lung disease — although this was not the situation in *Boomer*. Under traditional land use law, a property owner has no right to operate a nuisance on his property, and the government can enjoin the particular use under its police power to protect the public health, safety, welfare, and morals. Moreover, because a property owner has no right to operate a nuisance, preventing a use that amounts to a nuisance is not a taking under the Fifth Amendment to the U.S. Constitution. As a starting point, therefore, one must appreciate that nuisance law has long been a source of authority for government to limit the use rights of a property owner; it is a traditional background legal principle supporting the exercise of the police power.

Modern land use law now limits many more uses than those that rise to the level of a nuisance. Let us consider the *Boomer* situation in terms of externalities and the problem of transaction costs to suggest a further basis for government regulation of land uses. In the *Boomer* case, Atlantic Cement was making a use of its property that imposed costs and burdens on adjoining properties. The discharge of pollutants into the ambient air, resulting in dirt and dust on adjoining properties, is a classic spillover effect (also known as an externality), and because the spillover imposes burdens and costs on the adjoining properties, to the detriment of the owners, it is identified as a negative externality. In the language of property, Atlantic Cement is obtaining a free negative servitude over the adjoining properties because it is, in effect, using the adjoining property to deposit dust and dirt that it is unable to contain on its own property but that it must generate as part of its normal operations (dust and dirt are normal by-products of the production process). In other words, if Atlantic Cement wanted to avoid having a spillover effect on adjoining properties, it would need to acquire much more land to encircle its operations and "catch" all of the particles escaping from its facility. In the alternative, it would need to invest in a way to reduce and eliminate the discharge.

Determining if the negative servitude in this example is free might turn on the question of who was there first: Atlantic Cement or the adjoining property owners. If the adjoining property owners were there first, then Atlantic Cement moved in and its operations imposed costs on the adjoining property owners and diminished the value of their land. In this case, Atlantic Cement obtains the servitude for free, unless it pays the adjoining owners for the cost of the servitude — and the owners may be unwilling to sell. Conversely, if Atlantic Cement were located on its property prior to the arrival of adjoining property owners (a residential subdivision is built several years later), it could be argued that the adjoining owners moved to the nuisance and were able to acquire the property at a discounted price because of the presence of its operation next door. In the situation of moving to the nuisance, it might be held that the homeowners have already been compensated for the impact of the servitude at the time of purchase, as a result of the discounted purchase price. In other words, the negative effects of the Atlantic Cement operations result in a lower cost of acquiring the nearby property, and this lower acquisition price reflects an up-front compensation for the discharge of dust and dirt on surrounding lands. Situations such as this raise conflict among property owners, and the greater the number of property owners involved, the more complex and difficult an amicable resolution becomes.

The situation in *Boomer* is made more difficult for private parties to coordinate as the number of adjoining property owners increases and as the specificity of property rights and the costs and benefits on all sides become less clear. Government can sometimes assess the problem better than the immediately affected individuals and work out a regulatory arrangement that might be more tolerable than that which they might try to accomplish on their own. . . .

. . . .

The preceding example illustrates some of the issues involved in coordinating property development and land use. . . . Coordinating land uses does involve consideration of costs and benefits, but it frequently also involves a need to mediate deep and intense differences among people based on competing political, social, cultural, and aesthetic values. For these reasons, it may be difficult for individuals to achieve good community-wide outcomes when everyone simply seeks to pursue his own self-interest. Unlike the individual decision to purchase a home or to rent a particular apartment, the coordination of multiple and complex land uses across an entire community is difficult. Sometimes having access to experts and a little distance from an underlying relationship or conflict, as in being a kind of impartial spectator, is beneficial.

As a further prelude to addressing the *Euclid* case, it should be noted that . . . [a]n "invasion" of dust, dirt, noise, or something else is often an element of a classic spillover externality, but it is not a requirement. For example, an adjoining property owner may construct or modify a building in a way that is aesthetically undesirable, thus causing the value of surrounding property to fall. Similarly, a property owner might wish to place a series of large billboards on a residential lot, shelter numerous animals in a backyard, or use her building for a drug rehabilitation center. In a very real sense, these types of uses do not involve a physical "invasion" of adjoining property in the same way as dirt, dust, and noise might, but they do have a negative effect on the use and enjoyment of the surrounding property and likewise effect the public health, safety, welfare, and morals. Consider, too, a popular grocery store or restaurant that locates in a quiet residential neighborhood. Even if the store and restaurant are built with ample parking, and can be more or less self-contained on the property where they are located, it may be that the traffic generated by customers coming and going to these businesses creates a neighborhood impact that is akin to an externality or an associational spillover. Perhaps the roads in the neighborhood need to be widened to safely handle increased traffic loads, or perhaps because of increased automobile traffic, a need for new sidewalks is generated. The presence of these "attractor" uses can also create a type of neighborhood externality that land use professionals need to account for in seeking to effectively coordinate land uses. The point is that externalities in the land use context need not involve any sort of "invasion" or trespass to fall within the regulatory scope of the police power.

## Questions for Consideration

1) If a primary rationale for zoning is to advance the public health, safety, welfare, and morals by controlling externalities, spillover effects, and transaction costs, are there any easily identifiable limits on the scope and reach of such regulations?

2) Under contemporary U.S. law, do you think the limitations on the exercise of the police power are primarily substantive or procedural?

## Takeaway

- The important takeaway from the above discussion is one of recognizing that individuals acting on their own may have difficulty coordinating land uses in a way that minimizes conflict while promoting a wise use of resources. This may be due to incomplete or erroneous information; poorly defined property rights; coordination problems; wealth effects; and other types of transaction costs. When land use professionals can identify situations in which individuals may not be able to coordinate land uses in a way that protects and advances the public health, safety, welfare, and morals of the community, they have a foundation for regulating land through the exercise of the local police power.

- A related set of questions that run through land use and zoning law involve the deference owed to decision makers at various steps in the process. For example, if the police power is exercised to advance the public health, safety, welfare, and morals, who is to say a particular regulation serves this purpose? Similarly, if a regulation creates a zoning district defined by a particular geographic location on a zoning map, who decides where those district lines are drawn? These types of questions are really ones that recognize that the law involves many judgment calls. Thus, the question arises as to how much deference a reviewing body should give to these decisions and judgments. We analyze these issues in terms of the *standard of review*. So, as you work through the material in this chapter and the rest of the book, take account of the legal rules and policies addressed in each case, and pay attention to the standard of review applicable to the decisions and judgments. You will see that there are multiple standards of review addressed by the courts. The standards of review are important when you practice law in this area because they inform you about the level of evidence and justification that is needed to support a given judgment. For example, if a zoning board of appeal makes a decision in response to a petition by a property owner, the decision must be rational and supported by substantial competent evidence on the record. This is one form of the rational basis standard of review. In this situation, the judgment of the zoning board of appeal will be upheld by a reviewing body as long as the judgment meets the applicable rational basis standard of review. Consequently, even if a good case can be made for a different result, the zoning board of appeal "wins" as long as the decision it made was rational and based on the evidence. As you will learn, different standards of review apply to legislation, zoning board decisions, and to situations where local land regulations come into conflict with such things as First Amendment rights. It is important to be well informed on both the relevant substantive law and on the applicable standard of review.

# B. A Facial Challenge

A facial challenge to land regulation is one that asserts that the law in question is unconstitutional as written. A typical facial challenge asserts that the legislative body enacting a regulation lacked legal authority. Another way of looking at a facial challenge is that it is an assertion that there is no application of the regulation that is legal.

# Village of Euclid v. Ambler Realty Co.

Supreme Court of the United States

272 U.S. 365 (1926)

SUTHERLAND, Justice. The village of Euclid is an Ohio municipal corporation. It adjoins and practically is a suburb of the city of Cleveland. Its estimated population is between 5,000 and 10,000, and its area from 12 to 14 square miles, the greater part of which is farm lands or unimproved acreage. It lies, roughly, in the form of a parallelogram measuring approximately 3 1/2 miles each way. East and west it is traversed by three principal highways: Euclid avenue, through the southerly border, St. Clair avenue, through the central portion, and Lake Shore boulevard, through the northerly border, in close proximity to the shore of Lake Erie. The Nickel Plate Railroad lies from 1,500 to 1,800 feet north of Euclid avenue, and the Lake Shore Railroad 1,600 feet farther to the north. The three highways and the two railroads are substantially parallel.

Appellee is the owner of a tract of land containing 68 acres, situated in the westerly end of the village, abutting on Euclid avenue to the south and the Nickel Plate Railroad to the north. Adjoining this tract, both on the east and on the west, there have been laid out restricted residential plats upon which residences have been erected.

On November 13, 1922, an ordinance was adopted by the village council, establishing a comprehensive zoning plan for regulating and restricting the location of trades, industries, apartment houses, two-family houses, single family houses, etc., the lot area to be built upon, the size and height of buildings, etc.

The entire area of the village is divided by the ordinance into six classes of use districts, denominated U-1 to U-6, inclusive; three classes of height districts, denominated H-1 to H-3, inclusive; and four classes of area districts, denominated A-1 to A-4, inclusive. The use districts are classified in respect of the buildings which may be erected within their respective limits, as follows: U-1 is restricted to single family dwellings, public parks, water towers and reservoirs, suburban and interurban electric railway passenger stations and rights of way, and farming, non-commercial greenhouse nurseries, and truck gardening; U-2 is extended to include two-family dwellings; U-3 is further extended to include apartment houses, hotels, churches, schools, public libraries, museums, private clubs, community center buildings, hospitals, sanitariums, public playgrounds, and recreation buildings, and a city hall and courthouse; U-4 is further extended to include banks, offices, studios, telephone exchanges, fire and police stations, restaurants, theaters and moving picture shows, retail stores and shops, sales offices, sample rooms, wholesale stores for hardware, drugs, and groceries, stations for gasoline and oil (not exceeding 1,000 gallons storage) and for ice delivery, skating rinks and dance halls, electric substations, job and newspaper printing, public garages for motor vehicles, stables and wagon sheds (not exceeding five horses, wagons or motor trucks), and distributing stations for central store and commercial enterprises; U-5 is further extended to include billboards and advertising signs (if permitted), warehouses, ice and ice cream manufacturing and cold storage plants, bottling works milk bottling and central distribution stations, laundries, carpet cleaning, dry cleaning, and dyeing establishments, blacksmith, horseshoeing, wagon and motor vehicle repair shops, freight stations, street car barns, stables and wagon sheds (for more than five horses, wagons or motor trucks), and wholesale produce markets and salesroom; U-6 is further extended to include plants for sewage disposal and for producing gas, garbage and refuse incineration, scrap iron, junk, scrap paper, and rag storage, aviation fields, cemeteries, crematories, penal and correctional institutions, insane and feeble-minded institutions, storage of oil and gasoline (not to exceed 25,000 gallons), and manufacturing and industrial operations of any kind other than, and any public utility not included in, a class U-1, U-2, U-3, U-4, or U-5 use. There is a seventh class of uses which is prohibited altogether.

Class U-1 is the only district in which buildings are restricted to those enumerated. In the other classes the uses are cumulative; that is to say, uses in class U-2 include those enumerated in the preceding class U-1; class U-3 includes uses enumerated in the preceding classes, U-2, and U-1; and so on. In addition to the enumerated uses, the ordinance provides for accessory uses; that is, for uses customarily incident to the principal use, such as private garages. Many regulations are provided in respect of such accessory uses.

The height districts are classified as follows: In class H-1, buildings are limited to a height of 2 1/2 stories, or 35 feet; in class H-2, to 4 stories, or 50 feet; in class H-3, to 80 feet. To all of these, certain exceptions are made, as in the case of church spires, water tanks, etc.

The classification of area districts is: In A-1 districts, dwellings or apartment houses to accommodate more than one family must have at least 5,000 square feet for interior lots and at least 4,000 square feet for corner lots; in A-2 districts, the area must be at least 2,500 square feet for interior lots, and 2,000 square feet for corner lots; in A-3 districts, the limits are 1,250 and 1,000 square feet, respectively; in A-4 districts, the limits are 900 and 700 square feet, respectively. The ordinance contains, in great variety and detail, provisions in respect of width of lots, front, side, and rear yards, and other matters, including restrictions and regulations as to the use of billboards, signboards, and advertising signs.

A single family dwelling consists of a basement and not less than three rooms and a bathroom. A two-family dwelling consists of a basement and not less than four living rooms and a bathroom for each family, and is further described as a detached dwelling for the occupation of two families, one having its principal living rooms on the first floor and the other on the second floor.

Appellee's tract of land comes under U-2, U-3 and U-6. The first strip of 620 feet immediately north of Euclid avenue falls in class U-2, the next 130 feet to the north, in U-3, and the remainder in U-6. The uses of the first 620 feet, therefore, do not include apartment houses, hotels, churches, schools, or other public and semipublic buildings, or other uses enumerated in respect of U-3 to U-6, inclusive. The uses of the next 130 feet include all of these, but exclude industries, theaters, banks, shops, and the various other uses set forth in respect of U-4 to U-6, inclusive.

Annexed to the ordinance, and made a part of it, is a zone map, showing the location and limits of the various use, height, and area districts, from which it appears that the three classes overlap one another; that is to say, for example, both U-5 and U-6 use districts are in A-4 area district, but the former is in H-2 and the latter in H-3 height districts. The plan is a complicated one, and can be better understood by an inspection of the map, though it does not seem necessary to reproduce it for present purposes.

The lands lying between the two railroads for the entire length of the village area and extending some distance on either side to the north and south, having an average width of about 1,600 feet, are left open, with slight exceptions, for industrial and all other uses. This includes the larger part of appellee's tract. Approximately one-sixth of the area of the entire village is included in U-5 and U-6 use districts. That part of the village lying south of Euclid avenue is principally in U-1 districts. The lands lying north of Euclid avenue and bordering on the long strip just described are included in U-1, U-2, U-3, and U-4 districts, principally in U-2.

The enforcement of the ordinance is entrusted to the inspector of buildings, under rules and regulations of the board of zoning appeals. Meetings of the board are public, and minutes of its proceedings are kept. It is authorized to adopt rules and regulations to carry into effect provisions of the ordinance. Decisions of the inspector of buildings may be appealed to the board by any person claiming to be adversely affected by any such decision. The board is given power in specific cases of practical difficulty or unnecessary hardship to interpret the ordinance in harmony with its general purpose and intent, so that the public health, safety and general welfare may be secure and substantial justice done. Penalties are prescribed for violations, and it is provided that the various provisions are to be regarded as independent and the holding of any provision to be unconstitutional, void or ineffective shall not affect any of the others.

The ordinance is assailed on the grounds that it is in derogation of section 1 of the Fourteenth Amendment to the federal Constitution in that it deprives appellee of liberty and property without due process of law and denies it the equal protection of the law, and that it offends against certain provisions of the Constitution of the state of Ohio. The prayer of the bill is for an injunction restraining the enforcement of the ordinance and all attempts to impose or maintain as to appellee's property any of the restrictions, limitations or conditions. The court below held the ordinance to be unconstitutional and void, and enjoined its enforcement.

Before proceeding to a consideration of the case, it is necessary to determine the scope of the inquiry. The bill alleges that the tract of land in question is vacant and has been held for years for the purpose of selling and developing it for industrial uses, for which it is especially adapted, being immediately in the path of progressive industrial development; that for such uses it has a market value of about $10,000 per acre, but if the use be limited to residential purposes the market value is not in excess of $2,500 per acre; that the first 200 feet of the parcel back from Euclid avenue, if unrestricted in respect of use, has a value of $150 per front foot, but if limited to residential uses, and ordinary mercantile business be excluded therefrom, its value is not in excess of $50 per front foot.

It is specifically averred that the ordinance attempts to restrict and control the lawful uses of appellee's land, so as to confiscate and destroy a great part of its value; that it is being enforced in accordance with its terms; that prospective buyers of land for industrial, commercial, and residential uses in the metropolitan district of Cleveland are deterred from buying any part of this land because of the existence of the ordinance and the necessity thereby entailed of conducting burdensome and expensive litigation in order to vindicate the right to use the land for lawful and legitimate purposes; that the ordinance constitutes a cloud upon the land, reduces and destroys its value, and has the effect of diverting the normal industrial, commercial, and residential development thereof to other and less favorable locations.

The record goes no farther than to show, as the lower court found, that the normal and reasonably to be expected use and development of that part of appellee's land adjoining Euclid avenue is for general trade and commercial purposes, particularly retail stores and like establishments, and that the normal and reasonably to be expected use and development of the residue of the land is for industrial and trade purposes. Whatever injury is inflicted by the mere existence and threatened enforcement of the ordinance is due to restrictions in respect of these and similar uses, to which perhaps should be added — if not included in the foregoing — restrictions in respect of apartment houses. Specifically there is nothing in the record to suggest that any damage results from the presence in the ordinance of those restrictions relating to churches, schools, libraries, and other public and semipublic buildings. It is neither alleged nor proved that there is or may be a demand for any part of appellee's land for any of the last-named uses, and we cannot assume the existence of facts which would justify an injunction upon this record in respect to this class of restrictions. For present purposes the provisions of the ordinance in respect of these uses may therefore be put aside as unnecessary to be considered. It is also unnecessary to consider the effect of the restrictions in respect of U-1 districts, since none of appellee's land falls within that class.

We proceed, then, to a consideration of those provisions of the ordinance to which the case as it is made relates, first disposing of a preliminary matter.

A motion was made in the court below to dismiss the bill on the ground that, because complainant (appellee) had made no effort to obtain a building permit or apply to the zoning board of appeals for relief, as it might have done under the terms of the ordinance, the suit was premature. The motion was properly overruled, the effect of the allegations of the bill is that the ordinance of its own force operates greatly to reduce the value of appellee's lands and destroy their marketability for industrial, commercial and residential uses, and the attack is directed, not against any specific provision or provisions, but against the ordinance as an entirety. Assuming the premises, the existence and maintenance of the ordinance in effect constitutes a present invasion of appellee's property rights and a threat to continue it. Under these circumstances, the equitable jurisdiction is clear.

It is not necessary to set forth the provisions of the Ohio Constitution which are thought to be infringed. The question is the same under both Constitutions, namely, as stated by appellee: Is the ordinance invalid, in that it violates the constitutional protection "to the right of property in the appellee by attempted regulations under the guise of the police power, which are unreasonable and confiscatory?"

Building zone laws are of modern origin. They began in this country about 25 years ago. Until recent years, urban life was comparatively simple; but, with the great increase and concentration of population, problems have developed, and constantly are developing, which require, and will continue to require, additional restrictions in respect of the use and occupation of private lands in urban communities. Regulations, the wisdom, necessity, and validity of which, as applied to existing conditions, are so apparent that they are now uniformly sustained, a century ago, or even half a century ago, probably would have been rejected as arbitrary and oppressive. Such regulations are sustained, under the complex conditions of our day, for reasons analogous to those which justify traffic regulations, which, before the advent of automobiles and rapid transit street railways, would have been condemned as fatally arbitrary and unreasonable. And in this there is no inconsistency, for, while the meaning of constitutional guaranties never varies, the scope of their application must expand or contract to meet the new and different conditions which are constantly coming within the field of their operation. In a changing world it is impossible that it should be otherwise. But although a degree of elasticity is thus imparted, not to the meaning, but to the application of constitutional principles, statutes and ordinances, which, after giving due weight to the new conditions, are found clearly not to conform to the Constitution, of course, must fall.

The ordinance now under review, and all similar laws and regulations, must find their justification in some aspect of the police power, asserted for the public welfare. The line which in this field separates the legitimate from the illegitimate assumption of power is not capable of precise delimitation. It varies with circumstances and conditions. A regulatory zoning ordinance, which would be clearly valid as applied to the great cities, might be clearly invalid as applied to rural communities. In solving doubts, the maxim "sic utere tuo ut alienum non laedas," which lies at the foundation of so much of the common low of nuisances, ordinarily will furnish a fairly helpful clue. And the law of nuisances, likewise, may be consulted, not for the purpose of controlling, but for the helpful aid of its analogies in the process of ascertaining the scope of, the power. Thus the question whether the power exists to forbid the erection of a building of a particular kind or for a particular use, like the question whether a particular thing is a nuisance, is to be determined, not by an abstract consideration of the building or of the thing considered apart, but by considering it in connection with the circumstances and the locality. A nuisance may be merely a right thing in the wrong place, like a pig in the parlor instead of the barnyard. If the validity of the legislative classification for zoning purposes be fairly debatable, the legislative judgment must be allowed to control.

There is no serious difference of opinion in respect of the validity of laws and regulations fixing the height of buildings within reasonable limits, the character of materials and methods of construction, and the adjoining area which must be left open, in order to minimize the danger of fire or collapse, the evils of overcrowding and the like, and excluding from residential sections offensive trades, industries and structures likely to create nuisances.

Here, however, the exclusion is in general terms of all industrial establishments, and it may thereby happen that not only offensive or dangerous industries will be excluded, but those which are neither offensive nor dangerous will share the same fate. But this is no more than happens in respect of many practice-forbidding laws which this court has upheld, although drawn in general terms so as to include individual cases that may turn out to be innocuous in themselves. The inclusion of a reasonable margin, to insure effective enforcement, will not put upon a law, otherwise valid, the stamp of invalidity. Such laws may also find their justification in the fact that, in some fields, the bad fades into the good by such insensible degrees that the two are not capable of being readily distinguished and separated in terms of legislation. In the light of these considerations, we are not prepared to say that the end in view was not sufficient to justify the general rule of the ordinance, although some industries of an innocent character might fall within the proscribed class. It cannot be said that the ordinance in this respect "passes the bounds of reason and assumes the character of a merely arbitrary fiat." Moreover, the restrictive provisions of the ordinance in this particular may be sustained upon the principles applicable to the broader exclusion from residential districts of all business and trade structures, presently to be discussed.

It is said that the village of Euclid is a mere suburb of the city of Cleveland; that the industrial development of that city has now reached and in some degree extended into the village, and in the obvious course of things will soon absorb the entire area for industrial enterprises; that the effect of the ordinance is to divert this natural development elsewhere, with the consequent loss of increased values to the owners of the lands within the village borders. But the village, though physically a suburb of Cleveland, is politically a separate municipality, with powers of its own and authority to govern itself as it sees fit, within the limits of the organic law of its creation and the state and federal Constitutions. Its governing authorities, presumably representing a majority of its inhabitants and voicing their will, have determined, not that industrial development shall cease at its boundaries, but that the course of such development shall proceed within definitely fixed lines. If it be a proper exercise of the police power to relegate industrial establishments to localities separated from residential sections, it is not easy to find a sufficient reason for denying the power because the effect of its exercise is to divert an industrial flow from the course which it would follow, to the injury of the residential public, if left alone, to another course where such injury will be obviated. It is not meant by this, however, to exclude the possibility of cases where the general public interest would so far outweigh the interest of the municipality that the municipality would not be allowed to stand in the way.

We find no difficulty in sustaining restrictions of the kind thus far reviewed. The serious question in the case arises over the provisions of the ordinance excluding from residential districts apartment houses, business houses, retail stores and shops, and other like establishments. This question involves the validity of what is really the crux of the more recent zoning legislation, namely, the creation and maintenance of residential districts, from which business and trade of every sort, including hotels and apartment houses, are excluded. Upon that question this court has not thus far spoken. The decisions of the state courts are numerous and conflicting; but those which broadly sustain the power greatly outnumber those which deny it altogether or narrowly limit it, and it is very apparent that there is a constantly increasing tendency in the direction of the broader view....

The [cases expressing a broader view] ... agree that the exclusion of buildings devoted to business, trade, etc., from residential districts, bears a rational relation to the health and safety of the community. Some of the grounds for this conclusion are promotion of the health and security from injury of children and others by separating dwelling houses from territory devoted to trade and industry; suppression and prevention of disorder; facilitating the extinguishment of fires, and the enforcement of street traffic regulations and other general welfare ordinances; aiding the health and safety of the community, by excluding from residential areas the confusion and danger of fire, contagion, and disorder, which in greater or less degree attach to the location of stores, shops, and factories. Another ground is that the construction and repair of streets may be rendered easier and less expensive, by confining the greater part of the heavy traffic to the streets where business is carried on.

The Supreme Court of Illinois, in *City of Aurora v. Burns, supra*, pages 93–95 (149 N.E. 788), in sustaining a comprehensive building zone ordinance dividing the city into eight districts, including exclusive residential districts for one and two family dwellings, churches, educational institutions, and schools, said:

> "The constantly increasing density of our urban populations, the multiplying forms of industry and the growing complexity of our civilization make it necessary for the state, either directly or through some public agency by its sanction, to limit individual activities to a greater extent than formerly. With the growth and development of the state the police power necessarily develops, within reasonable bounds, to meet the changing conditions....

....

... "The exclusion of places of business from residential districts is not a declaration that such places are nuisances or that they are to be suppressed as such, but it is a part of the general plan by which the city's territory is allotted to different uses, in order to prevent, or at least to reduce, the congestion, disorder, and dangers which often inhere in unregulated municipal development."

The Supreme Court of Louisiana, in *State v. City of New Orleans, supra*, pages 282, 283 (97 So. 444), said:

"In the first place, the exclusion of business establishments from residence districts might enable the municipal government to give better police protection. Patrolmen's beats are larger, and therefore fewer, in residence neighborhoods than in business neighborhoods. A place of business in a residence neighborhood furnishes an excuse for any criminal to go into the neighborhood, where, otherwise, a stranger would be under the ban of suspicion. Besides, open shops invite loiterers and idlers to congregate; and the places of such congregations need police protection. In the second place, the zoning of a city into residence districts and commercial districts is a matter of economy is street paving. Heavy trucks, hauling freight to and from places of business in residence districts, require the city to maintain the same costly pavement in such districts that is required for business districts; whereas, in the residence districts, where business establishments are excluded, a cheaper pavement serves the purpose. . . .

"Aside from considerations of economic administration, in the matter of police and fire protection, street paving, etc., any business establishment is likely to be a genuine nuisance in a neighborhood of residences. Places of business are noisy; they are apt to be disturbing at night; some of them are malodorous; some are unsightly; some are apt to breed rats, mice, roaches, flies, ants, etc. . . .

"If the municipal council deemed any of the reasons which have been suggested, or any other substantial reason, a sufficient reason for adopting the ordinance in question, it is not the province of the courts to take issue with the council. We have nothing to do with the question of the wisdom or good policy of municipal ordinances. If they are not satisfying to a majority of the citizens, their recourse is to the ballot — not the courts."

The matter of zoning has received much attention at the hands of commissions and experts, and the results of their investigations have been set forth in comprehensive reports. These reports which bear every evidence of painstaking consideration, concur in the view that the segregation of residential, business and industrial buildings will make it easier to provide fire apparatus suitable for the character and intensity of the development in each section; that it will increase the safety and security of home life, greatly tend to prevent street accidents, especially to children, by reducing the traffic and resulting confusion in residential sections, decrease noise and other conditions which produce or intensify nervous disorders, preserve a more favorable environment in which to rear children, etc. With particular reference to apartment houses, it is pointed out that the development of detached house sections is greatly retarded by the coming of apartment houses, which has sometimes resulted in destroying the entire section for private house purposes; that in such sections very often the apartment house is a mere parasite, constructed in order to take advantage of the open spaces and attractive surroundings created by the residential character of the district. Moreover, the coming of one apartment house is followed by others, interfering by their height and bulk with the free circulation of air and monopolizing the rays of the sun which otherwise would fall upon the smaller homes, and bringing, as their necessary accompaniments, the disturbing noises incident to increased traffic and business, and the occupation, by means of moving and parked automobiles, of larger portions of the streets, thus detracting from their safety and depriving children of the privilege of quiet and open spaces for play, enjoyed by those in more favored localities — until, finally, the residential character of the neighborhood and its desirability as a place of detached residences are utterly destroyed. Under these circumstances, apartment houses, which in a different environment would be not only entirely unobjectionable but highly desirable, come very near to being nuisances.

If these reasons, thus summarized, do not demonstrate the wisdom or sound policy in all respects of those restrictions which we have indicated as pertinent to the inquiry, at least, the reasons are sufficiently cogent to preclude us from saying, as it must be said before the ordinance can be declared unconstitutional, that such provisions are clearly arbitrary and unreasonable, having no substantial relation to the public health, safety, morals, or general welfare.

It is true that when, if ever, the provisions set forth in the ordinance in tedious and minute detail, come to be concretely applied to particular premises, including those of the appellee, or to particular conditions, or to be considered in connection with specific complaints, some of them, or even many of them, may be found to be clearly arbitrary and unreasonable....

        . . . .

. . . In the realm of constitutional law, especially, this court has perceived the embarrassment which is likely to result from an attempt to formulate rules or decide questions beyond the necessities of the immediate issue. It has preferred to follow the method of a gradual approach to the general by a systematically guarded application and extension of constitutional principles to particular cases as they arise, rather than by out of hand attempts to establish general rules to which future cases must be fitted. This process applies with peculiar force to the solution of questions arising under the due process clause of the Constitution as applied to the exercise of the flexible powers of police, with which we are here concerned.

Decree reversed.

## Questions for Consideration

**EUCLID Case**

The above diagram may be helpful in answering questions about the *Euclid* case.

1) What is the relationship between the comprehensive plan, the zoning code, and the zoning map adopted by the Village of Euclid?

2) How did the Village of Euclid regulate land uses within its borders?

3) In the *Bove* case, the court adjusted property rights with reference to the belief that the homeowner should have anticipated the natural development of industrial uses in the area. Why didn't the Court in *Euclid* permit the property owner to rely on the natural direction of development of commercial uses extending from Cleveland into Euclid?

4) What are the economic consequences of the land use regulations on the property owner in this case? Should the property owner have alleged a takings claim?

5) How does the Court explain the relationship between nuisance law and zoning regulations?

6) What is the standard of review applied by the Court?

7) How does the use of experts fit into the Court's analysis?

8) How are apartment buildings treated in the Court's opinion? Why do you think the Court expressed this attitude?

## Takeaway

- Many people refer to the *Euclid* case to provide a baseline reference point for traditional zoning, which is referred to as Euclidian zoning. In fact, many modern zoning techniques are discussed and understood in terms of their deviation from traditional Euclidian zoning. Key elements of Euclidian zoning include:

    ° Dividing a jurisdiction into districts and regulating land uses in each district in accordance with a comprehensive plan.

    ° Establishing a hierarchy of uses. Typically, single-family residential use is placed at the top of the value hierarchy, and then one moves down into multi-family use; commercial use; and industrial use. There can be many districts and uses identified.

    ° Zones are cumulative. This means that a higher valued use (in terms of the zoning code) can be placed in a lower valued district, but a lower valued use cannot be placed in a higher valued district. For example, a single-family home (high value use) can be located in a commercial zone (lower value use), but a commercial use cannot be located in a single-family residential zone.

    ° Uses within a district are "as of right." This means that if the use is identified as permitted in the zoning district, the property owner has a right to engage in the use. Uses permitted within a district are not conditional or subject to discretionary approval. If a zoning code, for example, says that a person can operate a barber shop in this zone, then a property owner seeking to operate a barber shop has a right to locate in this area; assuming that he otherwise complies with local code requirements such as those related to setbacks.

- *Euclid* involves a facial challenge to the validity of local zoning legislation. Here, the property owner challenges the legal authority of the Village of Euclid to enact zoning regulations that restricted the otherwise lawful use of land. The standard of review for a facial challenge is the fairly debatable standard of rationality. Under this standard, if it is at least *fairly debatable* that the regulation advances the public health, safety, welfare, and morals, it will be upheld. The fairly debatable standard does not ask what the individual legislators had in mind when enacting legislation. Rather, upon review, the question is whether there is some rational basis that we can come up with for concluding that the legislation is not irrational; not arbitrary and capricious. As long as the matter is at least fairly debatable, the legislature is given deference as to the exercise of its judgment. Thus, it is not a question of whether the legislation in question reflects the best way to solve a problem, or is the way we might have chosen to solve a problem. The question is simply one of it being fairly debatable that we can at least imagine a rational basis for the legislation.

- In addition to regulating use, *Euclid* affirmed regulation of building height, lot coverage, and setback restrictions. Lot coverage is typically identified in terms of a restriction limiting a structure to covering no more than a set percentage of the lot, for example a limitation of 25%. In some cases, the regulation may be identified as a *floor area ratio* (FAR). A FAR for a particular property might be .5. This means that the structure placed on the lot can cover no more than 50% of the lot. This applies to a single-story building. If the property owner decides to build a two-story building with a FAR of .5, he will only be able to cover 25%

of the lot with the structure (25% lot coverage multiplied by two floors equals a FAR of .5).

- Setback regulations control the location of a structure relative to the lot lines. The diagram below illustrates the use of regulated setbacks from property lines. When reading a zoning code, make certain you locate the definition of front, side, and rear yard, as many codes will identify any part of a lot with its lot line abutting a street as a front yard. In such a situation, a corner lot will have two front yards.

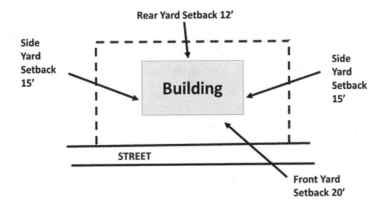

## Discussion Problem 3.1

Henderson is a fast-growing suburb on the outskirts of a large metropolitan area. Over time, the development of residential communities in Henderson, and its neighboring suburbs, has overwhelmed Henderson's ability to provide some basic public utilities, including street repairs, sewers, parks, and schools, but also other municipal services necessary to serve the increased population, like the fire, police, and health departments and the public transit system. As such, to address this situation, Henderson adopts a comprehensive plan for smart growth, to control development and discourage urban sprawl. The plan does not change any district's zoning classifications. Rather, it limits the number of development or construction permits granted annually based on the availability of necessary public services needed to serve the new population. A land developer challenges the ordinance under the state and federal constitutions claiming that it unfairly limits and rations development opportunities within the community. Who should prevail in this dispute?

# C. An "As Applied" Challenge

An "as applied" challenge is one that does not assert that the law or regulation is illegal in all circumstances. The argument is that, while there may be legal authority for the legislation, the application of the regulation in a given case is illegal. Thus, a city may have the authority to develop a zoning code dividing the city into different zoning districts; yet, a legal challenge may arise with respect to the treatment of a specific property under the zoning code. In such a case, a legal challenge is not that the city lacked authority to adopt a zoning code, but that the application of the code to a particular property is inappropriate.

## Nectow v. City of Cambridge

### Supreme Court of the United States
### 277 U.S. 183 (1928)

SUTHERLAND, Justice. A zoning ordinance of the city of Cambridge divides the city into three kinds of districts, residential, business, and unrestricted. Each of these districts is subclassified in respect of the kind of buildings which way be erected. The ordinance is an elaborate one, and of the same general character as that considered by this court in *Euclid v. Ambler Co.*, 272 U. S. 365, 47 S. Ct. 114, 71 L. Ed. 303. In its general scope it is conceded to be constitutional within that decision. The land of plaintiff in error was put in district R-3, in which are permitted only dwellings, hotels, clubs, churches, schools, philanthropic institutions, greenhouses and gardening, with customary incidental accessories. The attack upon the ordinance is that, as specifically applied to plaintiff in error, it deprived him of his property without due process of law in contravention of the Fourteenth Amendment.

The suit was for a mandatory injunction directing the city and its inspector of buildings to pass upon an application of the plaintiff in error for a permit to erect any lawful buildings upon a tract of land without regard to the provisions of the ordinance including such tract within a residential district. The case was referred to a master to make and report findings of fact. After a view of the premises and the surrounding territory, and a hearing, the master made and reported his findings. The case came on to be heard by a justice of the court, who, after confirming the master's report, reported the case for the determination of the full court. Upon consideration, that court sustained the ordinance as applied to plaintiff in error, and dismissed the bill.

A condensed statement of facts, taken from the master's report, is all that is necessary. When the zoning ordinance was enacted, plaintiff in error was and still is the owner of a tract of land containing 140,000 square feet, of which the locus here in question is a part. The locus contains about 29,000 square feet, with a frontage on Brookline street, lying west, of 304.75 feet, on Henry street, lying north, of 100 feet, on the other land of the plaintiff in error, lying east, of 264 feet, and on land of the Ford Motor Company, lying southerly, of 75 feet. The territory lying east and south is unrestricted. The lands beyond Henry street to the north and beyond Brookline street to the west are within a restricted residential district. The effect of the zoning is to separate from the west end of plaintiff in error's tract a strip 100 feet in width. The Ford Motor Company has a large auto assembling factory south of the locus; and a soap factory and the tracks of the Boston & Albany Railroad lie near. Opposite the locus, on Brookline street, and included in the same district, there are some residences; and opposite the locus, on Henry street, and in the same district, are other residences. The locus is now vacant, although it was once occupied by a mansion house. Before the passage of the ordinance in question, plaintiff in error had outstanding a contract for the sale of the greater part of his entire tract of land for the sum of $63,000. Because of the zoning restrictions, the purchaser refused to comply with the contract. Under the ordinance, business and industry of all sorts are excluded from the locus, while the remainder of the tract is unrestricted. It further appears that provision has been made for widening Brookline street, the effect of which, if carried out, will be to reduce the depth of the locus to 65 feet. After a statement at length of further facts, the master finds:

> "That no practical use can be made of the land in question for residential purposes, because among other reasons herein related, there would not be adequate return on the amount of any investment for the development of the property."

The last finding of the master is:

> "I am satisfied that the districting of the plaintiff's land in a residence district would not promote the health, safety, convenience, and general welfare of the inhabitants of that part of the defendant city, taking into account the natural development thereof and the character of the district and the resulting benefit to accrue to the whole city and I so find."

It is made pretty clear that because of the industrial and railroad purposes to which the immediately adjoining lands to the south and east have been devoted and for which they are zoned, the locus is of comparatively little value for the limited uses permitted by the ordinance.

We quite agree with the opinion expressed below that a court should not set aside the determination of public officers in such a matter unless it is clear that their action "has no foundation in reason and is a mere arbitrary or irrational exercise of power having no substantial relation to the public health, the public morals, the public safety or the public welfare in its proper sense." *Euclid v. Ambler Co., supra,* p. 395 (47 S. Ct. 121).

*An inspection of a plat of the city upon which the zoning districts are outlined,* taken in connection with the master's findings, shows with reasonable certainty that the inclusion of the locus in question is not indispensable to the general plan. The boundary line of the residential district before reaching the locus runs for some distance along the streets, and to exclude the locus from the residential district requires only that such line shall be continued 100 feet further along Henry street and thence south along Brookline street. There does not appear to be any reason why this should not be done. Nevertheless, if that were all, we should not be warranted in substituting our judgment for that of the zoning authorities primarily charged with the duty and responsibility of determining the question. But that is not all. The governmental power to interfere by zoning regulations with the general rights of the land owner by restricting the character of his use, is not unlimited, and, other questions aside, such restriction cannot be imposed if it does not bear a substantial relation to the public health, safety, morals, or general welfare. *Euclid v. Ambler Co., supra*, p. 395 (47 S. Ct. 114). Here, the express finding of the master, already quoted, confirmed by the court below, is that the health, safety, convenience, and general welfare of the inhabitants of the part of the city affected will not be promoted by the disposition made by the ordinance of the locus in question. This finding of the master, after a hearing and an inspection of the entire area affected, supported, as we think it is, by other findings of fact, is determinative of the case. That the invasion of the property of plaintiff in error was serious and highly injurious is clearly established; and, since a necessary basis for the support of that invasion is wanting, the action of the zoning authorities comes within the ban of the Fourteenth Amendment and cannot be sustained.

Judgment reversed.

## Questions for Consideration

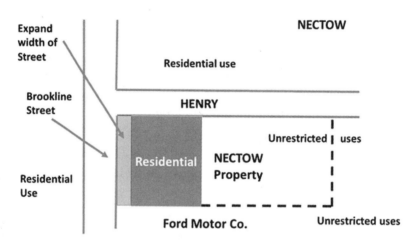

The diagram above may be useful in answering questions concerning the *Nectow* case.

1) How does the challenge to the applicable zoning regulations differ as between *Nectow* and *Euclid*?

2) What does the court say about the standard of review applicable in *Nectow* and how does this relate to the standard in *Euclid*?

3) How does the zoning regulation affect the value of the property?

4) Is this a takings case (a taking under the Fifth Amendment to the Constitution)? If not a takings claim, on what constitutional basis is the challenge made?

## Takeaway

- In *Nectow*, the property owner objected to the way the zoning district lines were drawn. *Nectow* involved an "as applied" challenge to the local zoning regulations. The applicable standard of review in an as applied case is the rational basis standard. This is not, however, the same as the rational basis standard using the fairly debatable test that was applied in the *Euclid* case. With the fairly debatable standard we inquire as to if there is *any* fairly debatable rationale for the regulation. In the as applied case, we ask if the regulation is rationally related to *the* stated objective. In the as applied situation, we want to inquire about the legislative intent.

- Later in the course, we will cover the topic of seeking a variance from the strict requirements of a zoning code. A variance is an exception from the zoning regulations. In *Nectow*, the property owner could have applied for a variance from the zoning requirements rather than challenging the regulations as a violation of due process applied to his property. After you learn about variances, ask yourself why a property owner might proceed on an as applied challenge rather than by seeking a variance.

## Figarsky v. Historic Dist. Com.

Supreme Court of Connecticut
368 A.2d 163 (Conn. 1976)

BARBER, Judge. The plaintiffs, owners of a house and lot located within the Norwich historic district, appealed to the Court of Common Pleas from a decision of the defendant commission denying their application for a certificate of appropriateness which would permit them to demolish the house. The court rendered judgment dismissing the appeal and the plaintiffs, upon the granting of certification, have appealed to this court.

The undisputed facts of the case are as follows: The Norwich historic district, established by the city of Norwich in 1967, . . . consists of the Norwichtown green, which dates back to colonial days, and about one hundred buildings and lots surrounding, or in close proximity to, the green. The plaintiffs' property, which they purchased in 1963, is a two-story building zoned for commercial uses and is located just inside the bounds of the district. The property faces the green but is bounded on two sides by a McDonald's hamburger stand and parking lot. The building is in need of some repairs, which the Norwich building inspector has ordered the plaintiffs to undertake. Rather than make the repairs, however, the plaintiffs would prefer to demolish the building. In August, 1972, the plaintiffs applied to the building inspector for a demolition permit. The building inspector informed the plaintiffs that before such a permit could be issued a certificate of appropriateness was required. The plaintiffs, therefore, applied to the defendant for a certificate, filing their application with the building inspector on November 29, 1972. The defendant held a public hearing on the application on January 25, 1973. The hearing was attended by more than 100 persons, none of whom, except for the plaintiffs and their attorney, spoke in favor of granting the application. On the following day, the commission voted unanimously to deny the plaintiffs' application.

The plaintiffs maintain that the costs of the repairs necessary for the building are prohibitive. The building inspector has ordered the plaintiffs to repair the foundation and replace a door sill and hall floor, and the health department has ordered the plaintiffs to tie in to a newly accessible public sewer. At the hearing before the commission, the plaintiffs offered the testimony of a local contractor to the effect that the cost of these repairs, together with the cost of reroofing the building, would amount to between $15,000 and $18,000. The plaintiffs offered no evidence of the value of the house without repairs, its value if repaired, or the value of the lot if the building were razed. Nor did the plaintiffs disclose to the commission the use which they intended to make of the lot if the building were razed.

The commission also received numerous opinions from the plaintiffs' neighbors and from the Connecticut historical commission, the southeastern Connecticut regional planning agency, and the Connecticut society of architects, as to the historic value of the premises. The consensus of these opinions was that although the building itself is of little historic value or interest, it does, by virtue of its location, perform an important screening function, separating the green from an encroaching commercial district, and its preservation is important in maintaining the character of the historic district.[1] The commission stated its reasons for denying the application as follows: "The Commission is of the opinion that the building in question significantly contributes to the importance of the Norwichtown Green as an historic landmark, and the Commission would have violated its responsibilities . . . to have permitted its demolition. In weighing all the considerations concerning this Application, the Commission was cognizant of . . . [permissible variations], but

---

1. A communication from the state historical commission stated, in part: "Competent authority has placed the date of construction in or about 1760 and identified the owner at that period as keeping an inn where lawyers at the nearby Court of Norwich were accommodated. On the exterior at least, the structure has undergone considerable alteration over the years but still retains its essential form and proportions, wholly in keeping with the scale and appearance of numerous other old buildings that border the Green area. Aside from the house proper, its site is of historic interest as occupying the original home lot of the Reverend James Fitch, religious leader of the first settlers. It often happens that buildings forming a recognizable grouping, as around a green, may not individually be especially notable for architecture or historical association. But together as a unified whole they constitute a significant entity, no part of which can be removed without a definite and usually adverse effect upon the character and appearance of the entire area. This is the condition that obtains in Norwichtown.

"The commercially zoned district south and southeast of the site under consideration exhibits the unattractive characteristics of so many such areas, with disparate structures of poor design uncoordinated with one another and obtrusive advertising signs. It stands close upon the boundaries of the local historic district. If the property at 86 Town Street were demolished, it would remove the most important screening element between these evidences of low-grade commercialism and the attractiveness of the largely unspoiled Green. State recognition of the importance of this land has recently been affirmed by the erection of an historical marker under auspices of this Commission, which details the history of early years in Norwich and the central role of the Green in that history. Nomination of the entire area has been made to the National Register of Historic Places maintained by the Office of Archeology and Historic Preservation, National Park Service, United States Department of the Interior, under the National Historic Preservation Act of 1966, Public Law 89-665."

concluded that the hardships presented by the Applicant were not of sufficient magnitude to warrant granting approval for demolition."

Procedure upon an appeal from any decision of a historic district commission is the same as that for appeals from zoning boards. . . . The controlling question which the trial court had to decide was whether the historic district commission had acted, as alleged in the appeal, illegally, arbitrarily and in abuse of the discretion vested in it. *Bogue v. Zoning Board of Appeals,* 165 Conn. 749, 752, 345 A.2d 9; *Byington v. Zoning Commission,* 162 Conn. 611, 613, 295 A.2d 553. Since the trial court decided the appeal solely on the record returned by the commission and made only a limited finding of facts on the issue of aggrievement, review by this court must be based on the record of the proceedings before the commission to determine whether the commission's decision is reasonably supported by the record. *Danseyar v. Zoning Board of Appeals,* 164 Conn. 325, 327, 321 A.2d 474; *Langer v. Planning & Zoning Commission,* 163 Conn. 453, 460, 313 A.2d 44.

In their appeal, the plaintiffs allege that they will be forced to undergo economic hardship and loss as a result of not being permitted to demolish their building, and that the historic district commission, in denying their application for a certificate of appropriateness, acted illegally, arbitrarily and in abuse of its discretion.

. . . .

The plaintiffs' principal claim is that the Norwich historic district ordinance, implementing the state enabling act, is unconstitutional as applied to them, and that the denial of their application for a certificate of appropriateness to demolish their building amounts to a taking of their property for public use without compensation. More specifically, they contend that the ordinance is "vague aesthetic legislation," incapable of application in accordance with mandates of due process, and that because of the denial of their application they will be forced to expend large sums in the maintenance of their property without being able to put it to any practical use.

Neither the constitution of the United States, amendments five and fourteen, nor the constitution of Connecticut, article first, §11, deny the state the power to regulate the uses to which an owner may devote his property.

"All property is held subject to the right of government to regulate its use in the exercise of the police power, so that it shall not be injurious to the rights of the community, or so that it may promote its health, morals, safety and welfare. The power of regulation by government is not unlimited; it cannot, as we have stated, be imposed unless it bears a rational relation to the subjects which fall fairly within the police power and unless the means used are not within constitutional inhibitions. The means used will fall within these inhibitions whenever they are destructive, confiscatory, or so unreasonable as to be arbitrary. *Euclid v. Ambler Realty Co.,* 272 U.S. 365, 47 Sup. Ct. 114 [71 L. Ed. 303]. Regulations may result to some extent, practically in the taking of property, or the restricting its uses, and yet not be deemed confiscatory or unreasonable. Courts will not substitute their judgment for the legislative judgment when these considerations are fairly debatable. They will regard their validity ... from the standpoint of existing conditions and present times." *State v. Hillman,* 110 Conn. 92, 105, 147 A. 294. When, as here, a legislative enactment is challenged in its application as beyond the scope or as an abuse of the state's police power, two issues are raised: first, whether the object of the legislation falls within the police power; and second, whether the means by which the legislation attempts to reach that object are reasonable. *Windsor v. Whitney,* 95 Conn. 357, 369, 111 A. 354.

"To be constitutionally valid, a regulation made under the police power must have a reasonable relation to the public health, safety, morality and welfare." *State v. Gordon,* 143 Conn. 698, 703, 125 A.2d 477; *DeMello v. Plainville,* 170 Conn. 675, 679, 368 A.2d 71. No contention is made that the historic district ordinance contributes to the health or safety of the public; our inquiry is limited to whether the preservation of historic areas in a static form serves the amorphous concept of "the public welfare." See *Opinion of the Justices,* 333 Mass. 773, 778, 128 N.E.2d 557. "The concept of the public welfare is broad and inclusive. . . . The values it represents are spiritual as well as physical, aesthetic as well as monetary. It is within the power of the legislature to determine that the community should be beautiful as well as healthy, spacious as well as clean, well-balanced as well as carefully patrolled." *Berman v. Parker,* 348 U.S. 26, 33, 75 S. Ct. 98, 99 L. Ed. 27. It is apparent from the language of the enabling statute[2] that the General Assembly, in enacting those statutes, was cognizant not only of the intangible benefits to be derived from historic districts, such as an increase in the public's awareness of its New England heritage, but of the economic benefits to be reaped as well, by augmenting the value of properties located within the old sections of the state's cities and towns, and encouraging tourism within the state. In a number of recent cases, it has been held that the preservation of a historical area or landmark as it was in the past falls within the meaning of general welfare and, consequently, the police power. See, e.g., *Maher v. New Orleans,* 516 F.2d 1051, 1060 (5th Cir.); *Annapolis v. Anne Arundel County,* 271 Md. 265, 316 A.2d 807; *Lutheran Church in America* v. *City of New York,* 35 N.Y.2d 121, 316 N.E.2d 305; *Rebman v. Springfield,* 111 Ill. App. 2d 430, 250 N.E.2d 282; *Opinion of the Justices,* supra, 773; see 1 Rathkopf, Zoning and Planning (4th Ed.), c. 15; 82 Am. Jur. 2d, Zoning and Planning, § 40. We cannot deny that the preservation of an area or cluster of buildings with exceptional historical and architectural significance may serve the public welfare.

The plaintiffs argue that the Norwich ordinance constitutes "vague aesthetic legislation," and point to our statement in *DeMaria v. Planning & Zoning Commission,* 159 Conn. 534, 541, 271 A.2d 105, that "vague and undefined aesthetic

---

2. "[General Statutes] Sec. 7-147a. HISTORIC DISTRICTS AUTHORIZED. . . . to promote the educational, cultural, economic and general welfare of the public through the preservation and protection of buildings, places and districts of historic interest by the maintenance of such as landmarks in the history of architecture, of the municipality, of the state or of the nation, and through the development of appropriate settings for such buildings, places and districts. . . ."

considerations alone are insufficient to support the invocation of the police power," and our dictum to the same effect. *Gionfriddo v. Windsor,* 137 Conn. 701, 704, 81 A.2d 266. The "aesthetic considerations" involved in the Norwich ordinance are not, however, "vague and undefined"; § 7-147f of the General Statutes, incorporated by reference into the ordinance, sets out with some specificity the factors to be considered by the commission in passing upon an application for a certificate of appropriateness.[3] Nor, as we pointed out in the preceding discussion, do "aesthetic considerations alone" provide the basis for the ordinance. Furthermore, as long ago as *Windsor v. Whitney,* 95 Conn. 357, 368, 111 A. 354, we commented that the question of the relationship between aesthetics and the police power was not a settled question. In *State v. Kievman,* 116 Conn. 458, 465, 165 A. 601, we stated that a land use regulation was not invalid simply because it was based in part on aesthetic considerations. And in *Murphy, Inc. v. Westport,* 131 Conn. 292, 302, 40 A.2d 177, we indicated that aesthetic considerations may have a definite relation to the public welfare. Although we need not directly decide the issue in the present case, we note that other jurisdictions have recognized that "aesthetic considerations alone may warrant an exercise of the police power." *People v. Stover,* 12 N.Y.2d 462, 467, 191 N.E.2d 272, appeal dismissed, 375 U.S. 42, 84 S. Ct. 147, 11 L. Ed. 2d 107; see 1 Rathkopf, op. cit., c. 14.

Having determined that the ordinance creating the Norwich historic district constitutes a valid exercise of the state's police power, we are left with the question of whether the application of that ordinance to the plaintiffs' property amounts to an unconstitutional deprivation of their property without compensation. In this context, it has often been noted that the police power, which regulates for the public good the uses to which private property may be put and requires no compensation, must be distinguished from the power of eminent domain, which takes private property for a public use and requires compensation to the owner. See, e.g., *DeMello v. Plainville,* 170 Conn. 675, 679-80, 368 A.2d 71, and cases cited therein. The difference is primarily one of degree, and the amount of the owner's loss is the basic criterion for determining whether a purported exercise of the police power is valid, or whether it amounts to a necessitating the use of the power

---

3. "[General Statutes] Sec. 7-147f. CONSIDERATIONS IN DETERMINING APPROPRIATE-NESS. If the commission determines that the proposed erection, construction, restoration, alteration, razing or parking will be appropriate, it shall issue a certificate of appropriateness. In passing upon appropriateness as to exterior architectural features the commission shall consider, in addition to any other pertinent factors, the historical and architectural value and significance, architectural style, general design, arrangement, texture and material of the architectural features involved and the relationship thereof to the exterior architectural style and pertinent features of other structures in the immediate neighborhood. In passing upon appropriateness as to parking, the commission shall take into consideration the size of such parking area, the visibility of cars parked therein, the closeness of such area to adjacent buildings and other similar factors. A certificate of appropriateness may be refused for any building or structure, the erection, reconstruction, restoration, alteration or razing of which, or any parking which, in the opinion of the commission, would be detrimental to the interest of the historic district."

of eminent domain. See Sax, "Takings and the Police Power," 74 Yale L.J. 36. "A regulation which otherwise constitutes a valid exercise of the police power may, as applied to a particular parcel of property, be confiscatory in that no reasonable use may be made of the property and it becomes of little or no value to the owner. . . . See, e.g., *Pennsylvania Coal Co. v. Mahon,* 260 U.S. 393, 43 S. Ct. 158, 67 L. Ed. 322; *Brecciaroli v. Commissioner of Environmental Protection,* 168 Conn. 349, 354, 362 A.2d 948; *Horwitz v. Waterford,* 151 Conn. 320, 323, 197 A.2d 636; *Dooley v. Town Plan & Zoning Commission,* 151 Conn. 304, 311-12, 197 A.2d 770; *Vartelas v. Water Resources Commission,* 146 Conn. 650, 657, 153 A.2d 822." *DeMello v. Plainville, supra,* 680; see *Penn Central Transportation Co. v. City of New York,* 50 App. Div. 2d 265, 377 N.Y.S.2d 20.

Whether the denial of the plaintiffs' application for a certificate of appropriateness to demolish their building has rendered the Norwich ordinance, as applied to them, confiscatory, must be determined in the light of their particular circumstances as they have been shown to exist. *Bartlett v. Zoning Commission,* 161 Conn. 24, 31, 282 A.2d 907; *Dooley v. Town Plan & Zoning Commission,* 151 Conn. 304, 311, 197 A.2d 770. In regulating the use of land under the police power, the maximum possible enrichment of a particular landowner is not a controlling purpose. *Goldblatt v. Hempstead,* 369 U.S. 590, 82 S. Ct. 987, 8 L. Ed. 2d 130; *Hyatt v. Zoning Board of Appeals,* 163 Conn. 379, 383, 311 A.2d 77; *Damick v. Planning & Zoning Commission,* 158 Conn. 78, 83, 256 A.2d 428. It is only when the regulation practically destroys or greatly decreases the value of a specific piece of property that relief may be granted, provided it promotes substantial justice. *Culinary Institute of America, Inc. v. Board of Zoning Appeals,* 143 Conn. 257, 261, 121 A.2d 637. "The extent of that deprivation must be considered in light of the evils which the regulation is designed to prevent." *Chevron Oil Co. v. Zoning Board of Appeals,* 170 Conn. 146, 152, 365 A.2d 387; see General Statutes § 7-147f.

The plaintiffs had the burden of proving that the historic district commission acted illegally, arbitrarily, in a confiscatory manner or in abuse of discretion. *Byington v. Zoning Commission,* 162 Conn. 611, 613, 295 A.2d 553. This the plaintiffs failed to do. See *Maher v. New Orleans,* 516 F.2d 1051, 1067 (5th Cir.); *Penn Central Transportation Co. v. City of New York, supra,* 274. The plaintiffs went no further than to present evidence that their house was unoccupied and in need of extensive repairs. There was no evidence offered that the house, if repaired, would not be of some value, or that the proximity of the McDonald's hamburger stand rendered the property of practically no value as a part of the historic district.

The Norwich historic district commission, after a full hearing, lawfully, reasonably and honestly exercised its judgment. The trial court was correct in not substituting its own judgment for that of the commission. *Bora v. Zoning Board of Appeals,* 161 Conn. 297, 300, 288 A.2d 89.

There is no error.

In this opinion the other judges concurred.

## *Questions for Consideration*

1) Why did the plaintiffs apply for a certificate of appropriateness to demolish the house?

2) What was the City of Norwich's Historic District Commission's rationale for denying the plaintiffs' application?

3) Why require a public hearing on an application for a certificate of appropriateness when a commission is considering whether to grant or deny such a permit? What role does the public play in the decision process?

4) The plaintiffs argued that the ordinance is unconstitutional as applied to them because the ordinance is "vague aesthetic legislation" incapable of application in accordance with mandates of due process. Why did the court conclude otherwise?

## *Takeaway*

- The possibility exists that in extraordinary situations, the impact of designating property as "historic" or as being in an "historic district" could be so economically severe as to amount to a taking; however, here the court confirmed that historic district regulations that are fairly and consistently applied do not amount to a taking of property.

- An ordinance requiring a permit before demolition of certain structures, and the fact that in some cases permits may not be obtained does not alone make out a case of a taking. This is the case if it serves a permissible goal in an otherwise reasonable fashion, and does not seem on its face constitutionally distinguishable from ordinances regulating other aspects of land ownership; such as building height, set back or limitations on use.

- Aesthetics are a valid basis for zoning. In this case, preserving the historic aesthetic of the village green was within the scope of the police power to regulate.

## Discussion Problem 3.2

Carolopolis is a city with an historic district — a neighborhood in which most of the buildings are over 200 years old; and many of the buildings are antebellum, a unique architectural style from the pre-Civil War era. The city's chamber of commerce markets the historic district's cultural heritage, which results in Carolopolis being a popular, world-wide tourist destination. The historic district showcases the unique aesthetic and architectural character of the buildings, and the international, historic significance of the locale. To preserve the distinctive, historic character of the district, Carolopolis has a city ordinance requiring a permit for all construction, renovations, alterations, and demolitions within the historic district. The city established a commission with the authority to grant or deny such permit requests.

Martha is the owner of a house within the district; her house itself is not of unique historic character. Martha seeks a permit to demolish the house and erect a new apartment building in its place; apartment buildings are otherwise authorized under the local zoning ordinance in this area. The commission denies Martha's permit request. The reason the commission gives for the denial is that, although Martha's house itself is not antebellum, the redevelopment of the property to an apartment building would tend to lessen the aesthetic appeal of the district and also detract from the distinctive, historic character of the district. Martha sues the city, seeking an injunction to stop the city from enforcing the ordinance or to compel the city to grant her a permit. Who should prevail in this dispute?

# D. Due Process and the Potential for a Regulatory Taking

Due process protection under the Constitution generally includes procedural and substantive due process. Procedural due process focuses on such things as getting notice, having an opportunity to be heard, and being able to submit supporting evidence in support of one's position. Historically, substantive due process includes protection of property rights. As the *Pennsylvania Coal* case illustrates, due process and Takings Clause concerns are closely related.

## Pennsylvania Coal Co. v. Mahon
### Supreme Court of the United States
### 260 U.S. 393 (1922)

HOLMES, Justice. This is a bill in equity brought by the defendants in error to prevent the Pennsylvania Coal Company from mining under their property in such way as to remove·the supports and cause a subsidence of the surface and of their house. The bill sets out a deed executed by the Coal Company in 1878, under which the plaintiffs claim. The deed conveys the surface but in express terms reserves the right to remove all the coal under the same and the grantee takes the premises with the risk and waives all claim for damages that may arise from mining out the coal. But the plaintiffs say that whatever may have been the Coal Company's rights, they were taken away by an Act of Pennsylvania, approved May 27, 1921 (P.L. 1198), commonly known there as the Kohler Act. The Court of Common Pleas found that if not restrained the defendant would cause the damage to prevent which the bill was brought but denied an injunction, holding that the statute if applied to this case would be unconstitutional. On appeal the Supreme Court of the State agreed that the defendant had contract and property rights protected by the Constitution of the United States, but held that the statute was a legitimate exercise of the police power and directed a decree for the plaintiffs, a writ of error was granted bringing the case to this Court.

The statute forbids the mining of anthracite coal in such way as to cause the subsidence of, among other things, any structure used as a human habitation, with certain exceptions, including among them land where the surface is owned by the owner of the underlying coal and is distant more than one hundred and fifty feet from any improved property belonging to any other person. As applied to this case the statute is admitted to destroy previously existing rights of property and contract. The question is whether the police power can be stretched so far.

Government hardly could go on if to some extent values incident to property could not be diminished without paying for every such change in the general law. As long recognized some values are enjoyed under an implied limitation and must yield to the police power. But obviously the implied limitation must have its limits or the contract and due process clauses are gone. One fact for consideration in determining such limits is the extent of the diminution. When it reaches a certain magnitude, in most if not in all cases there must be an exercise of eminent domain and compensation to sustain the act. So the question depends upon the particular facts. The greatest weight is given to the judgment of the legislature but it always is open to interested parties to contend that the legislature has gone beyond its constitutional power.

This is the case of a single private house. No doubt there is a public interest even in this, as there is in every purchase and sale and in all that happens within the commonwealth. Some existing rights may be modified even in such a case. But usually in ordinary private affairs the public interest does not warrant much of this kind of interference. A source of damage to such a house is not a public nuisance even if similar damage is inflicted on others in different places. The damage is not common or public. The extent of the public interest is shown by the statute to be limited, since the statute ordinarily does not apply to land when the surface is owned by the owner of the coal. Furthermore, it is not justified as a protection of personal safety. That could be provided for by notice. Indeed the very foundation of this bill is that the defendant gave timely notice of its intent to mine under the house. On the other hand the extent of the taking is great. It purports to abolish what is recognized in Pennsylvania as an estate in land — a very valuable estate — and what is declared by the Court below to be a contract hitherto binding the plaintiffs. If we were called upon to deal with the plaintiffs' position alone we should think it clear that the statute does not disclose a public interest sufficient to warrant so extensive a destruction of the defendant's constitutionally protected rights.

But the case has been treated as one in which the general validity of the act should be discussed. The Attorney General of the State, the City of Scranton and the representatives of other extensive interests were allowed to take part in the argument below and have submitted their contentions here. It seems, therefore, to be our duty to go farther in the statement of our opinion, in order that it may be known at once, and that further suits should not be brought in vain.

It is our opinion that the act cannot be sustained as an exercise of the police power, so far as it affects the mining of coal under streets or cities in places where the right to mine such coal has been reserved. As said in a Pennsylvania case, "For practical purposes, the right to coal consists in the right to mine it." *Commonwealth v. Clearview Coal Co.*, 256 Pa. 328, 331, 100 Atl. 820, L.R.A. 1917E, 672. What makes the right to mine coal valuable is that it can be exercised with profit. To make it commercially impracticable to mine certain coal has very nearly the same effect for constitutional purposes as appropriating or destroying it. Thus we think that we are warranted in assuming that the statute does.

It is true that in *Plymouth Coal Co. v. Pennsylvania*, 232 U.S. 531, 34 S. Ct. 359, 58 L. Ed. 713, it was held competent for the legislature to require a pillar of coal to be left along the line of adjoining property, that with the pillar on the other side of the line would be a barrier sufficient for the safety of the employees of either mine in case the other should be abandoned and allowed to fill with water. But that was a requirement for the safety of employees invited into the mine, and secured an average reciprocity of advantage that has been recognized as a justification of various laws.

The rights of the public in a street purchased or laid out by eminent domain are those that it has paid for. If in any case its representatives have been so short sighted as to acquire only surface rights without the right of support we see no more authority for supplying the latter without compensation than there was for taking the right of way in the first place and refusing to pay for it because the public wanted it very much. The protection of private property in the Fifth Amendment presupposes that it is wanted for public use, but provides that it shall not be taken for such use without compensation. A similar assumption is made in the decisions upon the Fourteenth Amendment. *Hairston v. Danville & Western Ry. Co.*, 208 U.S. 598, 605, 28 S. Ct. 331, 52 L. Ed. 637, 13 Ann. Cas. 1008. When this seemingly absolute protection is found to be qualified by the police power, the natural tendency of human nature is to extend the qualification more and more until at last private property disappears. But that cannot be accomplished in this way under the Constitution of the United States.

The general rule at least is that while property may be regulated to a certain extent, if regulation goes too far it will be recognized as a taking. It may be doubted how far exceptional cases, like the blowing up of a house to stop a conflagration, go — and if they go beyond the general rule, whether they do not stand as much upon tradition as upon principle. *Bowditch v. Boston*, 101 U.S. 16, 25 L. Ed. 980. In general it is not plain that a man's misfortunes or necessities will justify his shifting the damages to his neighbor's shoulders. *Spade v. Lynn & Boston Ry. Co.*, 172 Mass. 488, 489, 52 N.E. 747, 43 L.R.A. 832, 70 Am. St. Rep. 298. We are in danger of forgetting that a strong public desire to improve the public condition is not enough to warrant achieving the desire by a shorter cut than the constitutional way of paying for the change. As we already have said this is a question of degree — and therefore cannot be disposed of by general propositions. But we regard this as going beyond any of the cases decided by this Court. The late decisions upon laws dealing with the congestion of Washington and New York, caused by the war, dealt with laws intended to meet a temporary emergency and providing for compensation determined to be reasonable by an impartial board.

We assume, of course, that the statute was passed upon the conviction that an exigency existed that would warrant it, and we assume that an exigency exists that would warrant the exercise of eminent domain. But the question at bottom is upon whom the loss of the changes desired should fall. So far as private persons or communities have seen fit to take the risk of acquiring only surface rights, we cannot see that the fact that their risk has become a danger warrants the giving to them greater rights than they bought.

Decree reversed.

BRANDEIS, Justice. (dissenting). The Kohler Act prohibits, under certain conditions, the mining of anthracite coal within the limits of a city in such a manner or to such an extent "as to cause the subsidence of any dwelling or other structure used as a human habitation, or any factory, store, or other industrial or mercantile establishment in which human labor is employed." Act Pa. May 27, 1921, §1 (P.L. 1198). Coal in place is land, and the right of the owner to use his land is not absolute. He may not so use it as to create a public nuisance, and uses, once harmless, may, owing to changed conditions, seriously threaten the public welfare. Whenever they do, the Legislature has power to prohibit such uses without paying compensation; and the power to prohibit extends alike to the manner, the character and the purpose of the use. Are we justified in declaring that the Legislature of Pennsylvania has, in restricting the right to mine anthracite, exercised this power so arbitrarily as to violate the Fourteenth Amendment?

Every restriction upon the use of property imposed in the exercise of the police power deprives the owner of some right theretofore enjoyed, and is, in that sense, an abridgment by the state of rights in property without making compensation. But restriction imposed to protect the public health, safety or morals from dangers threatened is not a taking. The restriction here in question is merely the prohibition of a noxious use. The property so restricted remains in the possession of its owner. The state does not appropriate it or make any use of it. The state merely prevents the owner from making a use which interferes with paramount rights of the public. Whenever the use prohibited ceases to be noxious — as it may because of further change in local or social conditions — the restriction will have to be removed and the owner will again be free to enjoy his property as heretofore.

The restriction upon the use of this property cannot, of course, be lawfully imposed, unless its purpose is to protect the public. But the purpose of a restriction does not cease to be public, because incidentally some private persons may thereby receive gratuitously valuable special benefits. Thus, owners of low buildings may obtain, through statutory restrictions upon the height of neighboring structures, benefits equivalent to an easement of light and air. Furthermore, a restriction, though imposed for a public purpose, will not be lawful, unless the restriction is an appropriate means to the public end. But to keep coal in place is surely an appropriate means of preventing subsidence of the surface; and ordinarily it is the only available means. Restriction upon use does not become inappropriate as a means, merely because it deprives the owner of the only use to which the property can then be profitably put. . . . Nor is a restriction imposed through exercise of the police power inappropriate as a means, merely because the same end might be effected through exercise of the power of eminent domain, or otherwise at public expense.

Every restriction upon the height of buildings might be secured through acquiring by eminent domain the right of each owner to build above the limiting height; but it is settled that the state need not resort to that power. If by mining anthracite coal the owner would necessarily unloose poisonous gases, I suppose no one would doubt the power of the state to prevent the mining, without buying his coal fields. And why may not the state, likewise, without paying compensation, prohibit one from digging so deep or excavating so near the surface, as to expose the community to like dangers? In the latter case, as in the former, carrying on the business would be a public nuisance.

It is said that one fact for consideration in determining whether the limits of the police power have been exceeded is the extent of the resulting diminution in value, and that here the restriction destroys existing rights of property and contract. But values are relative. If we are to consider the value of the coal kept in place by the restriction, we should compare it with the value of all other parts of the land. That is, with the value not of the coal alone, but with the value of the whole property. The rights of an owner as against the public are not increased by dividing the interests in his property into surface and subsoil. The sum of the rights in the parts can not be greater than the rights in the whole. The estate of an owner in land is grandiloquently described as extending *ab orco usque ad coelum*. But I suppose no one would contend that by selling his interest above 100 feet from the surface he could prevent the state from limiting, by the police power, the height of structures in a city. And why should a sale of underground rights bar the state's power? For aught that appears the value of the coal kept in place by the restriction may be negligible as compared with the value of the whole property, or even as compared with that part of it which is represented by the coal remaining in place and which may be extracted despite the statute. Ordinarily a police regulation, general in operation, will not be held void as to a particular property, although proof is offered that owing to conditions peculiar to it the restriction could not reasonably be applied. But even if the particular facts are to govern, the statute should, in my opinion be upheld in this case. For the defendant has failed to adduce any evidence from which it appears that to restrict its mining operations was an unreasonable exercise of the police power. Where the surface and the coal belong to the same person, self-interest would ordinarily prevent mining to such an extent as to cause a subsidence. It was, doubtless, for this reason that the Legislature, estimating the degrees of danger, deemed statutory restriction unnecessary for the public safety under such conditions.

It is said that this is a case of a single dwelling house, that the restriction upon mining abolishes a valuable estate hitherto secured by a contract with the plaintiffs, and that the restriction upon mining cannot be justified as a protection of personal safety, since that could be provided for by notice. . . . The fact that this suit is brought by a private person is, of course, immaterial. To protect the community through invoking the aid, as litigant, of interested private citizens is not a novelty in our law. That it may be done in Pennsylvania was decided by its Supreme Court in this case. And it is for a state to say how its public policy shall be enforced.

This case involves only mining which causes subsidence of a dwelling house. But the Kohler Act contains provisions in addition to that quoted above; and as to these, also, an opinion is expressed. These provisions deal with mining under cities to such an extent as to cause subsidence of —

(a) Any public building or any structure customarily used by the public as a place of resort, assemblage, or amusement, including, but not limited to, churches, schools, hospitals, theaters, hotels, and railroad stations.

(b) Any street, road, bridge, or other public passageway, dedicated to public use or habitually used by the public.

(c) Any track, roadbed, right of way, pipe, conduit, wire, or other facility, used in the service of the public by any municipal corporation or public service company as defined by the Public Service Law, section 1.

A prohibition of mining which causes subsidence of such structures and facilities is obviously enacted for a public purpose; and it seems, likewise, clear that mere notice of intention to mine would not in this connection secure the public safety. Yet it is said that these provisions of the act cannot be sustained as an exercise of the police power where the right to mine such coal has been reserved. The conclusion seems to rest upon the assumption that in order to justify such exercise of the police power there must be "an average reciprocity of advantage" as between the owner of the property restricted and the rest of the community; and that here such reciprocity is absent. Reciprocity of advantage is an important consideration, and may even be an essential, where the state's power is exercised for the purpose of conferring benefits upon the property of a neighborhood, as in drainage projects. But where the police power is exercised, not to confer benefits upon property owners but to protect the public from detriment and danger, there is in my opinion, no room for considering reciprocity of advantage. . . .

## *Questions for Consideration*

1) In what ways does the majority opinion frame the nature of the case differently than the dissent? Address this question with particular reference to the nature of the underlying transaction and the exercise of the police power.

2) Is this case resolved based on due process or as a violation of the Takings Clause?

3) How does the majority opinion distinguish this case from *Plymouth Coal Co.*?

4) What is the concept of average reciprocity of advantage and how is it applicable to this case?

5) How does nuisance fit in with the analysis applied in this case?

6) This case discusses what is generally referred to as the "whole parcel" test. Explain the whole parcel test as it is used in the case.

7) In what ways does the opinion address the issue of diminution in property value as a result of regulation?

## *Takeaway*

- The state exercises the police power in order to protect and advance the *public* health, safety, welfare, and morals, not to benefit the parties to a single personal transaction.

- There are multiple factors to consider and balance when evaluating a case for a violation of due process or the Takings Clause. While there are no clear and simple answers in this area, there are well-defined issues that must be addressed. *Pennsylvania Coal* informs us of the need to consider such things as:

  ○ the character of the government action;

  ○ diminution in value;

  ○ average reciprocity of advantage;

  ○ harms and benefits; and

  ○ the whole parcel.

## Preseault v. United States

U.S. Court of Appeals, Federal Circuit
100 F.3d 1525 (Fed. Cir. 1996)

PLAGER, Circuit Judge. In this Takings case, the United States denies liability under the Fifth Amendment of the Constitution . . . for actions it took pursuant to the Federal legislation known as the Rails-to-Trails Act. . . . The original parties to the case were the property owners, J. Paul and Patricia Preseault, . . . plaintiffs, and the United States (the "Government"), defendant. The State of Vermont (the "State"), claiming an interest in the properties involved, intervened and, under the joinder rules of the Court of Federal Claims, entered its appearance as a co-defendant. The Court of Federal Claims, on summary judgment after hearings and argument, concluded that the law was on the Government's side, and rendered judgment against the complaining property owners. . . . The property owners appeal.

. . . .

[W]e conclude that, for the reasons we shall explain, the trial court erred in giving judgment for the Government; that judgment is reversed. The case is remanded to the trial court for further proceedings to determine the just compensation to which the property owners are entitled.

### A. Introduction and Summary

In brief, the issue in this case is whether the conversion, under the authority of the Rails-to-Trails Act and by order of the Interstate Commerce Commission, of a long unused railroad right-of-way to a public recreational hiking and biking trail constituted a taking of the property of the owners of the underlying fee simple estate. At this point we shall refer to the railroad's interest in the property by the term "right-of-way." That term is sufficient to indicate that the railroad had obtained a property interest allowing it to operate its equipment over the land involved. Later in the opinion it will become important to more precisely delineate the nature of the railroad's property interests, after which the use of the term "right-of-way" will refer only to those defined interests.

. . . .

In summary, we conclude that the trial court was correct in finding that the 1899 transfers to the railroad created easements for use for railroad purposes; the fee estates remained with the original property owners. (Part C.1.) We accept the Government's position that ultimately this is a matter to be decided under controlling federal law and Constitution, but we reject the Government's central thesis that general federal legislation providing for the governance of interstate railroads, enacted over the years of the Twentieth Century, somehow redefined state-created property rights and destroyed them without entitlement to compensation. (Part C.2.) The trial court erred in accepting that thesis.

As far as the Government's defenses based on the state's property law are concerned, we conclude that even if these easements were still in existence at the time the trail was created, there was no legal justification for the intrusion upon the Preseault's property. We find no support in Vermont law for the proposition, propounded by the defendants and accepted by the dissent, that the scope of an easement limited to railroad purposes should be read to include public recreational hiking and biking trails (Part D). But we find no clear error in the trial court's determination that in fact these easements had been abandoned years before the creation of the trail (Part E), and that determination is affirmed.

Finally, we conclude that the taking that resulted from the establishment of the recreational trail is properly laid at the doorstep of the Federal Government. Whether the State's role in the matter should have resulted in liability for the State, or whether the State could absolve itself by pointing to the Federal Government, as the State Court held, is immaterial. The Federal Government authorized and controlled the behavior of the State in this matter, and the consequences properly fall there. (Part E.)

### B. Factual Background

The Preseaults own a fee simple interest in a tract of land near the shore of Lake Champlain in Burlington, Vermont, on which they have a home. This tract of land is made up of several previously separate properties, the identities of which date back to before the turn of the century. The dispute centers on three parcels within this tract, areas over which the original railroad right-of-way ran. The areas are designated by the trial court as Parcels A, B, and C. Two of those parcels, A and B, derive from the old Barker Estate property. The third parcel, C, is part of what was the larger Manwell property.

The Rutland-Canadian Railroad Company, a corporation organized under the laws of Vermont, acquired in 1899 the rights-of-way at issue on Parcels A, B, and C, over which it laid its rails and operated its railroad. Over time the ownership interests of the Rutland-Canadian passed into the hands of several successor railroads with different names; except as it may be necessary to differentiate among them, they will be referred to collectively as the Railroad.

Meanwhile, ownership of the properties over which the rights-of-way ran passed through the hands of successors in interest, eventually arriving in the hands of the Preseaults. A map of the Preseault tract, showing the various parcels and the areas subject to the railroad's rights-of-way is reproduced here for the benefit of the reader:

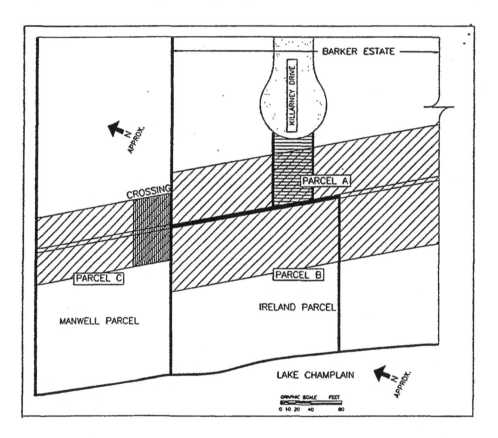

Image within *Preseault v. United States*, 100 F.3d at 1532.

### C. The Property Interests

In *Preseault II*, Justice Brennan writing for the Supreme Court noted the importance of determining the nature of the interests created by these turn-of-the-century transfers:

> The alternative chosen by Congress [the Rails-to-Trails program] is less costly than a program of direct federal trail acquisition because, under any view of takings law, only some rail-to-trail conversions will amount to takings. Some rights-of-way are held in fee simple. Others are held as easements that do not even as a matter of state law revert upon interim use as nature trails.

*Preseault II*, 494 U.S. 1, 16 [(1986)] (citation omitted).

Justice O'Connor, in a concurring opinion for herself and Justices Scalia and Kennedy, developed the point further:

> [T]he parties sharply dispute what interest, according to Vermont law, the State of Vermont acquired from the Rutland Railway Corporation and, correspondingly, whether petitioners possess the property interest that they claim has been taken. . . . Determining what interest petitioners would have enjoyed under Vermont law, in the absence of the ICC's recent actions, will establish whether petitioners possess the predicate property interest that must underlie any takings claim. We do not attempt to resolve that issue.

*Id.* at 20 (citation omitted).

Clearly, if the Railroad obtained fee simple title to the land over which it was to operate, and that title inures, as it would, to its successors, the Preseaults today would have no right or interest in those parcels and could have no claim related to those parcels for a taking. If, on the other hand, the Railroad acquired only easements for use, easements imposed on the property owners' underlying fee simple estates, and if those easements were limited to uses that did not include public recreational hiking and biking trails ("nature trails" as Justice Brennan referred to them), or if the easements prior to their conversion to trails had been extinguished by operation of law leaving the property owner with unfettered fee simples, the argument of the Preseaults becomes viable.

The determinative issues in the case, then, are three: (1) who owned the strips of land involved, specifically did the Railroad by the 1899 transfers acquire only easements, or did it obtain fee simple estates; (2) if the Railroad acquired only easements, were the terms of the easements limited to use for railroad purposes, or did they include future use as public recreational trails; and (3) even if the grants of the Railroad's easements were broad enough to encompass recreational trails, had these easements terminated prior to the alleged taking so that the property owners at that time held fee simples unencumbered by the easements.

The Government enriches the case with an argument that would have profound impact on future takings jurisprudence: that the general federal legislation providing for the Government's control over interstate railroad operations as enacted and amended over the years had the effect of redefining the private property rights of these owners, leaving them without a compensable interest in the land.

Before addressing these several issues, a preliminary matter. There is an alternative way, frequently used today including by the parties here, to describe property transactions involving easements. Instead of calling the property owner's retained interest a fee simple burdened by the easement, this alternative labels the property owner's retained interest following the creation of an easement as a "reversion" in fee. Upon the termination, however achieved, of the easement, the "reversion" is said to become fully possessory; it is sometimes loosely said that the estate "reverts" to the owner.

Under traditional common law estates terminology, a "reversion" is a future interest remaining in the transferor following the conveyance of certain lesser estates to a transferee, typically when the transferee takes a possessory estate of freehold, for example a life estate. An easement is not such a possessory estate of freehold. . . . Traditional characterization describes an easement as a "use" interest, sometimes an "incorporeal hereditament," but not a "possessory" interest in the land. . . . Therefore labeling the retained interest a "reversion" is not consistent with the traditional classification scheme, which views the retained interest as a present estate in fee simple, subject to the burden of the easement.

Be that as it may, whether the property owner's retained interest following the conveyance of an easement is denominated a fee simple estate or a reversion, it is uniformly treated at common law as a vested estate in fee. Under either characterization the result upon termination of the easement is the same. For consistency we use the traditional terminology which recognizes that the transferor remains seised of the freehold estate, and thus labels the owner's estate as a fee simple, burdened, during the life of the easement, by the easement-holder's rights.

### 1. The Interests Created

The question of what estates in property were created by these turn-of-the-century transfers to the Railroad requires a close examination of the conveying instruments, read in light of the common law and statutes of Vermont then in effect. Ideally that question would be decided by the State of Vermont's courts, utilizing their knowledge of and experience with their state's property law. However, when the question of the rights of the property owners vis-a-vis the successors of the Railroad was raised in the Vermont courts . . . , the Vermont Supreme Court took the position that the state courts were without subject matter jurisdiction due to the pervasive role of the Federal Government in railroad matters. See *Trustees of the Diocese of Vermont v. State*, 145 Vt. 510 (1985). The Vermont courts thus declined to address the question. . . . We have no choice, then, but to determine this question of state law ourselves.

In this undertaking we have the benefit of careful analysis by the trial judge. With regard to the two parcels, A and B, derived from the Barker Estate, the trial judge examined, as have we, the document referred to as a "Commissioner's Award," dated September 2, 1899, as well as the relevant cases and statutes of Vermont. The Commissioner's Award, which is the only document that memorializes the event, is unlike a deed in that it does not contain the usual premises (the clause describing the parties to and purposes of the transaction) or habendum clause (defining the extent of the ownership interest conveyed). Usually in a deed the habendum clause would define the exact interest to be conveyed, whether a fee simple or a lesser interest, although the premises clause sometimes serves as well.

Here, the Commissioner's Award simply confirms that "the Rutland-Canadian Railroad Company . . . for the purposes of its railroad has located, entered upon and occupied lands owned by [the Barkers] . . . described as follows [and here follows a metes and bounds description of the strip of land]." The document then states that the owners of the land and the Railroad have not agreed as to the damages to be paid to the owners, that upon application by the Railroad three disinterested commissioners were appointed by the Supreme Court of Vermont, and that "according to the provisions of the Act incorporating said Company and the Statutes of the State of Vermont" the commissioners "appraise and determine the damage to the said owners of said land occasioned by such location, entry and occupation by the said Company" to be a stated sum.

The references to the purposes of the Railroad, and to the provisions of the Act incorporating it, are to 1898 Vermont Acts No. 160, entitled "An Act to Incorporate the Rutland-Canadian Railroad Company," approved November 4, 1898. That Act provided that certain named individuals

> constituted and created a body politic and corporate by the name of the "Rutland-Canadian Railroad Company," for the purpose and with the right of constructing, maintaining and operating a railroad for public use in the conveyance of persons and property by the power of steam or otherwise. . . . Said Corporation shall have and enjoy the right of eminent domain . . . [and] may . . . take . . . such real and personal estate as is necessary or proper in the judgment of such corporation, for the construction, maintenance and accommodation of such railroad . . . as the purposes of the corporation may require. . . .

1898 Vt. Acts No. 160, §1. The Act goes on to state that the corporation shall have all privileges and rights given by the general law to railroad companies for acquiring title and possession to property covered by its location.

It is clear from the relevant documents and statutes that the actions of the Railroad in this case fall under well-established Vermont laws and procedures for acquisition of rights-of-way by companies incorporated for railroad purposes. . . . [T]he trial judge concluded that, in the context of the Vermont procedure for commissioners' awards for railroad rights-of-way, and in light of the Vermont case law, cited and discussed in the trial court's opinion, "[t]he portion of the right-of-way consisting of the parcel of land condemned from the Barker Estate and taken by commissioner's award is indisputably an easement under the law of the State of Vermont." . . .

As a result of our independent examination of the question we conclude that there is little real dispute about this. That was the rule in the early Vermont cases, and continues to be the rule today. . . . With few exceptions the Vermont cases are consistent in holding that, practically without regard to the documentation and manner of acquisition, when a railroad for its purposes acquires an estate in land for laying track and operating railroad equipment thereon, the estate acquired is no more than that needed for the purpose, and that typically means an easement, not a fee simple estate. . . . The trial court fully and correctly analyzed the matter; it hardly needs further elaboration. We find no error in the trial court's analysis and conclusion, and it is affirmed.

Determining the provenance of the third parcel, C, derived from the Manwell tract, tests the above stated proposition even further. The operative instrument is a warranty deed, dated August 2, 1899, from Frederick and Mary Manwell to the Railroad. The deed contains the usual habendum clause found in a warranty deed, and purports to convey the described strip of land to the grantee railroad "[t]o have and to hold the above granted and bargained premises . . . unto it the said grantee, its successors and assigns forever, to its and their own proper use, benefit and behoof forever." The deed further warrants that the grantors have "a good, indefeasible estate, in fee simple, and have good right to bargain and sell the same in manner and form as above written. . . ." In short, the deed appears to be the standard form used to convey a fee simple title from a grantor to a grantee.

But did it? At the outset it should be noted that the resolution of this issue will not moot the question of the Government's potential liability for its action in creating the recreational trail, since, as held above, the A and B parcels unquestionably involved conveyances of easements and not fee simple estates, and thus the question of a taking of the Preseaults' property remains to be decided. The issue of ownership of Parcel C does go to the question of damages, however. As noted earlier, if the Manwell transfer was a conveyance in fee simple, the Preseaults would have acquired no interest in that strip of land, and can claim no damages for its later use as a recreational trail.

At trial, the Preseaults argued that, although the Manwell deed purports to grant a fee simple, the deed was given following survey and location of the right-of-way and therefore it should be construed as conveying only an easement in accordance with Vermont railroad law. The Government responded that, while it was true that survey and location of the railroad's right-of-way had occurred, no "formal" eminent domain proceedings had taken place, and therefore the deed should be taken at its face as a conveyance in fee simple. Each side cited Vermont cases to support its position. The trial court, after reviewing and discussing at length the cases and other relevant materials, concluded that "[u]nder well-settled Vermont law, the property interests in the parcel . . . conveyed following survey and location by warranty deed, amounted to [an] easement[ ]. . . ." . . .

Our independent review of the state of Vermont law on this issue leads us to conclude, despite some uncertainties in the matter, that the trial court is correct. Part of the problem is that the Vermont cases that seem most on point are quite old. Assuming the Vermont courts would follow its precedents, a fair assumption, the probable outcome is that, despite the apparent terms of the deed indicating a transfer in fee, the legal effect was to convey only an easement. Two cases, from among others, will illustrate why.

In *Hill v. Western Vermont Railroad*, 32 Vt. 68 [(1859)], the railroad had a contract with one Josiah Burton to purchase some land for railroad purposes. The bond, or contract, entered into before the railroad had surveyed their right-of-way called for Burton to convey such lands "as shall be required" for the company's road. Plaintiff, a creditor of the railroad, attempted to levy on a part of the land potentially subject to the contract. The railroad defended against the levy by arguing that the tract at issue was not needed by the railroad for its purposes, and thus Burton could not have been made to sell it to the railroad. Since, it was argued, the claimed land was not subject to contract enforcement, it was not subject to the levying creditor.

The Vermont Supreme Court held for the railroad. The court observed that railroads acquire needed land either by order of a designated public body (through the exercise of eminent domain) or by consent of the landowner, although even in the latter case "the proceeding is, in some sense, compulsory." *Id.* at 75. Thus,

> [i]n either mode of appropriating land for the purposes of the company, there is this implied limitation upon the power, that the company will take only so much land or estate therein as is necessary for their public purposes. It does not seem to us to make much difference in regard to either the quantity or the estate whether the price is fixed by the commissioners or by the parties.

*Id.* at 76. The court held that the estate which Burton was to convey would be "a mere easement for a particular use," and under the governing statute would not be subject to a levy. *Id.* at 77.

Ten years later the Vermont Supreme Court decided *Troy & Boston Railroad v. Potter*, [42 Vt. 265 (1869)]. As noted, the right-of-way in that case had been surveyed and located, but there was some dispute over whether a conveying document had been properly executed and recorded. The court held that, regardless of the recording question, the survey and location of the road is what constitutes the taking of the land over which it was laid. *Id.*, 42 Vt. at 272. Consistent with *Hill*, the court deemed the railroad to have acquired only an easement and not a fee.

Thus it is that a railroad that proceeds to acquire a right-of-way for its road acquires only that estate, typically an easement, necessary for its limited purposes, and that the act of survey and location is the operative determinant, and not the particular form of transfer, if any. Here, the evidence is that the Railroad had obtained a survey and location of its right-of-way, after which the Manwell deed was executed confirming and memorializing the Railroad's action. On balance it would seem that, consistent with the view expressed in *Hill*, the proceeding retained its eminent domain flavor, and the railroad acquired only that which it needed, an easement for its roadway. Nothing the Government points to or that we can find in the later cases would seem to undermine that view of the case; the trial court's conclusion that the estate conveyed was an easement is affirmed.

We thus conclude that fee simple title to all three parcels in dispute remained with their original owners, subject only to the burden of the easements in favor of the Railroad. Those titles passed through various hands, coming to rest eventually in the hands of the Preseaults, where they lay in 1986 when the public recreational trail was created by the Government's action.

## 2. The Impact of Federal Legislation

The United States argues that the property interests in Parcels A, B, and C at the time the Preseaults acquired them are defined not by the original conveyances, as understood pursuant to state law, but by the evolving enactment and implementation of federal railroad law between 1899 and the date (1980 for parcels A and B; 1966 for parcel C) the Preseaults acquired the parcels. As a consequence, says the Government, when the Preseaults bought the land whatever rights might have existed in prior owners regarding possession following abandonment of the easements no longer existed, those rights having been modified or abolished by the Federal Government's plenary authority over rail operations. There are several flaws, both of logic and of law, in this argument.

There can be no denying that the Federal Government, beginning as early as 1920, has occupied the field of regulation of interstate railroad operations, preempting any pattern of conflicting state regulation. *See, e.g.,* Transportation Act of 1920, ch. 91, 41 Stat. 456 (1920); Rail Revitalization and Regulatory Reform Act of 1976, Pub.L. No. 94–210, 90 Stat. 31 (1976) ("4-R Act"); 49 U.S.C. §§ 101 et seq. And there can be no question that if the Federal Government wishes to create a national network of public recreational biking and hiking trails, it is within its power to do so. *See Preseault II*, 494 U.S. 1 [(1986)]. And that power includes the power to preempt state-created property rights, including the rights to possession of property when railroad easements terminate. *Id.* However, as Justice O'Connor succinctly pointed out in her concurring opinion, having and exercising the power of preemption is one thing; being free of the Constitutional obligation to pay just compensation for the state-created rights thus destroyed is another. *Id.* at 22.

The 1899 conveyances of Parcels A, B, and C established state-created rights in the owners of the underlying land to have unfettered possession upon the termination of the railroad's easements. If those rights were subsequently and sub rosa destroyed by Federal legislation, prior to the acquisition of the properties by the Preseaults, when did it happen? Could the Transportation Act of 1920 by itself have done it? Not very well. The passage of that Act, which in essence gave the ICC regulatory power over the conduct of railroads, including the establishment and cessation of service to any given community, in and of itself terminated no easements. The Act did not purport to address the rights of private property owners; indeed, it affected railroad operations themselves only with regard to future conduct and then only upon the issuance of individual orders of the ICC. And indeed, no change in the service use of Parcels A, B, and C occurred until 1970, some fifty years after enactment of the original Act.

If in 1920 the then-owners of these parcels had brought suit against the United States for a taking as a result of the enactment of the Transportation Act of 1920, it is difficult to imagine that any court would have granted them an award. The owner would have had to argue that the taking was a regulatory taking, since no actual physical occupation by the Government happened until fifty years later. But that was not a likely argument in 1920. The concept of regulatory takings as we know them today was not yet born; Justice Holmes did not utter his famous statement about regulation that "goes too far" until two years later. [*Pennsylvania Coal Co. v. Mahon*, 260 U.S. 393, 415 (1922) ("[I]f regulation goes too far it will be recognized as a taking.").]

Furthermore, enactment of broad general legislation authorizing a federal agency to engage in future regulatory activity is not the type of government action that alone supports a taking claim. *See, e.g., Hodel v. Virginia Surface Mining & Reclamation Ass'n*, 452 U.S. 264 (1981) (provisions of Surface Mining Control and Reclamation Act prescribing performance standards and authorizing variances for land development, including provisions prohibiting mining in certain locations, did not, on their face, violate the takings clause). If Congress intended the 1920 Act to have such an effect, contrary to all established assumptions about general legislation, and with the result of directly obligating the Government to a potentially enormous liability of unknown dimensions for takings throughout the United States, there surely would have been some indication of that intent in the legislative history, if not in the legislation itself. The Government points to none, because none exists.

The same problem prevails with regard to the enactment in 1976 of the 4-R Act, which contained authorization for the ICC to order a railroad, proposing to dispose of an unneeded right-of-way, to first offer it for sale for "public purposes." 49 U.S.C. § 10906 (1994). And even if the 1983 Rails-To-Trails Act was part of the evolving history pre-*Preseault* (which it was not since their ownership of all three parcels was vested by 1980), that Act also requires an administrative decision to apply the law to any given unused easement. Until the ICC makes the administrative decision to convert an unused right-of-way to a trail, rather than simply permit abandonment, and finds an appropriate public agency to operate the trail, a landowner's suit for a taking would run afoul of established requirements for exhaustion of administrative remedies. *See, e.g., Hodel*, 452 U.S. 264 [(1981)]; *Williamson County Regional Planning Comm'n v. Hamilton Bank*, 473 U.S. 172 (1985).

Thus any property owner who was prescient enough to allege a regulatory taking following the enactment of the Transportation Act of 1920, in addition to having some doctrinal explaining to do, presumably would have been met by an equally prescient Government with the defenses of absence of ripeness and failure to exhaust administrative remedies.

The Government attempts to evade this legal morass by not identifying any specific event that destroyed these property rights created back in 1899, but by instead invoking the broad concept that "background principles" define property rights, suggesting that there is nothing to preclude the use of federal law as well as state law in selecting the relevant "background principles." In support of this broad principle the Government relies heavily on phrases extracted from the Supreme Court's recent decision in *Lucas v. South Carolina Coastal Council*, 505 U.S. 1003 (1992).

But *Lucas* provides no such support. The background principles referred to by the Court in *Lucas* were state-defined nuisance rules. *Id.* at 1029–32. In *Lucas* the

Court took the position that if the State of South Carolina wished to control what it considered undesirable conduct by property owners (in that case building a house on beachfront property), a regulatory agency's order preventing the conduct was non-compensable under the Fifth Amendment if the imposition did little more than echo similar constraints available under the State's traditional nuisance law. In other words, the State could impose non-compensable restraints on property owners either through court-ordered injunctions or administrative agency orders, so long as either were within the scope of established state law principles of common law nuisance, principles which inhere in every property owner's title. *Id.*

Nothing in *Lucas* suggests that the background principles of a state's property law include the sweep of a century of federal regulatory legislation, and indeed much of what the Supreme Court said then, as well as in *Preseault II*, about property rights indicates to the contrary. Nor is there any suggestion in this case that the Preseaults' use of their property could be considered in any way to be a public nuisance under traditional nuisance concepts, justifying the intervention of state authorities.

The Government cites two recent cases by this court, *M & J Coal Co. v. United States*, 47 F.3d 1148 (Fed. Cir.), cert. denied, 516 U.S. 808 (1995), and *California Housing Securities, Inc. v. United States*, 959 F.2d 955 (Fed. Cir. 1992), as evidence that federal regulatory law generally modifies state property rights, and renders conflicting state-created property rights unenforceable and noncompensable. . . .

In both cases what was at issue was the reasonableness of the Government's actions in enforcing the law. Since no one has a property right to violate otherwise valid laws controlling social conduct, the claims that enforcement of the law, found to have been conducted reasonably under the circumstances, constituted a taking under the Fifth Amendment were unavailing. In the Preseaults' case, the occupation of their property by the Government was not in pursuance of an enforcement action to correct prohibited conduct on their part, unless it can be said that their desire to enjoy their private property without sharing it with the public falls under that rubric.

This argument, that the Preseaults' title somehow incorporates the federal transportation regulatory statutes enacted since the 19th Century, was made by the Government to the trial court, and again in its opening brief before the original panel, based on a different theory than the Lucas "background principles" concept presented to the in banc court. It is unclear whether the Government intended to abandon the earlier theory, but since it was the one accepted by the trial court in holding for the Government, it warrants examination. . . .

The argument goes as follows. These regulatory statutes governing railroad operations, at least the original statute enacted in 1920 authorizing ICC jurisdiction, were on the books when the Preseaults began buying the parcels at issue. As a consequence, the Preseaults should have anticipated that at some time in the future the Government might exercise its general regulatory powers in a way that could frustrate the Preseaults' interest in obtaining the land free of the easement upon its abandonment by the railroad. Thus the Preseaults could have no "reasonable expectations" that they would ever get the property free of the encumbering easement even if the railroad ceased to use it. Absent such an expectation, the Preseaults cannot complain that anything was taken from them; the title acquired by the Preseaults in effect has been modified by the history of federal regulatory enactments.

Support for this novel notion is found in two sentences lifted out of context from the Supreme Court's decision in *Loretto v. Teleprompter Manhattan CATV Corp.*, 458 U.S. 419 (1982), which ironically is the decision that definitively established the rights of a property owner to compensation whenever there is a physical taking, even a relatively minor one. In *Loretto*, Justice Marshall, writing for the Court, said: "We affirm the traditional rule that a permanent physical occupation of property is a taking. In such a case, the property owner entertains a historically rooted expectation of compensation. . . ." *Loretto*, 458 U.S. at 441. The Government reverses the order of the sentences, as if it read, "If the property owner has an expectation of compensation, then a permanent physical occupation of property is a taking." In effect, the Government argues that *Loretto* stands for the proposition that an owner's property rights are defined by what the owner might (should?) have believed the law to be at the time she acquired her property, and that that belief makes it so.

But what Justice Marshall clearly said was that a physical occupation of one's property by the Government, that is, a taking of a recognized property interest, invokes a general expectation of compensation. The Government's reading reverses the sentences, standing the law on its head. They read it to say that an owner's subjective expectations of keeping or losing her property under various possible scenarios define for that owner the extent of her title. Just the reverse is true. It is the law-created right to own private property, recognized and enforced by the Constitution, legislation, and common law, that gives the owner an historically rooted expectation of compensation. The expectations of the individual, however well- or ill-founded, do not define for the law what are that individual's compensable property rights.

This issue of title and ownership expectations must be distinguished from the question that arises when the Government restrains an owner's use of property, through zoning or other land use controls, without disturbing the owner's possession. Placing restraints on an owner's use of her property invokes the regulatory takings issue, rather than the question of the Government's physical occupation of private property, and both factually and legally raises significantly different issues. In the regulatory taking cases the owner's reasonable investment-backed expectations have been held to be relevant to the question of whether a regulatory imposition goes too far in constraining the owner's lawful uses of the property. *E.g., Penn Central Transp. Co. v. City of New York*, 438 U.S. 104, 124 (1978). As the Supreme Court makes clear, these two quite different situations call for quite different analyses. The Government's attempt to read the concept of "reasonable expectations" as used in regulatory takings law into the analysis of a physical occupation case would undermine, if not eviscerate, long-recognized understandings regarding protection of property rights; it is rejected categorically. . . .

The trial court erred in accepting the Government's effort to inject into the analysis of this physical taking case the question of the owner's "reasonable expectations." Under the governing law of the State, the Preseaults, successors in title to those who owned the property when the easements were created, owned the same title and interest as they, and are entitled to the same protections the law grants.

### D. The Scope of the Railroad's Easement

We turn then to the question of whether the easements granted to the Railroad, to which the Preseaults' title was subject, are sufficiently broad in their scope so that the use of the easements for a public recreational trail is not a violation of the Preseaults' rights as owners of the underlying fee estate. Both the Government and the State argue that under the doctrine of "shifting public use" the scope of the original easements, admittedly limited to railroad purposes, is properly construed today to include other public purposes as well, and that these other public purposes include a public recreational hiking and biking trail. Under that theory of the case, the establishment in 1986 of such a trail would be within the scope of the easements presumably now in the State's hands, and therefore the Preseaults would have no complaint. On the other hand, if the Government's use of the land for a recreational trail is not within the scope of the easements, then that use would constitute an unauthorized invasion of the land to which the Preseaults hold title. The argument on this issue assumes that the easements were still in existence in 1986, and for purposes of this part of the discussion we assume they were.

. . . .

In the absence of a Vermont case on point, we must seek the answer in traditional understandings of easement law, recognizing as we must that Vermont follows and applies common law property principles. The easements involved here are express easements, meaning that the scope of the easements are set out in express terms, either in the granting documents or as a matter of incorporation and legal construction of the terms of the relevant documents. "The extent of an easement created by a conveyance is fixed by the conveyance." 5 Restatement of Property § 482 (American Law Institute 1944). . . .

The general rule does not preclude the scope of an easement being adjusted in the face of changing times to serve the original purpose, so long as the change is consistent with the terms of the original grant:

> It is often said that the parties are to be presumed to have contemplated such a scope for the created easement as would reasonably serve the purposes of the grant. . . . This presumption often allows an expansion of use of the easement, but does not permit a change in use not reasonably foreseeable at the time of establishment of the easement.

Richard R. Powell, 3 Powell on Real Property § 34.12[2] (Patrick J. Rohan ed., 1996).

\* \* \* \*

When the easements here were granted to the Preseaults' predecessors in title at the turn of the century, specifically for transportation of goods and persons via railroad, could it be said that the parties contemplated that a century later the easements would be used for recreational hiking and biking trails, or that it was necessary to so construe them in order to give the grantee railroad that for which it bargained? We think not. Although a public recreational trail could be described as a roadway for the transportation of persons, the nature of the usage is clearly different. In the one case, the grantee is a commercial enterprise using the easement in its business, the transport of goods and people for compensation. In the other, the easement belongs to the public, and is open for use for recreational purposes, which happens to involve people engaged in exercise or recreation on foot or on bicycles. It is difficult to imagine that either party to the original transfers had anything remotely in mind that would resemble a public recreational trail.

Furthermore, there are differences in the degree and nature of the burden imposed on the servient estate. It is one thing to have occasional railroad trains crossing one's land. Noisy though they may be, they are limited in location, in number, and in frequency of occurrence. Particularly is this so on a relatively remote spur. When used for public recreational purposes, however, in a region that is environmentally attractive, the burden imposed by the use of the easement is at the whim of many individuals, and, as the record attests, has been impossible to contain in numbers or to keep strictly within the parameters of the easement. . . .

Most state courts that have been faced with the question of whether conversion to a nature trail falls within the scope of an original railroad easement have held that it does not.

. . . .

Given that the easements in this case are limited by their terms and as a matter of law to railroad purposes, we are unable to join the dissent's effort to read into Vermont law a breadth of scope for the easements that is well outside the parameters of traditional common law understanding. The concept of "shifting public use" must be anchored in established precedent, or it becomes little more than speculation about what a hypothetical Vermont court in 1996 might do. Our responsibility here is to apply established law, not to make new law. If a dramatic reinterpretation of the scope of the established terms by which railroad easements were historically granted is to be imposed upon Vermont and the parties to this case, it should not be at the hand of a federal appellate court.

### E. Abandonment

Even assuming for sake of argument that the Government and the State are correct and that the so-called "doctrine of shifting public use" is available to permit reading the original conveyances in the manner for which they argue, there remains yet a further obstacle to the Government's successful defense. The Preseaults contend that under Vermont law the original easements were abandoned, and thus extinguished, in 1975. If that is so, the State could not, over ten years later in 1986, have re-established the easement even for the narrow purposes provided in the original conveyances without payment of the just compensation required by the Constitution. *See, e.g., Loretto*, 458 U.S. at 441. It follows that if the State could not in 1986 use the parcels for railroad purposes without that use constituting a taking, then it surely could not claim the right to use the property for other purposes free of Constitutional requirements....

We have established that the effect of the turn-of-the-century transfers regarding Parcels A, B, and C was to create in the transferee Railroad an easement carrying the right to exclusive possession of the surface of the strips of land described in the conveyances for the limited purposes of railroad use, and to leave in the original owners of the property their fee simple estate, subject to the easement. An easement is not a possessory estate of freehold, but merely gives the easement holder a right to make use of the land over which the easement lies for the purposes for which it was granted....

Typically the grant under which such rights-of-way are created does not specify a termination date. The usual way in which such an easement ends is by abandonment, which causes the easement to be extinguished by operation of law. See generally Restatement of Property § 504. Upon an act of abandonment, the then owner of the fee estate, the "burdened" estate, is relieved of the burden of the easement. In most jurisdictions, including Vermont, this happens automatically when abandonment of the easement occurs....

Vermont law recognizes the well-established proposition that easements, like other property interests, are not extinguished by simple non-use. As was said in *Nelson v. Bacon*, 113 Vt. 161 (1943), "[o]ne who acquires title to an easement in this manner [by deed in that case] has the same right of property therein as an owner of the fee and it is not necessary that he should make use of his right in order to maintain his title." Thus in cases involving a passageway through an adjoining building (*Nelson*), or a shared driveway (*Sabins v. McAllister*, 116 Vt. 302 (1950), overruled in part on other grounds by *Lague v. Royea*, 152 Vt. 499 (1989)), the claimed easement was not extinguished merely because the owner had not made use of it regularly.

Something more is needed. The Vermont Supreme Court in *Nelson* summarized the rule in this way: "In order to establish an abandonment there must be in addition to nonuser, acts by the owner of the dominant tenement conclusively and unequivocally manifesting either a present intent to relinquish the easement or a purpose inconsistent with its future existence." *Nelson*, 32 A.2d at 146 (emphasis added); *see also Lague*, 152 Vt. at 503; *Barrett v. Kunz*, 158 Vt. 15 (1992). The record here establishes that these easements, along with the other assets of the railroad, came into the hands of the State of Vermont in the 1960s. The State then leased them to an entity called the Vermont Railway, which operated trains over them. In 1970, the Vermont Railway ceased active transport operations on the line which included the right-of-way over the parcels at issue, and used the line only to store railroad cars.

In 1975 the Railroad removed all of the railroad equipment, including switches and tracks, from the portion of the right-of-way running over the three parcels of land now owned by the Preseaults. . . . In light of these facts, the trial court concluded that under Vermont law this amounted to an abandonment of the easements, and adjudged that the easements were extinguished as a matter of law in 1975.

. . . .

The Government and the State argue that there are facts inconsistent with that determination, but we are not persuaded that any of them significantly undercut the trial court's conclusion. For example, when the Vermont Railway removed its tracks in 1975, it did not remove the two bridges or any of the culverts on the line, all of which remained "substantially intact." That is not surprising. The Railroad was under no obligation to restore the former easement to its original condition. Tearing out existing structures would simply add to its costs, whereas the rails that were taken up could be used for repairs of defective rails elsewhere on the line. It is further argued that, since the rail line continues to operate to a point approximately one and one-third miles south of the Preseaults' property, it is possible to restore the line to full operation. The fact that restoration of the northern portion of the line would be technically feasible tells us little. The question is not what is technically possible to do in the future, but what was done in the past.

Almost immediately after the tracks were removed, members of the public began crossing over the easement. Perhaps illustrating the difficulty in getting government paperwork to catch up with reality, or perhaps indicating that revenue collectors do not give up easily, the State of Vermont and Vermont Railway, as they had done before the removal of the tracks, continued to collect fees under various license and crossing agreements from persons wishing to establish fixed crossings. In January 1976, the Preseaults executed a crossing agreement with the Vermont Railway which gave the Preseaults permission to cross the right-of-way. In March 1976, the Preseaults entered into a license agreement with the State and the Vermont Railway to locate a driveway and underground utility service across the railroad right-of-way. As late as 1991, 985 Associates (through Paul Preseault) paid a $10 license fee to "Vermont Railroad" (sic), presumably pursuant to one of the 1976 agreements. The Preseaults paid "under protest." Much of this activity suggests that, initially at least, the adjacent property owners decided it was cheaper to pay a nominal license fee to the State than to litigate the question of whether the State had the right to extract the fee. . . . In view of all the contrary evidence of physical abandonment, we find this behavior by the State's revenue collectors unconvincing as persuasive evidence of a purpose or intent not to abandon the use of the right-of-way for actual railroad purposes.

One uncontrovertible piece of evidence in favor of abandonment is that, in the years following the shutting down of the line in 1970 and the 1975 removal of the tracks, no move has been made by the State or by the Railroad to reinstitute service over the line, or to undertake replacement of the removed tracks and other infrastructure necessary to return the line to service. The declarations in the 1985 lease between the State of Vermont, Vermont Railway, and the City of Burlington, which refer to the possible resumption of railroad operations at some undefined time in the future are of course self-serving and not indicative of the facts and circumstances in 1975. Other events occurring after 1975 are also of little probative value. [Here, the court notes that, since the 1950s, Rutland Railway and later the Vermont Railway have licensed the Burlington Electric Light Department, a municipal utility, to install and maintain electrical transmission and distribution lines within the right-of-way. The City of Burlington installed a water line on the property under an agreement with the Vermont Railway. The Government says this occurred in 1974, but the Preseaults say it was in 1976.]

. . . .

The trial judge in this case, after extensive recitation of the undisputed facts, and after reviewing cases . . . , concluded that as a fact the Railroad had effected in 1975 an abandonment of the easement running over parcels A, B, and C. Even without giving the trial judge the deference due her, our review of the facts and circumstances leading up to the events of 1975 persuades us that the trial judge is correct. . . . We affirm the determination of the trial court that abandonment of the easements took place in 1975. That determination provides an alternative ground for concluding that a governmental taking occurred.

### E. The Taking

The Preseaults had acquired Parcel C, the Manwell Parcel, in 1966. At that time it was still subject to the railroad's easement. In 1975, following the abandonment by the railroad of the easement across Parcel C, the Preseaults owned Parcel C in fee simple free of the encumbering easement. The Preseaults acquired Parcels A and B in 1980. At that time the easement had been extinguished for five years; the parcels they purchased were in fee simple, again free of the encumbrance.

. . . .

The ICC in a January 1986 Order authorized Vermont Railway ex post facto to discontinue service, and approved the agreement between the State and the City of Burlington for trail use of the former right-of-way. . . .

In due course an eight foot wide paved strip was established on the former right-of-way over Parcels A, B, and C. The path is some 60 feet from the Preseaults' front door. On each side of the Preseaults' driveway, where it crosses the easement, two concrete posts and one metal post were installed to block automobile traffic. The city also erected two stop signs on the path and built a water main under and along the path. The Preseaults have been unable to build on the land under the easement or to construct a driveway connecting their land through Parcels A and B to the nearest public street.

The path is used regularly by members of the public for walking, skating, and bicycle riding. On warm weekends up to two hundred people an hour go through the Preseaults' property. People using the path often trespass on the Preseaults' front yard. On one occasion Mr. Preseault was nearly run over by a cyclist as he walked across the path.

. . . .

Thus, if the Preseaults have interests under state property law that have traditionally been recognized and protected from governmental expropriation, and if, over their objection, the Government chooses to occupy or otherwise acquire those interests, the Fifth Amendment compels compensation. The record establishes two bases on which the Preseaults are entitled to recover. One, if the easements were in existence in 1986 when, pursuant to ICC Order, the City of Burlington established the public recreational trail, its establishment could not be justified under the terms and within the scope of the existing easements for railroad purposes. The taking of possession of the lands owned by the Preseaults for use as a public trail was in effect a taking of a new easement for that new use, for which the landowners are entitled to compensation. . . . [S]ome courts consider that the establishment of a use outside the scope of an existing easement has the effect of causing an abandonment, and thus termination, of the existing easement. *See, e.g., Lawson v. State*, 107 Wash. 2d 444 (1986). Either way, the result is the same — a new easement for the new use, constituting a physical taking of the right of exclusive possession that belonged to the Preseaults.

Two, as an alternative basis, in 1986 when the ICC issued its Order authorizing the City to establish a public recreational biking and pedestrian trail on Parcels A, B, and C, there was as a matter of state law no railroad easement in existence on those parcels, nor had there been for more than ten years. The easement had been abandoned in 1975, and the properties were held by the Preseaults in fee simple, unencumbered by any former property rights of the Railroad. When the City, pursuant to federal authorization, took possession of Parcels A, B, and C and opened them to public use, that was a physical taking of the right of exclusive possession that belonged to the Preseaults as an incident of their ownership of the land.

The Government argues that, since it was the City that actually established the trail, the United States should not be considered the responsible actor. If a taking occurred, says the Government, it was the City and the State who did it. In *Hendler v. United States*, 952 F.2d 1364 (Fed. Cir. 1991), the U.S. Environmental Protection Agency issued an Order which, among other things, authorized and directed the State of California to enter upon the land of the Hendlers, disregarding their objections, and establish monitoring wells. The State did so. In response to the Hendlers' takings claim against the United States, the Government argued, *inter alia*, that it could not be held responsible for what California did since the state could have entered under its own authority, and did not need the EPA Order.

We rejected the argument. We pointed out that pursuant to the Government's Order California entered on the property and dug and serviced deep wells. When

California acted pursuant to the Order, it acted under the aegis of the United States, and its actions were, for purposes of takings liability, the actions of the United States. That it could have acted on its own was immaterial.

In the case before us there was a similar physical entry upon the private lands of the Preseaults, acting under the Federal Government's authority pursuant to the ICC's Order. That it was for a valued public use is not the issue. We have here a straightforward taking of private property for a public use for which just compensation must be paid.

As previously noted, when the Preseaults and other affected landowners first sued in the Vermont state courts for a determination of ownership rights as between themselves and the Railroad (then owned by the State), the Vermont Supreme Court held that it was without subject matter jurisdiction since the matter was exclusively one within federal control. *Trustees of the Diocese of Vermont v. State*, 145 Vt. 510 (1985). In the subsequent litigation against the Federal Government, the Federal Government never denied its role, and indeed, as was previously explained, in arguing the case before us staked its position on the grounds of total federal control over railroads and railroad rights-of-way. Both the State and the Federal Governments were fully invested in the effort to create this public trail. It would be absurd to deny the Preseaults their Constitutional rights on the grounds that the State has concluded it was the Federal Government who did it, and the Federal Government has concluded it was the State. In sum, the Government cannot now point its finger at the State and say "they did it, not us." As in *Hendler*, when the Federal Government puts into play a series of events which result in a taking of private property, the fact that the Government acts through a state agent does not absolve it from the responsibility, and the consequences, of its actions.

A final argument made by defendants is based on a 1982 state statute which authorizes, indeed instructs, the State to retain any unused railroad rights-of-way it owns for future transportation uses, and in the meantime to use them for other public purposes not inconsistent with future transportation purposes. . . . That is what the State purports to have done, and presumably would have done with or without the statute. Defendants argue that the statute makes the action proper.

One can hardly fault the State government for complying with its law. However, the statute does not say that such actions are without consequences to the property owners, nor does it say that the property owners will not, or must not, be compensated for such actions. The statute is in fact wholly silent on the question of compensation. Obviously the State could not simply by enactment of a statute immunize itself from the salutary provisions of the Fifth Amendment. . . . The issue is not whether the State or Federal governments had the power or obligation to do what they did, but whether the Constitution requires that just compensation be paid as a consequence. The existence of the statute thus adds nothing to the Government's defense.

## Summary and Conclusion

... When state-defined property rights are destroyed by the Federal Government's preemptive power in circumstances such as those here before us, the owner of those rights is due just compensation.

We do not hold that every exercise of authority by the Government under the Rails-to-Trails Act necessarily will result in a compensable taking. Obviously if the railroad owns the right-of-way in fee simple, there is no owner of a separate underlying property interest to claim the rights of the servient estate holder. And even if an easement rather than fee title is the nature of the property interest held by the railroad at the time of the conversion to a public trail, if the terms of the easement when first granted are broad enough under then-existing state law to encompass trail use, the servient estate holder would not be in a position to complain about the use of the easement for a permitted purpose.

Whether, at the time a railroad applies to abandon its use of an easement limited to railroad purposes, a taking occurs under an ICC order to "railbank" the easement for possible future railroad use, and allowing in the interim for use of the easement for trail purposes, is a question not now before us. We offer no opinion at this time on that question. ... We conclude that the occupation of the Preseaults' property by the City of Burlington under the authority of the Federal Government constituted a taking of their property for which the Constitution requires that just compensation be paid. Neither the Government nor the State of Vermont have demonstrated a valid reason why the Preseaults are not entitled to what the Constitution mandates. The judgment of the Court of Federal Claims, holding the Government not liable, is reversed. The matter is remanded to that court for further proceedings consistent with this opinion.

REVERSED AND REMANDED.

RADER, Circuit Judge. (concurring). I too would reverse the Court of Federal Claims' holding that the Government is not liable for the uncompensated taking of the Preseaults' property. I write separately, however, to highlight the issues upon which I believe this case turns.

. . . .

While it is not disputed that an easement will not be extinguished through mere non-use, removing the tracks and switches from a railway cannot be termed non-use. Non-use of the easement began in 1970; abandonment occurred, as evidenced by the more permanent lack of operability, in 1975. I cannot say that the grant of summary judgment on that issue is in error.

Ultimately, and as a final indication of abandonment, I note the difference in the current use of the easement from that originally granted. The opinion of the court and the dissent dispute the applicability under Vermont law of the doctrine of shifting public use. However, even if the doctrine is applicable, a public trail is a use distinguishable from that of a railroad.

. . . .

While there is some dispute over the comparative burden of scheduled rumbling freight trains versus obnoxious in-line rollerskaters, the issue can be resolved on simpler terms. Realistically, nature trails are for recreation, not transportation. Thus, when the State sought to convert the easement into a recreational trail, it exceeded the scope of the original easement and caused a reversion.

As to the latter, otherwise known as railbanking, the dissent relies upon the 1982 Act to note the State's intention to keep the rights-of-way. However, the State's belated statement of intent, seven years after it exhibited an unequivocal intent to abandon the easement, cannot revive the property right. Moreover, the State's transparent attempt to retain property condemned for a narrow transportation use crumbled when it converted that property to a recreational use. The 1982 Act could not immunize the State from the consequences of exceeding the scope of the easement. As such, little by little, through federal regulation and state legislation, the United States and Vermont have converted a right to use the Preseaults' land for a railroad into a right to hold the land in perpetuity. The vague notion that the State may at some time in the future return the property to the use for which it was originally granted, does not override its present use of that property inconsistent with the easement. That conversion demands compensation. Moreover, the United States facilitated that conversion with its laws and regulatory approval.

For the reasons stated above, I would reverse the opinion of the Court of Federal Claims and remand for a proper assessment of damages.

CLEVENGER, Circuit Judge. (dissenting). . . . At the heart of this case is the use of a railroad right-of-way as a current walking and bicycle trail, pursuant to a contract which preserves the easement for future rail use (a concept known as "railbanking"), while allowing the interim trail use. The owners of the land over which the current trail crosses contend that the presence of the trail under color of federal law violates their rights under the takings clause of the Fifth Amendment to the U.S. Constitution. . . .

Whether the Preseaults presently have a justiciable Fifth Amendment claim, however, depends upon whether the right-of-way has been abandoned. This is so, because if the right-of-way still exists, and if the current use of the original right-of-way is permissible under Vermont law, then the Preseaults would have no present right to claim ownership of the underlying land, free of the burden on their property created by the trail. In short, their takings claim would be unripe and therefore moot.

. . . .

The Court of Federal Claims recognized that Vermont law requires more than nonuse of a railroad easement to extinguish it, and that some act by the owner of the dominant tenement beyond nonuse is required to establish abandonment. For the Court of Federal Claims, the removal of the tracks in 1975 was enough to hold, on the facts, that abandonment had occurred in 1975. . . . No other fact is cited by the court, or found in the record of the case, to sustain its conclusion.

During the pendency of the Preseaults' litigation in the Vermont state courts to declare that the easements had been abandoned by removal of the tracks, denominated as *Trustees of the Diocese of Vermont v. State*, [145 Vt. 510 (1985)] and decided in 1985, the State legislature passed in 1982 a specific enactment which required the State to retain, for future transportation purposes and for any other purpose not inconsistent with such future transportation purposes, all railroad rights-of-way it owned over which active rail service had been, or would be, terminated. The 1982 Act was made retroactive to apply to the easements that ran over the Preseaults' property.

In considering whether the Preseaults presently enjoy fee simple absolute ownership in their property, the Court of Federal Claims did not assess the impact of the 1982 Act. For the reasons stated in this opinion, the Court of Federal Claims thus erred.

. . . .

. . . I have concluded that the State has not abandoned its easements, the Preseaults can only show ownership of the servient tenements. No argument has been made that the current use of the easements imposes a greater burden on the servient tenement than would be imposed were the State to use the easements for railroad purposes. Also, no other argument has been made that would afford the Preseaults standing to maintain their takings complaint in the Court of Federal Claims at this time. Consequently, the decision granting the Preseaults' partial summary judgment motion against the State should be reversed and the case remanded to the Court of Federal Claims, with the instructions to grant the cross motion for summary judgment of the State and dismiss the Preseaults' complaint for failure to state a claim upon which relief can be granted. The second decision by the Court of Federal Claims granting summary judgment for the United States should be vacated as moot.

For these reasons, I respectfully dissent from the court's holding, without a majority supporting opinion, that the Preseaults are entitled to compensation from the United States.

## Questions for Consideration

1) Why did the railroad originally have an easement instead of a fee simple?

2) Why may an owner of a fee estate not abandon the property?

3) Why did the court conclude that the railway abandoned the easement by discontinuance of railroad use, relieving the servient tenement of the easement?

4) Should the scope of the original easement have included using the right of way for a public trail?

5) Why was the public use of right of way, authorized by the ICC, a taking of private property?

6) What amount of compensation would be "just" for this taking?

## *Takeaway*

- When a public entity takes private property for public use under the power of eminent domain, the public entity acquires only the property interests to the extent needed for the public use.

- Originally, the government took an easement rather than a fee estate, because the property right needed for the public use was merely an easement for laying a track and operating a railroad.

- This presumption of taking property interests only to the extent needed for the public use not only indicates a degree of protection for private property rights, but also minimizes the "just compensation" required to be paid by the government for the taking.

- Because the original taking was not in fee, then if the government abandoned its easement, it needed to re-take after such abandonment (a fee estate cannot be abandoned, whereas an easement may be abandoned).

- Sometimes surcharge (use exceeding the scope of an easement, where the scope is determined as what is reasonably foreseeable at the time of the creation of the easement) results in termination of the easement, but usually, if there is use beyond the scope of the original easement, then the servient tenement owner may seek an injunction to prevent the surcharge. When the user is the government, surcharge results in a taking because the government's use beyond the scope of the easement is the government taking more from the private landowner.

- Whether the railway easement was abandoned or whether the hiking trail exceeded the scope of the railway easement, a regulatory taking occurred either way, thus requiring just compensation to the Preseaults.

## Discussion Problem 3.3

The state enacts a new state statute, "The Tenant Protection Act" requiring landlords to provide "relocation assistance" when they terminate a tenancy. Specifically, if a tenant has lived at the property for more than twelve months and the owner terminates his or her tenancy, the landlord must either provide a direct payment to the tenant of one month's rent or waive the tenant's final month of rent. The landlord's failure to provide this relocation assistance renders any notice of termination void. The new state statute applies to all residential properties except those specifically exempted by statute, such as government-regulated affordable housing. Improve Housing, Inc., a nonprofit organization representing the interests of landlords in the state, brought an action against the Governor of the State because of the new state statute. Improve Housing contends that the new state statute violates the U.S. Constitution. Specifically, it has allegedly impacted landlords' ability to plan for the management and disposition of their units because they must now consider the financial penalty (the relocation payment) that they must pay for the right to repossess those units. Improve Housing claims landlords have been forced to incur significant costs to change their rental-business models. Who shall prevail in this dispute?

# E. Zoning for an Aging Population

As our population ages, many communities are seeing a demographic transition to having 20–25% of their population age 60 years or older. An aging population may require different services and different types of property development to meet the needs of elderly residents. An aging population is also a population with a much higher incidence of disability, and in particular mobility impairment, than is the general population. This triggers a need for land planning and zoning that accounts for aging in place. In the narrow sense, aging in place means that the person does not need to leave her current home as she ages and experiences difficulty with walking and other mobility issues. In the broad sense, aging in place can mean that a person can continue to reside in her familiar neighborhood and community as her needs change over time. Communities need to provide a range of affordable housing options so that people can age within their neighborhoods, and housing needs to be built with more attention to accessible design so that people can stay in their homes for a longer period of time. Prematurely relocating people to assisted living and nursing homes is generally much more expensive than making it possible for them to continue to live in their current homes.

## Maldini v. Ambro

Court of Appeals of New York
330 N.E.2d 403 (N.Y. 1975)

FUCHSBERG, Judge. The issues posed are (1) whether the Town Board of the Town of Huntington exceeded its powers by amending its zoning ordinance to create a residence district providing, among other uses, for a "Retirement Community District" and (2) whether a subsequent resolution of the town board granting an application of defendant Health Care Agencies of the New York Annual Conference of the Methodist Church, Inc. (Health Care Agencies), a nonprofit New York corporation, to rezone its 20-acre parcel of land from a "Residence B district" (single-family dwellings on minimum one-acre plots) to a "Retirement Community District" for the purpose of building residences designed for older people was valid.

This action, for declaratory judgment and injunctive relief, is brought by individual homeowners living in the area of the proposed retirement community. Following trial, the Supreme Court upheld both the amendment and the resolution. The Appellate Division unanimously affirmed. We hold that the town board's zoning power was validly exercised in its adoption of the amendment in question and that Health Care Agencies' subsequent application thereunder was properly granted.

The amendment, now chapter 62, section 4.9.01 of the Building Zone Ordinance of the Town of Huntington, was adopted following a public hearing. It reads as follows:

"In the R-RM Residence District a building or premises shall be used only for the following purposes:

"(1) Any use permitted in the R-80 Residence District [single-family dwellings on minimum two-acre plots and other uses including farms, churches, schools and libraries].

"(2) Multiple residences designed to provide living and dining accommodations, including social, health care, or other supportive services and facilities for aged persons to be owned and operated by a non-profit corporation organized for such purposes under the laws of the State of New York.

"(3) Any accessory use or structure permitted in the R-80 Residence District."

After the amendment was adopted, Health Care Agencies applied for a reclassification as "Retirement Community District" for its 20-acre parcel, presenting a plan which provided the facilities enumerated in the ordinance's amendment. The application was granted following a public hearing. None of the plaintiffs appeared or in any other way raised any objection at that hearing or at the earlier one that had preceded passage of the amendment itself. Plaintiffs now claim that the town board exceeded the zoning powers delegated it by the Legislature and impermissibly applied a classification based upon age.

The relevant enabling legislation pursuant to which the town board has the power to zone is section 261 of the Town Law. By that statute the State has empowered the town to regulate and restrict the use of land "[f]or the purpose of promoting the health, safety, morals, or the general welfare of the community." In our view, this grant provides a sufficient basis for the Town of Huntington's zoning law amendment to provide for multiple residences for elderly people.

The police power which provides the justification for zoning is not narrowly confined. (*Village of Belle Terre v. Boraas*, 416 U.S. 1.) As Judge Keating put it for this court, "[u]nderlying the entire concept of zoning is the assumption that zoning can be a vital tool for maintaining a civilized form of existence only if we employ the insights and the learning of the philosopher, the city planner, the economist, the sociologist, the public health expert and all the other professions concerned with urban problems." (*Udell v. Haas*, 21 N.Y.2d 463, 469.)

In view of the breadth of the grant of power and the presumption favoring constitutionality of zoning ordinances, we have concluded that the town board's amendment to Huntington's zoning ordinance has a rational basis. Its purpose — meeting the town's need for adequate housing for the aged — was within the town's police powers to regulate land use for the promotion of the community's health and general welfare. Not only was this an important goal of the Town's Comprehensive Plan, but a matter of general public concern not only to the locality but to the State and Nation as well.

Though the town has no burden to establish a need for the amendment, there was unrebutted testimony at trial that studies showed the town's elderly population was increasing at a substantially greater rate than had been anticipated and that there was considerable and justifiable community concern over the lack of available specialized housing for the aged.

It is also to be noted that the town's good faith effort to meet the special needs of its elderly, who otherwise would be likely to be excluded from enjoyment of adequate dwellings within the community, is inclusionary. The inclusionary, as distinguished from exclusionary, nature of such land use is made clear by the town board's conclusion (1) that there is a present shortage for housing for people when they get older, (2) that without the creation of the retirement district that need will go unredressed, and (3) that ameliorating the need in this way will impose no particular hardship on other groups of persons who suffer from significant lack of housing. Certainly, when a community is impelled, consistent with such criteria, to move to correct social and historical patterns of housing deprivation, it is acting well within its delegated "general welfare" power.

Plaintiffs do not claim they would suffer exclusion or disadvantage in their own housing. At trial, they merely offered one witness, a real estate appraiser, who testified that Health Care Agencies' proposed retirement community would increase traffic in the neighborhood and reduce the value of surrounding residential properties, which he valued at $75,000 to $100,000. But it is well-settled that a possible depreciation in value to particular property owners will not shield an existing zoning classification from adaptation to changing community needs (see, e.g., *Shepard v. Village of Skaneateles*, 300 N.Y. 115, 118, 120). In brief, plaintiffs fell far short of meeting their burden of showing that the amendment was arbitrary rather than rational.

Nor do plaintiffs suggest that Huntington was in error in assessing the need for suitable housing for its elderly population, or that the plan submitted by Health Care Agencies in any way fell short of the standards of the ordinance, requiring as they do "living and dining accommodations, including social, health care, or other supportive services and facilities for aged persons." While the amendment under attack makes express provision, among other uses, for suitable housing for the elderly, as with special zoning for schools it does no more in this case than implement the entirely supportable belief by the town that the aged require specially designed accommodations.

... [T]he instant case involves an ordinance enacted by the Huntington Town Board in its legislative capacity and providing standards for its application in a particular case, as well as a subsequent determination pursuant to that ordinance which is supported by substantial evidence.

It is one thing for a local zoning board to deny an application based solely upon the age of the intended residents; it is quite another for it to establish a zoning district allowing, among other things, residences designed for, but not necessarily limited to, aged persons. "Age" considerations are appropriately made if rationally related to the achievement of a proper governmental objective. Here, as already indicated, meeting the community shortage of suitable housing accommodations for its population, including an important segment of that population with special needs, is such an objective.

In the particular case before us, there is no indication whatever that the intent or effect of the ordinance is to segregate the community according to age or discriminate against younger people, or to benefit a particular building developer in the absence of community need for specialized housing for the elderly. Neither does the ordinance contain an arbitrary specific age limitation for residency. And the town's unimpeachable good faith has not given rise even to a suspicion that it was seeking to reap tax base benefits through multi-dwellings without the drain on municipal services created by families and children.

That the "users" of the retirement community district have been considered in creating the zoning classification does not necessarily render the amendment suspect, nor does it clash with traditional "use" concepts of zoning. Including the needs of potential "users" cannot be disassociated from sensible community planning based upon the "use" to which property is to be put. The line between legitimate and illegitimate exercise of the zoning power cannot be drawn by resort to formula, but as in other areas of the law, will vary with surrounding circumstances and conditions (*Euclid v. Ambler Co.*, 272 U.S. 365, 387). Therefore it cannot be said that the board acted unreasonably in this case in making special provision for housing designed for the elderly, one of the major groupings within our population.

"Senior citizenship" may be more appropriately regarded as a stage in life within the normal expectancy of most people than as an unalterable or obstinate classification like race, religion or economic status. Therefore, providing for land use suitable for the elderly may, as here, be viewed as a nondiscriminatory exercise of the power to provide for the general welfare of all people, especially since, even if the validity of that zoning classification were "fairly debatable, [the town board's] legislative judgment must be allowed to control." (*Euclid v Ambler Co., supra*, at p. 388).

Accordingly, the order of the Appellate Division should be affirmed.

JASEN, Judge. (dissenting). The question before us is not whether adequate housing should be provided for our aged citizens, but, rather, whether a town board may restrict the use of land solely for the benefit of the aged. While I fully agree with the majority that providing adequate housing for the aged is a matter of grave public concern, I believe that the town board, in attempting to alleviate this problem, exceeded its zoning powers by creating a land use classification based solely upon age.

It has long been the rule that a town's zoning power, if it is to be exercised lawfully, "must be founded upon a legislative delegation to so proceed, and in the absence of such a grant will be held *ultra vires* and void." Section 261 of the Town Law, the statutory grant of power to towns to enact and enforce zoning regulations, does, as the majority correctly notes, empower a town board to regulate and restrict the use of land "[f]or the purpose of promoting the health, safety, morals, or the general welfare of the community." However, a town board's powers under this section are not infinite. . . . The town law empowers a town board to regulate the *use*, not to specify the *users*. Nothing in the statute authorizes adoption of a zoning ordinance which restricts the age of those who may reside in a structure or which limits the use of a district to a particular class of persons. . . .

Moreover, not only is "age, in and of itself just as irrelevant a consideration insofar as zoning is concerned as is race, color, creed or physical condition," but it clearly favors a class without any apparent justification in violation of the equal protection clause of the Fourteenth Amendment. Not only is the record devoid of any need for such a limiting classification, but it is evident that adequate housing for the aged in the Town of Huntington can clearly be provided within the existing town zoning framework by constructing the necessary facilities for retired persons in an area already zoned for multiple dwellings, without creating an unauthorized land use classification based solely upon age.

Accordingly, I would reverse.

Chief Judge BREITEL and Judges GABRIELLI, JONES and COOKE concur with Judge FUCHSBERG; Judge JASEN dissents and votes to reverse in a separate opinion in which Judge WACHTLER concurs.

Order affirmed, with costs.

## *Questions for Consideration*

1) Who passed the zoning amendment at issue in this case?

2) What is the delegation issue in the case?

3) Was the amendment consistent with the comprehensive plan?

4) What studies, findings, and experts were referenced in support of the amendment?

5) What did the plaintiffs identify as potential negative externalities from the new development?

6) What standard of review is identified in the opinion?

## *Takeaway*

- Plaintiffs (property owners) have the burden of showing the amendment is arbitrary rather than rational.

- Zoning is supposed to regulate the use and not the user. Sometimes this distinction is difficult to sort out.

- Zoning regulations should not treat the elderly differently. For example, zoning regulations should not impose density standards on multi-family housing designed for seniors while not imposing similar standards on other types of multi-family housing. This issue was addressed in *Apfelbaum v. Clarkstown*,

428 N.Y.S.2d 387 (N.Y. Sup. Ct. 1980). In the *Apfelbaum* case, the zoning code prohibited construction of more than 106 dwelling units at any one senior citizens housing site, and it prohibited construction of senior citizens housing within 1,500 feet of each other. These restrictions were not imposed on any other type of multi-family housing. The court stated that reasonable regulations based upon differences in age are constitutional, but in this case, there was insufficient evidence to support a finding that the zoning restrictions applicable only to senior housing rationally furthered a legitimate interest.

## Allen v. Town of North Hempstead

Supreme Court of New York, Appellate Division, Second Department
478 N.Y.S.2d 919 (N.Y. App. Div. 1984)

PER CURIAM. Plaintiffs are nonresidents of the Town of North Hempstead who are interested in purchasing a condominium in a development constructed in a "Golden Age Residence District," a concept established in article X of chapter 70 of the Code of the Town of North Hempstead to enable private developers to build multifamily housing appropriate for the needs of senior citizens. Plaintiffs meet the age requirements for this special residence district contained in article X (§ 70-89, subd A) of chapter 70 of the Code of the Town of North Hempstead, as plaintiff Leonard P. Allen is over 62 years of age. They are precluded from purchasing a unit in this development, however, as they have not satisfied the one-year durational residency requirement imposed by subdivision B of section 70-89 of the Town Code as an additional condition precedent for applicants to occupy housing in a "Golden Age Residence District." Subdivision B of section 70-89, which plaintiffs have challenged in the instant declaratory judgment action, provides as follows: "Senior Citizens who apply for residence in a Golden Age Residence District shall have legally resided in the Town of North Hempstead for at least one (1) year previous to the date of said application."

We conclude that the above durational residency requirement is invalid and unconstitutional, but for different reasons than those articulated by Special Term (121 Misc. 2d 795). There is no need to reach the constitutional equal protection analysis employed by Special Term, as adequate bases for the invalidation of the challenged portion of the zoning ordinance of the Town of North Hempstead exist in the principles governing judicial review of such ordinances developed by the decisional authority of this State. Generally, a municipality will be allowed wide latitude in the exercise of its police power, as reflected in the enactment of local zoning ordinances (see *Village of Belle Terre v. Boraas*, 416 U.S. 1). Therefore, such zoning ordinances have normally been subject to the usual standard of judicial scrutiny for economic and social legislation, and will pass muster under both the Federal and State Constitutions if the restrictions contained therein are not arbitrary and bear a rational or substantial relationship to a legitimate governmental interest or objective. The permissible objectives of local zoning ordinances are broadly defined by section 261 of the Town Law as "promoting the health, safety, morals, or the general welfare of the community."

This is not to say that every zoning ordinance will survive even this liberal and deferential standard of judicial review.... "[While] the power to zone is a broad one, it is not without limit. It may be exercised only in pursuit of some valid public purpose and cannot serve to justify arbitrary exclusionary efforts." One such limitation on the power of municipalities to enact zoning ordinances recognized by the decisional authority is that such ordinances may regulate and restrict the uses of property, but may not place restraints upon the users or owners of that property.

There have been some limited exceptions to this general prohibition against zoning ordinances regulating the users or owners of property, most notably ordinances which create special residence districts for senior citizens similar to the "Golden Age Residence District" established by the Town of North Hempstead (see *Maldini v. Ambro*, 36 N.Y.2d 481, app dsmd & cert den 423 U.S. 993 . . . ). Senior citizens were held to constitute a category of persons who generally require more affordable housing suited to their particular needs and " '[s]enior citizenship' may be more appropriately regarded as a stage in life within the normal expectancy of most people than as an unalterable or obstinate classification like race" (*Maldini v. Ambro*). The same, however, is not true with respect to the durational residency requirement imposed by the Town of North Hempstead as an additional condition for senior citizens who wish to obtain housing in its "Golden Age Residence Districts." Unlike advanced age, residency within the Town of North Hempstead is not a status which people are likely to attain in the normal course of their lives. This is particularly true in the situation at bar, as the ordinance creating the "Golden Age Residence Districts" was based upon an implicit finding that appropriate, affordable housing for the elderly was not generally available within the Town of North Hempstead, whose housing stock is comprised predominantly of single-family residences. Therefore, plaintiffs and other similarly situated nonresident senior citizens are effectively prevented from moving to the Town of North Hempstead, altogether, if they are precluded from obtaining housing in a "Golden Age Residence District."

... The objectives of this durational residency requirement, reflected in statements made by the Town Supervisor and councilmen at the meeting of the Town Board at which it was adopted, include assisting local senior citizens adversely affected by inflation in housing costs and freeing single-family housing vacated by elderly persons who move to "Golden Age Residence Districts" for younger families. After registering his affirmative vote for the amendments to article X of chapter 70 of the town zoning ordinance which created the "Golden Age Residence District," North Hempstead Town Supervisor Michael J. Tully stated, "the Senior Citizen population will soon be equaling 25% of our population. They are the people that helped to make this Town what it is. They are entitled to our attention." These remarks reflect governmental objectives which have been held to be illegitimate in previous decisions, favoring long-term residents of a State or community in the allocation of government benefits or services, over nonresidents or recent migrants, based upon their past contributions to the jurisdiction. Moreover, the durational residency requirement bears no rational relationship to the laudable goal of providing appropriate and affordable housing for senior citizens, reflected in the ordinance creating the "Golden Age Residence Districts."

... [A] zoning ordinance must fulfill the dual objectives of providing a "properly balanced and well ordered plan" for the needs of the community involved and the giving of consideration to the housing needs of the region in which that community is located. In order to satisfy the latter requirement of giving proper consideration to regional needs, "[t]here must be a balancing of the local desire to maintain the *status quo* within the community and the greater public interest that regional needs be met." ... [A]n analysis of 1980 census data by the Nassau County Department of Senior Citizen Affairs indicat[ed] that the percentage increase in the elderly population of most of the neighboring municipalities equaled or exceeded the increase in the senior citizen population within the Town of North Hempstead. ... [T]he defendant town [has not] presented evidence that the surrounding municipalities have made sufficient provisions for the housing needs of senior citizens in the region so as to mitigate the exclusionary impact of the durational residency requirement for the "Golden Age Residence Districts."

Accordingly, for the foregoing reasons, we conclude that the one-year durational residency requirement contained in article X (§ 70-89, subd B) of chapter 70 of the Code of the Town of North Hempstead is invalid. ... Therefore, the judgment under review, declaring the above ordinance invalid and unconstitutional, should be affirmed.

THOMPSON, J.P., BRACKEN, BOYERS and LAWRENCE, JJ., concur.

Judgment of the Supreme Court, Nassau County, entered November 23, 1983, affirmed, with costs.

## Questions for Consideration

1) Explain the relationship between constitutional review of the substantive decision and the standard of review employed in resolving this case.

2) What is wrong with a residency requirement?

3) Why should the Town of North Hempstead have to consider the availability of senior housing in surrounding communities?

## Takeaway

- The court in *Allen* focuses on statements made by the Town Supervisor and by council members at the town meeting adopting the local residency provision. It is important to educate local government officials concerning what they say at meetings on the record, as their statements have legal implications. They must be clear and careful in their statements, making sure not to say anything that might be found to be illegal or discriminatory, and as we will see in some later cases, they should affirmatively counter discriminatory and impermissible considerations voiced by members of the public who might speak at such a meeting. Failure to reject or correct inappropriate comments from members of the public might potentially signal an implicit endorsement of such statements by the local officials.

### Discussion Problem 3.4

The Town of Southerly enacted a new local law, titled "Accessory Dwelling Allowance," permitting the maintenance of a single-bedroom apartment within a home situated in various specified single-family residence zoning districts upon obtaining a special permit. The purpose and intent underlying the new local law are to provide the opportunity and encouragement for the development of small rental housing units designed, in particular, to meet the special housing needs of single persons and couples of low and moderate income, both young and old, and of relatives of families presently living in Southerly. Furthermore, it is the purpose and intent of this new local law to allow the more efficient use of the town's limited space and existing dwellings to provide economic support of present resident families of limited income and to protect and preserve property values. Moreover, the new local law requires that the owner or owners of the lot upon which the accessory apartment is located shall reside within the principal dwelling building. Abigail is the owner of a parcel of property which has been improved with a single-family home and which is situated within one of the zoning districts to which the accessory apartments law applies. She does not occupy the residence, but resides elsewhere in Southerly. She applied to the appropriate town board for a permit to maintain an "Accessory Dwelling" apartment, but her application was denied because she did not occupy the subject premises. Abigail commenced an action against the Town of Southerly seeking a declaration that the new local law is void and unconstitutional insofar as it requires owner occupancy before an accessory apartment permit may be issued. Specifically, Abigail contends that the new local law draws an irrational distinction between owners who occupy their homes and those who do not, treating the two groups differently in violation of the plaintiff's rights to equal protection and due process of law, and impermissibly regulates the users of the property rather than the use of property. Who shall prevail in this dispute?

# F. Conditional Zoning

This section of the chapter explores two issues of conditional zoning. First, we address the issue of a zoning district that has no "as of right" uses. The zoning code in this case makes every use in the district a conditional use. Second, we explore a situation involving a zoning code that permits a use "as of right" while simultaneously permitting other uses only as conditional uses in the same zone.

## Town of Rhine v. Bizzell

Supreme Court of Wisconsin

751 N.W.2d 780 (Wis. 2008)

ZIEGLER, Judge. This case is before the court on certification by the court of appeals.... The court of appeals certified two issues to this court.

The first issue is whether Town of Rhine, Wis., Municipal Code § 4.08(2)(a) is unconstitutional on its face. We conclude that § 4.08(2)(a), the B-2 District, is unconstitutional on its face because it is arbitrary and unreasonable in that it precludes any use as of right in the B-2 District and such limitation bears no substantial relation to the public health, safety, morals or general welfare.

The second issue is whether the circuit court properly dismissed the defendants' nuisance ordinance violations. [This part of the decision is not included in the edited version used for this casebook.] ...

### I. Facts

On October 1, 2003, the Manitowoc Area Off Highway Vehicle Club, Inc., (hereinafter "the Club") purchased 77.2 acres of land in section twelve of the Town of Rhine, Sheboygan County. The zoning classification of this land has been "B-2 Commercial Manufacturing or Processing" for 20 years. Within this classification, "[t]here are no permitted uses in the B-2 District, except that those uses permitted in the Agricultural Land Districts A-1, A-2 and A-3 may be authorized in conjunction with any conditional uses.... All uses are conditional and shall comply with the provisions of Section 4.09 [Conditional Uses] of this ordinance." Town of Rhine, Wis., Municipal Code § 4.08(2)(a). Conditional uses in the "B-2 Commercial Manufacturing or Processing" district include: (1) fabrication of consumer or industrial commodities; (2) garbage, rubbish, offal, industrial waste and dead animal reduction or disposal; (3) quarrying; (4) mining and ore processing; (5) salvage yards for wood, metals, papers and clothing; and (6) stockyards.

After purchasing the property in 2003, club members used the property for riding all-terrain vehicles (ATVs) and hunting. On January 6, 2004, pursuant to a request by the Town of Rhine, the Club's president appeared at a Town of Rhine board meeting. At the meeting, the Club president was asked what activities were occurring on the property. The Club president responded that members "are a group of families that live in the city limits and don't own enough property to enjoy outdoor recreation such as hunting, horseback riding, bicycling, ATV riding etc."

Chairman Sager asked if the Club members were aware that the land was zoned B-2 when they purchased the land. The Club president responded that the Club's attorney informed them that "because it was zoned business and not residential[,] the manner in which they are using the land should not be an issue." Chairman Sager then related that B-2 zones require a conditional use permit "for any use of the land." He further stated that "an application should be directed to the Plan Commission for either a CUP [conditional use permit] or rezoning." The Club president then asked whether he needed to apply for specific uses or different zoning. Chairman Sager answered that it would depend on how they intended to use the land.

On May 19, 2004, the Club applied for a conditional use permit. In the conditional use application, the Club stated that it wanted to use the property for recreational activities, such as hunting and riding ATVs. The application stated, "[t]his IS NOT a request for a commercial or industrial operation." The conditional use permit was denied on September 7, 2004. Although the record is unclear as to when, the Club also applied for the B-2 zone to be rezoned to a B-1, "Neighborhood Business" district. That rezoning request was also denied, but it is unclear from the record when it was denied.

. . . .

The circuit court concluded "that a zoning ordinance which bars all uses within a district is unreasonable." It further stated that "a zoning ordinance which permits no uses within a district is confiscatory in nature and oppressive." Accordingly, the circuit court concluded that the zoning ordinance was unconstitutional. . . . The Town of Rhine appealed the circuit court's decision. Pursuant to Wis. Stat. § 809.61, the court of appeals certified this case to us for review and determination. We accepted the certification.

## II. Standard of Review

"The interpretation and application of an ordinance to an undisputed set of facts is a question of law, which this court decides de novo." The constitutionality of an ordinance is also a question of law, which this court reviews de novo.

## III. Analysis

The Club argues that Municipal Code § 4.08(2)(a), the B-2 District, is unconstitutional on its face because it violates due process in that any use of the property is prohibited unless the landowner obtains a conditional use permit. It further argues that there are no clear and objective standards for the landowner to obtain a conditional use permit. The Town of Rhine, on the other hand, argues that Municipal Code § 4.08(2)(a) is constitutional. It argues that the B-2 District does allow for certain uses of the property under a conditional use permit, and therefore, it is inaccurate to assert that B-2 zoning does not allow any use. The Town of Rhine also argues that Municipal Code § 4.01 sets forth adequate standards for obtaining a conditional use permit, and it asserts that a number of other municipalities have conditional use provisions similar to the Town of Rhine. We conclude that § 4.08(2)(a) is unconstitutional on its face.

### A. Zoning principles

Zoning ordinances and land use regulations have a useful, valid purpose, and the government has broad authority to enact such classifications for the purpose of promoting health, safety, morals or the general welfare of the community.

. . . .

In general, zoning ordinances provide landowners with permitted uses, which allow a landowner to use his or her land, in said manner, as of right. "Most ordinances impose a broad division of land uses, and, in addition, provide that specified uses may be established or maintained in named districts, only pursuant to a special permit. . . ." "Uses are permitted in designated districts because they are thought to be compatible with other uses permitted in such district."

In addition to permitted uses, ordinances may also provide for conditional uses by virtue of a special use or conditional use permit. A conditional use, however, is different than a permitted use. While a permitted use is as of right, a conditional use does not provide that certainty with respect to land use. Conditional uses are for those particular uses that a community recognizes as desirable or necessary but which the community will sanction only in a controlled manner.

A conditional use permit allows a property owner "to put his property to a use which the ordinance expressly permits when certain conditions [or standards] have been met." The degree of specificity of these standards may vary from ordinance to ordinance.

A zone that provides for use of property only when a landowner obtains a conditional use permit may face scrutiny. Conditional use permits, however remain a widely accepted tool of municipal planning.

Allowing for conditional uses, in addition to permitted uses as of right, makes sense when one considers the purpose of the conditional use permit. First, conditional uses are flexibility devices, "which are designed to cope with situations where a particular use, although not inherently inconsistent with the use classification of a particular zone, may well create special problems and hazards if allowed to develop and locate as a matter of right in [a] particular zone."

Second, conditional use permits are appropriate for "certain uses, considered by the local legislative body to be essential or desirable for the welfare of the community . . . but not at every or any location . . . or without conditions being imposed. . . ." Thus, those uses subject to a conditional use permit are necessary to the community, but because they often represent uses that may be problematic, their development is best governed more closely rather than as of right.

. . . .

## B. Constitutional principles

The role of courts in zoning matters is limited because zoning is a legislative function. An ordinance is presumed valid and must be liberally construed in favor of the municipality. The party challenging the constitutionality of an ordinance bears a heavy burden. In Wisconsin, "an ordinance will be held constitutional unless the contrary is shown beyond a reasonable doubt[,] and the ordinance is entitled to every presumption in favor of its validity." "Consequently, although a court may differ with the wisdom, or lack thereof, or the desirability of the zoning, the court, because of the fundamental nature of its power, cannot substitute its judgment for that of the zoning authority in the absence of statutory authorization."

Nonetheless, a properly enacted ordinance must satisfy constitutional requirements. Land use litigation generally arises out of the manner "in which zoning text and ordinance classify land into zoning districts." Constitutional challenges may arise, for example, under the takings, due process, or equal protection clauses of the state and federal constitutions. "The Constitutional Framework." Substantive due process claims with regard to land use regulation, as we see in this case, do not have high success rates. Under the due process clause, courts generally require that "land use controls must advance legitimate governmental interests that serve the public health, safety, morals, and general welfare."

"The Due Process Clause of the Fourteenth Amendment prohibits a state from depriving 'any person of life, liberty, or property without due process of law.'" "The substantive component of the Due Process Clause protects individuals from 'certain arbitrary, wrongful actions "regardless of the fairness of the procedures used to implement them."'" "Substantive due process forbids a government from exercising 'power without any reasonable justification in the service of a legitimate governmental objective.'"

The United States Supreme Court has recognized a landowner's right to substantive due process in zoning cases. *See . . . Nectow v. City of Cambridge*, 277 U.S. 183, 187, 48 S. Ct. 447, 72 L. Ed. 842 (1928); [*Village of*] *Euclid*[*, Ohio*] *v. Ambler Realty Co.*, 272 U.S. 365, 373, 47 S. Ct. 114, 71 L. Ed. 303 (1926). The Supreme Court has stated, "a zoning ordinance is unconstitutional when its 'provisions are clearly arbitrary and unreasonable having no substantial relation to the public health, safety, morals or general welfare.'"

. . . .

However, when evaluating a claim that a landowner's substantive due process rights have been violated, a plaintiff must show that he or she has been deprived of a property interest that is constitutionally protected. "A property interest is constitutionally protected if 'state law recognizes and protects that interest.'" "[I]t is well settled that the rights of ownership and use of property have long been recognized by this state." Additionally, Wis. Stat. § 62.23(7)(b) provides that "[a]ll such regulations shall be uniform . . . for the use of land throughout each district, but the regulations in one district may differ from those in other districts."

### C. Town of Rhine's B-2 District and conditional use ordinance

The Town of Rhine's Municipal Code § 4.08(2)(a) governs the permitted uses of the property at issue and provides:

(2) B-2 COMMERCIAL MANUFACTURING OR PROCESSING.

(a) *Permitted Uses.* There are no permitted uses in the B-2 District, except that those uses permitted in the Agricultural Land Districts A-1, A-2 and

A-3 may be authorized in conjunction with any conditional uses by express reference in the issued conditional use permit and upon such terms as the Plan Commission may recommend and the Town Board shall determine. All uses are conditional and shall comply with the provisions of Section 4.09 of this ordinance.

. . . .

Section 4.01(1), "Purpose," in relevant part outlines that "[t]he purpose of this ordinance is to promote the health, safety, morals and general welfare of the Town of Rhine by regulating and restricting" the use of land.

. . . .

### D. Constitutionality of the Town of Rhine, Wis., Municipal Code § 4.08(2)(a), "B-2 Commercial Manufacturing or Processing"

We conclude that Municipal Code § 4.08(2)(a), the B-2 District, is unconstitutional on its face because it is arbitrary and unreasonable in that it precludes any use as of right in the B-2 District and such limitation bears no substantial relation to the public health, safety, morals or general welfare.

A facial substantive due process challenge, as the landowners have made in this case, is only one of many ways in which a landowner can challenge a limitation on the use of his or her land. However, facial substantive due process challenges are rarely successful. The seminal zoning case, which involved a facial substantive due process challenge, is *Euclid.* In *Euclid,* the court upheld the constitutionality of a comprehensive zoning ordinance against a facial substantive due process challenge. The Village of Euclid adopted a comprehensive zoning ordinance that zoned the area in question so as to allow only residential use. *See Euclid*, 272 U.S. at 379–84, 47 S. Ct. 114. In so doing, it excluded all non-residential uses.

. . . .

In the wake of *Euclid*, other cases have helped to clarify the discussion regarding substantive due process challenges to zoning. Even so, the line between a valid or invalid exercise of police power remains less than clear. As the Court noted in *Euclid*, "[t]he line which in this field separates the legitimate from the illegitimate assumption of power is not capable of precise delimitation. It varies with circumstances and conditions. A regulatory zoning ordinance, which would be clearly valid as applied to the great cities, might be clearly invalid as applied to rural communities." *Euclid*, 272 U.S. at 387, 47 S. Ct. 114.

While the line between permissible and impermissible zoning may not always be readily ascertainable, the requisite standard that must be applied for a substantive due process challenge is clear: we must determine whether the ordinance is clearly arbitrary and unreasonable in the restricted sense that it has no substantial relation to the public health, safety, morals or general welfare.

. . . Municipalities have the power to zone property and restrict where particular undesirable uses may be developed within the municipality. However, zoning that restricts the land such that the landowner has no permitted use as of right must bear a substantial relation to the health, safety, morals or general welfare of the public in order to withstand constitutional scrutiny. In this case, the restricted use of the B-2 District land does not bear a substantial relation to the public health, safety, morals or general welfare.

We note that rather than precluding all uses as of right in a particular zone, the more common, acceptable practice is to provide for permitted uses as of right, and then in addition to permitted uses, the ordinance may provide for conditional uses. . . .

### Case law

Cases from Wisconsin and other jurisdictions support the conclusion that the common, accepted practice is to first outline permitted uses and then, in addition to permitted uses, the ordinance may provide for conditional uses.

. . . .

Here, we conclude that the B-2 District can be appropriately described as a "no permitted uses" zone, and we conclude that the no permitted uses B-2 District is arbitrary and unreasonable because it bears no substantial relation to public health, safety, morals or general welfare. However, we do recognize that there may be limited circumstances in which a "no permitted uses" zone is a valid exercise of power because the restriction bears substantial relation to the public health, safety, morals or general welfare. For example, in *Dur-Bar Realty Co. v. City of Utica*, 57 A.D.2d 51, 394 N.Y.S.2d 913, 918 (1977), the New York Supreme Court, Appellate Division, concluded that a "no permitted uses" zone was constitutional as the parcel at issue was in a "Land Conservation District and represented a zone located in the flood plain." *Id.* at 915–16, 918. The "Land Conservation District" "aimed to regulate the use" of land in a "flood prone area." *Id.* at 918. The ordinance at issue today does not include a similar purpose as in *Dur-Bar Realty*.

The court in *Dur-Bar Realty* identified several policy objectives for restricting use in a flood plain:

> (1) the protection of individuals who might choose, despite the flood dangers, to develop or occupy land on a flood plain; (2) the protection of other landowners from damages resulting from the development of a flood plain and the consequent obstruction of the flood flow; (3) the protection of the entire community from individual choices of land use which require subsequent public expenditures for public works and disaster relief.

*Id.* The court concluded, "[i]t is beyond question that these objectives, which correspond closely to the stated purposes of the present ordinance, may be the subject of a legitimate exercise of the police power." *Id.* The court further stated that, "'Land Conservation District' provisions do bear a substantial relation to legitimate governmental purpose and a reasonable relation to the goal of flood safety." *Id.* Thus, since the limitations related to flood safety, the restriction satisfied the relationship to the public health, safety, morals or general welfare.

. . . .

In the case at hand, we conclude that the ordinance governing the B-2 District is arbitrary and unreasonable, in that it precludes any use as of right in the B-2 District and such limitation bears no substantial relation to the public health, safety, morals or general welfare. Unlike in *Dur-Bar Realty* where restricting uses in a flood plain was directly tied to the health, safety, morals or general welfare of the public, no justification exists for precluding all uses as of right in the B-2 District.

. . . .

Precluding any permitted use and then only providing generalized standards for obtaining a conditional use permit opens the door to favoritism and discrimination. Under this scenario, a town, pursuant to the ordinance, may arbitrarily preclude any activity on the land in question because (1) there are no permitted uses as a matter of right; and (2) if obtaining a conditional use permit is completely within the discretion of a town, judicial review of a denial is significantly limited because of the non-specific nature of the conditional use standards. As a result, if such an ordinance was deemed acceptable, towns could preclude all uses at will and in a manner that virtually precludes any meaningful judicial review. Such a determination could open the door to abuse. If permitted uses exist as of right, the impact of denying conditional uses is significantly decreased because the landowner has permitted uses as of right.

The facial, constitutional challenge here is sustained. . . .

### V. Conclusion

We conclude that the Town of Rhine, Wis., Municipal Code § 4.08(2)(a), the B-2 District, is unconstitutional on its face because it is arbitrary and unreasonable in that it precludes any use as of right in the B-2 District and such limitation bears no substantial relation to the public health, safety, morals or general welfare. . . . As a result, we remand to the circuit court for a new hearing on the public nuisance claim.

The order of the circuit court is affirmed. . . .

## *Questions for Consideration*

1) Explain the basis of the constitutional challenge in this case.

2) What is an appropriate standard of review when such a challenge is filed?

3) How is the *Dur-Bar* case, discussed in the opinion, different from this case?

4) How does the court refer to and use the *Euclid* and *Nectow* opinions in its analysis?

5) If a community provides clear criteria for evaluating a request for a conditional use, must the zoning code fail if it provides no uses "as of right" in a particular zone? In other words, might a zone with only conditional uses permitted, comply with due process as long as the criteria for obtaining a conditional use permit are clearly stated and the local government is required

to make findings based on the established criteria? Under what kind of facts might such criteria be sufficient for purposes of due process?

## *Takeaway*

- Facial challenges to zoning regulations are extremely difficult for a property owner to win. Nonetheless, a violation of substantive due process is still a possibility. Unless a local government can identify very good reasons for establishing a zone that excludes all "as of right uses," it will be difficult to uphold. Generally, at least one "as of right" use should be identified for each zoning district.

- Even a voluntary offer to donate money to a town by a utility that sought rezoning of land to allow for previously prohibited development might not invalidate rezoning as arbitrary or unreasonable. In *Durand v. IDC Bellingham, L.L.C.*, 793 N.E.2d 359 (Mass. 2003), neighboring landowners brought an action challenging rezoning of a parcel to industrial use after the utility that sought rezoning offered to donate $8,000,000 to the town to allow a new high school to be built if rezoning was approved. The court stated:

  > In general, there is no reason to invalidate a legislative act on the basis of an "extraneous consideration," because we defer to legislative findings and choices without regard to motive. We see no reason to make an exception for legislative acts that are in the nature of zoning enactments, and find no persuasive authority for the proposition that an otherwise valid zoning enactment is invalid if it is in any way prompted or encouraged by a public benefit voluntarily offered. We conclude that the proper focus of review of a zoning enactment is whether it violates State law or constitutional provisions, is arbitrary or unreasonable, or is substantially unrelated to the public health, safety, or general welfare. In the absence of any infirmity other than the existence of a voluntary offer to make a gift to the town at some time in the future when the power plant became operational, we conclude that the [lower court] judge erred in holding the zoning ordinance invalid and granting summary judgment to the plaintiffs.

## Rise, Inc. v. Malheur County

United States District Court for the District of Oregon, Pendleton Division
2012 U.S. Dist. LEXIS 44994 (U.S. Dist. Ore. 2012)

SULLIVAN, Magistrate Judge. Rise, Inc. and Rise Legacy Development, LLC ("Rise") filed this action against Malheur County and the Malheur County Planning Commission ("the County") alleging violations of the federal Fair Housing Act, modified by the Fair Housing Amendments Act ("FHAA"), 42 U.S.C. § 3601, and Title II of the Americans with Disabilities Act ("ADA"), 42 U.S.C. § 12132. Specifically, Rise alleges the County intentionally discriminated against disabled persons by first requiring, and then denying, a conditional use permit for the operation of a residential home for the disabled in Malheur County....

## Factual Background

Rise, Inc. is a non-profit corporation offering support services for the developmentally disabled, including the operation of residential group homes for people with disabilities. Rise Legacy Development is the corporation that owns the properties on which Rise, Inc. operates its facilities. In March 2008, Rise Legacy Development purchased a house located on 1.73 acres at 650 Ontario Heights Road in Malheur County, Oregon, for the purposes of having Rise, Inc. open a residential home for developmentally disabled adults. Rise alleges that, after the property was purchased, it made repairs on the existing home, purchased furniture and equipment, hired and trained staff members, and selected the first residents of the residential home. On June 25, 2008, Rise was notified by the County that a conditional use permit was needed to operate a residential home in an exclusive farm use ("EFU") zone. . . .

Attorney Christ Troupis was hired by Rise sometime in 2008 to represent Rise in obtaining a conditional use permit. . . .

On July 23, 2009, the Malheur County Planning Commission ("the Commission") held a hearing on Rise's conditional use permit application. At the hearing, a number of county residents spoke in opposition to the opening of the residential home, a petition signed by individuals opposed to the application was submitted, and letters from the Malheur County Sheriff and Malheur County District Attorney were read into the record. The concerns of the neighbors focused on the safety of the residents who would be living in the house and the surrounding community, as well as a possible loss in property values for adjacent neighbors and the incompatibility of the residential home with farming in the area. At the close of testimony, the Chairperson of the Commission asked for more information from Rise, including a site plan showing fencing of the property, a traffic analysis, and a review by the Local Public Safety Coordinating Council regarding compatibility with farming. The hearing was continued pending the submission of the additional information.

On August 5, 2009, Troupis submitted an amended application for a conditional use permit. In the amended application, . . . Rise asserted that a traffic study was not undertaken, despite the Commission's request for such a study, as it would not provide useful information. The amended application addressed some of the concerns expressed by citizens at the July hearing but simply argued that there was no evidence to warrant such concerns. Rather, the amended application focused on the need for the residential facility in Malheur County and the value of Rise's services.

The Commission held a further hearing on September 24, 2009, when additional statements were made by county residents and letters were submitted in opposition to the opening of Rise's residential home. At the close of the meeting, Commission members openly deliberated on the conditional use permit application, discussing the potential residents — specifically referencing the letters submitted by the Sheriff and District Attorney — as well as compatibility with area farming practices and the possible impact on local traffic flow.

The Commission Chairman, Commissioner Findley, called for a vote on Rise's application. The Commission's preliminary decision to deny the conditional use permit, based on its incompatibility with area farm uses and traffic patterns, was unanimous.

On October 22, 2009, the Commission published its written Findings of Fact, Conclusions, and Decision ("the Decision") in the matter of Rise's application for a conditional use permit. The Decision referenced statements of neighbors and the letters from the Malheur County Sheriff and District Attorney. The Commission denied the application because it did "not meet all of the applicable approval criteria for a conditional use of a residential group home in an exclusive farm use zone. Applicant did not meet its burden of proof." . . .

After the Planning Commission's denial of their conditional use permit, Rise filed a notice of appeal to the Malheur County Commission and sought the assistance of a land use attorney to review the Planning Commission's decision. . . .

### Discussion

Rise alleges the County's decision to require, and subsequently deny, its application for a conditional use permit was motivated by intentional discrimination toward disabled persons. Rise also argues that, regardless of any alleged deficiencies in their application, the County should have granted them a conditional use permit as a reasonable accommodation under the FHAA and ADA. . . .

Rise alleges the County has intentionally discriminated against disabled persons by requiring, and then denying, a conditional use permit to operate a residential group home, which made unavailable a dwelling to disabled persons in violation of the FHAA. Similarly, Rise alleges the County intentionally discriminated against disabled individuals under the ADA. Rise also alleges that the County failed to reasonably accommodate disabled individuals in violation of the FHAA and the ADA.

### Statutory Framework

Both the FHAA and the ADA prohibit governmental entities from implementing or enforcing housing policies in a discriminatory manner against persons with disabilities. *See City of Edmonds v. Oxford House, Inc.*, 514 U.S. 725, 115 S. Ct. 1776, 131 L. Ed. 2d 801 (1995). Under the FHAA, it is unlawful to discriminate, or otherwise make unavailable, in the sale or rental of a dwelling because of the handicap of "a person residing in or intending to reside in that dwelling after it is sold, rented, or made available." 42 U.S.C. § 3604(f)(1). Similarly, the ADA provides, "no qualified individual with a disability shall, by reason of such disability, be excluded from participation in or be denied the benefits of the services, programs, or activities of a public entity, or be subject to discrimination by such entity." 42 U.S.C. § 12132. Both statutes require that "covered entities make reasonable accommodations in order to provide qualified individuals with an equal opportunity to receive benefits from or to participate in programs run by such entities." *Tsombanidis v. West Haven Fire Dept.*, 352 F.3d 565, 573 (2nd Cir. 2003) (quoting *Reg'l Econ. Cmty. Action Program, Inc. v.*

*City of Middletown*, 294 F.3d 35, 45 (2nd Cir. 2002), *cert. denied*, 537 U.S. 813, 123 S. Ct. 74, 154 L. Ed. 2d 16 (2002)). Because the statutes are similar, they may be interpreted together for purposes of the issues raised in this case. *Tsombanidis*, at 573; *see also Adam v. Linn-Benton Hous. Auth.*, 147 F.Supp.2d 1044, 1047–48 (D.Or. 2001).

. . . .

### Decision to deny the conditional use permit

Rise . . . claims the County is liable for damages as a result of its denial of the conditional use permit. The County asserts there is no evidence that the County intentionally discriminated against the disabled by denying the conditional use permit.

Rise seeks to establish a violation of the FHAA and ADA and asserts that it has "presented direct evidence of discrimination, in the form of discriminatory statements made by surrounding neighbors at the hearings on the conditional use application and discriminatory statements contained in letters opposing the conditional use permit submitted by the Malheur County Sheriff and Malheur County District Attorney." Rise alleges the views expressed by neighbors, the Sheriff, and the District Attorney "influenced" defendants' decision to deny plaintiffs' conditional use permit application, citing the Commission's written decision, which among other factors relied on "viewpoints of property owners in the surrounding area" and the letters submitted by the Sheriff and District Attorney. Plaintiffs argue that such evidence constitutes direct evidence of discrimination . . .

The Court agrees that some of the statements made by neighbors at the public hearings and submitted in letters were insensitive and offensive. However, such statements are not direct evidence of discrimination on the part of the actual decision makers. The Malheur County Zoning Ordinance and the Oregon Revised Statutes require the County to hold a public hearing on applications for a conditional use permit and to provide notice to potentially affected property owners. In addition, as Rise points out, the County Zoning Ordinance requires the Commission to consider the "viewpoints of property owners in the surrounding area." Thus, in holding a required public hearing, and in releasing a decision which acknowledges consideration of surrounding property owners' viewpoints, defendants acted in accordance with its zoning ordinances.

On Rise's motion for summary judgment, the burden is on Rise to provide evidence that animus toward the disabled "more likely than not" motivated the County to deny plaintiffs' application for a conditional use permit. The "direct evidence" in the form of statements made by third parties — specifically, Rise's neighbors, the Sheriff, and the District Attorney — are offered as proof of intentional discrimination in that the statements "influenced" the Commissioners' decision. While these statements made at the public hearing may be evidence of prejudicial beliefs, such beliefs may not be imputed to the Commissioners by the mere fact that the statements were made in their presence. See *Budnick* [*v. Town of Carefree*], 518 F.3d [1109] at 1117 [(9th Cir. 2008)] (". . . There is no evidence in the record to suggest that the cited comments . . . motivated the commissioners or Town Council members to vote against the [Special Use Permit], and we decline to make such an inference based solely on the fact that the comments were made.") . . . .

. . . [T]he County has proffered legitimate, nondiscriminatory reasons for denying Rise's application for a conditional use permit. At the final public hearing on Rise's application, as well as in its Decision denying plaintiffs' application, the Commission discussed the opposition of neighbors and county law enforcement officials as one of many other considerations, including the possible impact on neighboring farm operations, traffic patterns, and the stability of overall area land use. As discussed above, although the Commission acknowledged the opinions expressed by community members, that acknowledgment is a standard occurrence in such public forums and was in fact required by the County's own code under these circumstances. In addition, the County offers affidavits by each Commission member attesting that any prejudicial beliefs expressed before the Commission were not considered by the members in making its permit application decision.

If, as here, defendants have articulated a legitimate, nondiscriminatory reason for denying the conditional use permit, the burden shifts to plaintiffs to prove that defendants' asserted reason is a pretext for discrimination. . . .

. . . Rise has failed to provide adequate direct evidence of discrimination so as to preclude a grant of summary judgment in its favor. . . .

### Reasonable Accommodation

Under the FHAA and ADA, a municipality commits unlawful discrimination if it refuses to "make reasonable accommodations in rules, policies, practices, or services, when such accommodations may be necessary to afford [the disabled] equal opportunity to use and enjoy a dwelling." 42 U.S.C. § 3604(f)(3)(B); 28 C.F.R. § 35.130(b)(7). The FHAA and ADA apply identical standards whether the term used is reasonable accommodation or reasonable modification. *See Wong v. Regents of Univ. Of Calif.*, 192 F.3d 807, 816 n.26 (9th Cir. 1999). The FHAA and the ADA impose an affirmative duty on municipalities to reasonably accommodate disabled residents. Whether a municipality must alter its policies to accommodate the disabled is a question where "answers will vary depending on the facts of a given case." "The reasonable accommodation inquiry is highly fact-specific, requiring case-by-case determination."

To establish a claim of discrimination on a theory of failure to reasonably accommodate, a plaintiff must demonstrate that (1) plaintiff or his associate suffers from a disability; (2) defendants knew or reasonably should have known of the disability; (3) accommodation of the disability "may be necessary" to afford the disabled person an equal opportunity to use and enjoy the dwelling; (4) the accommodation is reasonable; and (5) defendants refused to make the requested accommodation.

Here, Rise argues that, even if its conditional use permit application was properly denied for noncompliance with applicable criteria for conditional use, defendants should have nonetheless granted Rise's application as a reasonable accommodation. As a preliminary issue, the County contends that Rise never actually requested a reasonable accommodation. Although at the July 23, 2009, hearing Rise submitted a summary of FHAA case law, including the statutory language requiring reasonable accommodations, Rise never submitted an explicit request that its application be approved as a reasonable accommodation. . . .

Given the generalized nature of the statement at issue, the Court cannot conclude that Rise made a request for a reasonable accommodation with sufficient particularity. . . .

Thus, because Rise cannot demonstrate that the County refused to make a requested accommodation, Rise is unable to establish a claim of discrimination on a theory of failure to reasonably accommodate under the FHAA or the ADA. As such, on this issue Rise's motion for summary judgment should be denied and defendants' motion for summary judgment should be granted.

## Questions for Consideration

1) How is the conditional use restriction in this case different from the one in the *Town of Rhine* case?

2) What kind of issues were raised in the first hearing, and what did the County want to see in support of an amended petition for the conditional use permit?

3) What reasons were given for the denial of the conditional use permit?

4) Do you think Rise has potential grounds for successfully asserting a violation of its substantive due process rights? Its procedural due process rights?

5) What is the nature of Rise's argument under the Fair Housing Act and the Americans with Disabilities Act?

6) Was Rise able to carry its burden on the claim of intentional discrimination?

7) Under the law, it is illegal discrimination when a local government fails to make a reasonable accommodation for a person entitled to an accommodation. What factors does the court consider in addressing the issue of a reasonable accommodation? How does the court resolve the matter of the reasonable accommodation?

## Takeaway

- The zoning code in this case included an "as of right" use in this zone (farming). Plaintiff's use was permitted as a conditional use. A conditional use has extra scrutiny and may or may not be permitted after review by a zoning board. A property owner seeking a conditional use will have to supply ample information to address the criteria for the granting of the condition. Granting or denying a conditional use permit is a judgment call by the zoning board. In later cases, we will learn about the standard of review applicable to these case specific determinations of a local zoning board.

- Rise sought a conditional use permit under the terms of the zoning code and was denied. The denial of the conditional use permit is reviewable. In addition to challenging the decision under the zoning code, Rise challenges the decision under the FHA and the ADA. As Rise represents people with disabilities protected under the referenced Acts, it can also challenge the decision as a violation of federal law. Rise asserts intentional discrimination and then asserts discrimination for failure to provide a reasonable accommodation. For intentional discrimination, one must show animus and additional factors might include not following the usual procedure in this case or reviewing the facts in light of earlier historical evidence that might suggest intent to discriminate in this situation.

- When a person makes a *prima facie* showing that they are covered under the FHA or ADA, and a reasonable accommodation is requested, it must be provided unless there are findings to support a conclusion that the request is: 1) unreasonable; 2) unnecessary; or 3) that if granted, the requested accommodation would fundamentally alter the comprehensive plan for the community zoning. These factors will be developed in more detail in later cases. For now, note that reasonableness is a question of costs and benefits. It is unreasonable to put an undue financial or administrative burden on the community. As to necessity, this is a "but for" test. "But for" making the accommodation, the plaintiff will not have a fair and equal opportunity to enjoy her property. Finally, the question must be answered as to if making the accommodation will fundamentally alter the comprehensive plan and the zoning regulations made pursuant to the plan. This is a balancing test, and a zoning board must consider and make findings on each of the factors. A zoning board's decision on the question of a reasonable accommodation must be rational and supported by substantial competent evidence on the record.

## Discussion Problem 3.5

George owns a parcel of property in a commercial zoning district. He operated a scrap metal recycling business on the property for decades. As the business grew, so did the amount of scrap metal on site, giving it the look of a junkyard. Recently, the City planning commission decided that the use of George's property had evolved into one not allowed under the zoning code. George was advised that with specified cleanup and modifications completed by certain deadlines, he could run a commercial recycling center if he obtained a conditional use permit. George promptly applied for a permit. Yet, before acting on George's application for a conditional use permit, the City council amended the ordinance under which George applied for the permit, with an aim to maintain a "pleasant viewshed." The amendment eliminated all permitted uses in his commercial district unless the property owner obtained a conditional use permit. Ultimately, the City council denied George's application because he did not complete the specified cleanup and modifications by the deadlines set by the City, and under the now amended ordinance, ordered him to cease all operations on his property. George brought an action against the City, contending that the City unconstitutionally eliminated all use of his property without a conditional use permit, resulting in a regulatory taking. Based on the cases in the chapter, who shall prevail in this dispute?

# G. Local Power to Zone and Accessibility

Legislation protecting people with disabilities is covered under federal law. State law also provides protection for people with disabilities. A question that arises is one concerning the extent to which local governments can enhance the protection that they wish to provide to residents by providing additional requirements for accessibility, particularly as it relates to home building.

## Washburn v. Pima County

Court of Appeals of Arizona, Division 2, Department B
81 P.3d 1030 (Ariz. Ct. App. 2003)

ECKERSTROM, Judge. Appellants Steven and Jeanette Washburn, the Southern Arizona Homebuilders Association (SAHBA), and Washburn Company, Inc. (collectively the Washburns), appeal from the trial court's order granting summary judgment in favor of appellee Pima County. The Washburns contend on appeal that the county lacked statutory authority to adopt an ordinance requiring builders of single-family homes to incorporate design features allowing for greater wheelchair access and that the ordinance violates the Arizona Constitution. We affirm [the decision in favor of Pima County].

### Background

On appeal from a grant of summary judgment, we view the facts and all reasonable inferences in the light most favorable to the party opposing the motion. In February 2002, the Pima County Board of Supervisors adopted Ordinance 2002-2, the Inclusive Home Design Ordinance, which was apparently modified by Pima County Ordinance 2002-72. Among its other effects, the ordinance promulgated building requirements applicable to the construction of new, single-family homes in unincorporated areas of Pima County. It did so by adopting selected construction standards found in the American National Standards Institute's (ANSI) publication A117.1, *Accessible and Usable Buildings and Facilities* (the ANSI standards), published by the International Code Council (ICC). The adopted provisions require that newly constructed homes incorporate design features that allow people in wheelchairs to more easily enter and use the homes. These features include "doorways wide enough to permit wheelchair access, electrical outlets reachable by a wheelchair-bound person, and bathroom walls reinforced to permit installation of grab bars." The Washburns admit that requiring these features in multi-family residential facilities and places of public accommodation serves an important government interest but challenge application of the requirements to single-family homes.

The Washburns applied for a permit to build a single-family home, but the proposed design failed to comply with the ordinance, and the county denied the application. They later filed a declaratory judgment and special action complaint in which they asked the trial court to declare that the county lacked statutory authority to adopt the ordinance and that it violated both the Equal Protection and Privacy Clauses of the Arizona Constitution. Ariz. Const. art. II, §§ 8, 13. . . . Our review focuses . . . on whether the trial court properly granted summary judgment in the county's favor.

## Standard of Review

Summary judgment is proper if the evidence presented by the party opposing the motion has so little probative value, given the required burden of proof, that reasonable jurors could not agree with the opposing party's conclusions. In reviewing a grant of summary judgment, we determine *de novo* whether any genuine issues of material fact exist and whether the trial court erred in applying the law.

. . . .

## Statutory Interpretation

The legislature authorized counties to adopt building codes but "limited [that authority] to the [adoption of] . . . [a]ny building, electrical or mechanical code that has been promulgated by any national organization or association that is organized and conducted for the purpose of developing codes." The Washburns challenge the county's adoption of the ANSI standards, which, through mandatory language, set forth a comprehensive collection of rules for builders to facilitate building access to people confined to wheelchairs. The Washburns contend that the county could not adopt the ANSI standards under § 11-861 because ICC neither titled nor classified those standards as a "code." Whether the legislature authorized the county to adopt requirements like the ANSI standards is a question of law subject to our *de novo* review.

The principal goal in interpreting a statute is to ascertain and give effect to the legislature's intent. To do so, we first examine the statute's language. Because § 11-861 is silent as to what the legislature intended a "code" to comprise, we find the statute ambiguous and consider other factors such as the statutory scheme, the statute's subject matter, historical context, effects and consequences, and spirit and purpose.

. . . .

Within the confines of guidelines promulgated by national associations organized and conducted for the purpose of developing codes, the legislature has enabled both counties and municipalities to determine regionally tailored building policy, to identify specific design elements that further policy objectives, and to require builders to incorporate those elements. Thus, cities' and counties' enabling statutes rest on the same underlying policy considerations.

. . . .

The Washburns also assert that, because § 11-861 requires counties to adopt building "codes" promulgated by nationally recognized organizations, we should interpret the term consistently with the term's meaning within the construction industry.

However, we attribute no specialized meaning to statutory language unless the legislature has clearly conveyed its intent that we do so. . . . Thus, the focus of our inquiry is not whether the terms "code" and "standard" have acquired an industry-specific meaning but whether the legislature intended the term "code" within § 11-861(C)(1) to convey an industry-specific meaning. Because there is nothing in the statutory history or the statute's language in § 11-861(C)(1) suggesting the legislature intended to imbue the terms "code" and "standards" with mutually exclusive, industry-specific definitions the Washburns proffer, we cannot agree with the Washburns' suggestion. If the legislature had intended to use the word "code" as an industry-specific term of art so as to substantially limit the options of county governments in their choice of nationally promulgated building specifications, it would have articulated that intention. Certainly, the legislature could not have expected counties to divine such an intent from a mere use of the word "code" in the statute.

Nor do we find any caveat in the ANSI standards themselves indicating they could not constitute a "code" within the meaning of § 11-861(C)(1). The foreword to the ANSI standards provides in part that the standards, "when adopted as a part of a building code, would be compatible with the building code and its enforcement." According to the Washburns, this language demonstrates that the ANSI standards were not intended to stand by themselves as a "code." But the Washburns' argument presupposes that a county could never amend or augment its current building code in a minor fashion without adopting a new comprehensive building code. We find nothing in § 11-861(C)(1) that prevents the county from amending or augmenting its comprehensive building regulations with self-contained "codes," promulgated by appropriate national organizations, that address discrete components of home construction. Moreover, the above-quoted foreword to the ANSI standards demonstrates ANSI's expectation that the standards would have an equal status to other parts of a pre-existing building code once adopted.

. . . .

We also find no policy-based explanation for why the legislature would have intended to limit the breadth of the word "code" as used in § 11-861(C)(1). Without question, counties are generally empowered to regulate the construction of homes consistent with specifications suggested by appropriate national bodies. A county's ability to do so depends upon its power to mandate the incorporation of particular design elements. . . .

. . . Accordingly, a governmental authority that enacts a tailored version of the ANSI standards operates in conformity with the intentions of the professional organization that promulgated the standards. In so doing, the county complies with the requirement of § 11-861(C)(1) that building regulations be consistent with standards set forth by a qualified "national organization." We therefore determine that § 11-861(C)(1) enables counties to adopt individual building design criterion "promulgated by any national organization or association that is organized and conducted for the purpose of developing codes" that the county determines advances the general health, safety, and welfare of its residents.

## Constitutional Claims

As they did below, the Washburns next claim the ordinance violates a homeowner's right to privacy in his or her home under the Privacy Clause, article II, § 8 of the Arizona Constitution. Although they concede that the government possesses the right to adopt building, fire, and mechanical codes that provide for the protection of the general population, they question whether the county can constitutionally impose costly design requirements on all new private homeowners "that have value to less than 1% of the population." They further assert the ordinance "deprives new homeowners and builders of the fundamental right to design private homes . . . by imposing design criteria that invade the exercise of personal, private, and aesthetic choices for personal private living spaces."

Homeowners do not have "a right to be completely free from governmental regulation of the use and occupancy of [their] real property." Our courts have already determined that building codes that affect the exercise of homeowners' "personal, private, and aesthetic choices" are a proper exercise of police power. Accordingly, we agree with the trial court that the ordinance does not unconstitutionally infringe on a homeowner's right to privacy.

In a related argument, the Washburns contend the ordinance violates their rights under Arizona's Equal Protection Clause, article II, § 13 of the Arizona Constitution, because it burdens only those people constructing new homes. The level of scrutiny we apply to a discriminatory law depends upon whether that law affects a fundamental right or a suspect class or enacts a gender-based classification. Other than pointing to their fundamental right to privacy, the Washburns point to nothing that would subject the ordinance to heightened scrutiny. Because we have already found that the ordinance does not unconstitutionally affect the right to privacy, and because the county has not engaged in any suspect classification in burdening builders of new homes, we uphold the ordinance "so long as there is a legitimate state interest to be served and the legislative classification rationally furthers that interest." The Washburns bear the burden of establishing the unconstitutionality of the ordinance.

To the extent the Washburns argue the Board of Supervisors had no rational basis for concluding that private home designs should facilitate access to people confined to wheelchairs, we disagree. "[I]f the court can hypothesize any rational reason why the legislative body made the choice it did, the statute or ordinance is constitutionally valid. This test validates statutes even if the legislative body did not consider the reasons articulated by the court." While reasonable minds might differ over whether government should impose these types of design criteria on those building new homes, the propriety of that public policy decision must be made through the political process by duly elected officials.

The uncontested evidence established that approximately one percent of the population is confined to wheelchairs, but the county points out that a much larger percentage will suffer a disability at some point in their lives. Although all age groups are affected by disability, the county introduced evidence that approximately forty-one percent of people over the age of sixty-five have some form of disability. Disability is a growing problem both nationally and locally, and the county also introduced evidence that Arizona's population of people over the age of sixty is expected to triple by 2025. Although many of these disabled people will not be confined to wheelchairs, the county concluded from these figures that the number of people confined to wheelchairs is rising. For these reasons, the county addressed a legitimate governmental interest when it adopted a building code designed to increase the number of homes accessible to those in wheelchairs.

The Washburns also argue that the ordinance is not rationally related to further the county's interests. Again, we disagree. "A perfect fit is not required; a statute that has a rational basis will not be overturned 'merely because it is not made with "mathematical nicety, or because in practice it results in some inequality."'" Although it is true that not all of the people affected by disabilities will benefit from the wheelchair access provisions of the ordinance and, although those conducting renovations of existing homes are not required to comply with the ordinance, a regulation may rationally advance a governmental interest despite the fact that it is underinclusive.

The Washburns lastly contend the ordinance does not rationally advance the county's interests because it places the financial design burdens on homeowners who will probably never be confined to wheelchairs. But the county submitted to the trial court the results of a study suggesting that complying with the ordinance would cost only about $100. In addition, § 103.1 of the ordinance provides that the county may waive any design requirement if a building official determines that the cost of complying with the requirement exceeds $200. Indeed, the Board of Supervisors found that the cost of including the ordinance's designs into a new home was substantially less than the cost of renovating a home to accommodate a person confined to a wheelchair. On this record, the Board of Supervisors could have rationally concluded that the benefit to the community in providing for the disabled justified the comparatively minimal cost of implementing the required design features. Although the Washburns now contest the accuracy of the county's assertions as to the costs of these renovations, they failed in the trial court to introduce controverting evidence regarding the cost of compliance. The Washburns, therefore, have failed to establish that there were genuine issues of material fact precluding summary judgment. Because the ordinance rationally advances a legitimate governmental interest, the trial court did not err in concluding that the ordinance does not violate Arizona's Equal Protection Clause.

Affirmed.

Philip G. Espinosa, Chief Judge and John Pelander, Presiding Judge, concurring.

## Questions for Consideration

1) How does the court approach the process of statutory interpretation?

2) What kind of building requirements are being added by the regulations?

3) Why would a builder object to these building standards?

4) Why would consumers of housing (buyers) not want a more accessible home?

5) Would a more accessible home be higher valued in a market where many people are elderly?

6) Does the lack of accessible housing in many communities (housing with steps and with narrow doorway bathrooms, for example) unfairly limit housing options for people with disabilities? Does this lack of accessible housing limit career opportunities in terms of being able to easily relocate and find accessible housing in a new job location?

7) What are the merits of the plaintiff's constitutional challenge?

8) What is the standard of review?

## *Takeaway*

- The starting place for many local zoning issues is the enabling legislation of the state. Remember that the police power is vested in the state, and the state can delegate police power within its jurisdiction. When local governments exercise their legislative authority, it must be done consistently with the authority they have been delegated by the enabling legislation of the state. Thus, a question in this case arises as to whether the adding of this code/regulation is properly within the authority delegated by the state.

- In this case, the state permitted local changes to the building code, and the issue was whether what was adopted was a code or not. Some states, such as New York, prohibit local governments from independently changing and adding to the state approved building code.

- As the court acknowledges in its opinion, America has an aging population with an increasing percentage of the population having mobility impairments. Planning and zoning professionals must take account of this so that people can safely age in place, and so that people of all ages and all abilities can easily and safely navigate our communities.

## Anderson v. City of Blue Ash

United States Court of Appeals for the Sixth Circuit
798 F.3d 338 (6th Cir. 2015)

COLE, Chief Judge. This appeal is the latest chapter in an ongoing dispute between Ingrid Anderson and the City of Blue Ash, Ohio, over whether Anderson can keep a miniature horse at her house as a service animal for her disabled minor daughter, C.A. C.A. suffers from a number of disabilities that affect her ability to walk and balance independently, and the horse enables her to play and get exercise in her backyard without assistance from an adult. Since Anderson first acquired a horse in 2010, she has struggled with the City for permission to keep it at her house. In 2013, the City passed a municipal ordinance banning horses from residential property and then criminally prosecuted Anderson for violating it. Anderson's defense was that the Americans with Disabilities Act ("ADA"), 42 U.S.C. 12101, et seq., and the Fair Housing Amendments Act ("FHAA"), 42 U.S.C. § 3601, et seq., both entitle her to keep the horse at her house as a service animal for C.A. Rejecting those arguments, the Hamilton County Municipal Court found Anderson guilty.

Anderson brought this action against the City in federal district court, again arguing that the ADA and FHAA entitle her to keep her horse as a service animal for C.A. She also claims that the City intentionally discriminated against her because of C.A.'s disabilities, in violation of both the ADA and the FHAA, and that the City's ordinance has had a disparate impact on C.A. and other disabled individuals, in violation of the FHAA. . . .

Because . . . there are significant factual disputes regarding whether the ADA or FHAA require the City to permit Anderson to keep her miniature horse at her house. We therefore reverse the district court's grant of summary judgment to the City on those claims.

### I. Background

### A. Factual Background

Ingrid Anderson lives in the City of Blue Ash, Ohio, with her disabled minor daughter, C.A. C.A. has a variety of disabilities, including autism, seizures, chronic lung disease, gastroesophageal reflux, feeding and vision problems, severe allergies, attention deficit hyperactivity disorder, developmental delay, autonomic dysfunction, and tachycardia, among others. Her disabilities make it difficult for C.A. to maintain her balance independently, particularly when she must change directions or navigate uneven surfaces. Consequently, C.A. cannot effectively use her backyard for recreation and exercise without assistance.

While the traditional service animal is a dog, miniature horses are often used to provide assistance to individuals with disabilities. *See generally* 28 C.F.R. § 35 app. A (2011) (specifically discussing miniature horses as service animals). Miniature horses can be trained to provide many of the services commonly associated with service dogs, such as guiding individuals with impaired vision. Like dogs, miniature horses can also be housebroken, and individuals with disabilities have taken them on trains and commercial flights. Miniature horses may be preferable to service dogs for "large stature individuals" and "individuals with allergies, or for those whose religious beliefs preclude the use of dogs." Additionally, because they are stronger than most dogs, miniature horses may be preferable for "providing stability and balance for individuals with disabilities that impair the ability to walk, and supplying leverage that enables a person with a mobility disability to get up after a fall." *Id.* Miniature horses also have significantly longer lifespans than dogs, and are able to provide service for more than twenty-five years while dogs can only provide service for approximately seven. This allows a disabled minor to have a single miniature horse throughout his or her childhood, without having to periodically replace aging service dogs. Therapy with miniature horses is sometimes referred to as "equine" or "hippotherapy."

In 2010, C.A. began working with miniature horses as a form of therapy at the Hamilton County Parks facility and in the backyard of her house. By gripping the mane of her horse, C.A. is able to move about outside for recreation and exercise. Dr. Ronald Levin — the physician who recommended that C.A. work with miniature horses as a form of therapy — described some of the benefits C.A. receives from working with a miniature horse in her backyard:

> Hippotherapy is beneficial for [C.A.] as it incorporates several avenues of traditional therapy including physical, occupational, speech and language. Specifically, this may address [C.A.'s] physical development through learning more about balance and control. Hippotherapy addresses many aspects of gross and fine motor skills that can be applied in everyday life. Cognitively [C.A.] may benefit from learning and practicing communication skills, as well as increase her social skills, self-esteem and independence.

C.A. fatigues easily: Dr. Levin stated that "just a drive across town to receive therapy can wipe her out leaving no energy to enjoy this therapeutic and recreational activity." As a result, Anderson began keeping a miniature horse at her Prospect Avenue residence in the City so that C.A. could benefit from this therapy at home.

In August 2010, Daniel Johnson, the City's Community Development Director and Zoning Administrator, began receiving complaints from Anderson's neighbors about the miniature horse at her house. Anderson's neighbors complained about excessive waste from the horse and other animals kept on the property. At least one complaint questioned whether C.A. was actually using the horse for therapeutic purposes, and noted that the condition of Anderson's property was devaluing the neighborhood because of "health issues" and an "extremely offensive . . . smell of horse manure that emanates from the piles in [her] backyard" so severe that the complaining neighbor's children could not play outside.

Johnson ordered Anderson to remove the horse from her property. Anderson appealed that order, first to the Blue Ash Board of Zoning Appeals ("BZA"), which affirmed, and then to the Blue Ash City Council. The Council ultimately decided not to enforce Johnson's order, citing a letter it received from Dr. Levin in which he supported "the housing of a miniature horse for in-home therapy support for [C.A.]" By "in-home therapy" Dr. Levin was not suggesting that the therapy take place indoors, but outdoors "at the home" so that the therapy "can be utilized in a schedule that is more conducive to [C.A.]"

. . . .

In August 2012 . . . Anderson and C.A. replaced their . . . miniature horse with Ellie, the miniature horse at issue in this appeal, and moved to their current residence on Myrtle Avenue. After completing several classes on how to train miniature horses for therapy, Anderson trained Ellie to assist C.A. in navigating her backyard, including by steadying C.A. while she is walking and helping her to stand after a fall.

On January 10, 2013, the Council passed Ordinance No. 2013-1, amending the City's municipal code "to prohibit keeping of farm animals at residences within the city." The ordinance specifically applied to horses, excepting those "[a]nimals which are otherwise specifically permitted elsewhere in the Municipal Code or permitted by Hamilton County, Ohio State, or Federal law." On January 31, 2013, Johnson sent a letter to Anderson informing her that the new ordinance would come into effect on February 20, 2013, and that she would be cited for violating it if the miniature horse was still present on her property on or after that date.

In responding to an anonymous complaint on February 21, 2013, a police officer observed a miniature horse in Anderson's backyard. The officer asked Anderson to remove the horse from her property. . . . [Anderson was issued citations for the violation.]

. . . .

Anderson responded to the . . . citations by email on July 24, 2013. She specifically asserted that both the FHAA and the United States Department of Housing and Urban Development ("HUD") guidelines on assistance animals (interpreting the FHAA and the ADA) entitled her to a "reasonable accommodation to keep the miniature horse for [C.A.]."

Anderson was tried on both citations in the Hamilton County Municipal Court on October 22, 2013. She did not deny that she kept the miniature horse, Ellie, at her house, but based her defense entirely on her position that the ADA and FHAA entitled her to keep the horse for C.A.'s therapy. . . .

On November 13, 2013, the Municipal Court found Anderson guilty on both citations. . . .

### B. Procedural Background

On February 18, 2014, Anderson, individually and on behalf of C.A., . . . filed this suit against the City. They alleged that the City's refusal to permit Anderson to keep the horse at her residence violated her rights under the ADA and the FHAA. . . .

. . . The district court . . . found for the City on the merits of the ADA and FHAA claims. The plaintiffs appealed.

### II. Analysis

. . . .

The issue before us is whether federal law entitles Anderson to keep Ellie at her house on Myrtle Avenue. . . .

. . . .

### ADA Claims

#### Reasonable Modification

Anderson contends that the ADA and its implementing regulations require the City to make a reasonable modification to its "policies, practices, and procedures" to permit her to keep Ellie at her residence. The ADA prohibits public entities from discriminating against individuals with disabilities, including by:

fail[ing] to make reasonable modifications in policies, practices, or procedures, when such modifications are necessary to afford such goods, services, facilities, privileges, advantages, or accommodations to individuals
with disabilities, unless the entity can demonstrate that making such modifications would fundamentally alter the nature of such goods, services,
facilities, privileges, advantages, or accommodations.

42 U.S.C. § 12182(b)(2)(A)(ii). Regulations implementing the ADA require a public
entity to make "reasonable modifications in policies, practices, or procedures to permit the use of a miniature horse by an individual with a disability if the miniature
horse has been individually trained to do work or perform tasks for the benefit of
the individual with a disability," provided that the horse and the requested modification also satisfy certain "[a]ssessment factors." 28 C.F.R. § 35.136(i)(1)–(2).

It is undisputed that C.A. is "an individual with a disability," but the district court
granted summary judgment to the City on Anderson's ADA claim for a reasonable
modification because it found that Ellie did not meet the ADA regulations' requirements and because it found that the regulations' "assessment factors" were not satisfied. On appeal, Anderson contends that there are disputed issues of fact material to
both the ADA regulatory requirements for miniature horses and the related assessment factors that preclude summary judgment in favor of the City.

### ADA Regulatory Requirements for Miniature Horses

The ADA regulations do not specify the amount or type of training that a miniature horse must undergo to qualify as a reasonable modification for a disabled
individual, nor the amount or type of work or assistance that the horse must provide
for his or her benefit. Courts have typically found that to qualify for a reasonable
modification, an animal must be specially trained to perform tasks directly related
to a disability, contrasted with animals that have received only general training,
provide only emotional support, or otherwise perform tasks not directly related to a
disability. *See, e.g., . . . Rose v. Springfield-Greene Cnty. Health Dep't*, 668 F. Supp. 2d
1206, 1215 (W.D. Mo. 2009) (finding that a monkey was not a service animal because
the tasks it performed did not "relate to [plaintiff's] disability" and merely provided
comfort to the plaintiff, whose disabilities did not require a monkey to perform day-
to-day activities).

On appeal, Anderson contends that her horse meets these requirements because
she has individually trained Ellie to assist C.A. by steadying her as she walks so
that she can enjoy independent recreation and exercise in her backyard. The City
first contends that the horse does not qualify for a reasonable modification under
the ADA and its implementing regulations because it does not help C.A. with her
daily life activities (such as going to school), C.A. can walk without the horse, and
the horse does not help C.A. inside the house. We are not persuaded by, nor do
we find any authority to support, the proposition that an animal must be needed
in all aspects of daily life or outside the house to qualify for a reasonable modification under the ADA. Many service animals are trained to provide specialized

assistance that may be necessary only at certain times or places. For example, C.A. has a seizure-response dog that is specifically trained to assist her if she has a seizure while sleeping. This dog indisputably qualifies as a service animal despite the fact that it does not provide assistance to C.A. with any of her daily activities while she is awake or outside the house. Anderson has produced evidence that Ellie is trained to assist C.A. with beneficial exercise in her backyard, and she is no less qualified for a reasonable modification under the ADA simply because C.A. does not need her horse's assistance for all of her daily activities or when traveling.

The City also contends that Ellie has not been "individually trained to do work or perform tasks for the benefit of" C.A. because Anderson, the horse's primary instructor, holds no certification in service-animal training. But the ADA regulations have no certification requirement. Rather, the ADA asks whether the horse has been instructed on how to perform a task that assists an individual with his or her disability, so the instructor's lack of certification at best creates a factual dispute as to whether a horse's training was adequate. Here, Anderson testified that Ellie is trained to assist C.A. to overcome her mobility limitations by steadying her as she walks and helping her stand after she falls, tasks specifically listed by the ADA regulations as examples of ways that miniature horses can assist the disabled. Construed in Anderson's favor, this evidence satisfies the ADA regulations' requirement that the miniature horse be "individually trained to do work or perform tasks for the benefit of the individual with a disability." 28 C.F.R. § 35.136(i)(1).

### Assessment Factors

In addition to the requirement that miniature horses be trained to assist an individual with his or her disability, the ADA regulations also provide four "assessment factors" that "shall [be] consider[ed]" when determining "whether reasonable modifications in policies, practices, or procedures can be made to allow a miniature horse into a specific facility":

(i) The type, size, and weight of the miniature horse and whether the facility can accommodate these features;

(ii) Whether the handler has sufficient control of the miniature horse;

(iii) Whether the miniature horse is housebroken; and

(iv) Whether the miniature horse's presence in a specific facility compromises legitimate safety requirements that are necessary for safe operation.

28 C.F.R. § 35.136(i)(2). The district court found that these factors weigh against Anderson, noting that her house is on a lot that is smaller than miniature horses typically require, that Ellie is not housebroken, and finding that health complaints lodged against Anderson over the past several years suggest that the horse's presence would compromise the City's "legitimate health and public safety concerns." On appeal, Anderson contends that she has produced evidence that at least creates disputed issues of fact as to each of these factors.

With regard to the first factor, the City contends that Anderson's residence is too small to accommodate her horse, pointing out that Anderson has admitted that her yard is significantly smaller than would be ideal for an average miniature horse. However, this factor calls for consideration of the "type, size, and weight" of the particular miniature horse at issue, not an average member of her species. *See* 28 C.F.R. § 35.136(i)(2)(i). Anderson has provided evidence that Ellie is uniquely suited for a smaller yard because her rear legs are deformed, thus reducing her need and ability to run. Furthermore, Anderson testified that her backyard includes a shed "of a size and dimension to accommodate three miniature horses comfortably, and thus houses Ellie very comfortably and keeps her safe from the elements." This evidence is sufficient to show a factual dispute regarding the first assessment factor.

The City contends that the second and third factors weigh against Anderson and C.A. because they did not have sufficient control over Ellie, and that she was not housebroken. Anderson testified that she has sufficient control over her horse because she has trained Ellie to perform specific tasks for C.A. In response, the City offered a sworn account of an incident in which C.A. attempted to demonstrate how she works with Ellie but was not able to do so, fell, and was stepped over by the horse. Given the conflicting affidavits concerning the extent of Anderson and C.A.'s control over their horse, there is a genuine factual dispute over the second assessment factor that cannot be resolved on summary judgment. Regarding the third factor, Anderson concedes that Ellie is not housebroken. However, this does not automatically relieve the City from its obligation to make a reasonable modification because the assessment factors are not *prerequisites* for a reasonable modification, but are independent *factors* that shall be considered when evaluating whether a particular modification is reasonable for a particular animal. The City provides no reason why Ellie's lack of control over producing waste indoors is relevant here, where the horse is never indoors and the requested accommodation is for the horse to assist C.A. and live outdoors in Anderson's backyard.

Finally, the City contends that the fourth factor weighs against Anderson. It points to multiple citizen complaints concerning unsanitary conditions related to a number of animals on Anderson's property. The City concludes from those complaints that the "miniature horse's presence" at her house "compromises legitimate safety requirements" of the City's health code. *See* 28 C.F.R. § 35.136(i)(2)(iv). Anderson responds that these complaints do not accurately reflect the condition of her residence and that she has now secured a service to regularly remove animal waste from her yard. Additionally, Anderson emphasizes that there are no complaints from her current neighbors, most whom have signed letters in support of her efforts to keep Ellie at her house. Anderson points out that those conditions complained of arose from the concurrent presence of multiple farm animals at her house, combined with her previous failure to clean up effectively after them. Indeed, she notes that some of the complaints the City cites concerned only dog waste and were made at times when no horses were present at Anderson's house. Taken together, this evidence shows that there is a factual dispute over whether a single miniature horse at Anderson's residence would threaten the City's "legitimate safety requirements."

Anderson has produced evidence that it would be reasonable for her to keep Ellie at her residence and that all the requirements and assessment factors of the ADA regulations have been satisfied. The City has produced conflicting evidence, such as health complaints, and draws a different conclusion from the record, but weighing the City's evidence against the plaintiffs' is inappropriate on summary judgment. The Ninth Circuit has observed that the "determination of what constitutes reasonable modification is highly fact-specific, requiring case-by-case inquiry." *Lentini v. Cal. Ctr. for the Arts, Escondido*, 370 F.3d 837, 844 (9th Cir. 2004). Viewing all facts and drawing all reasonable inferences in Anderson's favor, and given the "highly fact-specific" nature of the reasonableness inquiry, we conclude that there are disputed issues of material fact as to the reasonableness of Anderson's requested modification.

Because we find that disputed issues of fact preclude summary judgment in favor of the City on Anderson's ADA claim for a reasonable modification to keep Ellie at her house, we reverse the district court's judgment on that claim.

### Intentional Discrimination

The plaintiffs contend that the City intentionally discriminated against Anderson and her daughter when it passed Ordinance 2013-1 in violation of Title II of the ADA. Title II provides that "no qualified individual with a disability shall, by reason of such disability, be excluded from participation in or be denied the benefits of the services, programs, or activities of a public entity, or be subjected to discrimination by any such entity." 42 U.S.C. § 12132. "[T]he phrase 'services, programs, or activities' encompasses virtually everything a public entity does." *Tucker v. Tennessee*, 539 F.3d 526, 532 (6th Cir. 2008). . . .

To establish a prima facie case of intentional discrimination under Title II of the ADA, a plaintiff must show that: (1) she has a disability; (2) she is otherwise qualified; and (3) she was being excluded from participation in, denied the benefits of, or subjected to discrimination under the program because of her disability. . . .

Once a plaintiff establishes a prima facie case of discrimination, the defendant "must then offer a legitimate, nondiscriminatory reason for its" challenged action. . . .

Here, it is undisputed that C.A. is a qualified individual with a disability, but the parties dispute whether the plaintiffs can make out the third element of their prima facie case by showing that the City took action because of C.A.'s disability. The City maintains that its actions were motivated by the multiple citizen complaints against Anderson concerning unsanitary conditions at her house related to the presence of farm animals, and not by any discriminatory intent or animus against the disabled, while Anderson contends that the City was motivated to pass Ordinance 2013-1 because of C.A.'s disability. . . .

. . . .

We find that the evidence, even when viewed in the light most favorable to Anderson, shows that it was citizens' complaints that motivated the City's actions, and that there is no evidence to support an inference of discriminatory intent. . . .

. . . .

### FHAA Claims

The FHAA makes it unlawful to "discriminate against any person in the terms, conditions, or privileges of sale or rental of a dwelling, or in the provision of services or facilities in connection with such dwelling, because of a handicap." 42 U.S.C. § 3604(f)(2). Such discrimination includes a "refusal to make reasonable accommodations in rules, policies, practices, or services, when such accommodations may be necessary to afford such person equal opportunity to use and enjoy a dwelling[.]" *Id.* at § 3604(f)(3)(B). "Plaintiffs who allege a violation of 42 U.S.C. § 3604(f) may proceed under any or all of three theories: disparate treatment, disparate impact, and failure to make reasonable accommodations." *Smith & Lee Assocs. v. City of Taylor, Mich.*, 102 F.3d 781, 790 (6th Cir. 1996).

Anderson invokes all three theories. First, she contends that by refusing to permit her to keep Ellie at her dwelling the City failed to make a reasonable accommodation for C.A.'s disability as required by the FHAA. Second, as to her disparate treatment claim under the FHAA, Anderson repeats the assertion that she made under the ADA that the City intentionally discriminated against her because of C.A.'s disability. Third, Anderson alleges that, even if the City had no discriminatory animus, its actions have had a disparate impact on "C.A., and any disabled person within the City who may require the assistance of a miniature horse."

### Reasonable Accommodation

The plaintiffs contend that the FHAA, like the ADA, requires the City to make a reasonable accommodation to allow Anderson to keep her miniature horse at her residence. The FHAA "creates an affirmative duty on [a] municipalit[y] . . . to afford its disabled citizens reasonable accommodations in its municipal zoning practices if necessary to afford such persons equal opportunity in the use and enjoyment of their property." . . . The "three operative elements" of the FHAA's reasonable accommodation requirement are "equal opportunity," "necessary," and "reasonable." On appeal, Anderson contends that there are disputed issues of fact as to each of these elements that preclude summary judgment for the City.

### Equal Opportunity and Necessity

The first two elements are closely related. The first asks "whether the requested accommodation would afford the disabled resident an equal opportunity to enjoy the property." The FHAA "links the term 'necessary' to the goal of equal opportunity.

Plaintiffs must show that, but for the accommodation, they likely will be denied an equal opportunity to enjoy the housing of their choice." "The necessity element is, in other words, a causation inquiry that examines whether the requested accommodation or modification would redress injuries that otherwise would prevent a disabled resident from receiving the same enjoyment from the property as a non-disabled person would receive."

Equal use and enjoyment of a dwelling are achieved when an accommodation ameliorates the effects of the disability such that the disabled individual can use and enjoy his or her residence as a non-disabled person could. . . .

The district court found that permitting Anderson to keep a horse at her house was unnecessary because C.A. could obtain therapy with a horse by traveling to a local farm or stable. . . .

Regarding the assertion that C.A. can obtain therapy with a horse at a local farm or stable, . . . the availability of an alternative treatment away from the plaintiff's dwelling is irrelevant to the FHAA, which requires reasonable accommodations necessary for a disabled individual to receive the "*same* enjoyment from the property as a non-disabled person would receive," not merely those accommodations that the disabled individual cannot function without or for which no alternative is available away from the dwelling. For the same reason, the City's argument that "C.A. can ambulate and otherwise function without the horse" is likewise irrelevant because the FHAA requires accommodations that are necessary to achieve housing equality, not just those accommodations that are absolutely necessary for the disabled individual's treatment or basic ability to function.

The City's argument that the accommodation was not necessary because C.A. can continue to live in her house without it is also inapposite. . . . [T]he plaintiffs here do not contend that the accommodation is necessary for C.A. to continue to reside in her dwelling, but rather that the accommodation is necessary for her to have an equal opportunity to enjoy a particular use of her house — independent recreation and exercise in her backyard. . . . [T]he FHAA requires accommodations that are necessary for the same enjoyment of a dwelling that a non-disabled person would receive, not just those that are necessary to remain in the dwelling at all. . . .

Anderson testified that Ellie allows C.A. to play independently and exercise in her backyard and that, without the horse, C.A. cannot do so for any significant length of time, and would effectively be denied the equal opportunity to play in her own backyard as non-disabled children can. This evidence, viewed in a light most favorable to the plaintiffs, is sufficient for a reasonable jury to find that the requested accommodation of keeping the miniature horse at her house is necessary for C.A.'s equal use and enjoyment of her dwelling.

## Reasonability

The "crux of a reasonable-accommodation . . . claim typically will be [the third 'operative element,'] the question of reasonableness."

To determine the reasonableness of the requested modification, the burden that the requested modification would impose on the defendant (and perhaps on persons or interests whom the defendant represents) must be weighed against the benefits that would accrue to the plaintiff. This is a highly fact-specific inquiry. A modification should be deemed reasonable if it imposes no fundamental alteration in the nature of a program or undue financial and administrative burdens.

The district court held that the accommodation was unreasonable, reiterating its finding that C.A. did not need therapy at her house because she could obtain it elsewhere, and also finding that permitting a horse in a residential neighborhood would "fundamentally alter the nature of the [City's] zoning scheme." . . .

Factual disputes pervade the question of the accommodation's reasonableness and the "highly fact-specific" balancing of the City's interests against the plaintiffs' that it requires, precluding summary judgment for the City. . . . While the City's interests in public health, sanitation, and residential property values are clear, Anderson disputes the extent to which her requested accommodation would interfere with those interests, pointing to letters of support from her neighbors and the fact that she has secured a cleaning service to prevent the presence of a horse from creating unsanitary conditions at her house. . . .

. . . While protecting public health and property values are central to the City's interests, Anderson has produced evidence that the presence of one miniature horse at her house will not create unsanitary conditions or devalue her neighbors' property, supported not only by her own testimony but by signed letters of support from her current neighbors. . . . The fact that the City banned horses from residential property does not mean that any modification permitting a horse necessarily amounts to a fundamental alteration.

We conclude that there are genuine disputes of material fact as to whether Anderson's requested accommodation is reasonable and necessary to afford her and C.A. an equal opportunity to use and enjoy their dwelling, and so we reverse the district court's grant of summary judgment to the City on the plaintiffs' FHAA reasonable-accommodation claim.

### Disparate Treatment

"To prevail on a disparate treatment claim [brought under the FHAA], a plaintiff must show proof of intentional discrimination." *HDC, LLC v. City of Ann Arbor*, 675 F.3d 608, 612 (6th Cir. 2012). "Because a disparate-treatment claim requires the plaintiff to establish discriminatory animus, analysis of such a claim focuses on the defendant's intent." . . .

. . . [W]e find no evidence that the City acted because C.A. is an individual with a disability, nor that the City otherwise harbored discriminatory animus against the disabled. We therefore affirm the district court's grant of summary judgment to the City on the plaintiffs' FHAA disparate-treatment claim.

## Disparate Impact

Finally, the plaintiffs contend that the City violated the FHAA because its actions have had a disparate impact on C.A. and other disabled individuals who would benefit from the use of miniature horses at their houses. "To show disparate impact [in violation of the FHAA], a plaintiff must demonstrate that a facially neutral policy or practice has the effect of discriminating against a protected class of which the plaintiff is a member." A "disparate-impact claim . . . turns not on the defendant's intent but instead on the broader effects of the disputed housing practice." Plaintiffs alleging disparate-impact claims under the FHAA must first show that defendant's actions "caused handicapped individuals to suffer disproportionately more than other individuals."

Anderson and the other plaintiffs contend that Ordinance 2013-1 had a disparate impact on C.A. and other disabled individuals who are unable to benefit from the use of miniature horses at their houses. But Anderson fails to recognize that this ordinance specifically exempts any animals protected by federal law, including the FHAA. Thus, by its own terms, Ordinance 2013-1 has *less* of an impact on disabled individuals who rely on the assistance of miniature horses or other animals than it does on the general population. We therefore affirm the district court's grant of summary judgment to the City on the plaintiffs' FHAA disparate-impact claim.

### III. Conclusion

. . . We affirm the district court's grant of summary judgment to the City on the plaintiffs' intentional-discrimination ADA claim and disparate-treatment and disparate-impact FHAA claims. We reverse the district court's grant of summary judgment to the City in all other respects, and remand for further proceedings consistent with this opinion.

## *Questions for Consideration*

1) Why should people who bought homes in a single-family residential zone have to accommodate a neighbor moving in and having a horse, which is otherwise not permitted in this zone? In this case, the neighbors complained about the manure and the smell. In many communities, this situation will cause a number of complaints by homeowners to city and town officials. How should officials respond? Are the complaints understandable?

2) What did the city ordinance say?

3) Could a person keep an alpaca, llama, or a full-size horse on a single-family residential property by asserting it is a service animal or a therapy animal? What criteria might apply to this determination?

4) What is a reasonable modification and a reasonable accommodation?

5) Explain the difference between intentional discrimination and disparate treatment.

6) How does disparate impact relate to disparate treatment? What is the difference?

## *Takeaway*

- Federal legislation protecting people with disabilities applies to local planning and zoning. Local zoning codes must sometimes give way to the rights that people have under federal law related to disability. Statutes designed to protect people with disabilities work to limit the exercise of the local police power.

- Local planning and zoning officials must be able to interpret and apply the various criteria applicable to addressing the intersections between zoning law and disability law. In local zoning determinations, officials must review the appropriate evidence and make the appropriate findings on issues related to disability law. Thinking in terms of disability law is something local planning and zoning officials have not traditionally been asked to do.

### Discussion Problem 3.6

Tyler is an operator of residential substance-abuse rehabilitation facilities named New Day Centers. New Day Centers are residential facilities for recovering drug addicts and alcoholics. Tyler has been trying to open a New Day Center in the City of Northerly for over ten years. His facility in Northerly is located on the outskirts of a residential neighborhood. But the center's doors are currently closed on account of a dispute with Northerly's zoning board. Northerly, like many cities, regulates the number of non-traditional residences in or around neighborhoods that consist of mostly single-family homes. So, things like fraternity houses, multi-family dwellings, and residential substance-abuse rehabilitation centers all need to get a conditional use permit from the City before opening. Many years ago, Tyler applied for such a permit to open a New Day Center in Northerly, and the City's urban-planning departments approved. But residential neighbors to the New Day Center appealed the departments' decision to Northerly Board of Zoning Appeals, which then reversed the prior approval. Tyler sued the City and the Board, claiming that Northerly's zoning ordinance was invalid, and that the Board's decision was intentional discrimination against people with disabilities, including recovering addicts, in violation of three federal statutes: the Americans with Disabilities Act, the Fair Housing Act, and the Rehabilitation Act. Who shall prevail in this dispute? (In responding to this question, refer to your case materials and to the materials in the Appendix.)

# H. Takings: A Balancing Test

The police power is the source of local government authority to regulate land use and development. Traditionally, the limitations on the exercise of the police power have included due process, equal protection, and takings. We have already seen that disability law provides another limitation to the exercise of the police power. Now, however, we investigate more closely the Takings Clause as a limitation on the power to regulate and limit the lawful use of property.

## Penn Central Transportation Co. v. City of New York

Supreme Court of the United States

438 U.S. 104 (1978)

BRENNAN, Justice. The question presented is whether a city may, as part of a comprehensive program to preserve historic landmarks and historic districts, place restrictions on the development of individual historic landmarks — in addition to those imposed by applicable zoning ordinances — without effecting a "taking" requiring the payment of "just compensation." Specifically, we must decide whether the application of New York City's Landmarks Preservation Law to the parcel of land occupied by Grand Central Terminal has "taken" its owners' property in violation of the Fifth and Fourteenth Amendments.

### I.

### A.

Over the past 50 years, all 50 States and over 500 municipalities have enacted laws to encourage or require the preservation of buildings and areas with historic or aesthetic importance. These nationwide legislative efforts have been precipitated by two concerns. The first is recognition that, in recent years, large numbers of historic structures, landmarks, and areas have been destroyed without adequate consideration of either the values represented therein or the possibility of preserving the destroyed properties for use in economically productive ways. The second is a widely shared belief that structures with special historic, cultural, or architectural significance enhance the quality of life for all. Not only do these buildings and their workmanship represent the lessons of the past and embody precious features of our heritage, they serve as examples of quality for today. "[H]istoric conservation is but one aspect of the much larger problem, basically an environmental one, of enhancing — or perhaps developing for the first time — the quality of life for people."

New York City, responding to similar concerns and acting pursuant to a New York State enabling Act,[5] adopted its Landmarks Preservation Law in 1965. See N.Y.C. Admin. Code, ch. 8-A, § 205-1.0 et seq. (1976). The city acted from the conviction that "the standing of [New York City] as a world-wide tourist center and world capital of business, culture and government" would be threatened if legislation were not enacted to protect historic landmarks and neighborhoods from precipitate decisions to destroy or fundamentally alter their character. § 205-1.0(a). The city believed that comprehensive measures to safeguard desirable features of the existing urban fabric would benefit its citizens in a variety of ways: e.g., fostering "civic pride in the beauty and noble accomplishments of the past"; protecting and enhancing "the city's attractions to tourists and visitors"; "support[ing] and stimul[ating] business

---

5. See N.Y. Gen. Mun. Law § 96-a (McKinney 1977). It declares that it is the public policy of the State of New York to preserve structures and areas with special historical or aesthetic interest or value and authorizes local governments to impose reasonable restrictions to perpetuate such structures and areas.

and industry"; "strengthen[ing] the economy of the city"; and promoting "the use of historic districts, landmarks, interior landmarks and scenic landmarks for the education, pleasure and welfare of the people of the city." § 205-1.0(b).

The New York City law is typical of many urban landmark laws in that its primary method of achieving its goals is not by acquisitions of historic properties,[6] but rather by involving public entities in land-use decisions affecting these properties and providing services, standards, controls, and incentives that will encourage preservation by private owners and users. While the law does place special restrictions on landmark properties as a necessary feature to the attainment of its larger objectives, the major theme of the law is to ensure the owners of any such properties both a "reasonable return" on their investments and maximum latitude to use their parcels for purposes not inconsistent with the preservation goals.

The operation of the law can be briefly summarized. The primary responsibility for administering the law is vested in the Landmarks Preservation Commission (Commission), a broad based, 11-member agency[8] assisted by a technical staff. The Commission first performs the function, critical to any landmark preservation effort, of identifying properties and areas that have "a special character or special historical or aesthetic interest or value as part of the development, heritage or cultural characteristics of the city, state or nation." If the Commission determines, after giving all interested parties an opportunity to be heard, that a building or area satisfies the ordinance's criteria, it will designate a building to be a "landmark," situated on a particular "landmark site," or will designate an area to be a "historic district," § 207-1.0(h).[11] After the Commission makes a designation, New York City's Board of Estimate, after considering the relationship of the designated property "to the

---

6. The consensus is that widespread public ownership of historic properties in urban settings is neither feasible nor wise. Public ownership reduces the tax base, burdens the public budget with costs of acquisitions and maintenance, and results in the preservation of public buildings as museums and similar facilities, rather than as economically productive features of the urban scene. See Wilson & Winkler, *The Response of State Legislation to Historic Preservation*, 36 Law & Contemp. Prob. 329, 330–331, 339–340 (1971).

8. The ordinance creating the Commission requires that it include at least three architects, one historian qualified in the field, one city planner or landscape architect, one realtor, and at least one resident of each of the city's five boroughs. N.Y.C. Charter § 534 (1976). In addition to the ordinance's requirements concerning the composition of the Commission, there is, according to a former chairman, a "prudent tradition" that the Commission include one or two lawyers, preferably with experience in municipal government, and several laymen with no specialized qualifications other than concern for the good of the city. Goldstone, *Aesthetics in Historic Districts*, 36 Law & Contemp. Prob. 379, 384–385 (1971).

11. "'Historic district.' Any area which: (1) contains improvements which: (a) have a special character or special historical or aesthetic interest or value; and (b) represent one or more periods or styles of architecture typical of one or more eras in the history of the city; and (c) cause such area, by reason of such factors, to constitute a distinct section of the city; and (2) has been designated as a historic district pursuant to the provisions of this chapter." § 207-1.0(h). The Act also provides for the designation of a "scenic landmark," see § 207-1.0(w), and an "interior landmark." See § 207-1.0(m).

master plan, the zoning resolution, projected public improvements and any plans for the renewal of the area involved," may modify or disapprove the designation, and the owner may seek judicial review of the final designation decision. Thus far, 31 historic districts and over 400 individual landmarks have been finally designated, and the process is a continuing one.

Final designation as a landmark results in restrictions upon the property owner's options concerning use of the landmark site. First, the law imposes a duty upon the owner to keep the exterior features of the building "in good repair" to assure that the law's objectives not be defeated by the landmark's falling into a state of irremediable disrepair. See § 207-10.0(a). Second, the Commission must approve in advance any proposal to alter the exterior architectural features of the landmark or to construct any exterior improvement on the landmark site, thus ensuring that decisions concerning construction on the landmark site are made with due consideration of both the public interest in the maintenance of the structure and the landowner's interest in use of the property.

In the event an owner wishes to alter a landmark site, three separate procedures are available through which administrative approval may be obtained. First, the owner may apply to the Commission for a "certificate of no effect on protected architectural features": that is, for an order approving the improvement or alteration on the ground that it will not change or affect any architectural feature of the landmark and will be in harmony therewith. See § 207-5.0. Denial of the certificate is subject to judicial review.

Second, the owner may apply to the Commission for a certificate of "appropriateness." Such certificates will be granted if the Commission concludes — focusing upon aesthetic, historical, and architectural values — that the proposed construction on the landmark site would not unduly hinder the protection, enhancement, perpetuation, and use of the landmark. Again, denial of the certificate is subject to judicial review. Moreover, the owner who is denied either a certificate of no exterior effect or a certificate of appropriateness may submit an alternative or modified plan for approval. The final procedure — seeking a certificate of appropriateness on the ground of "insufficient return," see § 207-8.0 — provides special mechanisms, which vary depending on whether or not the landmark enjoys a tax exemption, to ensure that designation does not cause economic hardship.

Although the designation of a landmark and landmark site restricts the owner's control over the parcel, designation also enhances the economic position of the landmark owner in one significant respect. Under New York City's zoning laws, owners of real property who have not developed their property to the full extent permitted by the applicable zoning laws are allowed to transfer development rights to contiguous parcels on the same city block. See New York City, Zoning Resolution Art. I, ch. 2, § 12-10 (1978) (definition of "zoning lot"). A 1968 ordinance gave the owners of landmark sites additional opportunities to transfer development rights to other parcels. Subject to a restriction that the floor area of the transferee lot may not be increased by more than 20% above its authorized level, the ordinance permitted transfers from a landmark parcel to property across the street or across a street intersection. In 1969, the law governing the conditions under which transfers from landmark parcels could occur was liberalized, see New York City Zoning Resolutions 74-79 to 74-793, apparently to ensure that the Landmarks Law would not unduly restrict the development options of the owners of Grand Central Terminal. See Marcus, *Air Rights Transfers in New York City*, 36 Law & Contemp. Prob. 372, 375 (1971). The class of recipient lots was expanded to include lots "across a street and opposite to another lot or lots which except for the intervention of streets or street intersections f[or]m a series extending to the lot occupied by the landmark [building, provided that] all lots [are] in the same ownership." New York City Zoning Resolution 74-79 (emphasis deleted).[14] In addition, the 1969 amendment permits, in highly commercialized areas like midtown Manhattan, the transfer of all unused development rights to a single parcel. *Ibid.*

B.

This case involves the application of New York City's Landmarks Preservation Law to Grand Central Terminal ('Terminal). The Terminal, which is owned by the Penn Central Transportation Co. and its affiliates (Penn Central), is one of New York City's most famous buildings. Opened in 1913, it is regarded not only as providing an ingenious engineering solution to the problems presented by urban railroad stations, but also as a magnificent example of the French beaux-arts style.

The Terminal is located in midtown Manhattan. Its south facade faces 42d Street and that street's intersection with Park Avenue. At street level, the Terminal is bounded on the west by Vanderbilt Avenue, on the east by the Commodore Hotel, and on the north by the Pan-American Building. Although a 20-story office tower, to have been located above the Terminal, was part of the original design, the planned tower was never constructed.[15] The Terminal itself is an eight-story structure which Penn Central uses as a railroad station and in which it rents space not needed for railroad purposes to a variety of commercial interests. The Terminal is one of a number of properties owned by appellant Penn Central in this area of midtown Manhattan. The others include the Barclay, Biltmore, Commodore, Roosevelt, and Waldorf-Astoria Hotels, the Pan-American Building and other office buildings along Park Avenue, and the Yale Club. At least eight of these are eligible to

---

14. To obtain approval for a proposed transfer, the landmark owner must follow the following procedure. First, he must obtain the permission of the Commission which will examine the plans for the development of the transferee lot to determine whether the planned construction would be compatible with the landmark. Second, he must obtain the approbation of New York City's Planning Commission which will focus on the effects of the transfer on occupants of the buildings in the vicinity of the transferee lot and whether the landmark owner will preserve the landmark. Finally, the matter goes to the Board of Estimate, which has final authority to grant or deny the application. See also Costonis, [*The Chicago Plan: Incentive Zoning and the Preservation of Urban Landmarks*, 85 Harv.L.Rev. 574,] *supra* n.2, at 585–586 (1972).

15. The Terminal's present foundation includes columns, which were built into it for the express purpose of supporting the proposed 20-story tower.

be recipients of development rights afforded the Terminal by virtue of landmark designation.

On August 2, 1967, following a public hearing, the Commission designated the Terminal a "landmark" and designated the "city tax block" it occupies a "landmark site."[16] The Board of Estimate confirmed this action on September 21, 1967. Although appellant Penn Central had opposed the designation before the Commission, it did not seek judicial review of the final designation decision.

On January 22, 1968, appellant Penn Central, to increase its income, entered into a renewable 50-year lease and sublease agreement with appellant UGP Properties, Inc. (UGP), a wholly owned subsidiary of Union General Properties, Ltd., a United Kingdom corporation. Under the terms of the agreement, UGP was to construct a multistory office building above the Terminal. UGP promised to pay Penn Central $1 million annually during construction and at least $3 million annually thereafter. The rentals would be offset in part by a loss of some $700,000 to $1 million in net rentals presently received from concessionaires displaced by the new building.

Appellants UGP and Penn Central then applied to the Commission for permission to construct an office building atop the Terminal. Two separate plans, both designed by architect Marcel Breuer and both apparently satisfying the terms of the applicable zoning ordinance, were submitted to the Commission for approval. The first, Breuer I, provided for the construction of a 55-story office building, to be cantilevered above the existing facade and to rest on the roof of the Terminal. The second, Breuer II Revised,[17] called for tearing down a portion of the Terminal that included the 42d Street facade, stripping off some of the remaining features of the Terminal's facade, and constructing a 53-story office building. The Commission denied a certificate of no exterior effect on September 20, 1968. Appellants then applied for a certificate of "appropriateness" as to both proposals. After four days of hearings at which over 80 witnesses testified, the Commission denied this application as to both proposals.

The Commission's reasons for rejecting certificates respecting Breuer II Revised are summarized in the following statement: "To protect a Landmark, one does not tear it down. To perpetuate its architectural features, one does not strip them off." Breuer I, which would have preserved the existing vertical facades of the present

---

16. The Commission's report stated: "Grand Central Station, one of the great buildings of America, evokes a spirit that is unique in this City. It combines distinguished architecture with a brilliant engineering solution, wedded to one of the most fabulous railroad terminals of our time. Monumental in scale, this great building functions as well today as it did when built. In style, it represents the best of the French Beaux Arts." Record 2240.

17. Appellants also submitted a plan, denominated Breuer II, to the Commission. However, because appellants learned that Breuer II would have violated existing easements, they substituted Breuer II Revised for Breuer II, and the Commission evaluated the appropriateness only of Breuer II Revised.

structure, received more sympathetic consideration. The Commission first focused on the effect that the proposed tower would have on one desirable feature created by the present structure and its surroundings: the dramatic view of the Terminal from Park Avenue South. Although appellants had contended that the Pan-American Building had already destroyed the silhouette of the south facade and that one additional tower could do no further damage and might even provide a better background for the facade, the Commission disagreed, stating that it found the majestic approach from the south to be still unique in the city and that a 55-story tower atop the Terminal would be far more detrimental to its south facade than the Pan-American Building 375 feet away. Moreover, the Commission found that from closer vantage points the Pan Am Building and the other towers were largely cut off from view, which would not be the case of the mass on top of the Terminal planned under Breuer I. In conclusion, the Commission stated:

> "[We have] no fixed rule against making additions to designated buildings — it all depends on how they are done.... But to balance a 55-story office tower above a flamboyant Beaux-Arts facade seems nothing more than an aesthetic joke. Quite simply, the tower would overwhelm the Terminal by its sheer mass. The 'addition' would be four times as high as the existing structure and would reduce the Landmark itself to the status of a curiosity.

> "Landmarks cannot be divorced from their settings — particularly when the setting is a dramatic and integral part of the original concept. The Terminal, in its setting, is a great example of urban design. Such examples are not so plentiful in New York City that we can afford to lose any of the few we have. And we must preserve them in a meaningful way — with alterations and additions of such character, scale, materials and mass as will protect, enhance and perpetuate the original design rather than overwhelm it."

Appellants did not seek judicial review of the denial of either certificate. Because the Terminal site enjoyed a tax exemption, remained suitable for its present and future uses, and was not the subject of a contract of sale, there were no further administrative remedies available to appellants as to the Breuer I and Breuer II Revised plans. Further, appellants did not avail themselves of the opportunity to develop and submit other plans for the Commission's consideration and approval. Instead, appellants filed suit in New York Supreme Court, Trial Term, claiming, *inter alia*, that the application of the Landmarks Preservation Law had "taken" their property without just compensation in violation of the Fifth and Fourteenth Amendments and arbitrarily deprived them of their property without due process of law in violation of the Fourteenth Amendment. Appellants sought a declaratory judgment, injunctive relief barring the city from using the Landmarks Law to impede the construction of any structure that might otherwise lawfully be constructed on the Terminal site, and damages for the "temporary taking" that occurred between August 2, 1967, the designation date, and the date when the restrictions arising from the Landmarks

Law would be lifted. The trial court granted the injunctive and declaratory relief but severed the question of damages for a "temporary taking."[20]

Appellees appealed, and the New York Supreme Court, Appellate Division, reversed. 50 A.D.2d 265, 377 N.Y.S.2d 20 (1975). The Appellate Division held that the restrictions on the development of the Terminal site were necessary to promote the legitimate public purpose of protecting landmarks and therefore that appellants could sustain their constitutional claims only by proof that the regulation deprived them of all reasonable beneficial use of the property. The Appellate Division held that the evidence appellants introduced at trial—"Statements of Revenues and Costs," purporting to show a net operating loss for the years 1969 and 1971, which were prepared for the instant litigation—had not satisfied their burden.[21] First, the court rejected the claim that these statements showed that the Terminal was operating at a loss, for in the court's view, appellants had improperly attributed some railroad operating expenses and taxes to their real estate operations and compounded that error by failing to impute any rental value to the vast space in the Terminal devoted to railroad purposes. Further, the Appellate Division concluded that appellants had failed to establish either that they were unable to increase the Terminal's commercial income by transforming vacant or underutilized space to revenue-producing use, or that the unused development rights over the Terminal could not have been profitably transferred to one or more nearby sites.[22] The Appellate Division concluded that all appellants had succeeded in showing was that they had been deprived of the property's most profitable use, and that this showing did not establish that appellants had been unconstitutionally deprived of their property.

The New York Court of Appeals affirmed. 42 N.Y.2d 324, 397 N.Y.S.2d 914, 366 N.E.2d 1271 (1977). That court summarily rejected any claim that the Landmarks Law had "taken" property without "just compensation," indicating that there could be no "taking" since the law had not transferred control of the property to the city, but only restricted appellants' exploitation of it. In that circumstance, the Court of

---

20. Although that court suggested that any regulation of private property to protect landmark values was unconstitutional if "just compensation" were not afforded, it also appeared to rely upon its findings: first, that the cost to Penn Central of operating the Terminal building itself, exclusive of purely railroad operations, exceeded the revenues received from concessionaires and tenants in the Terminal; and second, that the special transferable development rights afforded Penn Central as an owner of a landmark site did not "provide compensation to plaintiffs or minimize the harm suffered by plaintiffs due to the designation of the Terminal as a landmark."

21. These statements appear to have reflected the costs of maintaining the exterior architectural features of the Terminal in "good repair" as required by the law. As would have been apparent in any case therefore, the existence of the duty to keep up the property was here—and will presumably always be—factored into the inquiry concerning the constitutionality of the landmark restrictions. The Appellate Division also rejected the claim that an agreement of Penn Central with the Metropolitan Transit Authority and the Connecticut Transit Authority provided a basis for invalidating the application of the Landmarks Law.

22. The record reflected that Penn Central had given serious consideration to transferring some of those rights to either the Biltmore Hotel or the Roosevelt Hotel.

Appeals held that appellants' attack on the law could prevail only if the law deprived appellants of their property in violation of the Due Process Clause of the Fourteenth Amendment. Whether or not there was a denial of substantive due process turned on whether the restrictions deprived Penn Central of a "reasonable return" on the "privately created and privately managed ingredient" of the Terminal. The Court of Appeals concluded that the Landmarks Law had not effected a denial of due process because: (1) the landmark regulation permitted the same use as had been made of the Terminal for more than half a century; (2) the appellants had failed to show that they could not earn a reasonable return on their investment in the Terminal itself; (3) even if the Terminal proper could never operate at a reasonable profit some of the income from Penn Central's extensive real estate holdings in the area, which include hotels and office buildings, must realistically be imputed to the Terminal; and (4) the development rights above the Terminal, which had been made transferable to numerous sites in the vicinity of the Terminal, one or two of which were suitable for the construction of office buildings, were valuable to appellants and provided "significant, perhaps 'fair,' compensation for the loss of rights above the terminal itself."

. . . We affirm.

## II.

The issues presented by appellants are (1) whether the restrictions imposed by New York City's law upon appellants' exploitation of the Terminal site effect a "taking" of appellants' property for a public use within the meaning of the Fifth Amendment, which of course is made applicable to the States through the Fourteenth Amendment, and, (2), if so, whether the transferable development rights afforded appellants constitute "just compensation" within the meaning of the Fifth Amendment.[24] We need only address the question whether a "taking" has occurred.[25]

---

24. Our statement of the issues is a distillation of four questions presented in the jurisdictional statement: "Does the social and cultural desirability of preserving historical landmarks through government regulation derogate from the constitutional requirement that just compensation be paid for private property taken for public use? "Is Penn Central entitled to no compensation for that large but unmeasurable portion of the value of its rights to construct an office building over the Grand Central Terminal that is said to have been created by the efforts of 'society as an organized entity'? "Does a finding that Penn Central has failed to establish that there is no possibility, without exercising its development rights, of earning a reasonable return on all of its remaining properties that benefit in any way from the operations of the Grand Central Terminal warrant the conclusion that no compensation need be paid for the taking of those rights? "Does the possibility accorded to Penn Central, under the landmark-preservation regulation, of realizing some value at some time by transferring the Terminal development rights to other buildings, under a procedure that is conceded to be defective, severely limited, procedurally complex and speculative, and that requires ultimate discretionary approval by governmental authorities, meet the constitutional requirements of just compensation as applied to landmarks?" Jurisdictional Statement 3–4. The first and fourth questions assume that there has been a taking and raise the problem whether, under the circumstances of this case, the transferable development rights constitute "just compensation." The second and third questions, on the other hand, are directed to the issue whether a taking has occurred.

25. As is implicit in our opinion, we do not embrace the proposition that a "taking" can never occur unless government has transferred physical control over a portion of a parcel.

## A.

Before considering appellants' specific contentions, it will be useful to review the factors that have shaped the jurisprudence of the Fifth Amendment injunction "nor shall private property be taken for public use, without just compensation." The question of what constitutes a "taking" for purposes of the Fifth Amendment has proved to be a problem of considerable difficulty. While this Court has recognized that the "Fifth Amendment's guarantee . . . [is] designed to bar Government from forcing some people alone to bear public burdens which, in all fairness and justice, should be borne by the public as a whole," *Armstrong v. United States*, 364 U.S. 40, 49, 80 S. Ct. 1563, 1569, 4 L. Ed. 2d 1554 (1960), this Court, quite simply, has been unable to develop any "set formula" for determining when "justice and fairness" require that economic injuries caused by public action be compensated by the government, rather than remain disproportionately concentrated on a few persons. See *Goldblatt v. Hempstead*, 369 U.S. 590, 594, 82 S. Ct. 987, 990, 8 L. Ed. 2d 130 (1962). Indeed, we have frequently observed that whether a particular restriction will be rendered invalid by the government's failure to pay for any losses proximately caused by it depends largely "upon the particular circumstances [in that] case." *United States v. Central Eureka Mining Co.*, 357 U.S. 155, 168, 78 S. Ct. 1097, 1104, 2 L. Ed. 2d 1228 (1958); see *United States v. Caltex, Inc.*, 344 U.S. 149, 156, 73 S. Ct. 200, 203, 97 L. Ed. 157 (1952).

In engaging in these essentially ad hoc, factual inquiries, the Court's decisions have identified several factors that have particular significance. The economic impact of the regulation on the claimant and, particularly, the extent to which the regulation has interfered with distinct investment-backed expectations are, of course, relevant considerations. See *Goldblatt v. Hempstead, supra*, 369 U.S., at 594, 82 S. Ct., at 990. So, too, is the character of the governmental action. A "taking" may more readily be found when the interference with property can be characterized as a physical invasion by government, see, *e.g., United States v. Causby*, 328 U.S. 256, 66 S. Ct. 1062, 90 L. Ed. 1206 (1946), than when interference arises from some public program adjusting the benefits and burdens of economic life to promote the common good.

"Government hardly could go on if to some extent values incident to property could not be diminished without paying for every such change in the general law," *Pennsylvania Coal Co. v. Mahon*, 260 U.S. 393, 413, 43 S. Ct. 158, 159, 67 L. Ed. 322 (1922), and this Court has accordingly recognized, in a wide variety of contexts, that government may execute laws or programs that adversely affect recognized economic values. Exercises of the taxing power are one obvious example. A second are the decisions in which this Court has dismissed "taking" challenges on the ground that, while the challenged government action caused economic harm, it did not interfere with interests that were sufficiently bound up with the reasonable expectations of the claimant to constitute "property" for Fifth Amendment purposes. *See, e.g., United States v. Willow River Power Co.*, 324 U.S. 499, 65 S. Ct. 761, 89 L. Ed. 1101 (1945) (interest in high-water level of river for runoff for tailwaters to maintain power head is not property); *United States v. Chandler-Dunbar Water Power Co.*, 229 U.S. 53, 33 S. Ct. 667, 57 L. Ed. 1063 (1913) (no property interest can exist in navigable waters); see also *Demorest v. City Bank Co.*, 321 U.S. 36, 64 S. Ct. 384, 88 L. Ed. 526 (1944); *Muhlker v. Harlem R. Co.*, 197 U.S. 544, 25 S. Ct. 522, 49 L. Ed. 872 (1905); Sax, *Takings and the Police Power*, 74 Yale L.J. 36, 61–62 (1964).

More importantly for the present case, in instances in which a state tribunal reasonably concluded that "the health, safety, morals, or general welfare" would be promoted by prohibiting particular contemplated uses of land, this Court has upheld land-use regulations that destroyed or adversely affected recognized real property interests. See *Nectow v. Cambridge*, 277 U.S. 183, 188, 48 S. Ct. 447, 448, 72 L. Ed. 842 (1928). Zoning laws are, of course, the classic example, see *Euclid v. Ambler Realty Co.*, 272 U.S. 365, 47 S. Ct. 114, 71 L. Ed. 303 (1926) (prohibition of industrial use); *Gorieb v. Fox*, 274 U.S. 603, 608, 47 S. Ct. 675, 677, 71 L. Ed. 1228 (1927) (requirement that portions of parcels be left unbuilt); *Welch v. Swasey*, 214 U.S. 91, 29 S. Ct. 567, 53 L. Ed. 923 (1909) (height restriction), which have been viewed as permissible governmental action even when prohibiting the most beneficial use of the property. See *Goldblatt v. Hempstead, supra*, 369 U.S., at 592–593, 82 S. Ct., at 988–989, and cases cited; see also *Eastlake v. Forest City Enterprises, Inc.*, 426 U.S. 668, 674, n. 8, 96 S. Ct. 2358, 2362 n. 8, 49 L. Ed. 2d 132 (1976).

Zoning laws generally do not affect existing uses of real property, but "taking" challenges have also been held to be without merit in a wide variety of situations when the challenged governmental actions prohibited a beneficial use to which individual parcels had previously been devoted and thus caused substantial individualized harm. *Miller v. Schoene*, 276 U.S. 272, 48 S. Ct. 246, 72 L. Ed. 568 (1928), is illustrative. In that case, a state entomologist, acting pursuant to a state statute, ordered the claimants to cut down a large number of ornamental red cedar trees because they produced cedar rust fatal to apple trees cultivated nearby. Although the statute provided for recovery of any expense incurred in removing the cedars, and permitted claimants to use the felled trees, it did not provide compensation for the value of the standing trees or for the resulting decrease in market value of the properties as a whole. A unanimous Court held that this latter omission did not render the statute invalid. The Court held that the State might properly make "a choice between the preservation of one class of property and that of the other" and since the apple industry was important in the State involved, concluded that the State had not exceeded "its constitutional powers by deciding upon the destruction of one class of property [without compensation] in order to save another which, in the judgment of the legislature, is of greater value to the public." *Id.*, at 279, 48 S. Ct., at 247.

Again, *Hadacheck v. Sebastian*, 239 U.S. 394, 36 S. Ct. 143, 60 L. Ed. 348 (1915), upheld a law prohibiting the claimant from continuing his otherwise lawful business of operating a brickyard in a particular physical community on the ground that the legislature had reasonably concluded that the presence of the brickyard was inconsistent with neighboring uses. See also *United States v. Central Eureka*

*Mining Co., supra* (Government order closing gold mines so that skilled miners would be available for other mining work held not a taking); *Atchison, T. & S.F. R. Co. v. Public Utilities Comm'n*, 346 U.S. 346, 74 S. Ct. 92, 98 L. Ed. 51 (1953) (railroad may be required to share cost of constructing railroad grade improvement); *Walls v. Midland Carbon Co.*, 254 U.S. 300, 41 S. Ct. 118, 65 L. Ed. 276 (1920) (law prohibiting manufacture of carbon black upheld); *Reinman v. Little Rock*, 237 U.S. 171, 35 S. Ct. 511, 59 L. Ed. 900 (1915) (law prohibiting livery stable upheld); *Mugler v. Kansas*, 123 U.S. 623, 8 S. Ct. 273, 31 L. Ed. 205 (1887) (law prohibiting liquor business upheld).

*Goldblatt v. Hempstead, supra*, is a recent example. There, a 1958 city safety ordinance banned any excavations below the water table and effectively prohibited the claimant from continuing a sand and gravel mining business that had been operated on the particular parcel since 1927. The Court upheld the ordinance against a "taking" challenge, although the ordinance prohibited the present and presumably most beneficial use of the property and had, like the regulations in *Miller* and *Hadacheck*, severely affected a particular owner. The Court assumed that the ordinance did not prevent the owner's reasonable use of the property since the owner made no showing of an adverse effect on the value of the land. Because the restriction served a substantial public purpose, the Court thus held no taking had occurred. It is, of course, implicit in *Goldblatt* that a use restriction on real property may constitute a "taking" if not reasonably necessary to the effectuation of a substantial public purpose, see *Nectow v. Cambridge, supra*; cf. *Moore v. East Cleveland*, 431 U.S. 494, 513–514, 97 S. Ct. 1932, 1943, 52 L. Ed. 2d 531 (1977) (Stevens, J., concurring), or perhaps if it has an unduly harsh impact upon the owner's use of the property.

*Pennsylvania Coal Co. v. Mahon*, 260 U.S. 393, 43 S. Ct. 158, 67 L. Ed. 322 (1922), is the leading case for the proposition that a state statute that substantially furthers important public policies may so frustrate distinct investment-backed expectations as to amount to a "taking." There the claimant had sold the surface rights to particular parcels of property, but expressly reserved the right to remove the coal thereunder. A Pennsylvania statute, enacted after the transactions, forbade any mining of coal that caused the subsidence of any house, unless the house was the property of the owner of the underlying coal and was more than 150 feet from the improved property of another. Because the statute made it commercially impracticable to mine the coal, *id.*, at 414, 43 S. Ct., at 159, and thus had nearly the same effect as the complete destruction of rights claimant had reserved from the owners of the surface land, see *id.*, at 414–415, 43 S. Ct., at 159–160, the Court held that the statute was invalid as effecting a "taking" without just compensation. See also *Armstrong v. United States*, 364 U.S. 40, 80 S. Ct. 1563, 4 L. Ed. 2d 1554 (1960) (Government's complete destruction of a materialman's lien in certain property held a "taking"); *Hudson Water Co. v. McCarter*, 209 U.S. 349, 355, 28 S. Ct. 529, 531, 52 L. Ed. 828 (1908) (if height restriction makes property wholly useless "the rights of property . . . prevail over the other public interest" and compensation is required).

Finally, government actions that may be characterized as acquisitions of resources to permit or facilitate uniquely public functions have often been held to constitute "takings." *United States v. Causby*, 328 U.S. 256, 66 S. Ct. 1062, 90 L. Ed. 1206 (1946), is illustrative. In holding that direct overflights above the claimant's land, that destroyed the present use of the land as a chicken farm, constituted a "taking," *Causby* emphasized that Government had not "merely destroyed property [but was] using a part of it for the flight of its planes."

**B.**

In contending that the New York City law has "taken" their property in violation of the Fifth and Fourteenth Amendments, appellants make a series of arguments, which, while tailored to the facts of this case, essentially urge that any substantial restriction imposed pursuant to a landmark law must be accompanied by just compensation if it is to be constitutional. Before considering these, we emphasize what is not in dispute. Because this Court has recognized, in a number of settings, that States and cities may enact land-use restrictions or controls to enhance the quality of life by preserving the character and desirable aesthetic features of a city, see *New Orleans v. Dukes*, 427 U.S. 297, 96 S. Ct. 2513, 49 L. Ed. 2d 511 (1976) . . . appellants do not contest that New York City's objective of preserving structures and areas with special historic, architectural, or cultural significance is an entirely permissible governmental goal. They also do not dispute that the restrictions imposed on its parcel are appropriate means of securing the purposes of the New York City law. Finally, appellants do not challenge any of the specific factual premises of the decision below. They accept for present purposes both that the parcel of land occupied by Grand Central Terminal must, in its present state, be regarded as capable of earning a reasonable return, and that the transferable development rights afforded appellants by virtue of the Terminal's designation as a landmark are valuable, even if not as valuable as the rights to construct above the Terminal. In appellants' view none of these factors derogate from their claim that New York City's law has effected a "taking."

They first observe that the airspace above the Terminal is a valuable property interest, citing *United States v. Causby, supra*. They urge that the Landmarks Law has deprived them of any gainful use of their "air rights" above the Terminal and that, irrespective of the value of the remainder of their parcel, the city has "taken" their right to this superadjacent airspace, thus entitling them to "just compensation" measured by the fair market value of these air rights.

Apart from our own disagreement with appellants' characterization of the effect of the New York City law, see *infra*, the submission that appellants may establish a "taking" simply by showing that they have been denied the ability to exploit a property interest that they heretofore had believed was available for development is quite simply untenable. Were this the rule, this Court would have erred not only in upholding laws restricting the development of air rights, see *Welch v. Swasey, supra*, but also in approving those prohibiting both the subjacent, see *Goldblatt v. Hempstead*, 369 U.S. 590, 82 S. Ct. 987, 8 L. Ed. 2d 130 (1962), and the lateral, see *Gorieb v.*

*Fox*, 274 U.S. 603, 47 S. Ct. 675, 71 L. Ed. 1228 (1927), development of particular parcels.[27] "Taking" jurisprudence does not divide a single parcel into discrete segments and attempt to determine whether rights in a particular segment have been entirely abrogated. In deciding whether a particular governmental action has effected a taking, this Court focuses rather both on the character of the action and on the nature and extent of the interference with rights in the parcel as a whole — here, the city tax block designated as the "landmark site."

Secondly, appellants, focusing on the character and impact of the New York City law, argue that it effects a "taking" because its operation has significantly diminished the value of the Terminal site. Appellants concede that the decisions sustaining other land-use regulations, which, like the New York City law, are reasonably related to the promotion of the general welfare, uniformly reject the proposition that diminution in property value, standing alone, can establish a "taking," see *Euclid v. Ambler Realty Co.*, 272 U.S. 365, 47 S. Ct. 114, 71 L. Ed. 303 (1926) (75% diminution in value caused by zoning law); *Hadacheck v. Sebastian*, 239 U.S. 394, 36 S. Ct. 143, 60 L. Ed. 348 (1915) (87 1/2 % diminution in value); cf. *Eastlake v. Forest City Enterprises, Inc.*, 426 U.S., at 674 n. 8, 96 S. Ct., at 2362 n. 8, and that the "taking" issue in these contexts is resolved by focusing on the uses the regulations permit. See also *Goldblatt v. Hempstead, supra*. Appellants, moreover, also do not dispute that a showing of diminution in property value would not establish a taking if the restriction had been imposed as a result of historic-district legislation, see generally *Maher v. New Orleans*, 516 F.2d 1051 (5th Cir. 1975), but appellants argue that New York City's regulation of individual landmarks is fundamentally different from zoning or from historic-district legislation because the controls imposed by New York City's law apply only to individuals who own selected properties.

Stated baldly, appellants' position appears to be that the only means of ensuring that selected owners are not singled out to endure financial hardship for no reason is to hold that any restriction imposed on individual landmarks pursuant to the New York City scheme is a "taking" requiring the payment of "just compensation." Agreement with this argument would, of course, invalidate not just New York City's law, but all comparable landmark legislation in the Nation. We find no merit in it.

It is true, as appellants emphasize, that both historic-district legislation and zoning laws regulate all properties within given physical communities whereas landmark laws apply only to selected parcels. But, contrary to appellants' suggestions, landmark laws are not like discriminatory, or "reverse spot," zoning: that is, a

---

27. These cases dispose of any contention that might be based on *Pennsylvania Coal Co. v. Mahon,* 260 U.S. 393, 43 S. Ct. 158, 67 L. Ed. 322 (1922), that full use of air rights is so bound up with the investment-backed expectations of appellants that governmental deprivation of these rights invariably — *i.e.,* irrespective of the impact of the restriction on the value of the parcel as a whole — constitutes a "taking." Similarly, *Welch, Goldblatt,* and *Gorieb* illustrate the fallacy of appellants' related contention that a "taking" must be found to have occurred whenever the land-use restriction may be characterized as imposing a "servitude" on the claimant's parcel.

land-use decision which arbitrarily singles out a particular parcel for different, less favorable treatment than the neighboring ones. In contrast to discriminatory zoning, which is the antithesis of land-use control as part of some comprehensive plan, the New York City law embodies a comprehensive plan to preserve structures of historic or aesthetic interest wherever they might be found in the city, and as noted, over 400 landmarks and 31 historic districts have been designated pursuant to this plan.

Equally without merit is the related argument that the decision to designate a structure as a landmark "is inevitably arbitrary or at least subjective, because it is basically a matter of taste," thus unavoidably singling out individual landowners for disparate and unfair treatment. The argument has a particularly hollow ring in this case. For appellants not only did not seek judicial review of either the designation or of the denials of the certificates of appropriateness and of no exterior effect, but do not even now suggest that the Commission's decisions concerning the Terminal were in any sense arbitrary or unprincipled. But, in any event, a landmark owner has a right to judicial review of any Commission decision, and, quite simply, there is no basis whatsoever for a conclusion that courts will have any greater difficulty identifying arbitrary or discriminatory action in the context of landmark regulation than in the context of classic zoning or indeed in any other context.[29]

Next, appellants observe that New York City's law differs from zoning laws and historic-district ordinances in that the Landmarks Law does not impose identical or similar restrictions on all structures located in particular physical communities. It follows, they argue, that New York City's law is inherently incapable of producing the fair and equitable distribution of benefits and burdens of governmental action which is characteristic of zoning laws and historic-district legislation and which they maintain is a constitutional requirement if "just compensation" is not to be afforded. It is, of course, true that the Landmarks Law has a more severe impact on some landowners than on others, but that in itself does not mean that the law effects a "taking." Legislation designed to promote the general welfare commonly burdens some more than others. The owners of the brickyard in *Hadacheck*, of the cedar trees in *Miller v. Schoene*, and of the gravel and sand mine in *Goldblatt v. Hempstead*, were uniquely burdened by the legislation sustained in those cases.[30] Simi-

---

29. When a property owner challenges the application of a zoning ordinance to his property, the judicial inquiry focuses upon whether the challenged restriction can reasonably be deemed to promote the objectives of the community land-use plan, and will include consideration of the treatment of similar parcels. See generally *Nectow v. Cambridge*, 277 U.S. 183, 48 S. Ct. 447, 72 L. Ed. 842 (1928). When a property owner challenges a landmark designation or restriction as arbitrary or discriminatory, a similar inquiry presumably will occur.

30. Appellants attempt to distinguish these cases on the ground that, in each, government was prohibiting a "noxious" use of land and that in the present case, in contrast, appellants' proposed construction above the Terminal would be beneficial. We observe that the uses in issue in *Hadacheck*, *Miller*, and *Goldblatt* were perfectly lawful in themselves. They involved no "blameworthiness,... moral wrongdoing or conscious act of dangerous risk-taking which induce[d society] to shift the cost to a pa[rt]icular individual." Sax, *Takings and the Police Power*, 74 Yale L.J. 36, 50

larly, zoning laws often affect some property owners more severely than others but have not been held to be invalid on that account. For example, the property owner in *Euclid* who wished to use its property for industrial purposes was affected far more severely by the ordinance than its neighbors who wished to use their land for residences.

In any event, appellants' repeated suggestions that they are solely burdened and unbenefited is factually inaccurate. This contention overlooks the fact that the New York City law applies to vast numbers of structures in the city in addition to the Terminal—all the structures contained in the 31 historic districts and over 400 individual landmarks, many of which are close to the Terminal.[31] Unless we are to reject the judgment of the New York City Council that the preservation of landmarks benefits all New York citizens and all structures, both economically and by improving the quality of life in the city as a whole—which we are unwilling to do—we cannot conclude that the owners of the Terminal have in no sense been benefited by the Landmarks Law. Doubtless appellants believe they are more burdened than benefited by the law, but that must have been true, too, of the property owners in *Miller, Hadacheck, Euclid,* and *Goldblatt.*[32]

Appellants' final broad-based attack would have us treat the law as an instance, like that in *United States v. Causby,* in which government, acting in an enterprise capacity, has appropriated part of their property for some strictly governmental purpose. Apart from the fact that *Causby* was a case of invasion of airspace that destroyed the use of the farm beneath and this New York City law has in nowise impaired the present use of the Terminal, the Landmarks Law neither exploits appellants' parcel for city purposes nor facilitates nor arises from any entrepreneurial operations of the city. The situation is not remotely like that in *Causby* where the airspace above the property was in the flight pattern for military aircraft. The Landmarks Law's effect is simply to prohibit appellants or anyone else from occupying

---

(1964). These cases are better understood as resting not on any supposed "noxious" quality of the prohibited uses but rather on the ground that the restrictions were reasonably related to the implementation of a policy—not unlike historic preservation—expected to produce a widespread public benefit and applicable to all similarly situated property.

Nor, correlatively, can it be asserted that the destruction or fundamental alteration of a historic landmark is not harmful. The suggestion that the beneficial quality of appellants' proposed construction is established by the fact that the construction would have been consistent with applicable zoning laws ignores the development in sensibilities and ideals reflected in landmark legislation like New York City's. Cf. *West Bros. Brick Co. v. Alexandria,* 169 Va. 271, 282–283, 192 S.E. 881, 885–886, *appeal dismissed for want of a substantial federal question,* 302 U.S. 658, 58 S. Ct. 369, 82 L. Ed. 508 (1937).

31. There are some 53 designated landmarks and 5 historic districts or scenic landmarks in Manhattan between 14th and 59th Streets. See Landmarks Preservation Commission, Landmarks and Historic Districts (1977).

32. It is, of course, true that the fact the duties imposed by zoning and historic-district legislation apply throughout particular physical communities provides assurances against arbitrariness, but the applicability of the Landmarks Law to a large number of parcels in the city, in our view, provides comparable, if not identical, assurances.

portions of the airspace above the Terminal, while permitting appellants to use the remainder of the parcel in a gainful fashion. This is no more an appropriation of property by government for its own uses than is a zoning law prohibiting, for "aesthetic" reasons, two or more adult theaters within a specified area, see *Young v. American Mini Theatres, Inc.*, 427 U.S. 50, 96 S. Ct. 2440, 49 L. Ed. 2d 310 (1976), or a safety regulation prohibiting excavations below a certain level. See *Goldblatt v. Hempstead.*

## C.

Rejection of appellants' broad arguments is not, however, the end of our inquiry, for all we thus far have established is that the New York City law is not rendered invalid by its failure to provide "just compensation" whenever a landmark owner is restricted in the exploitation of property interests, such as air rights, to a greater extent than provided for under applicable zoning laws. We now must consider whether the interference with appellants' property is of such a magnitude that "there must be an exercise of eminent domain and compensation to sustain [it]." *Pennsylvania Coal Co. v. Mahon*, 260 U.S., at 413, 43 S. Ct., at 159. That inquiry may be narrowed to the question of the severity of the impact of the law on appellants' parcel, and its resolution in turn requires a careful assessment of the impact of the regulation on the Terminal site.

Unlike the governmental acts in *Goldblatt*, *Miller*, *Causby*, *Griggs*, and *Hadacheck*, the New York City law does not interfere in any way with the present uses of the Terminal. Its designation as a landmark not only permits but contemplates that appellants may continue to use the property precisely as it has been used for the past 65 years: as a railroad terminal containing office space and concessions. So the law does not interfere with what must be regarded as Penn Central's primary expectation concerning the use of the parcel. More importantly, on this record, we must regard the New York City law as permitting Penn Central not only to profit from the Terminal but also to obtain a "reasonable return" on its investment.

Appellants, moreover, exaggerate the effect of the law on their ability to make use of the air rights above the Terminal in two respects.[33] First, it simply cannot be maintained, on this record, that appellants have been prohibited from occupying *any* portion of the airspace above the Terminal. While the Commission's actions in denying applications to construct an office building in excess of 50 stories above the Terminal may indicate that it will refuse to issue a certificate of appropriateness for any comparably sized structure, nothing the Commission has said or done suggests an intention to prohibit *any* construction above the Terminal. The Commission's report emphasized that whether any construction would be allowed depended upon whether the proposed addition "would harmonize in scale, material and character with [the Terminal]." Since appellants have not sought approval for the construction

---

33. Appellants, of course, argue at length that the transferable development rights, while valuable, do not constitute "just compensation." Brief for Appellants 36–43.

of a smaller structure, we do not know that appellants will be denied any use of any portion of the airspace above the Terminal.[34]

Second, to the extent appellants have been denied the right to build above the Terminal, it is not literally accurate to say that they have been denied *all* use of even those pre-existing air rights. Their ability to use these rights has not been abrogated; they are made transferable to at least eight parcels in the vicinity of the Terminal, one or two of which have been found suitable for the construction of new office buildings. Although appellants and others have argued that New York City's transferable development-rights program is far from ideal, the New York courts here supportably found that, at least in the case of the Terminal, the rights afforded are valuable. While these rights may well not have constituted "just compensation" if a "taking" had occurred, the rights nevertheless undoubtedly mitigate whatever financial burdens the law has imposed on appellants and, for that reason, are to be taken into account in considering the impact of regulation. Cf. *Goldblatt v. Hempstead*, 369 U.S., at 594 n. 3, 82 S. Ct., at 990 n. 3.

On this record, we conclude that the application of New York City's Landmarks Law has not effected a "taking" of appellants' property. The restrictions imposed are substantially related to the promotion of the general welfare and not only permit reasonable beneficial use of the landmark site but also afford appellants opportunities further to enhance not only the Terminal site proper but also other properties.[36]

Affirmed.

Rehnquist, Justice. (dissenting). Of the over one million buildings and structures in the city of New York, appellees have singled out 400 for designation as official landmarks.[1] The owner of a building might initially be pleased that his property has been chosen by a distinguished committee of architects, historians, and city

---

34. Counsel for appellants admitted at oral argument that the Commission has not suggested that it would not, for example, approve a 20-story office tower along the lines of that which was part of the original plan for the Terminal. See Tr. of Oral Arg. 19.

36. We emphasize that our holding today is on the present record, which in turn is based on Penn Central's present ability to use the Terminal for its intended purposes and in a gainful fashion. The city conceded at oral argument that if appellants can demonstrate at some point in the future that circumstances have so changed that the Terminal ceases to be "economically viable," appellants may obtain relief. See Tr. of Oral Arg. 42–43.

1. A large percentage of the designated landmarks are public structures (such as the Brooklyn Bridge, City Hall, the Statute of Liberty and the Municipal Asphalt Plant) and thus do not raise Fifth Amendment taking questions. See Landmarks Preservation Commission of the City of New York, Landmarks and Historic Districts (1977 and Jan. 10, 1978, Supplement). Although the Court refers to the New York ordinance as a *comprehensive* program to preserve *historic* landmarks, *ante*, at 2651, the ordinance is not limited to historic buildings and gives little guidance to the Landmarks Preservation Commission in its selection of landmark sites. Section 207-1.0(n) of the Landmarks Preservation Law, as set forth in N.Y.C. Admin. Code, ch. 8-A (1976), requires only that the selected landmark be at least 30 years old and possess "a special character or special historical or aesthetic interest or value as part of the development, heritage or cultural characteristics of the city, state or nation."

planners for such a singular distinction. But he may well discover, as appellant Penn Central Transportation Co. did here, that the landmark designation imposes upon him a substantial cost, with little or no offsetting benefit except for the honor of the designation. The question in this case is whether the cost associated with the city of New York's desire to preserve a limited number of "landmarks" within its borders must be borne by all of its taxpayers or whether it can instead be imposed entirely on the owners of the individual properties.

Only in the most superficial sense of the word can this case be said to involve "zoning."[2] Typical zoning restrictions may, it is true, so limit the prospective uses of a piece of property as to diminish the value of that property in the abstract because it may not be used for the forbidden purposes. But any such abstract decrease in value will more than likely be at least partially offset by an increase in value which flows from similar restrictions as to use on neighboring properties. All property owners in a designated area are placed under the same restrictions, not only for the benefit of the municipality as a whole but also for the common benefit of one another. In the words of Mr. Justice Holmes, speaking for the Court in *Pennsylvania Coal Co. v. Mahon*, 260 U.S. 393, 415, 43 S. Ct. 158, 160, 67 L. Ed. 322 (1922), there is "an average reciprocity of advantage."

Where a relatively few individual buildings, all separated from one another, are singled out and treated differently from surrounding buildings, no such reciprocity exists. The cost to the property owner which results from the imposition of restrictions applicable only to his property and not that of his neighbors may be substantial — in this case, several million dollars — with no comparable reciprocal benefits. And the cost associated with landmark legislation is likely to be of a completely different order of magnitude than that which results from the imposition of normal zoning restrictions. Unlike the regime affected by the latter, the landowner is not simply prohibited from using his property for certain purposes, while allowed to use it for all other purposes. Under the historic-landmark preservation scheme adopted by New York, the property owner is under an affirmative duty to *preserve* his property *as a landmark* at his own expense. To suggest that because traditional zoning results in some limitation of use of the property zoned, the New York City

---

2. Even the New York Court of Appeals conceded that "[t]his is not a zoning case.... Zoning restrictions operate to advance a comprehensive community plan for the common good. Each property owner in the zone is both benefited and restricted from exploitation, presumably without discrimination, except for permitted continuing nonconforming uses. The restrictions may be designed to maintain the general character of the area, or to assure orderly development, objectives inuring to the benefit of all, which property owners acting individually would find difficult or impossible to achieve...." Nor does this case involve landmark regulation of a historic district.... [In historic districting, as in traditional zoning,] owners although burdened by the restrictions also benefit, to some extent, from the furtherance of a general community plan." "Restrictions on alteration of individual landmarks are not designed to further a general community plan. Landmark restrictions are designed to prevent alteration or demolition of a single piece of property. To this extent, such restrictions resemble 'discriminatory' zoning restrictions, properly condemned...."42 N.Y.2d 324, 329–330, 397 N.Y.S.2d 914, 917–918, 366 N.E.2d 1271, 1274 (1977).

landmark preservation scheme should likewise be upheld, represents the ultimate in treating as alike things which are different. The rubric of "zoning" has not yet sufficed to avoid the well-established proposition that the Fifth Amendment bars the "Government from forcing some people alone to bear public burdens which, in all fairness and justice, should be borne by the public as a whole." *Armstrong v. United States*, 364 U.S. 40, 49, 80 S. Ct. 1563, 1569, 4 L. Ed. 2d 1554 (1960).

In August 1967, Grand Central Terminal was designated a landmark over the objections of its owner Penn Central. Immediately upon this designation, Penn Central, like all owners of a landmark site, was placed under an affirmative duty, backed by criminal fines and penalties, to keep "exterior portions" of the landmark "in good repair." Even more burdensome, however, were the strict limitations that were thereupon imposed on Penn Central's use of its property. At the time Grand Central was designated a landmark, Penn Central was in a precarious financial condition. In an effort to increase its sources of revenue, Penn Central had entered into a lease agreement with appellant UGP Properties, Inc., under which UGP would construct and operate a multistory office building cantilevered above the Terminal building. During the period of construction, UGP would pay Penn Central $1 million per year. Upon completion, UGP would rent the building for 50 years, with an option for another 25 years, at a guaranteed *minimum* rental of $3 million per year. The record is clear that the proposed office building was in full compliance with all New York zoning laws and height limitations. Under the Landmarks Preservation Law, however, appellants could not construct the proposed office building unless appellee Landmarks Preservation Commission issued either a "Certificate of No Exterior Effect" or a "Certificate of Appropriateness." Although appellants' architectural plan would have preserved the facade of the Terminal, the Landmarks Preservation Commission has refused to approve the construction.

## I.

The Fifth Amendment provides in part: "nor shall private property be taken for public use, without just compensation."[4] In a very literal sense, the actions of appellees violated this constitutional prohibition. Before the city of New York declared Grand Central Terminal to be a landmark, Penn Central could have used its "air rights" over the Terminal to build a multistory office building, at an apparent value of several million dollars per year. Today, the Terminal cannot be modified in *any* form, including the erection of additional stories, without the permission of the Landmark Preservation Commission, a permission which appellants, despite good-faith attempts, have so far been unable to obtain. Because the Taking Clause

---

4. The Court's opinion touches base with, or at least attempts to touch base with, most of the major eminent domain cases decided by this Court. Its use of them, however, is anything but meticulous. In citing to *United States v. Caltex, Inc.*, 344 U.S. 149, 156, 73 S. Ct. 200, 97 L. Ed. 157 (1952), for example, *ante*, at 2659, the only language remotely applicable to eminent domain is stated in terms of "the destruction of respondents' terminals by a trained team of engineers in the face of their impending seizure by the enemy." 344 U.S., at 156, 73 S. Ct., at 203.

of the Fifth Amendment has not always been read literally, however, the constitutionality of appellees' actions requires a closer scrutiny of this Court's interpretation of the three key words in the Taking Clause — "property," "taken," and "just compensation."[5]

### A.

Appellees do not dispute that valuable property rights have been destroyed. And the Court has frequently emphasized that the term "property" as used in the Taking Clause includes the entire "group of rights inhering in the citizen's [ownership]." *United States v. General Motors Corp.*, 323 U.S. 373, 65 S. Ct. 357, 89 L. Ed. 311 (1945). . . .

While neighboring landowners are free to use their land and "air rights" in any way consistent with the broad boundaries of New York zoning, Penn Central, absent the permission of appellees, must forever maintain its property in its present state.[6] The property has been thus subjected to a nonconsensual servitude not borne by any neighboring or similar properties.[8]

### B.

Appellees have thus destroyed — in a literal sense, "taken" — substantial property rights of Penn Central. While the term "taken" might have been narrowly interpreted to include only physical seizures of property rights, "the construction of the phrase has not been so narrow. . . .

### 1.

As early as 1887, the Court recognized that the government can prevent a property owner from using his property to injure others without having to compensate the owner for the value of the forbidden use. . . .

Thus, there is no "taking" where a city prohibits the operation of a brickyard within a residential area, see *Hadacheck v. Sebastian*, 239 U.S. 394, 36 S. Ct. 143,

---

5. In particular, Penn Central cannot increase the height of the Terminal. This Court has previously held that the "air rights" over an area of land are "property" for purposes of the Fifth Amendment. See *United States v. Causby*, 328 U.S. 256, 66 S. Ct. 1062, 90 L. Ed. 1206 (1946) ("air rights" taken by low-flying airplanes); *Griggs v. Allegheny County*, 369 U.S. 84, 82 S. Ct. 531, 7 L. Ed. 2d 585 (1962) (same); *Portsmouth Harbor Land & Hotel Co. v. United States*, 260 U.S. 327, 43 S. Ct. 135, 67 L. Ed. 287 (1922) (firing of projectiles over summer resort can constitute taking). See also *Butler v. Frontier Telephone Co.*, 186 N.Y. 486, 79 N.E. 716 (1906) (stringing of telephone wire across property constitutes a taking).

6. It is, of course, irrelevant that appellees interfered with or destroyed property rights that Penn Central had not yet physically used. The Fifth Amendment must be applied with "reference to the uses for which the property is suitable, having regard to the existing business or wants of the community, *or such as may be reasonably expected in the immediate future*." *Boom Co. v. Patterson*, 98 U.S. 403, 408, 25 L. Ed. 206 (1879) (emphasis added).

8. Each of the cases cited by the Court for the proposition that legislation which severely affects some landowners but not others does not effect a "taking" involved noxious uses of property. See *Hadacheck; Miller v. Schoene*, 276 U.S. 272, 48 S. Ct. 246, 72 L. Ed. 568 (1928); *Goldblatt*. See *ante*, at 2660–2661, 2664.

60 L. Ed. 348 (1915), or forbids excavation for sand and gravel below the water line, see *Goldblatt v. Hempstead*, 369 U.S. 590, 82 S. Ct. 987, 8 L. Ed. 2d 130 (1962). Nor is it relevant, where the government is merely prohibiting a noxious use of property, that the government would seem to be singling out a particular property owner. *Hadacheck, supra*, at 413, 36 S. Ct., at 146.[10]

The nuisance exception to the taking guarantee is not coterminous with the police power itself. The question is whether the forbidden use is dangerous to the safety, health, or welfare of others. . . .

Appellees are not prohibiting a nuisance. The record is clear that the proposed addition to the Grand Central Terminal would be in full compliance with zoning, height limitations, and other health and safety requirements. Instead, appellees are seeking to preserve what they believe to be an outstanding example of beaux-arts architecture. Penn Central is prevented from further developing its property basically because *too good* a job was done in designing and building it. The city of New York, because of its unadorned admiration for the design, has decided that the owners of the building must preserve it unchanged for the benefit of sightseeing New Yorkers and tourists.

Unlike land-use regulations, appellees' actions do not merely *prohibit* Penn Central from using its property in a narrow set of noxious ways. Instead, appellees have placed an *affirmative* duty on Penn Central to maintain the Terminal in its present state and in "good repair." Appellants are not free to use their property as they see fit within broad outer boundaries but must strictly adhere to their past use except where appellees conclude that alternative uses would not detract from the landmark. . . .

2.

Even where the government prohibits a noninjurious use, the Court has ruled that a taking does not take place if the prohibition applies over a broad cross section of land and thereby "secure[s] an average reciprocity of advantage." *Pennsylvania Coal Co. v. Mahon*, 260 U.S., at 415, 43 S. Ct., at 160.[11] It is for this reason that zoning

---

10. Appellants concede that the preservation of buildings of historical or aesthetic importance is a permissible objective of state action. Brief for Appellants 12. *Cf. Berman v. Parker*, 348 U.S. 26, 75 S. Ct. 98, 99 L. Ed. 27 (1954); *United States v. Gettysburg Electric R. Co.*, 160 U.S. 668, 16 S. Ct. 427, 40 L. Ed. 576 (1896). For the reasons noted in the text, historic *zoning*, as has been undertaken by cities, such as New Orleans, may well not require compensation under the Fifth Amendment.

11. "It is true that the police power embraces regulations designed to promote public convenience or the general welfare, and not merely those in the interest of public health, safety and morals. . . . But when particular individuals are singled out to bear the cost of advancing the public convenience, that imposition must bear some reasonable relation to the evils to be eradicated or the advantages to be secured. . . . While moneys raised by general taxation may constitutionally be applied to purposes from which the individual taxed may receive no benefit, and indeed, suffer serious detriment, . . . so-called assessments for public improvements laid upon particular property owners are ordinarily constitutional only if based on benefits received by them.

does not constitute a "taking." While zoning at times reduces *individual* property values, the burden is shared relatively evenly and it is reasonable to conclude that on the whole an individual who is harmed by one aspect of the zoning will be benefited by another.

Here, however, a multimillion dollar loss has been imposed on appellants; it is uniquely felt and is not offset by any benefits flowing from the preservation of some 400 other "landmarks" in New York City. Appellees have imposed a substantial cost on less than one one-tenth of one percent of the buildings in New York City for the general benefit of all its people. It is exactly this imposition of general costs on a few individuals at which the "taking" protection is directed. . . .

As Mr. Justice Holmes pointed out in *Pennsylvania Coal Co. v. Mahon*, "the question at bottom" in an eminent domain case "is upon whom the loss of the changes desired should fall." 260 U.S., at 416, 43 S. Ct., at 160. The benefits that appellees believe will flow from preservation of the Grand Central Terminal will accrue to all the citizens of New York City. There is no reason to believe that appellants will enjoy a substantially greater share of these benefits. If the cost of preserving Grand Central Terminal were spread evenly across the entire population of the city of New York, the burden per person would be in cents per year — a minor cost appellees would surely concede for the benefit accrued. Instead, however, appellees would impose the entire cost of several million dollars per year on Penn Central. But it is precisely this sort of discrimination that the Fifth Amendment prohibits.[12]

. . . .

## C.

Appellees, apparently recognizing that the constraints imposed on a landmark site constitute a taking for Fifth Amendment purposes, do not leave the property owner empty-handed. As the Court notes, *ante*, the property owner may theoretically "transfer" his previous right to develop the landmark property to adjacent properties if they are under his control. Appellees have coined this system "Transfer Development Rights," or TDR's.

Of all the terms used in the Taking Clause, "just compensation" has the strictest meaning. The Fifth Amendment does not allow simply an approximate compensation but requires "a full and perfect equivalent for the property taken." *Monongahela Navigation Co. v. United States*, 148 U.S., at 326, 13 S. Ct., at 626.

. . . The fact that *appellees* may believe that TDR's provide full compensation is irrelevant.

---

12. The fact that the Landmarks Preservation Commission may have allowed additions to a relatively few landmarks is of no comfort to appellants. *Ante*, at 2656 n. 18. Nor is it of any comfort that the Commission refuses to allow appellants to construct any additional stories because of their belief that such construction would not be aesthetic. *Ante*, at 2656.

"The legislature may determine what private property is needed for public purposes — that is a question of a political and legislative character; but when the taking has been ordered, then the question of compensation is judicial. It does not rest with the public, taking the property, through Congress or the legislature, its representative, to say what compensation shall be paid, or even what shall be the rule of compensation. The Constitution has declared that just compensation shall be paid, and the ascertainment of that is a judicial inquiry." *Monongahela Navigation Co. v. United States, supra*, 148 U.S., at 327, 13 S. Ct., at 626.

Appellees contend that, even if they have "taken" appellants' property, TDR's constitute "just compensation." Appellants, of course, argue that TDR's are highly imperfect compensation. Because the lower courts held that there was no "taking," they did not have to reach the question of whether or not just compensation has already been awarded.

## II.

Over 50 years ago, Mr. Justice Holmes, speaking for the Court, warned that the courts were "in danger of forgetting that a strong public desire to improve the public condition is not enough to warrant achieving the desire by a shorter cut than the constitutional way of paying for the change." *Pennsylvania Coal Co. v. Mahon*, 260 U.S., at 416, 43 S. Ct., at 160. The Court's opinion in this case demonstrates that the danger thus foreseen has not abated. The city of New York is in a precarious financial state, and some may believe that the costs of landmark preservation will be more easily borne by corporations such as Penn Central than the overburdened individual taxpayers of New York. But these concerns do not allow us to ignore past precedents construing the Eminent Domain Clause to the end that the desire to improve the public condition is, indeed, achieved by a shorter cut than the constitutional way of paying for the change.

## *Questions for Consideration*

1) What was Penn Central seeking to do with its property?

2) Did Penn Central's plan involve a permitted use? Were they going to develop the project in compliance with the zoning code?

3) New York City passed a landmark preservation act. How is this type of act similar and different from a zoning regulation?

4) On what authority did New York City pass the landmark legislation?

5) What provisions does the landmark law include as a way of protecting a property owner's procedural due process rights?

6) The landmark law restricted Penn Central's development plans. Did it also impose any affirmative obligations?

7) Considering all of the facts, do you think Penn Central was afforded due process?

8) Was Penn Central denied an opportunity to make significantly more money from its property because of the landmark law?

9) Was Penn Central successful in its takings claim?

10) How does a takings claim relate to eminent domain?

11) What was the role or purpose of the transferable development rights (TDRs) in this case?

12) The *Penn Central* case maps out a number of important factors to consider when evaluating a takings case. As between the majority opinion and the dissent; how are the following factors discussed and handled:

   a) The character of the government action;

   b) The diminution in value of the property;

   c) The property owner's reasonable investment backed expectations;

   d) The whole parcel;

   e) The average reciprocity of advantage; and,

   f) The consideration of the regulation in terms of its focus on preventing a harm as opposed to providing a benefit (the harm-benefit test).

13) If air rights are a property interest, are TDRs also property, or something else?

14) Are TDRs valuable in the absence of a well-functioning market in TDRs, with many sellers, buyers, and receiving property locations?

## *Takeaway*

- The first five factors identified in question 12 above remain important factors to discuss in contemporary takings cases. While the harm-benefit test has been criticized, it remains in the mix, and therefore all six factors should be discussed and balanced when doing a takings analysis.

- As observed in *Penn Central* and in the earlier case of *Euclid*, the value of one's property can be greatly diminished by regulation and still not rise to the level of being an unconstitutional taking of private property or a violation of due process.

- *Penn Central* provides us with six key factors to consider in evaluating a takings claim, but we still lack a clear jurisprudence of takings law, since it is often difficult to anticipate how the courts will weigh the various factors. Each case proceeds on its own facts, and the finding of a regulatory taking is a case-by-case determination.

- The whole parcel test mentioned in *Penn Central* is more complex than it may seem. A more current discussion of the whole parcel test can be found in *Murr v. Wisconsin*, 582 U.S. ___, 137 S. Ct. 1933 (2017).

## Murr v. Wisconsin

### 137 S. Ct. 1933 (2017)

KENNEDY, Justice. The classic example of a property taking by the government is when the property has been occupied or otherwise seized. In the case now before the Court, petitioners contend that governmental entities took their real property—an undeveloped residential lot—not by some physical occupation but instead by enacting burdensome regulations that forbid its improvement or separate sale because it is classified as substandard in size. The relevant governmental entities are the respondents.

Against the background justifications for the challenged restrictions, respondents contend there is no regulatory taking because petitioners own an adjacent lot. The regulations, in effecting a merger of the property, permit the continued residential use of the property including for a single improvement to extend over both lots. This retained right of the landowner, respondents urge, is of sufficient offsetting value that the regulation is not severe enough to be a regulatory taking. To resolve the issue whether the landowners can insist on confining the analysis just to the lot in question, without regard to their ownership of the adjacent lot, it is necessary to discuss the background principles that define regulatory takings.

### I.

### A.

The St. Croix River originates in northwest Wisconsin and flows approximately 170 miles until it joins the Mississippi River, forming the boundary between Minnesota and Wisconsin for much of its length. The lower portion of the river slows and widens to create a natural water area known as Lake St. Croix. Tourists and residents of the region have long extolled the picturesque grandeur of the river and surrounding area.....

Under the Wild and Scenic Rivers Act, the river was designated, by 1972, for federal protection.... The law required the States of Wisconsin and Minnesota to develop "a management and development program" for the river area.... In compliance, Wisconsin authorized the State Department of Natural Resources to promulgate rules limiting development in order to "guarantee the protection of the wild, scenic and recreational qualities of the river for present and future generations." ...

Petitioners are two sisters and two brothers in the Murr family. Petitioners' parents arranged for them to receive ownership of two lots the family used for recreation along the Lower St. Croix River in the town of Troy, Wisconsin. The lots are adjacent, but the parents purchased them separately, put the title of one in the name of the family business, and later arranged for transfer of the two lots, on different dates, to petitioners. The lots, which are referred to in this litigation as Lots E and F, are described in more detail below.

For the area where petitioners' property is located, the Wisconsin rules prevent the use of lots as separate building sites unless they have at least one acre of land suitable for development. . . . A grandfather clause relaxes this restriction for sub-standard lots which were "in separate ownership from abutting lands" on January 1, 1976, the effective date of the regulation. The clause permits the use of qualifying lots as separate building sites. The rules also include a merger provision, however, which provides that adjacent lots under common ownership may not be "sold or developed as separate lots" if they do not meet the size requirement. . . . The Wisconsin rules require localities to adopt parallel provisions, . . . so the St. Croix County zoning ordinance contains identical restrictions. . . . The Wisconsin rules also authorize the local zoning authority to grant variances from the regulations where enforcement would create "unnecessary hardship." . . .

## B.

Petitioners' parents purchased Lot F in 1960 and built a small recreational cabin on it. In 1961, they transferred title to Lot F to the family plumbing company. In 1963, they purchased neighboring Lot E, which they held in their own names.

The lots have the same topography. A steep bluff cuts through the middle of each, with level land suitable for development above the bluff and next to the water below it. The line dividing Lot E from Lot F runs from the riverfront to the far end of the property, crossing the blufftop along the way. Lot E has approximately 60 feet of river frontage, and Lot F has approximately 100 feet. Though each lot is approximately 1.25 acres in size, because of the waterline and the steep bank they each have less than one acre of land suitable for development. Even when combined, the lots' buildable land area is only 0.98 acres due to the steep terrain.

The lots remained under separate ownership, with Lot F owned by the plumbing company and Lot E owned by petitioners' parents, until transfers to petitioners. Lot F was conveyed to them in 1994, and Lot E was conveyed to them in 1995. . . .

A decade later, petitioners became interested in moving the cabin on Lot F to a different portion of the lot and selling Lot E to fund the project. The unification of the lots under common ownership, however, had implicated the state and local rules barring their separate sale or development. Petitioners then sought variances from the St. Croix County Board of Adjustment to enable their building and improve-ment plan, including a variance to allow the separate sale or use of the lots. The Board denied the requests, and the state courts affirmed in relevant part. In particu-lar, the Wisconsin Court of Appeals agreed with the Board's interpretation that the local ordinance "effectively merged" Lots E and F, so petitioners "could only sell or build on the single larger lot." . . .

Petitioners filed the present action in state court, alleging that the state and county regulations worked a regulatory taking by depriving them of "all, or practi-cally all, of the use of Lot E because the lot cannot be sold or developed as a separate lot." . . . The parties each submitted appraisal numbers to the trial court. Respon-dents' appraisal included values of $698,300 for the lots together as regulated; $771,000 for the lots as two distinct buildable properties; and $373,000 for Lot F as a single lot with improvements. . . . Petitioners' appraisal included an unrebutted, estimated value of $40,000 for Lot E as an undevelopable lot, based on the counter-factual assumption that it could be sold as a separate property.

The Circuit Court of St. Croix County granted summary judgment to the State, explaining that petitioners retained "several available options for the use and enjoyment of their property." . . . For example, they could preserve the existing cabin, relocate the cabin, or eliminate the cabin and build a new residence on Lot E, on Lot F, or across both lots. The court also found petitioners had not been deprived of all economic value of their property. Considering the valuation of the property as a single lot versus two separate lots, the court found the market value of the property was not significantly affected by the regulations because the decrease in value was less than 10 percent.

The Wisconsin Court of Appeals affirmed. The court explained that the regulatory takings inquiry required it to "'first determine what, precisely, is the property at issue.'" . . . Relying on Wisconsin Supreme Court precedent in *Zealy v. Waukesha*, 201 Wis.2d 365, 548 N.W.2d 528 (1996), the Court of Appeals rejected petitioners' request to analyze the effect of the regulations on Lot E only. Instead, the court held the takings analysis "properly focused" on the regulations' effect "on the Murrs' property as a whole" — that is, Lots E and F together.

Using this framework, the Court of Appeals concluded the merger regulations did not effect a taking. In particular, the court explained that petitioners could not reasonably have expected to use the lots separately because they were "'charged with knowledge of the existing zoning laws'" when they acquired the property. . . . Thus, "even if [petitioners] did intend to develop or sell Lot E separately, that expectation of separate treatment became unreasonable when they chose to acquire Lot E in 1995, after their having acquired Lot F in 1994." . . . The court also discounted the severity of the economic impact on petitioners' property, recognizing the Circuit Court's conclusion that the regulations diminished the property's combined value by less than 10 percent. The Supreme Court of Wisconsin denied discretionary review. This Court granted certiorari . . .

## II.

### A.

The Takings Clause of the Fifth Amendment provides that private property shall not "be taken for public use, without just compensation." The Clause is made applicable to the States through the Fourteenth Amendment. *Chicago, B. & Q.R. Co. v. Chicago*, 166 U.S. 226 (1897). As this Court has recognized, the plain language of the Takings Clause "requires the payment of compensation whenever the government acquires private property for a public purpose," see *Tahoe-Sierra Preservation Council, Inc. v. Tahoe Regional Planning Agency*, 535 U.S. 302, 321 (2002), but it does not address in specific terms the imposition of regulatory burdens on private property. Indeed, "[p]rior to Justice Holmes's exposition in *Pennsylvania Coal Co. v. Mahon*, 260 U.S. 393 (1922), it was generally thought that the Takings Clause reached only a direct appropriation of property, or the functional equivalent of a practical ouster of the owner's possession," like the permanent flooding of property. *Lucas v. South Carolina Coastal Council*, 505 U.S. 1003, 1014 (1992) (citation, brackets, and internal quotation marks omitted); . . . see also *Loretto v. Teleprompter Manhattan CATV Corp.*, 458 U.S. 419, 427 (1982). *Mahon*, however, initiated this Court's regulatory takings jurisprudence, declaring that "while property may be regulated to a certain extent, if regulation goes too far it will be recognized as a taking." 260 U.S., at 415. A regulation, then, can be so burdensome as to become a taking, yet the *Mahon* Court did not formulate more detailed guidance for determining when this limit is reached.

In the near century since *Mahon*, the Court for the most part has refrained from elaborating this principle through definitive rules. This area of the law has been characterized by "ad hoc, factual inquiries, designed to allow careful examination and weighing of all the relevant circumstances." *Tahoe-Sierra, supra*, at 322, (citation and internal quotation marks omitted). The Court has, however, stated two guidelines relevant here for determining when government regulation is so onerous that it constitutes a taking. First, "with certain qualifications . . . a regulation which 'denies all economically beneficial or productive use of land' will require compensation under the Takings Clause." *Palazzolo v. Rhode Island*, 533 U.S. 606, 617 (2001) (quoting *Lucas, supra*, at 1015). Second, when a regulation impedes the use of property without depriving the owner of all economically beneficial use, a taking still may be found based on "a complex of factors," including (1) the economic impact of the regulation on the claimant; (2) the extent to which the regulation has interfered with distinct investment-backed expectations; and (3) the character of the governmental action. *Palazzolo, supra*, at 617 (citing *Penn Central Transp. Co. v. New York City*, 438 U.S. 104, 124 (1978)).

. By declaring that the denial of all economically beneficial use of land constitutes a regulatory taking, *Lucas* stated what it called a "categorical" rule. See 505 U.S., at 1015. Even in *Lucas*, however, the Court included a caveat recognizing the relevance of state law and land-use customs: The complete deprivation of use will not require compensation if the challenged limitations "inhere . . . in the restrictions that background principles of the State's law of property and nuisance already placed upon land ownership." *Id.*, at 1029; see also *id.*, at 1030–1031 (listing factors for courts to consider in making this determination).

A central dynamic of the Court's regulatory takings jurisprudence, then, is its flexibility. This has been and remains a means to reconcile two competing objectives central to regulatory takings doctrine. One is the individual's right to retain the interests and exercise the freedoms at the core of private property ownership. Cf. *id.*, at 1028, 112 S. Ct. 2886 ("[T]he notion . . . that title is somehow held subject to the 'implied limitation' that the State may subsequently eliminate all economically valuable use is inconsistent with the historical compact recorded in the Takings Clause that has become part of our constitutional culture"). Property rights are necessary to preserve freedom, for property ownership empowers persons to shape and to plan their own destiny in a world where governments are always eager to do so for them.

The other persisting interest is the government's well-established power to "adjus[t] rights for the public good." *Andrus v. Allard*, 444 U.S. 51, 65 (1979). As Justice Holmes declared, "Government hardly could go on if to some extent values incident to property could not be diminished without paying for every such change in the general law." *Mahon, supra*, at 413. In adjudicating regulatory takings cases a proper balancing of these principles requires a careful inquiry informed by the specifics of the case. In all instances, the analysis must be driven "by the purpose of the Takings Clause, which is to prevent the government from 'forcing some people alone to bear public burdens which, in all fairness and justice, should be borne by the public as a whole.'" *Palazzolo, supra*, at 617–618 (quoting *Armstrong v. United States*, 364 U.S. 40, 49 (1960)).

B.

This case presents a question that is linked to the ultimate determination whether a regulatory taking has occurred: What is the proper unit of property against which to assess the effect of the challenged governmental action? Put another way, "[b]ecause our test for regulatory taking requires us to compare the value that has been taken from the property with the value that remains in the property, one of the critical questions is determining how to define the unit of property 'whose value is to furnish the denominator of the fraction.'" *Keystone Bituminous Coal Assn. v. DeBenedictis*, 480 U.S. 470, 497 (1987) (quoting Michelman, Property, Utility, and Fairness, 80 Harv. L. Rev. 1165, 1992 (1967)).

. . . [T]he answer to this question may be outcome determinative. . . . This Court . . . has explained that the question is important to the regulatory takings inquiry. "To the extent that any portion of property is taken, that portion is always taken in its entirety; the relevant question, however, is whether the property taken is all, or only a portion of, the parcel in question." *Concrete Pipe & Products of Cal., Inc. v. Construction Laborers Pension Trust for Southern Cal.*, 508 U.S. 602, 644 (1993).

Defining the property at the outset, however, should not necessarily preordain the outcome in every case. In some, though not all, cases the effect of the challenged regulation must be assessed and understood by the effect on the entire property held by the owner, rather than just some part of the property that, considered just on its own, has been diminished in value. This demonstrates the contrast between regulatory takings, where the goal is usually to determine how the challenged regulation affects the property's value to the owner, and physical takings, where the impact of physical appropriation or occupation of the property will be evident.

While the Court has not set forth specific guidance on how to identify the relevant parcel for the regulatory taking inquiry, there are two concepts which the Court has indicated can be unduly narrow.

First, the Court has declined to limit the parcel in an artificial manner to the portion of property targeted by the challenged regulation. In *Penn Central*, for example, the Court rejected a challenge to the denial of a permit to build an office tower above Grand Central Terminal. The Court refused to measure the effect of the denial only against the "air rights" above the terminal, cautioning that "'[t]aking' jurisprudence does not divide a single parcel into discrete segments and attempt to determine whether rights in a particular segment have been entirely abrogated." 438 U.S., at 130.

In a similar way, in *Tahoe-Sierra*, the Court refused to "effectively sever" the 32 months during which petitioners' property was restricted by temporary moratoria on development "and then ask whether that segment ha[d] been taken in its entirety." 535 U.S., at 331. That was because "defining the property interest taken in terms of the very regulation being challenged is circular." . . . That approach would overstate the effect of regulation on property, turning "every delay" into a "total ban." . . .

The second concept about which the Court has expressed caution is the view that property rights under the Takings Clause should be coextensive with those under state law. Although property interests have their foundations in state law, the *Palazzolo* Court reversed a state-court decision that rejected a takings challenge to regulations that predated the landowner's acquisition of title. 533 U.S., at 626–627. The Court explained that States do not have the unfettered authority to "shape and define property rights and reasonable investment-backed expectations," leaving landowners without recourse against unreasonable regulations. *Id.*, at 626.

By the same measure, defining the parcel by reference to state law could defeat a challenge even to a state enactment that alters permitted uses of property in ways inconsistent with reasonable investment-backed expectations. For example, a State might enact a law that consolidates nonadjacent property owned by a single person or entity in different parts of the State and then imposes development limits on the aggregate set. If a court defined the parcel according to the state law requiring consolidation, this improperly would fortify the state law against a takings claim, because the court would look to the retained value in the property as a whole rather than considering whether individual holdings had lost all value.

## III.

### A.

As the foregoing discussion makes clear, no single consideration can supply the exclusive test for determining the denominator. Instead, courts must consider a number of factors. These include the treatment of the land under state and local law; the physical characteristics of the land; and the prospective value of the regulated land. The endeavor should determine whether reasonable expectations about property ownership would lead a landowner to anticipate that his holdings would be treated as one parcel, or, instead, as separate tracts. The inquiry is objective, and the reasonable expectations at issue derive from background customs and the whole of our legal tradition. . . .

First, courts should give substantial weight to the treatment of the land, in particular how it is bounded or divided, under state and local law. The reasonable expectations of an acquirer of land must acknowledge legitimate restrictions affecting his or her subsequent use and dispensation of the property. See *Ballard v. Hunter*, 204 U.S. 241, 262 (1907) ("Of what concerns or may concern their real estate men usually keep informed, and on that probability the law may frame its proceedings"). A valid takings claim will not evaporate just because a purchaser took title after the law was enacted. See *Palazzolo*, 533 U.S., at 627 (some "enactments are unreasonable and do not become less so through passage of time or title"). A reasonable restriction that predates a landowner's acquisition, however, can be one of the objective factors that most landowners would reasonably consider in forming fair expectations about their property. See *ibid.* ("[A] prospective enactment, such as a new zoning ordinance, can limit the value of land without effecting a taking because it can be understood as reasonable by all concerned"). In a similar manner, a use restriction which is triggered only after, or because of, a change in ownership should also guide a court's assessment of reasonable private expectations.

Second, courts must look to the physical characteristics of the landowner's property. These include the physical relationship of any distinguishable tracts, the parcel's topography, and the surrounding human and ecological environment. In particular, it may be relevant that the property is located in an area that is subject to, or likely to become subject to, environmental or other regulation. . . .

Third, courts should assess the value of the property under the challenged regulation, with special attention to the effect of burdened land on the value of other holdings. Though a use restriction may decrease the market value of the property, the effect may be tempered if the regulated land adds value to the remaining property, such as by increasing privacy, expanding recreational space, or preserving surrounding natural beauty. A law that limits use of a landowner's small lot in one part of the city by reason of the landowner's nonadjacent holdings elsewhere may decrease the market value of the small lot in an unmitigated fashion. The absence of a special relationship between the holdings may counsel against consideration of all the holdings as a single parcel, making the restrictive law susceptible to a takings challenge. On the other hand, if the landowner's other property is adjacent to the small lot, the market value of the properties may well increase if their combination enables the expansion of a structure, or if development restraints for one part of the parcel protect the unobstructed skyline views of another part. That, in turn, may counsel in favor of treatment as a single parcel and may reveal the weakness of a regulatory takings challenge to the law.

State and federal courts have considerable experience in adjudicating regulatory takings claims that depart from these examples in various ways. The Court anticipates that in applying the test above they will continue to exercise care in this complex area.

## B.

The State of Wisconsin and petitioners each ask this Court to adopt a formalistic rule to guide the parcel inquiry. Neither proposal suffices to capture the central legal and factual principles that inform reasonable expectations about property interests.

Wisconsin would tie the definition of the parcel to state law, considering the two lots here as a single whole due to their merger under the challenged regulations. That approach, as already noted, simply assumes the answer to the question: May the State define the relevant parcel in a way that permits it to escape its responsibility to justify regulation in light of legitimate property expectations? It is, of course, unquestionable that the law must recognize those legitimate expectations in order to give proper weight to the rights of owners and the right of the State to pass reasonable laws and regulations. See *Palazzolo, supra*, at 627.

Wisconsin bases its position on a footnote in *Lucas*, which suggests the answer to the denominator question "may lie in how the owner's reasonable expectations have been shaped by the State's law of property — i.e., whether and to what degree the State's law has accorded legal recognition and protection to the particular interest in land with respect to which the takings claimant alleges a diminution in (or elimination of) value." 505 U.S., at 1017, n. 7. As an initial matter, *Lucas* referenced the parcel problem only in dicta, unnecessary to the announcement or application of the rule it established. See *ibid.* ("[W]e avoid th[e] difficulty" of determining the relevant parcel "in the present case"). In any event, the test the Court adopts today is consistent with the respect for state law described in *Lucas*. The test considers state law but in addition weighs whether the state enactments at issue accord with other indicia of reasonable expectations about property.

Petitioners propose a different test that is also flawed. They urge the Court to adopt a presumption that lot lines define the relevant parcel in every instance, making Lot E the necessary denominator. Petitioners' argument, however, ignores the fact that lot lines are themselves creatures of state law, which can be overridden by the State in the reasonable exercise of its power. In effect, petitioners ask this Court to credit the aspect of state law that favors their preferred result (lot lines) and ignore that which does not (merger provision).

This approach contravenes the Court's case law, which recognizes that reasonable land-use regulations do not work a taking. . . .

The merger provision here is likewise a legitimate exercise of government power, as reflected by its consistency with a long history of state and local merger regulations that originated nearly a century ago. . . . Merger provisions often form part of a regulatory scheme that establishes a minimum lot size in order to preserve open space while still allowing orderly development. . . .

When States or localities first set a minimum lot size, there often are existing lots that do not meet the new requirements, and so local governments will strive to reduce substandard lots in a gradual manner. The regulations here represent a classic way of doing this: by implementing a merger provision, which combines contiguous substandard lots under common ownership, alongside a grandfather clause, which preserves adjacent substandard lots that are in separate ownership. Also, as here, the harshness of a merger provision may be ameliorated by the availability of a variance from the local zoning authority for landowners in special circumstances. . . .

Petitioners' insistence that lot lines define the relevant parcel ignores the well-settled reliance on the merger provision as a common means of balancing the legitimate goals of regulation with the reasonable expectations of landowners. Petitioners' rule would frustrate municipalities' ability to implement minimum lot size regulations by casting doubt on the many merger provisions that exist nationwide today. . . .

Petitioners' reliance on lot lines also is problematic for another reason. Lot lines have varying degrees of formality across the States, so it is difficult to make them a standard measure of the reasonable expectations of property owners. Indeed, in some jurisdictions, lot lines may be subject to informal adjustment by property owners, with minimal government oversight. . . . The ease of modifying lot lines also creates the risk of gamesmanship by landowners, who might seek to alter the lines in anticipation of regulation that seems likely to affect only part of their property.

## IV.

Under the appropriate multifactor standard, it follows that for purposes of determining whether a regulatory taking has occurred here, petitioners' property should be evaluated as a single parcel consisting of Lots E and F together.

First, the treatment of the property under state and local law indicates petitioners' property should be treated as one when considering the effects of the restrictions. As the Wisconsin courts held, the state and local regulations merged Lots E and F. . . . ("The 1995 transfer of Lot E brought the lots under common ownership and resulted in a merger of the two lots under [the local ordinance]"). The decision to adopt the merger provision at issue here was for a specific and legitimate purpose, consistent with the widespread understanding that lot lines are not dominant or controlling in every case. . . . Petitioners' land was subject to this regulatory burden, moreover, only because of voluntary conduct in bringing the lots under common ownership after the regulations were enacted. As a result, the valid merger of the lots under state law informs the reasonable expectation they will be treated as a single property.

Second, the physical characteristics of the property support its treatment as a unified parcel. The lots are contiguous along their longest edge. Their rough terrain and narrow shape make it reasonable to expect their range of potential uses might be limited. . . . ("[Petitioners] asserted Lot E could not be put to alternative uses like agriculture or commerce due to its size, location and steep terrain"). The land's location along the river is also significant. Petitioners could have anticipated public regulation might affect their enjoyment of their property, as the Lower St. Croix was a regulated area under federal, state, and local law long before petitioners possessed the land.

Third, the prospective value that Lot E brings to Lot F supports considering the two as one parcel for purposes of determining if there is a regulatory taking. Petitioners are prohibited from selling Lots E and F separately or from building separate residential structures on each. Yet this restriction is mitigated by the benefits of using the property as an integrated whole, allowing increased privacy and recreational space, plus the optimal location of any improvements. . . . ("They have an elevated level of privacy because they do not have close neighbors and are able to swim and play volleyball at the property").

The special relationship of the lots is further shown by their combined valuation. Were Lot E separately saleable but still subject to the development restriction, petitioners' appraiser would value the property at only $40,000. We express no opinion on the validity of this figure. We also note the number is not particularly helpful for understanding petitioners' retained value in the properties because Lot E, under the regulations, cannot be sold without Lot F. The point that is useful for these purposes is that the combined lots are valued at $698,300, which is far greater than the summed value of the separate regulated lots (Lot F with its cabin at $373,000, according to respondents' appraiser, and Lot E as an undevelopable plot at $40,000, according to petitioners' appraiser). The value added by the lots' combination shows their complementarity and supports their treatment as one parcel.

The State Court of Appeals was correct in analyzing petitioners' property as a single unit. Petitioners allege that in doing so, the state court applied a categorical rule that all contiguous, commonly owned holdings must be combined for Takings Clause analysis. . . . This does not appear to be the case, however, for the precedent relied on by the Court of Appeals addressed multiple factors before treating contiguous properties as one parcel. . . . To the extent the state court treated the two lots as one parcel based on a bright-line rule, nothing in this opinion approves that methodology, as distinct from the result.

Considering petitioners' property as a whole, the state court was correct to conclude that petitioners cannot establish a compensable taking in these circumstances. Petitioners have not suffered a taking under *Lucas*, as they have not been deprived of all economically beneficial use of their property. See 505 U.S., at 1019. They can use the property for residential purposes, including an enhanced, larger residential improvement. See *Palazzolo*, 533 U.S., at 631 ("A regulation permitting a landowner to build a substantial residence . . . does not leave the property 'economically idle'"). The property has not lost all economic value, as its value has decreased by less than 10 percent. See *Lucas*, *supra*, at 1019, n. 8 (suggesting that even a landowner with 95 percent loss may not recover).

Petitioners furthermore have not suffered a taking under the more general test of *Penn Central*. See 438 U.S., at 124. The expert appraisal relied upon by the state courts refutes any claim that the economic impact of the regulation is severe. Petitioners cannot claim that they reasonably expected to sell or develop their lots separately given the regulations which predated their acquisition of both lots. Finally, the governmental action was a reasonable land-use regulation, enacted as part of a coordinated federal, state, and local effort to preserve the river and surrounding land.

. . . .

Like the ultimate question whether a regulation has gone too far, the question of the proper parcel in regulatory takings cases cannot be solved by any simple test. . . . Courts must instead define the parcel in a manner that reflects reasonable expectations about the property. Courts must strive for consistency with the central purpose of the Takings Clause: to "bar Government from forcing some people alone to bear public burdens which, in all fairness and justice, should be borne by the public as a whole." *Armstrong*, 364 U.S., at 49. Treating the lot in question as a single parcel is legitimate for purposes of this takings inquiry, and this supports the conclusion that no regulatory taking occurred here.

The judgment of the Wisconsin Court of Appeals is affirmed.

[Chief Justice Roberts filed a dissenting opinion, in which Justices Thomas and Alito joined. In this opinion, Chief Justice Roberts writes that, instead of the majority opinion's approach to defining "private property" by applying an elaborate test of factors, state law defines the boundaries of distinct parcels of land, and those boundaries should determine the "private property" at issue in regulatory takings cases. Whether a regulation effects a taking of that property is a separate question, one in which common ownership of adjacent property may be taken into account.]

[Justice Thomas filed a dissenting opinion. This opinion is omitted here.]

## Questions for Consideration

1) Does the "parcel as a whole" concept establish a rule that two legally distinct, but commonly owned, contiguous parcels must be combined for takings analysis purposes?

2) Why was there no *Lucas* taking? Why was there no *Penn Central* taking?

## Takeaway

- In this case, two lots were held to be subject to regulations limiting development as if they were one lot. The Court indicated that, for takings law purposes, the definition of a lot and of a whole parcel need not follow strict conformity with state law definitions. For takings law purposes, one looks at a variety of characteristics concerning the property, its history, and topography. The court considers: (1) "the physical characteristics of the land," (2) "the prospective value of the regulated land," (3) the "reasonable expectations" of the owner, and (4) "background customs and the whole of our legal tradition."

- A determination as to a whole parcel under federal takings law may not be the same as the determination of a parcel under state law. Consequently, regulations that limit the use of property and reduce its economic value must be viewed in accordance with federal law when evaluating the existence of an unconstitutional taking of property without just compensation under the Fifth Amendment.

## Discussion Problem 3.7

Clint owns undeveloped land on Seal Island. Beginning in the 1950s, land speculators purchased thousands of small lots on the island. Clint purchased over 200 of these undeveloped lots on the island. Clint built homes on some of the lots and hoped to develop the rest. His development plans were delayed because his lots could not accommodate septic systems. Seal Island had no sewer service, so every home required the construction of a septic system. Unfortunately, the soil on the island was not well-suited to septic systems, especially those built on small lots. Shortly after Clint began buying land, the County requirements for a septic system were tightened, forcing him to wait on his development plans until sewer was available on the island. County requirements also limited the construction of new septic systems, and thus the development of the small lots. However, the existing septic systems on Seal Island deteriorated, so the County adopted a plan to address the septic problems by extending sewer service to the homes with failing septic systems on Seal Island, while at the same time continuing to limit any new development. Specifically, the County's plan extended sewer service to all streets with failing septic systems; both developed and undeveloped lots on those streets would receive sewer service. However, to limit further development, there would be no sewer lines constructed on streets with only vacant land. The vacant lots on those streets would be excluded from service because no lots would abut a sewer line. The plan also prevents future connections outside the initial service area.

Further, to control excessive new development threatened by the sewer extension, the County enacted in 2014 a Grandfather/Merger Provision. Under this provision, the County would not grant a building permit for a lot smaller than the minimum size under the zoning regulations unless that lot was merged with any contiguous lots under common ownership. Many of the initial lots recorded on Seal Island did not meet the minimum size, and a developer who owned a group of those lots would have to merge them into fewer, larger lots to obtain a building permit. If a developer, though, owned an isolated undersized lot, he would still be able to obtain a building permit.

Taken together, the sewer extension and the Grandfather/Merger Provision would provide sewer service to the failing septic systems on Seal Island and hundreds of vacant lots, many of which could not have been developed without sewer service. The plan would also exclude hundreds of vacant lots, leaving them undevelopable. The impact on Clint mirrored the impact on the entire island — that is, he had several vacant lots that would receive sewer service and, subject to being merged with contiguous lots, will now be developable. However, Clint also owned a large tract of nearly two hundred vacant lots that would not receive sewer service, meaning that he will continue to be unable to build on this land.

Because Clint will not be able to build on nearly 200 of his lots as a result of the County's plan, Clint sued the County challenging the sewer extension and the

Grandfather/Merger Provision. He argued that the County had effected a regulatory taking, requiring compensation under the Fifth Amendment.

Who shall prevail in this dispute?

## Pinnock v. International House of Pancakes

United States District Court for the Southern District of California
844 F. Supp. 574 (S.D. Cal. 1993)

RHOADES, Judge. Plaintiff, Theodore A. Pinnock ("Pinnock") filed the complaint in this action against Defendant, Majid Zahedi, owner of an International House of Pancakes franchise ("Zahedi").[2] Pinnock, an attorney representing himself, is unable to walk and uses a wheelchair. Pinnock dined at the defendant's restaurant on June 21, 1992, and then attempted to use the restroom. The entrance to the restroom, however, was not wide enough to admit his wheelchair. Pinnock therefore removed himself from his wheelchair and crawled into the restroom. As a result of this encounter, Pinnock alleges nine causes of action against Zahedi. Five of the causes of action arise under state law, alleging violations of the state health and safety code, the Unruh Civil Rights Act, and infliction of emotional distress. The remaining four causes of action are alleged under the Americans with Disabilities Act of 1990, 42 U.S.C. §12101 *et seq.* ("ADA"), arising from Zahedi's alleged failure to comply with the statute's provisions governing access for disabled individuals in public accommodations ("title III").[3]

Zahedi presented twenty-five affirmative defenses in his answer to the complaint. Among these, and at issue here, are allegations that the ADA violates numerous provisions of the United States Constitution. Zahedi filed a compulsory counterclaim for Declaratory Judgment on the constitutional challenges pursuant to 28 U.S.C. §§1331 and 2201. The United States intervened pursuant to rule 24(a) of the Federal Rules of Civil Procedure and 28 U.S.C. §2403, to defend the constitutionality of the ADA, and filed a cross-motion for summary judgment on the constitutional issues. As no court has yet considered the constitutional challenges raised by Zahedi, these motions call upon the Court to decide questions of first impression.

---

2. On December 20, 1993, Zahedi's restaurant was destroyed by fire. Zahedi, along with two co-defendants, has been charged with Damaging and Destroying Property in and Affecting Interstate Commerce, in violation of 18 U.S.C. §844(i), and Using Fire to Commit a Felony, in violation of 18 U.S.C. §844(h).

3. The ADA is comprised of separate titles that regulate in the areas of employment (title I), Public Services (title II), and Public Accommodations (title III). Title III governs private businesses which meet the characteristics of a public accommodation as specified in section 12181(7) of the ADA. *See* 42 U.S.C. §12181(7).

### Zahedi is a Member of an Industry Which Affects Interstate Commerce and is Properly Regulated by Title III

Zahedi argues that Congress does not have constitutional authority to regulate his facility, asserting that title III of the ADA exceeds the powers granted Congress by the U.S. Constitution. Congress enacted title III pursuant to Article I, Section 8, of the United States Constitution, which grants Congress the power to "regulate Commerce . . . among the several States" and to enact all laws necessary and proper to this end. U.S. Const., art. I, § 8, cls. 3, 18; *Katzenbach v. McClung*, 379 U.S. 294, 301–02, 85 S. Ct. 377, 382, 13 L. Ed. 2d 290 (1964). The Supreme Court has consistently held that Congress is empowered under the Commerce Clause to regulate not only interstate activities, but also intrastate activities that substantially affect interstate commerce.

The Commerce Clause allows Congress to regulate any entity, regardless of its individual impact on interstate commerce, so long as the entity engages in a class of activities that affects interstate commerce. As the Supreme Court stated in *United States v. Darby*, Congress has "recognized that in present day industry, competition by a small party may affect the whole and that the total effect of the competition of many small producers may be great." 312 U.S. 100, 123, 85 L. Ed. 609, 61 S. Ct. 451 (1941).

Courts must defer to congressional findings that an activity affects commerce, so long as there is a rational basis for such a finding. As the Supreme Court recognized in the context of racial discrimination, the restaurant industry unquestionably affects interstate commerce in a substantial way. . . .

Even aside from its membership in an interstate industry, Zahedi's restaurant demonstrates characteristics which place it squarely in the category of interstate commerce. It is a franchise of a large, international, publicly traded corporation ("IHOP Corp."), organized under Delaware law. IHOP Corp. had total retail sales of $479 million in 1992, operates 547 franchises in thirty-five states, Canada, and Japan, and employs 16,000 persons. Furthermore, Zahedi's restaurant is located directly across the street from State Highway 163, and within two miles of two interstate highways. There are three hotels within walking distance, and three motels within one and one-half miles of the restaurant. The courts have found these facts to be indicia of a business operating in interstate commerce.

Congressional enactment of title III of the ADA was well within Congress' power to regulate interstate commerce under the Commerce Clause. As part of the restaurant industry, Zahedi is subject to the provisions of title III, which by its own terms, reaches as broadly as the Commerce Clause permits.[6]

---

6. Title III covers, *inter alia*, "public accommodations," which are defined by a list of type of facilities whose operations "affect commerce." 42 U.S.C. § 12181(7) (Supp. II 1990). In addition, the

As a member of the restaurant industry and as an individual enterprise which caters to travelers, Zahedi's restaurant is properly regulated by title III of the ADA.

. . . .

Title III's general prohibition against discrimination provides as follows:

No individual shall be discriminated against on the basis of disability in the full and equal enjoyment of the goods, services, facilities, privileges, advantages, or accommodations of any place of public accommodation. . . .

. . . These categories include denying a person with a disability public accommodations, or providing accommodations not equal to that afforded to other individuals.

Furthermore, the legislative history explains that

[f]ull and equal enjoyment does not encompass the notion that persons with disabilities must achieve the identical result or level of achievement of nondisabled persons, but does mean that persons with disabilities must be afforded equal opportunity to obtain the same result.

. . . .

Zahedi contends that the expenditure of funds necessary to make the restrooms in his facility accessible to individuals in wheelchairs, if required under the ADA, would constitute a taking of private property "for public use, without just compensation" in violation of the Fifth Amendment's Due Process Clause. In *Lucas v. South Carolina Coastal Council*, 505 U.S. 1003, 112 S. Ct. 2886, 120 L. Ed. 2d 798 (1992), the Supreme Court delineated . . . situations in which a governmental restraint is considered a taking, therefore requiring compensation. These [situations include]: 1) when the regulation compels a permanent physical invasion of the property; and 2) when the regulation denies an owner all economically beneficial or productive use of its land. . . . If either of the[se] two situations occur, the regulation will be considered a taking regardless of whether the action achieves an important public benefit or has only minimal impact on the owner. *Lucas*, 505 U.S. at —, 112 S. Ct. at 2893. The expenditure of funds required by Title III does not constitute a taking under the Fifth Amendment as defined in *Lucas*.

### Requiring Zahedi to Comply With the ADA Does Not Constitute A Physical Invasion of His Property.

The Fifth Amendment provides that private property may not be taken for public use without just compensation. A cornerstone of the law of takings is that if a regulation has the effect of establishing a permanent physical occupation, it will be a taking.

. . . .

---

ADA's statement of purpose states that it intends "to invoke the sweep of congressional authority, including the power . . . to regulate commerce." *Id.* § 12101(b)(4).

Zahedi argues that the remodeling required under the ADA may result in the loss of as many as 20 seating places in his restaurant. Zahedi [argues] that a regulation which requires a restaurant to widen restrooms and thereby restricts the use of part of his property, violates the Fifth Amendment. . . . This case . . . does not involve the granting of Zahedi's property to another party for its own exclusive use and profit. Rather, the ADA merely proscribes Zahedi's use of part of his *own* property and it therefore could be likened to a zoning regulation. Since the ADA merely regulates the use of property and does not give anyone physical occupation of Zahedi's property, it is not within the Supreme Court's first category of takings.

### The ADA Does not Deny Zahedi ALL Economically Beneficial or Productive Use of His Land.

Regulations which restrict the use of property will be upheld unless the economic impact of a challenged statute is so extreme that it denies the claimant any economically viable use of the property. . . . Zahedi does not, however, claim that the ADA would deny him all economic use of his property. To the contrary, Zahedi claims only that expenditures may be necessary to comply with the regulation.

. . . .

The remodeling which Zahedi claims is required under the ADA regulations could result in the loss of approximately 20 seating places in his restaurant. The mere loss of approximately 20 seating places surely will not deny Zahedi all economically viable use of his property.

The Court must also consider whether the requirements of the statute frustrate the property owner's reasonable investment backed expectations. A showing of frustration of investment-backed expectation is a very difficult one to make, and the impact of the ADA's barrier removal requirements pales in comparison to many of the regulations which the Supreme Court has upheld. . . .

. . . .

The legislative history of the Act (the ADA) reflects congressional concern over the deleterious effects of discrimination against people with disabilities.

> The large majority of people with disabilities do not go to movies, do not go to the theater, do not go to see musical performances, and do not go to sports events. A substantial minority of persons with disabilities never go to a restaurant, never go to a grocery store, and never go to a church or synagogue. . . . The extent of non-participation of individuals with disabilities in social and recreational activities [is] alarming.

Congress found that the exclusion of disabled individuals from public life was largely a result of the "lack of physical access to facilities." As a result, the legislative body elected to adopt the barrier removal requirements embodied in title III. These requirements directly address and remedy the problems which the Act aims to redress.

### Title III does not Intrude Upon State Sovereignty in Violation of the Tenth Amendment

Zahedi argues that the ADA constitutes a "national building code" which trespasses the regulatory area reserved to the states by the Tenth Amendment. It was once contended that the federal government had no police power, as such, except in the District of Columbia. It is now the law, however, that the federal government's implied powers under the "necessary and proper clause" of the Constitution (Art. I, § 8) provide for the passage of laws similar to legislation enacted by a state under its police power. Hence, it is recognized today that "in the exercise of its control over interstate commerce, the means employed by the Congress may have the quality of police regulations."

The Tenth Amendment does not insulate states from federal regulation simply because the regulation affects an area traditionally subject to state control. . . .

. . . .

. . . [T]itle III's statutory scheme does not displace local building codes. It is a federal civil rights act that sets forth accessibility standards that places of public accommodation and commercial facilities must follow. Departures from the ADA Standards are expressly permitted where "alternative designs and technologies used will provide substantially equivalent or greater access to and usability of the facility." State and local building codes remain in effect to be enforced by state officials. State officials are not required to adopt or enforce the ADA Standards for Accessible Design.

### Conclusion

. . . As Zahedi's brief illustrates, the public has grown increasingly weary of regulations which burden businesses and the court system with uncertain requirements. A district court, however, is limited to considering the constitutionality of the challenged regulations, rather than their political or economic desirability. . . .

Having carefully considered each of Zahedi's constitutional challenges, it is clear that none of these challenges can prevail. . . . Zahedi's motion for summary judgment is denied, and Zahedi's counterclaim is dismissed.

It is so ordered.

## Questions for Consideration

1)  How do the requirements of the ADA affect Zahedi's business?

2)  Why does Zahedi think the ADA requirements rise to the level of a taking?

3)  How might you apply the six-factor balancing test from *Penn Central* to an analysis of Zahedi's claim of a taking in this case?

## Takeaway

- Rational design requirements pursuant to the ADA are not going to be violations of the Takings Clause.

- From the above case: "The federal government's implied powers under the 'necessary and proper clause' of the Constitution (Art. I, § 8) provide for the passage of laws similar to legislation enacted by a state under its police power."

### D.O. Malagrinò, *Among Justice Stevens's Landmark Legacies:* Tahoe-Sierra Preservation Council, Inc. v. Tahoe Regional Planning Agency,

53 Creighton L. Rev. 77, 102–09 (2019)

(Footnotes have been omitted)

\* \* \*

### IV. Refocusing the Doctrinal Lens of Regulatory Takings

Takings analysis should take place not to determine if something is or is not a "taking" in situations where the government has indubitably taken away a right that was an incident of property. In such circumstances, it is a taking and the analysis described in *Penn Central* should be understood to determine what "just compensation" would be.

In *Lucas*, [*Lucas v. South Carolina Coastal Council*, 505 U.S. 1003 (1992) discussed *supra* Chap. 4] the court examined precedent and determined that a case specific inquiry has never been required when a regulation either compels a "property owner to suffer a physical 'invasion,'" or "denies all economically beneficial or productive use of land." The U.S. Supreme Court held that when a regulation intrudes so severely, market value compensation is always required. Because the trial court found that the regulation had extinguished the economic value of Lucas's lots, the Court applied the categorical rule to his claim.

The *Lucas* test is not flexible; market value compensation is owed when a regulation extinguishes the beneficial economic use of land, unless the restriction falls within a narrow exception. As such, a court that finds an owner has not suffered a total deprivation of economically viable use employs a partial takings analysis to determine if that owner has suffered a loss sufficient to warrant compensation. This analysis is what should happen in all cases, and it should be done through the lens of determining just compensation, regardless of whether there has been a partial or total deprivation of property.

We should concern ourselves with justice, not arbitrary classifications. In *Lucas*, the Court did not examine whether Lucas had reasonable, distinct investment-backed expectations at the time he purchased the property. Instead, the Court's reasoning was simplistic: Lucas proved that the regulation had extinguished the economically beneficial use of his property, and therefore the regulation effected a taking. Indeed it did, but then the Court held an automatic right to market value compensation — the investment-backed expectation of the owner did not have to factor into the just compensation analysis because it was a "total" taking.

Significantly, Justice Stevens attacked the categorical rule as being "wholly arbitrary," because "[a] landowner whose property is diminished in value 95% recovers nothing, while an owner whose property is diminished 100% recovers the land's full value." The majority responded by acknowledging that a landowner who has not been deprived of all economically viable use "might not be able to claim the benefit of [the Supreme Court's] categorical formulation"; however, the majority insisted that he would be able to bring a takings claim under the usual *Penn Central* balancing test.

*Lucas* contains an exception to its own categorical rule. If a regulation duplicates the result that could have been achieved in the courts by adjacent landowners under the State's general law of private nuisance then no taking has occurred. No taking has occurred not because of a lack of investment-backed expectations, as the owner's expectation is generally to make economically viable use of her property, but rather because background "principles of [state] nuisance and property law" demonstrate that the proscribed use was never part of the title. This analysis is consistent because nothing was taken from the titleholder, thus no analysis of what would be just compensation is necessary — unless state courts have evolved state nuisance law in the meantime to be more intrusive.

### A. Many More Takings are Had

Realistically, to be frank, in no way do we think that when courts interpret the common law in a new and different way that they are just newly discovering what it always was. On the contrary, they are simply changing it. Although one could say that rights are acquired against the backdrop of potential change in nuisance law, remember that rights are also acquired against the backdrop of potential change in legislation, too, and the U.S. Supreme Court skirts that issue.

And, the whole juridical perspective is to blame for this illogical analysis. Liberal jurists are mistaken to have the fight about just compensation under the rubric of takings. In doing so, they look conceptually incoherent. In each of these fights, of course a property interest — a power or freedom in the property bundle — is being taken. The interesting question is whether justice requires compensation.

Further, if the fight were had explicitly under the rubric of just compensation, then conservative jurists would look conceptually incoherent. Every new zoning ordinance, every law that imposes some new restriction on existing freedoms or powers over property takes. Even the most conservative minds must concede that compensation cannot be paid for all of these takings. Yet, the conservative view is that "just compensation" means "making the property owner whole." This view, taken literally, requires market value compensation whenever a power or freedom in the property bundle is restricted.

Liberal jurists, on the other hand, could cheerfully concede that all such restrictions are takings but then say that justice does not always require compensation, and instead requires some measure to determine what compensation, if any, is just. When would justice require compensation, and in what amount? That necessarily depends on the unique relation between the property interest and the regulation at issue in any particular case. So, then, what factors might be relevant to the analysis? The same *Penn Central* factors, which consider: (1) the economic impact of the taking on the claimant; (2) the investment-backed expectations; and, (3) the character of the taking.

## B. What is Just About Compensation?

The U.S. Supreme Court constructs its own set of principles for deciding when justice requires compensation, and the *Penn Central* analysis is effectively the Court trying to do just that. It is a vague standard risking inconsistent application by courts, but having bright-line rules makes inconsistency of application even more visible, thus bringing the law into even greater disrepute. If we have a bright-line rule, we can see the cases just on either side of the line; however, if we have a multi-factor standard, courts can look at what was awarded in one case, where a certain set of circumstances existed, and can consider how the circumstances in a case at bar differs; thus, overtime, a common law of property takings would evolve. The courts could come up with a theory of justice, and, through the process of concrete application by common-law method, this theory of justice would acquire a predictable content, sensitive to the range of factors relevant to whether justice requires compensation and, if so, how much.

Conservative jurists are left with the problem that they must define "takings" more narrowly than "any restriction of a right or freedom in the property bundle," because they plan on forcing the government to pay full, make-whole compensation for all takings. But, there is no principled other place to draw the "takings" line, so the conservative position ends up as arbitrary.

### V. Conclusion

To recap, the Takings Clause assures Americans that they will not be forced to sacrifice their property for a public good without just compensation. A categorical rule applies when a property owner has been denied all economically viable use of her property, while a balancing test applies when she loses something less. Determining just compensation is when we analyze policy, investment-backed expectations, etc., not to determine if something is a taking requiring just compensation. A total regulatory taking is analogous to a physical taking. The U.S. Supreme Court has generally held that physical invasions of any sort require market-value compensation. Fine, but any regulatory taking is analogous to a physical taking, too.

There is no principled distinction between outright acquisitions and regulatory takings — all are takings, and all should be subject to the *Penn Central* factor analysis to determine what counts as just compensation, what justice requires as compensation. Justice may require compensation without necessarily measuring that compensation as the market value of the right taken at some particular time, particularly because, since *Tahoe*, takings themselves are identified by the *Penn Central* ad hoc balancing test.

# I. Practice Problems

3.1 The police power is vested in the states. In turn, the individual states delegate police power authority to local government. With police powers, local governments can establish legislative bodies, a court system, and an executive. They also establish departments and entities such as the local planning and zoning authority. Importantly, the police powers of local government are expressed in the terms of the delegation of authority from the state. Review the questions below and outline your response to each so that you are prepared to answer them in a meeting where you will be reporting back to a more senior attorney.

a) In the state where you are located, find the statutory provisions that delegate authority to local and municipal governments.

b) Does your state make a distinction between cities of different size populations?

c) Does your state have any "home rule" provisions for local government? If you are unsure of what is meant by home rule, look it up and determine if any cities in your state have home rule.

d) Locate in your state statutes the obligation, if any, for local governments to engage in planning, and the state requirements for planning.

3.2 Most communities now have internet availability of their local comprehensive plan, zoning code, and applicable zoning map. Select your community or a nearby community and locate each of these three items. Select (or your instructor may select) a local landmark property or a particular building or home in your community. Then do the following and be prepared to report back on what you learn:

a) obtain the street address of the property;

b) view the property on Google Maps;

c) locate the property on the zoning map;

d) determine the zoning district of the property location;

e) determine the permitted uses in that district;

f) determine the required front, back, and side set-back requirements applicable to the property, and,

g) determine what, if anything, the comprehensive plan includes with respect to the property and its surrounding area.

3.3 Assume you are the attorney for the planning board of a small city. The chair of the planning board, a non-lawyer, returns from a planning conference and is excited about establishing a special zoning ordinance to preserve all of the Victorian architecture in the city. While at the conference, she heard a speaker talk about a similar zoning proposal for a nearby city. The speaker briefly mentioned that cities contemplating such a zoning ordinance need to consider the balancing test of *Penn Central*. Having mentioned this, the speaker did not elaborate. Consequently, when the chair of the planning board returns from the conference, she asks you to explain the *Penn Central* balancing test.

a) In a short memorandum addressed to the chair of your planning board, explain the *Penn Central* balancing test and how it might apply to a local ordinance protecting all of the Victorian architecture throughout the city.

# Chapter 4

# Comprehensive Plans

Planning and zoning are two different functions, or activities, of local government. These functions are interrelated. In common parlance, zoning is done pursuant to a comprehensive plan. Ideally, therefore, planning comes before zoning.

Studying and planning for the needs of a community establishes a rational basis for land regulation. The planning process typically addresses demographics, and a community's needs with respect to such things as transportation, housing, recreation, employment, water, schools, utilities, commerce, public services, sustainability, and accessibility. Zoning regulations are then enacted, pursuant to the plan, in order to facilitate local government in the management and coordination of uses designed to protect and promote the public health, safety, welfare, and morals. Generally, reference is made to a "comprehensive plan" for a community. This means the planning is comprehensive in terms of its elements (the types of needs provided for in the plan) and in terms of addressing the needs of the entire jurisdiction. Zoning ordinances are enacted pursuant to a comprehensive plan and facilitate the implementation of the plan. While it is generally agreed that zoning is to be done pursuant to a comprehensive plan, it is less clear as to what constitutes a comprehensive plan and how closely zoning decisions must follow the plan.

Some jurisdictions require a comprehensive plan to be a written document, whereas others refer to a process in which zoning is thought about holistically, without the necessity for a separate and identifiable document. Some comprehensive plans are very long and complex, and others are simple and short. Sometimes courts seem to discuss comprehensive plans in the abstract, such as considering if a zoning ordinance reflects a comprehensive approach to the regulation of land uses in a community. If it does, then it might lead to the conclusion that the zoning was pursuant to a comprehensive plan even if there is no actual written plan.

In addition to local planning, there can be regional and statewide planning. There can also be specialized planning for such purposes as preservation of agricultural lands, coastal land management, water resource protection, and economic development. Sometimes the implementation of a plan is challenged as a violation of due process or as a taking of property without just compensation.

# A. Consistency in Zoning Pursuant to a Comprehensive Plan

One issue that varies by jurisdiction involves the question of how closely zoning regulations and zoning decisions must fit with the comprehensive plan. This issue is referred to as one of *consistency*. In some states, state law treats the comprehensive plan as a general guide for zoning officials rather than as something that has to be closely followed. In other states, zoning is expected to closely follow the comprehensive plan and be strictly consistent with it.

## Fasano v. Board of County Commissioners of Washington County

Supreme Court of Oregon
507 P.2d 23 (Or. 1973)

HOWELL, Judge. The plaintiffs, homeowners in Washington county, unsuccessfully opposed a zone change before the Board of County Commissioners of Washington County. Plaintiffs applied for and received a writ of review of the action of the commissioners allowing the change. The trial court found in favor of plaintiffs, disallowed the zone change, and reversed the commissioners' order. The Court of Appeals affirmed, 489 P.2d 693 (1971), and this court granted review.

The defendants are the Board of County Commissioners and A.G.S. Development Company. A.G.S., the owner of 32 acres which had been zoned R-7 (Single Family Residential), applied for a zone change to P-R (Planned Residential), which allows for the construction of a mobile home park. The change failed to receive a majority vote of the Planning Commission. The Board of County Commissioners approved the change and found, among other matters, that the change allows for "increased densities and different types of housing to meet the needs of urbanization over that allowed by the existing zoning."

The trial court, relying on its interpretation of *Roseta v. County of Washington*, 254 Or. 161, 458 P.2d 405, 40 A.L.R.3d 364 (1969), reversed the order of the commissioners because the commissioners had not shown any change in the character of the neighborhood which would justify the rezoning. The Court of Appeals affirmed for the same reason, but added the additional ground that the defendants failed to show that the change was consistent with the comprehensive plan for Washington county.

According to the briefs, the comprehensive plan of development for Washington county was adopted in 1959 and included classifications in the county for residential, neighborhood commercial, retail commercial, general commercial, industrial park and light industry, general and heavy industry, and agricultural areas.

The land in question, which was designated 'residential' by the comprehensive plan, was zoned R-7, Single Family Residential.

Subsequent to the time the comprehensive plan was adopted, Washington county established a Planned Residential (P-R) zoning classification in 1963. The P-R classification was adopted by ordinance and provided that a planned residential unit development could be established and should include open space for utilities, access, and recreation; should not be less than 10 acres in size; and should be located in or adjacent to a residential zone. The P-R zone adopted by the 1963 ordinance is of the type known as a "floating zone," so-called because the ordinance creates a zone classification authorized for future use but not placed on the zoning map until its use at a particular location is approved by the governing body. The R-7 classification for the 32 acres continued until April 1970 when the classification was changed to P-R to permit the defendant A.G.S. to construct the mobile home park on the 32 acres involved.

The defendants argue that (1) the action of the county commissioners approving the change is presumptively valid, requiring plaintiffs to show that the commissioners acted arbitrarily in approving the zone change; (2) it was not necessary to show a change of conditions in the area before a zone change could be accomplished; and (3) the change from R-7 to P-R was in accordance with the Washington county comprehensive plan.

We granted review in this case to consider the questions — by what standards does a county commission exercise its authority in zoning matters; who has the burden of meeting those standards when a request for change of zone is made; and what is the scope of court review of such actions?

Any meaningful decision as to the proper scope of judicial review of a zoning decision must start with a characterization of the nature of that decision. The majority of jurisdictions state that a zoning ordinance is a legislative act and is thereby entitled to presumptive validity. This court made such a characterization of zoning decisions in *Smith v. County of Washington*, 241 Or. 380, 406 P.2d 545 (1965):

> "Inasmuch as ORS 215.110 specifically grants to the governing board of the county the power to amend zoning ordinances, a challenged amendment is a legislative act and is clothed with a presumption in its favor. . . ."

At this juncture we feel we would be ignoring reality to rigidly view all zoning decisions by local governing bodies as legislative acts to be accorded a full presumption of validity and shielded from less than constitutional scrutiny by the theory of separation of powers. Local and small decision groups are simply not the equivalent in all respects of state and national legislatures. There is a growing judicial recognition of this fact of life:

> "It is not a part of the legislative function to grant permits, make special exceptions, or decide particular cases. Such activities are not legislative but administrative, quasi-judicial, or judicial in character. To place them in the hands of legislative bodies, whose acts as such are not judicially reviewable, is to open the door completely to arbitrary government."

The Supreme Court of Washington, in reviewing a rezoning decision, recently stated:

"Whatever descriptive characterization may be otherwise attached to the role or function of the planning commission in zoning procedures, e.g., advisory, recommendatory, investigatory, administrative or legislative, it is manifest that it is a public agency, a principle (sic) and statutory duty of which is to conduct public hearings in specified planning and zoning matters, enter findings of fact — often on the basis of disputed facts — and make recommendations with reasons assigned thereto. Certainly, in its role as a hearing and fact-finding tribunal, the planning commission's function more nearly than not partakes of the nature of an administrative, quasi-judicial proceeding. . . ."

Ordinances laying down general policies without regard to a specific piece of property are usually an exercise of legislative authority, are subject to limited review, and may only be attacked upon constitutional grounds for an arbitrary abuse of authority. On the other hand, a determination whether the permissible use of a specific piece of property should be changed is usually an exercise of judicial authority and its propriety is subject to an altogether different test. An illustration of an exercise of legislative authority is the passage of the ordinance by the Washington County Commission in 1963 which provided for the formation of a planned residential classification to be located in or adjacent to any residential zone. An exercise of judicial authority is the county commissioners' determination in this particular matter to change the classification of A.G.S. Development Company's specific piece of property. The distinction is stated, as follows, in Comment, *Zoning Amendments — The Product of Judicial or Quasi-Judicial Action*, 33 Ohio St. L.J. 130 (1972):

"Basically, this test involves the determination of whether action produces a general rule or policy which is applicable to an open class of individuals, interest, or situations, or whether it entails the application of a general rule or policy to specific individuals, interests, or situations. If the former determination is satisfied, there is legislative action; if the latter determination is satisfied, the action is judicial." 33 Ohio St. L.J. at 137.

We reject the proposition that judicial review of the county commissioners' determination to change the zoning of the particular property in question is limited to a determination whether the change was arbitrary and capricious.

In order to establish a standard of review, it is necessary to delineate certain basic principles relating to land use regulation.

The basic instrument for county or municipal land use planning is the "comprehensive plan." The plan has been described as a general plan to control and direct the use and development of property in a municipality.

In Oregon the county planning commission is required by ORS 215.050 to adopt a comprehensive plan for the use of some or all of the land in the county. Under ORS 215.110(1), after the comprehensive plan has been adopted, the planning commission recommends to the governing body of the county the ordinances necessary to "carry out" the comprehensive plan. The purpose of the zoning ordinances, both under our statute and the general law of land use regulation, is to "carry out" or implement the comprehensive plan. Although we are aware of the analytical distinction between zoning and planning, it is clear that under our statutes the plan adopted by the planning commission and the zoning ordinances enacted by the county governing body are closely related; both are intended to be parts of a single integrated procedure for land use control. The plan embodies policy determinations and guiding principles; the zoning ordinances provide the detailed means of giving effect to those principles.

ORS 215.050 states county planning commissions "shall adopt and may from time to time revise a comprehensive plan." In a hearing of the Senate Committee on Local Government, the proponents of ORS 215.050 described its purpose as follows:

> "The intent here is to require a basic document, geared into population, land use, and economic forecasts, which should be the basis of any zoning or other regulations to be adopted by the county."

In addition, ORS 215.055 provides:

> "215.055 Standards for plan. (1) The plan and all legislation and regulations authorized by ORS 215.010 to 215.233 shall be designed to promote the public health, safety and general welfare and shall be based on the following considerations, among other: The various characteristics of the various areas in the county, the suitability of the areas for particular land uses and improvements, the land uses and improvements in the areas, trends in land improvement, density of development, property values, the needs of economic enterprises in the future development of the areas, needed access to particular sites in the areas, natural resources of the county and prospective needs for development thereof, and the public need for healthful, safe, aesthetic surroundings and conditions."

We believe that the state legislature has conditioned the county's power to zone upon the prerequisite that the zoning attempt to further the general welfare of the community through consciousness, in a prospective sense, of the factors mentioned above. In other words, except as noted later in this opinion, it must be proved that the change is in conformance with the comprehensive plan.

In proving that the change is in conformance with the comprehensive plan in this case, the proof, at a minimum, should show (1) there is a public need for a change of the kind in question, and (2) that need will be best served by changing the classification of the particular piece of property in question as compared with other available property.

In the instant case, the trial court and the Court of Appeals interpreted prior decisions of this court as requiring the county commissions to show a change of conditions within the immediate neighborhood in which the change was sought since the enactment of the comprehensive plan, or a mistake in the comprehensive plan as a condition precedent to the zone change.

In *Smith v. Washington County, supra,* the land in question was designated residential under the comprehensive plan, and the county commissioners enacted an amendatory ordinance changing the classification to manufacturing. This court held that the change constituted spot zoning and was invalid. We stated:

> "Once a [zoning scheme] is adopted, changes in it should be made only when such changes are consistent with the over-all objectives of the plan. And in keeping with changes in the character of the area or neighborhood to be covered thereby."

. . . .

. . . [A] physical change of circumstances within the rezoned neighborhood is [not] the only justification for rezoning. The county governing body is directed by ORS 215.055 to consider a number of other factors when enacting zoning ordinances, and the list there does not purport to be exclusive. The important issues . . . are compliance with the statutory directive and consideration of the proposed change in light of the comprehensive plan.

Because the action of the commission in this instance is an exercise of judicial authority, the burden of proof should be placed, as is usual in judicial proceedings, upon the one seeking change. The more drastic the change, the greater will be the burden of showing that it is in conformance with the comprehensive plan as implemented by the ordinance, that there is a public need for the kind of change in question, and that the need is best met by the proposal under consideration. As the degree of change increases, the burden of showing that the potential impact upon the area in question was carefully considered and weighed will also increase. If other areas have previously been designated for the particular type of development, it must be shown why it is necessary to introduce it into an area not previously contemplated and why the property owners there should bear the burden of the departure.

Although we have said . . . that zoning changes may be justified without a showing of a mistake in the original plan or ordinance, or of changes in the physical characteristics of an affected area, any of these factors which are present in a particular case would, of course, be relevant. Their importance would depend upon the nature of the precise change under consideration.

By treating the exercise of authority by the commission in this case as the exercise of judicial rather than of legislative authority and thus enlarging the scope of review on appeal, and by placing the burden of the above level of proof upon the one seeking change, we may lay the court open to criticism by legal scholars who think it desirable that planning authorities be vested with the ability to adjust more freely to changed conditions. However, having weighed the dangers of making desirable change more difficult against the dangers of the almost irresistible pressures that can be asserted by private economic interests on local government, we believe that the latter dangers are more to be feared.

What we have said above is necessarily general, as the approach we adopt contains no absolute standards or mechanical tests. We believe, however, that it is adequate to provide meaningful guidance for local governments making zoning decisions and for trial courts called upon to review them. With future cases in mind, it is appropriate to add some brief remarks on questions of procedure. Parties at the hearing before the county governing body are entitled to an opportunity to be heard, to an opportunity to present and rebut evidence, to a tribunal which is impartial in the matter — i.e., having had no pre-hearing or ex parte contacts concerning the question at issue-and to a record made and adequate findings executed.

When we apply the standards we have adopted to the present case, we find that the burden was not sustained before the commission. The record now before us is insufficient to ascertain whether there was a justifiable basis for the decision. The only evidence in the record, that of the staff report of the Washington County Planning Department, is too conclusory and superficial to support the zoning change. It merely states:

> "The staff finds that the requested use does conform to the residential designation of the Plan of Development. It further finds that the proposed use reflects the urbanization of the County and the necessity to provide increased densities and different types of housing to meet the needs of urbanization over that allowed by the existing zoning."

Such generalizations and conclusions, without any statement of the facts on which they are based, are insufficient to justify a change of use. Moreover, no portions of the comprehensive plan of Washington County are before us, and we feel it would be improper for us to take judicial notice of the plan without at least some reference to its specifics by counsel.

As there has not been an adequate showing that the change was in accord with the plan, or that the factors listed in ORS 215.055 were given proper consideration, the judgment is affirmed.

## Questions for Consideration

1) What zoning change was made by the County Commissioners?

2) Does a zoning change require a change in the character of a neighborhood?

3) How does the court address the relationship between the comprehensive plan and the zoning code?

4) With reference to the comprehensive plan, what factors should be evaluated in making a determination about the zoning of the land in question?

5) The court examines the legislative function and the adjudicative function of planning and zoning. What does it tell us about these functions in terms of the deference to be given to the decisions of local government when those decisions are reviewed on appeal?

6) If the local government body charged with making a zoning decision, concerning a particular parcel of land is composed of elected officials who perform legislative duties, does this mean that all of their decisions are legislative decisions?

7) What is a floating zone?

8) Is a floating zone consistent with traditional Euclidian zoning?

### *Takeaway*

- Zoning is done pursuant to a comprehensive plan.

- In evaluating the content of a comprehensive plan and the relationship between planning and zoning, one must look to the enabling provisions of state statutes.

- While the standard of review for legislative functions is one of great deference, the standard applied to quasi-adjudicative actions is different and less deferential. Usually when a quasi-adjudicative decision is made, it must be rational and supported by competent evidence on the record. Sometimes, courts will say it must be supported by *substantial* competent evidence on the record. This is a higher standard than that of the rational basis test using the fairly debatable standard set out in *Euclid*, and higher than that rational basis test applied in *Nectow*. This is a rational basis standard supported by substantial competent evidence on the record. This gives us three different tests for the rational basis standard of review: one for legislation generally; one for an as applied challenge; and one for quasi-adjudicative decision-making.

- A zoning board of appeal, when it makes decisions about the application of the zoning code to a specific property, is engaged in a quasi-adjudicative function. It is engaged in applying the law to a specific property, and its decisions will affect the legal rights of the property owner. Because this is a quasi-adjudicative process, the property owner's due process rights include such things as notice, an opportunity to be heard, an ability to present evidence, the right to ask questions, and an opportunity to review the record of the proceeding and the final decision. This is a "court-like" proceeding, and due process requires appropriate measures.

- Generally, adopting legislation authorizing a floating zone as part of a comprehensive plan is considered a legislative act, whereas the process of fixing the floating zone to a specific property location is considered a quasi-adjudicative act.

### Pinecrest Lakes, Inc. v. Shidel

Court of Appeal of Florida, Fourth District
795 So. 2d 191 (Fla. Dist. Ct. App. 2001)

Farmer, Judge. The ultimate issue raised in this case is unprecedented in Florida. The question is whether a trial court has the authority to order the complete demolition and removal of several multi-story buildings because the buildings are inconsistent with the County's comprehensive land use plan. We conclude that the court is so empowered and affirm the decision under review.

Some twenty years ago, a developer purchased a 500-acre parcel of land in Martin County and set out to develop it in phases. Development there is governed by the Martin County Comprehensive Plan (the Comprehensive Plan). Phase One of the property was designated under the Comprehensive Plan as "Residential Estate," meaning single-family homes on individual lots with a maximum density of 2 units per acre (UPA). The Comprehensive Plan provides that

> "[W]here single family structures comprise the dominant structure type within these areas, new development of undeveloped abutting lands *shall be required* to include compatible structure types of land immediately adjacent to existing single family development."

Phases One through Nine were developed as single-family homes on individual lots in very low densities.

The subject of this litigation, Phase Ten, is a 21-acre parcel between Phase One and Jensen Beach Boulevard, a divided highway designated both as "major" and "arterial." Phase Ten was designated by the Comprehensive Plan as "Medium Density Residential" with a maximum of 8 UPA. The developer sought approval of three different site plans before finally erecting the buildings that are the subject of this litigation. In 1988, the developer first sought approval for an initial scheme of 3-story apartment buildings with a density of just under 8 UPA. Karen Shidel, since 1986 an owner of a single-family residence in the adjoining area of Phase One, along with other residents, opposed the project proposed by the developer. This initial site plan for Phase Ten was approved by the County but never acted upon.

Five years later, the developer changed the proposed scheme to single family residences, and the County Commission approved a revised site plan for 29 single-family homes with a density of 1.37 UPA. Two years after that, however, the developer again changed its mind and returned to its original concept of multi-family structures. This time, the developer sought to develop 136 units in two-story buildings, with a density of 6.5 UPA. The County's growth management staff recommended that the County Commission approve this second revised site plan for Phase Ten. Following a hearing at which a number of people objected to the proposal, including Shidel, the County Commission approved the revision and issued a Development Order for Phase Ten permitting the construction of 19 two-story buildings.

Claiming statutory authority, Shidel and another Phase One homeowner, one Charles Brooks, along with the Homeowners Associations for Phases One through Nine, then filed a verified complaint with the Martin County Commission challenging the consistency of the Development Order with the Comprehensive Plan, requesting rescission of the Development Order. In response to the verified complaint, after a hearing the County Commission confirmed its previous decision to issue the Development Order.

Shidel and Brooks then filed a civil action in the Circuit Court against Martin County under the same statutory authority. They alleged that the Development Order was inconsistent with the Comprehensive Plan. The developer intervened. Shidel and Brooks argued that their statutory challenge was a de novo proceeding in which the court should decide in the first instance whether the Development Order was consistent with the Comprehensive Plan. Martin County and the developer argued that the proceeding was in the nature of appellate review in which the County's determination was entitled to deference and the court should consider only whether there was substantial competent evidence supporting the Development Order. Basing its decision solely on a review of the record created before the County Commission, the trial court found that the Development Order was consistent with the Comprehensive Plan and entered final judgment in favor of the developer.

At that point, the developer took stock of its position. It had prevailed before the County Commission and — at least initially — in the trial court. Technically, however, its approval for the project was not final. Developer considered whether to proceed to construct the buildings or instead await appellate review of the trial court's decision. Ultimately the developer decided to commence construction, notwithstanding the pendency of an appeal. Accordingly, it applied for and received building permits for construction of Buildings 8, 9, 10, 11 and 12, and started on each of those buildings while the case was under consideration in court. When construction was just beginning, Shidel and Brooks sent written notice to the developer of their intention, should they prove successful in court, to seek demolition and removal of any construction undertaken while judicial consideration of the consistency issue was pending.

Appellate review did not produce the outcome for which the developer had hoped. In 1997 we reversed the trial court's decision that the County's consistency determination complied with the Comprehensive Plan. . . . [The case was then remanded for further review.]

On remand, the trial judge proceeded in two stages: the first stage involved a determination whether the Development Order was consistent with the Comprehensive Plan; and the second stage, which became necessary, addressed the remedy. While the case was pending on remand, developer continued with construction. The County conducted final inspections of Building 11 and 12, issuing certificates of occupancy (CO), and residents moved into the buildings. At the end of the consistency phase, the trial court entered a partial judgment finding that the Development Order was not consistent with the Comprehensive Plan. The trial de novo then proceeded to the remedy.

At the conclusion of the remedy phase, the trial court entered a Final Judgment. The court found that the Comprehensive Plan established a hierarchy of land uses, paying deference to lower density residential uses and providing protection to those areas. The "tiering policy" required that, for structures immediately adjacent to each other, any new structures to be added to the area must be both comparable and compatible to those already built and occupied. The court then found significant differences between the northern tier of Phase One and the adjacent southern tier of Phase Ten. The structures in Phase One were single level, single family residences, while the structures in Phase Ten were two-story apartment buildings with eight residential units. Therefore, the court found, the 8-residential unit, two-story, apartment buildings in Phase Ten were not compatible or comparable types of dwelling units with the single family, single level residences in Phase One; nor were they of comparable density. Consequently, the court determined, the Development Order was inconsistent with the Comprehensive Plan.

As regards to the remedy, the Final Judgment found no evidence indicating that either Brooks or the Homeowners Association were damaged by any diminution in value. The court found that the Homeowners Association was not a person within the meaning of section 163.3215(2) and therefore had no standing to seek relief under section 163.3215. Accordingly, only plaintiff Shidel was entitled to seek injunctive relief under section 163.3215.

In granting such relief, the court found that the developer had acted in bad faith. Specifically, the court found that the developer continued construction during the pendency of the prior appeal and continued to build and lease during the trial — even after losing on the consistency issue. The court found that the developer "acted at [its] own peril in doing precisely what this lawsuit sought to prevent and now [is] subject to the power of the court to compel restoration of the status prior to construction." The relief awarded was:

> (1) the Court permanently enjoined Martin County from taking any further action on the subject Development Order for Phase Ten, other than to rescind it;

> (2) the Court permanently enjoined developer and its successors in interest from any further development of Phase Ten under the subject Development Order; and

> (3) the Court ordered developer to remove all apartment buildings from Phase Ten either through demolition or physical relocation by a date certain.

When the Final Judgment was entered, five of the eight-unit buildings had been constructed in Phase Ten (Buildings 8–12). Buildings 11 and 12 had already received their CO's, and fifteen of their sixteen units were actually occupied. Building 10 was fully completed and was awaiting final inspection as of the date the remedies stage of trial began. Buildings 8 and 9 were 50% and 66% completed, respectively, also as of that date.

Following the entry of Final Judgment, the developer filed this timely appeal and moved for a stay pending review. The trial court granted a stay only as to the demolition order, allowing lessees to continue in possession of those apartments in Buildings 9–12 under actual lease when the trial court entered final judgment, as well as to those leases in Building 8 in existence as of the date of filing of the notice of appeal. The developer was prohibited, however, from entering into any renewals of existing leases upon expiration of the original term or any new leases of any apartments. Upon review, we affirmed the stay order. We now explain our decision on the merits.

## I. The Consistency Issue

Initially the developer argues that the trial court erred in the consistency phase by failing to accord any deference to the County Commission's interpretation of its own Comprehensive Plan when the County approved the second revised site plan and its multi-story, multi-family buildings. Conceding that the proceedings are de novo and that the Development Order is subject to "strict scrutiny" under the Comprehensive Plan as to the consistency issue, the developer nevertheless argues that the courts must bow to the County's interpretation of its own Comprehensive Plan and the application of its many elements to the site plan. Developer argues that the statutes and cases accord such deference to a local government's interpretation of its own Comprehensive Plan and that it was reversible error for the trial court in this case to fail to do so. According to developer, these cases authorize the use of the highly deferential "fairly debatable" standard of review — customary with zoning decisions — to land use determinations such as the issue of consistency in this case. We disagree.

. . . .

. . . [T]here is but one basis for issuing the injunction: that the development order is not consistent with the Comprehensive Plan to the detriment of adjoining property owners. Hence the issuance of an injunction under section 163.3215(1) necessarily requires the judge to determine in the first instance whether a development order is consistent with the Comprehensive Plan. When a statute authorizes a citizen to bring an action to enjoin official conduct that is made improper by the statute, and that same statute necessitates a determination by the judge in the action as to whether the official's conduct was improper under the statute, as a general matter the requirement for a determination of the propriety of the official action should not be understood as requiring the court to defer to the official whose conduct is being judged. While the Legislature could nevertheless possibly have some reason to require judges to require some deference to the officials whose conduct was thus put in issue, we would certainly expect to see such a requirement of deference spelled out in the statute with unmistakable clarity. Here it is not a question of any lack of clarity; the statute is utterly silent on the notion of deference. It is thus apparent that the structure and text of the statute do not impliedly involve any deference to the decision of the county officials. So we necessarily presume none was intended.

Section 163.3194 requires that all development conform to the approved Comprehensive Plan, and that development orders be consistent with that Plan. The statute is framed as a rule, a command to cities and counties that they must comply with their own Comprehensive Plans after they have been approved by the State. The statute does not say that local governments shall have some discretion as to whether a proposed development should be consistent with the Comprehensive Plan. Consistency with a Comprehensive Plan is therefore not a discretionary matter. When the Legislature wants to give an agency discretion and then for the courts to defer to such discretion, it knows how to say that. Here it has not. We thus reject the developer's contention that the trial court erred in failing to defer to the County's interpretation of its own comprehensive plan.

Before we proceed to assess the trial court's determination on the consistency issue, we pause to consider the history of the land development statutes. The State of

Florida did not assert meaningful formal control over the explosive and unplanned development of land in this state until the passage of the first growth management statute, the Local Government Comprehensive Planning Act of 1975. Chapter 75-257, Laws of Fla. (the 1975 Act). The 1975 Act forced counties and cities to adopt comprehensive plans, but they were left to interpret such plans for themselves, largely free from effective oversight by the state. *See, e.g., City of Jacksonville Beach v. Grubbs*, 461 So. 2d 160, 163 (Fla. 1st DCA 1984) (determination of when to conform more restrictive zoning ordinances with Comprehensive Plan is legislative judgment to be made by local governing body, subject only to limited judicial review for patent arbitrariness). The requirement of adopting a Comprehensive Plan was, therefore, only a small step. Moreover nothing in the legislation required local governments to comply with their own Comprehensive Plans or that all development be consistent with the Plan.

. . . .

For another thing, the 1975 Act was criticized for failing to give affected property owners and citizen groups standing to challenge the land development decisions of local governments on the grounds that they were inconsistent with the Comprehensive Plan. . . .

. . . The result was the Growth Management Act of 1985. Chap. 85-55, Laws of Fla. . . . Its most important provision for our purposes was section 163.3215, the provision used by Shidel to bring this action into court.

. . . Affected citizens have been given a significantly enhanced standing to challenge the consistency of development decisions with the Comprehensive Plan.

The Growth Management Act of 1985 was discussed in what is now recognized as the most significant land use decision by the supreme court in the past decade, namely *Board of County Commissioners of Brevard County v. Snyder*, 627 So.2d 469 (Fla. 1993). *Snyder* involved a parcel then zoned only for single family homes and a proposed development of 5–6 units. The proposal also necessarily required a change of zoning. After substantial opposition, and in spite of a favorable staff recommendation, the County voted to deny the request without giving any reasons. Certiorari was denied in the circuit court, one judge dissenting. The Fifth District held that rezoning actions entailing the application of a general rule or policy to specific individuals, interests, or activities are quasi-judicial in nature and should be subjected to a stricter standard of judicial review. The court found that the proposed site plan was consistent with the Comprehensive Plan, that there was no evidence supporting the denial of any necessary rezoning, and that the denial of the request without giving any reasons was arbitrary and unreasonable.

. . . .

The court explained that in Florida the 1975 Act "was substantially strengthened by the Growth Management Act [of 1985]." 627 So. 2d at 473. After analyzing various provisions of the Growth Management Act of 1985, the court stated:

"We also agree with the court below that the review is *subject to strict scrutiny*. In practical effect, the review by strict scrutiny in zoning cases appears to be the same as that given in the review of other quasi-judicial decisions. . . . (The term 'strict scrutiny' arises from the *necessity of strict compliance with comprehensive plan*.) This term as used in the review of land use decisions must be distinguished from the type of strict scrutiny review afforded in some constitutional cases. . . ."

In the foregoing, quotation the supreme court drew a distinction between the use of strict scrutiny in land use cases and its use in other contexts. . . . [The court] explained that strict scrutiny of local government development orders is necessary to insure that the local governments comply with the duty imposed by section 163.3194 to make decisions consistent with the Comprehensive Plan. . . .

. . . .

Under section 163.3215 citizen enforcement is the primary tool for insuring consistency of development decisions with the Comprehensive Plan. . . . In light of the text of section 163.3215 and the foregoing history, we reject the developer's contention that the trial court erred in failing to defer to the County's interpretation of its own Comprehensive Plan.

Having thus decided that the trial court was correct in failing to accord any particular deference to the Martin County Commission in its interpretation of the Comprehensive Plan, we now proceed to consider the court's determination on the consistency issue. The trial court explained its decision as follows:

"The primary claim by [plaintiffs] is that the juxtaposition of multistory, multi-family apartments in Phase 10 directly next to the single family homes in Phase 1 violates a number of provisions in the Comprehensive Plan. The provision of the Comprehensive Plan that is central to their argument is section 4-5(A)(2)(b), known as the 'tiering policy.'

"The tiering policy was added to the Comprehensive Plan . . . to address how development would be added to existing single-family residential communities. There was a concern . . . over how existing single-family homes were being impacted by new, adjacent denser developments. . . .

"The tiering policy required . . . a transition zone along the southern portion of Phase 10 equal to 'the depth of the first block of single-family lots' within the northern portion of Phase 1. The section requires that development in the first tier of Phase 10 be limited to construction 'of comparable density and compatible dwelling unit types.' The court finds that the appropriate measure is 225 feet, using the shortest average depth method of computation.

"No transition zone was established for Phase 10. The buildings along the first tier of Phase 10 are multi-family, multi-story, and have balconies. The southern tier of Phase 10 has a density of 6.6 [UPA]. The overall density of Phase 10 is 6.5 [UPA]. There is no meaningful difference in density across the entire western portion of Phase 10. The northern tier of Phase 1, on the other hand, is comprised entirely of single-family homes on 0.75 acre to 1.2 acre lots, with a density of 0.94 [UPA].

"There was no first tier transition zone established for Phase 10 as mandated by section 4-5(A)(2)(b). That section is not the only provision of the Comprehensive Plan that mandated compatible structures within the first tier of Phase 10. Section 4-4(M)(1)(e)(2) provided:

> ... Where single family structures comprise the dominant structure type within [residential estate densities (RE-0.5A)], new development on undeveloped abutting lands shall be required to include compatible structure types of lands immediately adjacent to existing family development.

> ... Phase 1 is designated RE-0.5A.

. . . .

"It is impossible ... to examine the photographs of the homes in the northern tier of Phase 1, and the apartment buildings in the southern tier of Phase 10, and find that they are either 'compatible dwelling unit types' or 'compatible structure types.' The only residential structure that could be *less* compatible with the northern tier of Phase 1, would be a multi-story condominium building. There is no compatibility between the structures in the southern tier of Phase 10 and the northern tier of Phase 1. Further, an examination of the density of development in the two tiers at issue, precludes this court from finding that they are in any way comparable.

. . . .

"Based on the foregoing, the Court finds that the Development Order is inconsistent with the Comprehensive Plan. It is not compatible with, nor does it further the objective, policies, land uses, densities and intensities in the Comprehensive Plan. § 163.3194(3)(a)."

We have carefully reviewed the record of the trial and the evidence presented. It is apparent that there is substantial competent evidence to support these findings. Developer argues that the court erred in its interpretation of the "tiering policy," in deeming it a mandatory requirement rather than a discretionary guide. We conclude that the trial court's construction is consistent with the plain meaning of the text of the Comprehensive Plan.... Moreover, given the evidence as to Martin County's adoption of the tiering policy, the record clearly supports the finding that the policy was intended to be applied in all instances of projects abutting single-family residential areas. We therefore affirm the finding of inconsistency and proceed to explain our decision on the remedy.

## II. Remedy of Demolition

Developer challenges what it terms the "enormity and extremity of the injunctive remedy imposed by the trial court." It argues that the trial court's order requiring the demolition of 5 multi-family residential buildings is the most radical remedy ever mandated by a Florida court because of an inconsistency with a Comprehensive Plan. Specifically, the contention is that the trial judge failed to balance the equities between the parties and thus ignored the evidence of a $3.3 million dollar loss the developer will suffer from the demolition of the buildings. The court failed to consider alternative remedies in damages, it argues, that would have adequately remedied any harm resulting from the construction of structures inconsistent with the Comprehensive Plan.

. . . .

We disagree. . . . Here the Legislature has devised an entire statutory scheme to insure that all counties have a Comprehensive Plan for the development of land within their respective jurisdictions. The scheme creates mandatory duties to have a plan, mandatory duties to have the plan approved by the state, and once approved mandatory duties to limit all developments so that they are consistent with the plan's requirements. At the end of all these mandatory duties — all these *shalls* — comes a new relaxation of the requirements on standing for citizen suits to enforce comprehensive land use plans and providing for the issuance of injunctions when an inconsistency affects another land owner. . . .

Developer lays great stress on the size of the monetary loss that it claims it will suffer from demolition, as opposed to the much smaller diminution in value that the affected property owner bringing this action may have suffered. It contends that a $3.3 million loss far outweighs the evidence of diminution in the value of Shidel's property, less than $26,000. Its primary contention here is that the trial judge erred in failing to weigh these equities in its favor and deny any remedy of demolition. Instead, as developer sees it, the court should have awarded money damages to eliminate the objector's diminution in value. Developer argued that it should be allowed instead of demolition it should also be allowed to build environmental barriers, green areas of trees and shrubbery, between the apartment buildings and the adjoining area of single family homes.

Developer emphasizes that we deal here with an expensive development: "a high quality, upscale project;" "forty units of high-quality garden apartments;" "five upscale multi-family dwellings, housing 40 garden apartments, at a value of approximately $3 million." Developer concedes that there is evidence showing that plaintiff Shidel's property is diminished by $26,000. It also concedes that the total diminution for all the homes bordering its project is just under $300,000. Developer contends, however, that the real countervailing harm to all these affected property owners in the vicinity is not any diminution in the value of their homes, but instead is merely "knowing that there is an upscale apartment building approximately a football field away, partially visible through some trees behind the house."

Section 163.3215 says nothing about weighing these specific equities before granting an injunction. If the Legislature had intended that injunctive enforcement of comprehensive plans in the courts be limited to cases where such imbalances of equities were not present, we assume that it would have said so. As important, such balancing if applied generally would lead to substantial non-compliance with comprehensive plans. We doubt that there will be many instances where the cost of the newly allowed construction will be less than any diminution resulting from an inconsistency. Entire projects of the kind permitted here will frequently far exceed the monetary harms caused to individual neighbors affected by the inconsistency. In other words, if balancing the equities — that is, weighing the loss suffered by the developer against the diminution in value of the objecting party — were required before demolition could be ordered, then demolition will never be ordered.

Moreover, it is an argument that would allow those with financial resources to buy their way out of compliance with comprehensive plans. In all cases where the proposed use is for multiple acres and multiple buildings, the expenditures will be great. The greater will be its cost, and so will be a resulting loss from an after-the-fact demolition order. The more costly and elaborate the project, the greater will be the "imbalance in the equities." The more a developer is able to gild an inconsistency with nature's ornaments — trees, plants, flowers and their symbiotic fauna — the more certain under this argument will be the result that no court will enjoin an inconsistency and require its removal if already built.

In this case, the alleged inequity could have been entirely avoided if developer had simply awaited the exhaustion of all legal remedies before undertaking construction. It is therefore difficult to perceive from the record any great inequity in requiring demolition. Shidel let the developer know when it was just beginning construction of the first building that she would seek demolition if the court found the project inconsistent. When developer decided to proceed with construction in spite of the absence of a final decision as to the merits of the challenge under section 163.3215, the developer was quite able to foresee that it might lose the action in court. It could not have had a reasonable expectation that its right to build what it had proposed was finally settled. It may have thought the decision to build before the consistency question was settled in court a reasonable "business decision," but that hardly makes it inequitable to enforce the rule as written.

It also seems quite inappropriate, if balancing of equities were truly required by this statute, to focus on the relatively small financial impacts suffered by those adjoining an inconsistent land use. The real countervailing equity to any monetary loss of the developer is in the flouting of the legal requirements of the Comprehensive Plan. Every citizen in the community is intangibly harmed by a failure to comply with the Comprehensive Plan, even those whose properties may not have been directly diminished in value.

We claim to be a society of laws, not of individual eccentricities in attempting to evade the rule of law. A society of law must respect law, not its evasion. If the rule of law requires land uses to meet specific standards, then allowing those who develop land to escape its requirements by spending a project out of compliance would make the standards of growth management of little real consequence. It would allow developers such as this one to build in defiance of the limits and then escape compliance by making the cost of correction too high. That would render section 163.3215 meaningless and ineffectual.

. . . .

The statute says that an affected or aggrieved party may bring an action to enjoin an inconsistent development allowed by the County under its Comprehensive Plan. The statutory rule is that if you build it, and in court it later proves inconsistent, it will have to come down. The court's injunction enforces the statutory scheme as written. The County has been ordered to comply with its own Comprehensive Plan and restrained from allowing inconsistent development; and the developer has been found to have built an inconsistent land use and has been ordered to remove it. The rule of law has prevailed.

We therefore affirm the final judgment of the trial court in all respects.

GUNTHER and GROSS, JJ., concur.

## Questions for Consideration

1) What exactly is the developer doing with its development project that violates the comprehensive plan?

2) Were the development plans approved by the local planning and zoning officials, including the County Commission?

3) How far along was the project at the time of this court decision?

4) If the county was in agreement with the developer as to proceeding with the project, who brought this lawsuit?

5) As to the question of consistency with the comprehensive plan, what is the standard of review?

6) What is a key mechanism for ensuring that local planning and zoning officials will, in fact, act consistently with an approved comprehensive plan?

7) Does it make a difference if a state requires state approval of a local comprehensive plan, as contrasted with a state requirement that local communities engage in comprehensive planning without a need for state approval of the plans?

8) The court has four ways of addressing a remedy in this case. First, it can issue an injunction prohibiting all further development, and it could stop there. Second, it might issue the injunction and award damages to the property owners to compensate them for the diminution in value of their homes as a result of the new construction. Third, it can award damages for the diminished value of properties without granting an injunction. Fourth, it can order

the developer to take down the buildings and comply with the regulations. What approach to a remedy did the court take and why?

9) Is the remedy imposed by the court socially efficient?

## *Takeaway*

- Florida provides an example of a state that not only requires extensive planning at the local level but also requires coordination among local, regional, and state planning officials. Few states apply the same level of strict scrutiny to the question of consistency with the comprehensive plan, as Florida does. At the same time, consistency is an issue in every jurisdiction, and it is important to determine the level of consistency required in each locale.

## Foothill Communities Coalition v. County of Orange

Court of Appeal of California, Fourth Appellate District, Division Three
166 Cal. Rptr. 3d 627 (Cal. Ct. App. 2014)

FYBEL, Judge. The Roman Catholic Diocese of Orange (the Diocese) and Kisco Senior Living, LLC (Kisco), desire to build a living community for senior citizens on a parcel of real property, owned by the Diocese (the Project), which is located in an unincorporated area of Orange County (the County). The County Board of Supervisors (the Board) created a new zoning definition for senior residential housing, and applied it to the Project site; found the Project was consistent with the County's general plan and the "North Tustin Specific Plan" (sometimes referred to as NTSP); and found the Project complied with the California Environmental Quality Act (Pub. Resources Code, § 21000 et seq.) (CEQA). Foothill Communities Coalition, an unincorporated association of grassroots community groups and area homeowners (Foothill), challenged the Board's decisions by means of a petition for a peremptory writ of mandate. The trial court entered judgment in favor of Foothill, and issued the requested writ.

Appellants challenge the trial court's conclusion that the Board's acts constitute impermissible spot zoning. We publish this case to clarify the law regarding spot zoning in two respects. First, spot zoning may occur whether a small parcel of property is subject to *more or less restrictive* zoning than the surrounding properties. Second, to determine whether *impermissible* spot zoning has occurred, a court is required to conduct a two-part analysis. After determining that spot zoning has actually occurred, the court must determine whether the record shows the spot zoning is in the public interest.

In this case, applying the required standard of review, which is deferential to the Board, we conclude the Board's findings that the Project would be consistent with the County's general plan and with the North Tustin Specific Plan are supported by substantial evidence. The creation of the new senior residential housing zone and its application to the Project site were not arbitrary or capricious, or lacking in evidentiary support. Although the Board's actions constituted spot zoning, the spot zoning was permissible. The trial court erred in entering judgment in Foothill's favor and in issuing the writ of mandate. We therefore reverse. . . .

### Statement of Facts, Chronology, and Procedural History

In 1956, the Diocese received a gift of a 7.25-acre parcel of undeveloped property in the North Tustin area of the County. In 2003, the Diocese decided to develop the property as a senior residential community. The Diocese retained senior living communities developer Kisco to design and implement the Project. In January 2009, the Diocese and Kisco submitted to the County a project design proposing 153 senior living units.

The Project site is located within the area covered by the North Tustin Specific Plan, which regulates the development of property within its boundaries and was adopted by the Board in 1982. Under the North Tustin Specific Plan, the Project site is designated as a residential single-family district. In July 2009, the County issued a notice of preparation for the Project's environmental impact report (EIR). The draft EIR was released in May 2010 for a 45-day public comment period. The final EIR was released by the County in December 2010.

In January 2011, the County Planning Commission conducted a public hearing on the Project, at the end of which it recommended that the Board approve the Project and certify the final EIR. The Board conducted a public hearing on the Project, after which it issued one ordinance and two resolutions approving the Project and making necessary changes to the North Tustin Specific Plan to permit its development. In ordinance No. 11-008, the Board amended the North Tustin Specific Plan to add a new zoning district for senior residential housing and to change the land use district for the Project site to the new senior residential housing designation. In resolution No. 11-038, the Board certified the EIR for the Project as complete, accurate, and in compliance with the requirements of CEQA. And in resolution No. 11-039, the Board approved both a use permit for the Project as a senior living facility, and a site development permit. In March 2011, the Board amended the North Tustin Specific Plan to create a new zoning district — the senior residential housing land use district — which it applied to the Project site. The same month, the County filed a notice of determination of the Board's approval of the Project and certification of the final EIR.

In April 2011, Foothill filed a verified petition for a writ of mandate and complaint for declaratory relief against the County and the Board. . . .

### Discussion

### I.

### Standard of Review

"The 'rezoning of property, even a single parcel, is generally considered to be a quasi-legislative act' thus 'subject to review under ordinary mandamus.' The standard for review of a quasi-legislative act is whether the action was 'arbitrary or capricious or totally lacking in evidentiary support.'"

"'In a mandamus proceeding, the ultimate question, whether the agency's action was arbitrary or capricious, is a question of law. Trial and appellate courts therefore perform the same function and the trial court's statement of decision has no conclusive effect upon us.'"

The party challenging a zoning ordinance as arbitrary or capricious bears the burden of producing sufficient evidence from which the trier of fact may conclude that the ordinance is unreasonable and invalid. In this case, the burden of proof was on Foothill.

## II.

### Appellants' Appeals

### A. Zoning Decisions Are Exercises of the County's Police Power.

"It is well settled that zoning ordinances, when reasonable in object and not arbitrary in operation, constitute a justifiable exercise of police power, and that the establishment, as part of a comprehensive and systematic plan, of districts devoted to strictly private residences or single family dwellings, from which are excluded business or multiple dwelling structures, is a legitimate exercise of the police power."

The Project site is subject to both the County's general plan and a specific plan. "[T]he general plan [is] a '"constitution" for future development' located at the top of 'the hierarchy of local government law regulating land use.' The general plan consists of a 'statement of development policies . . . setting forth objectives, principles, standards, and plan proposals.' The plan must include seven elements—land use, circulation, conservation, housing, noise, safety and open space—and address each of these elements in whatever level of detail local conditions require. General plans are also required to be 'comprehensive [and] long term' as well as 'internally consistent.' The planning law thus compels cities and counties to undergo the discipline of drafting a master plan to guide future local land use decisions."

A specific plan, such as the North Tustin Specific Plan, is usually more detailed than a general plan, and covers specific parts of the community. The approval of a specific plan does not create a vested right to develop property in a manner consistent with the specific plan, or to prevent development inconsistent with it. A specific plan may be adopted or amended by resolution or ordinance of the appropriate legislative body. These sections of the Government Code recognize that "[a] county's needs necessarily change over time. . . . It follows that a county must have the power to modify its land use plans as circumstances require." Despite Foothill's argument to the contrary, the North Tustin Specific Plan does not constitute a contract entered into by the County. (See Gov. Code, § 65453, subd. (a) [specific plans "may be amended as often as deemed necessary by the legislative body"].)

A particular project must be "compatible with the objectives, policies, general land uses, and programs specified in" the general plan or any applicable, officially adopted specific plan. (Gov. Code, § 66473.5.) Government Code section 66473.5 has been interpreted "as requiring that a project be '"in agreement or harmony with"' the terms of the applicable plan, not in rigid conformity with every detail thereof."

The ordinance by which the new senior residential housing zoning district was created and applied to the Project site reads, in relevant part, as follows: "The County, after balancing the specific economic, legal, social, technological, and other benefits of the proposed Project, has determined that the unavoidable adverse environmental impacts identified . . . may be considered acceptable due to the following specific considerations which outweigh the unavoidable, adverse environmental impacts of the proposed Project, each of which standing alone is sufficient to support approval of the Project. . . ." The specific considerations identified by the County include (1) the Project addresses the housing element goals for senior housing set forth in the County's general plan, (2) the Project is compatible with the character of the surrounding neighborhood, (3) the Project addresses and remedies existing issues with storm drains and runoff, (4) the Project would provide for a deed restriction to be imposed on the property, so that future owners would be prohibited from other incompatible uses, and (5) the Project allows for implementation of policies set forth in the North Tustin Specific Plan.

### B. Spot Zoning

Foothill contends the zoning change created an instance of impermissible spot zoning. "The essence of spot zoning is irrational discrimination." "Spot zoning is one type of discriminatory zoning ordinance. 'Spot zoning occurs where a small parcel is restricted and given lesser rights than the surrounding property, as where a lot in the center of a business or commercial district is limited to uses for residential purposes thereby creating an "island" in the middle of a larger area devoted to other uses. Usually spot zoning involves a small parcel of land, the larger the property the more difficult it is to sustain an allegation of spot zoning. Likewise, where the "spot" is not an island but is connected on some sides to a like zone the allegation of spot zoning is more difficult to establish since lines must be drawn at some point. Even where a small island is created in the midst of less restrictive zoning, the zoning may be upheld where rational reason in the public benefit exists for such a classification.'"

Appellants correctly note that no published case in California has directly addressed the type of spot zoning at issue here — where the small parcel is given *greater rights* than the surrounding property. We reject Appellants' argument that this means the zoning change by the Board is not spot zoning. "A spot zone results when a small parcel of land is subject to more *or less* restrictive zoning than surrounding properties." . . .

    . . . .

The Supreme Court . . . [has] . . . set forth two clear rules of law applicable to challenges to zoning decisions. First, "[t]he courts cannot write the zoning laws and cannot say that the legislative body has erred in drawing the lines of the districts, or in restricting the territory devoted to business or to multiple dwellings, unless there is a clear showing of abuse of legislative discretion." Second, "[w]here it is claimed that the ordinance is unreasonable as applied to plaintiff's property, or that a change in conditions has rendered application of the ordinance unreasonable, it is incumbent on plaintiff to produce sufficient evidence from which the court can make such findings as to the physical facts involved as will justify it in concluding, as a matter of law, that the ordinance is unreasonable and invalid. It is not sufficient for him to show that it will be more profitable to him to make other use of his property, or that such other use will not cause injury to the public, but he must show an abuse of discretion on the part of the zoning authorities and that there has been an unreasonable and unwarranted exercise of the police power."

Many other jurisdictions have concluded that an amendment to a zoning ordinance that singles out a small parcel of land for a use different from that of the surrounding properties and for the benefit of the owner of the small parcel and to the detriment of other owners is spot zoning.

We hold the creation of an island of property with less restrictive zoning in the middle of properties with more restrictive zoning is spot zoning. This conclusion does not end our analysis, however, as spot zoning may or may not be impermissible, depending on the circumstances. "The rezoning ordinance may be justified, however, if a substantial public need exists, and this is so even if the private owner of the tract will also benefit." "[T]he term 'spot zoning' is merely shorthand for a certain arrangement of physical facts. When those facts exist, the zoning may or may not be warranted. . . . Spot zoning may well be in the public interest; it may even be in accordance with the requirements of a master plan."

### C. Were the Creation of the New Zoning District and Its Application to the Project Site in the Public Interest, and Were Those Decisions Arbitrary or Capricious, or Devoid of Evidentiary Support?

Foothill's overriding argument is that the change in zoning of the Project site was inconsistent with the North Tustin Specific Plan. "No . . . zoning ordinance may be adopted or amended within an area covered by a specific plan unless it is consistent with the adopted specific plan." Under the applicable standard of review, we consider the Board's factual findings of consistency and defer to them unless "no reasonable person could have reached the same conclusion on the evidence before it."

We note initially that the California Legislature has encouraged the development of senior citizen housing by creating a 20 percent density bonus for such projects. The Board's approval of the Project and change in zoning to permit the Project to be constructed are consistent with statewide priorities.

The creation of the senior residential housing zoning district is in the public interest and consistent with the County's general plan and with the North Tustin Specific Plan. In enacting resolution Nos. 11-038 and 11-039, the Board found, based on the facts in the administrative record, that "[t]he proposed Project would be consistent with the General Plan, NTSP, as amended, and Senior Living Ordinance." As defined in ordinance No. 11-008 creating the senior residential housing district, only senior housing units, not other types of multidwelling uses (such as apartment buildings), can be built on the Project site. Also, the development standards are consistent with the surrounding residential single-family zoning district. We reach this conclusion based on our review of the many factual findings of consistency with the applicable general and specific plans, which are included in the administrative record.

The housing element, one of nine elements of the County's general plan, provides, in relevant part: "The special housing needs of seniors are an important concern in Orange County. This is especially so since many retired persons are likely to be on fixed low incomes, at greater risk of impaction, or housing overpayment. In addition, the elderly maintain special needs related to housing construction and location. Seniors often require ramps, handrails, lower cupboards and counters to allow greater access and mobility. In terms of location, because of limited mobility the elderly also typically need access to public facilities (e.g., medical and shopping) and public transit facilities. . . . In general, every effort should be made to maintain the dignity, self-respect, and quality of life of mature residents in the County. . . . In 2000, there were 6,162 owner households and 606 renter households in unincorporated Orange County where the householder was 65 or older. . . . Of these, 1,235 elderly persons were living alone. Many elderly persons are dependent on fixed incomes and/or have a disability. Elderly homeowners may be physically unable to maintain their homes or cope with living alone. The housing needs of this group can be addressed through smaller units, second units on lots with existing homes, shared living arrangements, congregate housing and housing assistance programs."

The housing element of the County's general plan also states that the County's provision of housing for seniors involves the following: "Senior housing projects are a permitted use within any residential zoning district. The Zoning Code also provides a density bonus for the construction of senior housing projects through approval of an *Affordable Housing or Senior Citizen Housing Incentive Use Permit* (Section 7-9-140). The zoning ordinance is not considered to be a constraint to the development of senior housing because the regulations are the same as for other residential uses in the same districts."

The staff report of the communities planning unit to the County Planning Commission explains that the Project is consistent with the housing element of the general plan: "The County's General Plan includes a Housing Element. The Housing Needs Assessment . . . of the Housing Element acknowledges that the special housing needs of seniors are an important concern in the County of Orange. The elderly maintain special needs related to housing construction and location. The Housing Element states that every effort should be made to maintain the dignity, self-respect, and quality of life of mature residents in the County. This applies to mature citizens who prefer to stay in their own dwellings and those who relocate to a retirement community. According to the Housing Element, housing is one of the top five concerns among the senior population. According to the State of California, Department of Finance, in 2000 the total population of seniors in Orange

County, age 55 years and older, was at 509,043, which comprised about 17.8% of the total population. Orange County's senior population increased to 702,919, comprising 21.8% of the total population in 2010. It is anticipated to increase to 945,081 in 2020, which is an estimated 26.8% of the estimated total population. . . . This is approximately an 86% increase within ten years. The proposed project is for a 100 percent senior living community, and it will be deed restricted for those 55 years of age and older. There are two types of living arrangements proposed — independent living and assisted living. Some independent living units would be located in the main building. Additionally, the bungalows would serve as independent living units, and are a good transition for people moving from larger homes to a senior living campus. The independent residential units do not require licensing from the State of California. The proposed project would not be a nursing facility and would not offer nursing service. This project provides two different housing types, thus enabling residents to age in one place and not have to move as circumstances change."

The staff report also explains how the Project is consistent with the North Tustin Specific Plan. . . .

The Board's findings in support of the final EIR provide, in relevant part: "A modification of the land use in the NTSP would meet the intent of the land use design goals and policies, enhance the role of medium and high density housing, a stated goal of the NTSP, and permit additional variety of residential densities on the Project site and would fulfill the need for additional senior housing in the community, which is consistent with the County of Orange General Plan. The Project would be in substantial conformity with the goals and policies of the General Plan and the NTSP. Changing the land use designation within the NTSP of the Project site does not set a precedent for any future land use changes or rezones. The Project site would continue to be zoned only for residential uses. No Project-level or cumulative impacts are identified." Those findings also provide: "The proposed senior living community provides an opportunity to balance housing opportunities, promote innovative development concepts, provide landscaping buffers and maintain residential character as provided in the NTSP, which from a land use policy perspective allows for orderly implementation of the NTSP and County General Plan."

In the environmental analysis section of the draft EIR for the Project, the County provided a table explaining the Project's consistency with the land use design goals and policies of the North Tustin Specific Plan. In addition to being a residential development, consistent with the residential nature of the surrounding community, the Project was found to be consistent with the North Tustin Specific Plan's setback and landscape design criteria.

We conclude the Board's findings of consistency with the general plan and the North Tustin Specific Plan are supported by substantial evidence. The creation of the new senior residential housing zoning district and its application to the Project site were in the public interest and were not arbitrary or capricious. The trial court erred in entering judgment in Foothill's favor and in issuing the writ of mandate.

. . . .

Disposition

The judgment is reversed. . . .

## Questions for Consideration

1) What standard of consistency is applied in this case?

2) Who brought this lawsuit and on what grounds?

3) Part of the opinion discusses spot zoning. What is spot zoning and what are the legal concerns associated with it?

4) Can you speculate as to what the meaning of reverse spot zoning might be?

5) What process was followed and what steps were taken by local planning officials in pursuing the changes to the North Tustin Specific Plan?

6) What factors were to be considered in developing the county's general master plan?

7) What evidence does the court refer to in supporting the county's decision to amend the plan?

8) Do you think that Florida's strict scrutiny standard would have made a difference in the outcome of this case?

## Takeaway

• A primary situation in which spot zoning issues arise is when a zoning change or amendment is made outside of a comprehensive plan. Generally, when a zoning code or a plan is amended, a comprehensive review of the community or at least a significant area of the community is required as a basis for the change. Changes or adjustments as to specific properties are generally accomplished through *area* or *use* variances as provided for in the zoning code. Variances involve an appeal process seeking to obtain an exception from the strict compliance with the zoning code. Variances are discussed in detail later in the book. The main point for now is that changing the zoning on a single piece of property usually proceeds through a quasi-adjudicative process involving an application for a variance. When adjustments are made to a single piece of property by amending or changing the code itself, the issue of spot zoning arises.

## Discussion Problem 4.1

Fast Stop Gas Stations is a chain of twenty gas stations in a central region of the state. In the city of Tucan, Fast Stop has several stations. One of its stations is located at Dixie Corners. It is known as Dixie Corners because it is at the intersection of

Carolina and Alabama streets. This is an older urban neighborhood with many two story, two and three family residences on individual city lots. A gas station has been at the corner for many years, and Fast Stop acquired the location about five years ago. Under the zoning code, Fast Stop's gas station is a permitted use in this area that is zoned as Urban Multi-Family Residential. The neighborhood zoning also permits a drug store, barber shop, and beauty salon. No restaurants, grocery stores, bakeries, or retail food outlets are permitted in the zone.

Fast Stop petitions the City Council of Tucan to make a zoning change to permit it to add a convenience store at its gas station location at Dixie Corners. Fast Stop explains that convenience store sales make up over 30% of profits nation-wide at small gas stations. The company owner says that this revenue is vital to the continued success of this particular station. Fast Stop points out that a majority of gas stations in the central region of the state now include convenience stores and, in fact, two other Fast Stop gas stations in Tucan have such stores. The stores sell baked goods, dairy products, cooked hot dogs, pizza slices to go, drinks, beverages, and basic household grocery products. Fast Stop says it would be a great addition to the neighborhood. After a couple of meetings and some discussions with the planning board, the City approves a zoning amendment permitting the sale of groceries, beverages, baked goods, and other assorted food items and sundries at the Dixie corners location of Fast Stop, so long as a gas station continues to operate on the property and so long as the store does not exceed 1,000 square feet in size. The new zone that includes only the property owned by Fast Stop is now identified as a Special Service Commercial zone. This new zone is located right in the middle of the Urban Multi-Family Residential zone.

Six months after Fast Stop opens its new store at the Dixie Corners location, owners of another property in the Urban Multi-Family Residential zone, located two lots east of the corner (measuring 250 feet from the corner), apply to open a Whole Fruits store to sell fresh organic fruits, vegetables, and juices. The owners submit a plan for a store that will be 950 square feet in size. The owners of Whole Fruits are denied a permit to open with a statement that their proposed use is not permitted in the zone.

Whole Fruits hires you to explain the situation and to advise them on what they might do to obtain a permit for their store. Assess the City's position and the likelihood of success for Whole Fruits.

# B. Planning and Takings

The planning process sometimes raises legal challenges under federal law. The three cases that follow illustrate problems that can arise when the planning process generates results that property owners believe go "too far" in regulating the use of their property.

# City of Monterey v. Del Monte Dunes

Supreme Court of the United States
526 U.S. 687 (1999)

KENNEDY, Justice. This case began with attempts by the respondent, Del Monte Dunes, and its predecessor in interest to develop a parcel of land within the jurisdiction of the petitioner, the city of Monterey. The city, in a series of repeated rejections, denied proposals to develop the property, each time imposing more rigorous demands on the developers. Del Monte Dunes brought suit in the United States District Court for the Northern District of California, under Rev. Stat. § 1979, 42 U.S.C. § 1983. After protracted litigation, the case was submitted to the jury on Del Monte Dunes' theory that the city effected a regulatory taking or otherwise injured the property by unlawful acts, without paying compensation or providing an adequate post deprivation remedy for the loss. The jury found for Del Monte Dunes, and the Court of Appeals affirmed.

. . . .

The property which respondent and its predecessor in interest (landowners) sought to develop was a 37.6 acre ocean-front parcel located in the city of Monterey, at or near the city's boundary to the north, where Highway 1 enters. With the exception of the ocean and a state park located to the northeast, the parcel was virtually surrounded by a railroad right-of-way and properties devoted to industrial, commercial, and multifamily residential uses. The parcel itself was zoned for multifamily residential use under the city's general zoning ordinance.

The parcel· had not been untouched by its urban and industrial proximities. A sewer line housed in 15-foot man-made dunes covered with jute matting and surrounded by snow fencing traversed the property. Trash, dumped in violation of the law, had accumulated on the premises. The parcel had been used for many years by an oil company as a terminal and tank farm where large quantities of oil were delivered, stored, and reshipped. When the company stopped using the site, it had removed its oil tanks but left behind tank pads, an industrial complex, pieces of pipe, broken concrete, and oil-soaked sand. The company had introduced nonnative ice plant to prevent erosion and to control soil conditions around the oil tanks. Ice plant secretes a substance that forces out other plants and is not compatible with the parcel's natural flora. By the time the landowners sought to develop the property, ice plant had spread to some 25 percent of the parcel, and, absent human intervention, would continue to advance, endangering and perhaps eliminating the parcel's remaining natural vegetation.

The natural flora the ice plant encroached upon included buckwheat, the natural habitat of the endangered Smith's Blue Butterfly. The butterfly lives for one week, travels a maximum of 200 feet, and must land on a mature, flowering buckwheat plant to survive. Searches for the butterfly from 1981 through 1985 yielded but a single larva, discovered in 1984. No other specimens had been found on the property, and the parcel was quite isolated from other possible habitats of the butterfly.

In 1981, the landowners submitted an application to develop the property in conformance with the city's zoning and general plan requirements. Although the zoning requirements permitted the development of up to 29 housing units per acre, or more than 1,000 units for the entire parcel, the landowners' proposal was limited to 344 residential units. In 1982 the city's planning commission denied the application but stated that a proposal for 264 units would receive favorable consideration. In keeping with the suggestion, the landowners submitted a revised proposal for 264 units. In late 1983, however, the planning commission again denied the application. The commission once more requested a reduction in the scale of the development, this time saying a plan for 224 units would be received with favor. The landowners returned to the drawing board and prepared a proposal for 224 units, which, its previous statements notwithstanding, the planning commission denied in 1984. The landowners appealed to the city council, which overruled the planning commission's denial and referred the project back to the commission, with instructions to consider a proposal for 190 units.

The landowners once again reduced the scope of their development proposal to comply with the city's request, and submitted four specific, detailed site plans, each for a total of 190 units for the whole parcel. Even so, the planning commission rejected the landowners' proposal later in 1984. Once more the landowners appealed to the city council. The council again overruled the commission, finding the proposal conceptually satisfactory and in conformance with the city's previous decisions regarding, *inter alia*, density, number of units, location on the property, and access. The council then approved one of the site plans, subject to various specific conditions, and granted an 18-month conditional use permit for the proposed development.

The landowners spent most of the next year revising their proposal and taking other steps to fulfill the city's conditions. Their final plan, submitted in 1985, devoted 17.9 of the 37.6 acres to public open space (including a public beach and areas for the restoration and preservation of the buckwheat habitat), 7.9 acres to open, landscaped areas, and 6.7 acres to public and private streets (including public parking and access to the beach). Only 5.1 acres were allocated to buildings and patios. The plan was designed, in accordance with the city's demands, to provide the public with a beach, a buffer zone between the development and the adjoining state park, and view corridors so the buildings would not be visible to motorists on the nearby highway; the proposal also called for restoring and preserving as much of the sand dune structure and buckwheat habitat as possible consistent with development and the city's requirements.

After detailed review of the proposed buildings, roads, and parking facilities, the city's architectural review committee approved the plan. Following hearings before the planning commission, the commission's professional staff found the final plan addressed and substantially satisfied the city's conditions. It proposed the planning commission make specific findings to this effect and recommended the plan be approved.

In January 1986, less than two months before the landowners' conditional use permit was to expire, the planning commission rejected the recommendation of its staff and denied the development plan. The landowners appealed to the city council, also requesting a 12-month extension of their permit to allow them time to attempt to comply with any additional requirements the council might impose. The permit was extended until a hearing could be held before the city council in June 1986. After the hearing, the city council denied the final plan, not only declining to specify measures the landowners could take to satisfy the concerns raised by the council but also refusing to extend the conditional use permit to allow time to address those concerns. The council's decision, moreover, came at a time when a sewer moratorium issued by another agency would have prevented or at least delayed development based on a new plan.

The council did not base its decision on the landowners' failure to meet any of the specific conditions earlier prescribed by the city. Rather, the council made general findings that the landowners had not provided adequate access for the development (even though the landowners had twice changed the specific access plans to comply with the city's demands and maintained they could satisfy the city's new objections if granted an extension), that the plan's layout would damage the environment (even though the location of the development on the property was necessitated by the city's demands for a public beach, view corridors, and a buffer zone next to the state park), and that the plan would disrupt the habitat of the Smith's Blue Butterfly (even though the plan would remove the encroaching ice plant and preserve or restore buckwheat habitat on almost half of the property, and even though only one larva had ever been found on the property).

After five years, five formal decisions, and 19 different site plans, 10 Tr. 1294–1295 (Feb. 9, 1994), respondent Del Monte Dunes decided the city would not permit development of the property under any circumstances. Del Monte Dunes commenced suit against the city in the United States District Court for the Northern District of California under 42 U.S.C. §1983, alleging, *inter alia,* that denial of the final development proposal was a violation of the Due Process and Equal Protection provisions of the Fourteenth Amendment and an uncompensated, and so unconstitutional, regulatory taking.

. . . After reviewing at some length the history of attempts to develop the property, the court found that to require additional proposals would implicate the concerns about repetitive and unfair procedures expressed, and that the city's decision was sufficiently final to render Del Monte Dunes' claim ripe for review. . . .

. . . Del Monte Dunes argued to the jury that, although the city had a right to regulate its property, the combined effect of the city's various demands — that the development be invisible from the highway, that a buffer be provided between the development and the state park, and that the public be provided with a beach — was to force development into the "bowl" area of the parcel. As a result, Del Monte Dunes argued, the city's subsequent decision that the bowl contained sensitive buckwheat habitat which could not be disturbed blocked the development of any portion of the property. While conceding the legitimacy of the city's stated regulatory purposes, Del Monte Dunes emphasized the tortuous and protracted history of attempts to develop the property, as well as the shifting and sometimes inconsistent positions taken by the city throughout the process, and argued that it had been treated in an unfair and irrational manner. . . .

At the close of argument, the District Court instructed the jury it should find for Del Monte Dunes if it found either that Del Monte Dunes had been denied all economically viable use of its property or that "the city's decision to reject the plaintiff's 190 unit development proposal did not substantially advance a legitimate public purpose."

. . . .

The jury delivered a general verdict for Del Monte Dunes on its takings claim, a separate verdict for Del Monte Dunes on its equal protection claim, and a damages award of $ 1.45 million.

. . . .

The Court of Appeals affirmed. . . . The court ruled that sufficient evidence had been presented to the jury from which it reasonably could have decided each of these questions in Del Monte Dunes' favor. Because upholding the verdict on the regulatory takings claim was sufficient to support the award of damages, the court did not address the equal protection claim. . . .

. . . Although the government acts lawfully when, pursuant to proper authorization, it takes property and provides just compensation, the government's action is lawful solely because it assumes a duty, imposed by the Constitution, to provide just compensation. When the government repudiates this duty, either by denying just compensation in fact or by refusing to provide procedures through which compensation may be sought, it violates the Constitution. In those circumstances the government's actions are not only unconstitutional but unlawful and tortious as well.

. . . .

Almost from the inception of our regulatory takings doctrine, we have held that whether a regulation of property goes so far that "there must be an exercise of eminent domain and compensation to sustain the act . . . depends upon the particular facts." *Pennsylvania Coal Co. v. Mahon*, 260 U.S. 393, 413, 67 L. Ed. 322, 43 S. Ct. 158 (1922) . . . . Consistent with this understanding, we have described determinations of liability in regulatory takings cases as "'essentially ad hoc, factual inquiries,'" requiring "complex factual assessments of the purposes and economic effects of government actions."

In accordance with these pronouncements, we hold that the issue whether a landowner has been deprived of all economically viable use of his property is a predominantly factual question. . . .

The jury's role in determining whether a land-use decision substantially advances legitimate public interests within the meaning of our regulatory takings doctrine presents a more difficult question. . . .

In this case, the narrow question submitted to the jury was whether, when viewed in light of the context and protracted history of the development application process, the city's decision to reject a particular development plan bore a reasonable relationship to its proffered justifications. . . . Under these circumstances, we hold that it was proper to submit this narrow, fact bound question to the jury.

. . . .

. . . The city and its *amici* suggest that sustaining the judgment here will undermine the uniformity of the law and eviscerate state and local zoning authority by subjecting all land-use decisions to plenary, and potentially inconsistent, jury review. Our decision raises no such specter. Del Monte Dunes did not bring a broad challenge to the constitutionality of the city's general land-use ordinances or policies, and our holding does not extend to a challenge of that sort. . . . Rather, to the extent Del Monte Dunes' challenge was premised on unreasonable governmental action, the theory argued and tried to the jury was that the city's denial of the final development permit was inconsistent not only with the city's general ordinances and policies but even with the shifting ad hoc restrictions previously imposed by the city. These were questions for the jury. [The Court found no reason to set aside the findings of the jury.]

. . . [T]he judgment of the Court of Appeals is affirmed.

It is so ordered.

## Questions for Consideration

1) What was the nature of Del Monte's development project?

2) Was the proposed development consistent with zoning regulations?

3) What role did the planning officials play in approving the project?

4) What steps did Del Monte take in an effort to satisfy planning officials?

5) Relative to the description of the property provided at the outset of the opinion, do you think Del Monte's development plan would result in a net improvement?

6) At trial, Del Monte introduced evidence that planning officials had long been hoping to make the entire property a public park and beach but that lack of financial resources resulted in dropping this goal. Do you think this might have been a factor in the way this situation developed?

## Takeaway

- In many situations, property developers must not only address the requirements of a zoning code, but they must also work with a planning department. Planning officials may develop a number of suggestions and requirements for approval of a project. These suggestions and requirements may be imposed even if a project is otherwise fully compliant with the regulations in the applicable zoning code.

- Planning officials will typically have general criteria that are applied to the evaluation and approval of a development project. Generally, planning officials must act rationally in approving or denying a development project. This standard of review provides planning officials with a great degree of discretion when dealing with property developers.

- The discretion exercised by planning officials is not unlimited, however, as illustrated by the *Del Monte Dunes* case.

## Discussion Problem 4.2

The City of Carthage is developing a new comprehensive plan. The City and its planning department have spent three years gathering data and holding public hearings. The plan covers all major aspects of life within the City and is meant to be a ten-year plan for guiding the future growth and development of the community. Under the plan, certain large tracts of undeveloped land are designated as Green Zones and are set aside for green space that is not available for development. The only uses compatible with the designation under the new plan include: hiking, bicycling, cross-country skiing, bird watching, Frisbee golf, and family or group picnics. The only structures permitted are bike paths and open-sided pavilions for picnics. These paths and the pavilions are limited in size, location, and number, and must be approved by the planning board by going through site plan review. The comprehensive plan passed and was officially adopted by the City six months ago. It went into effect immediately. The zoning code has not yet been revised to reflect the changes made to the comprehensive plan.

One large tract of undeveloped land affected by the new comprehensive plan designations restricting future development is owned by Chester Logi. Chester's land is currently zoned to permit commercial and light industrial development, but under the newly adopted comprehensive plan, it is designated as a Green Zone and not available for development. Its use is limited as set out above. Chester had purchased this land ten years earlier with an investment strategy of holding it for development as the City grew. The City has been growing in the direction of Chester's land, and Chester feels that it is ripe for development within the next 1-2 years. The comprehensive plan has designated this land as within a Green Zone, and Chester is having trouble getting investors and lenders interested in his plans to develop the property because of the comprehensive plan.

a) Carthage is a city located in a state that, through judicial decisions, has held that while zoning must be consistent with the comprehensive plan, it need not be in strict compliance with the plan. Chester seeks your advice on suing the City of Carthage for a taking of his property under the plan. Will he be successful, and does it matter that the zoning code has not yet been updated?

What if Chester applies for a building permit for a commercial use after the plan is adopted but before an updated code is approved?

b) Same question as in part "a" above; except—Carthage is in a state that requires strict consistency between the comprehensive plan and the zoning code. Should this make a difference in the outcome, and if so, why do you believe that to be the case?

c) What if Carthage passes a new zoning code twelve months later and in the newly adopted code, uses within the Green Zone are described as those listed above, and including any other "appropriate recreational uses." Chester applies for a permit to operate a water park on the property. The water park will have multiple water slides, two swimming pools, a wave pool, and several splash pad areas. The permit officer denies the permit request, and Chester appeals this denial to the Carthage Zoning Board of Appeal. The Zoning Board of Appeal hears the appeal and decides that a water park fits within the meaning of the language of the code where it says, "and any other appropriate recreational uses." The City Board disagrees with the Zoning Board of Appeal and refuses to issue the permit. In a state that requires strict consistency between the comprehensive plan and the zoning code, what are the issues raised by this scenario and how do you think that they might best be resolved?

## Lucas v. South Carolina Coastal Council

Supreme Court of the United States
505 U.S. 1003 (1992)

SCALIA, Justice. In 1986, petitioner David H. Lucas paid $975,000 for two residential lots on the Isle of Palms in Charleston County, South Carolina, on which he intended to build single-family homes. In 1988, however, the South Carolina Legislature enacted the Beachfront Management Act, S.C. Code Ann. §48-39-250 *et seq.* (Supp.1990), which had the direct effect of barring petitioner from erecting any permanent habitable structures on his two parcels. A state trial court found that this prohibition rendered Lucas's parcels "valueless." This case requires us to decide whether the Act's dramatic effect on the economic value of Lucas's lots accomplished a taking of private property under the Fifth and Fourteenth Amendments requiring the payment of "just compensation." U.S. Const., amend. 5.

I

A

South Carolina's expressed interest in intensively managing development activities in the so-called "coastal zone" dates from 1977 when, in the aftermath of Congress's passage of the federal Coastal Zone Management Act of 1972, 86 Stat. 1280, as amended, 16 U.S.C. §1451 *et seq.*, the legislature enacted a Coastal Zone Management Act of its own. See S.C. Code Ann. §48-39-10 *et seq.* (1987). In its original form, the South Carolina Act required owners of coastal zone land that qualified as a "critical area" (defined in the legislation to include beaches and immediately adjacent sand dunes), to obtain a permit from the newly created South Carolina Coastal Council (Council) (respondent here) prior to committing the land to a "use other than the use the critical area was devoted to on [September 28, 1977]."

In the late 1970's, Lucas and others began extensive residential development of the Isle of Palms, a barrier island situated eastward of the city of Charleston. Toward the close of the development cycle for one residential subdivision known as "Beachwood East," Lucas in 1986 purchased the two lots at issue in this litigation for his own account. No portion of the lots, which were located approximately 300 feet from the beach, qualified as a "critical area" under the 1977 Act; accordingly, at the time Lucas acquired these parcels, he was not legally obliged to obtain a permit from the Council in advance of any development activity. His intention with respect to the lots was to do what the owners of the immediately adjacent parcels had already done: erect single-family residences. He commissioned architectural drawings for this purpose.

The Beachfront Management Act brought Lucas's plans to an abrupt end. Under that 1988 legislation, the Council was directed to establish a "baseline" connecting the landward-most "point[s] of erosion . . . during the past forty years" in the region of the Isle of Palms that includes Lucas's lots. S.C. Code Ann. § 48-39-280(A)(2) (Supp. 1988). In action not challenged here, the Council fixed this baseline landward of Lucas's parcels. That was significant, for under the Act construction of occupiable improvements was flatly prohibited seaward of a line drawn 20 feet landward of, and parallel to, the baseline. The Act provided no exceptions.

## B

Lucas promptly filed suit in the South Carolina Court of Common Pleas, contending that the Beachfront Management Act's construction bar effected a taking of his property without just compensation. Lucas did not take issue with the validity of the Act as a lawful exercise of South Carolina's police power, but contended that the Act's complete extinguishment of his property's value entitled him to compensation regardless of whether the legislature had acted in furtherance of legitimate police power objectives. Following a bench trial, the court agreed. Among its factual determinations was the finding that "at the time Lucas purchased the two lots, both were zoned for single-family residential construction and . . . there were no restrictions imposed upon such use of the property by either the State of South Carolina, the County of Charleston, or the Town of the Isle of Palms." The trial court further found that the Beachfront Management Act decreed a permanent ban on construction insofar as Lucas's lots were concerned, and that this prohibition "deprive[d] Lucas of any reasonable economic use of the lots, . . . eliminated the unrestricted right of use, and render[ed] them valueless." The court thus concluded that Lucas's properties had been "taken" by operation of the Act, and it ordered respondent to pay "just compensation" in the amount of $1,232,387.50.

The Supreme Court of South Carolina reversed. It found dispositive what it described as Lucas's concession "that the Beachfront Management Act [was] properly and validly designed to preserve . . . South Carolina's beaches." 304 S.C. 376, 379, 404 S.E.2d 895, 896 (1991). Failing an attack on the validity of the statute as such, the court believed itself bound to accept the "uncontested . . . findings" of the South Carolina Legislature that new construction in the coastal zone — such as petitioner intended — threatened this public resource. The court ruled that when a regulation respecting the use of property is designed "to prevent serious public harm," no compensation is owing under the Takings Clause regardless of the regulation's effect on the property's value.

Two justices dissented. They acknowledged that our . . . line of cases recognizes governmental power to prohibit "noxious" uses of property — *i.e.,* uses of property akin to "public nuisances" — without having to pay compensation. But they would not have characterized the Beachfront Management Act's "*primary* purpose [as] the prevention of a nuisance." To the dissenters, the chief purposes of the legislation, among them the promotion of tourism and the creation of a "habitat for indigenous flora and fauna," could not fairly be compared to nuisance abatement. As a consequence, they would have affirmed the trial court's conclusion that the Act's obliteration of the value of petitioner's lots accomplished a taking.

We granted certiorari.

### III

### A

Prior to Justice Holmes's exposition in *Pennsylvania Coal Co. v. Mahon*, 260 U.S. 393, 43 S. Ct. 158, 67 L. Ed. 322 (1922), it was generally thought that the Takings Clause reached only a "direct appropriation" of property, or the functional equivalent of a "practical ouster of [the owner's] possession." Justice Holmes recognized in *Mahon*, however, that if the protection against physical appropriations of private property was to be meaningfully enforced, the government's power to redefine the range of interests included in the ownership of property was necessarily constrained by constitutional limits. If, instead, the uses of private property were subject to unbridled, uncompensated qualification under the police power, "the natural tendency of human nature [would be] to extend the qualification more and more until at last private property disappear[ed]." These considerations gave birth in that case to the oft-cited maxim that, "while property may be regulated to a certain extent, if regulation goes too far it will be recognized as a taking."

Nevertheless, our decision in *Mahon* offered little insight into when, and under what circumstances, a given regulation would be seen as going "too far" for purposes of the Fifth Amendment. In 70-odd years of succeeding "regulatory takings" jurisprudence, we have generally eschewed any "'set formula'" for determining how far is too far, preferring to "engag[e] in . . . essentially ad hoc, factual inquiries." *Penn Central Transportation Co. v. New York City*, 438 U.S. 104, 124, 98 S. Ct. 2646, 2659, 57 L. Ed. 2d 631 (1978). We have, however, described at least two discrete categories of regulatory action as compensable without case-specific inquiry into the public interest advanced in support of the restraint. The first encompasses regulations that compel the property owner to suffer a physical "invasion" of his property. In general (at least with regard to permanent invasions), no matter how minute the intrusion, and no matter how weighty the public purpose behind it, we have required compensation. For example, in *Loretto v. Teleprompter Manhattan CATV Corp.*, 458 U.S. 419, 102 S. Ct. 3164, 73 L. Ed. 2d 868 (1982), we determined that New York's law requiring landlords to allow television cable companies to emplace cable facilities in their apartment buildings constituted a taking, even though the facilities occupied at most only 1 ½ cubic feet of the landlords' property.

The second situation in which we have found categorical treatment appropriate is where regulation denies all economically beneficial or productive use of land. . . .

We have never set forth the justification for this rule. Perhaps it is simply, as Justice Brennan suggested, that total deprivation of beneficial use is, from the landowner's point of view, the equivalent of a physical appropriation. Surely, at least, in the extraordinary circumstance when *no* productive or economically beneficial use of land is permitted, it is less realistic to indulge our usual assumption that the legislature is simply "adjusting the benefits and burdens of economic life," *Penn Central Transportation Co.*, 438 U.S., at 124, 98 S. Ct., at 2659, in a manner that secures an "average reciprocity of advantage" to everyone concerned, *Pennsylvania Coal Co. v. Mahon*, 260 U.S., at 415, 43 S. Ct., at 160. And the *functional* basis for permitting the government, by regulation, to affect property values without compensation — that "Government hardly could go on if to some extent values incident to property could not be diminished without paying for every such change in the general law," *id.*, at 413, 43 S. Ct., at 159 — does not apply to the relatively rare situations where the government has deprived a landowner of all economically beneficial uses.

On the other side of the balance, affirmatively supporting a compensation requirement, is the fact that regulations that leave the owner of land without economically beneficial or productive options for its use — typically, as here, by requiring land to be left substantially in its natural state — carry with them a heightened risk that private property is being pressed into some form of public service under the guise of mitigating serious public harm. . . .

We think, in short, that there are good reasons for our frequently expressed belief that when the owner of real property has been called upon to sacrifice *all* economically beneficial uses in the name of the common good, that is, to leave his property economically idle, he has suffered a taking.

### B

The trial court found Lucas's two beachfront lots to have been rendered valueless by respondent's enforcement of the coastal-zone construction ban. Under Lucas's theory of the case, which rested upon our "no economically viable use" statements, that finding entitled him to compensation. Lucas believed it unnecessary to take issue with either the purposes behind the Beachfront Management Act, or the means chosen by the South Carolina Legislature to effectuate those purposes. The South Carolina Supreme Court, however, thought otherwise. In its view, the Beachfront

Management Act was no ordinary enactment, but involved an exercise of South Carolina's "police powers" to mitigate the harm to the public interest that petitioner's use of his land might occasion. By neglecting to dispute the findings enumerated in the Act or otherwise to challenge the legislature's purposes, petitioner "concede[d] that the beach/dune area of South Carolina's shores is an extremely valuable public resource; that the erection of new construction, *inter alia*, contributes to the erosion and destruction of this public resource; and that discouraging new construction in close proximity to the beach/dune area is necessary to prevent a great public harm." In the court's view, these concessions brought petitioner's challenge within a long line of this Court's cases sustaining against Due Process and Takings Clause challenges the State's use of its "police powers" to enjoin a property owner from activities akin to public nuisances.

It is correct that many of our prior opinions have suggested that "harmful or noxious uses" of property may be proscribed by government regulation without the requirement of compensation. For a number of reasons, however, we think the South Carolina Supreme Court was too quick to conclude that that principle decides the present case. The "harmful or noxious uses" principle was the Court's early attempt to describe in theoretical terms why government may, consistent with the Takings Clause, affect property values by regulation without incurring an obligation to compensate — a reality we nowadays acknowledge explicitly with respect to the full scope of the State's police power. . . .

The transition from our early focus on control of "noxious" uses to our contemporary understanding of the broad realm within which government may regulate without compensation was an easy one, since the distinction between "harm-preventing" and "benefit-conferring" regulation is often in the eye of the beholder. It is quite possible, for example, to describe in *either* fashion the ecological, economic, and esthetic concerns that inspired the South Carolina Legislature in the present case. One could say that imposing a servitude on Lucas's land is necessary in order to prevent his use of it from "harming" South Carolina's ecological resources; or, instead, in order to achieve the "benefits" of an ecological preserve. . . . Whether one or the other of the competing characterizations will come to one's lips in a particular case depends primarily upon one's evaluation of the worth of competing uses of real estate. . . . Whether Lucas's construction of single-family residences on his parcels should be described as bringing "harm" to South Carolina's adjacent ecological resources thus depends principally upon whether the describer believes that the State's use interest in nurturing those resources is so important that *any* competing adjacent use must yield.

. . . .

Where the State seeks to sustain regulation that deprives land of all economically beneficial use, we think it may resist compensation only if the logically antecedent inquiry into the nature of the owner's estate shows that the proscribed use interests were not part of his title to begin with. This accords, we think, with our "takings" jurisprudence, which has traditionally been guided by the understandings of our citizens regarding the content of, and the State's power over, the "bundle of rights" that they acquire when they obtain title to property. It seems to us that the property owner necessarily expects the uses of his property to be restricted, from time to time, by various measures newly enacted by the State in legitimate exercise of its police powers; "[a]s long recognized, some values are enjoyed under an implied limitation and must yield to the police power." *Pennsylvania Coal Co. v. Mahon,* 260 U.S., at 413, 43 S. Ct., at 159. And in the case of personal property, by reason of the State's traditionally high degree of control over commercial dealings, he ought to be aware of the possibility that new regulation might even render his property economically worthless (at least if the property's only economically productive use is sale or manufacture for sale). In the case of land, however, we think the notion pressed by the Council that title is somehow held subject to the "implied limitation" that the State may subsequently eliminate all economically valuable use is inconsistent with the historical compact recorded in the Takings Clause that has become part of our constitutional culture.

Where "permanent physical occupation" of land is concerned, we have refused to allow the government to decree it anew (without compensation), no matter how weighty the asserted "public interests" involved.... We believe similar treatment must be accorded confiscatory regulations, *i.e.,* regulations that prohibit all economically beneficial use of land: Any limitation so severe cannot be newly legislated or decreed (without compensation), but must inhere in the title itself, in the restrictions that background principles of the State's law of property and nuisance already place upon land ownership. A law or decree with such an effect must, in other words, do no more than duplicate the result that could have been achieved in the courts — by adjacent landowners (or other uniquely affected persons) under the State's law of private nuisance, or by the State under its complementary power to abate nuisances that affect the public generally, or otherwise.

On this analysis, the owner of a lake-bed, for example, would not be entitled to compensation when he is denied the requisite permit to engage in a landfilling operation that would have the effect of flooding others' land. Nor the corporate owner of a nuclear generating plant, when it is directed to remove all improvements from its land upon discovery that the plant sits astride an earthquake fault. Such regulatory action may well have the effect of eliminating the land's only economically productive use, but it does not proscribe a productive use that was previously permissible under relevant property and nuisance principles. The use of these properties for what are now expressly prohibited purposes was *always* unlawful, and (subject to other constitutional limitations) it was open to the State at any point to make the implication of those background principles of nuisance and property law explicit.... When, however, a regulation that declares "off-limits" all economically productive or beneficial uses of land goes beyond what the relevant background principles would dictate, compensation must be paid to sustain it.

The "total taking" inquiry we require today will ordinarily entail (as the application of state nuisance law ordinarily entails) analysis of, among other things, the degree of harm to public lands and resources, or adjacent private property, posed by the claimant's proposed activities, the social value of the claimant's activities and their suitability to the locality in question, and the relative ease with which the alleged harm can be avoided through measures taken by the claimant and the government (or adjacent private landowners) alike. The fact that a particular use has long been engaged in by similarly situated owners ordinarily imports a lack of any common-law prohibition (though changed circumstances or new knowledge may make what was previously permissible no longer so. So also does the fact that other landowners, similarly situated, are permitted to continue the use denied to the claimant.

It seems unlikely that common-law principles would have prevented the erection of any habitable or productive improvements on petitioner's land; they rarely support prohibition of the "essential use" of land. The question, however, is one of state law to be dealt with on remand. We emphasize that to win its case South Carolina must do more than proffer the legislature's declaration that the uses Lucas desires are inconsistent with the public interest, or the conclusory assertion that they violate a common-law maxim such as *sic utere tuo ut alienum non laedas*. As we have said, a "State, by *ipse dixit*, may not transform private property into public property without compensation. . . ." Instead, as it would be required to do if it sought to restrain Lucas in a common-law action for public nuisance, South Carolina must identify background principles of nuisance and property law that prohibit the uses he now intends in the circumstances in which the property is presently found. Only on this showing can the State fairly claim that, in proscribing all such beneficial uses, the Beachfront Management Act is taking nothing.

The judgment is reversed, and the case is remanded for proceedings not inconsistent with this opinion.

So ordered.

## *Questions for Consideration*

1) What was the impact on Lucas from the state's comprehensive plan for coastal land management?

2) Does the state have a legitimate interest in regulating coastal lands for the benefit of the public health, safety, welfare, and morals?

3) What two situations are identified as categorical takings?

4) Assume the facts are different and that Lucas suffered an eighty percent loss in value because of the regulation in question; what test would be applicable to determine if a taking had occurred? Do you think Lucas would recover compensation for a taking under this test?

5) How does the opinion address the relationship between nuisance law and takings law?

## *Takeaway*

- *Lucas* establishes the two situations that trigger categorical takings under the Takings Clause. Generally, with the exception of exactions and unconstitutional conditions (to be discussed in a later chapter), *Lucas* and *Penn Central* establish the core elements of takings law jurisprudence.

- When doing a takings law analysis, one must also account for temporary takings. In *First English Evangelical Lutheran Church of Glendale v. County of Los Angeles*, 482 U.S. 304 (1987), the Court held that a temporary taking that denies a landowner of his property is not different in kind from a permanent taking, for which the Constitution requires compensation. This important case effected the dynamic of local regulation. Prior to *First English*, a local government could enact a regulation preventing land development, and if it eventually lost in litigation on the regulation going too far, the regulation would simply be dropped with no required compensation for the loss of the use of the property during the time period of the dispute and litigation. After *First English*, if the temporary loss of use amounts to a temporary taking, then compensation is due. Thus, attempts at over-regulations are not cost free, and local governments should be cautious in "overreaching" with regulation if they wish to avoid the potential of having to compensate a landowner for a temporary taking of property. In this setting, there is an incentive for local planning and zoning officials to negotiate with landowners when regulations and practices fall within a "gray area" that might arguably be a taking.

## Kelo v. City of New London

### Supreme Court of the United States
### 545 U.S. 469 (2005)

STEVENS, Justice. In 2000, the city of New London approved a development plan that, in the words of the Supreme Court of Connecticut, was "projected to create in excess of 1,000 jobs, to increase tax and other revenues, and to revitalize an economically distressed city, including its downtown and waterfront areas." In assembling the land needed for this project, the city's development agent has purchased property from willing sellers and proposes to use the power of eminent domain to acquire the remainder of the property from unwilling owners in exchange for just compensation. The question presented is whether the city's proposed disposition of this property qualifies as a "public use" within the meaning of the Takings Clause of the Fifth Amendment to the Constitution.

### I

The city of New London (hereinafter City) sits at the junction of the Thames River and the Long Island Sound in southeastern Connecticut. Decades of economic decline led a state agency in 1990 to designate the City a "distressed municipality." In 1996, the Federal Government closed the Naval Undersea Warfare Center, which had been located in the Fort Trumbull area of the City and had employed over 1,500 people. In 1998, the City's unemployment rate was nearly double that of the State, and its population of just under 24,000 residents was at its lowest since 1920.

These conditions prompted state and local officials to target New London, and particularly its Fort Trumbull area, for economic revitalization. To this end, respondent New London Development Corporation (NLDC), a private nonprofit entity established some years earlier to assist the City in planning economic development, was reactivated. In January 1998, the State authorized a $5.35 million bond issue to support the NLDC's planning activities and a $10 million bond issue toward the creation of a Fort Trumbull State Park. In February, the pharmaceutical company Pfizer Inc. announced that it would build a $300 million research facility on a site immediately adjacent to Fort Trumbull; local planners hoped that Pfizer would draw new business to the area, thereby serving as a catalyst to the area's rejuvenation. After receiving initial approval from the city council, the NLDC continued its planning activities and held a series of neighborhood meetings to educate the public about the process. In May, the city council authorized the NLDC to formally submit its plans to the relevant state agencies for review. Upon obtaining state-level approval, the NLDC finalized an integrated development plan focused on 90 acres of the Fort Trumbull area.

The Fort Trumbull area is situated on a peninsula that juts into the Thames River. The area comprises approximately 115 privately owned properties, as well as the 32 acres of land formerly occupied by the naval facility (Trumbull State Park now occupies 18 of those 32 acres). The development plan encompasses seven parcels. Parcel 1 is designated for a waterfront conference hotel at the center of a "small urban village" that will include restaurants and shopping. This parcel will also have marinas for both recreational and commercial uses. A pedestrian "riverwalk" will originate here and continue down the coast, connecting the waterfront areas of the development. Parcel 2 will be the site of approximately 80 new residences organized into an urban neighborhood and linked by public walkway to the remainder of the development, including the state park. This parcel also includes space reserved for a new U.S. Coast Guard Museum. Parcel 3, which is located immediately north of the Pfizer facility, will contain at least 90,000 square feet of research and development office space. Parcel 4A is a 2.4-acre site that will be used either to support the adjacent state park, by providing parking or retail services for visitors, or to support the nearby marina. Parcel 4B will include a renovated marina, as well as the final stretch of the riverwalk. Parcels 5, 6, and 7 will provide land for office and retail space, parking, and water-dependent commercial uses.

The NLDC intended the development plan to capitalize on the arrival of the Pfizer facility and the new commerce it was expected to attract. In addition to creating jobs, generating tax revenue, and helping to "build momentum for the revitalization of downtown New London," the plan was also designed to make the City more attractive and to create leisure and recreational opportunities on the waterfront and in the park.

The city council approved the plan in January 2000, and designated the NLDC as its development agent in charge of implementation. The city council also authorized the NLDC to purchase property or to acquire property by exercising eminent domain in the City's name. The NLDC successfully negotiated the purchase of most of the real estate in the 90-acre area, but its negotiations with petitioners failed. As a consequence, in November 2000, the NLDC initiated the condemnation proceedings that gave rise to this case.

## II

Petitioner Susette Kelo has lived in the Fort Trumbull area since 1997. She has made extensive improvements to her house, which she prizes for its water view. Petitioner Wilhelmina Dery was born in her Fort Trumbull house in 1918 and has lived there her entire life. Her husband Charles (also a petitioner) has lived in the house since they married some 60 years ago. In all, the nine petitioners own 15 properties in Fort Trumbull — 4 in parcel 3 of the development plan and 11 in parcel 4A. Ten of the parcels are occupied by the owner or a family member; the other five are held as investment properties. There is no allegation that any of these properties is blighted or otherwise in poor condition; rather, they were condemned only because they happen to be located in the development area.

In December 2000, petitioners brought this action in the New London Superior Court. They claimed, among other things, that the taking of their properties would violate the "public use" restriction in the Fifth Amendment. After a 7-day bench trial, the Superior Court granted a permanent restraining order prohibiting the taking of the properties located in parcel 4A (park or marina support). It, however, denied petitioners relief as to the properties located in parcel 3 (office space).

After the Superior Court ruled, both sides took appeals to the Supreme Court of Connecticut. That court held, over a dissent, that all of the City's proposed takings were valid. . . .

. . . .

We granted certiorari to determine whether a city's decision to take property for the purpose of economic development satisfies the "public use" requirement of the Fifth Amendment.

## III

Two polar propositions are perfectly clear. On the one hand, it has long been accepted that the sovereign may not take the property of A for the sole purpose of transferring it to another private party B, even though A is paid just compensation. On the other hand, it is equally clear that a State may transfer property from one private party to another if future "use by the public" is the purpose of the taking; the condemnation of land for a railroad with common-carrier duties is a familiar example. Neither of these propositions, however, determines the disposition of this case.

As for the first proposition, the City would no doubt be forbidden from taking petitioners' land for the purpose of conferring a private benefit on a particular private party. See [*Hawaii Housing Authority v.*] *Midkiff*, 467 U.S., at 245, 104 S. Ct. 2321 ("A purely private taking could not withstand the scrutiny of the public use requirement; it would serve no legitimate purpose of government and would thus be void"). Nor would the City be allowed to take property under the mere pretext of a public purpose, when its actual purpose was to bestow a private benefit. The takings before us, however, would be executed pursuant to a "carefully considered" development plan. 268 Conn., at 54, 843 A.2d, at 536. The trial judge and all the members of the Supreme Court of Connecticut agreed that there was no evidence of an illegitimate purpose in this case. Therefore, as was true of the statute challenged in *Midkiff*, 467 U.S., at 245, 104 S. Ct. 2321, the City's development plan was not adopted "to benefit a particular class of identifiable individuals."

On the other hand, this is not a case in which the City is planning to open the condemned land — at least not in its entirety — to use by the general public. Nor will the private lessees of the land in any sense be required to operate like common carriers, making their services available to all comers. But although such a projected use would be sufficient to satisfy the public use requirement, this "Court long ago rejected any literal requirement that condemned property be put into use for the general public." *Id.*, at 244, 104 S. Ct. 2321. Indeed, while many state courts in the mid-19th century endorsed "use by the public" as the proper definition of public use, that narrow view steadily eroded over time. Not only was the "use by the public" test difficult to administer (*e.g.*, what proportion of the public need have access to the property? at what price?), but it proved to be impractical given the diverse and always evolving needs of society. Accordingly, when this Court began applying the Fifth Amendment to the States at the close of the 19th century, it embraced the broader and more natural interpretation of public use as "public purpose." . . .

The disposition of this case therefore turns on the question whether the City's development plan serves a "public purpose." Without exception, our cases have defined that concept broadly, reflecting our longstanding policy of deference to legislative judgments in this field.

In *Berman v. Parker*, 348 U.S. 26, 75 S. Ct. 98, 99 L. Ed. 27 (1954), this Court upheld a redevelopment plan targeting a blighted area of Washington, D.C., in which most of the housing for the area's 5,000 inhabitants was beyond repair. Under the plan, the area would be condemned and part of it utilized for the construction of streets, schools, and other public facilities. The remainder of the land would be leased or sold to private parties for the purpose of redevelopment, including the construction of low-cost housing.

The owner of a department store located in the area challenged the condemnation, pointing out that his store was not itself blighted and arguing that the creation of a "better balanced, more attractive community" was not a valid public use. Writing for a unanimous Court, Justice Douglas refused to evaluate this claim in isolation, deferring instead to the legislative and agency judgment that the area "must be planned as a whole" for the plan to be successful. The Court explained that "community redevelopment programs need not, by force of the Constitution, be on a piecemeal basis — lot by lot, building by building." The public use underlying the taking was unequivocally affirmed:

> "We do not sit to determine whether a particular housing project is or is not desirable. The concept of the public welfare is broad and inclusive. . . . The values it represents are spiritual as well as physical, aesthetic as well as monetary. It is within the power of the legislature to determine that the community should be beautiful as well as healthy, spacious as well as clean, well-balanced as well as carefully patrolled. . . ."

In *Hawaii Housing Authority v. Midkiff*, 467 U.S. 229, 104 S. Ct. 2321, 81 L. Ed. 2d 186 (1984), the Court considered a Hawaii statute whereby fee title was taken from lessors and transferred to lessees (for just compensation) in order to reduce the concentration of land ownership. We unanimously upheld the statute and rejected the Ninth Circuit's view that it was "a naked attempt on the part of the state of Hawaii to take the property of A and transfer it to B solely for B's private use and benefit." Reaffirming *Berman*'s deferential approach to legislative judgments in this field, we concluded that the State's purpose of eliminating the "social and economic evils of a land oligopoly" qualified as a valid public use. Our opinion also rejected the contention that the mere fact that the State immediately transferred the properties to private individuals upon condemnation somehow diminished the public character of the taking. "[I]t is only the taking's purpose, and not its mechanics," we explained, that matters in determining public use.

. . . .

Viewed as a whole, our jurisprudence has recognized that the needs of society have varied between different parts of the Nation, just as they have evolved over time in response to changed circumstances. Our earliest cases in particular embodied a strong theme of federalism, emphasizing the "great respect" that we owe to state legislatures and state courts in discerning local public needs. . . .

## IV

Those who govern the City were not confronted with the need to remove blight in the Fort Trumbull area, but their determination that the area was sufficiently distressed to justify a program of economic rejuvenation is entitled to our deference. The City has carefully formulated an economic development plan that it believes will provide appreciable benefits to the community, including — but by no means limited to — new jobs and increased tax revenue. As with other exercises in urban planning and development, the City is endeavoring to coordinate a variety of commercial, residential, and recreational uses of land, with the hope that they will form a whole greater than the sum of its parts. To effectuate this plan, the City has invoked a state statute that specifically authorizes the use of eminent domain to promote economic development. Given the comprehensive character of the plan, the thorough deliberation that preceded its adoption, and the limited scope of our review, it is appropriate for us, as it was in *Berman*, to resolve the challenges of the individual owners, not on a piecemeal basis, but rather in light of the entire plan. Because that plan unquestionably serves a public purpose, the takings challenged here satisfy the public use requirement of the Fifth Amendment.

To avoid this result, petitioners urge us to adopt a new bright-line rule that economic development does not qualify as a public use. Putting aside the unpersuasive suggestion that the City's plan will provide only purely economic benefits, neither precedent nor logic supports petitioners' proposal. Promoting economic development is a traditional and long-accepted function of government. There is, moreover, no principled way of distinguishing economic development from the other public purposes that we have recognized. In our cases upholding takings that facilitated agriculture and mining, for example, we emphasized the importance of those industries to the welfare of the States in question, in *Berman*, we endorsed the purpose of transforming a blighted area into a "well-balanced" community through redevelopment, in *Midkiff*, we upheld the interest in breaking up a land oligopoly that "created artificial deterrents to the normal functioning of the State's residential land market," and in [*Ruckelshaus v.*] *Monsanto*, [467 U.S. 986, 81 L. Ed. 2d 815, 104 S. Ct. 2862 (1984),] we accepted Congress' purpose of eliminating a "significant barrier to entry in the pesticide market." It would be incongruous to hold that the City's interest in the economic benefits to be derived from the development of the Fort Trumbull area has less of a public character than any of those other interests. Clearly, there is no basis for exempting economic development from our traditionally broad understanding of public purpose.

Petitioners contend that using eminent domain for economic development impermissibly blurs the boundary between public and private takings. Again, our cases foreclose this objection. Quite simply, the government's pursuit of a public purpose will often benefit individual private parties. . . . "We cannot say that public ownership is the sole method of promoting the public purposes of community redevelopment projects."

It is further argued that without a bright-line rule nothing would stop a city from transferring citizen *A*'s property to citizen *B* for the sole reason that citizen *B* will put the property to a more productive use and thus pay more taxes. Such a one-to-one transfer of property, executed outside the confines of an integrated development plan, is not presented in this case. While such an unusual exercise of government power would certainly raise a suspicion that a private purpose was afoot, the hypothetical cases posited by petitioners can be confronted if and when they arise. They do not warrant the crafting of an artificial restriction on the concept of public use.

Alternatively, petitioners maintain that for takings of this kind we should require a "reasonable certainty" that the expected public benefits will actually accrue. Such a rule, however, would represent an even greater departure from our precedent. "When the legislature's purpose is legitimate and its means are not irrational, our cases make clear that empirical debates over the wisdom of takings—no less than debates over the wisdom of other kinds of socioeconomic legislation — are not to be carried out in the federal courts." . . .

Just as we decline to second-guess the City's considered judgments about the efficacy of its development plan, we also decline to second-guess the City's determinations as to what lands it needs to acquire in order to effectuate the project. "It is not for the courts to oversee the choice of the boundary line nor to sit in review on the size of a particular project area. Once the question of the public purpose has been decided, the amount and character of land to be taken for the project and the need for a particular tract to complete the integrated plan rests in the discretion of the legislative branch."

In affirming the City's authority to take petitioners' properties, we do not minimize the hardship that condemnations may entail, notwithstanding the payment of just compensation. We emphasize that nothing in our opinion precludes any State from placing further restrictions on its exercise of the takings power. This Court's authority, however, extends only to determining whether the City's proposed condemnations are for a "public use" within the meaning of the Fifth Amendment to the Federal Constitution. Because over a century of our case law interpreting that provision dictates an affirmative answer to that question, we may not grant petitioners the relief that they seek.

The judgment of the Supreme Court of Connecticut is affirmed.

It is so ordered.

## *Questions for Consideration*

1) What was the nature of the comprehensive development plan approved by the city of New London?

2) What did the city hope to accomplish with its development plan? What were the economic conditions of the city that the plan was designed to address and overcome?

3) Were the properties identified to be taken for the needs of the economic development plan blighted?

4) Was Susette Kelo living in a blighted or dilapidated building?

5) How does the Court refer to the *Berman* case and the *Midkiff* case?

6) Is economic development a "public purpose" for purposes of the Takings Clause?

7) Does the Fifth Amendment Takings Clause say that the taking must be for a "public purpose" or a "public use"? Does it make a difference, and should it make a difference?

8) How did the Court resolve the question of public or private purpose in this case?

## *Takeaway*

- Economic development is an important aspect of urban life. One issue with any major urban redevelopment project, such as the one envisioned by the plan in New London, is related to land assembly. Even if a developer is willing to pay for a large-scale urban development project completely funded by private investment, there often is still the need to acquire multiple contiguous parcels in order to complete it. The effort to assemble the property may result in some property owners refusing to sell. If a developer is unable to easily and cost effectively acquire and assemble all of the required property for the project, it will not be profitable. This problem can be solved if the government works with the developer to assemble all of the needed property by exercising its power of eminent domain as needed. This helps to eliminate the holdout problem.

- A problem with economic development, as a motivation for exercising the takings power, is that it is not always clear that certain undertakings will actually promote real economic growth. A great deal of faith must be placed in the economic projections of economists and others hoping to advance a project as a way to solve a number of complex urban development problems.

- In accordance with the *Kelo* decision, the individual states are empowered to have stronger protection for private property rights than that provided by the Fifth Amendment Takings Clause. A number of states responded to the *Kelo* decision by passing legislation constraining the use of their police powers for purposes of advancing economic development.

## Discussion Problem 4.3

Refer back to Discussion Problem 4.1, involving Fast Stop Gas Stations. Using the basic facts from that problem, consider a different situation. Assume Fast Stop is operating its gas station at Dixie Corners, as it has been done for many years (no convenience store). In this hypothetical, Fast Stop is not asking the City of Tucan for anything. Instead, the City is responding to federal and state regulations regarding fossil fuel emission levels. After a year of study by the planning board with input from a variety of environmental groups, the city adopts a new comprehensive plan. Likewise, they adopt a new city zoning code to implement the plan. Under the new code, the Fast Stop property at Dixie Corners is allowed to continue as a location for vehicle energy "refueling," but no fossil fuels can be sold on the property. Fast Stop is free to put in electric/battery charging stations or explore other alternatives for continuing to serve the public transportation needs in refueling. Under the regulations and the comprehensive plan, Fast Stop has eighteen months to completely transition away from fossil fuel sales.

The owner of Fast Stop comes to you for advice. The owner claims he will lose a lot of money under the new code and comprehensive plan. He also says no one will buy the property because it is in an Urban, Multi-Family, Residential zone and that none of the other permitted uses will generate enough value for a person to be willing to buy the Fast Stop property. This is because it will cost about $900,000 to repurpose the property and do the environmental cleanup of the location to eliminate any traces of fuel and other such contaminants on the property. On top of this expense, a buyer of the property would then have to build a structure for a permitted use. Houses in the neighborhood sell for $175,000–$275,000, and the other permitted uses, such as a small barber shop or salon, could not justify paying such a high start-up cost to open a new shop in the area.

Among other things, Fast Stop thinks his property is being taken in violation of the Fifth Amendment to the U.S. Constitution. What are the arguments for and against a taking, and what other legal issues might be involved?

# C. Planning for Accessibility

Local planning must include consideration of meeting the needs of people with disabilities and how best to ensure they have access to the programs, services, and activities otherwise available to all residents. With this in mind, consider the requirements of the *Olmstead* case and the cases that follow it in terms of local planning. These cases have significant implications for local planning. *Olmstead* raises questions of how best to facilitate an adequate supply of suitable housing to transition people out of institutions and into the community. It also raises issues of how best to make facilities, programs, services, and activities more accessible. Once in place, there are also issues of how to best maintain and improve accessibility going forward.

## Olmstead v. L.C.

Supreme Court of the United States
527 U.S. 581 (1999)

GINSBURG, Justice. This case concerns the proper construction of the antidiscrimination provision contained in the public services portion (Title II) of the Americans with Disabilities Act of 1990, 104 Stat. 337, 42 U.S.C. §12132. Specifically, we confront the question whether the proscription of discrimination may require placement of persons with mental disabilities in community settings rather than in institutions. The answer, we hold, is a qualified yes. Such action is in order when the State's treatment professionals have determined that community placement is appropriate, the transfer from institutional care to a less restrictive setting is not opposed by the affected individual, and the placement can be reasonably accommodated, taking into account the resources available to the State and the needs of others with mental disabilities. In so ruling, we affirm the decision of the Eleventh Circuit in substantial part. We remand the case, however, for further consideration of the appropriate relief, given the range of facilities the State maintains for the care and treatment of persons with diverse mental disabilities, and its obligation to administer services with an even hand.

I

This case, as it comes to us, presents no constitutional question. The complaints filed by plaintiffs-respondents L.C. and E.W. did include such an issue; L.C. and E.W. alleged that defendants-petitioners, Georgia health care officials, failed to afford them minimally adequate care and freedom from undue restraint, in violation of their rights under the Due Process Clause of the Fourteenth Amendment. Instead, the courts below resolved the case solely on statutory grounds. Our review is similarly confined. Cf. *Cleburne v. Cleburne Living Center, Inc.*, 473 U.S. 432, 450, 87 L. Ed. 2d 313, 105 S. Ct. 3249 (1985). Mindful that it is a statute we are construing, we set out first the legislative and regulatory prescriptions on which the case turns.

In the opening provisions of the ADA, Congress stated findings applicable to the statute in all its parts. Most relevant to this case, Congress determined that

"(2) historically, society has tended to isolate and segregate individuals with disabilities, and, despite some improvements, such forms of discrimination against individuals with disabilities continue to be a serious and pervasive social problem;

"(3) discrimination against individuals with disabilities persists in such critical areas as . . . institutionalization . . . ;

. . . . .

"(5) individuals with disabilities continually encounter various forms of discrimination, including outright intentional exclusion, . . . failure to make modifications to existing facilities and practices, . . . [and] segregation. . . ." 42 U.S.C. §§ 12101(a)(2), (3), (5).

Congress then set forth prohibitions against discrimination in employment (Title I, §§ 12111-12117), public services furnished by governmental entities (Title II, §§ 12131-12165), and public accommodations provided by private entities (Title III, §§ 12181-12189). The statute as a whole is intended "to provide a clear and comprehensive national mandate for the elimination of discrimination against individuals with disabilities." § 12101(b)(1).

This case concerns Title II, the public services portion of the ADA. The provision of Title II centrally at issue reads:

"Subject to the provisions of this subchapter, no qualified individual with a disability shall, by reason of such disability, be excluded from participation in or be denied the benefits of the services, programs, or activities of a public entity, or be subjected to discrimination by any such entity." § 12132.

Title II's definition section states that "public entity" includes "any State or local government," and "any department, agency, [or] special purpose district." §§ 12131(1)(A), (B). The same section defines "qualified individual with a disability" as

"an individual with a disability who, with or without reasonable modifications to rules, policies, or practices, the removal of architectural, communication, or transportation barriers, or the provision of auxiliary aids
and services, meets the essential eligibility requirements for the receipt of
services or the participation in programs or activities provided by a public
entity." § 12131(2).

On redress for violations of § 12132's discrimination prohibition, Congress
referred to remedies available under § 505 of the Rehabilitation Act of 1973, 92 Stat.
2982, 29 U.S.C. § 794a. See 42 U.S.C. § 12133 ("The remedies, procedures, and rights
set forth in [§ 505 of the Rehabilitation Act] shall be the remedies, procedures, and
rights this subchapter provides to any person alleging discrimination on the basis of
disability in violation of § 12132 of this title.").

Congress instructed the Attorney General to issue regulations implementing
provisions of Title II, including § 12132's discrimination proscription. See § 12134(a)
("The Attorney General shall promulgate regulations in an accessible format that
implement this part."). The Attorney General's regulations, Congress further
directed, "shall be consistent with this chapter and with the coordination regulations . . . applicable to recipients of Federal financial assistance under [§ 504 of the
Rehabilitation Act]." 42 U.S.C. § 12134(b). One of the § 504 regulations requires
recipients of federal funds to "administer programs and activities in the most integrated setting appropriate to the needs of qualified handicapped persons." 28 CFR
§ 41.51(d) (1998).

As Congress instructed, the Attorney General issued Title II regulations, see 28
CFR pt. 35 (1998), including one modeled on the § 504 regulation just quoted; called
the "integration regulation," it reads:

"A public entity shall administer services, programs, and activities in the
most integrated setting appropriate to the needs of qualified individuals
with disabilities." 28 CFR § 35.130(d) (1998).

The preamble to the Attorney General's Title II regulations defines "the most
integrated setting appropriate to the needs of qualified individuals with disabilities"
to mean "a setting that enables individuals with disabilities to interact with non-
disabled persons to the fullest extent possible." 28 CFR pt. 35, App. A, p. 450 (1998).
Another regulation requires public entities to "make reasonable modifications" to
avoid "discrimination on the basis of disability," unless those modifications would
entail a "fundamental alteration"; called here the "reasonable-modifications regulation," it provides:

"A public entity shall make reasonable modifications in policies, practices,
or procedures when the modifications are necessary to avoid discrimination on the basis of disability, unless the public entity can demonstrate that
making the modifications would fundamentally alter the nature of the service, program, or activity." 28 CFR § 35.130(b)(7) (1998).

We recite these regulations with the caveat that we do not here determine their validity. While the parties differ on the proper construction and enforcement of the regulations, we do not understand petitioners to challenge the regulatory formulations themselves as outside the congressional authorization.

## II

With the key legislative provisions in full view, we summarize the facts underlying this dispute. Respondents L.C. and E.W. are mentally retarded women; L.C. has also been diagnosed with schizophrenia, and E.W., with a personality disorder. Both women have a history of treatment in institutional settings. In May 1992, L.C. was voluntarily admitted to Georgia Regional Hospital at Atlanta (GRH), where she was confined for treatment in a psychiatric unit. By May 1993, her psychiatric condition had stabilized, and L.C.'s treatment team at GRH agreed that her needs could be met appropriately in one of the community-based programs the State supported. Despite this evaluation, L.C. remained institutionalized until February 1996, when the State placed her in a community-based treatment program.

E.W. was voluntarily admitted to GRH in February 1995; like L.C., E.W. was confined for treatment in a psychiatric unit. In March 1995, GRH sought to discharge E.W. to a homeless shelter, but abandoned that plan after her attorney filed an administrative complaint. By 1996, E.W.'s treating psychiatrist concluded that she could be treated appropriately in a community-based setting. She nonetheless remained institutionalized until a few months after the District Court issued its judgment in this case in 1997.

In May 1995, when she was still institutionalized at GRH, L.C. filed suit in the United States District Court for the Northern District of Georgia, challenging her continued confinement in a segregated environment. Her complaint invoked 42 U.S.C. § 1983 and provisions of the ADA, §§ 12131-12134, and named as defendants, now petitioners, the Commissioner of the Georgia Department of Human Resources, the Superintendent of GRH, and the Executive Director of the Fulton County Regional Board (collectively, the State). L.C. alleged that the State's failure to place her in a community-based program, once her treating professionals determined that such placement was appropriate, violated, *inter alia,* Title II of the ADA. L.C.'s pleading requested, among other things, that the State place her in a community care residential program, and that she receive treatment with the ultimate goal of integrating her into the mainstream of society. E.W. intervened in the action, stating an identical claim.

The District Court granted partial summary judgment in favor of L.C. and E.W. See App. to Pet. for Cert. 31a-42a. The court held that the State's failure to place L.C. and E.W. in an appropriate community-based treatment program violated Title II of the ADA. In so ruling, the court rejected the State's argument that inadequate funding, not discrimination against L.C. and E.W. "by reason of" their disabilities, accounted for their retention at GRH. Under Title II, the court concluded, "unnecessary institutional segregation of the disabled constitutes discrimination *per se*, which cannot be justified by a lack of funding."

In addition to contending that L.C. and E.W. had not shown discrimination "by reason of [their] disabilities," the State resisted court intervention on the ground that requiring immediate transfers in cases of this order would "fundamentally alter" the State's activity. The State reasserted that it was already using all available funds to provide services to other persons with disabilities. Rejecting the State's "fundamental alteration" defense, the court observed that existing state programs provided community-based treatment of the kind for which L.C. and E.W. qualified, and that the State could "provide services to plaintiffs in the community at considerably *less* cost than is required to maintain them in an institution."

The Court of Appeals for the Eleventh Circuit affirmed the judgment of the District Court, but remanded for reassessment of the State's cost-based defense. See 138 F.3d at 905. As the appeals court read the statute and regulations: When "a disabled individual's treating professionals find that a community-based placement is appropriate for that individual, the ADA imposes a duty to provide treatment in a community setting — the most integrated setting appropriate to that patient's needs"; "where there is no such finding [by the treating professionals], nothing in the ADA requires the deinstitutionalization of the patient." 138 F.3d at 902.

The Court of Appeals recognized that the State's duty to provide integrated services "is not absolute"; under the Attorney General's Title II regulation, "reasonable modifications" were required of the State, but fundamental alterations were not demanded. 138 F.3d at 904. The appeals court thought it clear, however, that "Congress wanted to permit a cost defense only in the most limited of circumstances." 138 F.3d at 902. In conclusion, the court stated that a cost justification would fail "unless the State can prove that requiring it to [expend additional funds in order to provide L.C. and E.W. with integrated services] would be so unreasonable given the demands of the State's mental health budget that it would fundamentally alter the service [the State] provides." 138 F.3d at 905. Because it appeared that the District Court had entirely ruled out a "lack of funding" justification, the appeals court remanded, repeating that the District Court should consider, among other things, "whether the additional expenditures necessary to treat L.C. and E.W. in community-based care would be unreasonable given the demands of the State's mental health budget." 138 F.3d at 905.

We granted certiorari in view of the importance of the question presented to the States and affected individuals.

### III

Endeavoring to carry out Congress' instruction to issue regulations implementing Title II, the Attorney General, in the integration and reasonable-modifications regulations made two key determinations. The first concerned the scope of the ADA's discrimination proscription, 42 U.S.C. §12132; the second concerned the obligation of the States to counter discrimination. As to the first, the Attorney General concluded that unjustified placement or retention of persons in institutions, severely limiting their exposure to the outside community, constitutes a form of discrimination based on disability prohibited by Title II. See 28 CFR § 35.130(d) (1998) ("A public entity shall administer services . . . in the most integrated setting appropriate to the needs of qualified individuals with disabilities."); Brief for United States as *Amicus Curiae* in *Helen L. v. DiDario*, 46 F.3d 325, 1995 U.S. App. LEXIS 2233, No. 94-1243 (CA3 1994), pp. 8, 15-16 (unnecessary segregation of persons with disabilities constitutes a form of discrimination prohibited by the ADA and the integration regulation). Regarding the States' obligation to avoid unjustified isolation of individuals with disabilities, the Attorney General provided that States could resist modifications that "would fundamentally alter the nature of the service, program, or activity." 28 CFR § 35.130(b)(7) (1998).

The Court of Appeals essentially upheld the Attorney General's construction of the ADA. As just recounted, see *supra*, at 9-10, the appeals court ruled that the unjustified institutionalization of persons with mental disabilities violated Title II; the court then remanded with instructions to measure the cost of caring for L.C. and E.W. in a community-based facility against the State's mental health budget.

We affirm the Court of Appeals' decision in substantial part. Unjustified isolation, we hold, is properly regarded as discrimination based on disability. But we recognize, as well, the States' need to maintain a range of facilities for the care and treatment of persons with diverse mental disabilities, and the States' obligation to administer services with an even hand. Accordingly, we further hold that the Court of Appeals' remand instruction was unduly restrictive. In evaluating a State's fundamental-alteration defense, the District Court must consider, in view of the resources available to the State, not only the cost of providing community-based care to the litigants, but also the range of services the State provides others with mental disabilities, and the State's obligation to mete out those services equitably.

## A

We examine first whether, as the Eleventh Circuit held, undue institutionalization qualifies as discrimination "by reason of . . . disability." The Department of Justice has consistently advocated that it does. Because the Department is the agency directed by Congress to issue regulations implementing Title II, its views warrant respect. We need not inquire whether the degree of deference described in *Chevron U.S.A. Inc. v. Natural Resources Defense Council, Inc.*, 467 U.S. 837, 844, 81 L. Ed. 2d 694, 104 S. Ct. 2778 (1984), is in order; "it is enough to observe that the well-reasoned views of the agencies implementing a statute 'constitute a body of experience and informed judgment to which courts and litigants may properly resort for guidance.'" *Bragdon v. Abbott*, 524 U.S. 624, 642, 141 L. Ed. 2d 540, 118 S. Ct. 2196 (1998) (quoting *Skidmore v. Swift & Co.*, 323 U.S. 134, 139-140, 89 L. Ed. 124, 65 S. Ct. 161 (1944)).

The State argues that L.C. and E.W. encountered no discrimination "by reason of" their disabilities because they were not denied community placement on account of those disabilities. Nor were they subjected to "discrimination," the State contends, because "'discrimination' necessarily requires uneven treatment of similarly situated individuals," and L.C. and E.W. had identified no comparison class, *i.e.*, no similarly situated individuals given preferential treatment. We are satisfied that Congress had a more comprehensive view of the concept of discrimination advanced in the ADA.

The ADA stepped up earlier measures to secure opportunities for people with developmental disabilities to enjoy the benefits of community living. The Developmentally Disabled Assistance and Bill of Rights Act (DDABRA), a 1975 measure, stated in aspirational terms that "the treatment, services, and habilitation for a person with developmental disabilities . . . *should be* provided in the setting that is least restrictive of the person's personal liberty." 89 Stat. 502, 42 U.S.C. § 6010(2) (1976 ed.). In a related legislative endeavor, the Rehabilitation Act of 1973, Congress used mandatory language to proscribe discrimination against persons with disabilities. See 87 Stat. 394, as amended, 29 U.S.C. § 794 (1976 ed.) ("No otherwise qualified individual with a disability in the United States . . . *shall*, solely by reason of her or his disability, be excluded from the participation in, be denied the benefits of, or be subjected to discrimination under any program or activity receiving Federal financial assistance." (Emphasis added)). Ultimately, in the ADA, enacted in 1990, Congress not only required all public entities to refrain from discrimination, see 42 U.S.C. § 12132; additionally, in findings applicable to the entire statute, Congress explicitly identified unjustified "segregation" of persons with disabilities as a "form of discrimination." See § 12101(a)(2) ("historically, society has tended to isolate and segregate individuals with disabilities, and, despite some improvements, such forms of discrimination against individuals with disabilities continue to be a serious and pervasive social problem"); § 12101(a)(5) ("individuals with disabilities continually encounter various forms of discrimination, including . . . segregation").

Recognition that unjustified institutional isolation of persons with disabilities is a form of discrimination reflects two evident judgments. First, institutional placement of persons who can handle and benefit from community settings perpetuates unwarranted assumptions that persons so isolated are incapable or unworthy of participating in community life. . . . Second, confinement in an institution severely diminishes the everyday life activities of individuals, including family relations, social contacts, work options, economic independence, educational advancement, and cultural enrichment. Dissimilar treatment correspondingly exists in this key respect: In order to receive needed medical services, persons with mental disabilities must, because of those disabilities, relinquish participation in community life they could enjoy given reasonable accommodations, while persons without mental disabilities can receive the medical services they need without similar sacrifice.

. . . .

We emphasize that nothing in the ADA or its implementing regulations condones termination of institutional settings for persons unable to handle or benefit from community settings. Title II provides only that "qualified individuals with a disability" may not "be subjected to discrimination." 42 U.S.C. § 12132. "Qualified individuals," the ADA further explains, are persons with disabilities who, "with or without reasonable modifications to rules, policies, or practices, . . . meet the essential eligibility requirements for the receipt of services or the participation in programs or activities provided by a public entity." § 12131(2).

Consistent with these provisions, the State generally may rely on the reasonable assessments of its own professionals in determining whether an individual "meets the essential eligibility requirements" for habilitation in a community-based program. Absent such qualification, it would be inappropriate to remove a patient from the more restrictive setting. See 28 CFR § 35.130(d) (1998) (public entity shall administer services and programs in "the most integrated setting *appropriate* to the needs of qualified individuals with disabilities" (emphasis added)); cf. *School Bd. of Nassau Cty. v. Arline*, 480 U.S. 273, 288, 94 L. Ed. 2d 307, 107 S. Ct. 1123 (1987) ("Courts normally should defer to the reasonable medical judgments of public health officials."). Nor is there any federal requirement that community-based treatment be imposed on patients who do not desire it. See 28 CFR § 35.130(e)(1) (1998) ("Nothing in this part shall be construed to require an individual with a disability to accept an accommodation . . . which such individual chooses not to accept."); 28 CFR pt. 35, App. A, p. 450 (1998) ("Persons with disabilities must be provided the option of declining to accept a particular accommodation."). In this case, however, there is no genuine dispute concerning the status of L.C. and E.W. as individuals "qualified" for non-institutional care: The State's own professionals determined that community-based treatment would be appropriate for L.C. and E.W., and neither woman opposed such treatment.

### B

The State's responsibility, once it provides community-based treatment to qualified persons with disabilities, is not boundless. The reasonable-modifications regulation speaks of "reasonable modifications" to avoid discrimination, and allows States to resist modifications that entail a "fundamental alteration" of the States' services and programs. 28 CFR § 35.130(b)(7) (1998). The Court of Appeals construed this regulation to permit a cost-based defense "only in the most limited of circumstances," 138 F.3d at 902, and remanded to the District Court to consider, among other things, "whether the additional expenditures necessary to treat L.C. and E.W. in community-based care would be unreasonable given the demands of the State's mental health budget," 138 F.3d at 905.

The Court of Appeals' construction of the reasonable-modifications regulation is unacceptable for it would leave the State virtually defenseless once it is shown that the plaintiff is qualified for the service or program she seeks. If the expense entailed in placing one or two people in a community-based treatment program is properly measured for reasonableness against the State's entire mental health budget, it is unlikely that a State, relying on the fundamental-alteration defense, could ever prevail. . . . Sensibly construed, the fundamental-alteration component of the reasonable-modifications regulation would allow the State to show that, in the allocation of available resources, immediate relief for the plaintiffs would be inequitable, given the responsibility the State has undertaken for the care and treatment of a large and diverse population of persons with mental disabilities.

When it granted summary judgment for plaintiffs in this case, the District Court compared the cost of caring for the plaintiffs in a community-based setting with the cost of caring for them in an institution. That simple comparison showed that community placements cost less than institutional confinements. As the United States recognizes, however, a comparison so simple overlooks costs the State cannot avoid; most notably, a "State . . . may experience increased overall expenses by funding community placements without being able to take advantage of the savings associated with the closure of institutions."

As already observed, the ADA is not reasonably read to impel States to phase out institutions, placing patients in need of close care at risk. (KENNEDY, J., concurring in judgment). Nor is it the ADA's mission to drive States to move institutionalized patients into an inappropriate setting, such as a homeless shelter, a placement the State proposed, then retracted, for E.W. See *supra,* at 8. Some individuals, like L.C. and E.W. in prior years, may need institutional care from time to time "to stabilize acute psychiatric symptoms." . . . For other individuals, no placement outside the institution may ever be appropriate. . . .

To maintain a range of facilities and to administer services with an even hand, the State must have more leeway than the courts below understood the fundamental-alteration defense to allow. If, for example, the State were to demonstrate that it had a comprehensive, effectively working plan for placing qualified persons with mental disabilities in less restrictive settings, and a waiting list that moved at a reasonable pace not controlled by the State's endeavors to keep its institutions fully populated, the reasonable-modifications standard would be met. In such circumstances, a court would have no warrant effectively to order displacement of persons at the top of the community-based treatment waiting list by individuals lower down who commenced civil actions.

. . . .

For the reasons stated, we conclude that, under Title II of the ADA, States are required to provide community-based treatment for persons with mental disabilities when the State's treatment professionals determine that such placement is appropriate, the affected persons do not oppose such treatment, and the placement can be reasonably accommodated, taking into account the resources available to the

State and the needs of others with mental disabilities. The judgment of the Eleventh Circuit is therefore affirmed in part and vacated in part, and the case is remanded for further proceedings consistent with this opinion.

It is so ordered.

STEVENS, Justice. (concurring in part and concurring in the judgment). Unjustified disparate treatment, in this case, "unjustified institutional isolation," constitutes discrimination under the Americans with Disabilities Act of 1990. . . .

KENNEDY, Justice. (joining Part I and concurring in the judgment). Despite remarkable advances and achievements by medical science, and agreement among many professionals that even severe mental illness is often treatable, the extent of public resources to devote to this cause remains controversial. Knowledgeable professionals tell us that our society, and the governments which reflect its attitudes and preferences, have yet to grasp the potential for treating mental disorders, especially severe mental illness. As a result, necessary resources for the endeavor often are not forthcoming. During the course of a year, about 5.6 million Americans will suffer from severe mental illness. E. Torrey, Out of the Shadows 4 (1997). Some 2.2 million of these persons receive no treatment. *Id.* at 6. Millions of other Americans suffer from mental disabilities of less serious degree, such as mild depression. These facts are part of the background against which this case arises. In addition, of course, persons with mental disabilities have been subject to historic mistreatment, indifference, and hostility.

Despite these obstacles, the States have acknowledged that the care of the mentally disabled is their special obligation. They operate and support facilities and programs, sometimes elaborate ones, to provide care. It is a continuing challenge, though, to provide the care in an effective and humane way, particularly because societal attitudes and the responses of public authorities have changed from time to time.

. . . .

THOMAS, Justice. [Dissenting in part, focusing on disparate impact analysis to prove discrimination.]

## *Questions for Consideration*

1) Does this case involve a constitutional or statutory challenge, or both?

2) Under Title II of the ADA, implementing regulations must be developed and applied to ensure that public programs and activities are delivered to recipients "in the most integrated setting appropriate to the needs of qualified handicapped persons." Who is responsible for developing these regulations, and where can we find these regulations?

3) In developing a comprehensive plan to integrate people with disabilities into the community, are there any defenses a local government may raise to a claim that the city has not met a request of a qualified person for a more integrated environment?

4) How, if at all, are costs to the state and local government considered in determining if they have met their obligation not to discriminate against a person with a disability in providing the most integrated setting?

5) In the context of local, regional, and statewide planning, what would be a fundamental alteration under the ADA? In other words, how might you advise state and local planning officials on the issue of when a change or exception rises to the level of a fundamental alteration?

## *Takeaway*

- Comprehensive planning must account for accessibility for people with disabilities. This goes beyond planning for changes in the built environment, such as planning for curb cuts, access ramps, and handicapped parking spaces. Planning must include a variety of housing options as well as planning for access and participation in programs and services for people of different mental and physical abilities.

- Planning must be "concrete" in the sense that a plan must include strategies for implementation and for adequate financing.

- The Court identified three criteria to consider in *Olmstead* planning. They concluded that; "under Title II of the ADA, States are required to provide community-based treatment for persons with mental disabilities when 1) the State's treatment professionals determine that such placement is appropriate, 2) the affected persons do not oppose such treatment, and 3) the placement can be reasonably accommodated, taking into account the resources available to the State and the needs of others with mental disabilities."

- If you represent state and local governments, you have to be sure that they comply with requirements found in 28 C.F.R. § 35.107.

  28 C.F.R. § 35.107 Designation of responsible employee and adoption of grievance procedures.

  (a) Designation of responsible employee. A public entity that employs 50 or more persons shall designate at least one employee to coordinate its efforts to comply with and carry out its responsibilities under this part, including any investigation of any complaint communicated to it alleging its noncompliance with this part or alleging any actions that would be prohibited by this part. The public entity shall make available to all interested individuals the name, office address, and telephone number of the employee or employees designated pursuant to this paragraph.

  (b) Complaint procedure. A public entity that employs 50 or more persons shall adopt and publish grievance procedures providing for prompt and equitable resolution of complaints alleging any action that would be prohibited by this part.

Planning must account for making our communities accessible. This includes planning as to facilities and as to programs, services, and activities of state and local government. The cases that follow provide guidance on the meaning of facilities, programs, services, and activities.

## Frame v. City of Arlington

U.S. Court of Appeals for the Fifth Circuit

657 F.3d 215 (5th Cir. 2011)

BENAVIDES and PRADO, Circuit Judges. Title II of the Americans with Disabilities Act (ADA), like § 504 of the Rehabilitation Act, provides that individuals with disabilities shall not "be denied the benefits of the services, programs, or activities of a public entity, or be subjected to discrimination by any such entity." For nearly two decades, Title II's implementing regulations have required cities to make newly built and altered sidewalks readily accessible to individuals with disabilities. The plaintiffs-appellants in this case, five individuals with disabilities, allege that defendant-appellee the City of Arlington (the City) has recently built and altered sidewalks that are not readily accessible to them. The plaintiffs brought this action for injunctive relief under Title II and § 504.

. . . [W]e must determine whether Title II and § 504 (and their implied private right of action) extend to newly built and altered public sidewalks. . . . We hold that the plaintiffs have a private right of action to enforce Title II and § 504 with respect to newly built and altered public sidewalks, and that the right accrued at the time the plaintiffs first knew or should have known they were being denied the benefits of those sidewalks.

The plaintiffs in this case depend on motorized wheelchairs for mobility. They allege that certain inaccessible sidewalks make it dangerous, difficult, or impossible for them to travel to a variety of public and private establishments throughout the City. Most of these sidewalks allegedly were built or altered by the City after Title II became effective on January 26, 1992. The plaintiffs sued the City on July 22, 2005, claiming that the inaccessible sidewalks violate Title II of the ADA and § 504 of the Rehabilitation Act. . . .

. . . .

It is established that Title II of the ADA and § 504 of the Rehabilitation Act are enforceable through an implied private right of action. The issue is whether these statutes (and their established private right of action) extend to newly built and altered public sidewalks. Based on statutory text and structure, we hold that Title II and § 504 unambiguously extend to newly built and altered public sidewalks. We further hold that the plaintiffs have a private right of action to enforce Title II and § 504 to the extent they would require the City to make reasonable modifications to such sidewalks.

The ADA is a "broad mandate" of "comprehensive character" and "sweeping purpose" intended "to eliminate discrimination against disabled individuals, and to integrate them into the economic and social mainstream of American life." Title II of the ADA focuses on disability discrimination in the provision of public services. Specifically, Title II, 42 U.S.C. § 12132, provides that "no qualified individual with a disability shall, by reason of such disability, be excluded from participation in or be denied the benefits of the services, programs, or activities of a public entity, or be subjected to discrimination by any such entity."

Section 504 of the Rehabilitation Act prohibits disability discrimination by recipients of federal funding. Like Title II, § 504 provides that no qualified individual with a disability "shall, solely by reason of her or his disability, be excluded from participation in, be denied the benefits of, or be subjected to discrimination under any program or activity receiving Federal financial assistance." The ADA and the Rehabilitation Act generally are interpreted in pari materia. Indeed, Congress has instructed courts that "nothing in [the ADA] shall be construed to apply a lesser standard than the standards applied under title V [i.e., § 504] of the Rehabilitation Act . . . or the regulations issued by Federal agencies pursuant to such title." The parties have not pointed to any reason why Title II and § 504 should be interpreted differently in this case. Although we focus primarily on Title II, our analysis is informed by the Rehabilitation Act, and our holding applies to both statutes.

. . . .

In interpreting the scope of Title II (and its implied private right of action), our starting point is the statute's plain meaning. In ascertaining the plain meaning of Title II, we "must look to the particular statutory language at issue, as well as the language and design of the statute as a whole."

If we determine that the plain meaning of Title II is ambiguous, we do not simply impose our own construction on the statute. When confronted with a statutory ambiguity, we refer to the responsible agency's reasonable interpretation of that statute. Here, because Congress directed the Department of Justice (DOJ) to elucidate Title II with implementing regulations, DOJ's views at least would "warrant respect" and might be entitled to even more deference.

. . . .

We begin by determining whether the plain meaning of Title II extends to newly built and altered sidewalks. As noted, Title II provides that disabled individuals shall not be denied the "benefits of the services, programs, or activities of a public entity, or be subjected to discrimination by any such entity." . . .

The ADA does not define the "services, programs, or activities of a public entity." The Rehabilitation Act, however, defines a "program or activity" as "all of the operations of . . . a local government." As already stated, we interpret Title II and the Rehabilitation Act in pari materia. Accordingly . . . we must determine whether newly built and altered city sidewalks are benefits of "all of the operations" and "services" of a public entity within the ordinary meaning of those terms.

. . . .

[W]hen a city decides to build or alter a sidewalk and makes that sidewalk inaccessible to individuals with disabilities without adequate justification, the city unnecessarily denies disabled individuals the benefits of its services in violation of Title II.

Building and altering city sidewalks unambiguously are "services" of a public entity under any reasonable understanding of that term. The Supreme Court has broadly understood a "service" to mean "the performance of work commanded or paid for by another," or "an act done for the benefit or at the command of another." Webster's Dictionary additionally defines a "service" as "the provision, organization, or apparatus for . . . meeting a general demand." For its part, Black's Law Dictionary defines a "public service" as work "provided or facilitated by the government for the general public's convenience and benefit."

Under each of these common understandings, building and altering public sidewalks unambiguously are services of a public entity. The construction or alteration of a city sidewalk is work commanded by another (i.e., voters and public officials), paid for by another (i.e., taxpayers), and done for the benefit of another (e.g., pedestrians and drivers). When a city builds or alters a sidewalk, it promotes the general public's convenience by overcoming a collective action problem and allowing citizens to focus on other ventures. [Moreover], when a city builds or alters a sidewalk, it helps meet a general demand for the safe movement of people and goods. In short, in common understanding, a city provides a service to its citizens when it builds or alters a public sidewalk.

A "service" also might be defined as "[t]he duties, work, or business performed or discharged by a public official." Under this definition too, newly built and altered public sidewalks are services of a public entity. Cities, through their officials, study, debate, plan, and ultimately authorize sidewalk construction. If a city official authorizes a public sidewalk to be built in a way that is not readily accessible to disabled individuals without adequate justification, the official denies disabled individuals the benefits of that sidewalk no less than if the official poured the concrete himself.

Furthermore, building and altering public sidewalks easily are among "all of the operations" (and thus also the "programs or activities") of a public entity. Webster's Dictionary broadly defines "operations" as "the whole process of planning for and operating a business or other organized unit," and defines "operation" as "a doing or performing esp[ecially] of action." In common understanding, the operations of a public entity would include the "whole process" of "planning" and "doing" that goes into building and altering public sidewalks.

In sum, in common understanding, building and altering public sidewalks are services, programs, or activities of a public entity. When a city decides to build or alter a sidewalk and makes that sidewalk inaccessible to individuals with disabilities without adequate justification, disabled individuals are denied the benefits of that city's services, programs, or activities. Newly built and altered sidewalks thus fit squarely within the plain, unambiguous text of Title II.

Even if we focus on a public sidewalk itself, we still find that a sidewalk unambiguously is a service, program, or activity of a public entity. A city sidewalk itself facilitates the public's "convenience and benefit" by affording a means of safe transportation. A city sidewalk itself is the "apparatus" that meets the public's general demand for safe transportation. As the Supreme Court has observed, sidewalks are "general government services" "provided in common to all citizens" to protect pedestrians from the "very real hazards of traffic." The Supreme Court also has recognized that public sidewalks are "traditional public fora" that "time out of mind" have facilitated the general demand for public assembly and discourse. When a newly built or altered city sidewalk is unnecessarily made inaccessible to individuals with disabilities, those individuals are denied the benefits of safe transportation and a venerable public forum.

. . . .

Additionally, in clarifying the requirements of Title II in the unique context of "designated public transportation services" (e.g., regular rail and bus services), Congress expressly provided that § 12132 requires new and altered "facilities" to be accessible. Although Congress did not define "facilities," the relevant Department of Transportation (DOT) regulations define the term to include, inter alia, "roads, walks, passageways, [and] parking lots." Congress's express statement that § 12132 extends to newly built and altered facilities is a good indication that Congress thought § 12132 would extend to newly built and altered sidewalks.

. . . .

. . . Congress intended Title II to extend to newly built and altered sidewalks. Congress anticipated that Title II would require local governments "to provide curb cuts on public streets" because the "employment, transportation, and public accommodation sections of [the ADA] would be meaningless if people who use wheelchairs were not afforded the opportunity to travel on and between streets." Implicit in this declaration is a premise that sidewalks are subject to Title II in the first place. Congress's specific application of Title II is consistent with its statutory findings. In enacting Title II, Congress found that individuals with disabilities suffer from "various forms of discrimination," including "isolat[ion] and segregat[ion]," and that inaccessible transportation is a "critical area[]" of discrimination. Moreover, Congress understood that accessible transportation is the "linchpin" that "promotes the self-reliance and self-sufficiency of people with disabilities." Continuing to build inaccessible sidewalks without adequate justification would unnecessarily entrench the types of discrimination Title II was designed to prohibit.

Title II does not only benefit individuals with disabilities. Congress recognized that isolating disabled individuals from the social and economic mainstream imposes tremendous costs on society. Congress specifically found that disability discrimination "costs the United States billions of dollars in unnecessary expenses resulting from dependency and nonproductivity." Congress also anticipated that "the mainstreaming of persons with disabilities will result in more persons with disabilities working, in increasing earnings, in less dependence on the Social Security system for financial support, in increased spending on consumer goods, and increased tax revenues." The Rehabilitation Act was passed with similar findings and purpose. Continuing to build inaccessible sidewalks without adequate justification would unnecessarily aggravate the social costs Congress sought to abate.

To conclude, . . . , we hold that Title II unambiguously extends to newly built and altered sidewalks. Because we interpret Title II and § 504 of the Rehabilitation Act in pari materia, we hold that § 504 extends to such sidewalks as well.

. . . .

For the reasons stated, we hold that the plaintiffs have a private right of action to enforce Title II of the ADA and § 504 of the Rehabilitation Act with respect to newly built and altered sidewalks.

## *Questions for Consideration*

1) What are several factors that go into determining if something is a program, service, or activity of a state or local government?

2) If a local government is patching a local road and then putting a new coat of tar sealer in the road surface, is this work an alteration, new construction, or simply upkeep and maintenance? What difference might it make?

3) If a local government decides to do new road construction along a roadway that already has an existing sidewalk, does it have to redo the sidewalks to upgrade them to current ADA standards, assuming that the existing sidewalks are not ADA compliant?

4) If a local government decides to construct a totally new road in a location where there was no road, is it required to build a sidewalk along that roadway in order to satisfy the ADA?

## *Takeaway*

- In making a case, one must look to legislative history and other sources to define and explain such terms as programs, services, and activities. It is not enough to just say something fits into one of these categories; an explanation must be offered.

- Interpretations of such things as facilities; programs, services, and activities; reasonable accommodations and modifications; and the various methods of demonstrating discrimination are similar across all of the different disability laws, even though details may differ. Therefore, you should be able to understand the similarities between and among the Americans with Disabilities Act (ADA), the Rehabilitation Act (RHA), and the Fair Housing Act (FHA).

- The difference between new construction, alterations, and upkeep and maintenance can be important, and you need to be able to identify and explain the differences and the consequences that may follow from such distinctions.

---

Sometimes, even with good planning, accessible services may be interrupted. What is the obligation to maintain such services, programs, and activities?

## Foley v. City of Lafayette

U.S. Court of Appeals for the Seventh Circuit

359 F.3d 925 (7th Cir. 2004)

KANNE, Circuit Judge. Robert Foley alleges that the City of Lafayette violated the Americans with Disabilities Act ("ADA") and the Rehabilitation Act of 1973 by failing to provide adequate egress from the city-owned train station platform. The district court, relying on 49 C.F.R. § 37.161, concluded that the inoperable elevators and snow-covered ramp that prevented Foley from an easy exit from the platform were non-actionable isolated or temporary conditions as a matter of law. Because we agree with the district court's conclusion, we affirm the grant of summary judgment to the City of Lafayette.

### I. History

Robert Foley, a lifetime resident of West Virginia, has suffered from significant pain in his legs and back since a work related injury in August of 2000. From the time of his injury, he has relied on a wheelchair because of intense pain caused by standing or walking. Robert's health problems are compounded by his morbid obesity — he weighs nearly four hundred pounds — and diabetes.

In December of 2000, Robert decided to travel to Indiana so that he could celebrate the holidays with his extended family. Robert's brother, Greg, hosting the proposed reunion at his home in Battle Ground (a town near Lafayette), made arrangements for Robert to travel from West Virginia to Indiana by train. Greg chose this means of transportation in part because the Lafayette train station is advertised by Amtrak as fully accessible to persons in wheelchairs. . . .

The sole Lafayette train station is owned and operated by the City of Lafayette. Amtrak, Grey-hound, the city bus system, and several other organizations utilize the station as a depot and/or for office space. Fred Taylor was the only City employee assigned to the station on a regular basis during the time period in question. Taylor performed maintenance and janitorial work. He worked from 6:00 a.m. to 3:00 p.m., Monday through Friday. Bill O'Connor, an employee of the Downtown Business Center, also worked at the station. His duties mirrored those of Taylor, he often followed orders given by Taylor, and he usually started work at 2:30 p.m. and ended work around 11:30 p.m. . . .

The train station is located at Riehle Plaza in downtown Lafayette and is situ-ated on the east side of the tracks. Passenger trains arriving in Lafayette unload at a ground level platform on the west side of the tracks. The facility has three levels.

In order to reach the parking lot . . . , passengers must go up to the third level, by way of stairs or an elevator, to a short bridge that crosses above the tracks. After crossing the short bridge, passengers can take the . . . stairs or elevator to descend to the middle or ground-floor levels of the station, where they can access the park-ing lot.

Alternatively, by taking either the stairs or a ramp [a person can exit the station]. . . .

It is undisputed that significant snowfall, up to nine inches, blanketed the Lafay-ette area over the weekend prior to Robert's arrival. It is also uncontested that it was extremely cold and that the wind was particularly strong on the morning of Decem-ber 18. In resolving all factual disputes in favor of Robert, we assume that the bulk of the snow fell early in the weekend, but . . . there is no dispute that blizzard-like conditions prevailed through Monday morning due to a large amount of snow on the ground and strong winds.

At 6:00 a.m. on December 18, Greg Foley set out with his brother-in-law, Mike Flagg, to pick up Robert. . . . When Greg arrived at the station, he discovered that neither of the elevators were working. Concerned, Greg notified Fred Taylor. Taylor was surprised and may have tried to fix the problem by switching a circuit breaker. At his deposition, Taylor recalled that the elevators were broken the previous week and stated that he had called his boss to report the problem. . . . Taylor, . . . spent most of the balance of his day shoveling snow, assisting other patrons of the depot, and attending to routine duties.

. . . .

. . . [R]ecords show [that a] . . . phone call for service regarding the train-station elevators was [made and] received at 9:13 a.m. At 9:31 a.m. . . . [In response to the call,] a Lafayette-area repairman [was dispatched] to the scene. He arrived at 10:00 a.m. In commencing the repairs, it was discovered that the heating elements neces-sary to maintain the proper temperature of the oil in the outdoor hydraulic eleva-tors were burned out. Because of the extremely cold temperatures, the elevators were rendered inoperable. Nothing further could be done that day, however, because parts were needed. . . .

In the meantime, . . .

Robert and his son, David, [arrived at the station and] were helped off the train by Amtrak employees but were left alone in the cold weather on the platform. Amtrak does not employ personnel at the Lafayette station and the individuals who assisted the Foleys returned to their posts on the northbound train. . . . Robert and David considered the option of going up the ramp to the pedestrian bridge. They decided that the snow, not yet removed from the ramp, made maneuvering the wheelchair up the incline too difficult and dangerous. . . .

[Around 11:30 a.m.] Robert, [with assistance] was able to leave the station [and met up with his brother, Greg]. . . .

The next day, Tuesday, December 19, repairs continued and one elevator was returned to service. Both elevators were made fully operational by December 22.

Robert made several trips to Lafayette's Home Hospital and visited other doctors in West Virginia. He complained of increased pain in his legs due to alleged frostbite caused by the cold air. Robert contends that the City of Lafayette discriminated against him on the basis of his disability in violation of Title II of the ADA and the Rehabilitation Act. He alleges that the lack of equal egress on the morning of December 18 constitutes a violation of these statutes. The district court granted Lafayette's motion for summary judgment and sent the state law claims to the Indiana courts.

## II. Analysis

. . . .

The ADA seeks to "provide a clear and comprehensive national mandate for the elimination of discrimination against individuals with disabilities[.]" 42 U.S.C. § 12101(b)(1) (2003). In pursuit of this goal, Title II of the ADA requires that "no qualified individual with a disability shall, by reason of such disability, be excluded from participation in or be denied the benefits of the services . . . of a public entity, or be subjected to discrimination by any such entity." 42 U.S.C. § 12132 (2003). For summary judgment purposes, the district court found that Robert was protected by the ADA as a "qualified individual" under 42 U.S.C. § 12131(2), and this finding was not challenged on appeal. Furthermore, the City of Lafayette is clearly a "public entity" under 42 U.S.C. § 12131(1). Thus, the issue before us under the ADA is whether the district court was correct in finding that the City, as a matter of law, did not unlawfully discriminate, exclude, or deny services to Robert." Since Rehabilitation Act claims are analyzed under the same standards as those used for ADA claims," *Ozlowski v. Henderson*, 237 F.3d 837, 842 (7th Cir. 2001), we will confine our analysis to the ADA.

The Lafayette train station is, in the normal course of operation, fully accessible to individuals with disabilities. The dispute in this case is whether the City of Lafayette did enough to prevent and/or remedy the elevator difficulties in December of 2000. It is in this context that the district court properly relied on a rule promulgated by the Department of Transportation ("DOT") that provides guidance on the particular issue of access to mass transit facilities. This rule states:

> (a) Public and private entities providing transportation services *shall maintain in operative condition* those features of facilities and vehicles that are required to make the vehicles and facilities readily accessible to and

usable by individuals with disabilities. These features include, but are not limited to . . . elevators.

(b) Accessibility features *shall be repaired promptly* if they are damaged or out of order. When an accessibility feature is out of order, the entity *shall take reasonable steps to accommodate* individuals with disabilities who would otherwise use the feature.

(c) This section *does not prohibit isolated or temporary interruptions* in service or access due to . . . repairs.

49 C.F.R. § 37.161 (emphasis added). Thus, Lafayette has three duties under this particular regulation: it must maintain the elevators in operative condition, it must repair the elevators promptly once an elevator malfunctions, and it must take reasonable steps to accommodate an individual who otherwise would have used the elevators when the elevators are out of order. But the regulation does not subject Lafayette to liability for isolated or temporary interruptions in service due to repairs.

The DOT provided further guidance regarding the regulations in the published commentary. On the issue of maintenance and prompt repair, the DOT noted:

The rule points out that temporary obstructions or isolated instances of mechanical failure would not be considered violations of the ADA or this rule. Repairs must be made "promptly." *The rule does not, and probably could not, state a time limit for making particular repairs, given the variety of circumstances involved.* However, repairing accessible features must be made a high priority.

Transportation for Individuals with Disabilities, 56 Fed. Reg. 45,621 (Sept. 6, 1991) app. D, subpt. G, § 37.161 (emphasis added).

The DOT's interpretation of its own regulation makes sense: the only way to apply 49 C.F.R. § 37.161 is to consider the unique circumstances inherent in any particular transportation service site. In other words, there are no universal definitions in the regulations for what is required to "maintain in operative condition" the accessibility features, to repair "promptly" such features, or to take "reasonable steps" to accommodate when the features are not accessible. The extent of inaccessibility covered by the terms "isolated or temporary" in 49 C.F.R. § 37.161 is likewise unclear and only determinable by considering the unique circumstances of the case.

Robert insists that Lafayette failed to maintain the elevators in operative condition. Furthermore, he argues that Lafayette did not repair the elevators promptly, and did not take reasonable steps to accommodate him – by clearing the ramp of snow, for instance. Lafayette argues that the elevator repairs, necessitated by the cold weather, led to a temporary or isolated interruption in service that should not be punished under the ADA.

Nothing in the record indicates frequent denial of access to disabled persons or a policy that neglects elevator maintenance.

. . . .

### III. Conclusion

Neither the interruption of elevator service nor the alternative ramp's snow-covered condition, under the circumstances of this case, constitutes a violation of the ADA or the Rehabilitation Act of 1973. The district court's grant of summary judgment is AFFIRMED.

## *Questions for Consideration*

1) What were the conditions at the train station in Lafayette, Indiana on the day of the alleged failure to comply with the ADA?

2) Should the train station have had more workers on duty during these conditions? Do we need to know about the availability of extra workers? Do we need to know about budget constraints that might affect services at the station? Would the ability to have more workers on hand to remove snow and ice make a difference if the elevators were not working correctly? Do we need to know if there are work rules such as union requirements that might affect use of workers and hours of work?

3) Could the city have done more to ensure that the train station would be fully accessible under these conditions? If so, what would you have advised them to do?

4) Assume you are local counsel to a small city. The elevators in city hall are out of order for two days. The offices for marriage licenses and handicap parking permits are located on the third floor. During this time, when the elevators are not working, several people with disabilities complain that they are unable to access important services in that they are unable to obtain marriage licenses and handicap parking permits. These claimants see others walking up the stairwells, but because of their disabilities, they are not able to walk up the stairs. Local city officials contact you and explain that the elevators may not be operable for several more days. What steps would you advise city officials to take in addressing this problem to ensure compliance with the ADA?

## *Takeaway*

- Even with the best planning, one must be prepared for things to go wrong. No one expects us to be perfect, but we must have back-up plans. We must have evidence of being prepared to respond to disruptions in access to facilities and to programs, services, and activities.

- Every situation is different. Each case turns on its own facts. Therefore, when handling a situation such as the one presented in the *Foley* case, it is important to master the facts and to relate these facts to specific elements of the law.

- Issues such as those that involve elevators, bus services, and the like, will have ongoing repair and upkeep concerns. Therefore, it is important to maintain records of all service calls and the time it takes to get the disruption corrected and repaired. In a given case, a past record of quick or slow responsiveness may influence an official determination as to the reasonableness of compliance with the requirements for maintaining accessibility for people with disabilities.

## Discussion Problem 4.4

Rebecca lives on the upper level of a two-family home in Mid-Town City. Mid-Town has a comprehensive plan with provisions for controlling the populations of animals within the city. The plan asserts that each year, many dogs are abandoned by their owners and are left roaming the streets. There is also a concern that having too many dogs in a neighborhood increases noise, animal waste, and conflicts between dog owners and others. The regulation is designed to help reduce complaints from neighbors regarding other people's dogs, and the underlying reasons given for this regulation are public health and safety related. The comprehensive plan responds to this identified problem by limiting the number of pets per household. The zoning code implements the plan with a regulation. The zoning code provides that each household may have a maximum of two dogs, and each dog must be registered with the city. Rebecca has three dogs. All three are trained house dogs. Two of her dogs are pets, and one is a service dog under the rules and regulations of the Americans with Disabilities Act (ADA). Acting in response to complaints from neighbors, Mid-Town planning and zoning officials inform Rebecca of the violation and order her to remove one of the dogs from the premises and to register the two she keeps. Rebecca responds, saying that she only has two pet dogs, and the other dog does not count under the local zoning code because it is protected by the federal ADA as a service animal. Mid-Town has given notice to Rebecca that they have filed an enforcement action against her and have ordered her to appear in local Mid-Town court to answer to the charge of non-compliance with the code. Rebecca comes to your law office and asks for advice. What advice do you give her?

# D. Practice Problems

4.1 The second case in this chapter, *Pinecrest Lakes, Inc. v. Shidel*, is an interesting and complicated case. Assume you are a summer law clerk in a small law firm, and one of the lawyers in the firm asks you to comment on this case and to do some follow up research. Prepare a memorandum to the lawyer addressing the points below. In doing this, you should begin by obtaining the full court opinion as reported rather than relying on the edited version in this casebook.

a) Give your opinion on the remedy applied in this case.

b) What has been the subsequent history of this case in Florida?

c) Has the case been followed or distinguished in opinions from any other states?

d) Can you identify other states that have a strict consistency requirement?

4.2 You are in-house counsel for Realty World, Inc., a large-scale real estate developer operating in New York. A year ago, Realty World acquired 150 acres of land for a 400-unit, single-family residential home development. Recently, the county where the property is located updated its comprehensive plan and its zoning ordinance. The new comprehensive plan calls for a "forever wild" greenbelt along the southern edge of Realty World's property. The greenbelt impacts approximately twenty acres of Realty World's property. The estimated financial impact involves the loss of 10% of the total land value and is equal to about $3 million. The president of Realty World is outraged and wants to sue the county for a taking of its property. The county says that Realty World will benefit from the greenbelt because it will add to the value of its remaining land. The county offers no evidence of the financial gain that might be added to Realty World's property as a result of the greenbelt. Realty World disagrees and argues that it is being asked to carry the full cost of a greenbelt on its own when the public should be paying to acquire his land since it is the public that benefits from such a prohibition on development.

a) Assume you have no additional information and that the company president wants your input in one hour. Write a memorandum of law to the president of Realty World addressing whether or not this is a taking in violation of the Takings Clause.

4.3 Euclidian zoning was the approach to zoning in the early 1900s. If you are involved in the contemporary practice of land use regulation, however, you are bound to encounter planning and zoning professionals who refer to a variety of other planning and zoning techniques. Several important concepts in planning and zoning are *performance zoning, form-based zoning, transect zoning, new urbanism,* and *concurrency.* Look up these terms and be prepared to discuss them with a planning and zoning colleague. Be able to compare and contrast these concepts with traditional Euclidian zoning concepts.

# Chapter 5

# Regulating Uses: Tension with other Fundamental Rights

As we have seen in prior chapters, the exercise of the police power is limited. Among the constraints imposed on the exercise of the police power are limitations relating to the protection of other important and fundamental rights. In this chapter, we deal directly with land use regulations that create tension with other fundamental rights, such as those of free speech, free association, and the rights of people with disabilities.

## A. Regulating Use Rather than Users

A fundamental principle of land use and zoning law is the law regulates uses and not people. Thus, it is important to focus on use, and on the coordination of uses for purposes of protecting and advancing the public health, safety, welfare, and morals; and not to focus on the race, ethnicity, religion, disability, or other characteristics of the users of the property.

### Sunrise Check Cashing v. Town of Hempstead

Court of Appeals of New York
986 N.E.2d 898 (N.Y. 2013)

SMITH, Judge. We hold that a zoning measure that prohibits check-cashing establishments in a town's business district is invalid, because it violates the principle that zoning is concerned with the use of land, not with the identity of the user.

The provision in question is section 302(K) of article XXXI of the Building Zone Ordinance of the Town of Hempstead, adopted January 10, 2006. It says in pertinent part: "In any use district except Y Industrial and LM Light Manufacturing Districts, check-cashing establishments are hereby expressly prohibited" (§ 302[K][1]).

The only document explaining the purpose of this enactment is a memorandum from a deputy town attorney dated December 13, 2005, the date of a public hearing held on the proposal that became section 302(K). The subject of the memorandum is *Public Policy behind Check Cashing Ordinance.* The memorandum says that the measure "represents sound public policy" because:

"Essentially, it serves the interest of encouraging young people and those of lower incomes to establish savings and checking accounts, do their banking at sound and reputable banking institutions, and develop credit ratings. It also eliminates predatory and exploitative finance enterprises from commercial areas, which is beneficial because these enterprises tend to keep a neighborhood down."

The memorandum consists of several pages criticizing check-cashing establishments on social policy grounds. It says that such establishments make it convenient for young and lower income people "to remain in the cash-only economy" and adds: "This is bad for society as a whole." The memorandum refers to studies finding that "check-cashing establishments actually exploit the poor and African Americans." It concludes that the proposal under consideration "encourages young and lower income people to open up bank accounts, save their money, and develop a credit rating" and "also removes a seedy type of operation, akin to pawnshops and strip clubs, from the commercial areas of the Town." Section 302(K) was adopted by the Town Board some four weeks after the memorandum was issued.

Several check-cashing establishments brought the present action, seeking a declaratory judgment that section 302(K) is invalid, and an injunction against its enforcement. . . .

A town's power to adopt zoning regulations derives from Town Law § 261, which authorizes town boards

"to regulate and restrict the height, number of stories and size of buildings and other structures, the percentage of lot that may be occupied, the size of yards, courts, and other open spaces, the density of population, and the location and use of buildings, structures and land for trade, industry, residence or other purposes" (*see also* Town Law § 263 [listing the purposes of zoning]).

Our cases make clear that the zoning power is not a general police power, but a power to regulate land use: "[I]t is a fundamental principle of zoning that a zoning board is charged with the regulation of land use and not with the person who owns or occupies it."

The provision at issue here contradicts this principle. It is clear from the memorandum of the deputy town attorney that section 302(K) was directed at the perceived social evil of check-cashing services, which were thought to exploit the younger and lower income people who are their main customers. Whatever the merits of this view as a policy matter, it cannot be implemented through zoning. Section 302(K) is obviously concerned not with the use of the land but with the business done by those who occupy it. It is true that there are cases in which the nature of the business is relevant to zoning because of the businesses' "negative secondary effects" on the surrounding community; this is true of so-called "adult entertainment" uses, but, despite the reference to "pawnshops and strip clubs" in the deputy town attorney's memorandum, the Town has not tried to show and does not argue that check-cashing services are in a similar category.

Indeed, the Town makes no attempt to defend the purposes advanced in the memorandum as legitimate objects of the zoning power. Instead, the Town tries to save section 302(K) by attributing to it a different purpose: protecting the health and safety of the community against the dangers created by armed robbery. The Town quotes the observation of the court in *American Broadcasting Cos. v Siebert* (110 Misc. 2d 744, 746, 747 [N.Y. Sup. Ct. 1981]) (a case arising under the Freedom of Information Law) that check-cashing facilities "are and have been over the years, the subject of robberies, kidnappings and murders" and that "the risk of robberies inherently exists in the check-cashing business." There is no evidence that the Town Board of Hempstead, when it enacted section 302(K), was worrying about armed robbery. . . .

We reject the Town's argument. . . . The record here clearly refutes the idea that section 302 (K) was a public safety measure. . . .

Accordingly, the [zoning] order [is not enforceable]. . . .

Chief Judge Lippman and Judges Graffeo, Read and Pigott concur; Judge Rivera taking no part.

Order affirmed, with costs.

## *Questions for Consideration*

1) Why isn't a regulation covering the location of cash checking services a regulation of land use?

2) How important is the memorandum of the deputy town attorney to the decision of the court?

3) What is a negative secondary effect?

4) What if the deputy town attorney had included with his memorandum evidence of crime statistics and of robberies that supported his position against permitting check cashing services in the zoning district?

## *Takeaway*

- Zoning is about regulating land *use*. It is not about regulating users. The race, religion, and other characteristics of users are not supposed to matter to use.

- In focusing on the regulation of land use, zoning is not concerned with who owns the property or how the ownership might be held (partnership, corporation, not-for-profit, individual ownership).

- It is sometimes difficult in practice to separate the use from the user, but as lawyers, we have to do our best to address a given situation in terms of the rules we have to work with. Consequently, when seeking to uphold a land regulation that seems to blend between use and user, be certain to focus on the language of regulating the use.

# B. Living Arrangements ("Family")

Land regulation typically identifies areas for single-family residential use. Such regulation seemingly requires a definition of family. In reading the case below, think about how a city might legally limit the number of unrelated people living in a single-family residential structure.

## Village of Belle Terre v. Boraas
### Supreme Court of the United States
### 416 U.S. 1 (1974)

Douglas, Justice. Belle Terre is a village on Long Island's north shore of about 220 homes inhabited by 700 people. Its total land area is less than one square mile. It has restricted land use to one-family dwellings excluding lodging houses, boarding houses, fraternity houses, or multiple-dwelling houses. The word "family" as used in the ordinance means, "(o)ne or more persons related by blood, adoption, or marriage, living and cooking together as a single housekeeping unit, exclusive of household servants. A number of persons but not exceeding two (2) living and cooking together as a single housekeeping unit through not related by blood, adoption, or marriage shall be deemed to constitute a family."

Appellees, the Dickmans, are owners of a house in the village and leased it in December 1971 for a term of 18 months to Michael Truman. Later Bruce Boraas became a co-lessee. Then Anne Parish moved into the house along with three others. These six are students at nearby State University at Stony Brook and none is related to the other by blood, adoption, or marriage. When the village served the Dickmans with an "Order to Remedy Violations" of the ordinance, the owners plus three tenants thereupon brought this action under 42 U.S.C. §1983 for an injunction and a judgment declaring the ordinance unconstitutional. The District Court held the ordinance constitutional, 367 F. Supp. 136, and the Court of Appeals reversed, one judge dissenting. 2 Cir., 476 F.2d 806. The case is here by appeal, 28 U.S.C. §1254(2); and we noted probable jurisdiction, 414 U.S. 907, 94 S. Ct. 234, 38 L. Ed. 2d 145.

This case brings to this Court a different phase of local zoning regulations from those we have previously reviewed. *Village of Euclid v. Ambler Realty Co.*, 272 U.S. 365, 47 S. Ct. 114, 71 L. Ed. 303, involved a zoning ordinance classifying land use in a given area into six categories. . . .

The Court [in *Euclid*] sustained the zoning ordinance under the police power of the State, saying that the line "which in this field separates the legitimate from the illegitimate assumption of power is not capable of precise delimitation. It varies with circumstances and conditions." And the Court added: "A nuisance may be merely a right thing in the wrong place, like a pig in the parlor instead of the barnyard. If the validity of the legislative classification for zoning purposes be fairly debatable, the legislative judgment must be allowed to control." The Court listed as considerations bearing on the constitutionality of zoning ordinances the danger of fire or collapse of buildings, the evils of overcrowding people, and the possibility that "offensive trades, industries, and structures" might "create nuisance" to residential sections. *Ibid.* But even those historic police power problems need not loom large or actually be existent in a given case. For the exclusion of "all industrial establishments" does not mean that "only offensive or dangerous industries will be excluded." *Ibid.* That fact does not invalidate the ordinance; the Court held:

> "The inclusion of a reasonable margin to insure effective enforcement, will not put upon a law, otherwise valid, the stamp of invalidity. Such laws may also find their justification in the fact that, in some fields, the bad fades into the good by such insensible degrees that the two are not capable of being readily distinguished and separated in terms of legislation."

The main thrust of the case in the mind of the Court was in the exclusion of industries and apartments, and as respects that it commented on the desire to keep residential areas free of "disturbing noises"; "increased traffic"; the hazard of "moving and parked automobiles"; the "depriving children of the privilege of quiet and open spaces for play, enjoyed by those in more favored localities." The ordinance was sanctioned because the validity of the legislative classification was "fairly debatable" and therefore could not be said to be wholly arbitrary.

Our decision in *Berman v. Parker*, 348 U.S. 26, 75 S. Ct. 98, 99 L. Ed. 27, sustained a land use project in the District of Columbia against a landowner's claim that the taking violated the Due Process Clause and the Just Compensation Clause of the Fifth Amendment. The essence of the argument against the law was, while taking property for ridding an area of slums was permissible, taking it "merely to develop a better balanced, more attractive community" was not, *id.*, at 31, 75 S. Ct., at 102. We refused to limit the concept of public welfare that may be enhanced by zoning regulations. We said:

> "Miserable and disreputable housing conditions may do more than spread disease and crime and immorality. They may also suffocate the spirit by reducing the people who live there to the status of cattle. They may indeed make living an almost insufferable burden. They may also be an ugly sore, a blight on the community which robs it of charm, which makes it a place from which men turn. The misery of housing may despoil a community as an open sewer may ruin a river.

> "We do not sit to determine whether a particular housing project is or is not desirable. The concept of the public welfare is broad and inclusive. . . . The values it represents are spiritual as well as physical, aesthetic as well as monetary. It is within the power of the legislature to determine that the

community should be beautiful as well as healthy, spacious as well as clean, well-balanced as well as carefully patrolled." *Id.,* at 32–33, 75 S. Ct., at 102.

If the ordinance segregated one area only for one race, it would immediately be suspect. . . .

In *Seattle Title Trust Co. v. Roberge,* 278 U.S. 116, 49 S. Ct. 50, 73 L. Ed. 210, Seattle had a zoning ordinance that permitted a "philanthropic home for children or for old people" in a particular district "when the written consent shall have been obtained of the owners of two-thirds of the property within four hundred (400) feet of the proposed building." *Id.,* at 118, 49 S. Ct., at 50. The Court held that provision of the ordinance unconstitutional, saying that the existing owners could "withhold consent for selfish reasons or arbitrarily and may subject the trustee (owner) to their will or caprice." *Id.,* at 122, 49 S. Ct., at 52. . . .

The present ordinance is challenged on several grounds: that it interferes with a person's right to travel; that it interferes with the right to migrate to and settle within a State; that it bars people who are uncongenial to the present residents; that it expresses the social preferences of the residents for groups that will be congenial to them; that social homogeneity is not a legitimate interest of government; that the restriction of those whom the neighbors do not like trenches on the newcomers' rights of privacy; that it is of no rightful concern to villagers whether the residents are married or unmarried; that the ordinance is antithetical to the Nation's experience, ideology, and self-perception as an open, egalitarian, and integrated society.

We find none of these reasons in the record before us. It is not aimed at transients. It involves no procedural disparity inflicted on some but not on others. . . . It involves no "fundamental" right guaranteed by the Constitution, such as voting; the right of association; the right of access to the courts; or any rights of privacy. We deal with economic and social legislation where legislatures have historically drawn lines which we respect against the charge of violation of the Equal Protection Clause if the law be "reasonable, not arbitrary" and bears "a rational relationship to a (permissible) state objective."

It is said, however, that if two unmarried people can constitute a "family," there is no reason why three or four may not. But every line drawn by a legislature leaves some out that might well have been included. That exercise of discretion, however, is a legislative, not a judicial, function.

It is said that the Belle Terre ordinance reeks with an animosity to unmarried couples who live together. There is no evidence so support it; and the provision of the ordinance bringing within the definition of a "family" two unmarried people belies the charge.

The ordinance places no ban on other forms of association, for a "family" may, so far as the ordinance is concerned, entertain whomever it likes.

The regimes of boarding houses, fraternity houses, and the like present urban problems. More people occupy a given space; more cars rather continuously pass by; more cars are parked; noise travels with crowds.

A quiet place where yards are wide, people few, and motor vehicles restricted are legitimate guidelines in a land-use project addressed to family needs. This goal is a permissible one within *Berman v. Parker, supra.* The police power is not confined to elimination of filth, stench, and unhealthy places. It is ample to lay out zones where family values, youth values, and the blessings of quiet seclusion and clean air make the area a sanctuary for people.

The suggestion that the case may be moot need not detain us. A zoning ordinance usually has an impact on the value of the property which it regulates. But in spite of the fact that the precise impact of the ordinance sustained in *Euclid* on a given piece of property was not known, 272 U.S., at 397, 47 S. Ct., at 121, the Court, considering the matter a controversy in the realm of city planning, sustained the ordinance. Here we are a step closer to the impact of the ordinance on the value of the lessor's property. He has not only lost six tenants and acquired only two in their place; it is obvious that the scale of rental values rides on what we decide today. When *Berman* reached us it was not certain whether an entire tract would be taken or only the buildings on it and a scenic easement. 348 U.S., at 36, 75 S. Ct., at 104. But that did not make the case any the less a controversy in the constitutional sense. When Mr. Justice Holmes said for the Court in *Block v. Hirsh*, 256 U.S. 135, 155, 41 S. Ct. 458, 459, 65 L. Ed. 865, "property rights may be cut down, and to that extent taken, without pay," he stated the issue here. As is true in most zoning cases, the precise impact on value may, at the threshold of litigation over validity, not yet be known.

Reversed.

BRENNAN, Justice. (dissenting). The constitutional challenge to the village ordinance is premised solely on alleged infringement of associational and other constitutional rights of tenants. But the named tenant appellees have quit the house, thus raising a serious question whether there now exists a cognizable "case or controversy" that satisfies that indispensable requisite of Art. III of the Constitution. . . .

MARSHALL, Justice. (dissenting). This case draws into question the constitutionality of a zoning ordinance of the incorporated village of Belle Terre, New York, which prohibits groups of more than two unrelated persons, as distinguished from groups consisting of any number of persons related by blood, adoption, or marriage, from occupying a residence within the confines of the township. Lessor-appellees, the two owners of a Belle Terre residence, and three unrelated student tenants challenged the ordinance on the ground that it establishes a classification between households of related and unrelated individuals, which deprives them of equal protection of the laws. In my view, the disputed classification burdens the students' fundamental rights of association and privacy guaranteed by the First and Fourteenth Amendments. Because the application of strict equal protection scrutiny is therefore required, I am at odds with my Brethren's conclusion that the ordinance may be sustained on a showing that it bears a rational relationship to the accomplishment of legitimate governmental objectives.

I am in full agreement with the majority that zoning is a complex and important function of the State. It may indeed be the most essential function performed by local government, for it is one of the primary means by which we protect that sometimes difficult to define concept of quality of life. I therefore continue to adhere to the principle of *Village of Euclid v. Ambler Realty Co.*, 272 U.S. 365, 47 S. Ct. 114, 71 L. Ed. 303 (1926), that deference should be given to governmental judgments concerning proper land-use allocation. . . .

I would also agree with the majority that local zoning authorities may properly act in furtherance of the objectives asserted to be served by the ordinance at issue here: restricting uncontrolled growth, solving traffic problems, keeping rental costs at a reasonable level, and making the community attractive to families. . . . But deference does not mean abdication. This Court has an obligation to ensure that zoning ordinances, even when adopted in furtherance of such legitimate aims, do not infringe upon fundamental constitutional rights.

When separate but equal was still accepted constitutional dogma, this Court struck down a racially restrictive zoning ordinance. *Buchanan v. Warley*, 245 U.S. 60, 38 S. Ct. 16, 62 L. Ed. 149 (1917). I am sure the Court would not be hesitant to invalidate that ordinance today. The lower federal courts have considered procedural aspects of zoning, and acted to insure that land-use controls are not used as means of confining minorities and the poor to the ghettos of our central cities. These are limited but necessary intrusions on the discretion of zoning authorities. By the same token, I think it clear that the First Amendment provides some limitation on zoning laws. It is inconceivable to me that we would allow the exercise of the zoning power to burden First Amendment freedoms, as by ordinances that restrict occupancy to individuals adhering to particular religious, political, or scientific beliefs. Zoning officials properly concern themselves with the uses of land — with, for example, the number and kind of dwellings to be constructed in a certain neighborhood or the number of persons who can reside in those dwellings. But zoning authorities cannot validly consider who those persons are, what they believe, or how they choose to live, whether they are Negro or white, Catholic or Jew, Republican or Democrat, married or unmarried.

My disagreement with the Court today is based upon my view that the ordinance in this case unnecessarily burdens appellees' First Amendment freedom of association and their constitutionally guaranteed right to privacy. Our decisions establish that the First and Fourteenth Amendments protect the freedom to choose one's associates. Constitutional protection is extended, not only to modes of association that are political in the usual sense, but also to those that pertain to the social and economic benefit of the members. The selection of one's living companions involves similar choices as to the emotional, social, or economic benefits to be derived from alternative living arrangements.

The freedom of association is often inextricably entwined with the constitutionally guaranteed right of privacy. The right to "establish a home" is an essential part of the liberty guaranteed by the Fourteenth Amendment. And the Constitution secures to an individual a freedom "to satisfy his intellectual and emotional needs in the privacy of his own home." Constitutionally protected privacy is, in Mr. Justice Brandeis' words, "as against the Government, the right to be let alone . . . the right most valued by civilized man." The choice of household companions — of whether a person's "intellectual and emotional needs" are best met by living with family, friends, professional associates, or others — involves deeply personal considerations as to the kind and quality of intimate relationships within the home. That decision surely falls within the ambit of the right to privacy protected by the Constitution.

The instant ordinance discriminates on the basis of just such a personal lifestyle choice as to household companions. It permits any number of persons related by blood or marriage, be it two or twenty, to live in a single household, but it limits to two the number of unrelated persons bound by profession, love, friendship, religious or political affiliation, or mere economics who can occupy a single home. Belle Terre imposes upon those who deviate from the community norm in their choice of living companions significantly greater restrictions than are applied to residential groups who are related by blood or marriage, and compose the established order within the community. The village has, in effect, acted to fence out those individuals whose choice of lifestyle differs from that of its current residents.

This is not a case where the Court is being asked to nullify a township's sincere efforts to maintain its residential character by preventing the operation of rooming houses, fraternity houses, or other commercial or high-density residential uses. Unquestionably, a town is free to restrict such uses. Moreover, as a general proposition, I see no constitutional infirmity in a town's limiting the density of use in residential areas by zoning regulations which do not discriminate on the basis of constitutionally suspect criteria. This ordinance, however, limits the density of occupancy of only those homes occupied by unrelated persons. It thus reaches beyond control of the use of land or the density of population, and undertakes to regulate the way people choose to associate with each other within the privacy of their own homes.

It is no answer to say, as does the majority that associational interests are not infringed because Belle Terre residents may entertain whomever they choose. Only last Term Mr. Justice Douglas indicated in concurrence that he saw the right of association protected by the First Amendment as involving far more than the right to entertain visitors. He found that right infringed by a restriction on food stamp assistance, penalizing households of "unrelated persons." As Mr. Justice Douglas there said, freedom of association encompasses the "right to invite the stranger into one's home" not only for "entertainment" but to join the household as well. I am still persuaded that the choice of those who will form one's household implicates constitutionally protected rights.

Because I believe that this zoning ordinance creates a classification which impinges upon fundamental personal rights, it can withstand constitutional scrutiny only upon a clear showing that the burden imposed is necessary to protect a compelling and substantial governmental interest. And, once it be determined that a burden has been placed upon a constitutional right, the onus of demonstrating that no less intrusive means will adequately protect the compelling state interest and that the challenged statute is sufficiently narrowly drawn, is upon the party seeking to justify the burden.

A variety of justifications have been proffered in support of the village's ordinance. It is claimed that the ordinance controls population density, prevents noise, traffic and parking problems, and preserves the rent structure of the community and its attractiveness to families. As I noted earlier, these are all legitimate and substantial interests of government. But I think it clear that the means chosen to accomplish these purposes are both overinclusive and underinclusive, and that the asserted goals could be as effectively achieved by means of an ordinance that did not discriminate on the basis of constitutionally protected choices of lifestyle. The ordinance imposes no restriction whatsoever on the number of persons who may live in a house, as long as they are related by marital or sanguinary bonds — presumably no matter how distant their relationship. Nor does the ordinance restrict the number of income earners who may contribute to rent in such a household, or the number of automobiles that may be maintained by its occupants. In that sense the ordinance is under inclusive. On the other hand, the statute restricts the number of unrelated persons who may live in a home to no more than two. It would therefore prevent three unrelated people from occupying a dwelling even if among them they had but one income and no vehicles. While an extended family of a dozen or more might live in a small bungalow, three elderly and retired persons could not occupy the large manor house next door. Thus the statute is also grossly over inclusive to accomplish its intended purposes.

There are some 220 residences in Belle Terre occupied by about 700 persons. The density is therefore just above three per household. The village is justifiably concerned with density of population and the related problems of noise, traffic, and the like. It could deal with those problems by limiting each household to a specified number of adults, two or three perhaps, without limitation on the number of dependent children. The burden of such an ordinance would fall equally upon all segments of the community. It would surely be better tailored to the goals asserted by the village than the ordinance before us today, for it would more realistically restrict population density and growth and their attendant environmental costs. Various other statutory mechanisms also suggest themselves as solutions to Belle Terre's problems — rent control, limits on the number of vehicles per household, and so forth, but, of course, such schemes are matters of legislative judgment and not for this Court. Appellants also refer to the necessity of maintaining the family character of the village. There is not a shred of evidence in the record indicating that if Belle Terre permitted a limited number of unrelated persons to live together, the residential, familial character of the community would be fundamentally affected.

By limiting unrelated households to two persons while placing no limitation on households of related individuals, the village has embarked upon its commendable course in a constitutionally faulty vessel. Cf. *Marshall v. United States*, 414 U.S. 417,

94 S. Ct. 700, 38 L. Ed. 2d 618 (1974) (dissenting opinion). I would find the challenged ordinance unconstitutional. But I would not ask the village to abandon its goal of providing quiet streets, little traffic, and a pleasant and reasonably priced environment in which families might raise their children. Rather, I would commend the village to continue to pursue those purposes but by means of more carefully drawn and even-handed legislation.

I respectfully dissent.

## Questions for Consideration

1) Is the Village of Belle Terre regulating the use of property or the definition of "family"?

2) How does the majority opinion make use of the *Euclid* case?

3) How does the majority opinion make use of the *Berman v. Parker* case?

4) How does the majority opinion frame the case differently than Marshall's dissent?

5) Under the Marshall dissent, how would a "university town" be able to limit the number of college students living in one house?

## Takeaway

- In recent years, changing attitudes have moved the law closer to the views expressed in Marshall's dissent and further away from the positions articulated in the majority.

- *Village of Belle Terre* illustrates the way that fundamental rights may limit the exercise of the police power and the ability of local officials to regulate land use. This is particularly true, when one considers that legal values have shifted in favor of Marshall's dissent since the time that this case was decided.

## Keys Youth Servs. v. City of Olathe

United States Court of Appeals for the Tenth Circuit
248 F.3d 1267 (2001)

McKay, Circuit Judge. Defendant Olathe City, Kansas, appeals from the district court's summary judgment determination that it denied a zoning permit to Plaintiff Keys Youth Services, Inc., based on Keys' familial status in violation of the Fair Housing Act (FHA), 42 U.S.C. § 3604. Keys cross-appeals from the court's bench trial ruling that Olathe's denial of the zoning permit was not based on Keys' handicap status under the FHA and that the permit denial did not violate state law. We have jurisdiction under 28 U.S.C. § 1291.

I.

Keys operates several youth group homes. It purchased a house in an Olathe neighborhood zoned for single-family residential use for the purpose of establishing another group home for ten troubled adolescent males. Unable to qualify as a "family" by Olathe's definition, Keys applied for a special use permit from the city council in order to run the proposed home. In response, the neighbors filed a protest petition with the Olathe Planning Commission. At the subsequent hearings on the matter, they argued that the troubled juveniles would increase area crime and pose a threat to the many children in the area, and that surrounding property values would decrease. At some of these same hearings, Keys supplied the Commission with evidence suggesting the neighbors' fears were unjustified. In the end, the Planning Commission recommended to the Olathe City Council that Keys be denied a special use permit. By a 4-3 vote, the City Council agreed and Keys subsequently sued.

Keys alleged in its suit that Olathe and four city council members denied it a special use permit for its juvenile group home based on the potential occupants' "familial status" and "handicaps" in violation of the FHA. Keys also alleged that Olathe's permit denial violated Kansas state law. The district court dismissed the claims against the individual council members on qualified immunity grounds. . . .

## II.

### A. Familial Status Discrimination

We review de novo the district court's grant of summary judgment and apply the same legal standard employed by that court. To wit, summary judgment should be granted if the evidence submitted shows "that there is no genuine issue of material fact and that the moving party is entitled to judgment as a matter of law." Fed. R. Civ. P. 56(c). "When applying this standard, we view the evidence and draw reasonable inferences therefrom in the light most favorable to the nonmoving party." *Simms* [*v. Oklahoma ex rel. Dep't of Mental Health & Substance Abuse Servs.*], 165 F.3d [1321] at 1326 [(10 Cir. 1999)]. In the instant case, both parties sought summary judgment on the familial status issue.

Since its amendment in 1988, the FHA has prohibited discriminatory housing practices based on familial status. *See* 42 U.S.C. § 3604(a)-(e). The FHA defines "familial status" as (1) one or more minors (2) "domiciled with" (3) a parent or legal custodian or the designee of a parent or custodian. *Id.* § 3602(k). Keys' group home satisfies the first element: there are one or more minors.

Regarding the second element, Olathe intimated to the district court that Keys' living arrangements did not satisfy the "domiciled with" requirement. . . .

There is no material dispute regarding the "living" arrangements at Keys' proposed youth group home. Ten minors would live at the home. They would be supervised twenty-four hours a day by a rotating staff of Keys' employees. Though by no means dispositive, we note that Dr. Edward Neufeld, a licensed psychologist who counsels Keys' existing group home occupants, characterized the Keys' homes as "therapeutic milieus" rather than a "family environment" because, in his view, "these are not group homes that are characterized by a foster parent or two foster parents who are there all the time. It's more a staffing situation."

More specifically, the summary judgment record indicates that in the proposed home in question a "manager" would work from 7:00 a.m. to 3:00 p.m., Monday through Friday; an "assistant manager" and a "staff number 3" employee would work from 2:00 p.m. to 10:00 p.m., Monday through Friday; and an "additional staff member" would work from either 10:00 p.m. to 6:00 a.m. or 11:00 p.m. to 7:00 a.m. each night. In addition, one "teaching parent" ("shift number 1") would work from 6:00 a.m. Monday morning to 2:00 p.m. Tuesday afternoon, and from 2:00 p.m. Wednesday to 2:00 p.m. Thursday; another "teaching parent" ("shift number 2") would work from 2:00 p.m. Tuesday to 2:00 p.m. Wednesday, and from 2:00 p.m. Thursday to 10:00 p.m. Friday; a "weekend staff person" would work 10:00 p.m. Friday until 6:00 a.m. Monday morning; and a "part-time staff person" would work 10:00 a.m. to 10:00 p.m. Saturday and Sunday. In sum, as the district court put it, "The staff works on day and night shifts and does not reside at the home."

"Familial status" requires that the minors be domiciled "with" their caretaker. This means that the youths and Keys' staff must be domiciled together, at the same dwelling. . . . The question thus becomes whether any Keys' staff members would be "domiciled" at the proposed home with the youths.

The FHA does not define "domiciled," nor are we aware of a federal or state court that has done so in the "familial status" context. We therefore look "both to the generally accepted meaning of the term 'domicile' and to the purpose of the statute" for the appropriate definition. . . .

A "domicile" is an individual's "'true, fixed, and permanent home and principal establishment.'" *Eastman v. Univ. of Mich.*, 30 F.3d 670, 672–73 (6th Cir. 1994) (quoting *Black's Law Dictionary* 484 (6th ed. 1990)). Traditionally, an individual has only one domicile at a time. *See Williamson v. Osenton*, 232 U.S. 619, 625, 58 L. Ed. 758, 34 S. Ct. 442 (1914). An adult establishes a domicile "by physical presence in a place [i.e., a dwelling] in connection with a certain state of mind concerning one's intent to remain there." [*Mississippi Band of Choctaw Indians v.*] *Holyfield*, 490 U.S. [30] at 48 [(1988)]; *see also Crowley v. Glaze*, 710 F.2d 676, 678 (10th Cir. 1983); Restatement (Second) of Conflict of Laws § 15. There is no question that Keys' staff would be physically present in the group home during their respective shifts. To establish it as their domicile, however, they must also intend to remain — to make that dwelling their home. *See* Restatement (Second) of Conflict of Laws § 18; . . .

In light of the FHA context of our inquiry, the definition of "home" given in the Restatement (Second) of Conflict of Laws seems particularly applicable: "The place where a person dwells and which is the center of his domestic, social and civil life." Restatement (Second) of Conflict of Laws § 12. While many facts may aid in determining one's home, an individual's employment at the site is not one of them. *See* Restatement (Second) of Conflict of Laws § 12 cmt. f. Absent other indicia, one's workplace is not one's home and, thus, not where one is domiciled for purposes of the FHA.

Based on our review of the summary judgment record in the instant case, it appears the sole connection between Keys' staff and the group home is the fact that the staff works there. No other reason for their presence in the house is given. Since the staff members clearly do not live at the group home, they must of necessity be residing someplace else, presumably at their actual homes/domiciles. The fact that some of Keys' employees work a night shift or a twenty-four or thirty-six hour shift does not alter our conclusion. The critical fact remains that the only proffered reason these employees occupy the home is for employment. As a matter of law under these circumstances, we cannot conclude that Keys' employees, collectively or individually, are domiciled at the group home. Thus, the youths cannot be "domiciled with" them, and Keys' proposed group home therefore cannot qualify for "familial status" under the FHA. Any other conclusion stretches the meaning of "domiciled" and the scope of "familial status" protection beyond sensible bounds. We reverse the grant of summary judgment for Keys and order summary judgment entered for Olathe on Keys' "familial status" discrimination claim.

### B. Handicap Discrimination

The FHA also forbids discriminatory housing practices based on a potential occupant's handicap(s). *See* 42 U.S.C. § 3604(f). Prohibited handicap discrimination may take several forms, including (1) disparate treatment, i.e., intentional discrimination; (2) disparate impact, i.e., the discriminatory effect of a facially neutral practice or policy; (3) a refusal to permit "reasonable modifications of existing premises"; (4) a "refusal to make reasonable accommodations in rules, policies, practices, or services"; or (5) a failure to "design and construct" handicap accessible buildings. 42 U.S.C. § 3604(f)(3) (outlining reasonable modification and accommodation claims and failure to design and construct claim); *see also Bangerter v. Orem City Corp.*, 46 F.3d 1491, 1500–01 (10th Cir. 1995) (discussing disparate treatment and impact claims).

In the instant case, Keys has made out two discrimination claims. First, Keys alleges that Olathe intentionally denied the permit because of the juveniles' handicaps. [The second claim of discrimination is based on failure to provide an accommodation and is discussed later in the opinion.]

Olathe countered [the first claim, saying] that it denied the permit because the troubled juveniles would pose a legitimate threat to neighborhood safety, not because they were handicapped. Because Keys presented no direct evidence of intentional discrimination,

. . . .

"Weighing all of the evidence," the district court determined that "the City Council denied the permit because it reasonably determined that the residents of the [group] home would pose a safety threat to residents of the neighborhood." In short, the court found that Olathe's justification was not "mere pretext" for handicap discrimination.

In an appeal from a bench trial, we review the district court's factual findings for clear error and its legal conclusions de novo. Whether Olathe's public safety concerns were mere pretext for handicap discrimination is a factual issue. Thus, we will reverse the district court's finding only "if it is without factual support in the record" or if, "after reviewing all the evidence," we are "left with a definite and firm conviction that a mistake has been made." The court reached its decision after weighing the following evidence.

Keys operates group homes for youths between the ages of twelve and seventeen who have been abused, neglected, or abandoned. The Kansas Department of Social and Rehabilitation Services, which places most of Keys' youth, categorizes juvenile behavioral problems from level III to level VI. Keys applied for a permit in order to open a level V home for ten males in a single-family residential neighborhood. Level V teenagers are typically antisocial and aggressive, engaging in assaults, batteries, thefts, and vandalism. Parents and teachers describe level V youths as cruel, aggressive, moody, argumentative, uncooperative, disruptive, and occasionally assaultive. At the time of the permit application, Keys was already managing a level V home elsewhere in Olathe. Unlike that existing home, however, the proposed home in question would sit in close proximity to numerous residences and within walking distance of several schools and day care centers. At public hearings regarding the proposed home, neighbors voiced their concerns about the safety of area children. They also reported that Keys' youths had once escaped the existing group home in Olathe and had gone on a crime spree that included setting a car on fire, burglarizing cars, defecating on a car, shoplifting, and vandalizing. Moreover, neighbors furnished Olathe with information about the numerous phone calls made to police from other Keys' homes reporting various criminal conduct and provided anecdotal accounts of their own negative experiences with, or perceptions of, level V juveniles.

In its own presentations to Olathe, Keys attempted to downplay much of the neighbors' evidence. For instance, Keys showed that after the crime-spree incident it had hired additional nighttime staff at level V homes, which thus far had prevented similar break-outs. In addition, Keys explained that a vast majority of the police calls originating from Keys' homes involved in-house incidents only; no neighbors were affected. Dr. Neufeld also opined that Keys' residents posed less of a public threat than their less supervised peers. In the end, however, the Olathe City Council voted 4-3 to deny Keys' request for a special use permit, despite legal advice urging that the request be granted. All four council members who voted to deny the permit testified that they did so due to public safety concerns.

On appeal, Keys essentially argues that its evidence conclusively establishes that a level V home does not create a public danger. To be sure, Keys' evidence might lead a reasonable person to that conclusion. However, Olathe's fears are not groundless. Level V youths are undisputedly dangerous and have caused problems of real concern in the past. It is not unreasonable to think that they are capable of causing similar problems in the future. In short, the district court, acting as the factfinder, reasonably could have chosen either of two plausible interpretations of the facts. Under the clearly erroneous standard of review, we must therefore affirm the court's choice....

We turn now to Keys' second handicap discrimination claim.

As noted *supra*, handicap discrimination includes "a refusal to make reasonable accommodations in rules, policies, practices, or services, when such accommodations may be necessary to afford such person equal opportunity to use and enjoy a dwelling." 42 U.S.C. §3604(f)(3)(B). For zoning purposes, Olathe's ordinances define "family," in relevant part, as "a group of eight (8) or fewer unrelated disabled persons including two (2) additional persons acting as houseparents or guardians who need not be related to each other or to any of the disabled persons in residence." Keys claims that when Olathe denied it a special use permit to house ten youths plus staff in a single-family neighborhood, the City refused to reasonably accommodate its ordinances to Keys' needs.

The crux of Keys' argument is that it must house no less than ten youths in order to generate enough funds to survive. Following the bench trial, the court stated that the ten-resident minimum may be "necessary," but nevertheless ruled for Olathe because Keys had failed to demonstrate its economic need for the accommodation to the City. The court based its decision on the principle that Olathe cannot be liable for refusing to grant a reasonable and necessary accommodation if the City never knew the accommodation was in fact necessary. We agree.... Hence, the issue on appeal is whether Olathe realized Keys' need to house ten youths instead of eight. Keys does not point to any evidence suggesting that its economic need argument was presented to the Planning Commission or the City Council. In fact, Keys' executive director testified at trial that she did not believe "the economics of the situation came up at the Planning Commission."

In addition, we can affirm the court's reasonable accommodation ruling for a separate reason. Even assuming that Keys presented its economic necessity argument to the City Council, we conclude that the requested accommodation — housing ten troubled adolescents instead of eight — is not "reasonable" in light of Olathe's legitimate public safety concerns. Common sense dictates that when a defendant possesses a legitimate nondiscriminatory reason for a housing decision, a plaintiff's requested accommodation must substantially negate the defendant's concern in order to be considered reasonable. For example, if the evidence in the instant case showed that housing ten juveniles instead of eight actually resolved the safety problem, then Keys' request would be reasonable. However, we see nothing in the record so indicating. We therefore affirm the district court's reasonable accommodation ruling.

### C. State Law Claim

Finally, Keys appeals the district court's rejection of its state law claim. Keys had asserted that Olathe's denial of the permit violated chapter 12, article 736 of the Kansas Statutes Annotated. This provision explains that it is the policy of Kansas that "persons with a disability shall not be excluded from the benefits of single family residential surroundings by any municipal zoning ordinance, resolution or regulation." Kan. Stat. Ann. §12-736(a). The statute further mandates that "no municipality shall prohibit the location of a group home in any zone or area where single family dwellings are permitted." *Id.* §12-736(e). However, the statute defines "group home" as "any dwelling occupied by not more than 10 persons, including eight or fewer persons with a disability who need not be related by blood or marriage and not to exceed two staff residents who need not be related by blood or marriage to each other or to the residents of the home, which dwelling is licensed by a regulatory agency of this state." *Id.* §12-736(b)(1).

In considering Olathe's summary judgment motion on this claim, the court noted its uncertainty concerning article 12-736's meaning and its asserted applicability to Keys' juvenile group home. . . .

We agree that article 12-736 may not be the clearest statute in some respects. Nonetheless, it plainly limits group homes to "any dwelling occupied by not more than 10 persons." Kan. Stat. Ann. §12-736(b)(1). In the instant case, the proposed home, by Keys' own admission, would be occupied by *more* than ten persons — ten juveniles plus staff. Thus, it would not qualify as a group home under article 12-736, and Keys has no basis upon which to assert an article 12-736 violation. We affirm the district court's rejection of Key's state law claim.

### IV.

In sum, we Reverse the district court's summary judgment decision on Keys' "familial status" claim and order summary judgment entered for Olathe. We Affirm the court's bench trial decisions on Keys' intentional discrimination, reasonable accommodation, and state law claims. The qualified immunity issues are now Moot.

## *Questions for Consideration*

1) How does the City of Olathe define "family"?

2) How does the FHA define "family"?

3) How does the court define domiciled?

4) What facts influenced the determination of whether the members of the group home constituted a "family" within the definition of the FHA? Within the definition of the Olathe city ordinance?

5) What facts are relied on in determining whether the City of Olathe discriminated against Keys Youth Services in violation of the FHA?

6) How does the court handle the state law claim?

## *Takeaway*

- Efforts to define family may raise constitutional concerns as observed in *Village of Belle Terre*. Here, we learn that resolving a local zoning question may also involve dealing with multiple definitions of family arising under different statutory authorities.

# C. Group Homes for People with Disabilities

*Key Youth Services* dealt with group homes and defining family. The case below is the leading U.S. Supreme Court case on group homes for people with disabilities where "the residents' disability is alleged to be the grounds for different treatment." The case was decided before the enactment of our modern ADA.

## City of Cleburne v. Cleburne Living Center

Supreme Court of the United States
473 U.S. 432 (1985)

WHITE, Justice. A Texas city denied a special use permit for the operation of a group home for the mentally retarded, acting pursuant to a municipal zoning ordinance requiring permits for such homes. The Court of Appeals for the Fifth Circuit held that mental retardation is a "quasi-suspect" classification and that the ordinance violated the Equal Protection Clause because it did not substantially further an important governmental purpose. We hold that a lesser standard of scrutiny is appropriate, but conclude that under that standard the ordinance is invalid as applied in this case.

I

In July 1980, respondent Jan Hannah purchased a building at 201 Featherston Street in the city of Cleburne, Texas, with the intention of leasing it to Cleburne Living Center, Inc. (CLC), for the operation of a group home for the mentally retarded. It was anticipated that the home would house 13 retarded men and women, who would be under the constant supervision of CLC staff members. The house had four bedrooms and two baths, with a half bath to be added. CLC planned to comply with all applicable state and federal regulations.

The city informed CLC that a special use permit would be required for the operation of a group home at the site, and CLC accordingly submitted a permit application. In response to a subsequent inquiry from CLC, the city explained that under the zoning regulations applicable to the site, a special use permit, renewable annually, was required for the construction of "[h]ospitals for the insane or feebleminded, or alcoholic [*sic*] or drug addicts, or penal or correctional institutions." The city had determined that the proposed group home should be classified as a "hospital for the feebleminded." After holding a public hearing on CLC's application, the City Council voted 3 to 1 to deny a special use permit.

CLC then filed suit in Federal District Court against the city and a number of its officials, alleging, *inter alia,* that the zoning ordinance was invalid on its face and as applied because it discriminated against the mentally retarded in violation of the equal protection rights of CLC and its potential residents. The District Court found that "[i]f the potential residents of the Featherston Street home were not mentally retarded, but the home was the same in all other respects, its use would be permitted under the city's zoning ordinance," and that the City Counsel's decision "was motivated primarily by the fact that the residents of the home would be persons who are mentally retarded." Even so, the District Court held the ordinance and its application constitutional. Concluding that no fundamental right was implicated and that mental retardation was neither a suspect nor a quasi-suspect classification, the court employed the minimum level of judicial scrutiny applicable to equal protection claims. The court deemed the ordinance, as written and applied, to be rationally related to the city's legitimate interests in "the legal responsibility of CLC and its residents . . . the safety and fears of residents in the adjoining neighborhood," and the number of people to be housed in the home.

The Court of Appeals for the Fifth Circuit reversed, determining that mental retardation was a quasi-suspect classification and that it should assess the validity of the ordinance under intermediate-level scrutiny. Because mental retardation was in fact relevant to many legislative actions, strict scrutiny was not appropriate. But in light of the history of "unfair and often grotesque mistreatment" of the retarded, discrimination against them was "likely to reflect deep-seated prejudice." In addition, the mentally retarded lacked political power, and their condition was immutable. The court considered heightened scrutiny to be particularly appropriate in this case, because the city's ordinance withheld a benefit which, although not fundamental, was very important to the mentally retarded. Without group homes, the court stated, the retarded could never hope to integrate themselves into the community. Applying the test that it considered appropriate, the court held that the ordinance was invalid on its face because it did not substantially further any important governmental interests. The Court of Appeals went on to hold that the ordinance was also invalid as applied. Rehearing en banc was denied with six judges dissenting in an opinion urging en banc consideration of the panel's adoption of a heightened standard of review. We granted certiorari.

## II

The Equal Protection Clause of the Fourteenth Amendment commands that no State shall "deny to any person within its jurisdiction the equal protection of the laws," which is essentially a direction that all persons similarly situated should be treated alike. Section 5 of the Amendment empowers Congress to enforce this mandate, but absent controlling congressional direction, the courts have themselves devised standards for determining the validity of state legislation or other official action that is challenged as denying equal protection. The general rule is that legislation is presumed to be valid and will be sustained if the classification drawn by the statute is rationally related to a legitimate state interest.

The general rule gives way, however, when a statute classifies by race, alienage, or national origin. These factors are so seldom relevant to the achievement of any legitimate state interest that laws grounded in such considerations are deemed to reflect prejudice and antipathy — a view that those in the burdened class are not as worthy or deserving as others. For these reasons and because such discrimination is unlikely to be soon rectified by legislative means, these laws are subjected to strict scrutiny and will be sustained only if they are suitably tailored to serve a compelling state interest. . . .

Legislative classifications based on gender also call for a heightened standard of review. That factor generally provides no sensible ground for differential treatment. "[W]hat differentiates sex from such nonsuspect statuses as intelligence or physical disability . . . is that the sex characteristic frequently bears no relation to ability to perform or contribute to society." Rather than resting on meaningful considerations, statutes distributing benefits and burdens between the sexes in different ways very likely reflect outmoded notions of the relative capabilities of men and women. A gender classification fails unless it is substantially related to a sufficiently important governmental interest. Because illegitimacy is beyond the individual's control and bears "no relation to the individual's ability to participate in and contribute to society," official discriminations resting on that characteristic are also subject to somewhat heightened review. Those restrictions "will survive equal protection scrutiny to the extent they are substantially related to a legitimate state interest."

We have declined, however, to extend heightened review to differential treatment based on age:

> "While the treatment of the aged in this Nation has not been wholly free of discrimination, such persons, unlike, say, those who have been discriminated against on the basis of race or national origin, have not experienced a 'history of purposeful unequal treatment' or been subjected to unique disabilities on the basis of stereotyped characteristics not truly indicative of their abilities."

. . . .

### III

Against this background, we conclude for several reasons that the Court of Appeals erred in holding mental retardation a quasi-suspect classification calling for a more exacting standard of judicial review than is normally accorded economic and social legislation. First, it is undeniable, and it is not argued otherwise here, that those who are mentally retarded have a reduced ability to cope with and function in the everyday world. Nor are they all cut from the same pattern: as the testimony in this record indicates, they range from those whose disability is not immediately evident to those who must be constantly cared for. They are thus different, immutably so, in relevant respects, and the States' interest in dealing with and providing for them is plainly a legitimate one. How this large and diversified group is to be treated under the law is a difficult and often a technical matter, very much a task for legislators guided by qualified professionals and not by the perhaps ill-informed opinions of the judiciary. Heightened scrutiny inevitably involves substantive judgments about legislative decisions, and we doubt that the predicate for such judicial oversight is present where the classification deals with mental retardation.

Second, the distinctive legislative response, both national and state, to the plight of those who are mentally retarded demonstrates not only that they have unique problems, but also that the lawmakers have been addressing their difficulties in a manner that belies a continuing antipathy or prejudice and a corresponding need for more intrusive oversight by the judiciary. Thus, the Federal Government has not only outlawed discrimination against the mentally retarded in federally funded programs, see § 504 of the Rehabilitation Act of 1973, 29 U.S.C. § 794, but it has also provided the retarded with the right to receive "appropriate treatment, services, and habilitation" in a setting that is "least restrictive of [their] personal liberty." Developmental Disabilities Assistance and Bill of Rights Act, 42 U.S.C. §§ 6010(1), (2). In addition, the Government has conditioned federal education funds on a State's assurance that retarded children will enjoy an education that, "to the maximum extent appropriate," is integrated with that of nonmentally retarded children. Education of the Handicapped Act, 20 U.S.C. § 1412(5)(B). The Government has also facilitated the hiring of the mentally retarded into the federal civil service by exempting them from the requirement of competitive examination. See 5 C.F.R. § 213.3102(t) (1984). The State of Texas has similarly enacted legislation that acknowledges the special status of the mentally retarded by conferring certain rights upon them, such as "the right to live in the least restrictive setting appropriate to [their] individual needs and abilities," including "the right to live . . . in a group home."

Such legislation thus singling out the retarded for special treatment reflects the real and undeniable differences between the retarded and others. That a civilized and decent society expects and approves such legislation indicates that governmental consideration of those differences in the vast majority of situations is not only legitimate but also desirable. It may be, as CLC contends, that legislation designed to benefit, rather than disadvantage, the retarded would generally withstand examination under a test of heightened scrutiny. . . .

Third, the legislative response, which could hardly have occurred and survived without public support, negates any claim that the mentally retarded are politically powerless in the sense that they have no ability to attract the attention of the lawmakers. Any minority can be said to be powerless to assert direct control over the legislature, but if that were a criterion for higher level scrutiny by the courts, much economic and social legislation would now be suspect.

Fourth, if the large and amorphous class of the mentally retarded were deemed quasi-suspect for the reasons given by the Court of Appeals, it would be difficult to find a principled way to distinguish a variety of other groups who have perhaps immutable disabilities setting them off from others, who cannot themselves mandate the desired legislative responses, and who can claim some degree of prejudice from at least part of the public at large. One need mention in this respect only the aging, the disabled, the mentally ill, and the infirm. We are reluctant to set out on that course, and we decline to do so.

Doubtless, there have been and there will continue to be instances of discrimination against the retarded that are in fact invidious, and that are properly subject to judicial correction under constitutional norms. But the appropriate method of reaching such instances is not to create a new quasi-suspect classification and subject all governmental action based on that classification to more searching evaluation. Rather, we should look to the likelihood that governmental action premised on a particular classification is valid as a general matter, not merely to the specifics of the case before us. Because mental retardation is a characteristic that the government may legitimately take into account in a wide range of decisions, and because both State and Federal Governments have recently committed themselves to assisting the retarded, we will not presume that any given legislative action, even one that disadvantages retarded individuals, is rooted in considerations that the Constitution will not tolerate.

Our refusal to recognize the retarded as a quasi-suspect class does not leave them entirely unprotected from invidious discrimination. To withstand equal protection review, legislation that distinguishes between the mentally retarded and others must be rationally related to a legitimate governmental purpose. This standard, we believe, affords government the latitude necessary both to pursue policies designed to assist the retarded in realizing their full potential, and to freely and efficiently engage in activities that burden the retarded in what is essentially an incidental manner. The State may not rely on a classification whose relationship to an asserted goal is so attenuated as to render the distinction arbitrary or irrational. Beyond that, the mentally retarded, like others, have and retain their substantive constitutional rights in addition to the right to be treated equally by the law.

## IV

We turn to the issue of the validity of the zoning ordinance insofar as it requires a special use permit for homes for the mentally retarded. We inquire first whether requiring a special use permit for the Featherston home in the circumstances here deprives respondents of the equal protection of the laws. If it does, there will be no occasion to decide whether the special use permit provision is facially invalid where the mentally retarded are involved, or to put it another way, whether the city may never insist on a special use permit for a home for the mentally retarded in an R-3 zone. This is the preferred course of adjudication since it enables courts to avoid making unnecessarily broad constitutional judgments.

The constitutional issue is clearly posed. The city does not require a special use permit in an R-3 zone for apartment houses, multiple dwellings, boarding and lodging houses, fraternity or sorority houses, dormitories, apartment hotels, hospitals, sanitariums, nursing homes for convalescents or the aged (other than for the insane or feebleminded or alcoholics or drug addicts), private clubs or fraternal orders, and other specified uses. It does, however, insist on a special permit for the Featherston home, and it does so, as the District Court found, because it would be a facility for the mentally retarded. May the city require the permit for this facility when other care and multiple-dwelling facilities are freely permitted?

It is true, as already pointed out, that the mentally retarded as a group are indeed different from others not sharing their misfortune, and in this respect they may be different from those who would occupy other facilities that would be permitted in an R-3 zone without a special permit. But this difference is largely irrelevant unless the Featherston home and those who would occupy it would threaten legitimate interests of the city in a way that other permitted uses such as boarding houses and hospitals would not. Because in our view the record does not reveal any rational basis for believing that the Featherston home would pose any special threat to the city's legitimate interests, we affirm the judgment below insofar as it holds the ordinance invalid as applied in this case.

The District Court found that the City Council's insistence on the permit rested on several factors. First, the Council was concerned with the negative attitude of the majority of property owners located within 200 feet of the Featherston facility, as well as with the fears of elderly residents of the neighborhood. But mere negative attitudes, or fear, unsubstantiated by factors which are properly cognizable in a zoning proceeding, are not permissible bases for treating a home for the mentally retarded differently from apartment houses, multiple dwellings, and the like. It is plain that the electorate as a whole, whether by referendum or otherwise, could not order city action violative of the Equal Protection Clause, and the City may not avoid the strictures of that Clause by deferring to the wishes or objections of some fraction of the body politic. "Private biases may be outside the reach of the law, but the law cannot, directly or indirectly, give them effect."

Second, the Council had two objections to the location of the facility. It was concerned that the facility was across the street from a junior high school, and it feared that the students might harass the occupants of the Featherston home. But the school itself is attended by about 30 mentally retarded students, and denying a permit based on such vague, undifferentiated fears is again permitting some portion of the community to validate what would otherwise be an equal protection violation. The other objection to the home's location was that it was located on "a five hundred year flood plain." This concern with the possibility of a flood, however, can hardly be based on a distinction between the Featherston home and, for example, nursing homes, homes for convalescents or the aged, or sanitariums or hospitals, any of which could be located on the Featherston site without obtaining a special use permit. The same may be said of another concern of the Council — doubts about the legal responsibility for actions which the mentally retarded might take. If there is no concern about legal responsibility with respect to other uses that would be permitted in the area, such as boarding and fraternity houses, it is difficult to believe that the groups of mildly or moderately mentally retarded individuals who would live at 201 Featherston would present any different or special hazard.

Fourth, the Council was concerned with the size of the home and the number of people that would occupy it. The District Court found, and the Court of Appeals repeated, that "[i]f the potential residents of the Featherston Street home were not mentally retarded, but the home was the same in all other respects, its use would be permitted under the city's zoning ordinance." Given this finding, there would be no restrictions on the number of people who could occupy this home as a boarding house, nursing home, family dwelling, fraternity house, or dormitory. The question is whether it is rational to treat the mentally retarded differently. It is true that they suffer disability not shared by others; but why this difference warrants a density regulation that others need not observe is not at all apparent. At least this record does not clarify how, in this connection, the characteristics of the intended occupants of the Featherston home rationally justify denying to those occupants what would be permitted to groups occupying the same site for different purposes. Those who would live in the Featherston home are the type of individuals who, with supporting staff, satisfy federal and state standards for group housing in the community; and there is no dispute that the home would meet the federal square-footage-per-resident requirement for facilities of this type. In the words of the Court of Appeals, "[t]he City never justifies its apparent view that other people can live under such 'crowded' conditions when mentally retarded persons cannot."

In the courts below the city also urged that the ordinance is aimed at avoiding concentration of population and at lessening congestion of the streets. These concerns obviously fail to explain why apartment houses, fraternity and sorority houses, hospitals and the like, may freely locate in the area without a permit. So, too, the expressed worry about fire hazards, the serenity of the neighborhood, and the avoidance of danger to other residents fail rationally to justify singling out a home such as 201 Featherston for the special use permit, yet imposing no such restrictions on the many other uses freely permitted in the neighborhood.

The short of it is that requiring the permit in this case appears to us to rest on an irrational prejudice against the mentally retarded, including those who would occupy the Featherston facility and who would live under the closely supervised and highly regulated conditions expressly provided for by state and federal law.

The judgment of the Court of Appeals is affirmed insofar as it invalidates the zoning ordinance as applied to the Featherston home. The judgment is otherwise vacated, and the case is remanded.

It is so ordered.

Justice STEVENS, with whom THE CHIEF JUSTICE joins, concurring.

STEVENS, Justice. (concurring). The Court of Appeals disposed of this case as if a critical question to be decided were which of three clearly defined standards of equal protection review should be applied to a legislative classification discriminating against the mentally retarded. In fact, our cases have not delineated three — or even one or two — such well-defined standards. Rather, our cases reflect a continuum of judgmental responses to differing classifications which have been explained in opinions by terms ranging from "strict scrutiny" at one extreme to "rational basis" at the other. I have never been persuaded that these so-called "standards" adequately explain the decisional process. Cases involving classifications based on alienage, illegal residency, illegitimacy, gender, age, or — as in this case — mental retardation, do not fit well into sharply defined classifications.

. . . .

Accordingly, I join the opinion of the Court.

Justice MARSHALL, with whom Justice BRENNAN and Justice BLACKMUN join, concurring in the judgment in part and dissenting in part.

MARSHALL, Justice. (concurring). The Court holds that all retarded individuals cannot be grouped together as the "feebleminded" and deemed presumptively unfit to live in a community. Underlying this holding is the principle that mental retardation *per se* cannot be a proxy for depriving retarded people of their rights and interests without regard to variations in individual ability. With this holding and principle I agree. The Equal Protection Clause requires attention to the capacities and needs of retarded people as individuals.

I cannot agree, however, with the way in which the Court reaches its result or with the narrow, as-applied remedy it provides for the city of Cleburne's equal protection violation. The Court holds the ordinance invalid on rational-basis grounds and disclaims that anything special, in the form of heightened scrutiny, is taking place. Yet Cleburne's ordinance surely would be valid under the traditional rational-basis test applicable to economic and commercial regulation. In my view, it is important to articulate, as the Court does not, the facts and principles that justify subjecting this zoning ordinance to the searching review — the heightened scrutiny — that actually leads to its invalidation. . . . Because I dissent from this novel and truncated remedy, and because I cannot accept the Court's disclaimer that no "more exacting standard" than ordinary rational-basis review is being applied, I write separately.

. . . .

I have long believed the level of scrutiny employed in an equal protection case should vary with "the constitutional and societal importance of the interest adversely affected and the recognized invidiousness of the basis upon which the particular classification is drawn." When a zoning ordinance works to exclude the retarded from all residential districts in a community, [it] . . . require[s] that the ordinance be convincingly justified as substantially furthering legitimate and important purposes.

First, the interest of the retarded in establishing group homes is substantial. The right to "establish a home" has long been cherished as one of the fundamental liberties embraced by the Due Process Clause. For retarded adults, this right means living together in group homes, for as deinstitutionalization has progressed, group homes have become the primary means by which retarded adults can enter life in the community. . . .

Second, the mentally retarded have been subject to a "lengthy and tragic history," of segregation and discrimination that can only be called grotesque. During much of the 19th century, mental retardation was viewed as neither curable nor danger-ous and the retarded were largely left to their own devices. By the latter part of the century and during the first decades of the new one, however, social views of the retarded underwent a radical transformation. Fueled by the rising tide of Social Darwinism, the "science" of eugenics, and the extreme xenophobia of those years, leading medical authorities and others began to portray the "feeble-minded" as a "menace to society and civilization . . . responsible in a large degree for many, if not all, of our social problems." A regime of state-mandated segregation and degrada-tion soon emerged that in its virulence and bigotry rivaled, and indeed paralleled, the worst excesses of Jim Crow. . . .

Segregation was accompanied by eugenic marriage and sterilization laws that extinguished for the retarded one of the "basic civil rights of man"—the right to marry and procreate. . . .

Prejudice, once let loose, is not easily cabined. . . .

In light of the importance of the interest at stake and the history of discrimi-nation the retarded have suffered, the Equal Protection Clause requires us to do more than review the distinctions drawn by Cleburne's zoning ordinance as if they appeared in a taxing statute or in economic or commercial legislation.

. . . .

For the retarded, just as for Negroes and women, much has changed in recent years, but much remains the same; outdated statutes are still on the books, and irra-tional fears or ignorance, traceable to the prolonged social and cultural isolation of the retarded, continue to stymie recognition of the dignity and individuality of retarded people. Heightened judicial scrutiny of action appearing to impose unnec-essary barriers to the retarded is required in light of increasing recognition that such barriers are inconsistent with evolving principles of equality embedded in the Fourteenth Amendment.

. . . Heightened scrutiny does not allow courts to second-guess reasoned legis-lative or professional judgments tailored to the unique needs of a group like the retarded, but it does seek to assure that the hostility or thoughtlessness with which there is reason to be concerned has not carried the day. By invoking heightened scrutiny, the Court recognizes, and compels lower courts to recognize, that a group may well be the target of the sort of prejudiced, thoughtless, or stereotyped action that offends principles of equality found in the Fourteenth Amendment. Where classifications based on a particular characteristic have done so in the past, and the threat that they may do so remains, heightened scrutiny is appropriate.

As the history of discrimination against the retarded and its continuing legacy amply attest, the mentally retarded have been, and in some areas may still be, the targets of action the Equal Protection Clause condemns. With respect to a liberty so valued as the right to establish a home in the community, and so likely to be denied on the basis of irrational fears and outright hostility, heightened scrutiny is surely appropriate.

. . . .

... [T]he Court's narrow, as-applied remedy fails to deal adequately with the overbroad presumption that lies at the heart of this case. Rather than leaving future retarded individuals to run the gauntlet of this overbroad presumption, I would affirm the judgment of the Court of Appeals in its entirety and would strike down on its face the provision at issue. I therefore concur in the judgment in part and dissent in part.

## Questions for Consideration

1) In this case, Cleburne Living Center (CLC) seeks a permit to operate a group home for people with mental disabilities. The City of Cleburne informs CLC that it will need to seek a special use permit. Explain the difference between a use requiring a special use permit, and a use that is expressly permitted under the zoning code without the need for a special use permit.

2) Are special use permits consistent with traditional Euclidian zoning?

3) How was CLC's proposed use classified under the zoning ordinance?

4) Was the proposed classification and regulation of CLC's use consistent with other uses identified in the ordinance? Was CLC's use treated in a similar way as other similar uses under the ordinance?

5) The majority opinion in the case differs from the opinion of the Fifth Circuit court in what ways?

6) The majority opinion in the case differs from the dissenting opinion in what ways?

7) In terms of outcome in the particular case, how does the use of heightened scrutiny differ from simply reviewing the case as an "as applied" challenge to the zoning regulations?

8) How would you explain to a non-lawyer friend the Court's analysis of people with disabilities as members of a quasi-suspect class?

## Takeaway

- In *Nectow*, we learned that the drawing of zoning district lines will be upheld as long as the decision about where those lines are placed meets a rational basis standard of review. This is the standard of review for an "as applied challenge." Here, we see that the definitions and classifications of the permitted uses within the zoning district lines must also be rational under an "as applied" test.

- In discussing the standard of review applicable to a quasi-suspect classification, the case provides an opportunity to identify several key standards of review which are important in zoning law. First, we have the rational basis test. As we have already learned, there are three different ways of approaching the rational basis standard. For general legislative acts, the standard is "fairly debatable" (we do not consider the intent of the legislators); for "as applied" challenges, the standard is rational basis (we do consider the intent of the legislators); and, for quasi-adjudicative actions, the standard is one of a rational basis supported by substantial competent evidence on the record. In *Cleburne*, we learn that if the regulation affects members of a *quasi-suspect class* (a class based on sex and gender, or on age for example), it must be reviewed with a *heightened level of scrutiny*. Finally, if the regulation affects members of a *suspect class* (a class based on race, for example), it must be reviewed under *strict scrutiny*. The higher the level of scrutiny, the less deference is given to the judgments and decisions of local land use regulators.

• *Cleburne* is an older case and does not involve the ADA. Today, a case such as *Cleburne* would probably be decided under the ADA, and an opinion in such a case would likely provide stronger language in support of the rights of people with disabilities. The outcomes would likely be the same, but the reasoning and applicable law would be different.

### Discussion Problem 5.1

Dr. Tiffany McKale and her husband buy a house in a single-family residential zone. The house is a ranch style home, meaning it is a single level house. There are three bedrooms and 1 ½ bathrooms on the first/main level of the house. Additionally, the house has a finished "walkout" basement with a door opening to the backyard. In the basement, there is also one bedroom and one full bathroom. The basement also features a required escape window for safety purposes. Dr. McKale and her husband occupy the house with their married daughter, the daughter's husband, and their little girl. Also occupying the house is Dr. McKale's son, his wife, and their little girl. Dr. McKale and each of her children have two cars for a total of six cars. There is a two-car garage, but it is used for storage of personal items and not for housing the automobiles. Dr. McKale and each of her children have a dog, so there are three dogs at the property. Neighbors complain to the town that the house has three families living there and that it is undermining the nature of the neighborhood and lowering house values and prices. To demonstrate their claim, the neighbors cite the six cars parked in the McKale's driveway and on the street, the numerous garbage cans lining the street on garbage pick-up days, and the lawn chairs, children's toys, and other objects scattered around the lawn. The McKales contend everyone in the house belongs to one family. You are the town attorney. How do you advise the town in dealing with this complaint signed by 26 neighbors?

# D. Speech

Land use regulation may cause tension with the right of free expression. When there is a conflict between land regulation and free expression, there are special factors that need to be considered in reviewing the legality of the regulation. A primary concern in such cases is that the regulation must not be focused on the users or the content of their speech or expression. The regulation must be focused on the use and the secondary effects of the use.

# City of Renton v. Playtime Theaters, Inc.

Supreme Court of the United States
475 U.S. 41 (1986)

REHNQUIST, Justice. This case involves a constitutional challenge to a zoning ordinance, enacted by appellant city of Renton, Washington, that prohibits adult motion picture theaters from locating within 1,000 feet of any residential zone, single- or multiple-family dwelling, church, park, or school. Appellees, Playtime Theatres, Inc., and Sea-First Properties, Inc., filed an action in the United States District Court for the Western District of Washington seeking a declaratory judgment that the Renton ordinance violated the First and Fourteenth Amendments and a permanent injunction against its enforcement. The District Court ruled in favor of Renton and denied the permanent injunction, but the Court of Appeals for the Ninth Circuit reversed and remanded for reconsideration. We noted probable jurisdiction, and now reverse the judgment of the Ninth Circuit.

In May 1980, the Mayor of Renton, a city of approximately 32,000 people located just south of Seattle, suggested to the Renton City Council that it consider the advisability of enacting zoning legislation dealing with adult entertainment uses. No such uses existed in the city at that time. Upon the Mayor's suggestion, the City Council referred the matter to the city's Planning and Development Committee. The Committee held public hearings, reviewed the experiences of Seattle and other cities, and received a report from the City Attorney's Office advising as to developments in other cities. The City Council, meanwhile, adopted Resolution No. 2368, which imposed a moratorium on the licensing of "any business . . . which . . . has as its primary purpose the selling, renting or showing of sexually explicit materials." The resolution contained a clause explaining that such businesses "would have a severe impact upon surrounding businesses and residences."

In April 1981, acting on the basis of the Planning and Development Committee's recommendation, the City Council enacted Ordinance No. 3526. The ordinance prohibited any "adult motion picture theater" from locating within 1,000 feet of any residential zone, single- or multiple-family dwelling, church, or park, and within one mile of any school. The term "adult motion picture theater" was defined as "[a]n enclosed building used for presenting motion picture films, video cassettes, cable television, or any other such visual media, distinguished or characteri[zed] by an emphasis on matter depicting, describing or relating to 'specified sexual activities' or 'specified anatomical areas' . . . for observation by patrons therein." *Id.*, at 78.

In early 1982, respondents acquired two existing theaters in downtown Renton, with the intention of using them to exhibit feature-length adult films. The theaters were located within the area proscribed by Ordinance No. 3526. At about the same time, respondents filed the previously mentioned lawsuit challenging the ordinance on First and Fourteenth Amendment grounds, and seeking declaratory and injunctive relief. While the federal action was pending, the City Council amended the ordinance in several respects, adding a statement of reasons for its enactment and reducing the minimum distance from any school to 1,000 feet.

In November 1982, the Federal Magistrate to whom respondents' action had been referred recommended the entry of a preliminary injunction against enforcement of the Renton ordinance and the denial of Renton's motions to dismiss and for summary judgment. The District Court adopted the Magistrate's recommendations and entered the preliminary injunction, and respondents began showing adult films at their two theaters in Renton. Shortly thereafter, the parties agreed to submit the case for a final decision on whether a permanent injunction should issue on the basis of the record as already developed.

The District Court then vacated the preliminary injunction, denied respondents' requested permanent injunction, and entered summary judgment in favor of Renton. The court found that the Renton ordinance did not substantially restrict First Amendment interests, that Renton was not required to show specific adverse impact on Renton from the operation of adult theaters but could rely on the experiences of other cities, that the purposes of the ordinance were unrelated to the suppression of speech, and that the restrictions on speech imposed by the ordinance were no greater than necessary to further the governmental interests involved. Relying on *Young v. American Mini Theatres, Inc.*, 427 U.S. 50, 96 S. Ct. 2440, 49 L. Ed. 2d 310 (1976), and *United States v. O'Brien*, 391 U.S. 367, 88 S. Ct. 1673, 20 L. Ed. 2d 672 (1968), the court held that the Renton ordinance did not violate the First Amendment.

The Court of Appeals for the Ninth Circuit reversed. The Court of Appeals first concluded, contrary to the finding of the District Court, that the Renton ordinance constituted a substantial restriction on First Amendment interests. Then, using the standards set forth in *United States v. O'Brien, supra*, the Court of Appeals held that Renton had improperly relied on the experiences of other cities in lieu of evidence about the effects of adult theaters on Renton, that Renton had thus failed to establish adequately the existence of a substantial governmental interest in support of its ordinance, and that in any event Renton's asserted interests had not been shown to be unrelated to the suppression of expression. The Court of Appeals remanded the case to the District Court for reconsideration of Renton's asserted interests.

In our view, the resolution of this case is largely dictated by our decision in *Young v. American Mini Theatres, Inc., supra*. There, although five Members of the Court did not agree on a single rationale for the decision, we held that the city of Detroit's zoning ordinance, which prohibited locating an adult theater within 1,000 feet of any two other "regulated uses" or within 500 feet of any residential zone, did not violate the First and Fourteenth Amendments. *Id.*, 427 U.S., at 72–73, 96 S. Ct., at 2453 (plurality opinion of Stevens, J., joined by Burger, C.J., and White and Rehnquist, JJ.); *id.*, at 84, 96 S. Ct., at 2459 (Powell, J., concurring). The Renton ordinance, like the one in *American Mini Theatres*, does not ban adult theaters altogether, but merely provides that such theaters may not be located within 1,000 feet of any residential zone, single- or multiple-family dwelling, church, park, or school. The ordinance is therefore properly analyzed as a form of time, place, and manner regulation.

Describing the ordinance as a time, place, and manner regulation is, of course, only the first step in our inquiry. This Court has long held that regulations enacted for the purpose of restraining speech on the basis of its content presumptively violate the First Amendment. On the other hand, so-called "content-neutral" time, place, and manner regulations are acceptable so long as they are designed to serve a substantial governmental interest and do not unreasonably limit alternative avenues of communication.

At first glance, the Renton ordinance, like the ordinance in *American Mini Theatres*, does not appear to fit neatly into either the "content-based" or the "content-neutral" category. To be sure, the ordinance treats theaters that specialize in adult films differently from other kinds of theaters. Nevertheless, as the District Court concluded, the Renton ordinance is aimed not at the *content* of the films shown at "adult motion picture theatres," but rather at the *secondary effects* of such theaters on the surrounding community. The District Court found that the City Council's *"predominate* concerns" were with the secondary effects of adult theaters, and not with the content of adult films themselves. But the Court of Appeals, relying on its decision in *Tovar v. Billmeyer*, 721 F.2d 1260, 1266 (9th Cir. 1983), held that this was not enough to sustain the ordinance. According to the Court of Appeals, if *"a motivating factor"* in enacting the ordinance was to restrict respondents' exercise of First Amendment rights the ordinance would be invalid, apparently no matter how small a part this motivating factor may have played in the City Council's decision. 748 F.2d, at 537 (emphasis in original). This view of the law was rejected in *United States v. O'Brien*, 391 U.S., at 382–386, 88 S. Ct., at 1681–1684, the very case that the Court of Appeals said it was applying:

> "It is a familiar principle of constitutional law that this Court will not strike down an otherwise constitutional statute on the basis of an alleged illicit legislative motive. . . ."
>
>      . . . .
>
> ". . . What motivates one legislator to make a speech about a statute is not necessarily what motivates scores of others to enact it, and the stakes are sufficiently high for us to eschew guesswork." *Id.,* at 383–384, 88 S. Ct., at 1683.

The District Court's finding as to "predominate" intent, left undisturbed by the Court of Appeals, is more than adequate to establish that the city's pursuit of its zoning interests here was unrelated to the suppression of free expression. The ordinance by its terms is designed to prevent crime, protect the city's retail trade, maintain property values, and generally "protec[t] and preserv[e] the quality of [the city's] neighborhoods, commercial districts, and the quality of urban life," not to suppress the expression of unpopular views. As Justice Powell observed in *American Mini*

*Theatres,* "[i]f [the city] had been concerned with restricting the message purveyed by adult theaters, it would have tried to close them or restrict their number rather than circumscribe their choice as to location." 427 U.S., at 82, n. 4, 96 S. Ct., at 2458, n. 4.

In short, the Renton ordinance is completely consistent with our definition of "content-neutral" speech regulations as those that "are *justified* without reference to the content of the regulated speech." The ordinance does not contravene the fundamental principle that underlies our concern about "content-based" speech regulations: that "government may not grant the use of a forum to people whose views it finds acceptable, but deny use to those wishing to express less favored or more controversial views." [*Police Department of Chicago v.*] *Mosley, supra,* 408 U.S., at 95–96, 92 S. Ct., at 2289–2290.

It was with this understanding in mind that, in *American Mini Theatres,* a majority of this Court decided that, at least with respect to businesses that purvey sexually explicit materials, zoning ordinances designed to combat the undesirable secondary effects of such businesses are to be reviewed under the standards applicable to "content-neutral" time, place, and manner regulations. Justice Stevens, writing for the plurality, concluded that the city of Detroit was entitled to draw a distinction between adult theaters and other kinds of theaters "without violating the government's paramount obligation of neutrality in its regulation of protected communication," 427 U.S., at 70, 96 S. Ct., at 2452, noting that "[it] is [the] secondary effect which these zoning ordinances attempt to avoid, not the dissemination of 'offensive' speech." Justice Powell, in concurrence, elaborated:

> "[The] dissent misconceives the issue in this case by insisting that it involves an impermissible time, place, and manner restriction based on the content of expression. It involves nothing of the kind. We have here merely a decision by the city to treat certain movie theaters differently because they have markedly different effects upon their surroundings.... Moreover, even if this were a case involving a special governmental response to the content of one type of movie, it is possible that the result would be supported by a line of cases recognizing that the government can tailor its reaction to different types of speech according to the degree to which its special and overriding interests are implicated."

The appropriate inquiry in this case, then, is whether the Renton ordinance is designed to serve a substantial governmental interest and allows for reasonable alternative avenues of communication. See [*Clark v.*] *Community for Creative Non-Violence,* 468 U.S., at 293, 104 S. Ct., at 3069; [*Heffron v.*] *International Society for Krishna Consciousness,* 452 U.S., at 649, 654, 101 S. Ct., at 2564, 2567. It is clear that the ordinance meets such a standard. As a majority of this Court recognized in *American Mini Theatres,* a city's "interest in attempting to preserve the quality of urban life is one that must be accorded high respect." 427 U.S., at 71, 96 S. Ct., at 2453 (plurality opinion); see *id.,* at 80, 96 S. Ct., at 2457 (Powell, J., concurring) ("Nor is there doubt that the interests furthered by this ordinance are both important and substantial"). Exactly the same vital governmental interests are at stake here.

The Court of Appeals ruled, however, that because the Renton ordinance was enacted without the benefit of studies specifically relating to "the particular problems or needs of Renton," the city's justifications for the ordinance were "conclusory and speculative." We think the Court of Appeals imposed on the city an unnecessarily rigid burden of proof. The record in this case reveals that Renton relied heavily on the experience of, and studies produced by, the city of Seattle. In Seattle, as in Renton, the adult theater zoning ordinance was aimed at preventing the secondary effects caused by the presence of even one such theater in a given neighborhood. See *Northend Cinema, Inc. v. Seattle*, 90 Wash. 2d 709, 585 P.2d 1153 (1978). The opinion of the Supreme Court of Washington in *Northend Cinema*, which was before the Renton City Council when it enacted the ordinance in question here, described Seattle's experience as follows:

> "The amendments to the City's zoning code which are at issue here are the culmination of a long period of study and discussion of the problems of adult movie theaters in residential areas of the City. . . . [T]he City's Department of Community Development made a study of the need for zoning controls of adult theaters. . . . The study analyzed the City's zoning scheme, comprehensive plan, and land uses around existing adult motion picture theaters. . . ." *Id.*, at 711, 585 P.2d, at 1155.

> "[T]he [trial] court heard extensive testimony regarding the history and purpose of these ordinances. It heard expert testimony on the adverse effects of the presence of adult motion picture theaters on neighborhood children and community improvement efforts. The court's detailed findings, which include a finding that the location of adult theaters has a harmful effect on the area and contribute to neighborhood blight, are supported by substantial evidence in the record." *Id.*, at 713, 585 P.2d, at 1156.

> "The record is replete with testimony regarding the effects of adult movie theater locations on residential neighborhoods." *Id.*, at 719, 585 P.2d, at 1159.

We hold that Renton was entitled to rely on the experiences of Seattle and other cities, and in particular on the "detailed findings" summarized in the Washington Supreme Court's *Northend Cinema* opinion, in enacting its adult theater zoning ordinance. The First Amendment does not require a city, before enacting such an ordinance, to conduct new studies or produce evidence independent of that already generated by other cities, so long as whatever evidence the city relies upon is reasonably believed to be relevant to the problem that the city addresses. That was the case here. Nor is our holding affected by the fact that Seattle ultimately chose a different method of adult theater zoning than that chosen by Renton, since Seattle's choice of a different remedy to combat the secondary effects of adult theaters does not call into question either Seattle's identification of those secondary effects or the relevance of Seattle's experience to Renton.

We also find no constitutional defect in the method chosen by Renton to further its substantial interests. Cities may regulate adult theaters by dispersing them, as in Detroit, or by effectively concentrating them, as in Renton. "It is not our function to appraise the wisdom of [the city's] decision to require adult theaters to be separated rather than concentrated in the same areas. . . . [T]he city must be allowed a reasonable opportunity to experiment with solutions to admittedly serious problems." *American Mini Theatres*, 427 U.S., at 71, 96 S. Ct., at 2453 (plurality opinion). Moreover, the Renton ordinance is "narrowly tailored" to affect only that category of theaters shown to produce the unwanted secondary effects, thus avoiding the flaw that proved fatal to the regulations in *Schad v. Mount Ephraim*, 452 U.S. 61, 101 S. Ct. 2176, 68 L .Ed. 2d 671 (1981), and *Erznoznik v. City of Jacksonville*, 422 U.S. 205, 95 S. Ct. 2268, 45 L. Ed. 2d 125 (1975).

Respondents contend that the Renton ordinance is "under-inclusive," in that it fails to regulate other kinds of adult businesses that are likely to produce secondary effects similar to those produced by adult theaters. On this record the contention must fail. There is no evidence that, at the time the Renton ordinance was enacted, any other adult business was located in, or was contemplating moving into, Renton. In fact, Resolution No. 2368, enacted in October 1980, states that "the City of Renton does not, at the present time, have any business whose primary purpose is the sale, rental, or showing of sexually explicit materials." That Renton chose first to address the potential problems created by one particular kind of adult business in no way suggests that the city has "singled out" adult theaters for discriminatory treatment. We simply have no basis on this record for assuming that Renton will not, in the future, amend its ordinance to include other kinds of adult businesses that have been shown to produce the same kinds of secondary effects as adult theaters.

Finally, turning to the question whether the Renton ordinance allows for reasonable alternative avenues of communication, we note that the ordinance leaves some 520 acres, or more than five percent of the entire land area of Renton, open to use as adult theater sites. The District Court found, and the Court of Appeals did not dispute the finding, that the 520 acres of land consists of "[a]mple, accessible real estate," including "acreage in all stages of development from raw land to developed, industrial, warehouse, office, and shopping space that is criss-crossed by freeways, highways, and roads." App. to Juris. Statement 28a.

Respondents argue, however, that some of the land in question is already occupied by existing businesses, that "practically none" of the undeveloped land is currently for sale or lease, and that in general there are no "commercially viable" adult theater sites within the 520 acres left open by the Renton ordinance. The Court of Appeals accepted these arguments, concluded that the 520 acres was not truly "available" land, and therefore held that the Renton ordinance "would result in a substantial restriction" on speech.

We disagree with both the reasoning and the conclusion of the Court of Appeals. That respondents must fend for themselves in the real estate market, on an equal footing with other prospective purchasers and lessees, does not give rise to a First Amendment violation. And although we have cautioned against the enactment of zoning regulations that have "the effect of suppressing, or greatly restricting access to, lawful speech," *American Mini Theatres*, 427 U.S., at 71, n. 35, 96 S. Ct., at 2453, n. 35 (plurality opinion), we have never suggested that the First Amendment compels the Government to ensure that adult theaters, or any other kinds of speech-related businesses for that matter, will be able to obtain sites at bargain prices.) ("The inquiry for First Amendment purposes is not concerned with economic impact"). In our view, the First Amendment requires only that Renton refrain from effectively denying respondents a reasonable opportunity to open and operate an adult theater within the city, and the ordinance before us easily meets this requirement.

In sum, we find that the Renton ordinance represents a valid governmental response to the "admittedly serious problems" created by adult theaters. Renton has not used "the power to zone as a pretext for suppressing expression," but rather has sought to make some areas available for adult theaters and their patrons, while at the same time preserving the quality of life in the community at large by preventing those theaters from locating in other areas. This, after all, is the essence of zoning. Here, as in *American Mini Theatres*, the city has enacted a zoning ordinance that meets these goals while also satisfying the dictates of the First Amendment. The judgment of the Court of Appeals is therefore

Reversed.

Justice BLACKMUN concurs in the result.

Justice BRENNAN, with whom Justice MARSHALL joins, dissenting.

BRENNAN, Justice. (dissenting). Renton's zoning ordinance selectively imposes limitations on the location of a movie theater based exclusively on the content of the films shown there. The constitutionality of the ordinance is therefore not correctly analyzed under standards applied to content-neutral time, place, and manner restrictions.

## I

"[A] constitutionally permissible time, place, or manner restriction may not be based upon either the content or subject matter of speech." The Court asserts that the ordinance is "aimed not at the *content* of the films shown at 'adult motion picture theatres,' but rather at the *secondary effects* of such theaters on the surrounding community," *ante*, and thus is simply a time, place, and manner regulation. This analysis is misguided.

The fact that adult movie theaters may cause harmful "secondary" land-use effects may arguably give Renton a compelling reason to regulate such establishments; it does not mean, however, that such regulations are content neutral. Because the ordinance imposes special restrictions on certain kinds of speech on the basis of *content*, I cannot simply accept, as the Court does, Renton's claim that the ordinance was not designed to suppress the content of adult movies. "[W]hen regulation is based on the content of speech, governmental action must be scrutinized more carefully to ensure that communication has not been prohibited 'merely because public officials disapprove the speaker's views.'" ...

. . . .

. . . The City Council conducted no studies, and heard no expert testimony, on how the protected uses would be affected by the presence of an adult movie theater, and never considered whether residents' concerns could be met by "restrictions that are less intrusive on protected forms of expression." As a result, any "findings" regarding "secondary effects" caused by adult movie theaters, or the need to adopt specific locational requirements to combat such effects, were not "findings" at all, but purely speculative conclusions. Such "findings" were not such as are required to justify the burdens the ordinance imposed upon constitutionally protected expression.

The Court holds that Renton was entitled to rely on the experiences of cities like Detroit and Seattle, which had enacted special zoning regulations for adult entertainment businesses after studying the adverse effects caused by such establishments. However, even assuming that Renton was concerned with the same problems as Seattle and Detroit, it never actually reviewed any of the studies conducted by those cities. Renton had no basis for determining if any of the "findings" made by these cities were relevant to *Renton's* problems or needs. . . .

In sum, the circumstances here strongly suggest that the ordinance was designed to suppress expression, even that constitutionally protected, and thus was not to be analyzed as a content-neutral time, place, and manner restriction. The Court allows Renton to conceal its illicit motives, however, by reliance on the fact that other communities adopted similar restrictions. The Court's approach largely immunizes such measures from judicial scrutiny, since a municipality can readily find other municipal ordinances to rely upon, thus always retrospectively justifying special zoning regulations for adult theaters. Rather than speculate about Renton's motives for adopting such measures, our cases require the conclusion that the ordinance, like any other content-based restriction on speech, is constitutional "only if the [city] can show that [it] is a precisely drawn means of serving a compelling [governmental] interest." Only this strict approach can insure that cities will not use their zoning powers as a pretext for suppressing constitutionally protected expression.

Applying this standard to the facts of this case, the ordinance is patently unconstitutional. Renton has not shown that locating adult movie theaters in proximity to its churches, schools, parks, and residences will necessarily result in undesirable "secondary effects," or that these problems could not be effectively addressed by less intrusive restrictions.

II

. . . .

A

The Court finds that the ordinance was designed to further Renton's substantial interest in "preserv[ing] the quality of urban life." As explained above, the record here is simply insufficient to support this assertion. The city made no showing as to how uses "protected" by the ordinance would be affected by the presence of an adult movie theater. . . .

### B

Finally, the ordinance is invalid because it does not provide for reasonable alternative avenues of communication. The District Court found that the ordinance left 520 acres in Renton available for adult theater sites, an area comprising about five percent of the city. However, the Court of Appeals found that because much of this land was already occupied, "[l]imiting adult theater uses to these areas is a substantial restriction on speech." . . .

Despite the evidence in the record, the Court reasons that the fact "[t]hat respondents must fend for themselves in the real estate market, on an equal footing with other prospective purchasers and lessees, does not give rise to a First Amendment violation." However, respondents are not on equal footing with other prospective purchasers and lessees, but must conduct business under severe restrictions not imposed upon other establishments. The Court also argues that the First Amendment does not compel "the government to ensure that adult theaters, or any other kinds of speech-related businesses for that matter, will be able to obtain sites at bargain prices." However, respondents do not ask Renton to guarantee low-price sites for their businesses, but seek only a reasonable opportunity to operate adult theaters in the city. By denying them this opportunity, Renton can effectively ban a form of protected speech from its borders. The ordinance "greatly restrict[s] access to . . . lawful speech."

### *Questions for Consideration*

1) Can you identify any significant differences in the way the case is framed in the majority opinion in comparison to how it is framed by the dissent?

2) What studies were done by the City of Renton prior to passing its regulation regarding the location of adult entertainment venues?

3) How can a local city government establish a substantial government interest in regulating a particular use such as adult entertainment?

4) How does a local city government demonstrate that the predominant intent in passing a regulation such as the one in *Renton*, is not to restrict speech?

5) How is the prior case of *Young v. American Mini Theaters, Inc.* discussed in this case?

6) Might a small city or town be able to lawfully ban all adult entertainment within its jurisdiction if adult entertainment was available in a nearby community?

7) The majority opinion provides the language used by Renton to define an adult motion picture theater.

> The term "adult motion picture theater" was defined as "[a]n enclosed building used for presenting motion picture films, video cassettes,

cable television, or any other such visual media, distinguished or characteri[zed] by an emphasis on matter depicting, describing or relating to 'specified sexual activities' or 'specified anatomical areas' . . . for observation by patrons therein."

Do you think that this applies to modern hotels providing adult video images and movies on television sets in a patron's room; or to the provision of free Wi-Fi to patrons who use the provided internet services to access and view the regulated adult movie content on their personal computers?

8) How do the majority opinion and the dissent deal with each of these questions?

    a) Does the regulation regulate speech?

    b) Is it content neutral? (focused on secondary effects rather than the content of the speech)

    c) If it is content neutral, does it focus on time, place, and manner restrictions?

    d) Does the regulation serve a substantial government interest?

    e) Is the regulation narrowly tailored to achieve the goals of the substantial government interest?

    f) Are other alternative avenues of communication available?

## *Takeaway*

- The police power to regulate land use is limited when it conflicts with protected First Amendment rights such as the right to free speech.

- In evaluating land use regulations that conflict with free speech, one must address the points raised above in question 8 of the Questions for Consideration.

- The standard applied to commercial speech is lower than that applied to other varieties of speech. *Central Hudson Gas & Electric Corp. v. Public Service Commission*, 447 U.S. 557 (1980), established this different standard for commercial speech. In that opinion the Court said:

  In commercial speech cases, then, a four-part analysis has developed. At the outset, we must determine whether the expression is protected by the First Amendment. For commercial speech to come within that provision, it at least must concern lawful activity and not be misleading. Next, we ask whether the asserted governmental interest is substantial. If both inquiries yield positive answers, we must determine whether the regulation directly advances the governmental interest asserted, and whether it is not more extensive than is necessary to serve that interest.

- Compare the *Central Hudson* case test to that set out in *Renton*. *Central Hudson* gives more discretion to local regulations of commercial speech than is permitted with respect to regulation of non-commercial speech. In local land regulation, this is important for regulation of business signs, billboards, and advertisements. Issues related to the regulation of signage is a matter of major importance to many businesses.

- Many cities and towns are unable to afford detailed studies addressing topics such as the secondary effects of adult entertainment and they therefore rely on studies done by other cities or on studies that provide general and generic information on the subject. Generally, this reliance is permissible provided that the local officials make some findings with respect to the reasons they conclude that such studies are useful and applicable to their own community.

## Reed v. Town of Gilbert

### Supreme Court of the United States
### 135 S. Ct. 2218 (2015)

THOMAS, Justice. The town of Gilbert, Arizona (or Town), has adopted a comprehensive code governing the manner in which people may display outdoor signs. Gilbert, Ariz., Land Development Code (Sign Code or Code), ch. 1, § 4.402 (2005).[1] The Sign Code identifies various categories of signs based on the type of information they convey, then subjects each category to different restrictions. One of the categories is "Temporary Directional Signs Relating to a Qualifying Event," loosely defined as signs directing the public to a meeting of a nonprofit group. § 4.402(P). The Code imposes more stringent restrictions on these signs than it does on signs conveying other messages. We hold that these provisions are content-based regulations of speech that cannot survive strict scrutiny.

### I

### A

The Sign Code prohibits the display of outdoor signs anywhere within the Town without a permit, but it then exempts 23 categories of signs from that requirement. These exemptions include everything from bazaar signs to flying banners. Three categories of exempt signs are particularly relevant here.

The first is "Ideological Sign[s]." This category includes any "sign communicating a message or ideas for noncommercial purposes that is not a Construction Sign, Directional Sign, Temporary Directional Sign Relating to a Qualifying Event, Political Sign, Garage Sale Sign, or a sign owned or required by a governmental agency." Sign Code, Glossary of General Terms. Of the three categories discussed here, the Code treats ideological signs most favorably, allowing them to be up to 20 square feet in area and to be placed in all "zoning districts" without time limits.

The second category is "Political Sign[s]." This includes any "temporary sign designed to influence the outcome of an election called by a public body." The

---

1. The Town's Sign Code is available online at http://www.gilbertaz.gov/departments /development-service/planning-development/land development-code (as visited June 16, 2015, and available in Clerk of Court's case file).

Code treats these signs less favorably than ideological signs. The Code allows the placement of political signs up to 16 square feet on residential property and up to 32 square feet on nonresidential property, undeveloped municipal property, and "rights-of-way." § 4.402(I). These signs may be displayed up to 60 days before a primary election and up to 15 days following a general election.

The third category is "Temporary Directional Signs Relating to a Qualifying Event." This includes any "Temporary Sign intended to direct pedestrians, motorists, and other passersby to a 'qualifying event.'" A "qualifying event" is defined as any "assembly, gathering, activity, or meeting sponsored, arranged, or promoted by a religious, charitable, community service, educational, or other similar non-profit organization." The Code treats temporary directional signs even less favorably than political signs. Temporary directional signs may be no larger than six square feet. They may be placed on private property or on a public right-of-way, but no more than four signs may be placed on a single property at any time. And, they may be displayed no more than 12 hours before the "qualifying event" and no more than 1 hour afterward.

## B

Petitioners Good News Community Church (Church) and its pastor, Clyde Reed, wish to advertise the time and location of their Sunday church services. The Church is a small, cash-strapped entity that owns no building, so it holds its services at elementary schools or other locations in or near the Town. In order to inform the public about its services, which are held in a variety of different locations, the Church began placing 15 to 20 temporary signs around the Town, frequently in the public right-of-way abutting the street. The signs typically displayed the Church's name, along with the time and location of the upcoming service. Church members would post the signs early in the day on Saturday and then remove them around midday on Sunday. The display of these signs requires little money and manpower, and thus has proved to be an economical and effective way for the Church to let the community know where its services are being held each week.

This practice caught the attention of the Town's Sign Code compliance manager, who twice cited the Church for violating the Code. The first citation noted that the Church exceeded the time limits for displaying its temporary directional signs. The second citation referred to the same problem, along with the Church's failure to include the date of the event on the signs. Town officials even confiscated one of the Church's signs, which Reed had to retrieve from the municipal offices.

Reed contacted the Sign Code Compliance Department in an attempt to reach an accommodation. His efforts proved unsuccessful. The Town's Code compliance manager informed the Church that there would be "no leniency under the Code" and promised to punish any future violations.

Shortly thereafter, petitioners filed a complaint in the United States District Court for the District of Arizona, arguing that the Sign Code abridged their freedom of speech in violation of the First and Fourteenth Amendments. The District

Court denied the petitioners' motion for a preliminary injunction. The Court of Appeals for the Ninth Circuit affirmed, holding that the Sign Code's provision regulating temporary directional signs did not regulate speech on the basis of content. It reasoned that, even though an enforcement officer would have to read the sign to determine what provisions of the Sign Code applied to it, the "'kind of cursory examination'" that would be necessary for an officer to classify it as a temporary directional sign was "not akin to an officer synthesizing the expressive content of the sign." It then remanded for the District Court to determine in the first instance whether the Sign Code's distinctions among temporary directional signs, political signs, and ideological signs nevertheless constituted a content-based regulation of speech.

On remand, the District Court granted summary judgment in favor of the Town. The Court of Appeals again affirmed, holding that the Code's sign categories were content neutral. The court concluded that "the distinctions between Temporary Directional Signs, Ideological Signs, and Political Signs ... are based on objective factors relevant to Gilbert's creation of the specific exemption from the permit requirement and do not otherwise consider the substance of the sign." Relying on this Court's decision in *Hill v. Colorado*, 530 U.S. 703, 120 S. Ct. 2480, 147 L. Ed. 2d 597 (2000), the Court of Appeals concluded that the Sign Code is content neutral. 707 F.3d, at 1071–1072. As the court explained, "Gilbert did not adopt its regulation of speech because it disagreed with the message conveyed" and its "interests in regulat[ing] temporary signs are unrelated to the content of the sign." Accordingly, the court believed that the Code was "content-neutral as that term [has been] defined by the Supreme Court." In light of that determination, it applied a lower level of scrutiny to the Sign Code and concluded that the law did not violate the First Amendment.

We granted certiorari, 573 U.S. ___, 134 S. Ct. 2900, 189 L. Ed. 2d 854 (2014), and now reverse.

## II

### A

The First Amendment, applicable to the States through the Fourteenth Amendment, prohibits the enactment of laws "abridging the freedom of speech." U. S. Const., Amdt. 1. Under that Clause, a government, including a municipal government vested with state authority, "has no power to restrict expression because of its message, its ideas, its subject matter, or its content." Content-based laws — those that target speech based on its communicative content — are presumptively unconstitutional and may be justified only if the government proves that they are narrowly tailored to serve compelling state interests.

Government regulation of speech is content based if a law applies to particular speech because of the topic discussed or the idea or message expressed. This commonsense meaning of the phrase "content based" requires a court to consider whether a regulation of speech "on its face" draws distinctions based on the message a speaker conveys. Some facial distinctions based on a message are obvious, defining regulated speech by particular subject matter, and others are more subtle, defining regulated speech by its function or purpose. Both are distinctions drawn based on the message a speaker conveys, and, therefore, are subject to strict scrutiny.

Our precedents have also recognized a separate and additional category of laws that, though facially content neutral, will be considered content-based regulations of speech: laws that cannot be "'justified without reference to the content of the regulated speech,'" or that were adopted by the government "because of disagreement with the message [the speech] conveys." Those laws, like those that are content based on their face, must also satisfy strict scrutiny.

## B

The Town's Sign Code is content based on its face. It defines "Temporary Directional Signs" on the basis of whether a sign conveys the message of directing the public to church or some other "qualifying event." It defines "Political Signs" on the basis of whether a sign's message is "designed to influence the outcome of an election." And it defines "Ideological Signs" on the basis of whether a sign "communicat[es] a message or ideas" that do not fit within the Code's other categories. It then subjects each of these categories to different restrictions.

The restrictions in the Sign Code that apply to any given sign thus depend entirely on the communicative content of the sign. If a sign informs its reader of the time and place a book club will discuss John Locke's Two Treatises of Government, that sign will be treated differently from a sign expressing the view that one should vote for one of Locke's followers in an upcoming election, and both signs will be treated differently from a sign expressing an ideological view rooted in Locke's theory of government. More to the point, the Church's signs inviting people to attend its worship services are treated differently from signs conveying other types of ideas. On its face, the Sign Code is a content-based regulation of speech. We thus have no need to consider the government's justifications or purposes for enacting the Code to determine whether it is subject to strict scrutiny.

## C

In reaching the contrary conclusion, the Court of Appeals offered several theories to explain why the Town's Sign Code should be deemed content neutral. None is persuasive.

### 1

The Court of Appeals first determined that the Sign Code was content neutral because the Town "did not adopt its regulation of speech [based on] disagree[ment] with the message conveyed," and its justifications for regulating temporary directional signs were "unrelated to the content of the sign." . . .

But this analysis skips the crucial first step in the content-neutrality analysis: determining whether the law is content neutral on its face. A law that is content based on its face is subject to strict scrutiny regardless of the government's benign motive, content-neutral justification, or lack of "animus toward the ideas contained" in the regulated speech. . . .

That is why we have repeatedly considered whether a law is content neutral on its face *before* turning to the law's justification or purpose. . . .

. . . Because strict scrutiny applies either when a law is content based on its face or when the purpose and justification for the law are content based, a court must evaluate each question before it concludes that the law is content neutral and thus subject to a lower level of scrutiny.

. . . Innocent motives do not eliminate the danger of censorship presented by a facially content-based statute, as future government officials may one day wield such statutes to suppress disfavored speech. That is why the First Amendment expressly targets the operation of the laws — *i.e.,* the "abridg[ement] of speech" — rather than merely the motives of those who enacted them. "'The vice of content-based legislation . . . is not that it is always used for invidious, thought-control purposes, but that it lends itself to use for those purposes.'"

. . . .

2

The Court of Appeals next reasoned that the Sign Code was content neutral because it "does not mention any idea or viewpoint, let alone single one out for differential treatment." It reasoned that, for the purpose of the Code provisions, "[i]t makes no difference which candidate is supported, who sponsors the event, or what ideological perspective is asserted."

. . . But it is well established that "[t]he First Amendment's hostility to content-based regulation extends not only to restrictions on particular viewpoints, but also to prohibition of public discussion of an entire topic."

Thus, a speech regulation targeted at specific subject matter is content based even if it does not discriminate among viewpoints within that subject matter. For example, a law banning the use of sound trucks for political speech — and only political speech — would be a content-based regulation, even if it imposed no limits on the political viewpoints that could be expressed. The Town's Sign Code likewise singles out specific subject matter for differential treatment, even if it does not target viewpoints within that subject matter. Ideological messages are given more favorable treatment than messages concerning a political candidate, which are themselves given more favorable treatment than messages announcing an assembly of like-minded individuals. That is a paradigmatic example of content-based discrimination.

3

. . . .

. . . [A] speech regulation is content based if the law applies to particular speech because of the topic discussed or the idea or message expressed. A regulation that targets a sign because it conveys an idea about a specific event is no less content based than a regulation that targets a sign because it conveys some other idea. Here, the Code singles out signs bearing a particular message: the time and location of a specific event. This type of ordinance may seem like a perfectly rational way to regulate signs, but a clear and firm rule governing content neutrality is an essential means of protecting the freedom of speech, even if laws that might seem "entirely reasonable" will sometimes be "struck down because of their content-based nature."

## III

Because the Town's Sign Code imposes content-based restrictions on speech, those provisions can stand only if they survive strict scrutiny, "'which requires the Government to prove that the restriction furthers a compelling interest and is narrowly tailored to achieve that interest,'" Thus, it is the Town's burden to demonstrate that the Code's differentiation between temporary directional signs and other types of signs, such as political signs and ideological signs, furthers a compelling governmental interest and is narrowly tailored to that end.

The Town cannot do so. It has offered only two governmental interests in support of the distinctions the Sign Code draws: preserving the Town's aesthetic appeal and traffic safety. Assuming for the sake of argument that those are compelling governmental interests, the Code's distinctions fail as hopelessly underinclusive.

Starting with the preservation of aesthetics, temporary directional signs are "no greater an eyesore," [*City of Cincinnati v.*] *Discovery Network*, 507 U. S., at 425, 113 S. Ct. 1505, 123 L. Ed. 2d 99, than ideological or political ones. Yet the Code allows unlimited proliferation of larger ideological signs while strictly limiting the number, size, and duration of smaller directional ones. The Town cannot claim that placing strict limits on temporary directional signs is necessary to beautify the Town while at the same time allowing unlimited numbers of other types of signs that create the same problem.

The Town similarly has not shown that limiting temporary directional signs is necessary to eliminate threats to traffic safety, but that limiting other types of signs is not. The Town has offered no reason to believe that directional signs pose a greater threat to safety than do ideological or political signs. If anything, a sharply worded ideological sign seems more likely to distract a driver than a sign directing the public to a nearby church meeting.

In light of this under inclusiveness, the Town has not met its burden to prove that its Sign Code is narrowly tailored to further a compelling government interest. Because a "'law cannot be regarded as protecting an interest of the highest order, and thus as justifying a restriction on truthful speech, when it leaves appreciable damage to that supposedly vital interest unprohibited,'" the Sign Code fails strict scrutiny.

## IV

Our decision today will not prevent governments from enacting effective sign laws. The Town asserts that an "'absolutist'" content-neutrality rule would render "virtually all distinctions in sign laws . . . subject to strict scrutiny," but that is not the case. Not "all distinctions" are subject to strict scrutiny, only *content-based* ones are. Laws that are *content neutral* are instead subject to lesser scrutiny.

The Town has ample content-neutral options available to resolve problems with safety and aesthetics. For example, its current Code regulates many aspects of signs that have nothing to do with a sign's message: size, building materials, lighting, moving parts, and portability. And on public property, the Town may go a long way toward entirely forbidding the posting of signs, so long as it does so in an even-handed, content-neutral manner. . . .

We acknowledge that a city might reasonably view the general regulation of signs as necessary because signs "take up space and may obstruct views, distract motorists, displace alternative uses for land, and pose other problems that legitimately call for regulation." At the same time, the presence of certain signs may be essential, both for vehicles and pedestrians, to guide traffic or to identify hazards and ensure safety. A sign ordinance narrowly tailored to the challenges of protecting the safety of pedestrians, drivers, and passengers — such as warning signs marking hazards on private property, signs directing traffic, or street numbers associated with private houses — well might survive strict scrutiny. The signs at issue in this case, including political and ideological signs and signs for events, are far removed from those purposes. As discussed above, they are facially content based and are neither justified by traditional safety concerns nor narrowly tailored.

We reverse the judgment of the Court of Appeals and remand the case for proceedings consistent with this opinion.

It is so ordered.

Justice ALITO, with whom Justice KENNEDY and Justice SOTOMAYOR join, concurring.

ALITO, Justice. (concurring). I join the opinion of the Court but add a few words of further explanation.

As the Court holds, what we have termed "content-based" laws must satisfy strict scrutiny. Content-based laws merit this protection because they present, albeit sometimes in a subtler form, the same dangers as laws that regulate speech based on viewpoint. Limiting speech based on its "topic" or "subject" favors those who do not want to disturb the status quo. Such regulations may interfere with democratic self-government and the search for truth.

As the Court shows, the regulations at issue in this case are replete with content-based distinctions, and as a result they must satisfy strict scrutiny. This does not mean, however, that municipalities are powerless to enact and enforce reasonable sign regulations. I will not attempt to provide anything like a comprehensive list, but here are some rules that would not be content based:

Rules regulating the size of signs. These rules may distinguish among signs based on any content-neutral criteria, including any relevant criteria listed below.

Rules regulating the locations in which signs may be placed. These rules may distinguish between free-standing signs and those attached to buildings.

Rules distinguishing between lighted and unlighted signs.

Rules distinguishing between signs with fixed messages and electronic signs with messages that change.

Rules that distinguish between the placement of signs on private and public property.

Rules distinguishing between the placement of signs on commercial and residential property.

Rules distinguishing between on-premises and off-premises signs.

Rules restricting the total number of signs allowed per mile of roadway.

Rules imposing time restrictions on signs advertising a one-time event. Rules of this nature do not discriminate based on topic or subject and are akin to rules restricting the times within which oral speech or music is allowed.

In addition to regulating signs put up by private actors, government entities may also erect their own signs consistent with the principles that allow governmental speech. They may put up all manner of signs to promote safety, as well as directional signs and signs pointing out historic sites and scenic spots.

Properly understood, today's decision will not prevent cities from regulating signs in a way that fully protects public safety and serves legitimate esthetic objectives.

BREYER, Justice. (concurring). I join Justice Kagan's separate opinion. Like Justice Kagan I believe that categories alone cannot satisfactorily resolve the legal problem before us. The First Amendment requires greater judicial sensitivity both to the Amendment's expressive objectives and to the public's legitimate need for regulation than a simple recitation of categories, such as "content discrimination" and "strict scrutiny," would permit. In my view, the category "content discrimination" is better considered in many contexts, including here, as a rule of thumb, rather than as an automatic "strict scrutiny" trigger, leading to almost certain legal condemnation.

To use content discrimination to trigger strict scrutiny sometimes makes perfect sense. There are cases in which the Court has found content discrimination an unconstitutional method for suppressing a viewpoint. And there are cases where the Court has found content discrimination to reveal that rules governing a traditional public forum are, in fact, not a neutral way of fairly managing the forum in the interest of all speakers. In these types of cases, strict scrutiny is often appropriate, and content discrimination has thus served a useful purpose.

. . . .

. . . Regulatory programs almost always require content discrimination. And to hold that such content discrimination triggers strict scrutiny is to write a recipe for judicial management of ordinary government regulatory activity.

. . . .

. . . The Court has said, for example, that we should apply less strict standards to "commercial speech." *Central Hudson Gas & Elec. Corp. v. Public Service Comm'n*, 447 U.S. 557, 562–563, 100 S. Ct. 2343, 65 L. Ed. 2d 341 (1980). But I have great concern that many justifiable instances of "content-based" regulation are noncommercial. And, worse than that, the Court has applied the heightened "strict scrutiny" standard even in cases where the less stringent "commercial speech" standard was appropriate. . . .

Here, regulation of signage along the roadside, for purposes of safety and beautification is at issue. There is no traditional public forum nor do I find any general effort to censor a particular viewpoint. Consequently, the specific regulation at issue does not warrant "strict scrutiny." Nonetheless, for the reasons that Justice Kagan sets forth, I believe that the Town of Gilbert's regulatory rules violate the First Amendment. I consequently concur in the Court's judgment only.

KAGAN, Justice. (concurring). Countless cities and towns across America have adopted ordinances regulating the posting of signs, while exempting certain categories of signs based on their subject matter. For example, some municipalities generally prohibit illuminated signs in residential neighborhoods, but lift that ban for signs that identify the address of a home or the name of its owner or occupant. In other municipalities, safety signs such as "Blind Pedestrian Crossing" and "Hidden Driveway" can be posted without a permit, even as other permanent signs require one. Elsewhere, historic site markers — for example, "George Washington Slept Here" — are also exempt from general regulations. And similarly, the federal Highway Beautification Act limits signs along interstate highways unless, for instance, they direct travelers to "scenic and historical attractions" or advertise free coffee.

Given the Court's analysis, many sign ordinances of that kind are now in jeopardy. See *ante*, at 14 (acknowledging that "entirely reasonable" sign laws "will sometimes be struck down" under its approach (internal quotation marks omitted)). Says the majority: When laws "single[] out specific subject matter," they are "facially content based"; and when they are facially content based, they are automatically subject to strict scrutiny. And although the majority holds out hope that some sign laws with subject-matter exemptions "might survive" that stringent review, the likelihood is that most will be struck down. After all, it is the "rare case[] in which a speech restriction withstands strict scrutiny." To clear that high bar, the government must show that a content-based distinction "is necessary to serve a compelling state interest and is narrowly drawn to achieve that end." So on the majority's view, courts would have to determine that a town has a compelling interest in informing passersby where George Washington slept. And likewise, courts would have to find that a town has no other way to prevent hidden-driveway mishaps than by specially treating hidden-driveway signs. (Well-placed speed bumps? Lower speed limits? Or how about just a ban on hidden driveways?) The consequence — unless courts water down strict scrutiny to something unrecognizable — is that our communities will find themselves in an unenviable bind: They will have to either repeal the exemptions that allow for helpful signs on streets and sidewalks, or else lift their sign restrictions altogether and resign themselves to the resulting clutter.

. . . .

. . . The Town, for example, provides no reason at all for prohibiting more than four directional signs on a property while placing no limits on the number of other types of signs. Similarly, the Town offers no coherent justification for restricting the size of directional signs to 6 square feet while allowing other signs to reach 20 square feet. The best the Town could come up with at oral argument was that directional signs "need to be smaller because they need to guide travelers along a route." Why exactly a smaller sign better helps travelers get to where they are going is left a mystery. The absence of any sensible basis for these and other distinctions dooms the Town's ordinance under even the intermediate scrutiny that the Court typically applies to "time, place, or manner" speech regulations. Accordingly, there is no need to decide in this case whether strict scrutiny applies to every sign ordinance in every town across this country containing a subject-matter exemption.

I suspect this Court and others will regret the majority's insistence today on answering that question in the affirmative. As the years go by, courts will discover that thousands of towns have such ordinances, many of them "entirely reasonable." And as the challenges to them mount, courts will have to invalidate one after the other. (This Court may soon find itself a veritable Supreme Board of Sign Review.) . . . Because I see no reason why such an easy case calls for us to cast a constitutional pall on reasonable regulations quite unlike the law before us, I concur only in the judgment.

## Questions for Consideration

1) After *Reed*, how do we know when a regulation focuses on the content of the speech?

2) After *Reed*, in what ways can a community regulate signs?

3) According to *Reed*, how does the standard of review vary as between a land use regulation that regulates the content of speech and one that is content neutral?

4) Do you think a community could have a land use regulation requiring all signs to be in English only?

5) The regulation of signs is a subject that occupies a significant amount of space in local zoning codes. What advice might you give to a local community seeking to draft regulations controlling signs after the *Reed* decision?

6) Do you think that a local zoning code can lawfully prohibit the flying of the flag of the Unites States in a residential neighborhood? In a commercial or industrial neighborhood? If a community permits the flying of the flag of the United States, can it nonetheless prohibit the flying of the national flag of another country, of the Confederate flag, or of the Rainbow flag?

## *Takeaway*

- *Reed* makes it clear that when applying strict scrutiny review, the government must prove that the regulation furthers a compelling state interest and that the regulation is narrowly tailored to achieve that interest.

- Signs can be regulated for purposes of safety and aesthetics.

- Refer back to the Takeaway section after the *Renton* case for a reference to the *Hudson* case and the lower standard of review typically given to commercial speech. The issue for contemporary zoning is; to what extent *Hudson* is changed by *Reed*.

## Burns v. Town of Palm Beach

United States Court of Appeals for the Eleventh Circuit

999 F.3d 1317 (2021)

Luck, Circuit Judge. Donald Burns wants to knock down his "traditional" beachfront mansion and build a new one, almost twice its size, in the midcentury modern style. The new mansion, Burns says, will reflect his evolved philosophy of simplicity in lifestyle and living with an emphasis on fewer personal possessions. The new two-story mansion will have a basement garage, outdoor pool and spa, cabana, and exercise room.

To build his new mansion, Burns had to get the approval of the Town of Palm Beach's architectural review commission. Palm Beach created the commission to review building permit applications to make sure new structures were "in harmony with the proposed developments on land in the general area" and "not excessively dissimilar in relation to any other structure existing . . . within 200 feet of the proposed site in respect to . . . [a]rchitectural compatibility[,] . . . [a]rrangement of the components of the structure[,] . . . [a]ppearance of mass from the street," and "[d]iversity of design that is complimentary with the size and massing of adjacent properties." In other words, the town doesn't want elephants next to poodles. Or, as the town explained in its findings creating the commission, Palm Beach "has become a worldwide synonym for beauty, quality and value" and the "essential foundation of beauty in communities is harmony." "The task of the architectural commission is . . . to preserve various elements of urban beauty and require that new projects enhance the existing elements" in order "to achieve a pleasant and comprehensive cohesiveness in community development."

Applying its criteria, the architectural review commission denied Burns's building permit. The commission found that his new mansion was not in harmony with the proposed developments on land in the general area and was excessively dissimilar to other homes within 200 feet in terms of its architecture, arrangement, mass, and size.

Burns sued the town, claiming that the criteria the commission used to deny his building permit violated his First Amendment free speech rights and his

Fourteenth Amendment rights to due process and equal protection. The district court granted summary judgment for the town. We conclude that summary judgment was not granted too early and affirm on the First Amendment claim because there was no great likelihood that some sort of message would be understood by those who viewed Burns's new beachfront mansion. We also affirm the summary judgment on the Fourteenth Amendment claims because the commission's criteria were not unconstitutionally vague and Burns has not presented evidence that the commission applied its criteria differently for him than for other similarly situated mansion-builders.

### Factual Background and Procedural History

### Palm Beach's Architectural Review Commission

Palm Beach created its architectural review commission because the town is "internationally known . . . for beauty, quality and value" and "beautiful communities can be created only through a deliberate search for beauty on the part of the community leadership, architects, planners, realtors and the building industry." Town of Palm Beach, Fla., Code § 18-146(a)-(b).[1] The "essential foundation of beauty in communities," the town found, "is harmony." *Id.* § 18-146(e). "The plan for achieving beauty must grow out of special local characteristics of site, aesthetic tradition and development potential." *Id.* The commission was directed to "preserve various elements of urban beauty and require that new projects enhance the existing elements." *Id.* § 18-146(d). Palm Beach's "intent," it made clear, was "to achieve a pleasant and comprehensive cohesiveness in community development." *Id.* § 18-146(e).

There are seven commissioners on the architectural review commission. *Id.* § 18-166(a). The commissioners must be "specially qualified" by "training or experience in art, architecture, community planning, land development, real estate, landscape architecture, or other relevant business or profession, or by reason of civic interest and sound judgment to judge the effects of a proposed building upon the desirability, property values and development of surrounding areas." *Id.* § 18-167(a). No less than two, but no more than three, commissioners must be Florida-registered architects. *Id.* § 18-166(a). And one commissioner must be a landscape architect or a "master gardener." *Id.*

Except for minor changes and changes to historic buildings, all applications for demolition and construction in the town must be approved by the commission. *Id.* § 18-175(a). The commission reviews an application for a building permit based on the criteria in section 18-205(a) of the town's code. *Id.* If an applicant meets

---

1. The dissenting opinion uses the name "ARCOM" for the architectural review commission and then calls the name it uses "Orwellian." If by Orwellian the dissenting opinion means any government agency that administers regulations impacting our lives, then the architectural review commission is as Orwellian as the state board of therapeutic massage, the local dog catcher, and every one of the alphabet soup of departments and agencies and bureaus in Washington, D.C.

the criteria, the commission "shall" approve the application. *Id.* §18-205(b). Section 18-205(a) identifies ten criteria for the commission to consider:

(1) The plan for the proposed building or structure is in conformity with good taste and design and in general contributes to the image of the town as a place of beauty, spaciousness, balance, taste, fitness, charm and high quality.

(2) The plan for the proposed building or structure indicates the manner in which the structures are reasonably protected against external and internal noise, vibrations, and other factors that may tend to make the environment less desirable.

(3) The proposed building or structure is not, in its exterior design and appearance, of inferior quality such as to cause the nature of the local environment to materially depreciate in appearance and value.

(4) The proposed building or structure is in harmony with the proposed developments on land in the general area, with the comprehensive plan for the town, and with any precise plans adopted pursuant to the comprehensive plan.

(5) The proposed building or structure is not excessively similar to any other structure existing or for which a permit has been issued or to any other structure included in the same permit application within 200 feet of the proposed site in respect to one or more of the following features of exterior design and appearance:

> a. Apparently visibly identical front or side elevations;
>
> b. Substantially identical size and arrangement of either doors, windows, porticos or other openings or breaks in the elevation facing the street, including reverse arrangement; or
>
> c. Other significant identical features of design such as, but not limited to, material, roof line and height of other design elements.

(6) The proposed building or structure is not excessively dissimilar in relation to any other structure existing or for which a permit has been issued or to any other structure included in the same permit application within 200 feet of the proposed site in respect to one or more of the following features:

> a. Height of building or height of roof.
>
> b. Other significant design features including, but not limited to, materials or quality of architectural design.
>
> c. Architectural compatibility.
>
> d. Arrangement of the components of the structure.
>
> e. Appearance of mass from the street or from any perspective visible to the public or adjoining property owners.

f. Diversity of design that is complimentary with size and massing of adjacent properties.

g. Design features that will avoid the appearance of mass through improper proportions.

h. Design elements that protect the privacy of neighboring property.

(7) The proposed addition or accessory structure is subservient in style and massing to the principal or main structure.

(8) The proposed building or structure is appropriate in relation to the established character of other structures in the immediate area or neighboring areas in respect to significant design features such as material or quality or architectural design as viewed from any public or private way (except alleys).

(9) The proposed development is in conformity with the standards of this Code and other applicable ordinances insofar as the location and appearance of the buildings and structures are involved.

(10) The project's location and design adequately protects unique site characteristics such as those related to scenic views, rock outcroppings, natural vistas, waterways, and similar features.

*Id.* § 18-205(a).

### Burns's New Mansion

For the last eighteen years, Burns has been living in his 10,063 square foot mansion — which he describes as a "traditional home" — on the Atlantic Ocean in Palm Beach.

*Photo of Burn's "Traditional Home"*

But in 2013, Burns decided he wanted to knock down the "traditional home" so he could build a new mansion in the midcentury modern style to convey the evolution of his personal philosophy. He wanted his new mansion "to be a means of communication and expression of the person inside: Me." He picked a design of international or midcentury modern architecture because it emphasized simple lines, minimal decorative elements, and open spaces built of solid, quality materials. According to Burns, the midcentury modern design communicated that the new home was clean, fresh, independent, and modern — a reflection of his evolved philosophy of simplicity in lifestyle and living with an emphasis on fewer personal possessions. It also communicated Burns's message that he was unique and different from his neighbors.

*Photo of Burn's New Proposed Home*

Burns initially submitted a plan to the town council that proposed demolishing his existing 10,063 square foot mansion and building in its place a 25,198 square foot mansion in the midcentury modern design. His emphasis on fewer personal possessions included two stories and a basement containing a five-car garage, wine storage area, and steam room. The first floor would have an open-air entry, guest rooms, dining room, kitchen, family room, powder rooms, and living room. The open-air entry would lead to the pool, spa, and cabana. The second floor would have more guest rooms, an exercise room, and the master bedroom.

At the council's meeting on the application, Burns's landscape architect testified that the "most important design criteri[on]," as directed by Burns, was "to screen th[e] house properly, and more than adequate." The landscaper proposed curtaining the house from the public road with heavy landscaping, including a sixteen-to-eighteen-foot-tall hedge and a large specimen of trees. The design also called for landscaping to buffer the new mansion from Burns's northern and southern neighbors. After some of Burns's neighbors opposed the plan, the town council deferred action until the architectural review commission considered the building permit.

At the commission's May 25, 2016 meeting, Burns presented the testimony of his landscaper, attorney, architects, and expert architectural witness, David Chase. The landscaper told the commission about the "much more dense" landscaping that the new design would implement compared with Burns's current mansion. Facing the street, Burns proposed planting a "tall, green callifolium wall or hedge" to "separate" the "street from the house and provide screening and a buffer." The design would also stagger coconut palms in between the house and the street. To "block views from the neighbors to the north," Burns would plant a fourteen-to-sixteen-foot-tall hedge, coconut palms at least thirty-two feet tall, and eighteen-to-twenty-two-foot-tall grey wood trees. The design called for similar landscaping on the south side.

Burns's architectural expert, Chase, submitted a report and testified about the architectural styles in Palm Beach and previous applications that the commission had approved. The report identified fifteen midcentury modern design applications, other than Burns's, that the commission considered from 1979 to 2016. Chase documented the commission's deliberations on each application and some of the individual commissioners' statements about the designs. He compared the commissioners' observations to the eight design features in section 18-205(a)(6) and categorized the commission's reception as good, bad, or no comment for each criterion. He also identified where a commissioner found a design feature "excessively dissimilar" in relation to nearby structures. The commission had approved fourteen applications and denied one. Chase gave his professional opinion that Burns's design met the commission's criteria in section 18-205(a)(6).

At the meeting, Burns's neighbors told the commission that the new mansion was too large for the lot, too dissimilar with the neighborhood, had inappropriate glass-to-mass ratios, and invaded their privacy. The commission approved the demolition but voted to defer its decision on the building permit.

At the commission's August 24, 2016 meeting, Burns presented a revised design. Burns reduced the square footage of his new mansion by twenty-two percent — to 19,594 square feet — but kept similar plans for the landscaping. His neighbors again testified in opposition to the plan. And the commission again deferred its decision.

At the commission's next meeting, on September 28, 2016, Burns presented another revised plan. . . .

Among other changes, and to alleviate some of the concerns, he added a limestone wall between the front of the mansion and Ocean Boulevard (the residential street in front of the home) with a louvered gate. The gate had angled vertical slats (the louvers) spaced at regular intervals across its length to allow for air and light to come through. The angle of the louvers prevented anyone driving north on Ocean Boulevard from seeing the house. Drivers headed south would not see the house because of the heavy landscaping on the other side of the gate. Even with the changes, the commission voted five-to-two to deny his application. The commission explained why it denied the building permit based on the section 18-205(a) criteria:

> (4) The proposed building or structure is not in harmony with the proposed developments on land in the general area, with the comprehensive plan for the town, and with any precise plans adopted pursuant to the Comprehensive Plan.

. . .

(6) The proposed building or structure is excessively dissimilar in relation to any other structure . . . within 200 feet of the proposed site in respect to . . .

(c) Architectural compatibility.

(d) Arrangement of the components of the structure.

(e) Appearance of mass from the street or from any perspective visible to the public or adjoining property owners.

(f) Diversity of design that is complimentary with size and massing of adjacent properties.

. . . [and]

(8) The proposed development is not in conformity with the standards of this Code and other applicable ordinances insofar as the location and appearance of the buildings and structures are involved.

### Burns Sues Palm Beach in Federal District Court

Burns could have appealed the commission's decision to the town council and then the state circuit court. See Town of Palm Beach, Fla., Code §§ 18-177, 134-173. Instead, Burns sued Palm Beach in federal district court under 42 U.S.C. section 1983. In his two-count complaint, Burns brought a Fourteenth Amendment due process void-for-vagueness challenge and an equal protection challenge to section 18-146 (the section explaining the town's findings and purpose for creating the architectural review commission) and section 18-205(a) (the section with the commission's criteria for approving building permits) of the town's ordinances. Burns also alleged that the two ordinances violated his First Amendment right to speak through the midcentury modern design of his new mansion. Burns claimed that the ordinances violated his constitutional rights both on their face and as applied to him.

[The matter] was referred to the magistrate judge. . . .

As to Burns's First Amendment claim against the commission's criteria in section 18-205(a), the magistrate judge adopted the three-part predominant-purpose test from *Mastrovincenzo v. City of New York*, 435 F.3d 78 (2d Cir. 2006) for determining whether the new mansion was constitutionally protected speech. The predominant-purpose test asks whether: (1) the owner of the structure subjectively intended to communicate a message; (2) the predominant purpose of the structure was to communicate a message; and (3) a reasonable observer viewing the structure in its surrounding context had a great likelihood of understanding it to be predominantly communicating some message.

The town conceded that Burns intended to communicate a message, so that wasn't an issue. After reviewing the summary judgment evidence, the magistrate judge found that the predominant purpose of Burns's mansion was nonexpressive because the design — with its two stories, basement garage, numerous bedrooms and bathrooms, pool, oceanfront views, privacy wall, and heavy landscaping — demonstrated that the "structure [was] to serve as a residence, not as a piece of visual art." And any message from the mansion would be ambiguous, according to the magistrate judge, because of its residential features and because, even though the mansion was a custom design, a reasonable viewer would not infer that the design sent a message. Rather, a viewer might think that the owner liked the architecture, wanted a different style from his neighbors, or believed the house would be more hurricane resistant. Because the design was nonexpressive, the magistrate judge found that the First Amendment did not apply.

As to Burns's vagueness claim, . . . the magistrate judge explained that the commission's criteria were not vague because the ordinance listed specific design elements to compare a proposed structure to others in the area and identified "architectural compatibility" and "harmony" with nearby structures as guidelines for a design. As to Burns's equal protection claim, the magistrate judge said that Burns had failed to present evidence of similarly situated building permit applications that Palm Beach treated differently than his, so his class-of-one claim failed.

. . . .

The district court overruled Burns's objections and adopted the magistrate judge's report. . . .

As to Burns's First Amendment claim, the district court agreed that the three-part predominant-purpose test applied and that the primary purpose of Burns's new mansion was to be his residence. Because Burns designed the residence to be concealed from the public by a privacy wall and heavy landscaping, the district court also concluded that a reasonable observer would not have a great likelihood of understanding that the mansion communicated a message. As to Burns's vagueness claim, the district court agreed that section 18-205(a)'s criteria and reference to design elements were understandable to an ordinary person and prevented arbitrary and discriminatory enforcement. Finally, as to Burns's equal protection claim, the district court agreed with the magistrate judge that Burns had not presented evidence of comparator mansions, "identical in all relevant respects" to his design, that were approved by the commission.

Burns appeals the summary judgment for Palm Beach.

. . . .

### First Amendment Claim

The parties raise three issues with Burns's First Amendment claim: (1) Can residential architecture ever be expressive conduct protected by the First Amendment? (2) If so, what First Amendment test do we use to analyze whether a home is expressive conduct? And (3) applying the proper test, is Burns's new mansion expressive conduct protected by the First Amendment? Burns contends that custom-designed residential architecture communicates a form of expressive conduct unique to the homeowner, like his lifestyle choices, political stances, and individuality. Because the commission's criteria in section 18-205(a) restricted his expressive conduct, Burns argues that they had to meet the Supreme Court's two-part test in *Texas v. Johnson*, 491 U.S. 397, 109 S. Ct. 2533, 105 L. Ed. 2d 342 (1989). Applying the *Johnson* test, Burns contends that building his new mansion was expressive conduct entitled to First Amendment protection.

Palm Beach, on the other hand, argues that residential architecture is not expressive conduct because, whatever its artistic elements, those elements can't be separated from the home's predominant and primary purpose as a place to sleep, eat, and live. To the extent that it can be expressive conduct, Palm Beach asks us to apply the district court's three-part predominant purpose test adopted from *Mastrovincenzo*. Under that test, Burns's mansion was not expressive because its predominant purpose, as shown by its location, design, and use, was to serve as a residence.

Because we conclude that, even under the easier-to-meet *Johnson* test, Burns's new mansion was not expressive conduct protected by the First Amendment, we do not decide, and save for another day, the harder issues of whether residential architecture can ever be expressive conduct and, if so, what is the proper First Amendment test. We assume that *Johnson* controls and apply it here to Burns's new mansion.

. . . .

. . . [W]e emphasize . . . that we are *not* deciding whether residential architecture can ever be expressive conduct protected by the First Amendment.

Burns's First Amendment claim challenges the criteria the architectural review commission used to deny the building permit for his new beachfront mansion. As part of our independent examination of the actual record in this case, we will dig deeply into Burns's plans for his new mansion and his dealings with the commission to see whether the new mansion meets the *Johnson* test for expressive conduct (it doesn't). Because our review is limited to the actual record in this case, which is about Burns's proposed mansion, this opinion says nothing about the expressive conduct of national historical landmarks, the homes of our founding fathers and mothers, and the world's most iconic skyscrapers.

"In determining whether the government has violated free speech rights, the initial inquiry is whether the speech or conduct affected by the government action comes within the ambit of the First Amendment." *One World One Fam. Now v. City of Miami Beach*, 175 F.3d 1282, 1285 (11th Cir. 1999). "Constitutional protection for freedom of speech 'does not end at the spoken or written word.'" [*Fort Lauderdale Food Not Bombs v. City of*] *Fort Lauderdale*, 901 F.3d at 1240 (quoting *Johnson*, 491 U.S. at 404). Rather, the First Amendment offers safeguards for "expressive conduct, as well." *Holloman ex rel. Holloman v. Harland*, 370 F.3d 1252, 1270 (11th Cir. 2004) (internal quotation marks omitted).

To determine "whether particular conduct possesses sufficient communicative elements to bring the First Amendment into play," the two-part *Johnson* test asks:

(1) "whether '[a]n intent to convey a particularized message was present,'" and (2) whether "the likelihood was great that the message would be understood by those who viewed it." *Johnson*, 491 U.S. at 404 (quoting *Spence v. Washington*, 418 U.S. 405, 410-11, 94 S. Ct. 2727, 41 L. Ed. 2d 842 (1974)); *see also Fort Lauderdale*, 901 F.3d at 1240. . . .

Palm Beach conceded to the magistrate judge, and does not dispute on appeal, that Burns had the intent to convey a message. But Burns cannot meet *Johnson*'s second element. A reasonable viewer would not infer some sort of message from Burns's new mansion because, quite simply, a viewer can't see it.

As the second factor of the *Johnson* test indicates, the Supreme Court's cases (and ours) have focused on the perspective of those who "view" the expressive conduct. *See Johnson*, 491 U.S. at 404. There has to be a viewer for there to be a great likelihood that the expressive conduct will be understood by those who view it. Expressive conduct has a "communicative" element, but only insofar as it, "in context, would reasonably be understood by the viewer to be communicative." . . . All of the Supreme Court's expressive conduct cases have dealt with conduct that was and could be seen by viewers.

. . . .

The many other cases in which the Supreme Court and this Court have identified protected expressive conduct all share a common element: the expressive conduct in each of those cases was or could be viewed. The conduct was not like the proverbial tree, which was out of view because it was deep in the forest. . . .

Here, Burns sought to express a message through his new mansion's simple lines, minimal decorative elements, and open spaces built of solid, quality materials, but his design calls for carefully shielding those purportedly expressive elements from any viewer. A limestone wall and louvered gate prevent a person driving or walking north along Ocean Boulevard from seeing the design at all. While a person driving or walking south may be able to see through the gaps in the louvred gate, the viewer's gaze would be met not by a midcentury modern design, but by heavy landscaping. Private properties close off the north and south view of the new mansion, further reducing the opportunity for an observer to see the design. Even Burns's neighbors could not see his house because he purposely blocked it from their view with a fourteen-to-sixteen-foot-tall hedge and trees at least eighteen feet tall. . . . A viewer cannot infer a message from something the viewer cannot view.

. . . .

But even if potential viewers could see through the trees, shrubbery, and other landscaping (put there at Burns's direction to block the view) and could catch a glimpse of some part of the backside of the proposed new mansion, there still would be no great likelihood they would understand that it conveyed some sort of message. *See Fort Lauderdale*, 901 F.3d at 1240. In expressive conduct cases, "context matters." *Id.* at 1237. Context separates "the physical activity of walking from the expressive conduct associated with a picket line or a parade"; the act of sitting down to read at a library from sit-ins protesting segregation; and nude dancing from private dressing. *Id.* at 1241. The "circumstances surrounding an event" help a reasonable observer discern the dividing line between expressive conduct and everyday conduct. *See id.*

. . . .

One day, we may even find some residential architecture to be expressive conduct. But Burns's proposed new mansion is not Monticello or Versailles, no matter how much the dissenting opinion wants to compare it to those historic homes. It's just a really big beachfront house that can't be seen, located on a quiet residential street in Palm Beach, Florida.

. . . .

### Fourteenth Amendment Equal Protection Claim

Burns argues that the district court erred in granting summary judgment on his class-of-one equal protection claim because he offered evidence that the commission reviewed fifteen midcentury modern designs (before Burns's) and approved all of them except one. This evidence, Burns says, showed that he was treated differently than similar homeowners.

. . . .

. . . Because "[d]ifferent treatment of dissimilarly situated persons does not violate the equal protection clause," the plaintiff must show that those "others similarly situated" are "prima facie identical in all relevant respects." *Id.* In evaluating the similarly situated requirement, we look at the state action "in light of the full variety of factors that an objectively reasonable governmental decisionmaker would have found relevant in making the challenged decision." *Griffin Indus., Inc. v. Irvin*, 496 F.3d 1189, 1203 (11th Cir. 2007).

Palm Beach has given us "the full variety of factors that an objectively reasonable governmental decisionmaker would have found relevant" in the form of the statutory criteria it uses to review building permits — section 18-205(a). *See id.* The statutory criteria are mandatory and apply to every application the commission reviews. Town of Palm Beach, Fla., Code § 18-205(b). So, to show an equal protection violation, Burns must offer evidence of similar mansions that the commission approved based on the same criteria in section 18-205(a) that the commission cited in rejecting his application.

The only evidence Burns points to in order to meet this burden is the report his expert David Chase made for the commission. But Chase's report does not show that the mansions the commission approved were similar to Burns's new mansion in all relevant respects. Chase's report identifies homeowners who had midcentury modern designs that were approved, but his report does not say that the other midcentury modern designs were "not in harmony with the proposed developments on land in the general area" but approved nonetheless. And Chase's report did not compare the architectural compatibility, massing, and size of Burns's property to the mansions the commission approved. Instead, the report provided summaries of the commissioners' thoughts on each application. But those summaries do not establish that the fourteen midcentury modern designs the commission approved were excessively dissimilar to nearby homes in the same way that the commission found Burns's new mansion excessively dissimilar to his neighbors' homes. Chase's report does not show comparators that are "prima facie identical in all relevant respects." *See Campbell* [*Rainbow City*], 434 F.3d at 1314 (emphasis omitted). Given the absence of evidence of other similarly situated designs, Burns has not shown any difference in treatment. . . .

### Conclusion

We conclude that the district court did not grant summary judgment too early, Burns's proposed new mansion is not expressive conduct protected by the First Amendment, section 18-205(a) is not unconstitutionally vague, and Burns was not treated differently from other Palm Beach homeowners. . . . We affirm the district court's summary judgment for the town in all respects.

AFFIRMED.

Marcus, Circuit Judge. (dissenting). Outside of Chicago there is a home called the Farnsworth House, nestled in the woods along the Fox River. Or it was a home. Now it is a museum, a National Historic Landmark, and a piece of our common cultural heritage. Designed by the renowned architect Ludwig Mies van der Rohe, the Farnsworth House is a striking piece of art. A single rectangular prism, two-thirds of which is enclosed by glass, the remainder an open-air porch, elevated five feet above the ground by the white steel beams that form its structure, the house blends seamlessly into its sylvan surroundings. When the river floods, the water flows beneath the house; in the snow its white beams and glass panes are nearly invisible; from within it is as though one stands unsheltered in the forest. The house expresses the view of Mies — and of the home's first owner, Dr. Edith Farnsworth — that the modern world has strayed too far from nature and lost the potential for individual fulfillment hidden therein.

Donald Burns has lived in Palm Beach for many years. His current home is built in a traditional style that matches that of his immediate neighbors. Seven years ago, Burns decided that his house no longer   reflected his identity and he decided to build a house like the Farnsworth House, in the International Style. He wants to do that because of the message he believes the International Style conveys — minimalism, individuality, and the pursuit of fulfillment in harmony with nature. He also might just find the style beautiful. Many do. The question in this case is whether a government commission created by the Town of Palm Beach with the Orwellian moniker "ARCOM" may prevent Burns from expressing his philosophy and taste through the architecture of his home and create a work of art on land he owns solely because a majority of the members of the Commission do not like the way it looks.

In my view, the First Amendment — the most powerful commitment to think, speak, and express in the history of the world — does not permit the government to impose its majoritarian aesthetic whims on Burns without a substantial reason. The

First Amendment's protection of the freedom of speech is not limited to the polite exchange of words or pamphlets. It is not limited — as the majority suggests — to public displays clearly related to the narrow issues of the day. It protects art, like architecture, and it protects artistic expression in a person's home as powerfully as in the public sphere, if not more so.

. . . .

Today's case is not an easy case, but it is an important one. Although we are one of the first courts to address the issue of First Amendment protection for residential architecture, this should not dissuade us from our task. *Cf. Masterpiece Cakeshop, Ltd. v. Colorado Civil Rights Comm'n*, 138 S. Ct. 1719, 1723, 201 L. Ed. 2d 35 (2018) ("[T]he application of constitutional freedoms in new contexts can deepen our understanding of their meaning."). The First Amendment represents a powerful commitment to free expression, a commitment that does not stop at the edge of the printed page or the painted canvas. When that freedom is in jeopardy, the courts must step in to preserve it. Because the majority shies away from this task, I respectfully dissent.

## *Questions for Consideration*

1) What is the required make-up of the Architectural Review Commission? Is the make-up of the Commission important to the validity of its decision making?

2) On what basis did the Commission deny Burns's application to construct his new home?

3) Do you believe that the criteria for approval or denial permits Commission members to exercise a great deal of subjective discretion in the decision-making process? If there is a great deal of discretion, does this make the local zoning code provision arbitrary, even if not vague?

4) What is the difference between the two-part *Johnson* test and the three-part predominant purpose test of *Mastovincenzo*?

5) If it is agreed that Burns was making a statement with his home design, why isn't his architectural plan protected as free expression under the First Amendment?

6) The court leaves unanswered the question of whether a residential home design may ever be protected under the free expression provisions of the First Amendment. It also leaves open the question of whether the First Amendment applies to national landmarks, the homes of the founders, and iconic skyscrapers. How do you think the court should handle these questions if directly presented with the matter in a future case?

7) Why wasn't Burns successful on his claim that he was being treated differently from other similarly situated property owners (the equal protection claim)?

8) The home that Burns wishes to construct is in Palm Beach, Florida. In a 2021 Wall Street Journal report on Palm Beach housing, it was revealed that homes in the area near this home site were priced at between $40–$140 million

dollars each. Should the value of the properties, wealth of owners, and custom designs of the houses, make a difference in a community's ability to impose architectural review standards? In other words, do wealthy home buyers, such as Burns, with homes priced in the tens of millions of dollars, get stronger zoning restrictions than might be enforceable or acceptable in neighborhoods where homes are priced at $200,000–$500,000? Why or why not?

## *Takeaway*

- Note that the criteria for protection of free expression in art and architecture is different from that of free speech (e.g., adult entertainment). You can see this more clearly by reviewing the free speech cases earlier in the chapter with the *Burns* case.

- *Burns* involves decision making by an Architectural Review Commission. In this case, the Commission is a public body acting pursuant to a zoning code. Private subdivisions and gated communities also often have private requirements for homeowners to get approvals from private architectural review boards. In both cases, it is important that these review commissions and boards have a set of enumerated criteria for decision making, otherwise their decisions are likely to be considered arbitrary. Even with enumerated criteria, they must make decisions based on a rational application of the criteria to the facts of each specific case.

- When zoning boards and architectural review boards make decisions, they affect property rights. Under requirements of due process, they should keep a record of their decisions, and their decisions should explain the justification and rationale for their decisions. Note that these decisions are not only important in a given case, for an appeal. They also serve as a record of how other property owners have been treated in prior similar situations. Burns uses the record of prior decisions and the comments of Commission members in those earlier cases in presenting his own case. This means that attorneys must not only read prior case law in pursuing a zoning matter, but they must also read prior decisions of local zoning boards and commissions. In addition, when representing a zoning board or a commission, it is important to educate members that any comments that they make on the record may be used in a later case. Thus, they should be cautious in making comments. Likewise, when making a decision, it is sometimes important to make very specific findings so that a current case decision can be distinguished from a potential future case. In other words, specific factual findings related to a given property will reduce its potential precedential authority and make it easier to treat future property petitions as distinguishable, and then treat them differently.

## Discussion Problem 5.2

Tupper Lake, New York is a tourist town in the Adirondack Mountains of New York State. It is a small community, but it garners a significant amount of tourism with summertime hikers, fishermen, and campers. In the fall, people come to enjoy the color of the leaves changing and to hunt, and in winter, tourists come to ride snowmobiles and ski. There are probably two dozen shops and at least a dozen restaurants in the center of town. More than 80% of their revenue derives from tourists. Tourism supports other businesses as well, such as gas stations, the local movie house, a liquor store and two grocery stores. The Town's local business association has collected signatures demanding that a new provision be added to the zoning code. The petition states, in order to appeal to the changing demographics of people visiting the Adirondacks, the town must appeal to a more diverse population. In an effort to do this, the town should adopt a zoning provision preventing the flying of the Confederate flag at any location within the downtown business zone. It has been observed that several gift shops, the local gas station, and a few homeowners in the downtown zone regularly display the Confederate Battle flag on their properties. Most of the shops that display this flag are shops that sell a collection of flags. Others are displayed as a protest of big government. The business association presents evidence from several tourist trade associations demonstrating that many people, including people of all races, have negative feelings about communities that display the Confederate Battle flag, and these feelings translate into fewer tourists and fewer tourists' dollars.

In considering this petition, the Town Board asks for your legal advice on whether they can enforce such a zoning provision if passed; and, if they do proceed to pass such a provision, how might they best draft it so as to minimize the chances of any successful legal challenges from residents.

## Discussion Problem 5.3

In Sag Harbor, Long Island, N.Y., there is a 16 foot 1-inch-tall sculpture by artist Larry Rivers. The sculpture is of a woman's legs. You can see an image of the sculpture at:

> https://www.wsj.com/articles/SB100014240527487043125045756187732349009064

or by doing an online search for Larry Rivers sculpture, Legs.

The sculpture was placed along the side of a building in downtown Sag Harbor that was used as an art gallery. The legs were located within a narrow strip of grass between the sidewalk and the building. Some people thought the legs were delightful; others thought they were completely inappropriate for display in a public place. The town faced multiple requests to remove the legs. Ultimately, the dispute came down to one of classifying the legs. The town had zoning code provisions regulating the size and placement of structures on a lot. If the legs were considered a "structure," they violated these regulations. The owner of the art gallery argued the legs were either a sign, attracting art lovers to her gallery, or an art installation itself. Although local sign law covered what could be on a sign, and even stipulated the size of lettering, it offered little guidance about something such as these legs. As art itself, the town had no current regulations on art displayed as viewable from public places. The owner said that "while this may not be a masterpiece, it is the work of a master." She argues that art has a special place in the community. Others argue that it was difficult to regulate art because the appreciation and qualifications of something as "art" are seemingly subjective.

The town has hired you to assist them with this problem. Provide your best arguments for holding the legs to be a structure and able to be regulated under these zoning code provisions. What are the best arguments for treating them as a sign? Finally, are the legs art? Do they deserve special protection as art? If one were to regulate art with provisions in a zoning code, how would such provisions need to be drafted in order to be rational and applied fairly? How might one treat public art, purchased by a public entity and displayed on public property, as compared to private art, bought and displayed on private property but visible to the public. Would it make a difference if the art was sexually explicit but done by a famous and well-established artist?

# E. Disability and "RLUIPA"

The last case in this chapter provides an opportunity to examine a number of important zoning issues, including: addressing the application of the Americans with Disabilities Act ("ADA"), the Fair Housing Act ("FHA"), and the Religious Land Use and Institutionalized Persons Act ("RLUIPA"). Each of these statutes provides protections that limit the police power of local communities with respect to zoning.

## Candlehouse, Inc. v. Town of Vestal

United States District Court for the Northern District of New York
2013 WL 1867114 (N.D.N.Y. 2013)

PEEBLES, Judge. Plaintiff Candlehouse, Inc. ("Candlehouse"), the owner of residentially zoned property located in the Town of Vestal, New York ("Town"), has commenced this action against the Town based upon the refusal of its Code Enforcement Officer and Zoning Board of Appeals to find that plaintiff's anticipated use of the property, as a Christian faith-based residential treatment facility for young women struggling with addiction or emotional disorders, is a permitted use of the property under the Town's zoning ordinances. In its complaint, Candlehouse asserts that the Town's refusal to allow its intended use of the property violated the Americans with Disabilities Act ("ADA"), 42 U.S.C. § 12101, and the Fair Housing Act ("FHA"), 42 U.S.C. § 3601. Plaintiff also alleges that the Town's restriction on its use of the premises constitutes an unlawful burden on its residents' religious exercise, in violation of the Religious Land Use and Institutionalized Persons Act of 2000 ("RLUIPA"), 42 U.S.C. § 2000cc(a).

... For the reasons set forth below, I conclude that the defendant is entitled to the entry of summary judgment dismissing plaintiff's disparate impact claim under the ADA and the FHA, and its RLUIPA cause of action, but that the existence of material disputes of fact preclude the entry of summary judgment in either party's favor with regard to plaintiff's intentional discrimination and reasonable accommodation claims under the ADA and FHA. . . .

## Background

Plaintiff, which operates as Candlehouse Teen Challenge, is a Christian non-profit organization whose avowed function is "to restore individuals who struggle with life controlling problems such as alcohol abuse and/or who struggle with emotional disorders." According to its mission statement, Candlehouse's purpose is to permit its residents "to live life together with freedom, peace and joy." Candlehouse is one of 234 accredited Teen Challenge programs operating nationwide, utilizing a program pioneered in 1958 by Rev. David Wilkerson. Candlehouse has operated as a Teen Challenge-affiliated residential center in New York for more than seventeen years, and for eight years prior to that as a non-affiliated center, assisting women to recover from the negative impacts of substance abuse and emotional disabilities. While students eligible for participation in the Candlehouse program who struggle with substance abuse are no longer chemically dependent, "they have demonstrated an inability to live independently and abstain from addiction in the long-term and/or live without support as a result of an emotional disability or illness."

Students who enroll in the program typically reside at a Candlehouse facility between twelve and thirty-six months, depending upon their needs. During their stay, the students live in a family-like environment, in which they experience a daily regimen of activities that include Bible study, life skills classes, work assignments, community projects, religious worship, and free time. The goal of the Candlehouse program is to restore students suffering from the disabling affects of addiction or mental health issues to a point where they are capable of living independently, finding and maintaining employment, mending relationships with family members, and caring for themselves.

Students enrolled in the Candlehouse program live, sleep, cook and eat together, and spend much of their days interacting with other students. The operators of Candlehouse prefer to locate the program's facilities in residential neighborhoods. According to Candlehouse's director, Richard Mecklenborg, being situated in a residential neighborhood allows participating students to go outdoors, and motivates them to abstain from drug or alcohol abuse.

In or about September 2008, Candlehouse purchased from the Episcopal Diocese of Syracuse two properties located at 400 Mirador Drive and 401 Mirador Drive, Vestal, New York ("Mirador property"). For the last fifty years, the Mirador property had been utilized as a church and accompanying church campus. Candlehouse's intent in acquiring the Mirador property was to combine its residential campus and work training programs with the religious component of the Teen Challenge programs, which includes Bible study and other classes. It was contemplated that the residential program would support up to twelve students, plus two staff employees and a housemother.

The Mirador property is located in a portion of the Town of Vestal designated as RA-1 residential district for zoning purposes. In pertinent part, Article IV, Section 25-151 of the Town's Zoning Code permits the following uses for such properties:

> Boarding and/or rooming house providing accommodations, for not more than two (2) transient roomers, provided that off-street parking requirements can be met . . .

> Church and other place of worship, including Sunday school building and rectory, provided said lot has a minimum frontage of one hundred fifty (150) feet, a minimum depth of one hundred fifty (150) feet, and contains a minimum of twenty-two thousand five hundred (22,500) square feet . . .

> Cultivation of plants and plantings when conducted by the occupants of the premises and incidental to the principal use . . .

> One-family detached dwelling . . .

> One-family detached modular home . . .

> Park, playground and other open recreational area when operated by the town . . .

> Public elementary or secondary school; parochial school . . .

> Temporary structure incidental to the development of land or to the erection of a permanent structure[.]

That same provision prohibits, *inter alia,* the following uses in RA-1 residential districts:

> Boarding house or rooming house . . .

> Boarding and/or rooming house providing accommodations for not more than four (4) nontransient roomers and provided that off-street parking requirements are met . . .

> Eleemosynary institution . . .

> Multiple family dwelling . . .

> Nursing or convalescent home or sanitarium . . .

> Two-family dwelling or modular home[.]

On September 23, 2008, Mecklenborg approached Mark Dedrick, the Town's Code Enforcement Officer ("CEO"), to discuss Candlehouse's interest in the Mirador property, and inquire as to whether it would be permitted to use the property as a church and residence for its students in light of the fact that the property is zoned as RA-1 residential. The next day, Mecklenborg sent a letter to Dedrick indicating that the proposed use of the property was "to continue to use it as a church," and that Candlehouse's "regular services . . . offer women a temporary residence with counseling." In response, Dedrick wrote Mecklenborg a letter dated September 30, 2008, requesting additional information and advising Mecklenborg that temporary housing is not permitted in an RA-1 zoned district.

On October 12, 2008, Mecklenborg again wrote a letter to Dedrick providing the requested details concerning Candlehouse's proposed use of the Mirador property. More specifically, Mecklenborg explained that "temporary residents" could be anticipated to stay an average of thirteen months, and live together with three or more assigned to each bedroom.

On December 17, 2008, the Vestal Town Board discussed the proposed use of the Mirador property by Candlehouse during a public meeting. In that meeting, the Town's attorney stated that Candlehouse's proposed dormitory living quarters would be inconsistent with the RA-1 zoning regulation. Following that meeting, residents in the neighborhood surrounding the Mirador property began to voice their concerns over Candlehouse's proposed use. In an effort to assuage those concerns, Candlehouse held a neighborhood meeting on December 22, 2008, for the purpose of providing attendees with information concerning the contemplated use. At that meeting, both supporters and opponents to the proposed use spoke, although there was significantly more opposition than support voiced for the program. Four members of the Vestal Town Board attended that neighborhood meeting.

The topic of Candlehouse's plans for the Mirador property arose again during a Vestal Town Board meeting, held on January 14, 2009. At that meeting, five Town residents spoke out against the proposed use.

On January 21, 2009, Sara G. Campbell, Esq., an attorney for Candlehouse, wrote to CEO Dedrick, stating that her client proposed to use the Mirador property as a church and rectory only, defining rectory as "a residence for church personnel." By letter dated February 5, 2009, Dedrick responded to Attorney Campbell by indicating that, while use as a church was consistent with the property's RA-1 residential district zoning, the proposed use as a residence with twenty-four hour, supervised, community-living accommodations and parental style leadership for students, did not qualify as a rectory.

On February 6, 2009, Attorney Campbell again wrote to Dedrick, claiming that Candlehouse's proposed use of the Mirador property constituted a "family/functional equivalent of a family under the Town of Vestal Code."

Dedrick responded by letter dated February 11, 2009, explaining that how, in his view, Candlehouse's proposed use does not comport with any of the seven definitional paragraphs provided for in the Town's zoning Code related to family. He concluded by stating that "the definition within the context of the Code of the Town of Vestal does not allow me to affirm that the Candlehouse use, as presented in written and oral information meets the criterial of a family."

On March 25, 2010, the Town's Zoning Board of Appeals ("ZBA") entertained an appeal by Candlehouse concerning its proposed use of the Mirador property. During the ZBA hearing, Candlehouse representatives made a presentation concerning their proposed use of the Mirador property and were questioned by ZBA members regarding Candlehouse's program. Time was then allotted for public comments, of which there were many. Following that hearing, the ZBA issued a decision, dated May 10, 2010, unanimously concluding that Candlehouse does not meet the definition of the functional equivalent of a family, and setting out the reasoning for [] its determination. In its decision, the ZBA considered and applied the attributes of a family as set out in the governing ordinance, concluding that (1) the proposed assembly of students does not resemble a traditional family unit; (2) it is anticipated that the group will live and cook together as a single housekeeping unit; (3) Candlehouse students are anticipated to be transient in nature, rather than permanent, entering and leaving as they are either rehabilitated or expelled; and (4) the proposed bedroom would not be a "conventional" bedroom but instead would contain rows of bunks for all students in one large room.

On May 5, 2010, through counsel, Candlehouse argued to the Town Board that its program is protected by the FHA and ADA, and formally requested that the Town make a reasonable accommodation to its zoning rules and policies in the form of either a waiver of the family requirement, or, alternatively, an amendment of the Town's zoning ordinance to permit the desired use. The parties dispute whether, and when, the Town Board decided Candlehouse's reasonable accommodation request.

During the pendency of this action, Candlehouse has utilized the Mirador property for various church related uses. However, it has had to carry out the residential portion of its program elsewhere, requiring that its students be transported on a daily basis to the Mirador property for programming.

. . . .

## Discussion

### A. Summary Judgment Standard

Summary judgment motions are governed by Rule 56 of the Federal Rules of Civil Procedure. Under that provision, the entry of summary judgment is warranted "if the movant shows that there is no genuine dispute as to any material facts and the movant is entitled to judgment as a matter of law." . . .

### B. Overview of Plaintiff's Remaining Claims: The Statutory Framework

The claims remaining in this case allege violations of three statutory provisions. Specifically, Candlehouse alleges that the Town's actions violate the FHA and ADA, both of which prohibit discrimination in housing based upon handicap or disability. In addition, Candlehouse alleges that the Town's actions have unreasonably burdened its exercise of religion, in violation of the RLUIPA.

Under the FHA, it is unlawful "[t]o discriminate in the sale or rental, or to otherwise make unavailable or deny, a dwelling to any buyer or renter because of a handicap[.]" 42 U.S.C. §3604(f)(1). Discrimination is defined to include "a refusal to make reasonable accommodations in rules, policies, practices, or services, when such accommodations may be necessary to afford [a handicapped] person equal opportunity to use and enjoy a dwelling[.]" 42 U.S.C. §3604(f)(3)(b). Similarly, Title II of the ADA prohibits discrimination on the basis of disability by public entities, providing that "no qualified individual with a disability shall, by reason of such disability, be excluded from participation in or be denied the benefits of the services, programs, or activities of a public entity, or be subjected to discrimination by any such entity." Both the ADA and FHA apply to municipal zoning determinations. Discrimination is actionable under the ADA and FHA pursuant to one of three distinct theories, including (1) intentional discrimination, or disparate treatment; (2) disparate impact; and (3) failure to make a reasonable accommodation.

Plaintiff's third remaining claim arises under the RLUIPA, which provides, in pertinent part, that

> [n]o government shall impose or implement a land use regulation in a manner that imposes a substantial burden on a religious exercise of a person, including a religious assembly or institution, unless the government demonstrates that imposition of the burden on that . . . institution —
>
> (A) is in furtherance of a compelling governmental interest; and
>
> (B) is the least restrictive means of furthering that compelling governmental interest.

42 U.S.C. §2000cc(a)(1). In a land-use context, a substantial burden is interposed when "government action . . . *coerces* the religious institution to change its behavior[.]"

### C. Standing

"In every federal case, the party bringing the suit must establish standing to prosecute the action." . . . To establish standing for purposes of the constitutional "case or controversy" requirement, a plaintiff must show that he personally has suffered an injury that is "concrete, particularized, and actual or imminent; fairly traceable to the challenged action; and redressable by a favorable ruling." Before proceeding to the merits of the pending motions, I must first determine *sua sponte* whether plaintiff has standing to litigate the claims asserted in its complaint.

For two reasons, I find that Candlehouse possesses the requisite standing necessary to pursue its claims. First, Candlehouse suffered a concrete injury when the ZBA decided that its program failed to qualify as the "functional equivalent of a family" under the relevant zoning provisions. In addition, because Candlehouse's students comprise a class of individuals, all or some of whom possess discrimination claims of their own right, and those interests are closely aligned with those of Candlehouse, plaintiff also meets the requirements for organizational standing.

## D. Disability/Handicap

To succeed under FHA and ADA claims, the plaintiff must establish that its students are "handicapped" under the FHA, or "disabled" as defined in the ADA. "To demonstrate a disability under [the FHA and ADA], a plaintiff must show: (1) a physical or mental impairment which substantially limits one or more major life activities; (2) a record of having such an impairment; or (3) that [he is] regarded as having such an impairment."

The Supreme Court has articulated a three-step test for determining whether an individual's alleged impairment constitutes a disability or handicap under the ADA and FHA. The first inquiry focuses upon whether the plaintiff suffers from an impairment. If so, then the court must next identify any major life activity potentially limited by the impairment. In the third step, "tying the two statutory phrases together, [the court] ask[s] whether the impairment substantially limit[s] the major life activity."

. . . .

... In this case, Candlehouse serves women struggling with a variety of impairments. Indeed, it is abundantly clear from the record that a potential Candlehouse student need not suffer from alcoholism or drug addiction in order to qualify for admission. ("A few students at Candlehouse are admitted because of their struggle with a mental illness or diagnosis[.]"); ("[Since its inception,] hundreds of women have been helped to overcome emotional problems, such as anxiety and depression, and addictions to drugs[,] alcohol and behaviors."). Instead, the record now before the court suggests that admission into Candlehouse depends only on whether a candidate suffers from a "life controlling issue," a phrase that is not explicitly defined anywhere in the record. . . .

Accordingly, by virtue of their pending motions, the parties in essence have asked the court to determine how many of Candlehouse's students must be found "disabled" or "handicapped" under the ADA and FHA in order for Candlehouse to seek relief under those statutes. Plaintiff contends that the inclusion of some non-disabled students into its program does not preclude it from seeking the protections offered by the FHA and ADA (citing *Innovative Health Sys., Inc. v. City of White Plains*, 117 F.3d 37, 48 (2d Cir. 1997). The primary case offered by Candlehouse in support of this argument, however, is not directly on point.

In *Innovative Health Sys., Inc.,* the Second Circuit considered whether a drug rehabilitation program is protected by the ADA when some of its clients are not drug-free and, therefore, are excluded from the definition of "disability" under the ADA based upon their unlawful use of drugs. *Innovative Health Sys., Inc.,* 117 F.3d at 48–49. The court held that "[a]n inevitable, small percentage of failures should not defeat the rights of the majority of participants in the rehabilitation program who are drug-free and therefore disabled under both statutes." In this case, however, Candlehouse assists women with "life controlling issues," a term that is not defined in the record, but does not exclusively require a woman to be suffering from a condition recognized as a *per se* impairment under the definition of disability. ("A few students at Candlehouse are admitted because of their struggle with a mental illness or diagnosis[.]")

In any event, even assuming that *Innovative Health Sys., Inc.* stands for the proposition that a mixed-population of disabled and non-disabled students would not necessarily disqualify a program sponsor from the protections of the FHA and ADA, that case held only that a "small percentage" of non-disabled participants would not deprive the organization from the benefit of those protections. *Innovative Health Sys., Inc.*, 117 F.3d at 49. The question of what constitutes a "small percentage," however, is left unanswered by the Second Circuit's decision.

Without further guidance from controlling authority, and in consideration of the broad remedial purposes to be achieved by the ADA and FHA, I find that, to succeed in any of its claims under those statutes, Candlehouse must establish that a majority of its students are disabled. This finding is consistent with the sparse case law that has addressed whether an organization that serves a mixed group of disabled and nondisabled participants is protected by the FHA and ADA. *See Innovative Health Sys., Inc.*, 117 F.3d at 49 (holding that, to the extent that "a small percentage" of residents at a drug rehabilitation program were not drug free, the program was not precluded from the protections of the ADA and Rehabilitation Act). . . .

Having determined the threshold question of how many of Candlehouse's residents must be found disabled for it to seek protection under the ADA and FHA, the next question is whether the record evidence supports a finding that the majority of Candlehouse's residents are disabled. In connection with the pending motions, the parties collectively have submitted only partial information concerning eleven of the 110 students that have participated in Candlehouse's program. . . .

In summary, based on the record now before me, I find that there remain genuine disputes of material fact to be resolved in connection with whether Candlehouse serves a sufficient number of disabled students to extend the protections of the ADA and FHA to its program. As a result, this material threshold issue thus precludes the entry of summary judgment in favor of plaintiff on any of its ADA and FHA claims.

### D. Intentional Discrimination

One of the theories of discrimination advanced by Candlehouse under the ADA and FHA is the claim that the Town engaged in intentional discrimination by denying the application to have its proposed use of the Mirador property be considered the functional equivalent of a family under the Town's relevant zoning laws. Both parties seek the entry of summary judgment with respect to this claim.

Claims of intentional discrimination under the ADA and FHA are properly analyzed utilizing the familiar, burden-shifting model developed by the courts for use in employment discrimination settings dating back to the Supreme Court's decision in *McDonnell Douglas Corp. v. Green*, 411 U.S. 792, 93 S. Ct. 1817, 36 L. Ed. 2d 668 (1973). Under that analysis, a plaintiff must first establish a *prima facie* case of intentional discrimination under the FHA and ADA by "present[ing] evidence that animus against the protected group was *a* significant factor in the position taken by the municipal decision-makers themselves or by those to whom the decision-makers were knowingly responsive." Once a plaintiff makes out its *prima facie* case, "the burden of production shifts to the defendants to provide a legitimate, nondiscriminatory reason for their decision." "The plaintiff must then prove that the defendants intentionally discriminated against them on a prohibited ground." The factfinder is permitted "to infer the ultimate fact of discrimination" if the plaintiff has made "a substantial showing that the defendants' proffered explanation was false."

The key inquiry in the intentional discrimination analysis is whether discriminatory animus was a motivating factor behind the decision at issue. The Second Circuit has identified the following five factors a factfinder may consider in evaluating a claim of intentional discrimination:

> (1) the discriminatory impact of the governmental decision; (2) the decision's historical background; (3) the specific sequence of events leading up to the challenged decision; (4) departures from the normal procedural sequences; and (5) departures from normal substantive criteria.

In this case, there is considerable record evidence reflecting that many Town residents, including members of the Town Board, were unsupportive of the prospect of Candlehouse moving into the Mirador property. While potentially relevant, the intent of the Town residents is not the focus of the intentional discrimination inquiry, nor is the motivation of the Town Board, as an entity distinct from the ZBA. Instead, to prevail, plaintiff must demonstrate that the decisions by the Town's CEO, Dedrick, and ZBA were discriminatorily motivated.

The record evidence now before the court discloses the existence of a sharp dispute as to whether the CEO Dedrick and ZBA were, in fact, influenced by community animus in their decisionmaking. The record does not definitively reveal the extent of interaction between members of the Town Board, some of whom were clearly opposed to the project, and CEO Dedrick, who made the initial decision to deny Candlehouse's proposal for use of the Mirador property. Town Board member Bielecki testified during his deposition that he spoke with Dedrick regarding Candlehouse on different occasions, including prior to the board meeting on December 17, 2008, and after the neighborhood meeting held on December 22, 2008. In contrast, Dedrick denies speaking with any Town officials regarding the Candlehouse matter between at least October 12, 2008, and January 1, 2009.

Turning to the ZBA's motivation, in his affidavit Acting ZBA Chairman Mark Tomko states that the packet of information received by the ZBA when a party appeals a decision by CEO Dedrick typically contains only the appellant's submissions, as well as any responses to those submissions from Town officials. He also states that "[t]his packet does not contain any letters or correspondence from town officials regarding their feelings or interpretations of the Zoning Code." Moreover, the transcript of the ZBA's hearing on Candlehouse's appeal does not reflect that any of the ZBA board members engaged in discriminatory questioning, or were influenced by the public comments that followed the formal presentation by plaintiff and the question-and-answer period from the ZBA board members. The ZBA board members' questions were objective in nature, and focused on the question of whether plaintiff's organization operates as the functional equivalent of a family. The ZBA's written decision is facially neutral, and focuses on the zoning ordinance's definition of family. All of this evidence suggests that the ZBA was not influenced by discriminatory intent in denying plaintiff's appeal.

As a counterweight to this evidence, the record discloses that, before accepting any public comment at the ZBA hearing, Chairman Tomko acknowledged that whether plaintiff may establish itself in the area has created some "a lot of issues" for the community. Although in his affidavit Tomko attempts to distance himself and the ZBA from the community's outcry, this acknowledgment at the hearing indicates that he possessed at least some awareness of the community sentiment opposed to Candlehouse's program. The fact that the ZBA heard public comment and received letters from the public in lieu of live testimony at the ZBA hearing, and made a record of the proceeding, further suggests that the ZBA was not entirely insulated from the community's disapproval of Candlehouse.

For all of these reasons, I conclude that there remain genuine disputes of material fact as to whether CEO Dedrick or the ZBA were motivated by discriminatory intent in denying Candlehouse's request to find that its program meets the functional equivalent of a family under the Town's zoning laws. As a result, the parties' motions for summary judgment, as they relate to plaintiff's intentional discrimination claim, are denied.

### E. Disparate Impact

Candlehouse also claims that the Town's application of its zoning ordinance and decision not to find that its proposed use of the Mirador property constitutes the functional equivalent of a family resulted in a disparate impact upon Candlehouse's disabled residents. Only defendant has moved for summary judgment with respect to this claim.

"To establish a *prima facie* case under this theory, the plaintiff must show: (1) the occurrence of certain outwardly neutral practices, and (2) a significantly adverse or disproportionate impact on persons of a particular type produced by the defendant's facially neutral acts or practices." "A plaintiff need not show the defendant's action was based on any discriminatory intent." To prove that a neutral practice has a significantly adverse or disproportionate impact "on a protected group, a plaintiff must prove the practice actually or predictably results in discrimination." In addition, a plaintiff must prove "a causal connection between the facially neutral policy and the alleged discriminatory effect." Once a plaintiff establishes its *prima facie* case, "the burden shifts to the defendant to prove that its actions furthered, in theory and in practice, a legitimate, bona fide governmental interest and that no alternative would serve that interest with less discriminatory effect."

"The basis for a successful disparate impact claim involves a comparison between two groups — those affected and those unaffected by the facially neutral policy. This comparison must reveal that although neutral, the policy in question imposes a significantly adverse or disproportionate impact on a protected group of individuals."

"Statistical evidence is . . . normally used in cases involving fair housing disparate impact claims." "Although there may be cases where statistics are not necessary, *there must be some analytical mechanism to determine disproportionate impact.*" A plaintiff may choose to undertake a "qualitative comparison" to demonstrate adverse or disproportionate impact. . . .

. . . .

In this case, to prevail on its disparate impact claim, Candlehouse must do more than merely show that the Town's enforcement of its facially neutral zoning provisions has adversely affected its students. It must also establish, through statistics or some other reliable analytical mechanism, that defendant's neutral policy actually or predictably created a shortage of housing for the individuals served by Candlehouse's program. . . .

Here, the parties agree that the zoning ordinance at issue is facially neutral. . . . They are at odds, however, over whether it disproportionally affects the group of individuals served by Candlehouse. Plaintiff has not provided any statistical evidence demonstrating that potential candidates for its program suffer from a shortage of housing as a result of defendant's policies. Nor has plaintiff undergone a qualitative comparison between that group and one that does not suffer from any of the same impairments, and evaluated whether there is a greater need of residential housing for its group of students.

. . . .

. . . [T]o prevail on a disparate impact claim, plaintiff must show that defendant's admittedly facially neutral ordinances predictably discriminates against plaintiff's students as a whole, and not a group of, for instance, *only* alcoholics or *only* drug addicts. Because it serves a mixed population of students, suffering from potentially diverse impairments, Candlehouse cannot establish that the facially neutral ordinance will predictably discriminate against that group, comprised of students with varying needs.

In light of the lack of statistical or other evidence reliably demonstrating a dispute of material fact regarding the existence of the required disparate impact as a result of the Town's facially neutral zoning ordinance and its application, I conclude that no reasonable factfinder could rule in favor of the plaintiff with respect to plaintiff's disparate impact cause of action. Accordingly, summary judgment is granted in the Town's favor dismissing this claim.

## G. Reasonable Accommodation

Plaintiff has also asserted a reasonable accommodation claim under the FHA and ADA against the Town. Both parties seek the entry of summary judgment on this cause of action.

Under the FHA and ADA, "a governmental entity engages in a discriminatory practice if it refuses to make a 'reasonable accommodation' to 'rules, policies, practices or services when such accommodation may be necessary to afford a handicapped person equal opportunity to use and enjoy a dwelling.'" . . .

To prevail under a reasonable accommodation theory in this type of case, a plaintiff "must show that, but for the accommodation, [its residents] likely will be denied an equal opportunity to enjoy the housing of their choice." "A defendant must incur reasonable costs and take modest, affirmative steps to accommodate the handicapped as long as the accommodations sought do not pose an undue hardship or a substantial burden." In addition, "[t]he [defendant] is not required to grant an exception for a group of people to live as a single family, but it cannot deny the variance request based solely on plaintiffs' handicap where the requested accommodation is reasonable."

In this instance, there is a dispute of material fact as to whether defendant's denial of plaintiff's request for a reasonable accommodation was based on the impairments of its students. . . .

In response to an interrogatory, the Town has offered the following explanation for its decision to deny plaintiff's request for an accommodation:

> The defendant has a legitimate interest in creating single-family neighborhoods comprised of single family residences. The plaintiff's proposed use of a nonconforming structure as a one family residence would cause a fundamental alteration in the zoning scheme of the town. Furthermore, the proposed use and the proposed density of such use also seems contrary to the long-standing zoning scheme involved herein. record is not clear why defendant denied plaintiff's request for a reasonable accommodation.

This rationale does not implicate the impairments of Candlehouse students as the basis for defendant's denial of the reasonable accommodation.

In contrast to this evidence, however, there is evidence that at least some of the Town Board members were biased against Candlehouse and its proposal. For example, a review of the recording of the neighborhood meeting held on December 22, 2008, demonstrates that at least two of the Town Board members spoke out against the prospect of Candlehouse moving into the neighborhood. Indeed, as was previously noted, one Town Board member went so far as to seemingly threaten to have the area rezoned so that Candlehouse could not move into the Mirador property. Because there is conflicting evidence as to the basis for the Town Board's denial of plaintiff's reasonable accommodation, defendant's motion for summary judgment, as it relates to this claim, is denied.

## H. Plaintiff's RLUIPA Substantial Burden Claim

In its sole remaining non-ADA/FHA claim, plaintiff alleges that, through its conduct, the Town has placed an undue substantial burden on its religious exercise rights guaranteed under the RLUIPA. Only defendant has moved for summary judgment on this claim.

Section 2000cc(a)(1) of the RLUIPA provides, in pertinent part, as follows:

> No government shall impose or implement a land use regulation in a manner that imposes a substantial burden on the religious exercise of a person, including a religious assembly or institution, unless the ... imposition of the burden ... is in furtherance of a compelling governmental interest; and ... is the least restrictive means of furthering that compelling governmental interest.

42 U.S.C. § 2000cc(a)(1). In land-use contexts, the Second Circuit has held that a "substantial burden" occurs when "a government action ... *coerces* the religious institution to change its behavior." "[A] burden need not be found insuperable to be held substantial."

"[T]o establish a prima facie violation of RLUIPA, a plaintiff must show that the land use regulation at issue as implemented: (1) imposes a substantial burden, (2) on the religious exercise, (3) of a person, institution, or assembly." *Roman Catholic Diocese of Rockville Ctr., N.Y. v. Inc. Vill. of Old Westbury*, No. 09-CV-5195, 2012 WL 1392365 (E.D.N.Y. Apr.23, 2012). Once a plaintiff has established a *prima facie* case, "the burden shifts to the government to demonstrate that the regulation furthers a compelling governmental interest and is the least restrictive means of furthering that compelling interest."

While the RLUIPA generally forbids governmental action that substantially burdens religious exercise and lacks a compelling interest, "a law that is neutral and of general applicability need not be justified by a compelling governmental interest even if the law has the incidental effect of burdening a particular religious practice." "[E]ven if the [neutral and generally applicable] statute has the effect of incidentally burdening [the plaintiff's] religious exercise, the statute is constitutional so long as it satisfies a rational basis review." "Under rational basis review, the statute must be reasonable and not arbitrary, and it must bear a rational relationship to a permissible state objective."

In this case, Candlehouse argues that, because the Town's ordinance defining family and its functional equivalent restricts its full use of the Mirador property by precluding it from operating a residence with twelve students, the Town has placed a substantial burden on its religious exercise. This argument, however, ignores the Second Circuit's requirement that "[t]here must exist a close nexus between the coerced or impeded conduct and the institution's religious exercise for such conduct to be a substantial burden on that religion." Accordingly, for its RLUIPA claim to survive defendant's motion for summary judgment, Candlehouse must demonstrate the existence of a genuine dispute of material fact as to whether there is a close nexus between the Town's decision to deny its proposed use of the Mirador property as a residence for more than five unrelated people ("the coerced or impeded conduct") and its religious exercise. A careful review of the record reflects that plaintiff has satisfied this burden.

The record reveals that Candlehouse is a Teen Challenge-affiliated program; Teen Challenge operates as a Christian faith-based program that offers "a balance of Bible classes, work assignments, and recreation." There is evidence that the Christian faith-based program is separate from the residential program. ("Along with the Christian faith-based program, the other important component of Teen Challenge's program is the family like residential living arrangement each center provides to its students.") ... Although Mecklenborg states that Candlehouse's inability to operate a residence at the Mirador property precludes students from participating in evening activities, he does not include any support for a finding that these evening activities implement or incorporate religious teachings. In addition, Mecklenborg and Cheryl Clever, a former student and graduate of Candlehouse, explain that having a residence on the Mirador property, which is located in a residential neighborhood, provides students a "unique opportunity to bond," allows them to "develop and maintain relationships," provides a safe environment with access to the outdoors, and "enhances the spiritual element of the program." These explanations, however, provide the court with little guidance as to what types of, if any, religious activity occurs at the residence, as distinct from the church property, which plaintiff is permitted to utilize for religious purposes.

At the ZBA hearing, however, counsel for plaintiff stated that "the emphasis through [the] program is ... to increase their faith and their intimacy with God through a disciplined Christ-centered approach to a family living experience[.]" ... [T]hat the Candlehouse program incorporates religious components in every aspect of a student's experience. . . . As a result, I find that there is a dispute of fact as to whether the Town's denial of its proposed use of the Mirador property has affected Candlehouse's religious exercise.

Notwithstanding whether there is a nexus between Town's conduct and Candlehouse's religious exercise, there is nothing in the record to support a finding that the Town's conduct substantially burdened its religious exercise. . . . Accordingly, because plaintiff has failed to submit evidence giving rise to a dispute of fact as to whether its religious exercise has been substantially burdened, defendant's motion for summary judgment on this claim is granted.

. . . .

## Summary and Recommendation

Based upon the record now before the court, I conclude that there remains a genuine dispute of material fact as to whether Candlehouse serves a disabled or handicapped population under the ADA and FHA, a threshold determination that must be made in order to resolve any claim of discrimination under those provisions. Similarly, issues of fact preclude a finding as a matter of law that defendant intentionally discriminated against the plaintiff and its students, and in denying plaintiff's request for a reasonable accommodation. I do, however, find that no reasonable factfinder could conclude, based upon the existing record, that the requirements to establish a disparate impact claim under the FHA and the ADA have been satisfied. For this reason, defendant's motion for summary judgment on that claim is granted. Similarly, I conclude that plaintiff has failed to demonstrate that a reasonable fact finder could find the requisite burden upon plaintiff and its students in their religious exercise, sufficient to support a claim under the RLUIPA.

## Questions for Consideration

1) In this case, how does the court address the definition of a family?

2) In this case, how does the court address the definition of a rectory?

3) In this case, how does the court address the definition of a transient?

4) What role, if any, did correspondence, records of public meetings, and comments by Town Board members, play in the court's analysis of the case?

5) How does Candlehouse have standing to bring this action?

6) What is a "life controlling issue," and is it the same as a disability protected under the ADA?

7) Does everyone residing at the Candlehouse facility have to have a disability in order for the ADA or FHA to apply?

8) Under the ADA and the FHA, discrimination can be shown in three different ways. Identify the three approaches to proving discrimination and explain the elements of each approach.

9) Under RLUIPA, local planning and zoning regulations cannot impose a substantial burden on the religious exercise of a person. What are the elements of the RLUIPA requirements, and how does the court rule on the matter in this case?

## Takeaway

- Contemporary zoning cases can involve a mix of state and federal law.

- In this chapter, we have seen the exercise of the police power limited by federal laws protecting people with disabilities and by constitutional protections for other fundamental rights. These limitations are in addition to limitations imposed by due process, equal protection, and by the Takings Clause.

- RLUIPA, 42 U.S.C. §2000cc et seq., addresses a specialized area of land use regulation focused on religious liberty. In general, RLUIPA provides protections for places of worship, faith-based social service providers, religious schools, and individuals using land for religious purposes. More specifically, RLUIPA restricts land use regulation by providing:

  ○ Protection against substantial burdens on religious exercise;

- ○ Protection against unequal treatment for religious assemblies and institutions;

- ○ Protection against religious or denominational discrimination;

- ○ Protection against total exclusion of religious assemblies; and

- ○ Protection against unreasonable limitation of religious assemblies.

- For a helpful outline explaining RLUIPA, with examples, see an excellent explanatory letter issued by Vanita Gupta (Principal Deputy Assistant Attorney General, Civil Rights Division), on December 15, 2016, from the U.S. Justice Department, Civil Rights Division, Office of the Assistant Attorney General, titled: The Religious Land Use and Institutionalized Persons Act, https://www .justice.gov/crt/page/file/918596/download.

## Discussion Problem 5.4

The City of Lafayette has a zoning code regulation restricting the locations of schools, daycare centers, and senior centers to specific areas of the city as designated on the zoning map. Recently, complaints have been filed with the City regarding "group-based" homeschooling, also known as "Homeschool Pods." The issue involves members of a religious group identified as The New Reform Judaism Movement ("NRJM"). The members of the group promote homeschooling as the proper setting for religiously informed education. The homeschool curriculum integrates elements of Reformed Judaism into all aspects of the grade school through high school program. Jewish beliefs, practices, and holidays are celebrated and form a part of the daily routine. In an effort to share the burden of schooling and in order to build a strong sense of their religious community, parents rotate holding classes for a group or "pod" of students each month. Usually, a pod is made up of twelve students. Students are dropped off at the host home at 7:30 AM and picked up at 4:30 PM each weekday, with one exception — on Fridays, they are dismissed and picked up at 3:00 PM. The complaints from neighbors are that these parents are using their homes as schools in residential neighborhoods where schools are not permitted. The complaining neighbors want the City to shut down the in-home schools. They argue that this is not a case of parents homeschooling their own children. They also argue that these children should be in the public schools learning the values promoted by the public school system.

Members of the New Reform Judaism Movement contact you to assist them in preventing their neighbors and the City from shutting down their homeschooling program. With primary reference to the Religious Land Use and Institutionalized Persons Act (RLUIPA), advise the NRJM on how you will advance their cause. Explain what you will need to prove, who will have the burden in the case, and what kind of evidence you will want to gather and present at a hearing, if a hearing is required. Also advise them as to the probable position to be taken by the City of Lafayette. Finally, provide an assessment of the likelihood of success should the NRJM engage you as their lawyer to represent them in this matter.

# F. Practice Problems

5.1 World Families, Inc. is a not-for-profit organization that settles immigrant and refugee families in the United States. One program of World Families involves acquiring single-family residential homes to house their clients near a college, university, or other similar institution. World Families believes that such a setting in a single-family residential neighborhood is beneficial for resettlement and that it is important not to cluster immigrants and refugees in crowed multi-family buildings. World Families typically houses people with 2–4 people per bedroom in a house. Ideally, they seek a four-bedroom home but sometimes manage with a three-bedroom structure. Part of how they determine the number of people in a bedroom is based on if they are immediate family members. A home may house 8–16 people. Often times, many of these people are unrelated and strangers to each other prior to being resettled in a home by World Families. It is the practice of World Families to make all best efforts to have the residents of a home be people of a common country and background. In addition, all people in the home share housekeeping duties and share the same kitchen. Members of a household are encouraged to share shopping and meals together. Housing costs, utilities, and a monthly allowance for food and for necessaries are provided for the residential household group by World Families.

a) Assume World Families has come to you for legal advice as it plans to acquire its first residential property in your community. As is its practice, it seeks a four-bedroom home in a single-family residential neighborhood. It wants your advice on the potential issues that may arise under your local zoning code with respect to opening and operating a house for a group of immigrants and refugees from certain areas of the Middle East and North Africa. Review your local zoning code in light of the cases and provide a written response to World Families.

b) Assume alternate facts, and that you are not asked to work for World Families. Instead, assume that your local town or city has heard that a group identified as World Families is interested in opening one of its resettlement homes in the community. Members of the local government planning and zoning authority have come to you, as the local city attorney, and they seek your legal advice on how they can keep World Families out of all of their residential neighborhoods; both single-family and multi-family neighborhoods. They assert that the World Families operation produces over-crowding, brings more crime to a community, and causes a decline in neighborhood property values. The members of the local government planning and zoning authority want your advice on the best way to use the local zoning code to keep World Families out of the community.

5.2 Assume that you are an associate attorney in a small law firm. The firm has a new client, Live Jive, Inc., that is interested in opening an adult entertainment club. The club will feature live male and female dancers performing in the nude. When live performances are not taking place, the club will provide nude music video entertainment on large-screen televisions. There will be a bar serving soft-drinks, beer, wine, and alcohol, in addition to a food service providing "pub food." All entertainment occurs in the main room of the club. There are no private rooms. The typical size of a Live Jive club is 9,000 square feet. Live Jive hires your firm to explain the requirements and limitation on adult entertainment in your community. You have been assigned to prepare the information for Live Jive.

a) Live Jive needs to know all of the restrictions under your local zoning code. It needs to know where it can locate, what kind of signage it can use to identify and promote its business location, the types of lighting permitted, and the number of parking spaces required.

5.3 In light of the decision in the *Reed* case, your local community has asked for your legal opinion regarding its zoning code. It asks you to review its zoning code and to opine on the legality and enforceability of all of its various sign regulations. Furthermore, to the extent that you identify any problems, you are asked to suggest how these problems might best be corrected.

# Chapter 6

# Additional Zoning Concepts

Up to this point, we have focused primarily on understanding planning and zoning law as an exercise of the police power. The police power permits regulation of property for purposes of protecting and advancing the public health, safety, welfare, and morals. The exercise of the police power has its limits, however. We have seen various limitations on the police power such as those provided by the requirements of due process, equal protection, and the Takings Clause, as well as limitations imposed by tensions with other fundamental and constitutional rights.

In this chapter, we focus on typical concerns related specifically to a land use and zoning law practice. Some of the zoning issues addressed in this chapter you will recognize from cases that have already been covered in this book. The cases included here cover a broad range of fundamental land use and zoning law topics designed to provide the reader with additional core knowledge needed to practice in this area.

## A. Use Permit

Under a typical land use regulation and zoning code, all uses must be approved. This means that a new use must be permitted and approved usually through a permit process. In the language of traditional Euclidian zoning: if the use is a permitted use, a permit should be issued, *as of right*. When a property owner applies for a permit, the permit is either issued or denied based on the administrator's interpretation of the zoning code and the requested use. If the use is denied, the property owner may appeal to the zoning board of appeal in an attempt to receive the permit. Many of these disputes are straightforward disagreements concerning the classification of a particular use within the language of permitted uses identified in the zoning code.

# Innovative Health Systems, Inc. v. City of White Plains

United States Court of Appeals for the Second Circuit

117 F.3d 37 (2d Cir. 1997)

HEANEY, Judge. In December 1992, plaintiff-appellee Innovative Health Systems, Inc. ("IHS"), an outpatient drug and alcohol rehabilitation treatment center, began efforts to relocate to a building in downtown White Plains. After over a year of seeking permission from the city, IHS was ultimately denied the necessary building permit by the White Plains Zoning Board of Appeals ("ZBA"). On November 14, 1995, plaintiffs-appellees, IHS and five individual clients, initiated this action against the City of White Plains; Mayor S.J. Schulmann; the ZBA; Chair of the ZBA, Terrence Guerrier; the White Plains Planning Board; and Chair of the Planning Board, Mary Cavallero, (collectively, "the City"), alleging that the ZBA's zoning decision violated both Title II of the Americans with Disabilities Act, 42 U.S.C. §§ 12131-12165 (1994), and section 504 of the Rehabilitation Act of 1973, 29 U.S.C. § 794 (1994). The plaintiffs-appellees moved for a preliminary injunction to prevent the City from interfering with IHS's occupation of the new site. The City cross-moved to dismiss the complaint. In a detailed and thorough opinion, the United States District Court for the Southern District of New York (Barrington D. Parker, Jr., Judge) granted the preliminary injunction and denied the motion to dismiss, except with respect to Mayor Schulmann. *Innovative Health Sys. v. City of White Plains*, 931 F. Supp. 222 (S.D.N.Y. 1996). The remaining defendants appeal. We affirm except with respect to one individual client, Martin A.

## Background

In 1992, Dr. Ross Fishman, Executive Director of IHS, decided that the program should move from its current facility to a building located in downtown White Plains. The new site was more than five times as large as the current site and was closer to a bus line and to other service providers that IHS clients frequently visit. Dr. Fishman planned to expand the services offered by IHS at the new site to include a program for children of chemically dependent persons. Therefore, IHS predicted an increase in the number of clients it would serve.

In December 1992, the Deputy Commissioner of Building for the City of White Plains informed IHS that its proposed use of the downtown site — counseling offices with no physicians on staff for physical examinations or dispensing of medication — qualified as a business or professional office under White Plains' zoning ordinance and thus would be permissible in the zoning district. In January 1994, Dr. Fishman signed a lease for the new space. IHS paid a monthly rent of $8,500 from July 1, 1994 to June 30, 1995, and has paid $6,000 per month since July 1995. The leased space includes a section that formerly had been used as retail space. Dr. Fishman initially intended to renovate the former retail space for the treatment program and sub-lease the remaining space, which had previously been used as an office. In April 1994, IHS filed an application with the White Plains Department of Building for a building permit. Because the application requested a change of use from "retail" to "office," the Commissioner of Building ("Commissioner") referred it to the Planning Board for approval as required by the local zoning ordinance.

The application provoked tremendous opposition from the surrounding community, including Cameo House Owners, Inc. ("Cameo House"), a co-operative association representing resident-owners who lived in the remainder of the downtown building in which IHS sought to relocate, and Fashion Mall Partners, L.P. ("Fashion Mall"), the owner of a shopping mall located near the proposed IHS site. The Planning Board held two public meetings on the proposed use at which the opponents expressed their concern about the condition and appearance of people who attend alcohol- and drug-dependence treatment programs and the effect such a program would have on property values. Opponents also argued that the proposed use constituted a "clinic" and that, therefore, under the zoning ordinance, the use was a "hospital or sanitarium," an impermissible use in the zoning district. In response to this argument, at the Planning Board's request, the Commissioner reconsidered and reaffirmed his previous determination that the proposed site constituted permitted "office" use.

Because continued opposition caused delay and additional costs, IHS withdrew its application from the Planning Board. It instead applied to the Commissioner for a permit to renovate the former retail section of the downtown site, which did not involve a change of use or the Planning Board's approval. Again, however, the application was vehemently opposed by members of the surrounding community.

To resolve the dispute, the Commissioner sought review of his decision by the White Plains Corporation Counsel. In his written opinion, the Corporation Counsel stated that, absent compelling authority to the contrary, the Commissioner's decision should stand. The Corporation Counsel considered the opponents' argument under the zoning ordinance and concluded that the Commissioner's interpretation was correct. Accordingly, the Commissioner issued his final determination that the use was permitted and the Department of Building issued the building permit to IHS.

Cameo House and Fashion Mall immediately appealed the Commissioner's decision to the ZBA, requesting an interpretation of the zoning ordinance that an alcohol-treatment facility is not permitted in the relevant zoning district. The ZBA conducted a two-day public hearing on the matter, at which community members continued to voice strong opposition to having a drug- and alcohol-dependency treatment center in the downtown location. They again focused largely on fears of jeopardized safety and falling property values. The opposition also pressed the same zoning arguments rejected by the Commissioner and the Corporation Counsel. IHS relied on the reasoning of the previous decisions and urged the ZBA to consider their consistency with already-permitted uses in the same zoning district. Specifically, IHS reminded the board that the zoning district of its former location also excludes "hospitals and sanitaria" and that several other mental health professionals and social workers practiced in the district of the proposed site.

On July 5, 1995, the ZBA voted four-to-one to reverse the Commissioner's decision. The Board did not issue a written resolution, as required by the zoning ordinance, but rather stated on the record that, based on its understanding of the services IHS provides, it is better classified as a clinic than an office. Absent in their discussion, however, was any reference to the zoning ordinance or the Commissioner's interpretation.

IHS and five individual clients initiated this action against the City, alleging that the revocation of the building permit constituted discrimination and differential treatment based on a disability as against both the individual clients and the program that assisted them. They also claimed that even if the zoning decision was not discriminatory, the City should have permitted the relocation as a reasonable accommodation. In February 1996, they moved for a preliminary injunction against the City to prevent it from interfering with the occupation of the downtown site.

The City opposed the motion and moved for dismissal, arguing: (1) zoning decisions do not fall within the scope of the ADA or the Rehabilitation Act, (2) the appellees lack standing under the ADA, (3) the federal statutes do not accord preferential treatment to persons with disabilities, and (4) neither IHS nor the individual clients have demonstrated irreparable harm or a likelihood of success on the merits. The district court granted the preliminary injunction and denied the motion to dismiss, except as against the Mayor. The City now appeals, raising essentially the same arguments.

### Preliminary Injunction

We have jurisdiction to consider an appeal from the grant of a preliminary injunction as an appeal as of right under 28 U.S.C. §1292(a). The district court found, as is required for the grant of a preliminary injunction, that the appellees demonstrated that they would suffer irreparable harm absent the injunction and that they are likely to succeed on the merits of their discrimination claim. . . .

### 1. Application of Discrimination Statutes to Zoning

Both Title II of the ADA and section 508 of the Rehabilitation Act prohibit discrimination based on a disability by a public entity. The ADA provides:

> [N]o qualified individual with a disability shall, by reason of such disability, be excluded from participation in or be denied the benefits of the services, programs, or activities of a public entity, or be subjected to discrimination by any such entity.

42 U.S.C. §12132 (1994). The Rehabilitation Act contains the following similar prohibition:

> No otherwise qualified individual with a disability . . . shall, solely by reason of her or his disability, be excluded from the participation in, be denied the benefits of, or be subjected to discrimination under any program or activity receiving Federal financial assistance. . . .

29 U.S.C. §794(a) (1994). It is undisputed that both anti-discrimination provisions govern the City. What the City contests is the application of either statute to its

zoning decisions because it contends that zoning does not constitute a "service, program, or activity." We disagree.

The ADA does not explicitly define "services, programs, or activities." Section 508 of the Rehabilitation Act, however, defines "program or activity" as "all of the operations" of specific entities, including "a department, agency, special purpose district, or other instrumentality of a State or of a local government." 29 U.S.C. § 794(b)(1)(A) (1994). Further, as the district court recognized, the plain meaning of "activity" is a "natural or normal function or operation." *Innovative Health Sys.*, 931 F.Supp. at 232 (quoting Webster's Third New International Dictionary (1993)). Thus, as the district court held, both the ADA and the Rehabilitation Act clearly encompass zoning decisions by the City because making such decisions is a normal function of a governmental entity. *Id.* Moreover, as the district court also noted, the language of Title II's anti-discrimination provision does not limit the ADA's coverage to conduct that occurs in the "programs, services, or activities" of the City. Rather, it is a catch-all phrase that prohibits all discrimination by a public entity, regardless of the context, and that should avoid the very type of hair-splitting arguments the City attempts to make here.

In its analysis, the district court also looked to the ADA's legislative history and the Department of Justice's regulations and Technical Assistance Manual, all of which support the court's interpretation of the plain language of the statute. With respect to Title II of the ADA, the House Committee on Education and Labor stated:

> The Committee has chosen not to list all the types of actions that are included within the term "discrimination", as was done in titles I and III, because this title essentially simply extends the anti-discrimination prohibition embodied in section 504 to *all actions of state and local governments*.
>
> . . . .
>
> Title II of the bill makes *all activities of State and local governments* subject to the types of prohibitions against discrimination against a qualified individual with a disability included in section 504 (nondiscrimination).

H.R.Rep. No. 101-485(II), at 84, 151 (1990), *reprinted in* 1990 U.S.C.C.A.N. 303, 367, 434 (emphasis added). As the preamble to the Department of Justice regulations explains, "[T]itle II applies to anything a public entity does. . . . All governmental activities of public entities are covered." The Department of Justice's Technical Assistance Manual, which interprets its regulations, specifically refers to zoning as an example of a public entity's obligation to modify its policies, practices, and procedures to avoid discrimination. The Americans with Disabilities Act: Title II Technical Assistance Manual § II-3.6100, illus. 1 (1993) ("TA Manual").

Although it gives lip service to the importance of looking to the statutory language to glean legislative intent, the City does not point to specific language in either statute to explain the exemption it seeks to create for zoning decisions. We decline to draw an arbitrary distinction — to prohibit public entities from discriminating against persons with disabilities in some of their activities and not in others — without a reasoned basis for such a distinction. . . .

### 2. Standing

The City also challenges IHS's standing to sue under either the ADA or the Rehabilitation Act. . . .

Looking to the enforcement provisions of each statute, we agree with the district court that IHS has standing under both Title II of the ADA and the Rehabilitation Act. Title II's enforcement provision extends relief to "*any person* alleging discrimination on the basis of disability." 42 U.S.C. § 12133 (1994). Similarly, the Rehabilitation Act extends its remedies to "any person aggrieved" by the discrimination of a person on the basis of his or her disability. 29 U.S.C. § 794a(a)(2). As the district court noted, the use of such broad language in the enforcement provisions of the statutes "evinces a congressional intention to define standing to bring a private action under 504 [and Title II] as broadly as is permitted by Article III of the Constitution." . . .

. . . .

### 3. Appellees' Discrimination Claims

. . . .

The City claims that IHS has admitted that some of its clients are not drug-free and that therefore, under either statute the clients are excluded from the definition of "qualified individuals with a disability." *See* 42 U.S.C. § 12210(a) (term "does not include an individual who is currently engaging in the illegal use of drugs, when the covered entity acts on the basis of such use"); 29 U.S.C. § 706(8)(C)(i) (same). Although, we are not convinced that IHS has admitted that its clients are not drug-free, the program indisputably does not tolerate drug use by its participants. An inevitable, small percentage of failures should not defeat the rights of the majority of participants in the rehabilitation program who are drug-free and therefore disabled under both statutes. *See* 42 U.S.C. § 12210(b)(2); 29 U.S.C. § 706(8)(C)(ii)(II).

The City also argues that the appellees have not been denied the benefits of the City's zoning activity because they were able to participate in every step of the process: They were given full consideration by the Commissioner, the Corporation Counsel, the Planning Board, and the ZBA. In so arguing, the City has misconstrued the nature of the appellees' complaint. The appellees' claim is not premised on the denial of the right to participate in the zoning approval process. Rather, they allege that they have been denied the benefit of having the City make a zoning decision without regard to the disabilities of IHS's clients. They have therefore made a claim cognizable under both statutes of discrimination. The City additionally contends that the appellees have not produced any evidence of the City's discriminatory motives in denying the building permit to IHS. There is little evidence in the record to support the ZBA's decision on any ground other than the need to alleviate the intense political pressure from the surrounding community brought on by the prospect of drug- and alcohol-addicted neighbors. The public hearings and submitted letters were replete with discriminatory comments about drug- and alcohol-dependent persons based on stereotypes and general, unsupported fears. Although the City certainly may consider legitimate safety concerns in its zoning decisions, it may not base its decisions on the perceived harm from such stereotypes and generalized fears. As the district court found, a decision made in the context of strong, discriminatory opposition becomes tainted with discriminatory intent even if the decision makers personally have no strong views on the matter.

We also find the ZBA's decision to be highly suspect in light of the requirements set forth in the zoning ordinance. The Commissioner and the Corporation Counsel carefully reviewed IHS's application and gave detailed explanations for their approval. The Corporation Counsel analyzed the definition of "hospital or sanitaria" and concluded that because IHS was not an "institution for the purpose of serving general medical, surgical, psychiatric, physical therapy and rehabilitation purposes," it did not fall under this classification. The ZBA, on the other hand, simply stated, without explanation, that IHS was a clinic and thus an impermissible use in the downtown site. The ZBA ignored the requirements of the "hospital or sanitaria" classification and did not explain why it declined to follow the Corporation Counsel's straightforward analysis. Further, although made aware of other similar uses in the same district, the ZBA did not explain the distinction between IHS's proposed use and the other mental health professionals and social workers who do not work exclusively with chemically-dependent persons. On appeal, the City states that the ZBA's decision was "amply supported by legal arguments" without setting forth any of the supposed "legal arguments" for our consideration. The lack of a credible justification for the zoning decision raises an additional inference that the decision was based on impermissible factors, namely the chemical-dependent status of IHS's clients. Accordingly, we see no reason to disturb the district court's finding of likelihood of success on the merits.

. . . .

## Conclusion

Accordingly, we affirm the district court's grant of a preliminary injunction in favor of appellees, except with respect to Martin A., who lacks standing to pursue this claim.

## *Questions for Consideration*

1) What was Innovative Health Systems seeking to do in this case?

2) What was the "classification" issue with respect to the application for a use permit?

3) What was the public reaction to the permit request?

4) What reasons did planning and zoning officials give for denial of the permit?

5) What did the court say with respect to the issue of standing in the case?

### *Takeaway*

- Zoning Boards of Appeal must sometimes make determinations as to the interpretation of a zoning code provision or definition. These interpretations must be rational and reasonable.

- The ADA and the RHA apply to planning and zoning because they are "programs, services, and activities" of local government, as covered under the acts.

- The zoning process must be open to participation by people with disabilities, and the substantive application of the zoning code must comply with regulations protecting the rights of people with disabilities.

# B. Special Use Permit

Many zoning codes provide for a *special use permit* or what is sometimes referred to as a *conditional use permit*. These relate to uses that are generally considered compatible with other uses in a zoning district but are ones that require special and conditional consideration. For example, fast food restaurants with drive-thru windows may be permitted in a zoning district, but they may require a special or conditional use permit so the planning authorities may evaluate the suitability of a location with respect to safe traffic patterns and ingress and egress. If the requested location lacks adequate ingress and egress, or if it poses other traffic issues, it may be denied even though it is otherwise considered an acceptable use in that zoning district. The criteria for evaluating a special use permit and a conditional use permit should be located in the zoning code.

## Wisconsin Community Services, Inc. v. City of Milwaukee

United States Court of Appeals for the Seventh Circuit
465 F.3d 737 (7th Cir. 2006)

RIPPLE, Judge. Wisconsin Community Services ("WCS"), a provider of treatment to mentally ill patients, brought this action under Title II of the Americans with Disabilities Act ("ADA"), 42 U.S.C. §§ 12131–12134, and section 504 of the Rehabilitation Act of 1973, *id.* § 794. The WCS sought an injunction ordering the City of Milwaukee ("the City") to issue a zoning permit that would allow it to move its mental health clinic to an area of Milwaukee, Wisconsin, where health clinics are permitted only on a case-by-case basis. The district court granted partial summary judgment to WCS, concluding that the ADA and the Rehabilitation Act obligated the City to accommodate the disabilities of WCS' patients by allowing WCS to move to its desired location. For the reasons set forth in this opinion, we reverse the judgment of the district court and remand for proceedings consistent with this opinion.

## I. Background

### A. Wisconsin Community Services

WCS is a private, non-profit organization that provides a variety of inpatient and outpatient services to individuals afflicted with severe mental illnesses. WCS provides patients, who cannot live alone without substantial assistance, with psychiatric treatment, counseling, medication monitoring, transportation and help in finding housing and employment. A number of WCS' patients have a history of substance abuse, and a majority have had previous run-ins with the criminal justice system; WCS often accepts patient referrals from court-related agencies such as the United States Probation Service. Although WCS staff sometimes will treat patients in their homes, most of WCS' services are administered in a 7,500 square-foot mental health clinic located at 2023 West Wisconsin Avenue in the City of Milwaukee. Originally, WCS shared this facility with other non-profit organizations, but, as its clientele grew, WCS expanded to occupy the entire building. In 1994, at the time of this initial expansion, WCS employed twenty full-time employees and served 250 patients.

By 1998, the staff at WCS' 2023 West Wisconsin Avenue facility had grown to approximately forty full-time employees serving approximately 400 patients. This increase in clients, services and personnel had caused a shortage in space available for employee parking, client treatment, group therapy sessions and other services. Faced with the shortage, WCS at first considered remodeling, but finally concluded that such a project would be too costly and would interfere with client care. WCS then began searching for a new building. Despite having a limited budget, WCS needed a facility that was located in a safe neighborhood and had adequate floor space, parking and access to public transit. After searching for three years, WCS was able to find two buildings that met its criteria. Neither property, unfortunately, was located in a neighborhood zoned for health clinics. Both were in areas where health clinics are permitted only as "special uses" that require issuance of a permit by the Milwaukee zoning authorities.

WCS previously had received this type of special use permit for some of its other facilities. It therefore made an offer of purchase for one of the properties, contingent on obtaining the necessary special use permit from the Milwaukee zoning board. The seller of this property, concerned about this contingency, declined to accept the offer. WCS then abandoned its efforts to purchase that property and instead made a similar contingent offer on the other identified property. This facility was an 81,000 square-foot building located about one mile from its current facility at 3716 West Wisconsin Avenue. The larger facility is located in an area zoned as a "local business district." Milwaukee, Wis. Code § 295-703-1. According to the City Code's "use table," health care clinics, except for nursing homes, are deemed "special uses" for this zone. Incidentally, the same zone allows foster homes, shelter care facilities, community living arrangements and animal hospitals either as "permitted" or "limited" (no special approval required) uses. The seller accepted WCS' offer.

### B. The First Proceeding Before the Board of Zoning Appeals

Milwaukee's City Code defines "special use" as "[a] use which is generally acceptable in a particular zoning district but which, because of its characteristics and the characteristics of the zoning district in which it would be located, requires review on a case by case basis to determine whether it should be permitted, conditionally permitted, or denied." Milwaukee, Wis.Code § 295-7-166. Special use designations are instruments of municipal planning that allow city officials to retain review power over land uses that, although presumptively allowed, may pose special problems or hazards to a neighborhood.

In Milwaukee, an applicant for a special use permit must present its plans to the Department of City Development ("the DCD"), where they are reviewed by a plan examiner. If the DCD denies the special use application, the applicant may appeal the decision to the Milwaukee Board of Zoning Appeals ("BOZA"), where the application is reviewed, a public hearing is held and evidence is heard. Consistent with this procedure, WCS submitted a plan to DCD, outlining its intent to relocate the mental health clinic and several of its administrative offices to the new building. The plan stated that WCS would occupy 32,000 out of the 81,000 square feet of space in the building. An additional 12,000 square feet, according to the plan, would be occupied by two existing tenants, a Walgreens pharmacy and an office of the Social Security Administration. The remaining 37,000 square feet, the plan stated, would be rented out for use as office space or for other commercial purposes.

Under Wisconsin law, in deciding whether to issue a special use permit, the City's zoning officials are guided by four statutory considerations: (1) protection of public health, safety and welfare; (2) protection of the use, value and enjoyment of other property in the neighborhood; (3) traffic and pedestrian safety; and (4) consistency with the City's comprehensive plan. *See* Milwaukee, Wis. Code § 295-59-5.5. After reviewing WCS' plan, DCD concluded that these criteria had not been met. Specifically, DCD expressed concern over the second factor, protection of neighboring property value. It stated that use of the property as a mental health clinic would jeopardize the commercial revitalization that the neighborhood currently was undergoing. WCS, availing itself of its right to administrative review, then appealed the DCD's decision to Milwaukee's BOZA.

On March 22, 2001, BOZA held a hearing on WCS' appeal. At the outset, WCS argued that, even if its proposal did not meet the special-use criteria, the ADA required BOZA to modify these criteria so that WCS would have the same opportunity to obtain a permit as would a clinic serving non-disabled individuals. BOZA denied this request because it did not believe that it had the authority to deviate from the City's zoning code. Indeed, BOZA prohibited WCS from introducing evidence on the issue. Confined to making its case under the unmodified special use considerations, WCS presented evidence in an effort to refute the perception that the mental health clinic posed a safety threat and would discourage businesses from locating in the neighborhood. This evidence included testimony from a security official who told BOZA that, based on his own investigation, WCS' patients had not been the source of any safety problems in WCS' current neighborhood. WCS also presented letters from its current neighbors to the same effect. Finally, WCS submitted evidence of an award it had received from the National Institute of Justice for exemplary care of previously institutionalized individuals with mental health needs. BOZA then heard testimony in opposition to the permit. An attorney representing several area businesses testified that opening a mental health clinic that serves a large number of young, unemployed males with histories of mental illness and illegal behavior substantially increases the chance of crime and anti-social behavior in the neighborhood. In a similar vein, a nearby high school voiced its fear that WCS' clients would be riding public transit alongside its "young and vulnerable" students. Additionally, a neighborhood organization encouraged residents to object to WCS' request; it circulated leaflets that argued that the clustering of WCS' clientele "in one location on a daily basis raises a serious risk for the health and well being of people living and working in surrounding neighborhoods."

On May 9, 2001, BOZA voted unanimously to deny WCS' application for a special use permit. The accompanying written decision said only that the proposed use was inconsistent with the considerations set forth in the zoning code. However, several board members orally announced the reasoning behind their decision. One member noted that the "overwhelming" opposition from neighborhood residents convinced him that the WCS clinic would have "a damaging effect upon neighboring business." Another member stated that WCS' clientele, with its large number of convicted criminals, raised "red flags" for local residents. These board members did not think that BOZA had the duty to question the "perceptions" of local residents regarding the possible dangers presented by WCS' patients.

### C. The First Federal Court Proceeding

Although Wisconsin law allows for direct review by a Wisconsin state court of adverse BOZA decisions, WCS instead filed the present action in the United States District Court for the Eastern District of Wisconsin. Its complaint alleged that BOZA had violated the ADA and the Rehabilitation Act by failing to make reasonable modifications to its methods for determining whether to issue a special use permit. . . .

The district court held that BOZA had violated the federal disability laws when it failed even to consider making a reasonable modification to its policies to accommodate WCS' request. . . . The court directed that BOZA hear evidence on WCS' accommodation claim and determine: (1) whether WCS' patients are "disabled"; (2) whether the requested accommodation is "reasonable" and "necessary"; and (3) whether the requested relief would work a "fundamental change" to the services being rendered.

### D. The Second Proceeding Before the Board of Zoning Appeals

On September 12, 2002, BOZA reconvened a public hearing to decide whether, and to what extent, the ADA and the Rehabilitation Act required it to modify its zoning policies in considering WCS' application for a special use permit. BOZA heard testimony regarding the necessity of a modification, whether such modification was a reasonable accommodation and whether it might work any fundamental change on the City's zoning practices.

Jill Fuller, WCS' clinic administrator, was the first to testify. She described the state of overcrowding at WCS' current facility and the effect that these conditions were having on WCS' patients. . . . Overcrowding in the common area of WCS' facility—a room described by another WCS administrator as noisy, smoky and packed—created an extremely stressful environment for these patients and caused their symptoms to become more acute. Additionally, Fuller testified that overcrowding compromised the privacy of one-on-one therapy sessions, which represent a primary component of WCS' treatment.

WCS then presented testimony from its executive director, Stephen Swigart. He described the search process under-taken by WCS to find a new facility that, in addition to being of adequate size, would satisfy the clinic's need for a central location, access to public transit, a serviceable floor plan, low renovation costs and a safe neighborhood. Swigart testified that, after being denied the special use permit, WCS had worked with city planners to locate a suitably zoned property, but that its efforts had been unsuccessful. Any potential alternatives, Swigart explained, were either unavailable or too costly.

Finally, WCS presented expert testimony from Dr. Nancy Frank, the Chair and Associate Dean of the Department of Architecture and Urban Planning at the University of Wisconsin-Milwaukee. She opined that locating the mental health clinic at WCS' desired location, 3716 West Wisconsin Avenue, would have a positive rather than an adverse effect on the surrounding neighborhood. Pointing out that a properly zoned health clinic already was located directly across the street from the proposed site, Frank noted that WCS' clinic would be a consistent addition to the neighborhood and encourage commercial uses of a similar nature. In addition, Frank testified that the building at 3716 West Wisconsin Avenue had been mostly vacant for some time. According to Frank, the goal of city planners seeking to revitalize a commercial area should be to fill vacant space as quickly as possible. Frank predicted that relocating WCS and all of its employees to the area would attract businesses such as "restaurants, dry cleaners [and] coffee shops" eager to serve the new influx of professionals. . . . When asked about safety concerns, Frank stated that four of the six parole offices in the City of Milwaukee were located in areas zoned for business use. Frank saw no reason why WCS' clinic would present any more of a safety risk than these offices.

BOZA then heard testimony from Michael Murphy, an alderman representing the area in which WCS was seeking to relocate its clinic. Steadfastly opposed to

WCS' plans, Alderman Murphy stated that "WCS' thrust to rip an 81,000 square foot building out of the heart of this emerging business district could be fatal to this area." When pressed on whether the new clinic conceivably could bring economic benefits to the neighborhood, Alderman Murphy conceded that the influx of professionals potentially could draw new businesses. He stated, nevertheless, that he objected to the plan because it meant that WCS, as a non-profit, would not pay tax on the space used for its clinic and operations; Alderman Murphy preferred a tax-paying commercial tenant in the space. Notably, the only submission on whether WCS' patients were a safety risk to the community were affidavits from business owners near the proposed site. None of these opinions, however, was supported by actual evidence.

On December 22, 2002, BOZA issued a written decision denying the special use permit to WCS. It concluded that WCS' claim for an accommodation under the disabilities laws failed because such an accommodation was neither reasonable nor necessary. On the question of necessity, BOZA framed the inquiry as "whether the requested accommodation will ameliorate, that is, directly improve the burden of the mental illnesses from which [WCS' patients] suffer." Concluding that WCS had not satisfied its burden on this issue, BOZA noted that mental illness, unlike a physical impairment, "is not a one size fits all handicap or disability within the ADA." Rather, in BOZA's view, the mental disabilities suffered by WCS' patients were likely to vary dramatically across the patient population. It was therefore, according to BOZA, a "gross overgeneralization and speculation" for WCS to contend that each of its patients would respond favorably to treatment in the new, larger facility. Moreover, in BOZA's estimation, the factors considered by WCS in seeking out a new facility were not linked to its patients' disabilities. According to BOZA, "[t]he WCS search criteria resemble those of many other commercial businesses, profit or non profit, which have outgrown their physical premises and want to move into a larger setting."

BOZA concluded that, in addition to being unnecessary, the requested accommodation also was unreasonable. In making this determination, BOZA stressed that the relocation of WCS' clinic to its proposed site would "place an undue financial burden on the district," threatening "the economic survival [of] this already shaky neighborhood." According to BOZA, these costs to the City were not outweighed by the needs of WCS because WCS apparently had other relocation options available in other neighborhoods.

Finally, BOZA determined that the requested accommodation, in addition to being unreasonable and unnecessary, fundamentally would alter the City's zoning scheme:

> Every time a social service agency, AA club, homeless shelter serving mentally ill homeless people; hospital, psychologists or psychiatrists [sic] office, therapists' office, etc. wanted to locate their business in a zoning district requiring a special use to do so, the City or this Board would have to automatically consider giving them an accommodation under ADA regardless of the special use criteria in the City's ordinance.

### E. The Second Federal Court Proceeding

On January 24, 2003, WCS reinstated its action in federal court challenging the second BOZA ruling. It alleged that the City's refusal to grant WCS a special use permit violated the ADA and the Rehabilitation Act. In determining the standard that it ought to employ in assessing WCS' accommodation claim, the district court declined, despite the parties' recommendation, to apply the test that governs cases arising under the Fair Housing Amendments Act of 1988 ("FHAA"). The FHAA requires a reasonable accommodation to zoning rules when necessary to afford a handicapped person the "equal opportunity" to obtain housing. 42 U.S.C. § 3604(f) (3)(B). In the district court's view, this standard did not apply to the present case because WCS sought its accommodation not to obtain housing but to provide mental health services to its patients. Moreover, the court continued, "unlike housing, the general public does not require mental health services; thus, in the present case, it makes little sense to inquire whether the disabled are entitled to equal opportunity to such services."

Instead, relying upon our decision in *Oconomowoc Residential Programs, Inc. v. City of Milwaukee*, 300 F.3d 775 (7th Cir. 2002), the court held that, to satisfy its initial burden, WCS must show that its requested accommodation is (1) reasonable and (2) necessary to enhance affirmatively its disabled patients' "'quality of life by ameliorating the effects of the disability.'" Once WCS had made this showing, according to the district court, the City then must "demonstrate unreasonableness or undue hardship in the particular circumstances."

### II. Discussion

### A.

The legal question before us is whether, and to what extent, a city must modify its zoning standards to prevent them from discriminating against the disabled. The statutes relevant to answering that question are three separate but interrelated federal laws that protect persons with disabilities from discrimination. The first two laws chronologically were the Rehabilitation Act of 1973 and the FHAA. Enactment of the ADA followed in 1990. All three statutory schemes embrace the concept that, in certain instances, the policies and practices of covered entities must be modified to accommodate the needs of the disabled. We now shall examine each statute's accommodation requirement in detail.

### 1. The Rehabilitation Act of 1973

The Rehabilitation Act, 29 U.S.C. § 701 et seq., applies to federal government agencies as well as organizations that receive federal funds. The parties in this case stipulated that the City receives federal funding and is therefore covered by the Rehabilitation Act. Much of the Rehabilitation Act focuses on employment, but section 504 broadly covers other types of programs and activities as well. Section 504(a) provides that "[n]o otherwise qualified individual with a disability in the United States . . . shall, solely by reason of her or his disability, be excluded from the participation in, be denied the benefits of, or be subjected to discrimination under any program or activity receiving Federal financial assistance. . . ." 29 U.S.C. § 794(a).

. . . .

. . . [T]he Supreme Court has located a duty to accommodate in the statute generally. . . .

. . . .

. . . [S]everal courts of appeals have adopted the view that the Rehabilitation Act requires public entities to modify federally assisted programs if such a modification is necessary to ensure that the disabled have equal access to the benefits of that program. . . .

### 2. The Fair Housing Amendments Act

The duty to accommodate imposed by the FHAA, 42 U.S.C. § 3601 et seq., mirrors in large part the modification obligations under the Rehabilitation Act. Enacted in 1988, the FHAA extended the scope of other federal housing laws to cover persons with disabilities. Under these amendments, disabled individuals may not be prevented from buying or renting private housing because of their disabilities. *See id.* § 3604. They also must be provided reasonable "accommodation in rules, policies, practices, or services when such accommodation may be necessary to afford [them] equal opportunity to use and enjoy a dwelling." *Id.* § 3604(f)(3)(B).

. . . The basic elements of an FHAA accommodation claim are well-settled. First, the requested accommodation must be reasonable, which, as we have stated, is a "highly fact-specific inquiry and requires balancing the needs of the parties. An accommodation is reasonable if it is both efficacious and proportional to the costs to implement it." In the zoning context, a municipality may show that a modification to its policy is "unreasonable if it is so at odds with the purpose behind the rule that it would be a fundamental and unreasonable change."

Second, the requested accommodation must be "necessary," meaning that, without the accommodation, the plaintiff will be denied an equal opportunity to obtain the housing of her choice. . . .

In addition, the FHAA links the term "necessary" to the goal of "equal opportunity." 42 U.S.C. § 3604(f)(3)(B). The "equal opportunity" element limits the accommodation duty so that not every rule that creates a general inconvenience or expense to the disabled needs to be modified. Instead, the statute requires only accommodations necessary to ameliorate the effect of the plaintiff's disability so that she may compete equally with the non-disabled in the housing market. . . .

. . . .

### 3. Title II of the Americans with Disabilities Act

The ADA was built on the Rehabilitation Act and the FHAA, but extends the reach of those laws substantially. Invoking "the sweep of congressional authority, including the power to enforce the fourteenth amendment and to regulate commerce," the ADA was designed "to provide a clear and comprehensive national mandate for the elimination of discrimination against individuals with disabilities." 42 U.S.C. § 12101(b)(1), (b)(4). It forbids discrimination against persons with disabilities in three major areas of public life: (1) employment, which is covered by Title I of the statute; (2) public services, programs and activities, which are the subjects of Title II; and (3) public and private lodging, which is covered by Title III.

This case concerns Title II, commonly referred to as the public services portion of the ADA. Title II provides that "no qualified individual with a disability shall, by reason of such disability, be excluded from participation in or be denied the benefits of the services, programs, or activities of a public entity." 42 U.S.C. § 12132.

As courts have held, municipal zoning qualifies as a public "program" or "service," as those terms are employed in the ADA, and the enforcement of those rules is an "activity" of a local government. . . .

Unlike Title I and Title III, Title II of the ADA does not contain a specific accommodation requirement. Instead, the Attorney General, at the instruction of Congress, has issued an implementing regulation that outlines the duty of a public entity to accommodate reasonably the needs of the disabled. The Title II regulation reads:

> A public entity shall make reasonable modifications in policies, practices, or procedures when the modifications are necessary to avoid discrimination on the basis of disability, unless the public entity can demonstrate that making the modifications would fundamentally alter the nature of the service, program, or activity.

28 C.F.R. § 35.130(b)(7).

. . . First, as our cases already hold, failure to accommodate is an *independent* basis for liability under the ADA. Second, the plain language of the regulation also makes clear that an accommodation only is required when *necessary* to avoid discrimination *on the basis of* a disability. Third, the regulation states, in its plain language, that any accommodation must be a *reasonable* one. We shall now examine each of these features of the regulation, keeping in mind that Congress has expressed its desire that interpretation of the ADA be compatible with interpretation of the other federal disability statutes, a point also made clear in several holdings of the Supreme Court.

Under the Title II regulation, a modification must be "necessary to avoid discrimination on the basis of disability." . . .

. . . .

The regulation also requires that any accommodation be a reasonable one. In the context of the FHAA, we have interpreted this requirement to mandate an inquiry into whether the accommodation is "both efficacious and proportional to the costs to implement it." In the zoning context, a municipality may show that a modification to its policy is "unreasonable if it is so at odds with the purpose behind the rule that it would be a fundamental and unreasonable change." This assessment is "a highly fact-specific inquiry and requires balancing the needs of both parties." In this regard, we think it is important to note that, in undertaking this highly fact-specific assessment, it is necessary that the court take into consideration *all* of the costs to *both* parties. Some of these costs may be objective and easily ascertainable. Others may be more subjective and require that the court demonstrate a good deal of wisdom in appreciating the intangible but very real human costs associated with the disability in question. On the other side of the equation, some governmental costs associated with the specific program at issue may be a matter of simply looking at a balance sheet. Others, however, may be those intangible values of community life that are very important if that community is to thrive and is to address the needs of its citizenry.

We pause to emphasize one other important feature of the Title II regulation. We think that the regulation makes clear that the duty to accommodate is an independent basis of liability under the ADA. The language of the regulation itself certainly supports this view. By requiring measures that are "necessary to avoid discrimination on the basis of disability," 28 C.F.R. § 35.130(b)(7), the regulation clearly contemplates that prophylactic steps must be taken to avoid discrimination. . . .

Under the law of this circuit, a plaintiff need not allege either disparate treatment or disparate impact in order to state a reasonable accommodation claim under Title II of the ADA. In sum, a Title II claim under the ADA "may be established by evidence that (1) the defendant intentionally acted on the basis of the disability, (2) the defendant refused to provide a reasonable modification, or (3) the defendant's rule disproportionally impacts disabled people."

### B.

. . . In essence, we must decide whether, and to what extent, the Rehabilitation Act and Title II require the City to modify its zoning practices in order to accommodate the needs of the disabled individuals served by WCS.

WCS submits that the City must waive application of its normal special-use criteria for WCS because it has shown that granting the permit will ameliorate overcrowding, a condition that particularly affects its disabled clients. Before accepting this position, however, we must ask whether WCS has satisfied the "necessity" element contained in the Rehabilitation Act. . . . WCS contends that the necessity element is satisfied simply when a modification *helps* the disabled, regardless of whether it is *necessary* to alleviate discrimination. Implicit in this position is that the federal accommodation obligation reaches not only rules that create barriers "on the basis of" a person's disability, but also rules that are not disability-based and create obstacles to persons because of some factor unrelated to disability.

. . . [W]ith respect to the Rehabilitation Act, . . . a modification is "necessary" only when it allows the disabled to obtain benefits that they ordinarily could not have by reason of their disabilities, and not because of some quality that they share with the public generally. . . . (asking whether the rule in question, if left unmodified, hurts "handicapped people *by reason of their handicap*, rather than . . . by virtue of what they have in common with other people, such as a limited amount of money to spend on housing"). The inquiry is the same under the ADA regulation, . . . the element is satisfied only when the plaintiff shows that, "but for" his disability, he would have been able to access the services or benefits desired.

On the present record, WCS' inability to meet the City's special use criteria appears due not to its client's disabilities but to its plan to open a non-profit health clinic in a location where the City desired a commercial, taxpaying tenant instead. As far as this record indicates, the City would have rejected similar proposals from non-profit health clinics serving the non-disabled. WCS contends that Title II's accommodation requirement calls, in such a situation, for "'preferential' treatment and 'is not limited only to lowering barriers created by the disability itself.'" WCS' view, however, is inconsistent with the "necessity" element as it has been defined under the Rehabilitation Act, the FHAA and Title II of the ADA. On this record, because the mental illness of WCS' patients is not the cause-in-fact of WCS' inability to obtain a suitable facility, the program that it seeks modified does not hurt persons with disabilities "*by reason of their handicap.*"

. . . .

. . . [T]o satisfy Title II's necessity element, a plaintiff must show that, "but for" its disability, it would have received the ultimate benefit being sought — which, in WCS' case, is a larger facility. The same is true under the Rehabilitation Act. . . . WCS must demonstrate that, *because* of its clients' disabilities, it cannot relocate to a suitable site. Only then will the unmodified policy hurt the disabled *on account of* their disability. Only then will the modification be "necessary to avoid discrimination on the basis of disability."

The district court assumed that the proposed modification could be deemed "necessary" even if the disabilities suffered by WCS' patients were not the cause-in-fact of its inability to find a larger building. The district court failed to apply a "but for" causation standard in determining the necessity element of WCS' accommodation claim. Choosing this course was error in light of the prevailing standards under our case law. We therefore must remand to the district court so that it may afford the parties the opportunity to develop the question of whether WCS has been prevented, *because of its clients' disabilities*, from locating a satisfactory new facility.

### Conclusion

For the foregoing reasons, we reverse the judgment of the district court and remand for proceedings consistent with this opinion. The City may recover its costs in this court.

Reversed and Remanded.

## *Questions for Consideration*

1) What services does Wisconsin Community Services (WCS) provide and what is it seeking to do in this case?

2) How does a special use permit application differ from the use permit request in the *Innovative Health Systems* case?

3) What are the criteria to be satisfied for a special use permit under the applicable zoning code?

4) What type of evidence is introduced in the proceedings?

5) What were the factors considered by the court regarding the classification of WCS's use in this case?

6) Are there identifiable alternative locations for the proposed use?

7) What reasons did the zoning board give for its decision?

8) What are the criteria for a reasonable accommodation and what was the discussion concerning each of the criteria?

9) What does the court say about the RHA, FHA, and ADA as applicable to this case?

## Takeaway

- Even though the RHA, FHA, and ADA do not directly state that they apply to planning and zoning, this case along with others included in this book show that the courts have clearly concluded that planning and zoning are covered by each of these acts.

- It is important for a zoning board to make a clear record of the reasons and justifications for its decisions, because their decisions must be supported by competent evidence on the record.

- It is the job of the attorneys representing the parties to make sure that there is ample evidence submitted, on the record, to support a decision in their client's favor.

# C. Variances

Variances are exceptions to the strict requirements of the zoning code. A petition for a variance can be for either an *area variance* or a *use variance*. An area variance involves a request for an exception from regulations covering such things as the setback distance between a structure and a road or a property line, the amount of lot coverage occupied by a structure, and the height of a structure. A use variance involves a petition to allow *a use* that is otherwise not permitted by the zoning code. A use variance is more difficult to obtain. Traditionally, an area variance requires a property owner to demonstrate a *practical difficulty* with complying with the code, and a use variance requires a *unique or undue hardship*. There may be specific criteria arising from case law or as provided in a statute or ordinance that apply to variance requests in specific situations and jurisdictions. An appropriate party may challenge the granting of a variance as well as the denial of a variance.

Traditionally a variance, once granted, *runs with the land.* This means that the variance continues for the benefit of subsequent owners of the property.

As an example of a state that has sought to clarify the criteria for granting an area and a use variance, consider New York. (*See, e.g.,* N.Y. Town Law section 267-b(2) & (3).) In granting a petition for an *area variance* under New York law, the applicant must address five criteria (identified below). The applicant should present evidence in support of the petition for a *variance.* This evidence should include photos of the property and surrounding neighborhood, letters from neighbors, land surveys, and whatever other evidence might be appropriate in terms of addressing each of the criteria. In granting an area variance, a zoning board of appeal must determine that, "on balance," the benefits to the applicant outweigh the detriments to the community. The five criteria for an *area variance* are:

1) Whether an undesirable change will be produced in the character of the neighborhood or a detriment to nearby properties will be created by granting the area variance;

2) Whether the benefits sought by the applicant can be achieved by some method feasible for the applicant to pursue, other than the area variance;

3) Whether the requested variance is substantial;

4) Whether the proposed variance will have an adverse effect or impact on the physical or environmental conditions in the neighborhood or district; and,

5) Whether the alleged difficulty was self-created, which consideration shall be relevant to the decision of the board of appeals, but shall not necessarily preclude the granting of the area variance.

While each of the criteria must be addressed, the area variance involves a balancing test and no single criteria is determinative.

A *use variance* generally requires that a property owner demonstrate that the permitted uses under the zoning code impose an undue hardship with respect to her property. In New York, there are four established criteria used to evaluate a petition for a use variance. In order to obtain a use variance under New York law, a zoning board of appeal must find in favor of the property owner on each and every one of the four identified criteria. This is not a balancing test as used for an area variance. The criteria for a *use variance* in New York are:

1) The applicant cannot realize a reasonable return [for every permitted use of the property], provided that lack of return is substantial as demonstrated by competent financial evidence;

2) The alleged hardship relating to the property in question is unique and does not apply to a substantial portion of the district or neighborhood;

3) The required use variance, if granted will not alter the essential character of the neighborhood; and

4) The alleged hardship has not been self-created.

Only if a favorable determination is made for the property owner as to each and every one of the four criteria can a use variance be granted.

## Mastandrea v. North

Court of Appeals of Maryland
760 A.2d 677 (Md. 2000)

HARRELL, Judge. We issued a writ of certiorari on our own initiative in this appeal, before it was considered by the Court of Special Appeals, primarily to consider the question of whether Title II of the Americans With Disabilities Act (42 U.S.C. §§ 12131–12134) applies to the administration and enforcement of the Talbot County Zoning Ordinance (the Zoning Ordinance or Z.O.), and specifically its provisions governing variances for property within the Chesapeake Bay Critical Area lying within Talbot County. . . . [W]e . . . conclude that the Board's grant of the variance was supported by substantial evidence on the record before the Board.

### I.

Dr. and Mrs. John P. Mastandrea (Appellants) purchased in December 1992 an approximately 12 acre undeveloped, but subdivided, lot with frontage on Glebe Creek in Talbot County. Over the next 4 years or so, the Mastandreas, for themselves and their family, constructed on the lot a home, swimming pool, tennis court, pier, garden, and an extensive set of pathways connecting these improvements. Included in the pathway system, installed personally in 1996 by Dr. Mastandrea and his three eldest sons, were a brick-in-cement path connecting the house and pier and a brick-in-sand path roughly parallel to and within 20–25 feet of the bulkheaded edge of Glebe Creek. A primary reason given for installing the extensive, connecting path system was that the Mastandreas' daughter, Leah, suffered from muscular dystrophy (a progressively degenerative neurological and muscular disease) and was confined to a motorized wheelchair for mobility purposes. In order that she might access all of the property's amenities, and partake of them to some extent with her siblings, the pathways were designed to facilitate her movement by wheelchair. Much of the design and construction of the improvements on the lot also considered wheelchair access as an integral goal.

The Mastandreas installed the pathways without the benefit of a required building permit from Talbot County (or any form of prior governmental blessing or review) and heedless of the fact that a portion of the pathways were placed within the 100 foot buffer of the Chesapeake Bay Critical Area adjacent to Glebe Creek. The brick-in-cement portion of that path within the Critical Area buffer comprised 711 square feet of surface area. The brick-in-sand portion covered 4486 square feet of the surface of the Critical Area buffer. Together, the surface areas of these two components of the overall path system represented 4% of the total Critical Area buffer identified on the lot. Discovery by the authorities of the unauthorized installation led, among other things, to the Mastandreas filing on 29 January 1998 a variance application with the Board in an effort to validate the pathways constructed within the Critical Area buffer.

Zoning Ordinance § 19.12(b)(5)(iii)(b) defines the Critical Area buffer as being "at least 100 feet wide, measured landward from the Mean Highwater Line of tidal waters and tidal wetlands, and from tributary streams." The need for a variance for those portions of the pathways located within 100 feet of the shore of Glebe Creek is necessitated by Z.O. § 19.12(b)(5)(iii)(c), which prohibits "[n]ew development activities, including structures, roads, parking areas and other impervious surfaces" in the buffer.

At the time the Mastandreas filed their variance application, Z.O. § 19.14(b)(3)(iv) required the following favorable findings to be made by the Board before it could grant a variance from the Critical Area regulations:

(iv) In order to vary or modify the Talbot County Critical Area provisions of this Ordinance, the Board of Appeals must determine that the application meets all of the criteria set forth below.

[a] Special conditions or circumstances exist that are peculiar to the land or structure such that a literal enforcement of the provisions of this Ordinance would result in unwarranted hardship to the property owner;

[b] A literal interpretation of this Ordinance will deprive the property owner of rights commonly enjoyed by other property owners in the same zone;

[c] The granting of a variance will not confer upon the property owner any special privilege that would be denied by this Ordinance to other owners of lands or structures within the same zone;

[d] The variance request is not based on conditions or circumstances which are the result of actions by the property owner nor does the request arise from any condition relating to land or building use, either permitted or nonconforming, on any neighboring property;

[e] The granting of a variance within the Critical Area will not adversely affect water quality or adversely impact fish, wildlife, or plant habitat and the granting of the variance will be in harmony with the general spirit and intent of the Critical Area Law, the Talbot County Critical Area Plan and the regulations adopted in this Ordinance;

[f] The variance shall not exceed the minimum adjustment necessary to relieve the unwarranted hardship; and

[g] The granting of the variance will not adversely affect water quality or adversely impact fish, wildlife or plant habitat, and the granting of the variance will be in harmony with the general spirit and intent of the Critical Area Law, the Talbot County Critical Area Program and the Critical Area provisions of this Ordinance.

At the Board's 11 May 1998 hearing on the Mastandreas' application, the applicants, in support of their principal theme that the variance should be granted as a reasonable accommodation of Leah's disability so that she could access the pier and enjoy the shoreline of Glebe Creek, mustered both testimony and exhibits. They explained that the pathways were located to allow a wheelchair to get close enough that Leah could enjoy the waterfront, but not so close as to be dangerous. According to the Mastandreas, the natural slope and the soil composition of the lot near the shoreline (except for the direct pier access) did not permit wheelchair access directly to the waterfront. Placing the pathways outside the 100 foot buffer, however, would deny a wheelchair occupant access to and enjoyment of the waterfront, they contended. The pathways permitted Leah to enjoy the natural and recreational aspects of her family's waterfront lot and were the only means by which Leah could accompany her brothers and sisters on walks and other activities on the lot. Mrs. Mastandrea testified that her daughter's ability to have access to the waterfront is one of the few pleasures that she still is able to enjoy due to the physical effects of her disorder.

The (brick-in-concrete) pier access pathway was designed to prevent a wheelchair from gaining momentum on the natural downslope from the house to the water. A pathway constructed in a straight line from the house to the pier, without the slope break provided by the Mastandreas' construction, would create a dangerous situation for a person confined to a wheelchair.

Dr. Mastandrea testified that in constructing the brick-in-sand pathway parallel to Glebe Creek his sons removed about six inches of turf, surface soil, and clay, and replaced it with three to five inches of sand. An environmental consultant, Ronald Gatton, testified that he was familiar with the Mastandreas' property and the intent of the Critical Area laws to reduce the amount of runoff into the Chesapeake Bay and its tributaries. Mr. Gatton testified that the soil of the lot was one of the heaviest clay soils that he had ever tested. He conducted an infiltration test on the brick-in-sand path and determined that water permeated the brick-in-sand pathway faster than the surrounding undisturbed soil, making the path three times as permeable as the surrounding lawn. Mr. Gatton stated that because the natural soil conditions in the area tended to be very stiff, with a "plastic" quality, it was his opinion that the pathway parallel to the creek actually intercepts much of the runoff from the lawn between the house and the path before entering Glebe Creek.

Dr. Mastandrea explained that during the initial construction of the home he removed a number of trees, mainly from the shoreline, to allow bulkheading. Prior to bulkheading, the shoreline was eroding under the bordering trees. The Mastandreas replaced the removed trees and vegetation with approximately 100 eight-to-twelve foot trees and approximately 1000 three-foot seedlings planted throughout the lot. Overall, they installed approximately 2000 new plantings on the property.

The Critical Area Commission (the Commission) presented one witness in opposition to the variance request. Mr. Gregory L. Schaner, a Natural Resources Planner for the Commission, opined that the requirements for granting a variance were not met by the Mastandreas. Mr. Schaner re-stated the position of the Commission, previously set forth in a 9 April 1998 letter to the Talbot County Planning Commission, that the Commission recommended denial of the variance request and that the Mastandreas be required to remove all portions of the pertinent pathways, except for an immediate perpendicular access from the house to the pier. As to the house-to-pier connection, Mr. Schaner recommended that the Board require that the Mastandreas remove all portions of the pathway, including the circular, wheelchair "break" areas designed to reduce a wheelchair's momentum on the way toward the pier, and suggested that the Board allow only a single, straight-line path from the house to the pier. He acknowledged that the Commission had not conducted any environmental impact studies or tests to ascertain the actual impact, if any, of the relevant pathways in the Critical Area buffer on the lot or the water quality of Glebe Creek. Mr. Schaner also acknowledged that there were, at that time, no provisions in the Critical Area regulations (State or county) or the Z.O. variance provisions expressly taking into account handicapped access considerations.

The Board, in split decisions rendered on 27 July 1998, voted to grant legitimizing variances for the existing pathway from the house to the pier (by a 4-1 vote) and for the existing pathway parallel to Glebe Creek (by a 3-2 vote). Essentially, the Board majority in each instance concluded that the paths provided reasonable access to the waterfront for handicapped persons and were reasonable accommodations for Leah's disability. The Board majority was impressed also with the mitigation effects of the Mastandreas' plantings and the permeability enhancement of the brick-in-sand pathway. Accordingly, the Board made written findings on 21 October 1998 favorable to the Mastandreas' application, as required by Z.O. §19.14(b)(3)(iv).

The Commission (Appellee) timely sought judicial review of the Board's decision in the Circuit Court for Talbot County. The Mastandreas, in their memorandum of law supporting affirmance of the Board's decision, offered their now flagship legal argument that Title II of the federal Americans With Disabilities Act (ADA) not only applied to the Board's consideration of their variance application, but compelled its approval on the evidence before the Board. In essence, the Mastandreas argued that public entities, such as the Board, are required by the ADA to make reasonable modifications to their policies, practices, and procedures (such as the Z.O. provisions prohibiting new impervious surfaces within the Critical Area buffer), when necessary to avoid discrimination on the basis of a disability, unless it is shown that the modifications sought would alter fundamentally the nature of the service, program, or activity. Therefore, as Appellants' argument went, the Board's grant of the variance on the record before it, especially in light of the absence in the record of any contrary evidence that the variance would affirmatively harm the water quality of Glebe Creek or the Critical Area buffer on the lot, resulted in the reasonable accommodation of Leah's disability, as directed by the ADA and extant case law interpreting its application to land use regulations.

Appellee's response to Appellants' ADA argument in the Circuit Court, delivered at oral argument on 4 June 1999, was that the ADA did not apply to the present case. The Commission asserted that the most that could be gleaned from the case law interpreting Title II was that "zoning authorities must make their decisions in a neutral manner, that is without regard to the disabilities of the applicant." The environmentally-justified, all-embracing prohibition against the development of new impervious surfaces within the Critical Area buffer was not a law that discriminated, argued the Commission's attorney. Moreover, as the argument continued, the ADA did not trump or compel the grant of variances in the present case merely because each resident of the house on the lot could not enjoy unfettered access to every part of the lot, i.e., "there is no . . . fundamental right to lateral shoreline access on the part of anyone with private property."

. . . .

## II.

### A.

. . . [T]he Mastandreas contend that the Circuit Court erred in concluding that Title II of the ADA is limited to places of public accommodation and does not apply to local land use regulatory actions. . . .

Even though there was scant reference to the ADA in the record before the Board and no express reliance on the ADA in the Board's written findings of fact and conclusions of law granting the variance, it is clear that the Board considered and relied on Leah's disability in its application of the Critical Area variance standards in Z.O. § 19.14(b)(3)(iv). The Board's pertinent conclusions of law stated:

[1. The first conclusion is omitted.]

2. There are special conditions or circumstances which exist that are peculiar to the subject property such a literal enforcement of the provisions of the ordinance would result in unwarranted hardship to the property owner. The property is a large parcel with a substantial amount of waterfront. A walkway only to the pier on this property does not provide reasonable access to the entire waterfront area of the property if a walkway is the only means by which a resident can gain access to the waterfront. Part of the reasonable use of such a property is access to the entire waterfront, not just the pier. The lateral walkways within the buffer providing such access to a handicapped resident of the property amount to only about four percent of the entire surface area of the buffer, an amount which can easily be offset by mitigating plantings on the property and the Applicant appears to have already mitigated much of the potential increase in runoff from the lateral walkway by existing and planned landscaping. (The property was previously cultivated annually as farm property.)

3. A literal interpretation of the ordinance will deprive the property owner of rights commonly enjoyed by other property owners in the

same zone. Access to the waterfront of the property for the Applicant's daughter is limited by her disability. Most people fortunate enough to live on waterfront property have access to the entire waterfront without having special walkways disturbing the buffer zone vegetation. The special circumstances of this resident will deprive her of that access commonly enjoyed by others.

4. The granting of the variance will not confer upon the property owner any special privilege that would be denied by the ordinance to other owners of lands or structures within the same zone. The walkways constructed by the Applicants are a reasonable accommodation for the special circumstances of the Applicants and should be granted to all owners of land in similar circumstances.

5. The variance request is not based on conditions or circumstances which are the result of actions by the property owner. By their actions, the Applicants purchased the property and placed the walkways where they are. However, they simply desire equal access to as much of the enjoyment of the property for their handicapped daughter as reasonably possible. The walkways are the least objectionable means to that end to accommodate her special circumstance which, of course, is not a result of their choice. The request does not arise from any condition relating to land or building use, either permitted or nonconforming, on any neighboring property.

6. The proposed variance will not adversely affect water quality or adversely impact fish, wildlife, or plant habitat and the granting of the variance will be in harmony with the general spirit and intent of the Critical Area Law, the Talbot County Critical Area Plan and the regulations adopted in the Ordinance. While the walkways exceed that which is normally required to provide direct access to a pier on the property the excess is minimal and can easily be mitigated.

In this appeal, neither side argues that the Board should not have considered Leah's disability. Rather, Appellants would have us affirm the Board because, on this record, the ADA compels that result. . . .

. . . .

## B.

. . . .

The pith of the Mastandreas argument is that the Board of Appeals implicitly recognized the need to accommodate disabled persons despite restrictions imposed by the neutral Critical Area zoning criteria and that reasonable accommodations were possible without fundamentally altering the nature of the Critical Area program. We find this argument to be persuasive given the record evidence supporting the Board's conclusion that the pathway in question provides Leah with reasonable and significant use of the lot, but does not impact adversely the Chesapeake Bay. Given the unique dependence many disabled persons have on wheelchairs, the path constitutes a reasonable modification to the relevant zoning ordinance requirement and enables such a disabled person to enjoy the waterfront within the Critical Area buffer equally with a non-disabled person. . . .

### C.

. . . .

In this case, we find no practical reason to remand the case for further consideration by the Board. Review of the record and the Board's written findings of fact and conclusions of law makes clear that the Board took Leah's disability into consideration when making each required finding under Z.O. § 19.14(b)(3)(iv). By both accommodating Leah's needs and satisfying the requirements of the Zoning Ordinance, the Board acted within the scope of both Title II of the ADA and Bill No. 741. The Board, in effect, applied the correct standard in considering the Mastandreas' variance application. . . . Therefore, there is no purpose to be served by a remand, if the Board's findings and conclusions are sustainable otherwise on the record before it.

### III.

. . . .

. . . In our opinion, the intent of the Zoning Ordinance is aimed at the cautious and thoughtful consideration and, where appropriate, granting of variances within the Critical Area on a case-by-case basis. Under Talbot County law, such variances are appropriate when their applications meet the Critical Area criteria and, where necessary, create reasonable accommodations for the needs of disabled citizens.

Although the Mastandreas' paths did create some 5000 square feet of new impervious surface area within the buffer, the evidence indicated that the brick-in-sand path was actually three times as permeable as the surrounding natural lawn, and that much of the potential increase in runoff from the other pertinent pathways was mitigated by landscaping. The Board's conclusion that these extensive mitigating factors do not impact adversely fish, wildlife, or plant habitat and are in harmony with the Zoning Ordinance's intent was supported by the record evidence. . . .

### Conclusion

In conclusion, we find that the Board considered all of the factors required under Talbot County Zoning Ordinance § 19.14(b)(3)(iv) and, after weighing the evidence before it, permissibly decided to make a reasonable accommodation of Leah Mastandreas' disability in granting the variance for the pathway in the Critical Area buffer parallel to Glebe Creek. Given the substantial evidence before the Board and the Board's application of the variance criteria to that evidence, we hold that there was no basis for the Circuit Court's reversal. The Mastandreas and the Board have met generally the requirements of the Talbot County Zoning Ordinance.

Judgment of the circuit court for Talbot county reversed; case remanded to the circuit court with directions to affirm the decision of the board of appeals of Talbot county.

## Questions for Consideration

1) Who objected to the granting of the variance in this case?

2) What special criteria were applicable to the granting of a variance in this situation?

3) What evidence was presented with respect to the hearing regarding the granting or denial of the variance?

4) What findings were made as to each criterion considered in evaluating the request for a variance in this case?

## Takeaway

• Mastandrea constructed the various walkways on his property without approval. After the fact, he sought an area variance. This is problematic. A zoning board, in such a situation, is supposed to consider the various criteria for the granting of a variance without being swayed by the fact that the work has already been done. This means that the zoning board is not supposed to give any special equity to the fact that a lot of money may have already been spent by the property owner, and that it may cost even more money to undo the work completed.

• Granting of a variance may be challenged by an interested party with standing if there is a belief that the granting of the variance was improper.

• A zoning board decision will be upheld when the zoning board provides justification for its decision, and the decision is rational and supported by competent evidence on the record.

## Bryant Woods Inn, Inc. v. Howard County

### United States Court of Appeals for the Fourth Circuit
### 124 F.3d 597 (4th Cir. 1997)

NIEMEYER, Judge. Bryant Woods Inn, Inc., a group home for handicapped persons, seeks to expand from 8 residents to 15 residents. When Howard County, Maryland, refused to waive its neutral zoning regulation to allow this expansion, Bryant Woods Inn sued the county, contending that it had violated the Fair Housing Act, 42 U.S.C. § 3601 *et seq.*, by refusing to make a reasonable accommodation. Because Bryant Woods Inn has not shown that its proposed expansion relates to the accommodation of disabled residents in seeking equality of housing opportunities, we affirm the district court's summary judgment entered in favor of the county.

### I

Richard Colandrea, the owner and resident of an 11-bedroom house in Columbia, Maryland, rents portions of his house to 8 elderly persons who suffer from Alzheimers disease and other forms of dementia and disability. Colandrea, together with his mother, operates the licensed group home through a for-profit corporation, Bryant

Woods Inn, Inc. The applicable zoning regulations issued by Howard County, where the house is located, permit this use of Colandrea's house as a matter of right. *See* Howard County, Md., Zoning Regulations § 110.C.4.b.

Seeking to expand his group home from 8 to 15 disabled or elderly residents, Colandrea filed an application with the appropriate Maryland state licensing agencies. The agencies denied Colandrea's request, however, until Colandrea had obtained zoning approval for the expansion from Howard County.

Colandrea filed an application with Howard County for a zoning variance, locally called an amendment to the neighborhood's Final Development Plan, to use his house as a "group care facility" limited to 15 disabled residents who will benefit from "the opportunity to live in a smaller, supervised home that provides some daily care in a structured social environment." The proposed expansion would include two daytime employees and one employee at other times. Colandrea proposed to provide existing off-street parking for five to six vehicles for use by employees and occasional visitors. The application indicates that the residents themselves generally do not drive and therefore the facility would not need to provide parking for eight vehicles as required by the applicable zoning regulations.

Applicable regulations provide generally for approval of requests "only if [the Planning Board] finds that: (1) the use is consistent with the land use designation of the property . . . and compatible with existing or proposed development in the vicinity, [and] (2) the use will not adversely affect vicinal properties." Howard County, Md., Zoning Regulations § 125.D.2.c. More specifically, any group care facility for more than 8 persons is deemed a nursing home, *see id.* § 103.A.55, and requires one parking space for every 2 beds, or at least 8 spaces for the 15 residents anticipated in Colandrea's application, *see id.* § 133.D.7.f. A residential group home with up to eight residents is required to have only four parking spaces. *See id.* §§ 133.D.1.c & 133.D.2.a.

The staff at the Howard County Department of Planning and Zoning recommended denial of Colandrea's application because it lacked the information necessary for a decision and the county received no response to its requests for information. Colandrea did respond, however, after the staff recommended denial. The Howard County Planning Board decided to proceed with a hearing and to receive Colandrea's response at the hearing.

The Howard County Planning Board conducted a full public hearing on Colandrea's application in February 1994 at which persons testified both for and against the zoning change. Speaking for the expansion were persons representing Colandrea, the Howard County Office of Aging, and the county's Alzheimer Association, and speaking against it were neighbors and three neighborhood associations, as well as the Department of Planning and Zoning staff.

The board received information that only 3 of more than 32 licensed group homes in Howard County had more than 8 residents and that the smaller homes seemed to be functioning "reasonably well" so that "there is a viable position for a facility of up to 8 patients." It received letters from residents reporting that the Colandrea family had operated several businesses from their house which "seem[ed] to include a junk hauling business and a rooming house." One neighbor commented at the hearing:

> This kind of thing, this institutional use needs to be in a different area. As it is now, I don't think anybody has a problem with it. It's this expansion and the construction and the additional parking that's really going to throw it over. The real reason that I think more than eight is needed . . . is the pure economies of scale. I had heard the number quoted twenty-five hundred dollars a month is what each resident pays. Well if you multiply that by 12 months times 8 residents, you're talking about a quarter of a million dollars of receipts in a year. That's a pretty good size in-home business and we as the neighbors feel like we're struggling against a business in this case.

Other neighbors expressed concern about traffic and congestion. One board member added her own comments that when looking at the property at about 9:30 in the morning and again at 4:30 in the afternoon she observed "parking all over the place and also parking in the driveway" and concluded that given the relatively small lot size in the rest of the neighborhood, an expansion of the facility would be too "intense to use on this particular lot" and would result in overflow parking onto the residential street.

In a unanimous written opinion dated March 31, 1994, the Planning Board denied Colandrea's request for a variance to enable him to expand his facility. In its opinion it found as fact that the proposed parking plan "accommodates between four and six vehicles on the site," but "does not allow for easy circulation of the accommodated vehicles and would likely result in fewer cars actually using on-site parking, thus forcing overflow parking onto the street." The board determined that this adverse effect would be aggravated by the wedged shape of the property which gives it a narrow road frontage available for on-street parking. It also found that "even the existing use generates parking congestion on the street. This situation would be exacerbated by Petitioner's proposed expansion." Observing that current zoning requires provision for 8 off-street parking spaces for a group home having 15 residents, the board decided not to waive the minimum requirement because it would "undermine the basic purpose of that requirement and the legitimate interest of the county in reducing the parking and traffic congestion associated with an intensified land use in a residential setting, particularly where the existing use already generates congestion." The board also found that denial of the amendment would not limit housing opportunities for the disabled in contravention of the Fair Housing Act. The board observed that more than 30 assisted-living facilities with 8 or fewer residents exist in Howard County to provide housing opportunity for the elderly and disabled and concluded that 8 residents is a reasonable breakpoint for economic viability and for requiring additional scrutiny of specific impacts. Observing that only 3 group care facilities have 15 residents, the board noted that each one of those facilities has between one and three acres of property, whereas Colandrea's has roughly one-third an acre.

Colandrea moved for reconsideration of the board's decision based on his assurance that none of the disabled residents would park a car and that his expansion would definitely be limited to 15 persons. No further evidence was provided, however, and the board denied Colandrea's motion for reconsideration.

The Planning Board's decision and order became final because Colandrea did not appeal to the Howard County Board of Appeals as provided for in Howard County Code § 16.900(j)(2)(iii), or to the Circuit Court for Howard County. Instead, he filed this action through his corporation, Bryant Woods Inn, Inc., alleging that Howard County intentionally discriminated against Bryant Woods Inn and failed to make a reasonable accommodation for the handicapped in violation of the Fair Housing Act.

On cross-motions for summary judgment, the district court ruled that plaintiffs had failed to present evidence on which a finder of fact could base a conclusion of intentional discrimination. The court also concluded that Howard County's refusal to make an accommodation was justified because the requested accommodation would "fundamentally alter the nature of Howard County's system of land use regulation." Moreover, the court found, any accommodation was not "necessary" under the Fair Housing Act because numerous other group homes existed in Columbia, Maryland, having from 18 to 23% vacancy rates. . . .

. . . On its appeal, Bryant Woods Inn argues only that the county denied it reasonable accommodation, abandoning its claim of intentional discrimination. . . .

## II

. . . .

. . . Howard County . . . argues that this case is analogous to "the routine land-use disputes that inevitably and constantly arise among developers, local residents, and municipal officials [which are] simply not the business of the federal courts." . . . This argument, however, fails to recognize that . . . Bryant Woods Inn does not contest the interpretation of local law, but argues that a federal antidiscrimination statute requires the county to make accommodation to its properly interpreted zoning ordinance. Hence, we are not in danger of misapplying local laws because of the impossibility of unraveling the skein of federal claims and the interpretation of local law.

## III

Howard County zoning regulations allow any resident family to house up to eight handicapped or elderly persons in its principal residence, provided state approval is obtained. Group care facilities for more than eight persons are defined as nursing homes for which zoning approval is required. In connection with its application to change the zoning to house 15 handicapped or elderly residents, Bryant Woods Inn was unable to satisfy Howard County's traffic and parking requirements and therefore sought a waiver of the requirements on the ground that its residents would not need additional parking. Howard County denied the request. Bryant Woods Inn contends that Howard County's refusal to change its zoning for the Colandrea property to accommodate expansion from 8 to 15 residents violates the Fair Housing Act ("FHA"), as amended by the Fair Housing Amendments Act of 1988, Pub.L. No. 100-430, 102 Stat. 1619 (adding handicap and familial status to list of impermissible bases of discrimination). . . . Discrimination is defined to include "a refusal to make reasonable accommodations in rules, policies, practices, or services, when such accommodations may be necessary to afford such person equal opportunity to use and enjoy a dwelling." 42 U.S.C. § 3604(f)(3)(B).

. . . .

Land use planning and the adoption of land use restrictions constitute some of the most important functions performed by local government. Local land use restrictions seek to prevent the problems arising from the proverbial "pig in the parlor instead of the barnyard," *Village of Euclid v. Ambler Realty Co.*, 272 U.S. 365, 388, 47 S. Ct. 114, 118, 71 L. Ed. 303 (1926), and to preserve "the character of neighborhoods, securing 'zones where family values, youth values, and the blessings of quiet seclusion and clean air make the area a sanctuary for people.'" In *Euclid*, the Court upheld the constitutionality of local land use restrictions, observing that "apartment houses which in a different environment would be not only entirely unobjectionable but highly desirable, come very near to being nuisances" in residential neighborhoods of detached houses. *Euclid*, 272 U.S. at 395, 47 S. Ct. at 121.

In enacting the FHA, Congress clearly did not contemplate abandoning the deference that courts have traditionally shown to such local zoning codes. And the FHA does not provide a "blanket waiver of all facially neutral zoning policies and rules, regardless of the facts," which would give the disabled "carte blanche to determine where and how they would live regardless of zoning ordinances to the contrary." Seeking to recognize local authorities' ability to regulate land use and without unnecessarily undermining the benign purposes of such neutral regulations, Congress required only that local government make "reasonable accommodation" to afford persons with handicaps "equal opportunity to use and enjoy" housing in those communities. 42 U.S.C. § 3604(f)(3)(B).

The FHA thus requires an accommodation for persons with handicaps if the accommodation is (1) reasonable and (2) necessary (3) to afford handicapped persons equal opportunity to use and enjoy housing. *See* 42 U.S.C. § 3604(f)(3). Because the FHA's text evidences no intent to alter normal burdens, the plaintiff bears the burden of proving each of these three elements by a preponderance of the evidence. *See Elderhaven, Inc. v. City of Lubbock*, 98 F.3d 175, 178 (5th Cir. 1996). *But see Hovsons[, Inc. v. Township of Brick]*, 89 F.3d at 1103 (placing the burden of proving that a proposed accommodation is not reasonable on the defendant).

In determining whether the reasonableness requirement has been met, a court may consider as factors the extent to which the accommodation would undermine the legitimate purposes and effects of existing zoning regulations and the benefits that the accommodation would provide to the handicapped. It may also consider whether alternatives exist to accomplish the benefits more efficiently. And in measuring the effects of an accommodation, the court may look not only to its functional and administrative aspects, but also to its costs. "Reasonable accommodations" do not require accommodations which impose "undue financial and administrative burdens," or "changes, adjustments, or modifications to existing programs that would be substantial, or that would constitute fundamental alterations in the nature of the program." Thus, for example, even though a prohibition of pets in apartments is common, facially neutral, and indeed reasonable, the FHA requires a relaxation of it to accommodate a hearing dog for a deaf person because such an accommodation does not unduly burden or fundamentally alter the nature of the apartment complex.

The "necessary" element — the FHA provision mandating reasonable accommodations which are *necessary* to afford an equal opportunity — requires the demonstration of a direct linkage between the proposed accommodation and the "equal opportunity" to be provided to the handicapped person. This requirement has attributes of a causation requirement. And if the proposed accommodation provides no direct amelioration of a disability's effect, it cannot be said to be "necessary."

And finally, the "equal opportunity" requirement mandates not only the level of benefit that must be sought by a reasonable accommodation but also provides a limitation on what is required. The FHA does not require accommodations that increase a benefit to a handicapped person above that provided to a nonhandicapped person with respect to matters unrelated to the handicap.... [T]he requirement of even-handed treatment of handicapped persons does not include affirmative action by which handicapped persons would have a greater opportunity than nonhandicapped persons.

With this background in hand, we determine whether Bryant Woods Inn's request to expand its facility from 8 to 15 residents is a reasonable accommodation required by the FHA.

Bryant Woods Inn argues in this case that its requested zoning variance is reasonable because the expansion of its group home would not increase traffic congestion since its residents do not drive. Unrefuted testimony, however, was presented to the Howard County Planning Board by a member who observed vehicles parked "all over the place and also in the driveway" even under Bryant Woods Inn's current level of occupancy. The board also received unrefuted evidence that Bryant Woods Inn's wedge-shaped parcel affords minimal frontage and that the parcel is less than one-third of the size of other Howard County group homes which have 15 residents. Following a full public hearing where the board heard the evidence of all parties, the board found that "even the existing use generates parking congestion on the street. This situation would be exacerbated by Petitioner's proposed expansion." Bryant Woods Inn elected not to appeal the board's decision and is now bound by its findings on this point. Thus, Bryant Woods Inn has failed, as a matter of law, to establish in this case that its requested accommodation is reasonable.

The more serious inadequacy of Bryant Woods Inn's position, however, appears in connection with its effort to show that its zoning change is "necessary." Howard

County's existing zoning regulations do not prohibit group housing for individuals with handicaps. Indeed, the regulations permit such group housing.

The zoning variance that Bryant Woods Inn seeks is not aimed at permitting handicapped persons to live in group homes in residential communities — that, as we have noted, is already permitted — but at *expanding* its group home size from 8 to 15 persons. While "some minimum size may be essential to the success" of group homes, the Inn has introduced no evidence that group homes are not financially viable with eight residents. On the contrary, the record before the board shows that almost 30 such homes operate viably in Howard County with 8 or fewer residents. Moreover, while it is uncontested that group homes are often therapeutically valuable in providing patients with a higher quality of life and thereby helping to avoid the functional decline which is frequently consequent to institutionalization in a traditional nursing home. Bryant Woods Inn has also presented no evidence in this case that expansion from 8 to 15 residents would be therapeutically meaningful. Thus, nothing in the record that we can find suggests that a group home of 15 residents, as opposed to one of 8, is necessary to accommodate individuals with handicaps. If Bryant Woods Inn's position were taken to its limit, it would be entitled to construct a 10-story building housing 75 residents, on the rationale that the residents had handicaps.

The only suggestion in the record of advantage from the proposed expansion is that it will financially assist Bryant Woods Inn as a for-profit corporation. But the proper inquiry is not whether "a particular profit-making company needs such an accommodation, but, rather do such businesses as a whole need this accommodation. Otherwise, by unreasonably inflating costs, one business would get such an accommodation while another, better run, did not."

A handicapped person desiring to live in a group home in a residential community in Howard County can do so now at Bryant Woods Inn under existing zoning regulations, and, if no vacancy exists, can do so at the numerous other group homes at which vacancies exist. The unrefuted evidence is that the vacancy rate was between 18 to 23% within Howard County. We hold that in these circumstances, Bryant Woods Inn's demand that it be allowed to expand its facility from 8 to 15 residents is not "necessary," as used in the FHA, to accommodate handicapped persons.

Were we to require Howard County to grant a zoning variance to allow Bryant Woods Inn to expand its group home from 8 to 15 residents without providing adequate parking and not to require the county to grant a similar waiver for group homes not involving handicapped persons, the benefit would advantage Bryant Woods Inn on a matter unrelated to the amelioration of the effects of a handicap. This would provide not an *equal* opportunity to Bryant Woods Inn's residents but a financial advantage to Bryant Woods Inn. Yet, the FHA only requires an "equal opportunity," not a superior *advantage*. . . .

In short, Bryant Woods Inn has failed to satisfy any of the three requirements imposed by the FHA for accommodation of the handicapped persons.

## IV

. . . .

For the foregoing reasons, we affirm the judgment of the district court.

Affirmed.

## *Questions for Consideration*

1) What is Bryant Woods intended use?

2) Why does Bryant Woods need a variance?

3) What are the identified criteria applicable in this case for a zoning variance?

4) What evidence was presented, and what findings of fact were made in this case?

5) What classification issue was involved in going from a house with 8 residents to a house with 15 residents?

6) What were the issues under the FHA and how did the court resolve them?

7) What economic considerations were considered to be relevant to the decision?

## *Takeaway*

- In *Bryant Woods*, the board provided a written opinion detailing its findings and the justification for its decision. This facilitated a favorable review of its action.

- *Bryant Woods* provides further clarity on the elements needed to be determined under the FHA.

## Loren v. Sasser

United States Court of Appeals for the Eleventh Circuit
309 F.3d 1296 (11th Cir. 2002)

PER CURIAM. This appeal presents the issue of whether a deed-restricted subdivision must accommodate handicapped individuals under federal and state fair housing statutes. . . .

### I. Background

In 1997, plaintiff-appellant Nicole Loren jointly bought and moved into a home located at 4065 Jewfish Drive in Hernando Beach South, a deed-restricted subdivision, consisting of approximately 425 lots, in Hernando Beach, Florida. Loren resided in the house with her handicapped mother, plaintiff-appellant Bettie J. Newbold, who suffers from chronic osteoarthritis, high blood pressure, and has two artificial knees that cause her difficulty in using stairs, and plaintiff-appellant Charlene Janke, her step-aunt, who is severely mentally retarded, blind, and has a guide dog. Loren provides caretaking services for both her mother and her step-aunt. Prior to purchasing the house, Loren was given a copy of the deed restrictions for Hernando

Beach South. Specifically, the deed restrictions provide as to improvements to the house and lot:

> IMPROVEMENTS. No building, addition, accessory, *fence*, television antenna or signal receiver, landscaping or other structure or improvement shall be commenced, erected, placed or maintained upon any lot, nor shall *any exterior addition* to or change or alteration be made until *complete written plans and specifications* showing the nature, kind, size (including the size and square footage of each separate room or area), driveway layout, shape, color, height, floor plan, materials, location and approximate costs of same have been submitted and *approved in writing.* . . . (emphasis added)

After moving into the house, appellants requested permission to construct a four-foot, chain-link fence in the front yard. The purposes for requesting the fence were "allowing Janke to begin adjusting to her outdoor surroundings and feel secure and safe outdoors as well as indoors, to enjoy the sun and fresh air, to have her dog nearby without fear that the dog would run off or bite someone approaching the property; and affording Newbold and Loren a respite from continuous supervision without fear of Janke wandering off." R1-1-9. Defendant-appellee Hernando Beach, Inc., the corporate developer of Hernando Beach South, through its president, defendant-appellee Charles M. Sasser, Jr., denied the request and advised Loren that fences were not permitted on the front of homes but could be constructed on the side or back of a house consistent with the deed restrictions and approvals accorded other property owners in the subdivision. Because appellants' residence was a corner lot, Sasser further informed that such a fence might inhibit visibility of drivers at that intersection and, consequently, be a safety hazard.

Loren subsequently requested permission to construct a deck and wheelchair ramp on the front of the house. Appellees initially denied the request for a deck and wheelchair ramp because Loren failed to provide an adequate drawing. After submitting a more detailed drawing, appellees denied Loren's second request for a deck and wheelchair ramp because of safety concerns for Newbold and Janke. Sasser suggested that, for the safety of the handicapped individuals, the deck and ramp should be built in the garage, which would be the safest and most appropriate place for the ramp. Because the deck and wheelchair ramp were intended for the front of the house, Sasser further informed Loren that her proposed deck and wheelchair ramp did not conform with other approved decks in the subdivision, which were on the back of the houses. Shortly after making the requests for the chain-link fence, deck, and wheelchair ramp, Newbold and Janke fell down the stairs leading to the garage and sustained various injuries.

The denials of Loren's requests, combined with Newbold and Janke's fall, prompted Loren to decide to move from the subdivision. . . .

Loren, Newbold, and Janke, who originally were represented by counsel, filed a six-count complaint against Sasser, Hernando Beach, Inc., and HBSPOA. Counts I and II allege discrimination in violation of the Fair Housing Act, 42 U.S.C. § 3601 et seq., and the Florida Fair Housing Act, Fla. Stat. § 760.20 et seq. for refusing permission to construct a chain-link fence in the front yard. Specifically, they alleged that the requested front-yard fence was a reasonable modification necessary to afford Newbold and Janke safe and full enjoyment of the property. Counts III and IV alleged discrimination in violation of federal and state fair housing statutes for refusing permission to construct a deck and wheelchair ramp on the front of the house....

. . . .

The district judge ... addressed the reasonable-accommodation claims. Regarding the chain-link fence claims, appellees argued that they were entitled to summary judgment because (1) appellants failed to submit complete written plans of the proposed fence for approval as required by the deed restrictions; and (2) the denial of the request for a chain-link fence in the front yard was not unreasonable and did not discriminate against handicapped persons because they could put a chain-link fence in their back yard. As required, the district judge viewed the evidence most favorably toward appellants and presumed that Loren correctly filed the request for the front-yard, chain-link fence. Nonetheless, the district judge found that appellees were entitled to summary judgment on the chain-link fence counts, Counts I and II, because Loren, Newbold, and Janke "ha[d] not established that this accommodation, even if reasonable, was denied with discriminatory intent or was necessary to afford Plaintiffs 'equal opportunity to use and enjoy' their dwelling." Regarding the deck-and-ramp counts, the district judge found that plaintiffs had produced some evidence from which a factfinder could conclude that denial of appellants' application to construct a deck and wheelchair ramp was discriminatory. Accordingly, the district judge denied appellees' motion for summary judgment regarding the deck-and-ramp counts, Counts III and IV, which proceeded to trial.

Following a four-day trial, the jury returned a verdict in favor of appellees and determined that they did not discriminate by refusing to approve the request for a deck and wheelchair ramp on the front of the house.... On appeal, appellants ... argue that there was insufficient evidence for the jury to conclude that appellees did not discriminate by refusing to approve appellants' application for a wheelchair ramp and deck.

## II. Discussion

. . . .

Loren, Newbold, and Janke argue that appellees discriminated against them by denying their application for a chain-link fence in their front yard because this fence was a reasonable modification of their property to permit the handicapped residents, Newbold and Janke, a safe and equal opportunity for full enjoyment of the premises under the Fair Housing Act. They assert that the chain-link fence was reasonable to allow Janke time outdoors with her guide dog without the possibility of her wandering from the premises and to prevent her guide dog from biting individuals who might come onto the property. They further represent that the front yard provides a more scenic space for her time outside than other parts of the lot.

Under the Fair Housing Act, a handicapped individual is one who has "(1) a physical or mental impairment which substantially limits one or more of such person's major life activities, (2) a record of having such an impairment, or (3) be[en] regarded as having such an impairment." 42 U.S.C. §3602(h)(1)-(3). The district judge correctly considered Newbold and Janke to be handicapped under the Fair Housing Act, which prohibits

> (A) a refusal to permit, at the expense of the handicapped person, *reasonable modifications* of existing premises occupied or to be occupied by such person if such modifications may be necessary to afford such person full enjoyment of the premises. . . . [or]

> (B) a refusal to make reasonable accommodations in rules, policies, practices, or services, when such accommodations may be necessary *to afford such person equal opportunity to use and enjoy a dwelling. . . .*

42 U.S.C. §3604(f)(3)(A) & (B) (emphasis added); Fla. Stat. §760.23(9)(a) & (b) (identical statutory wording).

The Supreme Court has decided that discrimination under the Fair Housing Act includes a refusal to make a "reasonable accommodation" for handicapped persons. *City of Edmonds v. Oxford House, Inc.*, 514 U.S. 725, 729–30, 115 S. Ct. 1776, 1779, 131 L. Ed.2d 801 (1995). "Whether a requested accommodation is required by law is 'highly fact-specific, requiring case-by-case determination.'" *Groner v. Golden Gate Gardens Apartments*, 250 F.3d 1039, 1044 (6th Cir. 2001) (citation omitted). Under the Fair Housing Act, plaintiffs have the burden of proving that a proposed accommodation is reasonable. *Groner*, 250 F.3d at 1045; *Bryant Woods Inn, Inc. v. Howard County, Md.*, 124 F.3d 597, 603–04 (4th Cir. 1997); *Elderhaven, Inc. v. City of Lubbock, Tex.*, 98 F.3d 175, 178 (5th Cir. 1996).

There is no evidence in this record that Hernando Beach, Inc., HBSPOA, or Sasser discriminated against appellants by denying their request for a chain-link fence in their front yard. Appellants failed to introduce any evidence that other houses in the deed-restricted subdivision have been permitted to construct fences on the front of their lots. Appellees informed appellants that they would approve construction of a chain-link fence on the back or the side of their house. For the specific reasons of preventing Janke from wandering from the premises, prohibiting her guide dog from biting anyone entering onto the premises, and enabling Newbold and Janke the ability to be outside unsupervised, a chain-link fence on the back or side of the house would accomplish the same purposes by providing an opportunity to be outdoors safely in accordance with the deed restrictions of the subdivision. While a chain-link fence on the back or side yard of their property may not be appellants' preference, it nevertheless would be a reasonable accommodation for the asserted needs of the handicapped appellants. We conclude that the district judge properly granted summary judgment to appellees on Counts I and II relating to the front-yard, chain-link fence because appellants have not established a genuine issue of material fact to show that appellees discriminated against them in violation of the

Fair Housing Act by denying their application for a front-yard, chain-link fence. Significantly, a reasonable accommodation, compliant with the deed restrictions of the subdivision, was available to serve the stated purposes of appellants.

. . . .

### III. Conclusion

In this appeal, Loren, Newbold, and Janke have contested the district judge's granting summary judgment to Sasser, Hernando Beach, Inc., and HBSPOA on their allegations of violations of federal and state fair housing statutes relating to their application to construct a chain-link fence on the front of their premises. . . . As we have explained, . . . summary judgment for appellees was appropriate because appellants failed to show that appellees violated the federal or state fair housing statutes by acting with discrimination in denying appellants' application for a chain-link fence in their front yard. . . . Accordingly, the district court's . . . verdict in favor of appellees [is] . . . affirmed.

## *Questions for Consideration*

1) What is the basis of the property restriction in this case?

2) Who lived on the property?

3) What was Loren seeking permission to do on her property?

4) What was the claim under the FHA?

5) What was the outcome of the FHA claim?

## *Takeaway*

- *Loren v. Sasser* involves a private land restriction and therefore does not come within Title II of the ADA. This is the reason that the case focuses on the FHA.

- A person may request a reasonable accommodation or modification, but they are not necessarily entitled to what they request. They are entitled to a reasonable accommodation and modification, and this may be different from what is requested.

## Austin v. Town of Farmington

United States Court of Appeals for the Second Circuit
826 F.3d 622 (2016)

WINTER, Circuit Judge. The complaint alleges that, in 2009, Colleen and John Austin decided to move from North Carolina to up-state New York, with their two sons. Their older son, Cole, has multiple serious disabilities as a result of being born prematurely, including cerebral palsy and global developmental delays. He is non-verbal and visually impaired.

Appellants sought to move to an area with good public schools and chose the Town of Farmington. Appellants became interested in a newly-constructed home in the Town's Auburn Meadows development. Appellants wanted to install a fence in order to keep their son safely within their yard and to build an above-ground pool because of the benefits aquatic therapy affords to children with cerebral palsy.

Before purchasing the home, appellants learned that there was a Town ordinance restricting "patio lots," like that of the house in question, in the subdivision. The restriction in question was passed as part of the rezoning and authorization necessary to the Auburn Meadows development. The authorization contained numerous provisions relating to open space, trails, etc. The provision at issue here prohibited accessory structures, such as pools and fences, "within the patio home portion of the site" but allowed such structures on other (larger) lots "within the rear yard portion of the site provided that such rear yards are screened from adjacent public rights-of-ways." Appellants' lot was subject to the full prohibition.

Upon learning of the land-use restriction on the property, Colleen Austin called the Farmington Town building department to seek a variance. The Code Enforcement Officer told her that appellants would have to request such a variance from the Town Board. Appellants bought the home confident that they would be able to secure the necessary permission.

In June 2012, after negotiations with appellants, the Town Board passed a Resolution entitled "Granting a Temporary Accommodation to install a Fence and an Above-Ground Swimming Pool to the Owners of 1685 Lillybrook Court ... in the Auburn Meadows Subdivision...." However, the Resolution also stated that the fence and swimming pool must "be wholly removed" from the property "within 21 days" of the disabled child ceasing to live on the property, of appellants ceasing to own the property "whether by conveyance, death or any other reason," or of anyone being added as an additional owner of the property. The Resolution further stated that the fence and pool were to be removed "at the expense of the Austin's [sic] or of the new owners of [the property]."

During the summer of 2012, appellants installed the fence and pool. After the Town granted appellants' request for a second variance, they added a deck to the pool. The second Resolution contained the same Restoration Provision. The total cost for installing the fence, pool, and deck, as well as accompanying landscaping work, was over $27,000. Appellants have been quoted a price of $6,630 to remove the fence, pool, and deck and repair the damage to the yard.

On June 11, 2014, appellants filed the present action challenging the Restoration Provisions and seeking declaratory and injunctive relief against their enforcement. Appellants alleged ... based on the FHA, discrimination by the Town's denial of "a reasonable modification pursuant to 42 U.S.C. Section 3604(f)(3)(A)" ....

On June 8, 2015, the district court dismissed appellants' complaint pursuant to the Town's Fed. R. Civ. P. 12(b)(6) motion. The court concluded that there were "simply no facts alleged that evince a discriminatory intent in requiring that plaintiffs restore their property to its original condition once the need for the modifications is no longer present." Further, the court held that "[p]laintiffs fail[ed] to support, beyond their conclusory assertions, that requiring them to bear the cost of removal of the fence and pool is in some way based upon their son's disability when the initial grant of a variance to build the pool along with a fence was granted knowing that plaintiffs' son was disabled." Finally, the court stated that "plaintiffs have not sufficiently alleged a violation of the FHA under the disparate-impact analysis.... Here, there has been no showing that the restoration requirement does not apply to non-disabled individuals."

### Discussion

. . . .

In 1988, Congress amended the Fair Housing Act of 1968 to extend its coverage to housing discrimination based on an individual's disability.

Section 3604(f)(3) provides:

For purposes of this subsection, discrimination includes —

(A) a refusal to permit, at the expense of the handicapped person, reasonable modifications of existing premises occupied or to be occupied by such person if such modifications may be necessary to afford such person full enjoyment of the premises except that, in the case of a rental, the landlord may where it is reasonable to do so condition permission for a modification on the renter agreeing to restore the interior of the premises to the condition that existed before the modification, reasonable wear and tear excepted.

(B) a refusal to make reasonable accommodations in rules, policies, practices, or services, when such accommodations may be necessary to afford such person equal opportunity to use and enjoy a dwelling; or. . . .

42 U.S.C. §3604(f)(3). Neither Subsection (A) nor Subsection (B) requires that the denial of modifications or accommodations be the result of a discriminatory animus toward the disabled. Both require only that the requested modification or accommodation be reasonable and that the denial(s) result, in the case of Section 3604(f)(3)(A), in diminishing the disabled person's full enjoyment of the premises or, in the case of Section 3604(f)(3)(B), in so diminishing that person's use and enjoyment of the premises as to constitute a denial of equal opportunity.

The Town does not challenge the applicability of the FHA to the ordinance prohibiting accessory structures on patio lots in the Auburn Meadows development. Indeed, the House Report accompanying the 1998 Amendments to the FHA specifically stated that the Act was intended "to prohibit the application of special requirements through land-use regulations, restrictive covenants, and conditional or special use permits that have the effect of limiting the ability of such individuals [disabled persons] to live in the residence of their choice in the community." H.R. Rep. No. 100-711, at 24 (1988), reprinted in 1988 U.S.C.C.A.N. 2173, 2185; *see, e.g., City of Edmonds v. Oxford House, Inc.*, 514 U.S. 725, 729–30, 115 S. Ct. 1776, 131 L. Ed. 2d 801 (1995) (applying FHA provisions to a city zoning code).

. . . .

. . . [A] plain reading of the statute reveals that there is no *per se* rule against land-use regulators including restoration provisions in zoning variances or other land-use accommodations. . . .

Appellants rely heavily upon a "Joint Statement of the Department of Housing and Urban Development and the Department of Justice" regarding "Reasonable Modifications under the Fair House Act." . . . This reliance is misplaced. The Joint Statement on Reasonable Modifications is inapplicable because the instant appeal concerns an accommodation, not a modification. Nonetheless, the document's description . . . remains informative, and is described as follows:

> [A] reasonable *modification* is a structural change made to the premises whereas a reasonable *accommodation* is a change, exception, or adjustment to a rule, policy, practice, or service. A person with a disability may need either a reasonable accommodation or a reasonable modification, or both, in order to have an equal opportunity to use and enjoy a dwelling. . . .

. . . In dismissing appellants' complaint, the district court concluded, seemingly as a matter of law, that the Town's "refusal to remove the restoration condition [did] not constitute a refusal to make a reasonable accommodation for plaintiffs' disabled son in its zoning policy." The court also determined that appellants failed to state a claim under the FHA because they alleged neither an intent to discriminate, nor facts sufficient to constitute disparate-impact discrimination. Because of these failures, and the fact that appellants were not excluded from purchasing or using the housing of their choice because of the restoration requirement, the court granted appellees' motion to dismiss the complaint.

The language of Section 3604(f)(3)(A), (B) compels a different conclusion. The subsections define unlawful discrimination, in the present context, as refusing a reasonable accommodation allowing appellants to make reasonable modifications to their property to afford their disabled child an equal opportunity to enjoy fully the use of the property. The unlawful act, therefore, is the refusal to make a reasonable accommodation without regard to the state of mind underlying the refusal.

Appellants do not challenge the accommodation made by the Town to the extent it allowed them, as they requested, to build a fence, install a pool, and add a deck to the pool. Their challenge is simply to the portion of the Town's Resolutions requiring the removal of these modifications. The Town, in short, does not want the variance to "run with the land" — to be taken advantage of by later occupants without a disability — while appellants want to avoid the cost of removal and to capture any increase in the value of the property caused by the modifications and/or by permanently freeing the lot in question from the restrictions applicable to the neighborhood in question.

It is certainly true, as the district court reasoned, that the Restoration Provisions did not directly deprive the disabled child of his rights under the FHA. However, we believe that a trier of fact might find that a restoration requirement in some circumstances so burdens a party wanting to modify a property to accommodate a disabled person that it amounts to a refusal of a reasonable accommodation. *See Logan v. Matveevskii*, 57 F. Supp. 3d 234, 257 (S.D.N.Y. 2014) (asserting that "a refusal of a request for a reasonable accommodation can be both actual or constructive," such as where request for accommodation is met with indeterminate delay instead of outright denial (internal quotation mark omitted)). This would violate the FHA even though the authority imposing a restoration requirement believed in good faith that it was fully accommodating the disabled individual.

The issue of whether the failure of the Town to allow the modifications to continue in place after the child left the property was reasonable therefore can neither be avoided nor decided as a matter of law on the pleadings. . . . Whether the Town's Resolutions are reasonable in light of appellants' needs requires a complex balancing of factors. Reasonableness analysis is "highly fact-specific, requiring a case-by-case determination."

The reasonableness issue here cannot be determined on the pleadings because the relevant factors are numerous and balancing them requires a full evidentiary record. A requested accommodation is reasonable where the cost is modest and it does not pose an undue hardship or substantial burden on the rule maker. . . . ([An] accommodation is not reasonable "if it would impose an undue financial and administrative burden on the [rule maker] or it would fundamentally alter the nature of the [rule maker's] operations"). Applied to the context of land-use regulations, relevant factors may include the purposes of the restriction, the strength of the Town's interest in the land-use regulation at issue, the need for uniformity, the effect of allowing later landowners without a disability to enjoy the lack of a restriction on pools, decks, and fences, while all their neighbors are subject to it, the likelihood that a permanent variance will cause other landowners subject to the regulation to seek similar variances, etc. Balanced against those factors is the cost of removal—again, whether out of pocket or in a reduced sale price.

We say no more because there are undoubtedly a host of relevant factors looking in both directions to be considered. . . .

. . .

### Conclusion

For the foregoing reasons, the judgment granting the Town's motion to dismiss [as to the restoration requirement] is . . . vacated. Each party should bear its own costs.

## *Questions for Consideration*

1) After buying their home, what accommodations and modifications did the Austins request?

2) Were the Austins granted their requests?

3) What condition was imposed on the granting of the exceptions to the zoning code?

4) Do you think it is fair to require a property owner to restore the property to its earlier condition after the person being accommodated is no longer residing on the property?

5) What factors might one need to consider in evaluating the ability of a local government to enforce a restoration provision?

### *Takeaway*

- Traditionally, variances run with the land. This means that the variance continues for the benefit of subsequent owners.

- If a local government makes an accommodation to a person with a disability by granting a variance, the variance will run with the land. This means that the accommodation or variance in the code requirements will continue even after the person being accommodated is no longer present at the property. Sometimes a zoning board may be concerned about granting an accommodation that will run with the land. One possible way to address this issue is for local planning and zoning officials to deny the request for a variance and then do an interpretation of their zoning code in light of the RHA, ADA, and FHA, as applicable. In such a situation, it may be argued that a variance is not being granted, but that the code is being interpreted in light of making a reasonable accommodation or modification. If it is an interpretation and not a variance then, arguably, it should not run with the land.

## Discussion Problem 6.1

Francesco and Silvia own a home in a suburban community. They have a lovely older home with a wraparound front porch. Entry to the house includes having to take five steps up from the ground level to the porch and then an additional step up into the doorway. Angelina, Francesco's mother, also lives with them. Angelina is getting older and is now using a wheelchair to get around because of problems with her legs when walking. The house is currently in compliance with the 25-foot setback from the street requirement in place under the zoning code. Francesco and Silvia, however, seek to add a ramp to the front of the home for Angelina to get in and out of the house. An appropriate ramp would extend ten feet into the front yard setback.

Francesco and Silvia purchase some lumber down at the local hardware store and build a ramp at a cost of about $400. After setting up the ramp and firmly securing it to the house, a neighbor files a complaint with the city. The city investigates and gives Francesco and Silvia a notice of zoning code violation requiring them to remove the ramping structure from intruding into the front yard setback. Consider the following issues, assuming that Francesco and Silvia appeal the matter to the zoning board of appeal.

1) What factors will you consider if they request an area or a use variance [using New York criteria discussed at the beginning of Section C, *supra*]?

2) What factors should you consider on a disability claim for a reasonable accommodation?

3) Can a zoning board of appeal require removal of the current ramp and replacement with a more expensive ramp using materials and design features that match the house (estimated cost $3,000)?

4) Can the zoning board grant permission for the ramp but require that it be removed when Angelina is no longer residing in the home?

5) What difference should it make if there is a secondary, or as Francesco calls it, a "less desirable" rear entrance to the house where a ramp can be placed without interfering with or violating any setback requirements? What if the rear entrance option requires extending a walking path around the side of the house so that a wheelchair could more easily get to the rear entrance (estimated cost $800)?

# D. Accessory Dwelling and Use

Accessory uses are uses that are *customary* and *incidental* to a permitted primary use, the primary use being a use permitted in the zoning code. Traditionally, accessory uses are permitted along with the primary use without need for a variance. A typical example of an accessory use might be a garage for a house in a zone that permits only single-family residential homes. Likewise, a shed for a lawn mower and garden tools may be an accessory use to a residential home. Just because something may qualify as an accessory use and not require a variance, it may require a permit and may need to meet certain design, placement, and safety specifications to be built. Under many contemporary zoning codes, accessory uses may be subject to their own regulations and may not simply be permitted as of right.

## Mortimer v. New Britain Township Zoning Hearing Board

Commonwealth Court of Pennsylvania
93 A.3d 936 (Pa. Commw. Ct. 2014)

LEADBETTER, Judge. On May 6, 2010, Edward Mortimer (Applicant) appealed the Decision of the New Britain Township Zoning Hearing Board (ZHB) dated April 16, 2010 denying his "Application for a Variance and/or Interpretations of the Zoning Ordinance." The ZHB upheld the Zoning Officer's determination that the improvements to the second floor of Applicant's detached garage constituted an accessory dwelling use (use H14) which is not a permitted use in the SR-2 (Suburban Residential) Zoning District where Applicant's property is located. The ZHB also denied Applicant's request for a variance from Zoning Ordinance Section 27-801(a) to permit an accessory dwelling use (use H14) in the SR-2 Zoning District. Finally, the ZHB upheld the Zoning Officer's determination that Applicant's proposal to construct a so-called "great room" to connect the garage to Applicant's house would constitute a two-family detached dwelling use (use B4) which is not a permitted use in an SR-2 Zoning District. Following a review of the certified record of the proceedings before the ZHB, this court found that the ZHB did not abuse its discretion or commit an error of law and, therefore, by order dated June 28, 2013, affirmed the ZHB's decision. Applicant subsequently filed Notice of Appeal.

Applicant is the owner of the property located at 55 Curley Mill Road, Chalfont, New Britain Township, Bucks County, Pennsylvania (Property). The Property is approximately nine and three quarter acres in size. Applicant is a construction manager for a residential home builder. After he purchased the land, Applicant built a house and a detached garage on the Property in May 2007. The house has approximately 5,400 square feet of living space, including four bedrooms and a finished basement. The garage is two stories and has approximately 1,600 square feet of usable space on each floor. The Property is zoned SR-2 (Suburban Residential) under the New Britain Township Zoning Ordinance (Zoning Ordinance). The detached single family dwelling (use B1) and a detached residential accessory garage structure (use H1) are permitted by right in the SR-2 zoning district.

In May 2009, Applicant made improvements to the second floor of the garage without submitting any building plans and without obtaining any of the necessary building permits. Applicant installed a bedroom, office, kitchen, living room, dining room, full bathroom, laundry room and utility space with all related electrical, plumbing, heating and other utilities necessary to support those improvements.

The Township issued a Violation Notice on May 28, 2009 advising him that he had illegally constructed an apartment in the detached garage without obtaining the necessary permits: and further advising him that an apartment is not a permitted use within the SR-2 Zoning District. On July 2, 2009, the New Britain Township Zoning Officer (the Zoning Officer) inspected the property and concluded that the second floor living space in the detached garage constituted a "dwelling unit" and an "accessory dwelling" in a detached structure (use H14) under the Zoning Ordinance. An "accessory dwelling" (use H14) is not a permitted use in the SR-2, Suburban Residential, zoning district where Applicant's property is located. Applicant was notified of this determination by letter dated July 20, 2009. He was advised in that letter that he had a right to appeal the Zoning Officer's determination to the ZHB within thirty days of the date of the letter.

On October 12, 2009, Applicant submitted an application (the Application) to the ZHB requesting the following:

> 1. An interpretation of section 27-801(a) of the Zoning Ordinance to permit an accessory dwelling use (use H14) in a detached garage residential accessory structure; or,
>
> 2. a variance from the Zoning Ordinance to permit said use; or
>
> 3. an interpretation of the Zoning Ordinance that construction of "a great room" (attaching the garage to the single-family house) would bring the

existing illegal apartment into compliance with the Zoning Ordinance as an "in-law suite" and would not, as the Zoning Officer concluded, constitute a prohibited two-family detached dwelling use (use B4).

A hearing on the application was held on March 18, 2010. On April 16, 2010, the ZHB issued its Findings of Fact, Conclusions of Law and Decision denying the Application.

In land use and zoning appeals, the scope of this court's review is limited. Where a Court of Common Pleas does not conduct a *de novo* hearing nor receive additional evidence that was not before the zoning board, as in this case, the applicable standard of review is whether the zoning board committed an abuse of discretion or an error of law in denying the variance. An abuse of discretion will the found only where the Board's findings are not supported by substantial evidence. "Substantial evidence" means such relevant evidence as a reasonable mind might accept as adequate to support a conclusion.

In denying the Application, the ZHB found that the extensive living space created by Applicant on the second floor of the detached garage constituted a "Dwelling Unit" under the Zoning Ordinance. The Zoning Ordinance defines a "Dwelling Unit" as "any room or group of rooms located within a residential building and forming a single, habitable unit with facilities used or intended for living, sleeping, cooking and eating, by one family." The ZHB's finding is clearly consistent with the plain language of the Zoning Ordinance. Given the undisputed nature of the improvement the Applicant made to the building, there is no question that the factual basis for the finding is supported by substantial evidence.

The ZHB further found that living space constituted an "Accessory Dwelling" use under the Zoning Ordinance which is not a permitted use in the SR-2 (Suburban Residential) Zoning District where Applicant's property is located. The Zoning Ordinance defines a "Dwelling" as "a structure or portion thereof that is used exclusively for human habitation." The Zoning ordinance defines an "Accessory Dwelling" (use H14) as a "single family dwelling used as a residence by relatives, tenant farmers or employees of a farm or estate." The ZHB's finding is clearly consistent with the plain language of the Zoning Ordinance. Moreover, the undisputed evidence regarding the living space improvement and its use as a residence by Applicant's niece provide a substantial factual basis for the ZHB's finding.

Applicant argued that the extensive living space he constructed in his detached garage is an "in-law suite." . . . The Zoning Ordinance in the instant case does not identify an "in-law suite" as a separate use. . . . The ZHB properly concluded that because the detached garage is a separate structure and is not part of the principal dwelling, Applicants is not entitled to convert the garage into an "in-law suite."

By letter dated November 23, 2009, the Zoning Officer informed Applicant of her determination that the proposed construction of a "great room" connecting the garage to the house would create a "Two-Family Detached Dwelling" (use B4). The ZHB upheld the decision of the Zoning Officer. The Zoning Ordinance defines a

"Two-Family Detached Dwelling" as "two dwelling units within one building, and both dwelling units within one lot and without the dwelling units being completely separated by vertical and horizontal fire walls." As stated above, the ZHB properly concluded that the extensive living space created by the Applicant constituted a "Dwelling Unit." The ZHB therefore, did not abuse its discretion or commit an error of law in concluding that concerning two separate structures, both of which contain dwelling units, would create a "Two-Family Detached Dwelling."

Applicant argued that his proposal to connect the two buildings would create one principal dwelling, thereby transforming the impermissible. "Accessory Dwelling" use into a permissible principal dwelling use. The ZHB properly found that connecting the two buildings would not create one principal dwelling but rather would create a "Two-Family Detached Dwelling" which is not permitted in a SR-2 (Suburban Residential) Zoning District. As explained above, the ZHB found that the property has two separate dwelling units, the primary residence and the apartment above the detached garage each with separate and complete living facilities, each supported by their own electrical, plumbing, heating and other utilities. Merely connecting these two buildings does not alter their designation as separate dwellings. To hold otherwise would completely blur the distinction between single family residence and multiple family housing.

Finally, Applicant challenges the denial of his request for a variance. . . . [T]o qualify for a variance an applicant must establish that (1) an unnecessary hardship stemming from unique physical characteristics or conditions will result if the variance is denied; (2) because of such physical circumstances or condition, there is no possibility that the property can be developed in strict conformity with the provisions of the zoning ordinance and a variance is necessary to enable the reasonable use of the property; (3) the hardship has not been created by the applicant; (4) granting the variance will not alter the essential character of the neighborhood nor be detrimental to the public welfare; and (5) the variance sought is the minimum variance that will afford relief. To obtain a variance, a landowner bears the heavy burden of proving that he suffers from an unnecessary hardship, which hardship is not self-imposed, and that granting the variance will not adversely affect the public health, safety, and welfare.

Applicant claims that he sought a *dimensional* [area] variance. The ZHB found Applicant's request to conduct an accessory dwelling use (an "in-law suite") in a detached structure constituted a request for a use variance. . . . A use variance involves a request to use property in a manner that is wholly outside zoning regulations. There is a more relaxed standard for establishing unnecessary hardship for a dimensional [area] variance, as opposed to a use variance. The courts may consider multiple factors to determine whether an applicant established unnecessary hardship for a dimensional variance including the cost of the strict compliance with the zoning ordinance the economic hardship that will result from denial of a variance, and the characteristics and conditions of the surrounding neighborhood. "Where no hardship is shown or where the asserted hardship amounts to a landowner's desire to increase profitability or maximize development potential, the unnecessary hardship criterion required to obtain a variance is not satisfied even under the relaxed standard. . . ." In the instant case, Applicant failed to establish any hardship, economic or otherwise. He failed to establish that a variance was necessary to enable the reasonable use of his property. It is undisputed that Applicant initially developed and enjoyed the use of the Property within the parameters of the Zoning Ordinance. The ZHB, therefore, did not abuse its discretion or commit an error of law in denying Applicant's request for a variance.

For the reasons set forth above, this court affirmed the decision of the New Britain Township Zoning Hearing Board.

By The Court: Diane E. Gibbons, J.

## Questions for Consideration

1) Was Mortimer seeking an area variance or a use variance?

2) What is the accessory use in this case?

3) What two strategies or lines of argument did Mortimer make use of in an effort to get what he wanted?

4) Where does this decision leave the property owner in terms of the structure that he has already built?

## Takeaway

- Generally, accessory uses have to be located on the same lot as the primary use. This is what makes them accessory uses, permitted without a variance. Some people may have two small residential lots and may think that if they have a single-family home on one lot, they can place a detached garage on the adjoining lot. This is not the case if the zoning dictates that a lot in a given zone can be used for a single-family home; the garage might be an accessory use to the home when located on the same lot, but is not an accessory use to the home if it is located on its own lot.

- An accessory use must be both *incidental* and *customary*. If a gas station owner seeks to add a small convenience store to his property, he might assert that it is permitted as an accessory use. He would need to show that it is customary for contemporary gas stations to have a convenience store attached, and that the store will be incidental. Showing that the store is incidental, might include estimates of the expected sales or profits from store activities compared to gasoline sales. It might also be based on square feet of space devoted to the different activities.

- A significant feature of an accessory use is that the use does not require a variance. This is the general understanding unless the code in a particular jurisdiction expressly states otherwise.

## Discussion Problem 6.2

Dominique and her husband live with their three children in a nice home on a large two-acre lot in a suburban neighborhood. The zoning code applicable to their home limits the use to single-family residential with one dwelling unit on a lot. Dominique's oldest daughter, Tina, is age 21. Tina has a disability which requires the availability of 24-hour care and supervision, but Tina is also reasonably functional in taking care of herself, within a structured and supervised environment. Tina has been acting out because she knows that other people her age have independence and do not live at home with their mom, dad, and younger siblings. She wants her own space. Plus, she met a person that she wants to live with. Dominique wants to find a way for Tina to live with her friend and to have some independence while still being able to be supervised and cared for by her family. Dominique seeks to have an additional dwelling unit (ADU) on her property. This would be a small unit with minimal space. It would not have a full kitchen, and Tina and her friend would have access to the kitchen in the main house. The ADU would have a sink and a microwave but no oven or stove top. The tiny house would be placed on a part of the lot that has a number of mature trees and shrubs such that the ADU would not be visible from the street or from adjoining properties. The only alternatives to the ADU would be for the family to move to a neighborhood with different zoning, but they have been in this neighborhood for years and everyone knows them. Buying and moving to a new multi-family home is also very expensive. The other alternative is to find a group home willing and able to take Tina. This is also expensive, and it is highly unlikely that Tina will be able to be in the same group home as her friend. Moreover, Tina does not do well when she is away from family members. For all of these reasons, Dominique seeks to have an ADU on her property. What do you suggest to Dominique? Consider this alternatively as a request for an accessory use, an area and use variance [using the New York criteria, discussed at the beginning of Section C, *supra*], and a request for a reasonable accommodation under an appropriate part of federal disability law. Assess the chances of winning under each approach. What standard of review should a reviewing court apply to a decision on appeal from a zoning board of appeal determination?

# E. Nonconforming Use

A nonconforming use, as the term implies, is a use that does not conform to the zoning code. Sometimes a property becomes nonconforming when the zoning code is updated. For example, in time period one, a city zoning code may require all structures to be built at least twenty feet set back from the edge of the road. In time period two, the city may decide that a greater setback is desirable, and thus it updates the code to require at least a forty-foot set back from the edge of the road. Such an update in the code requirements would make all of the homes that were previously in compliance, nonconforming. This type of nonconforming use is generally permitted to continue as a "legal nonconforming use" (this is some-times referred to as being "grandfathered"). Another situation that results in a nonconforming use is when someone does something not permitted by the code, such as expanding a deck into a required set back without a variance, or adding an enclosed porch without a required permit. These activities would result in illegal nonconforming uses.

Legal nonconforming uses may continue but are subject to certain limitations. These limitations may typically include an inability to expand the use, to rebuild it if it is destroyed, and to make improvements to the legal nonconforming use. A legal nonconforming use may also be subject to elimination under an authorized *amortization* law.

## Cigarrilha v. City of Providence

Supreme Court of Rhode Island

64 A.3d 1208 (R.I. 2013)

ROBINSON, Justice. On appeal, the plaintiffs, Cecilia and Manuel Cigarrilha, con-tend that the trial justice in the Superior Court erred in declining to declare that their three-family rental property, which is located in an area of the city of Provi-dence that is zoned for no more than two-family dwelling units, was a pre-existing legal nonconforming use. This case came before the Supreme Court pursuant to an order directing the parties to appear and show cause why the issues raised in this appeal should not be summarily decided. After a close review of the record and careful consideration of the parties' arguments (both written and oral), we are satisfied that cause has not been shown and that this appeal may be decided at this time. For the reasons set forth in this opinion, we affirm the judgment of the Superior Court.

### Facts and Travel

It is undisputed that plaintiffs own real estate located at 24–26 Farragut Avenue in Providence (the property) and that they have owned the property jointly since 2000. The parties agree that the subject dwelling units at 24–26 Farragut Avenue were constructed in approximately 1911 — several years prior to 1923, the year in which Providence adopted its first zoning ordinance. Pursuant to the terms of the 1923 zoning ordinance, any uses established prior to the enactment of that ordinance were deemed to be grandfathered unless abandoned. Neither party disputes the fact that the property owned by plaintiffs is currently situated in a Residential R-2 zone, which zone is defined by the current zoning ordinance as being one "intended for low density residential areas comprising single-family dwelling units and two-family dwelling units in detached structures located on lots with a minimum land area of five thousand (5,000) square feet."

In 2008, plaintiffs sought permits from the city so that they might restore electri-cal meters at the Farragut Avenue property. Before issuing the requested permits, the city conducted an inspection of the property, during which plaintiffs were found to be in violation of several provisions of the city's housing code and Rhode Island's building code. Most pertinently, the inspection revealed that the property was being used as a three-family dwelling and that, therefore, it was not in compliance with the above-quoted provision of the zoning ordinance. The city maintains that the area in which the property is located is zoned for single- and two-family residences, and it contests plaintiffs' contention that they should benefit from the grandfathering provision.

On May 1, 2008, plaintiffs commenced this action in the Superior Court for Providence County by filing a verified complaint as well as a motion for a temporary restraining order. In that motion, plaintiffs sought to enjoin the city from enforcing the city's codes based upon the above-referenced violations; in addition, they sought to compel the city's building official to issue all permits necessary with respect to restoring the electrical meters. . . .

Following the May 1, 2008 hearing in the Superior Court, plaintiffs filed with the city's zoning board an appeal of the city official's determination that their property was an illegal three-family dwelling. After a hearing on July 22, the zoning board affirmed the city official's determination that using the property as a three-family dwelling was illegal.

Thereafter, plaintiffs filed an amended verified complaint in their pending Superior Court action, in which they appealed the zoning board's decision and sought a declaration that their use of the property as a three-family dwelling was a legal nonconforming use. . . .

. . . [T]he trial justice issued a written decision, in which he found that plaintiffs had failed to meet their burden of proving that the property was used as a three-family dwelling prior to the enactment of the city's first zoning ordinance in 1923. He therefore declined to declare that the property constituted a legal nonconforming use. The trial justice also ruled that plaintiffs had failed to establish that either equitable estoppel or the equitable doctrine of laches precluded the city from enforcing its zoning ordinance.

The plaintiffs filed a timely notice of appeal. . . .

### The Merits of the Nonconforming Use Contention

We have previously noted that a "nonconforming use is a particular use of property that does not conform to the zoning restrictions applicable to that property but which use is protected because it existed lawfully before the effective date of the enactment of the zoning restrictions and has continued unabated since then." It is axiomatic that the "burden of proving a nonconforming use is upon the person or corporation asserting the nonconforming use." . . . The proponent of a nonconforming use must shoulder that burden because the law views nonconforming uses as "thorn[s] in the side of proper zoning [which] should not be perpetuated any longer than necessary." Indeed, . . . "[t]he policy of zoning is to abolish nonconforming uses as speedily as justice will permit."

The plaintiffs contend that the trial justice erred when he declined to sufficiently consider the tax assessment records because of his view that they constituted inadmissible hearsay. In order to succeed in having their property declared a legal nonconforming use, plaintiffs were required to prove that the Farragut Avenue property was used as a three-family dwelling at the time of the enactment of the zoning ordinance in 1923. We note that all evidence in the record, including the tax assessment records, postdate 1923. Bearing in mind the previously described burden of proof that the law imposes upon plaintiffs, it is our view that we need not address plaintiffs' above-referenced contention because the evidence of any use of the property after 1923 is irrelevant to the determination of legal nonconforming use. As the trial justice correctly noted, the record is silent as to the use of the property in 1923; accordingly, we perceive no error in the trial justice's conclusion that plaintiffs failed to sustain their burden of proof. Therefore, in our view, the trial justice did not abuse his discretion in declining to declare that plaintiffs' property was a legal nonconforming use, nor did he misinterpret the applicable law, overlook facts, or otherwise exceed his authority.

. . . .

### Conclusion

For the reasons set forth in this opinion, the judgment of the Superior Court is affirmed.

## *Questions for Consideration*

1) What is the alleged nonconforming use?

2) Is the alleged nonconforming use a legal or illegal nonconforming use?

3) What was the problem with Cigarrilha's submitted evidence in support of his use?

4) Who has the burden of proof in establishing a legal nonconforming use?

## *Takeaway*

- Nonconforming uses are disfavored.

- Generally, nonconforming uses may not be enlarged or expanded.

- Generally, nonconforming uses cannot be rebuilt. For example, if a nonconforming structure burns down, the property owner will generally not be permitted to rebuild it.

- Generally, remodeling and upgrading a nonconforming use is not permitted.

- Generally, if a nonconforming use is abandoned (not used for a certain period of time), it will cease to be a legal nonconforming use.

## Edelhertz v. City of Middletown

United States District Court for the Southern District of New York

943 F. Supp. 2d 388 (S.D.N.Y. 2012)

RAMOS, Judge. The Melvyn Edelhertz and Helaine Edelhertz Revocable Living Trust ("Plaintiff" or "Edelhertz") brings this action against the City of Middletown ("Defendant" or the "City") pursuant to 42 U.S.C. §1983, alleging violations of its procedural due process rights guaranteed by the Fourteenth Amendment to the U.S. Constitution. Plaintiff now moves for partial summary judgment on the issue of liability only and Defendant cross-moves for summary judgment. For the reasons stated below, Plaintiff's motion is denied and Defendant's cross-motion is granted.

### I. Factual Background

The following facts are undisputed unless otherwise indicated. Plaintiff is the owner of a multiple-dwelling building located at 57 Beattie Avenue in the City of Middletown, New York (the "Beattie Avenue property"). Melvyn and Helaine Edelhertz acquired the Beattie Avenue property in 1993 and transferred title to it to Plaintiff in 1995. The building has four units, and is a non-owner occupied nonconforming use located in the City's R-1 zoning district. As an owner of a non-owner occupied multiple dwelling in zone R-1, the City required Plaintiff to apply for and obtain a permit from the Commissioner of Public Works, which he obtained annually and which contained Plaintiff's correct name and address.

On July 13, 2009, the Common Council of the City enacted an amendment to Chapter 475 of the Zoning Code of the City of Middletown to eliminate non-owner occupied multiple dwellings in various zoning districts, including zone R-1. The amendment (the "Amortization Law") provided the following:

> Any multiple dwelling in existence in any R-1, R-2, or OR-2 zoning district as of the date of enactment of this Subsection . . . shall, at the expiration of five years from such date, become a prohibited and unlawful use and shall be discontinued, excepting, however, that this Subsection . . . shall not apply to any multiple dwelling which is owner-occupied, and further excepting that this Subsection . . . shall not apply to any multiple dwelling for which it is structurally unreasonable to convert into a lawful use in the subject zoning district. The determination as to whether it is structurally unreasonable to convert a particular multiple dwelling into a lawful use shall be made by the Commissioner of Public Works.

The zoning districts affected by the Amortization Law contained a total of 142 multiple dwellings. Since 1995, 128 of them were cited for code violations, and between 2005 and 2010, there were police calls to 140 of those 142 dwellings-accounting for a total of 3,790 police calls. The Common Council determined that the prevalence of boardinghouses and apartments in multiple dwellings in those areas was the cause of increased code violations and criminal activity. Consequently, the Council enacted the Amortization Law to eliminate multiple dwellings, finding that they were undesirable, out of character, and impaired the orderly development and general welfare of the affected zoning districts.

The Common Council gave notice of the proposed enactment of the Amortization Law to any interested person through a "Public Hearing Notice" published in the legal classified advertisements of the Times Herald Record, the primary newspaper of Middletown and Orange Counties, on May 29 and 30, 2009. The public hearing was held on June 8, 2009. Only one person appeared at the hearing and spoke in favor of the Amortization Law; no one appeared to speak against it. The Council did not mail or deliver the notice to the Plaintiff or to any owner of the affected multiple dwellings, despite having knowledge of Plaintiff's correct name and mailing address.

On August 12, 2010, more than one year after the enactment of the Amortization Law, Plaintiff entered into a contract to sell the Beattie Avenue property to Composite LLC for $215,000. In the contract, Plaintiff represented to Composite that the Beattie Avenue property was a lawful multiple dwelling, but through a title report, Composite's attorney became aware of the existence of the Amortization Law. Both Edelhertz's attorney and Composite's attorney attempted to secure verification from the City that the Beattie Avenue property was a lawful nonconforming use and would be allowed to continue as such notwithstanding the Amortization Law, but never received a response. In early October 2010, Edelhertz's attorney further sought a specific determination from the City that the Beattie Avenue property could not be structurally altered to a conforming use, to which the Commissioner of Public Works did not respond. On October 6, 2010, the Commissioner sent Plaintiff a form-letter notifying him of the enactment of the Amortization Law. On October 26, 2010, Composite withdrew its offer to purchase the Beattie Avenue property.

Defendant does not dispute any material fact . . . nor does Plaintiff dispute any material fact. . . . [As to the Amortization Law,] Plaintiff argues that the City was required to provide him with notice by mail, while Defendant contends that notice by publication was sufficient.

## II. Summary Judgment Standard

Summary judgment is only appropriate where "the pleadings, depositions, answers to interrogatories, and admissions on file, together with the affidavits, if any, show that there is no genuine issue as to any material fact and that the moving party is entitled to judgment as a matter of law." . . .

 . . . .

## III. Discussion

Section 1983 [42 U.S.C.] protects against state action that violates a property owner's right to due process under the Fourteenth Amendment to the U.S. Constitution. To determine whether a procedural due process violation has occurred, courts must engage in a two-step analysis: first, a court must determine whether there exists a property interest of which a person has been deprived; and if so, a court must next determine if the procedures followed by the state were constitutionally sufficient.

## A. Constitutionally Protected Property Right

To possess a federally protected property interest, a person must have a legitimate claim of entitlement to it. Such a claim does not arise from the Constitution, but rather from an independent source such as state or local law. Under New York law, a nonconforming use that predates the enactment of a restrictive zoning ordinance is a vested right and is entitled to constitutional protection. A vested nonconforming use is defined as one that came into existence before enactment of the zoning ordinance that prohibits its use, and that is continuously maintained after the zoning changes take effect.

In the instant matter, it is undisputed that Plaintiff had a vested property right in the nonconforming use of his property as a non-owner occupied multiple dwelling. Though it is unclear from the record when exactly the Beattie Avenue property became a nonconforming use, it is clear that a non-owner occupied multiple dwelling is a nonconforming use in zone R-1, and that Plaintiff has maintained the property as such since obtaining title to it in 1993. Plaintiff's nonconforming use remained in effect upon enactment of the Amortization Law, which mandated its discontinuance within five years. Thus, Plaintiff had a vested property right in the maintenance of the Beattie Avenue property as a nonconforming use.

## B. The Amortization Law Was Legislative Action

Before a deprivation of a property interest occurs, the Due Process Clause requires, at a minimum, that the government provide "notice reasonably calculated, under all the circumstances, to apprise interested parties of the pendency of the action and afford them an opportunity to present their objections." However, due process protections are not required when the government takes action that is legislative rather than adjudicative. The Supreme Court has not recognized a constitutional right to participate directly in legislative action because of the "massive intrusion into state and federal policymaking" that would result. "Government makes so many policy decisions affecting so many people that it would likely grind to a halt were policymaking constrained by constitutional requirements on whose voices must be heard." "Instead, the public may influence the legislative process by effectuating its power over those elected officials through, *inter alia*, the electoral process." Thus, due process "does not require any hearing or participation in legislative decision making other than that afforded by judicial review after rule promulgation."

In the Second Circuit, "the test for determining whether official action is adjudicative or legislative focuses on the function performed by the decisionmaker, not on the method of selecting the decisionmaker, or on the form in which the decision is announced." Action is adjudicative when it is based on "facts about the parties and their activities, businesses, and properties," and "designed to adjudicate disputed facts in particular cases." On the other hand, government action is legislative when it considers "general facts which help the tribunal decide questions of law and policy and discretion," and when it has "general application and look[s] to the future."

Adjudicative decisions apply a statute or legal standard "to a given fact situation involving particular individuals," whereas legislative action entails "the formulation of a general rule to be applied . . . at a subsequent time." Procedural due process claims "must be dismissed when they challenge purely legislative action."

Plaintiff argues that enacting the Amortization Law was adjudicative — and not legislative — action as to him because it was "based on a host of targeted facts" and was "retrospective in nature looking back over several years of examined activity." Therefore, he asserts that he was entitled to individual notification of the proposed legislation. However, the Common Council's decision to enact the Amortization Law "did not attempt to adjudicate particular facts as to any one [landowner] or group of [landowners]," nor was it enacted to single out any individual "for special consideration based on [her] own peculiar circumstances." Rather, the Common Council, acting in a policy-making capacity, considered facts relating generally to non-owner occupied multiple dwellings in the relevant zoning districts. . . . Here, the Council found that non-owner occupied multiple dwellings *generally* impaired the orderly development and general welfare of certain zoning districts. These findings were based on data indicating that the prevalence of non-owner occupied multiple dwellings was the cause of increased housing and sanitary code violations as well as criminal activity.

As the Amortization Law applies "across the board to all" non-owner occupied multiple dwellings in the affected zoning districts, and does "not seek to impose any retroactive penalty," but rather is forward looking, it cannot be considered an adjudicative decision by the Common Council. Accordingly, because the City's enactment of the Amortization Law constitutes legislative action, Plaintiff was not entitled to due process protection before its enactment.

. . . .

### IV. Conclusion

. . . The Clerk of the Court is respectfully directed to . . . enter judgment in favor of Defendant.

It is so ordered.

### *Questions for Consideration*

1) What is the purpose of amortization?

2) What was the purported reason (justification) for the amortization law in this case?

3) Edelhertz brought this case under 42 U.S.C. §1983; what needs to be determined in order to conclude that a violation of Edelhertz's due process rights occurred?

4) How does the court explain the difference between legislative and adjudicative functions?

5) Does the court determine that the amortization law is legislative or adjudicative, and why?

6) What kind of notice did due process require in this situation?

## *Takeaway*

- Amortization provides a means for eliminating a nonconforming use.

- An amortization time period must be reasonable and provide some opportunity for the property owner to realize a return on her investment in the property.

- If an amortization statute does not permit a property owner to earn a reasonable return on her investment, it may be challenged as a taking of property without just compensation.

## Giurleo v. McCusker

Massachusetts Land Court

2010 Mass. LCR LEXIS 44 (Mass. Land Ct. 2010)

LONG, Justice. In this case, plaintiffs James and Elaine Giurleo appeal from a decision of the defendant Town of Westwood Zoning Board of Appeals' (the "ZBA") granting defendant Belle Soloway a special permit to construct an accessory apartment addition to her single-family home. . . .

A trial was held before me, jury-waived, . . . . I find and rule that the ZBA's decision was neither arbitrary nor capricious and, accordingly, must be upheld. The ZBA's decision is thus affirmed and the plaintiffs' claims are dismissed. . . .

### Facts

Defendant Belle Soloway applied for and received a special permit to construct an addition to her existing home for an accessory apartment. Ms. Soloway's home, located at 109 Cobleigh Street in Westwood in a Single Residence A ("SRA") district, is a preexisting nonconforming structure. In an SRA district, the minimum dimensional requirements include the following: a lot area of 12,000 square feet, a lot frontage of 90 feet, a lot width of 90 feet, a non-wetland area of 12,000 square feet, a front setback of 25 feet, a side yard setback of 15 feet, and a rear yard setback of 30 feet. The Bylaw also has a maximum building coverage requirement of 25 percent. Ms. Soloway's property, however, only contains 9,849 square feet and does not conform to the minimum lot area, lot frontage, lot width, and non-wetland area requirements. It also appears, based upon plans submitted into evidence, that Ms. Soloway's originally existing home also was nonconforming with respect to minimum side yard setback requirements.

Ms. Soloway applied for a building permit to construct the addition (an apartment intended for her elderly father). The plot plan filed with the application indicated that the proposed apartment would be constructed along the boundary line between Ms. Soloway's and the plaintiffs' properties — varying in distance from that line between 3.6 and 3.9 feet. That application was denied by the building inspector because he believed that the addition required special permits under Bylaw §§ 4.4.3 (Accessory Apartments) and 4.5.6 (Special Permit for Nonconforming Uses and Structures). Based upon that determination, Ms. Soloway filed an application with the ZBA seeking special permits.

A hearing on Ms. Soloway's application was held on June 21, 2006, at which the plaintiffs testified in opposition to the proposal. In two separate decisions, the ZBA granted Ms. Soloway's special permits. In its decision regarding the nonconforming structure, the ZBA indicated that the applicable sections of the Bylaw included §§ 4.5.3 (Nonconforming Structures), 4.5.4 (New or Expansion of Nonconformity), and 4.5.6 (Special Permit). Those sections of the Bylaw provide for the following:

> 4.5.3 Nonconforming Structures. The Board of Appeals may grant a special permit to reconstruct, extend, alter or change a nonconforming structure in accordance with this Section only if it determines that such reconstruction, extension, alteration or change shall not be substantially more detrimental than the existing nonconforming structure to the neighborhood. The following types of changes to nonconforming structures may be considered by the Board of Appeals:
>
> > 4.5.3.1 Reconstructed, extended or structurally changed.
> >
> > 4.5.3.2 Altered to provide for a substantially different purpose or for the same purpose in a substantially different manner or to a substantially greater extent.
>
> 4.5.4 New or Expansion of Nonconformity. The reconstruction, extension or structural change of a nonconforming structure in such a manner as to increase an existing nonconformity, or create a new nonconformity, including the extension of an exterior wall at or along the same nonconforming distance within a required setback, shall require the issuance of a special permit from the Board of Appeals.
>
> 4.5.6 Special Permit. In the event that the Building Inspector determines that the nonconforming nature of such structure would be increased by the proposed reconstruction, extension, alteration or change, the Board of Appeals may, by special permit, allow such reconstruction, extension, alteration or change where it determines that the proposed modification will not be substantially more detrimental to the neighborhood than the existing nonconforming structure.

In reaching its decision, the ZBA made the following findings:

1. The Petitioner proposes to construct an addition to the right rear section of the house located at 109 Cobleigh Street. The addition would be used as an Accessory Apartment for the applicant's elderly father. The addition will consist of a living and

kitchen area, bedroom, and full bathroom. The project will require a special permit pursuant to Section 4.5.6 because the lot area is non-conforming. The Board of Appeals is the Special Permit granting authority.

2. The side yard setback of the existing garage section of the house, to which the accessory apartment will be attached, is 11.0 feet from the lot line tapering to 10 feet in the back. The addition will be at 3.9 feet from the lot line tapering to 3.6 feet in the rear.

3. There is a fence between the Petitioner's property and the abutter to the right facing the side of the property. The side windows of the proposed structure will be set at such a height that they will not interfere with the privacy of the abutter. The proposed accessory apartment will have a height of less than fifteen (15) feet.

4. A letter signed by twenty-five neighbors and abutters of the Petitioner in support of the request for a special permit to build an Accessory Apartment was submitted to the Board.

5. Any adverse effects of the Petitioner's proposed construction will not outweigh its beneficial impact to the Town, or the neighborhood, in view of the particular characteristics of the site and the proposal in relation to that site. The proposed addition will be situated so that it is minimally visible from the street.

6. The Petitioner's proposed construction will not have a material adverse effect on the value of the land and buildings in the neighborhood, or on the amenities thereof, or be detrimental to the normal use of the adjacent property, and it will not be injurious or dangerous to the public health or hazardous because of traffic congestion, or other reason, and any adverse effects of the proposed use do not outweigh its beneficial aspects, all in view of the particular characteristics of the site and of the proposal in relation to that site.

7. The Petitioner has met all the requirements for a Special Permit pursuant to the Westwood Zoning Bylaw.

Based on these findings, the ZBA unanimously voted to grant the special permit and allowed the construction of the accessory apartment so long as, among other conditions, it was "constructed in strict conformity with the submitted plan entitled 'Renovations and Additions to the Soloway Residence', consisting of two (2) pages, prepared by Ira Rakatansky . . . and the submitted plot plan. . . ."

The plaintiffs timely appealed from the ZBA's decision regarding the special permit for the nonconforming structure. Subsequently, Ms. Soloway was granted a building permit and construction began. . . . As constructed, the addition is located 16 feet from the rear lot line and between 3.4 and 4.2 feet from the side lot line adjacent to the plaintiffs' property.

At trial, Ms. Soloway and Mr. Giurleo testified. In addition, Thomas C. Houston (an engineer) and Richard Kattman (a landscape architect) were called by Ms. Soloway to offer expert testimony and Elizabete Fekete (a real estate appraiser) was called by the plaintiff to offer expert testimony. Relevant details of their testimony, as well as other pertinent facts, are included in the analysis section below.

## Analysis

### Standing

Ms. Soloway challenged the plaintiffs' standing to bring this action. Standing is a jurisdictional prerequisite. In order to obtain standing, a plaintiff must "assert a plausible claim of a definite violation of a private right, a private property interest, or a private legal interest." The injury claimed by the plaintiff must also be "legitimately within the scope of the zoning laws."

As abutters to Ms. Soloway, the plaintiffs "enjoy a rebuttable presumption that they are 'persons aggrieved.'" ... Specifically, the plaintiffs allege that due to the "looming" apartment building being constructed within three feet of their property line, they have suffered because of a decrease in privacy, decrease in their property value, and an increase in noise and artificial lights shining into their residence.

These alleged injuries clearly relate to "density interests protected by applicable zoning laws." ... Without question, Ms. Soloway's apartment addition increased the nonconformities of her property since the addition to the building is located 3.6 feet from the side yard lot line and 16 feet from the rear lot line, and it now violates maximum building coverage (the total lot coverage is now 27.4% and the maximum coverage is 25%).... The trial testimony and exhibits admitted into evidence (as also confirmed by my observations on the site view) clearly revealed that the addition, built so close to the plaintiffs' property line, has a significant impact on the plaintiffs' property and constitutes a harm sufficient to provide standing.

.... The court's "function on appeal," ... is "to ascertain whether the reasons given by the [ZBA] had a substantial basis in fact, or were, on the contrary, mere pretexts for arbitrary action or veils for reasons not related to the purposes of the zoning law." The ZBA must have acted "fairly and reasonably on the evidence presented to it," and have "set forth clearly the reason or reasons for its decisions," in order to be upheld.

. . . .

Based on the evidence and testimony at trial, I find that the ZBA's determination was *not* arbitrary and capricious. While the *plaintiffs* obviously are impacted by the size and location of the addition, there is little to no impact to the *neighborhood*. Indeed, even the plaintiffs' own expert, Ms. Fekete, testified that the addition did *not* have a "significant negative impact" on the property values in the neighborhood. Similarly, Ms. Soloway's witnesses testified that the addition is consistent in style and size to both the primary residence and to the neighborhood in general. Ms. Soloway's home still has the appearance of a single-family home and, indeed, the addition can barely be seen from Cobleigh Street (the view from the neighborhood's perspective). There also was no testimony to indicate that the addition will add undue traffic congestion to the neighborhood roads, would negatively impact the environment, or would negatively impact the health and welfare of the neighborhood.

. . . Evidence submitted at trial supports the ZBA's conclusion and indicates that the ZBA was neither arbitrary nor capricious in issuing the special permit. Therefore, the decision must be upheld.

### Conclusion

For the foregoing reasons, the ZBA's decision granting Ms. Soloway a special permit pursuant to Bylaw § 4.5.6 is neither arbitrary nor capricious and is hereby affirmed. The plaintiffs' claims are accordingly dismissed.

So ordered.

### *Questions for Consideration*

1) Why was Soloway seeking to expand a nonconforming use?

2) Did the zoning code provide authority for granting the expansion of a nonconforming use?

3) What findings were made by the ZBA with respect to the application for expanding the nonconforming use?

4) Was there any expert testimony in support of or against the application to expand the nonconforming use?

5) How does the court deal with Ms. Soloway's challenge to plaintiff's standing to bring this lawsuit?

6) What standard of review does the court apply to the ZBA decision in this case?

### *Takeaway*

- While the general rule is that nonconforming uses may not be enlarged, one must read the applicable zoning code and law to determine if there are exceptions to the general rule in a given jurisdiction.

- The case illustrates a situation combining both an accessory use issue with a nonconforming use issue.

- As we have seen elsewhere, it is important for the ZBA to make findings that support the rationality of its decision-making.

# F. Spot Zoning

Spot zoning is generally not permitted. Spot zoning happens when one or a few properties are singled out for zoning changes that are not applied to surrounding properties. Spot zoning raises concerns because it generally does not occur in the context of a broad review of the comprehensive plan for a community. Instead, spot zoning generally represents a piecemeal adjustment to zoning that is not necessarily pursuant to a comprehensive plan. Spot zoning also raises questions of due process, and equal protection.

For more on spot zoning, revisit *Foothill Communities Coalition v. County of Orange* (Chapter 4).

## Discussion Problem 6.3

Big Tractor and Truck Company has a business location just off the local interstate highway. In order to make the business more noticeable to potential customers, Big Tractor engages a sign company to design a 4-feet by 5-feet lighted sign that can be placed on a 14-foot sign pole. The design work, manufacturing and installation of the sign pole and the mounted sign with electricity for the lighting cost Big Tractor $23,000. The sign was up and in use for about four months before another business, located next to Big Tractor, went to the town for a permit to put in a similar sign for its business. This brought the attention of town officials to the sign installed by Big Tractor. Big Tractor never came in to apply for and obtain the required permit for placing a structure and sign on the property as required by the code. When Cheryl, the town code enforcement officer, went to examine the Big Tractor sign, she discovered that Big Tractor not only did not apply for the required permit, Big Tractor's sign violates the zoning code. The code restricts signs in a commercial zone such as the one applicable to Big Tractor. The code limits the height of signs to 10 feet and a size of three feet by four feet or of a height and width specifically approved by the planning board not to exceed 12 square feet. Lighting, pole material, and sign placement must all be approved by the planning board prior to issuing a permit. Because Big Tractor is in non-compliance with the code, it must file for a permit (pay the permit fees) and now go to the zoning board of appeal if it wishes to ask for a variance so as not to have to take down and replace the sign that it recently purchased for $23,000. The sign company that designed and delivered the sign to Big Tractor has a clause in its contract that says the property owner is responsible for compliance with local planning and zoning code requirements. Thus, the sign company asserts that it has no liability. Nonetheless, the sign company plans to appear at the zoning board of appeal hearing with Big Tractor so that it can explain why, in its opinion, the sign needs to be the size and of the design they created, in order to be safely visible to potential customers driving at high speed on the nearby interstate highway. They make assertions in support of the need for the size and design of the sign without any studies to support their claim that the sign has to be larger than the code requirements to be safely visible to nearby drivers on the interstate. Big Tractor and the sign company also have no studies to support the claim that potential customers of Big Tractor actually drive on the nearby interstate. Nonetheless, this is their testimony to the zoning board of appeal.

Technically, a zoning board of appeal should review the Big Tractor case in the light of the work not yet having been done. At the same time, everyone knows the work has been done and Big Tractor spent $23,000 on it. Big Tractor claims it did not know it needed a permit to put a sign up on its own property. As the attorney for the zoning board, how will you advise the board with respect to granting a variance for Big Tractor so that it can keep its sign even though it did not file for a permit and did not follow the rules applicable to all businesses in a commercial zone. Would it make any difference if Big Tractor intentionally did not file for a permit because it wanted a sign bigger than the code allowed, and it figured that if they built it first, they would not have to take it down? Should intent matter when the zoning code does not say anything about intent? [For this problem, use the New York criteria for a variance found at the beginning of Section C, *supra*.]

## Discussion Problem 6.4

Wilbert Johnson owns a small convenience store in the City of Fansville, across the street from the law school on the campus of Big University. He calls his store Wilbert's, and he has operated the store for over 30 years. When he opened the store, it was in a neighborhood on the far edges of the Big University campus. The store is located in what a lot of people call a rundown building, and it has a dirt parking lot. Since it opened up, the neighborhood has continued to grow, and when the university placed a new law school building on property across the street from Wilbert's, business really took off. As the neighborhood grew and roads were developed, the zoning code was dramatically changed. There were now zoning requirements that made Wilbert's building and operation non-conforming uses. If the new code is applied to Wilbert's, Wilbert's would be in violation because Wilbert's building is: 1) too large for the lot, 2) in violation of the requirements for accessibility under the zoning code and the Americans with Disabilities Act, 3) is placed too close to the road in violation of current setback requirements, and 4) it has an unpaved dirt parking lot. Wilbert has defended against city enforcement of the code requirements on the grounds that his property is "grandfathered" under earlier zoning code requirements. Recently, there was a fire at Wilbert's, and the damage destroyed about 20% of his store. Wilbert had insurance on the building and plans to use the insurance proceeds to restore the damaged part of the store to its prior condition.

Develop the best arguments for Wilbert in support of rebuilding his store to what it was prior to the fire. Also develop the best arguments for the City of Fansville to use the fire as an opportunity to eliminate Wilbert's store as a nonconforming use.

# G. Floating Zone

A floating zone is an approved zoning district that is, at the time of its creation, "unanchored" to a specific location on the zoning map. When a use is identified that meets the requirements of the floating zone, an application can be made to locate the zone on the zoning map.

## Beyer v. Burns

Supreme Court of New York, Albany County
567 N.Y.S.2d 599 (N.Y. Sup. Ct. 1991)

HUGHES, Judge. Petitioners seek judgment annulling Local Laws, 1990, No. 6 which established a Senior Citizen Residence District (SCRD) in the zoning code of the Town of Bethlehem by use of a "floating zone."

The petition alleges that petitioners reside on or near North Street in the Town of Bethlehem, the proposed site of a 50-unit senior citizen housing project. The area is presently zoned "A" residential. It is alleged that on June 1, 1990, Bethlehem Town Supervisor Kenneth Ringler submitted a letter to the United States Department of Housing and Urban Development (HUD) seeking financial aid for the project. Local Law No. 6 was enacted on November 28, 1990, to facilitate the project. Petitioners assert that Local Law No. 6 creates a "floating zone" in which the only permitted use would be multifamily dwelling arranged as individual units for the occupancy of elderly families, with 12% of the units allowed to be occupied by nonelderly physically handicapped families. HUD did not fund the project during 1990, but the sponsors of the project intend to reapply.

. . . .

Zoning provisions creating a district limited to elderly people and the creation of a five-acre "floating zone." It is against that background that the causes of action must be examined. . . .

[It is] . . . allege[d] that the "sunset" provision of the local law which has the property revert to its original zoning classification if a building permit is not applied for and actual construction commenced within two years of the rezoning of the parcel violates Town Law. The argument appears to be that the creation of a temporary district is not permissible under the Town Law. The court disagrees. . . . The court noted: "In enacting the challenged amendments, the Town Board has sought to control subdivision in all residential districts, pending the provision (public or private) at some future date of various services and facilities. A reading of the relevant statutory provisions reveals that there is no specific authorization for the 'sequential' and 'timing' controls adopted here. That, of course, cannot be said to end the matter, for the additional inquiry remains as to whether the challenged amendments find their basis within the perimeters of the devices authorized and purposes sanctioned under current enabling legislation. Our concern is, as it should be, with the effects of the statutory scheme taken as a whole and its role in the propagation of a viable policy of land use and planning."

The Court of Appeals determined that even though the timing controls placed in the zoning ordinance were not specifically authorized in the Town Law, they were still sustainable as a reasonable method of controlling development pursuant to the comprehensive plan. The reason advanced by the Town Board for the "sunset" provision in issue is set forth at paragraph 10 of the affidavit of Kenneth J. Ringler, Jr., as follows: "In the past, the Town Board had granted zoning changes for Planned Residence Districts which had remained on the map for years but were never built. As the years passed, the neighborhoods and character of the community surrounding them changed so that the initial project approval was no longer appropriate for the area. It was only then, that the developer sought to pursue such project. To avoid this zoning dilemma, the Town Board determined to place a time restriction for the commencement of the project."

This court can find nothing in the Town Law prohibiting the timing device enacted by the Town Board. Furthermore, the "sunset" provision appears to be a reasonable method of controlling development in furtherance of the town's over-all zoning plan. . . .

. . . .

> "Whatever the final conclusion as to the hazards of the floating-zone technique, it seems clear that it does not necessarily constitute spot zoning, and it will be approved if it is employed as a part of the community's comprehensive plan.
>
> "The floating zone described in this section, and approved in the cases cited herein, is a single use zone."

The . . . cause of action [also] asserts that the "floating zone" constitutes illegal "spot zoning." "Spot zoning is the singling out of a small parcel of land for a use classification totally different from that of the surrounding area, for the benefit of the owner of the property and to the detriment of the other owners." Petitioners have the burden of proof upon the charge that the "floating zone" constitutes illegal "spot" zoning and have failed to meet that burden. Simply put, the petitioners have not established that the purpose behind the SCRD is to benefit the owners of the proposed location on North Street, rather than to benefit the community by providing low-cost senior citizen housing pursuant to a comprehensive plan.

. . . .

The respondents are entitled to a judgment dismissing the petition and declaring that Local Law No. 6 of the year 1990 is a valid enactment.

## Questions for Consideration

1) What is the purpose of this floating zone; that is, what use does it permit? Why use a floating zone in planning a zoning map? What are the benefits of planning for a floating zone? What are the potential issues?

2) In addition to being a floating zone, this zone has a *sunset* provision. What is the purpose of the sunset provision?

3) What is the legal concern with respect to the validity of the sunset provision?

4) Why doesn't a floating zone such as the one in this case violate the prohibition against illegal spot zoning?

## *Takeaway*

- Floating zones are permitted when established pursuant to a comprehensive plan and in accordance with authority delegated to the local planning and zoning authority.

- "Sunset" provisions are a useful way of limiting the duration of floating zones.

# H. Vesting

When a property right becomes fixed, it is said to be vested. Vested property rights are protected by the Fifth Amendment's Takings Clause. A significant issue in a planning and zoning context concerns determining when a property interest becomes vested with respect to planning and zoning regulations. The development of land often takes a considerable amount of time and money, especially in the case of large-scale real estate development projects. Many resources must be invested in property development over extended time periods. The question and risk that arises is one of figuring out how best to deal with the possibility of changes in the zoning and planning code during the development process.

### Western Land Equities v. City of Logan

Supreme Court of Utah

617 P.2d 388 (Utah 1980)

STEWART, Justice. Defendants appeal from a ruling of the district court that the City of Logan unlawfully withheld approval of plaintiffs' proposed residential plan and was estopped from enforcing a zoning change that prohibits plaintiffs' proposed use. We affirm the trial court's order.

In February 1969 plaintiffs purchased 18.53 acres of property within the City of Logan. In April 1976, pursuant to a new land use ordinance, the property was zoned M-1, a manufacturing zone which permitted single-family dwellings. Plaintiffs' intent was to use the property for moderately priced single-family housing.

The procedure for securing approval of single-family residential subdivisions is established by city ordinance. The ordinance requires consultation with the city planning commission, preparation and submittal of a preliminary plan showing compliance with minimum requirements of the subdivision ordinance, and approval of both preliminary and final plans by the city planning commission. . . . Plaintiffs' project was introduced on July 13, 1977. . . .

[The City of Logan changed its zoning code on January 19, 1978, and denied the Plaintiff's project.]

In connection with plaintiffs' motion for summary judgment, the parties submitted stipulated statements of facts and issues. The issues submitted to the court were:

1. Did the M1 Land Use Description as set forth in the Logan City Land Use Ordinance of 1976, prior to the January 31, 1978 amendment, permit the

development of subdivisions consisting of single family dwelling units on property zoned M1? [M1 zones are for manufacturing and permit single-family dwellings.]

2. Does the amendment to the M1 Land Use Description of the Logan City Land Use Ordinance of 1976, which was adopted January 31, 1978 and which prohibits the development of single-family dwelling units in the M1 zone except by special use permit, give Defendants the authority to deny approval of Plaintiff's Willow Creek subdivision which was submitted prior to the amendment . . . ?

Plaintiffs sought a determination, as a matter of law, that they had a vested right to develop a subdivision of single-family dwellings on their property and that defendants were estopped from withholding approval of the subdivision.

The trial court in its findings of fact and conclusions of law held that plaintiffs' proposed development was permissible under the zoning regulations in existence prior to January 31, 1978, that plaintiffs had substantially complied with procedural requirements and had a vested right to develop the proposed subdivision, and that defendants were estopped from withholding approval of plaintiffs' subdivision on the basis of the amended ordinance enacted after the application for subdivision approval had been submitted.

On appeal defendants argue that the planning commission was justified in its disapproval of plaintiffs' proposed subdivision because of its undesirable or non-conforming aspects. . . .

. . . .

Defendants also contend that, in any event, the application for approval of a subdivision does not create vested rights in the owner which immunize him from subsequent zoning changes. Since the decision of the court below was based on a finding that plaintiffs did have such a vested right, . . . we deal only with the issue of whether the amendment to the zoning ordinance enacted by the city could be retroactively applied to plaintiffs' application for subdivision approval.

It is established that an owner of property holds it subject to zoning ordinances enacted pursuant to a state's police power. *Euclid v. Ambler Realty Co.,* 272 U.S. 365, 47 S. Ct. 114, 71 L. Ed. 303 (1926). With various exceptions legislative enactments, other than those defining criminal offenses, are not generally subject to the constitutional prohibitions against retroactive application. The legality of retroactive civil legislation is tested by general principles of fairness and by due process considerations.

This Court has previously dealt with the issue of retroactive application of zoning laws in *Contracts Funding & Mortgage Exchange v. Maynes,* Utah, 527 P.2d 1073 (1974). . . .

The holding of Contracts Funding is not in accord with the rule generally accepted in other jurisdictions that an applicant for a building permit or subdivision approval does not acquire any vested right under existing zoning regulations prior to the issuance of the permit or official approval of a proposed subdivision. Generally, denial of an application may be based on subsequently-enacted zoning regulations.

However, for the reasons discussed below, we are of the view that the majority rule fails to strike a proper balance between public and private interests and opens the area to so many variables as to result in unnecessary litigation. We hold instead that an applicant for subdivision approval or a building permit is entitled to favorable action if the application conforms to the zoning ordinance in effect at the time of the application, unless changes in the zoning ordinances are pending which would prohibit the use applied for, or unless the municipality can show a compelling reason for exercising its police power retroactively to the date of application.

In the present case, the trial court found that plaintiffs had acquired a vested development right by their substantial compliance with procedural requirements and that the city was estopped from withholding approval of the proposed subdivision. The court used the language of zoning estoppel, a principle that is widely followed. That principle estops a government entity from exercising its zoning powers to prohibit a proposed land use when a property owner, relying reasonably and in good faith on some governmental act or omission, has made a substantial change in position or incurred such extensive obligations or expenses that it would be highly inequitable to deprive the owner of his right to complete his proposed development.

The focus of zoning estoppel is primarily upon the conduct and interests of the property owner. The main inquiry is whether there has been substantial reliance by the owner on governmental actions related to the superseded zoning that permitted the proposed use. The concern underlying this approach is the economic hardship that would be imposed on a property owner whose development plans are thwarted. Some courts hold that before a permit is issued no action of the owner is sufficient reliance to bar application of changes in zoning ordinances because there has been no governmental act sufficient to support an estoppel. Accordingly, a landowner is held to have no vested right in existing or anticipated zoning. . . .

Generally, "substantial reliance" is determined by various tests employed by the courts-for example, the set quantum test, the proportionate test, and a balancing test. The set quantum test, used by the majority of courts, determines that an owner is entitled to relief from new, prohibitory zoning if he has changed his position beyond a certain point, measured quantitatively. A related test is the proportionate test, which determines the percentage of money spent or obligations incurred before the zoning change as compared with the total cost. The problem with both of these tests is that there is no predictable point short of adjudication which separates reliance that is less than "substantial" from the reliance sufficient to result in a vested right or to support an estoppel.

The balancing test, although likely to produce a more fair outcome in a particular case, also results in little predictability. The test weighs the owner's interest in developing his property and the reasonableness of his proposed use against the interests of public health, safety, morals, or general welfare. If the gain to the public is small when compared to the hardship that would accrue to the property owner, the actions of the owner in preparation for development according to a formerly permitted use may be seen as sufficiently substantial to justify the issuance of a permit or continuation of development despite an amendment to the zoning ordinances.

An additional requirement generally considered in zoning estoppel cases is that of the existence of some physical construction as an element of substantial reliance. Preconstruction activities such as the execution of architectural drawings or the clearing of land and widening of roads are not sufficient to create a vested right, nor generally are activities that are not exclusively related to the proposed project.

If the substantial reliance requirement of zoning estoppel were applied to the facts of the present case, we could not agree with the trial court that plaintiffs' "substantial compliance" with procedural requirements justified the estoppel of the city's enforcement of a new zoning ordinance. Although plaintiffs allege they proceeded with subdivision plans and incurred significant costs with the encouragement of certain city officials, they had not yet received official approval of their plan, and their expenditures were merely for surveying and preliminary plans. The record indicates that plaintiffs spent $1,335 for a boundary survey and $890 for the preparation of a preliminary subdivision plat. The boundary survey has value regardless of the city's approval or disapproval of the plaintiffs' proposal. The expenditure of $890 for the plat is not significant in relation to the size of the parcel and is not substantial enough to justify an estoppel with regard to the enforcement of valid zoning ordinances that became effective before official approval of plaintiffs' proposed subdivision.

In rejecting the zoning estoppel approach in this matter, we are not prepared to state that it would never be relevant to a determination of the validity of the retroactive application of a zoning ordinance. We are of the view, however, that the relevant public and private interests are better accommodated in the first instance by a different approach.

. . . .

Courts in several states have adopted the view, not unlike that stated in *Contract Funding & Mortgage Exchange v. Maynes, Utah,* 527 P.2d 1073 (1974), that an application for a building permit creates a vested right as of the time of application. Pennsylvania, one of these states, initially followed the general rule that a vested right accrued when an owner could show substantial reliance, made in good faith, on a validly issued permit. In 1968 the Pennsylvania court in *Gallagher v. Building Inspector, City of Erie,* 432 Pa. 301, 247 A.2d 572 (1968), eliminated the need to show reliance on a permit to create a vested right when the amendment to the zoning ordinance was not considered by the city council until after a permit had been issued. At the present time Pennsylvania follows what is termed the "pending ordinance rule." This rule provides that an application for a permitted use cannot be refused unless a prohibiting ordinance is pending at the time of application.

. . . .

Idaho has also adopted the view that an applicant is entitled to a building permit upon compliance with the zoning ordinance in effect at the time of the application, at least where no zoning change is pending. . . .

. . . .

The State of Washington has also refused to follow the general rule that building permits are not protected against revocation by subsequent zoning change unless a permittee has gained a vested right through a substantial change in position in reliance on the permit. . . .

> Notwithstanding the weight of authority, we prefer to have a date certain upon which the right vests to construct in accordance with the building permit. . . . The more practical rule to administer, we feel, is that the right vests when the party, property owner or not, applies for his building permit, if that permit is thereafter issued. This rule, of course, assumes that the permit applied for and granted be consistent with the zoning ordinances and building codes in force at the time of application for the permit.

. . . .

A vested right in a particular development scheme may [also] be created by statute. For example, in Pennsylvania, § 508(4) of the Municipalities Planning Code confers a vested right on property owners who have previously received approval of a subdivision plan in which the lots are too small to conform to the requirements of a newly-enacted ordinance. This vested right has a three-year duration. The California Legislature has also considered bills which would grant a limited expansion of vested rights.

In our view the tests employed by most other jurisdictions tend to subject landowners to undue and even calamitous expense because of changing city councils or zoning boards or their dilatory action and to the unpredictable results of burdensome litigation. The majority rule permits an unlimited right to deny permits when ordinances are amended after application and preliminary work. It allows government in many cases broader power with regard to land regulation than may be justified by the public interests involved. A balancing test, though geared toward promoting fairness, must be applied on a case-by-case basis and offers no predictable guidelines on which landowners can intelligently base their decisions regarding extensive development projects. Tests currently followed by the majority of states are particularly unsatisfactory in dealing with the large multistage projects. The threat of denial of a permit at a late stage of development makes a developer vulnerable to shifting governmental policies and tempts him to manipulate the process by prematurely engaging in activities that would establish the substantial reliance required to vest his right to develop when inappropriate.

The economic waste that occurs when a project is halted after substantial costs have been incurred in its commencement is of no benefit either to the public or to landowners. In a day when housing costs have severely escalated beyond the means of many prospective buyers, governmental actions should not be based on policies that exacerbate a severe economic problem without compelling justification. Governmental powers should be exercised in a manner that is reasonable and, to the extent possible, predictable.

On the other hand, a rule which vests a right unconditionally at the time application for a permit is made affords no protection for important public interests that may legitimately require interference with planned private development. If a proposal met zoning requirements at the time of application but seriously threatens public health, safety, or welfare, the interests of the public should not be thwarted.

The above competing interests are best accommodated in our view by adopting the rule that an applicant is entitled to a building permit or subdivision approval if his proposed development meets the zoning requirements in existence at the time of his application and if he proceeds with reasonable diligence, absent a compelling, countervailing public interest. Furthermore, if a city or county has initiated proceedings to amend its zoning ordinances, a landowner who subsequently makes application for a permit is not entitled to rely on the original zoning classification.

. . . .

At the same time, compelling public interests may, when appropriate, be given priority over individual economic interests. A city should not be unduly restricted in effectuating legitimate policy changes when they are grounded in recognized legislative police powers. There may be instances when an application would for the first time draw attention to a serious problem that calls for an immediate amendment to a zoning ordinance, and such an amendment would be entitled to valid retroactive effect. It is incumbent upon a city, however, to act in good faith and not to reject an application because the application itself triggers zoning reconsiderations that result in a substitution of the judgment of current city officials for that of their predecessors. Regardless of the circumstances, a court must be cognizant of legitimate public concerns in considering whether a particular development should be protected from the effects of a desirable new law.

In the present case, the zoning of the property in question was found by the trial court to have permitted the proposed use at the time of the application. The owners had received encouragement from city officials, although no official approval was rendered. After the application, the city council members decided to reexamine the pertinent zoning regulation and thereafter voted to amend or "clarify" the zoning ordinance to disallow subdivisions in an M-1 zone and permit residences only by special permit. Their actions may have had a reasonable basis. It was argued that fire protection would be undermined because of limited access roads, but it does not appear the problem would be any less serious if the unarguably-permitted manufacturing facilities were erected instead of single-family houses. Objections as to inadequate sidewalks and other problems can be handled by requiring modification of specifications that do not meet city subdivision requirements. Indeed, the order of the trial court stated that the developers must comply with all the reasonable requirements of the city's subdivision ordinance.

We do not find the reasons given by the city for withholding approval of plaintiffs' proposed subdivision to be so compelling as to overcome the presumption that an applicant for a building permit or subdivision approval is entitled to affirmative official action if he meets the zoning requirements in force at the time of his application.

The order of the trial court is affirmed. No costs awarded.

Maughan, Wilkins and Hall, JJ., concur.

Crockett, C.J., concurs in result.

## Questions for Consideration

1) What is the nature of Western Land's real estate development project? What are they trying to build, and what is their difficulty?

2) What is zoning estoppel?

3) In determining substantial reliance, courts generally use one of three tests; the set quantum test, the proportionate test, and the balancing test. Explain each of these tests.

4) What is the "pending ordinance" rule discussed in the court's opinion?

5) What are some of the economic factors to consider in determining when a development right has vested?

6) If a development right is vested at the start of a major real estate development project, and in the interim the zoning laws change, does the completed project end up being a legal nonconforming use?

## Takeaway

- In addition to the various tests for vesting discussed in this case, many planning and zoning professionals will speak in terms of an *early vesting* jurisdiction or a *late vesting* jurisdiction. An early vesting jurisdiction might be one that has a rule that vesting occurs when a proper application is filed. A late vesting jurisdiction might be one that holds that vesting does not occur until the final certificate of occupancy is issued. There are different events along the timeline of a real estate development project that can be identified and used as a "time certain" event at which vesting occurs. As this case points out, these rules are easier to work with than balancing tests and trying to figure out when a developer has demonstrated substantial reliance. A jurisdiction that picks a specific event, such as filing an application, an event that comes early in the process, is a jurisdiction with early vesting. A jurisdiction that picks an event that comes late in the process, such as issuing a final certificate of occupancy, is a late vesting jurisdiction. The earlier vesting takes place, the lower the risk of change to the real estate developer.

- Local governments, in many cases, retain the power to change the zoning if doing so is important to the public health, safety, welfare, and morals. Generally, this would be based on new information developed after vesting, or as a result of changed circumstances.

# I. Contract Zoning

Sometimes property owners undertake long-term projects that may be subject to zoning changes and amendments during the time needed to complete the development project. When zoning requirements change during the development process, it can disrupt plans and destroy investment expectations. The possibility of zoning changes during development involves risk, and risk is a cost. Consequently, property owners will try to reduce the risk of zoning changes and amendments. One idea is to contract with local government authorities in order to obtain a promise that the local government will not make changes to the zoning requirements after a date certain. The question that arises is one of the legality of such contracts.

## Carlino v. Whitpain Investors

### Supreme Court of Pennsylvania
### 453 A.2d 1385 (Pa. 1982)

FLAHERTY, Judge. This equity action was commenced . . . by the appellants, Peter Carlino and Elizabeth Carlino, seeking a preliminary injunction against the appellees, Whitpain Investors (hereinafter Developer), Whitpain Township (hereinafter Township), and Pennsylvania Department of Transportation (hereinafter PennDOT). . . .

. . . The facts as alleged by appellants' complaint establish the following. Developer is constructing an apartment complex in the Township on a 47 acre tract of land situated between three roads, one of which, Stenton Avenue, is a state highway. Appellants' residence lies directly across Stenton Avenue from the construction site. Developer's predecessor in title sought to have the 47 acre tract rezoned from an R-1 (single-family) classification to an R-3 (multi-family) classification to permit construction of residential rental units. At the hearing on rezoning of the tract, the then owner stipulated that a 300 foot buffer would be provided from the right-of-way line of Stenton Avenue, and further specified that no access road from the apartment complex to Stenton Avenue would be built. In 1973, the requested zoning change was adopted by the Township. In 1979, however, construction of an access road from the apartment complex to Stenton Avenue commenced, and appellants became aware that the land development plan finally approved by the Township had, at the insistence of the Township, included a provision for access to Stenton Avenue, and that in 1978, a driveway permit authorizing construction of the access road to Stenton Avenue had been issued by Penn DOT. [In other words, the Township changed its position as to the desirability of an access road.]

. . . .

Appellants [argue that the] . . . presence of the access road immediately adjacent to their property will cause inconvenience and annoyance, thereby impairing the value of their property in a manner not compensable in damages. . . .

With respect to Township and Developer, appellants seek an injunction requiring the former to refrain from conditioning Developer's construction permit upon provision of the access road in question, and requiring the latter to eliminate that road and restore the 300 foot buffer zone along Stenton Avenue. The complaint alleges that Developer's predecessor in title, pursuant [to] an agreement with the Township, stipulated as to plans to preserve the buffer area and forego an access road to Stenton Avenue, thereby rendering the 1973 rezoning contractually conditioned upon there being no access route traversing the buffer zone. [Appellants seek to hold the Township to the 1973 contractual condition.]

The concept of contractually conditioned zoning advanced by appellants lacks precedent in this Commonwealth, and authorities elsewhere differ with respect to whether to accord the concept validity. The proposition has long been recognized in this Commonwealth that individuals cannot, by contract, abridge police powers which protect the general welfare and public interest. "Where the rights of individuals under a contract which would otherwise be perfectly valid are in conflict with the 'general well-being of the State,' the rights of the individuals must give way to the general welfare." The police power of municipalities cannot be subjected to agreements which restrict or condition zoning district classifications as to particular properties. . . .

> Zoning is an exercise of the police power to serve the common good and general welfare. It is elementary that the legislative function may not be surrendered or curtailed by bargain or its exercise controlled by the considerations which enter into the law of contracts. . . .

Accordingly, we reject the view that agreements, and concomitant representations or stipulations, which induce changes in zoning district classifications limit the effect of those changes once enacted. Thus, . . . proceedings to enforce the restrictions were properly dismissed by the court below.

Order affirmed.

## Questions for Consideration

1) What did the Township do that prompted this lawsuit by Carlino?

2) What is the concept of contract zoning, and should it be permitted?

## Takeaway

- As the case reminds us, zoning involves the exercise of the police power to protect and advance the public, health, safety, welfare, and morals. This is an inherent power of sovereignty, and the government cannot contract away its authority to act for the public health, safety, welfare and morals. Limitations on the exercise of the police power include those we have discussed in this book, such as, due process, equal protection, takings, and limitations imposed by the protection of other fundamental rights (including free speech, and rights of people with disabilities, for example).

# J. Development Agreements

In many ways, development agreements have similarities to contract zoning, but development agreements are permitted. These agreements provide some degree of certainty to a property owner/developer while preserving the police power.

## Santa Margarita Area Residents Together v. San Luis Obispo County

### Court of Appeal of California, Second Appellate District, Division Six
### 100 Cal. Rptr. 2d 740 (Cal. Ct. App. 2000)

PERREN, Judge. Santa Margarita Area Residents Together, an association; Kenneth Haggard; and Otto Schmidt appeal the judgment denying their petition for writ of mandate to set aside a development agreement between defendant San Luis Obispo County (County) and real party in interest Santa Margarita Limited. To develop its property, Santa Margarita Limited needs to be certain that the law governing local development will not change during the development process. Relying on the development agreement statute, [Gov. Code section 65864 et. seq.], the landowner and County agreed to a development plan. Appellants contend that the agreement is invalid under the statute because it covers the planning stage of a real estate development before buildings or other structures have been designed or approved. Appellants also contend that, under these circumstances, the zoning "freeze" in the agreement unconstitutionally contracts away the County's police power. We conclude that this agreement, which assigns rights and obligations to both government and developer concerning the planning of a large real estate project, complies with the statute and does not contract away the County's police power. We affirm.

### Facts and Procedural History

The Santa Margarita Ranch (Ranch) consists of approximately 13,800 acres of real property in San Luis Obispo County. The owner of the Ranch, Santa Margarita Limited, has long desired to develop the Ranch. Santa Margarita Area Advisory Council, a community organization, has opposed the development. After Santa Margarita Limited sued the County to facilitate development by increasing the number of legal parcels in the Ranch, Santa Margarita Limited, the County, and representatives of the Santa Margarita Area Advisory Council agreed to mediate their differences over long-range development of the Ranch. The mediation achieved a consensus among most of the participants, including representatives from the Santa Margarita Area Advisory Council. A mediation report reflecting the consensus recommended approval of a project which would include 550 housing units and nonresidential improvements in an 1,800-acre area, devote at least 8,400 acres to permanent open space easements, and place a minimum of 3,600 acres under 40-year . . . contracts for preservation of agricultural land. The report also recommended use of a development agreement to guarantee that the 550 residential units would be "subject to applicable laws and regulations."

Shortly after the mediation, the County began preparing a development agreement with Santa Margarita Limited for the specific planning of a project which would include the improvements and other land uses specified in the mediation report and which also designated a golf course, guest lodge, equestrian center, bikeways, and parklands as nonresidential improvements (Project). At the same time, the County amended part of its general plan, the Salinas River Area Plan, to describe the Project and establish certain criteria for its ultimate implementation.

After lengthy negotiations and a public hearing, the County enacted an ordinance authorizing it to enter into the development agreement (Agreement). The next day, the chairperson of the County's board of supervisors signed the Agreement.

### Discussion

### Santa Margarita Agreement

In general, the Agreement freezes zoning on the Project property in return for the developer's commitment to submit a specific plan for construction in compliance with County land use requirements. Contingencies and further approvals remain, but the Agreement commits the County and Santa Margarita Limited to the Project, including its public improvements and amenities.

Specifically, the Agreement provides that Santa Margarita Limited will file a comprehensive application for approval of the Project, including a specific plan, a vesting tentative map, and an environmental impact report. The specific plan must incorporate the standards set forth in the Salinas River Area Plan. The application must state that Santa Margarita Limited will commit itself to develop the Project in its entirety and to engage in all necessary environmental review. The Agreement also provides that Santa Margarita Limited will dedicate land for a public swimming pool, sewer treatment plant, and cemetery expansion.

In return for these commitments, the County agrees to process, review, and approve or disapprove the specific plan, and to apply its current zoning and other land use regulations to the plan without change for up to five years during the review and approval period. The Agreement is entered into under the authority of the Development Agreement Statute and satisfies its technical requirements.

. . . .

. . . [T]he Agreement was approved by an ordinance duly enacted by the County Board of Supervisors and we defer to that body in matters pertaining to the merits, usefulness and public advantages of the Agreement. One of the purposes of development agreements is to obtain benefits for the public, and the record shows that the

County believed that an agreement was required as an incentive to the developer to engage in the comprehensive planning desired by the County, and also as an incentive to expand the public facilities and benefits included in the Project.

The Agreement also represents the resolution of a protracted dispute and balances the interests of all concerned parties. Santa Margarita Limited sought a more comprehensive agreement but, according to a planning commission staff report, the County decided to "lock in" the Salinas River Area Plan standards while deferring construction approval. The record reveals that the County's decision resulted from careful assessment of the importance of the Ranch to the region.

The record also reveals that the Agreement resulted from a mediation by parties interested in the future of the Ranch. The mediation did not result in unanimity but produced an agreement among most participants, including representatives of the public. As such, the mediation and Agreement reflect an inclusive and open governmental process.

### Surrender of Police Power

... [The] appellants argue that [the Agreement] does too much to avoid constitutional infirmity. Appellants contend that the freeze on Ranch zoning before a project that is ready for construction constitutes the contracting away of the County's zoning authority and, therefore, a surrender of the right to exercise its police power in the future. We disagree. If anything, case law concerning a municipality's "surrender" of its regulatory authority supports the conclusion that the Agreement ... satisfies all constitutional mandates concerning a city or county's exercise of its regulatory authority.

It is established that a city or county may not contract away its right to exercise police power in the future and that the power to enact, modify, and amend zoning and other land use regulations constitutes a part of a county's police power. Therefore, the development agreement statute must be construed in a manner that does not permit the County to surrender its police power in the name of planning efficiency.

The Agreement in this case presents no such constitutional infirmity. Land use regulation is an established function of local government and the County has authority to enter into contracts to carry out this function. A contract which "appears to have been fair, just, and reasonable at the time of its execution, and prompted by the necessities of the situation or in its nature advantageous to the municipality at the time it was entered into, is neither void nor voidable merely because some of its executory features may extend beyond the terms of office of the members" of the legislative body which entered into the contract.

A governmental entity does not contract away its police power unless the contract amounts to the "surrender" or "abnegation" of a proper governmental function. The zoning freeze in the Agreement is not such a surrender or abnegation. The Project must be developed in accordance with the County's general plan (§ 65867.5), and the Agreement does not permit construction until the County has approved detailed building plans. The Agreement retains the County's discretionary authority in the future and, in any event, the zoning freeze is for five years. It is not of unlimited duration.

The County concluded that the zoning freeze in the Agreement advances the public interest by preserving future options. This type of action by the County is more accurately described as a legitimate exercise of governmental police power in the public interest than as a surrender of police power to a special interest.

### Conclusion

. . . .

It is true that local government may not surrender its regulatory power through ad hoc commitments. It may, however, act in partnership with private enterprise, as authorized by the development agreement statute and the Agreement. The Agreement addresses recurring land use issues without limiting the County's regulatory discretion. Through the Agreement, the County tailors the exercise of its legislative power to the complex issues involved in regulating a major real estate project in the public interest. By requiring expeditious Project planning and preserving future options, the Agreement enhances the County's power to regulate land use to achieve its Salinas River Area Plan and other land use goals.

The judgment is affirmed. Costs on appeal are awarded to Santa Margarita Limited.

## Questions for Consideration

1) Who is bringing this lawsuit, and who is being sued?

2) What did the local government do that formed the basis of this lawsuit?

3) What is the nature of Santa Margarita Limited's development project?

4) What did Santa Margarita Limited agree to do for the public under the terms of the development agreement?

5) What factors did the court consider in determining that the development agreement was not impermissible contract zoning?

## Takeaway

- In drafting a development agreement, it is important to avoid identifying your agreement as a contract. While development agreements are in some ways very similar to contract zoning, it is important to refer to them as development agreements in order to avoid giving a court any added opportunity for characterizing your agreement as impermissible "contract" zoning. In other words, if the courts do not like contract zoning, you should not identify what you are doing by using such language. It just does not help to use wording that a court might point to if they are looking for a reason to invalidate your agreement.

- Development agreements usually require property owners/developers to provide some benefits to the community in exchange for beneficial approvals and permits granted by the local government. The nature of the benefits provided and offered are up for negotiation. From the local government's perspective, the benefits given and offered must be in furtherance of the public health, safety, welfare, and morals.

- In practice, development agreements may also be used to clarify vesting and to offer an alternative basis for fixing the development rights of a property owner/developer with respect to applicable planning and zoning regulations.

# K. Subdivisions

Subdividing land involves taking a single parcel of land and dividing it into two or more parcels that can be individually conveyed. Many zoning regulations prohibit the subdividing of land without local government approval. Zoning codes will typically have code sections governing subdivision of land and will require that certain criteria be met before subdividing is approved.

Every state has enabling legislation for subdivision of land. While these regulations can apply to relatively small parcels of land, they are generally used when a property owner seeks to develop a larger parcel by subdividing it into smaller lots. A developer, for instance, may acquire a large parcel of land and seek to develop twenty housing lots on that parcel. Special subdivision regulations will govern the layout of the lots in terms of size and shape. The regulations will also require provisions for infrastructure, roads, and utilities. There will be the need to evaluate the impact on traffic, and to assess the impact of new housing on schools and public services. The property owner will be required to submit plans and drawings for the subdivision. In obtaining approval for a subdivision, a local government may also require the dedication of property, easements, and a right of way for public purposes such as utilities and sidewalks. Subdivisions usually include a set of private restrictive covenants that control land uses within the subdivision in ways that go beyond the public regulations of the local zoning code. Once a subdivision is finally approved, a formal plat of the subdivision is recorded in the public records. Below is a sample subdivision plat as recorded in the public records in Onondaga County, New York. The plat shows the location of all lots and streets. All of the lots are numbered. Once the plat is filed, the legal description for each lot in the subdivision will refer to the indicated lot number shown on the Lewiston Manor Subdivision plat as recorded at a specified book and page number in the public land records. As the plat indicates, this subdivision (Lewiston Manor) was once part of lot 70 in the Town of DeWitt. The plat shows the division of the former lot 70 into a significant number of individual lots. Each lot is designed for a single-family residential home. The plat also indicates the portions of the original lot 70 dedicated to roadways and to park space.

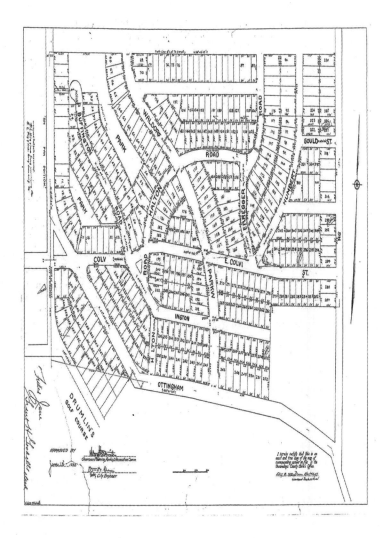

## Town of Hollywood v. Floyd

Supreme Court of South Carolina
744 S.E.2d 161 (S.C. 2013)

TOAL, Chief Justice. The Town of Hollywood (the Town) filed this action against William Floyd, Troy Readen, and Edward McCracken (collectively, the developers) seeking a declaration that the developers may not subdivide their property without approval from the Town's Planning Commission and an injunction prohibiting subdivision of the property until such approval is obtained. The developers filed counterclaims under 42 U.S.C. §1983 (2006), alleging equal protection and due process violations as well as various state law claims. . . . The jury returned a verdict in favor of the Town on the developers' due process claim, but awarded the developers $450,000 in actual damages on their equal protection claim. Both parties appealed. The Town argues the circuit court erred in denying its motions for a directed verdict and judgment notwithstanding the verdict (JNOV) on the developers' equal protection claim, and in granting the developers' motion for attorney's fees and costs. The developers argue the circuit court erred in granting summary judgment in favor of the Town on its claims for [being able to go forward with the subdivision]. . . .

## Factual/Procedural History

In February 2007, the developers entered into a contract to purchase a thirteen-acre tract located on Bryan Road in the Town of Hollywood. Thereafter, the developers filed an application with the Town's Planning Commission to rezone the property for residential use. The Planning Commission heard the matter on June 14, 2007, at which time the developers presented a "preliminary lot sketch" and indicated their intent to subdivide and develop the property into seventeen residential lots. Commissioner Matthew Wolf informed the developers their plans did not require rezoning; instead, Wolf instructed the developers to file for approval with the Planning Commission to subdivide their property. Wolf further stated that before the Planning Commission could hear a subdivision application, the developers needed to give notice to all landowners within a 300-foot radius of their property and gather information about roadways, drainage, and timber removal. . . .

. . . .

The Planning Commission then opened the floor for public comments. Councilwoman Annette Sausser stated she did not support the developers' subdivision. Sausser stated Bryan Road was too narrow to handle any additional traffic without improvement and noted the developers' property was located near a dangerous curve where multiple accidents had occurred. Sausser also cited drainage and environmental concerns associated with a nearby marshland and stated the Town's constituents did not support the developers' subdivision.

Other constituents also expressed concern about drainage issues and Bryan Road's ability to withstand additional traffic. One constituent stated, "Bryan Road is a one-car road. You cannot get two large vehicles past each other. And the idea that there might be another 30 cars coming down through there is just so difficult to imagine." Another constituent stated ingress and egress for residents along Bryan Road would not be satisfactory with additional traffic, and also expressed concern about the ability of emergency vehicles to access the road.

Subsequent to the meeting, the developers . . . closed on the property[,] . . . recorded the plats in the Charleston County [public land records] . . . office, [and commenced work on the subdivision.].

When the developers began working on the subdivision, the Town issued a stop-work order. After the developers indicated they would not comply with the stop-work order, the Town filed this action seeking declaratory and injunctive relief. Specifically, the Town sought a declaration that the developers could not subdivide their property without approval from the Town's Planning Commission and an injunction prohibiting subdivision of the property until such approval was obtained. The developers filed equal protection, due process, and state law counterclaims. . . .

On August 14, 2008, the developers appeared before the Planning Commission a second time to discuss the "preliminary subdivision" of their property. During the meeting, the Planning Commission informed the developers of multiple issues they needed to address before the Commission could approve the subdivision, including an acceptable septic system, a wetlands certification letter, and a traffic study of Bryan Road. Again, constituents expressed concern about Bryan Road's ability to handle a heightened level of traffic and the effect it would have on the dangerous curve adjacent to the developers' property.

In reference to the traffic study, Commissioner Wolf stated, "[N]o one's denying access to the [developers'] lot. No one has ever suggested that there be no access to that lot." Instead, Wolf stated, it is a matter of "commonsense and safety for the Town of Hollywood." Wolf stated Bryan Road is "one of the most dangerous roads in Hollywood" with a high density of traffic. Consequently, Wolf explained, the Planning Commission requested a traffic study to ensure Bryan Road could withstand a heightened level of traffic and that it would not hinder emergency vehicles' access to the properties along Bryan Road. The Planning Commission ultimately tabled the subdivision request until the developers addressed all necessary issues.

[The developer challenged the failure to approve the subdivision.]

. . . .

### Law/Analysis

. . . .

Section 30-7 of the Town's Code states no subdivision plat may be filed or recorded in the [public records office] . . . and no building permits may be issued "until the plat . . . has been submitted to and approved by the town planning commission according to the procedures set forth in this chapter." Section 30–34 provides the Planning Commission's procedure for review and approval of subdivision plats shall consist of two separate steps: (1) review and approval of a preliminary plat, and (2) review and approval of a final plat. That section further provides that "the developer may submit a sketch plan for the planning commission's informal review prior to step one." However, as an exception to the general rule that subdivision plats must be approved by the Planning Commission, section 30-12 states the Town's zoning administrator may approve and sign plats without referring them to the Planning Commission upon a finding that all requirements have been met and the property is being subdivided into "three or fewer lots."

We find the circuit court properly granted summary judgment in favor of the Town with respect to its claims for declaratory and injunctive relief. The Town's ordinances clearly state the Planning Commission . . . must approve subdivision plats if the property is subdivided into more than three lots. . . . [T]he developers intended to subdivide their property into seventeen lots. . . .

[On appeal, this court finds that the circuit court properly granted summary judgment in favor of the town.]

[As to the circuit court ruling that there was an equal protection violation;] [t]he Town argues [that] the circuit court erred in denying its motions for a directed verdict and JNOV on the developers' equal protection claim because they failed to demonstrate that the Planning Commission treated them differently than other similarly situated developers. . . .

When reviewing the trial court's ruling on a motion for a directed verdict or JNOV, this Court applies the same standard as the trial court by viewing the evidence and all reasonable inferences in the light most favorable to the nonmoving party. . . .

No person shall be denied equal protection of the law. U.S. Const. Amend. XIV, § 1; S.C. Const. Art. I, § 3. "The *sine qua non* of an equal protection claim is a showing that similarly situated persons received disparate treatment." Where an alleged equal protection violation does not implicate a suspect class or abridge a fundamental right, the rational basis test is used. To prevail under the rational basis standard, a claimant must show similarly situated persons received disparate treatment, and that the disparate treatment did not bear a rational relationship to a legitimate government purpose.

. . . [T]he equal protection clause does not prohibit different treatment of people in different circumstances under the law. . . .

We find the circuit court erred in denying the Town's motions for a directed verdict and JNOV because the developers failed to show the Planning Commission treated them differently than other similarly situated developers in the subdivision application process. Instead, the developers claim "this case is not the traditional equal protection case" and cite arguments in support of their due process claim. Specifically, the developers argue Councilwoman Sausser acted improperly by making a throat-cutting gesture and stating their development would "never happen." The developers further contend Commissioner Wolf should not have participated in the Planning Commission hearings because he lives in the adjoining subdivision. However, while the developers assert these actions alone demonstrate a denial of equal protection, the alleged misconduct relates only to the developers' due process claim, which the jury rejected and the developers did not appeal. The developers' confusion is further highlighted by the fact that they quote *due process* law in support of their equal protection argument.

The pertinent issue before this Court is whether the developers presented evidence that the Planning Commission treated them differently than other similarly situated developers. We find that . . . the developers failed to meet their burden of proof.

In response to the Town's motion for a directed verdict during trial, the developers argued the Planning Commission treated the developers of Stono Plantation differently because it did not require a traffic study despite the fact that Stono Plantation is adjacent to the developers' property. However, Stono Plantation is not a "similarly situated" comparator because it was approved for subdivision in 1985, long before the Town adopted its ordinances and created the Planning Commission in 1998.

The developers also argued the Planning Commission treated them differently than the developers of Wide Awake Park and Holly Grove because the Commission did not require traffic studies for those projects. However, there are material differences between those projects and the developers' subdivision. Wide Awake Park is a public park rather than a residential subdivision, was already developed when the Town acquired it, and required consolidation rather than subdivision of lots. Holly Grove is a low-income, "planned development" subject to a different approval process than residential subdivisions. Moreover, unlike the developers' subdivision, the community did not oppose either of those projects.

Additionally, neither Wide Awake Park nor Holly Grove is located on Bryan Road and the developers failed to present evidence suggesting the projects posed the same traffic and safety concerns as the developers' proposed subdivision. The Town presented evidence that Bryan Road is "one of the most dangerous roads in Hollywood" and that the developers' property is located along a dangerous curve where multiple accidents have occurred. Commissioner Wolf testified the Planning Commission's purpose behind requiring a traffic study was to ensure Bryan Road could safely support additional travelers. Because the addition of a new residential subdivision on Bryan Road would create a heightened level of traffic, we find the Planning Commission's decision to require a traffic study was rationally related to the legitimate goal of maintaining the safety of its citizens living and traveling along Bryan Road. We further find there are material differences between the developers' subdivision and its alleged comparators — Wide Awake Park and Holly Grove — which demonstrate a rational basis for treating them differently.

Accordingly, we find the circuit court erred in denying the Town's motions for a directed verdict and JNOV on the developers' equal protection claim. Because the developers are no longer the "prevailing party," we also find the circuit court erred in awarding attorney's fees and costs to the developers.

### Conclusion

We affirm the circuit court's grant of summary judgment in favor of the Town on its claims for declaratory and injunctive relief, reverse the circuit court's denial of the Town's motions for a directed verdict and JNOV on the developers' equal protection claim, and reverse the circuit court's award of attorney's fees and costs to the developers.

## Questions for Consideration

1)  How many lots did the developers intend to subdivide their property into?

2)  Who had to approve the subdivision? Was a different process available for subdividing a single parcel into fewer lots than what was proposed by the developers?

3) The developers asserted that the Town denied them due process and equal protection. How does the court address these claims in its opinion?

## *Takeaway*

- In a basic property law course, one often encounters fact patterns where the owner of one parcel of land decides to convey portions of the land to different people. These conveyances divide the original parcel into two or more smaller parcels. While property law may readily permit these conveyances, modern planning and zoning law typically subjects them to subdivision regulations. This means that while a conveyance may satisfy the requirements of property law, it may result in a violation of local land regulations and subject an owner to legal action.

- The merger or combining of lots will also typically be regulated by local planning and zoning laws.

- In addition to subdivisions, there will often be regulations for *planned unit developments* (P.U.D.s). A P.U.D. is another way of regulating real estate development and is typically used with larger scale projects. A zoning code will specifically provide requirements and a process for reviewing and approving a P.U.D. As with a subdivision, much work will be done working with the local planning department to address the requirements of the development and the specifics of the project. One objective of P.U.D.s is to create planned neighborhoods within a local community. The P.U.D. will involve private covenants and restrictions to supplement public zoning regulations governing land use. Often, the regulations will provide for *mixed use development*; for example, multifamily and single-family residential homes in different price ranges and perhaps the inclusion of rental units. Provisions are made for internal roads, utilities, and infrastructure. Likewise, there are typically provisions for community areas that include park-like green space, playgrounds, walking and bike paths. A common feature of P.U.D.s is *clustering* of housing. Consider a zoning code that requires one residential unit per acre of land. In a normal development or subdivision, a property owner might have ten acres of land and seek to subdivide it into ten lots with one house on each lot. Each lot might have a nice size yard, but it would be difficult to create large green spaces that can be shared by all of the lot owners in the development. Under the rules of a P.U.D., the developer might be able to cluster all of the housing together on one corner of the ten acres, placing four houses per acre. This means that ten houses can be built on two and one-half acres of land and that six and one-half acres remain available for such things as greenspace, a playground, a run-off water pond, and other shared uses. The P.U.D. permits flexibility in development provided certain criteria are met.

- Subdivisions and P.U.D.s are governed by their own planning and zoning ordinances, but understanding these ordinances should be straightforward once a person has a basic understanding of zoning law. In addition, subdivisions and

P.U.D.s are often covered in course materials on real estate transactions and on property law.

# L. Linkage Programs and Inclusionary Zoning

One concern arising from local land use planning and zoning law is that local regulations may be used to exclude people from certain communities. Exclusions may take any number of forms and be based on various characteristics or factors. A significant concern in many communities has to do with excluding people because of a lack of affordable housing. Local zoning regulations can drive up the cost of housing by requiring large lot sizes and large homes. This increases the cost of a home and drives low-income people out of the market. In this way, current residents can influence the development of planning and zoning regulations that exclude low-income people from "their" community. This practice is known as *exclusionary zoning*. An offsetting effort to increase access to a community by a cross section of people in different income groups is referred to as *inclusionary zoning*.

Two important state court decisions have shaped much of the conversation and law involving inclusionary zoning. These two cases are: *Southern Burlington County NAACP v. Mount Laurel Township*, 67 N.J. 151, 336 A.2d 713, *cert. denied*, 423 U.S. 808, 96 S. Ct. 18, 46 L. Ed.2d 28 (1975) (*Mt. Laurel I*), and *Southern Burlington County NAACP v. Mount Laurel Township*, 92 N.J. 158, 456 A.2d 390 (1983) (*Mt. Laurel II*). In general, these cases promoted a nationwide movement to advance affordable housing, and to require every community to plan for and provide its fair share of the affordable housing needed in a given region. In attempting to meet the challenge of inclusionary zoning, many communities have *linkage programs* to encourage or require construction of affordable housing with the granting of development approvals or the relaxation of zoning regulations. Programs that do this are commonly referred to as employing *incentive zoning*.

## Home Builders Ass'n v. City of Napa

Court of Appeal, First District, Division 5, California
90 Cal. App. 4th 188 (2001)

JONES, P.J. Home Builders Association of Northern California (HBA) appeals from a judgment entered after the trial court sustained a demurrer and dismissed its complaint asserting a facial challenge to an inclusionary zoning ordinance that was enacted by the City of Napa (City). HBA contends primarily that the trial court erroneously applied federal and California takings law. We disagree and will affirm the judgment.

### I. Factual and Procedural Background

City, like many other localities in California, has a shortage of affordable housing. This shortage has negative consequences for all of City's population, but causes particularly severe problems for those on the lower end of the economic spectrum. Manual laborers, some of whom work in the region's wine or leisure industries, are forced to live in crowded, substandard housing. There is a large and growing population of homeless, including many families and teenagers. Workers from low-income families increasingly are forced to live greater distances from their places of employment, which causes increased traffic congestion and pollution.

City formed the Napa Affordable Housing Task Force to address these problems. The task force was a broad based community group that included representatives from nonprofit agencies, environmental groups, religious institutions, local industries, for-profit developers, and the local chamber of commerce. The purpose of the task force was to "study the issues surrounding affordable housing in the City of Napa and . . . make recommendations to the Housing Authority Commission."

The task force studied housing issues for several months. It formed subcommittees, conducted public hearings, and evaluated affordable housing solutions that had been enacted by other communities. Ultimately the task force recommended that City enact an inclusionary housing ordinance[1] modeled after one that had been enacted by Napa County.

City responded by enacting the inclusionary zoning ordinance[2] that is at issue in the present appeal. The ordinance applies to all development in the city, including residential and nonresidential.

The primary mandate imposed by the ordinance on residential developers is a requirement that 10 percent of all newly constructed units must be "affordable" as that term is defined.[3] The ordinance offers developers two alternatives. First, developers of single-family units may, at their option, satisfy the so called inclusionary requirement through an "alternative equivalent proposal" such as a dedication of land, or the construction of affordable units on another site. Developers of multi-family units may also satisfy the 10 percent requirement through an "alternative equivalent proposal" if the city council, in its sole discretion, determines that the proposed alternative results in affordable housing opportunities equal to or greater than those created by the basic inclusionary requirement.

---

1. An "inclusionary zoning" or "inclusionary housing" ordinance is one that requires a residential developer to set aside a specified percentage of new units for lower moderate income housing. (See Padilla, *Reflections on Inclusionary Housing and a Renewed Look at its Viability* (1995) 23 Hofstra L.Rev. 539, 540.)

2. In fact, City enacted two ordinances to address the inclusionary housing problem. We will refer to the ordinances collectively as the inclusionary zoning ordinance or simply, the ordinance.

3. The definition of "affordable" in the ordinance is complex. In general, the term refers to an amount that could be paid by persons who live in a household that earns significantly less than the area median income.

As a second alternative, a residential developer may choose to satisfy the inclusionary requirement by paying an in-lieu fee. Developers of single-family units may choose this option by right, while developers of multi-family units are permitted this option if the city council, again in its sole discretion, approves. All fees generated through this option are deposited into a housing trust fund, and may only be used to increase and improve the supply of affordable housing in City.

Developments that include affordable housing are eligible for a variety of benefits including expedited processing, fee deferrals, loans or grants, and density bonuses that allow more intensive development than otherwise would be allowed. In addition, the ordinance permits a developer to appeal for a reduction, adjustment, or *complete waiver* of obligations under the ordinance "based upon the absence of any reasonable relationship or nexus between the impact of the development and . . . the inclusionary requirement."

HBA is a nonprofit corporation and association of builders, contractors, and related trades and professionals involved in the residential construction industry. In September 1999, HBA filed a complaint against City seeking to have the inclusionary zoning ordinance declared facially invalid. As is relevant here, HBA alleged the ordinance violated (1) the takings clauses of the federal and state Constitutions, (2) the Mitigation Fee Act (Gov. Code, § 66000 et seq.), (3) the due process clause of the federal Constitution, and (4) Proposition 218.

City demurred to the complaint, arguing it was entitled to prevail as a matter of law. City supported its demurrer with nearly 700 pages of reports and materials that it had relied upon when adopting the ordinance.

In December 1999, the trial court allowed a group of persons and entities to intervene in the action in support of the ordinance.[4] The interveners joined City's demurrer.

The trial court sustained the demurrer without leave to amend, and entered judgment in favor of City and the interveners. This appeal followed.

## II. Discussion

### A. Introduction and Standard of Review

HBA contends the trial court erred when it sustained the demurrer to its complaint. In arguing City's inclusionary zoning ordinance is facially invalid, HBA again asserts the ordinance violates (1) the takings clauses of the federal and state Constitutions, (2) the Mitigation Fee Act (Gov. Code, § 66000 et seq.), (3) the due process clause of the federal Constitution, and (4) Proposition 218.

---

4. The interveners were Napa Valley Community Housing, Non-Profit Housing Association of Northern California, Housing California, Patricia Domingo, Heather Clayton, Donna Simon, Hilda Avia, Rainy Stegall, and Hector Candelario.

The standard of review we apply is familiar. On appeal from a judgment of dismissal after an order sustaining a demurrer, the appellate court reviews the record de novo, to determine whether the complaint states a cause of action as a matter of law. (*Moore v. Regents of University of California* (1990) 51 Cal. 3d 120, 125 [271 Cal. Rptr. 146, 793 P.2d 479, 16 A.L.R.5th 903].) All facts properly pleaded are deemed to be true. (*Ibid.*)

With these principles in mind, we consider the arguments that have been advanced concerning each claim.

## B. Takings Issues

### 1. Is the Ordinance Facially Invalid?

HBA contends that City's inclusionary zoning ordinance is facially invalid because it violates the taking clauses of the federal and state Constitutions.

A claimant who advances a facial challenge faces an "uphill battle." (*Keystone Bituminous Coal Assn. v. DeBenedictis* (1987) 480 U.S. 470, 495 [107 S. Ct. 1232, 1247, 94 L. Ed. 2d 472].) "'A claim that a regulation is *facially* invalid is only tenable if the terms of the regulation will not permit those who administer it to avoid an unconstitutional *application* to the complaining parties.'" (*San Mateo County Coastal Landowners' Assn. v. County of San Mateo* (1995) 38 Cal. App. 4th 523, 547 [45 Cal. Rptr. 2d 117], quoting *Tahoe-Sierra Preservation Council v. State Water Resources Control Bd.* (1989) 210 Cal. App. 3d 1421, 1442 [259 Cal. Rptr. 132].) This is because a facial challenge is predicated on the theory that "the mere enactment of the . . . ordinance worked a taking of plaintiff's property. . . ." (*Hensler v. City of Glendale* (1994) 8 Cal. 4th 1, 24 [32 Cal. Rptr. 2d 244, 876 P.2d 1043].)

Here, City's inclusionary zoning ordinance imposes significant burdens on those who wish to develop their property. However the ordinance also provides significant benefits to those who comply with its terms. Developments that include affordable housing are eligible for expedited processing, fee deferrals, loans or grants, and density bonuses. More critically, the ordinance permits a developer to appeal for a reduction, adjustment, or *complete waiver* of the ordinance's requirements. Since City has the ability to waive the requirements imposed by the ordinance, the ordinance cannot and does not, on its face, result in a taking.

HBA contends the ordinance's waiver clause does not preclude a facial challenge because that clause improperly places the burden on the developer to prove that a waiver would be appropriate when the City has not established a justification for the exactions mandated by the ordinance. According to HBA, allocating the burden in this way is inconsistent with *Dolan v. City of Tigard* (1994) 512 U.S. 374, 391, footnote 8 [114 S. Ct. 2309, 2320, 129 L. Ed. 2d 304]. HBA misreads *Dolan.* Quite to the contrary, the Supreme Court stated in *Dolan,* that when evaluating the validity of generally applicable zoning regulations, it is appropriate to place the burden on the party who is challenging the regulation. (*Ibid.*) As we will discuss below, City's inclusionary zoning ordinance is a generally applicable legislative enactment rather than an individualized assessment imposed as a condition of development. Thus, the burden shifting standard described in *Dolan* does not apply.

### 2. Does the Ordinance Substantially Advance a Legitimate Interest?

The Fifth Amendment to the United States Constitution states that "private property [shall not] be taken for public use without just compensation." Article I, section 19 of the California Constitution contains similar language, stating that governmental entities must pay just compensation when they "take" private property for public use.

In *Agins v. Tiburon* (1980) 447 U.S. 255 [100 S. Ct. 2138, 65 L. Ed. 2d 106], the Supreme Court provided a test to determine whether a taking has occurred. The court said, "the application of a general zoning law to particular property effects a taking if the ordinance does not substantially advance legitimate state interests . . . or denies an owner economically viable use of his land. . . ." (*Id.* at p. 260 [100 S. Ct. at p. 2141].)

Here, HBA contends that City's inclusionary zoning ordinance effects a taking under the first of these tests; i.e., that the ordinance is invalid because it fails to substantially advance legitimate state interests. We are unpersuaded.

First, we have no doubt that creating affordable housing for low and moderate income families is a legitimate state interest. Our Supreme Court has said that the "assistance of moderate-income households with their housing needs is recognized in this state as a legitimate governmental purpose." (*Santa Monica Beach, Ltd. v. Superior Court* (1999) 19 Cal. 4th 952, 970 [81 Cal. Rptr. 2d 93, 968 P.2d 993].) This conclusion is consistent with repeated pronouncements from the state Legislature which has declared that "the development of a sufficient supply of housing to meet the needs of *all Californians* is a matter of statewide concern," (Gov. Code, § 65913.9, italics added) and that local governments have "a responsibility to use the powers vested in them to facilitate the improvement and development of housing to make adequate provision for the housing needs of *all economic segments of the community*." (Gov. Code, § 65580, subd. (d), italics added.) Indeed, Witkin lists 12 separate statutes that are "designed to stimulate the construction of low and moderate income housing by the private sector." (4 Witkin, Summary of Cal. Law (9th ed. 1987) Real Property, § 54, p. 275; *id.* (2000 supp.) § 54, p. 134.)

Second, it is beyond question that City's inclusionary zoning ordinance will "substantially advance" the important governmental interest of providing affordable housing for low and moderate-income families. By requiring developers in City to create a modest amount of affordable housing (or to comply with one of the alternatives) the ordinance will necessarily increase the supply of affordable housing. We conclude City's ordinance "substantially advance[s] legitimate state interests." (*Agins v. Tiburon, supra,* 447 U.S. at p. 260 [100 S. Ct. at p. 2141].)

HBA's principal constitutional claim is that City's ordinance is invalid under *Nollan v. California Coastal Comm'n* (1987) 483 U.S. 825 [107 S. Ct. 3141, 97 L. Ed. 2d 677], and *Dolan v. City of Tigard, supra,* 512 U.S. 374.

In *Nollan* the court discussed the "substantially advance" test in the context of a governmental requirement that appellant property owners dedicate a portion of their beachfront property to the public as a condition for obtaining a rebuilding permit. In the course of its discussion, the court said there must be an "essential nexus" between a condition imposed on the use of land, and the impacts caused by the proposed use. (*Nollan v. California Coastal Comm'n, supra*, 483 U.S. at p. 837 [107 S. Ct. at p. 3148].)

*Dolan* also involved dedications of property that were a condition for granting a development permit. There the court said that a "rough proportionality" standard "best encapsulates what we hold to be the requirement of the Fifth Amendment. No precise mathematical calculation is required, but the city must make some sort of individualized determination that the required dedication is related both in nature and extent to the impact of the proposed development." (*Dolan v. City of Tigard, supra*, 512 U.S. at p. 391 [114 S. Ct. at pp. 2319-2320].)

HBA contends City's ordinance is invalid under *Nollan* and *Dolan* because there is no "essential nexus" or "rough proportionality" between the exaction required by the ordinance, and the impacts caused by development of property.

We reject this argument because *Nollan* and *Dolan* are inapplicable under the facts of this case. "The intermediate standard of judicial scrutiny formulated by the high court in *Nollan* and *Dolan* is intended to address . . . land use 'bargains' between property owners and regulatory bodies — those in which the local government conditions permit approval for a given use on the owner's surrender of benefits which *purportedly* offset the impact of the proposed development. It is in this paradigmatic permit context — where the individual property owner-developer seeks to negotiate approval of a planned development — that the combined *Nollan* and *Dolan* test quintessentially applies." (*Ehrlich v. City of Culver City* (1996) 12 Cal. 4th 854, 868 [50 Cal. Rptr. 2d 242, 911 P.2d 429].) "But a different standard of scrutiny [applies] to development fees that are generally applicable through legislative action 'because the heightened risk of the "extortionate" use of the police power to exact unconstitutional conditions is not present.'"[5] (*Santa Monica Beach, Ltd. v. Superior Court, supra*, 19 Cal. 4th at p. 966, quoting *Ehrlich v. City of Culver City, supra*, 12 Cal. 4th at p. 876.) "[I]ndividualized development fees warrant a type of review akin to the conditional conveyances at issue in *Nollan* and *Dolan*, whereas generally applicable development fees warrant the more deferential review that the *Dolan* court recognized is generally accorded to legislative determinations." (*Santa Monica Beach, Ltd. v. Superior Court, supra*, 19 Cal. 4th at pp. 966-967.) The justification for these varying levels of scrutiny is founded in the nature of the two types of exactions. "It is one thing for courts to make a government agency adhere to its

---

5. While the court in *Santa Monica Beach*, discussed the scope of *Nollan* and *Dolan* in the context of "development fees," the court has made clear that the same analysis applies whether a governmental entity requires the conveyance of property, or the payment of a fee. (See *Ehrlich v. City of Culver City, supra*, 12 Cal. 4th at p. 876.)

own justification for requiring the dedication of a particular portion of property as a condition of development; such adherence safeguards against the possibility that the justification is merely a pretext for taking the property without paying compensation. . . . But it is another thing for courts to require that a complex, generally applicable piece of economic legislation that will have many effects on many different persons and entities accomplish precisely the goals stated in a legislative preamble in order to preserve its constitutionality." (*Santa Monica Beach, Ltd. v. Superior Court, supra,* 19 Cal. 4th at p. 972, 81 Cal. Rptr. 2d 93, 968 P.2d 993.)

Here, we are not called upon to determine the validity of a particular land use bargain between a governmental agency and a person who wants to develop his or her land. Instead we are faced with a facial challenge to economic legislation that is generally applicable to *all* development in City. We conclude the heightened standard of review described in *Nollan* and *Dolan* is inapplicable under these facts.

### 3. Other Takings Issues

HBA advances two additional arguments on the takings issue.

First HBA contends that even if the heightened level of scrutiny set forth in *Nollan* and *Dolan* are inapplicable, City's inclusionary zoning ordinance is still invalid under California cases such as *Rohn v. City of Visalia* (1989) 214 Cal. App. 3d 1463 [263 Cal. Rptr. 319], *Whaler's Village Club v. California Coastal Com.* (1985) 173 Cal. App. 3d 240 [220 Cal. Rptr. 2], and *Liberty v. California Coastal Com.* (1980) 113 Cal. App. 3d 491 [170 Cal. Rptr. 247]. These decisions are inapposite. The issue in each was the validity of an ad hoc condition that was imposed on an individual developer. None of them involved a facial challenge to a generally applicable zoning ordinance that imposed obligations on all development in a given area. We conclude *Rohn, Whaler's Village,* and *Liberty* are not applicable under the facts of this case.

HBA also contends that the inclusionary zoning ordinance is invalid because the lack of housing for low and moderate income families in City is the product of City's own prior restrictive land use policies.

HBA has not cited any authority to support the proposition that a zoning ordinance which tries to solve problems caused by prior legislative decisions is invalid, and case law is directly to the contrary. For example, in *Penn Central Transp. Co. v. New York City* (1978) 438 U.S. 104 [98 S. Ct. 2646, 57 L. Ed. 2d 631], the Supreme Court ruled that New York could enact a landmark preservation law that was designed to mitigate the effects of prior policies that permitted "large numbers of historic structures, landmarks, and areas" to be destroyed. (*Id.* at p. 108 [98 S. Ct. at p. 2651].) If New York can enact a landmark preservation law to remedy a shortage of historic buildings created by its prior policies, City can enact an inclusionary zoning ordinance even if its prior policies contributed to a scarcity of available land and a shortage of affordable housing.

. . . .

## D. Due Process

HBA contends the inclusionary zoning ordinance is facially invalid under the due process clause of the Federal Constitution because it "requires property owners who develop residential housing to sell or rent 10 of their units at prices or rents that are based entirely upon certain fixed percentages of the income levels of lower and very low income households." Imposing such a requirement violates the due process clause, HBA argues, because "the inclusionary zoning law provides no mechanism to make a fair return for property owners who are forced to sell or rent units at an amount unrelated to market prices."

We doubt seriously that HBA is entitled to a "fair return" under the due process clause. The "fair return" standard is commonly used to evaluate restrictions placed on historically regulated industries such as railroads and public utilities. (See, e.g., *Power Comm'n v. Pipeline Co.* (1942) 315 U.S. 575 [62 S. Ct. 736, 86 L. Ed. 1037].) It has also been used to evaluate rent control ordinances. (See, e.g., *Fisher v. City of Berkeley* (1984) 37 Cal. 3d 644, 679 [209 Cal. Rptr. 682, 693 P.2d 261].) However HBA has not cited, and we are not aware of, any case that holds a housing developer is entitled to "fair return" on his or her investment.

However we need not base our decision on this ground. First, it is not literally correct to say that City's ordinance "requires property owners who develop residential housing to sell or rent 10 of their units [to low income individuals]." Under the ordinance, any person who does not want to sell or rent a portion of his or her housing units to low income individuals may choose one of the alternatives, such as donating vacant land or paying an in-lieu fee. Thus HBA's argument is based on an incorrect premise.

Second, and more importantly, HBA's facial due process challenge must necessarily fail. As we have said, "'A claim that a regulation is *facially* invalid is only tenable if the terms of the regulation will not permit those who administer it to avoid an unconstitutional *application* to the complaining parties. . . .'" (*San Mateo County Coastal Landowners' Assn. v. County of San Mateo, supra,* 38 Cal. App. 4th at p. 547, citation omitted.) When an ordinance contains provisions that allow for administrative relief, we must presume the implementing authorities will exercise their authority in conformity with the Constitution. (See *Fisher v. City of Berkeley, supra,* 37 Cal. 3d at p. 684.)

Here, as we have noted, City's ordinance includes a clause that allows city officials to reduce, modify or waive the requirements contained in the ordinance "based upon the absence of any reasonable relationship or nexus between the impact of the development and . . . the inclusionary requirement." Since City has the authority to completely waive a developer's obligations, a facial challenge under the due process clause must necessarily fail.

HBA contends the waiver clause does not preclude a facial challenge because it does not state expressly that a waiver may be granted based on a lack of a "fair return." However the power of an agency to make adjustments to guarantee a fair return is "not limited to those literally granted by the ordinance. . . ." (*City of Berkeley v. City of Berkeley Rent Stabilization Bd.* (1994) 27 Cal. App. 4th 951, 962 [33 Cal. Rptr. 2d 317].) When this standard is not expressly stated, it is "present by implication." (*Ibid.*)

\* \* \* \*

### III. Disposition

The judgment is affirmed.

STEVENS, J., and SIMONS, J., concurred.

## *Questions for Consideration*

1) What was the City of Napa's rationale for enacting the inclusionary zoning ordinance? What policy was the City advancing by enacting the ordinance?

2) Why did the Home Builders Association file a complaint against the City? What harms did the HBA identify that its members have suffered or would suffer under this inclusionary zoning ordinance?

3) When is an ordinance inclusionary instead of exclusionary? Does its characterization rely on the identity of the groups being included/excluded?

4) The HBA argued that the lack of housing for low- and moderate-income families in the City is the product of the City's own prior restrictive land use policies. The court's opinion does not explore in any detail this contention. What do you think is the basis for this argument the HBA makes?

## *Takeaway*

- The court affirms the trial court decision that the City of Napa's inclusionary zoning ordinance, which required affordable housing, does not violate the federal or state Takings Clauses, and does not violate the federal Due Process Clause.

- The ordinance required 10% of all newly constructed residential units in the City be affordable. To meet that, developers may dedicate land for affordable housing, construct affordable units on an alternate site, or pay an in-lieu-of fee to a trust for affordable housing. The City may also waive the affordable housing requirement.

- Developers challenge inclusionary housing ordinances because they arguably take property rights from the developers. Such ordinances require developers to accommodate low- to moderate-income housing programs, where presumably the developers could otherwise choose to establish high-priced units.

- The court held that, because the City may waive the ordinance's affordable housing requirement, the ordinance cannot, on its face, violate the Takings Clauses.

- Also, the court held that by creating affordable housing, the inclusionary zoning ordinance advances a legitimate state interest, and is not subject to the heightened judicial review of the essential nexus and rough proportionality tests required of exactions under *Nollan* and *Dolan*, and instead should be afforded deference as a legislative land use regulation.

## Holmdel Builders Ass'n v. Township of Holmdel

· Supreme Court of New Jersey
583 A.2d 277 (N.J. 1990)

HANDLER, Judge. In 1975, this Court held that developing municipalities are constitutionally required to provide a realistic opportunity for the development of low- and moderate-income housing. *Southern Burlington County NAACP v. Mount Laurel Township*, 67 N.J. 151, 336 A.2d 713, *cert. denied*, 423 U.S. 808, 96 S. Ct. 18, 46 L. Ed.2d 28 (1975) (*Mt. Laurel I*). In the years following, many municipalities failed to comply with the clear mandate of *Mt. Laurel I*. The failure to provide the necessary opportunity for affordable housing led to a new legal challenge. We clarified and reaffirmed the constitutional mandate set forth in *Mt. Laurel I*, imposing an affirmative obligation on every municipality to provide its fair share of affordable housing. *Southern Burlington County NAACP v. Mount Laurel Township*, 92 N.J. 158, 456 A.2d 390 (1983) (*Mt. Laurel II*). We enumerated several possible approaches by which municipalities could comply with the constitutional obligation, including lower-income density bonuses and mandatory set-asides. We stressed that "municipalities and trial courts are encouraged to create other devices and methods for meeting fair share obligations." *Id.* at 265–66, 456 A.2d 390. Subsequently, the Legislature codified the *Mt. Laurel* doctrine, including its available compliance measures, by enacting the Fair Housing Act, L.1985, c. 222; N.J.S.A. 52:27D-301 to -329 (FHA). We have since upheld the constitutionality of the FHA. *Hills Dev. Co. v. Bernards Township*, 103 N.J. 1, 25, 510 A.2d 621 (1986).

The cases that comprise this appeal arise out of attempts by several municipalities to comply with their obligation to provide a realistic opportunity for the construction of affordable housing under our ruling in *Mt. Laurel II* and the provisions of the FHA. The ordinances, in varying forms, impose fees on developers as a condition for development approval. The fees are dedicated to an affordable-housing trust fund to be used in satisfying the municipality's *Mt. Laurel* obligation.

. . . .

This appeal raises two major substantive issues. One is whether there is statutory authority, derived from the FHA, the Municipal Land Use Law (MLUL), N.J.S.A. 40:55D-1 to -129, and the general police power of government, N.J.S.A. 40:48-2, that enables a municipality to impose affordable-housing development fees as a condition for development approval. That issue raises the related questions whether the development-fee ordinances constitute an impermissible taking of property or violate substantive due process or equal protection. The second major issue is whether affordable-housing development fees are an unconstitutional form of taxation. . . .

## I.

Resolution of these several issues requires initially a presentation of the municipal ordinances involved in this case. It is also important to explain the statutory and administrative framework structured by the FHA within which these ordinances were adopted and the role of the Council on Affordable Housing (COAH or the Council), the administrative agency created under the FHA, in the adoption of local ordinances designed to fulfill a municipal fair-share affordable-housing obligation.

Chester Township's *Mt. Laurel* obligation is limited to indigenous need. Accordingly, the Township amended its zoning ordinance to address its *Mt. Laurel* obligation. The purpose of the ordinance is to require all new development to share in the cost of *Mt. Laurel* compliance. The ordinance creates an affordable-housing trust fund and imposes a mandatory development fee on all new commercial and residential development as a condition for receiving a certificate of occupancy. . . .

The amount of the fee varies in accordance with the proposed size of the development, ranging from twenty-five cents to seventy-five cents per square foot. . . .

South Brunswick Township concluded that "the constitutional obligation to provide affordable housing should apply not merely to those owners of tracts specifically rezoned for meeting this obligation, but rather to the developers of other residential, commercial or industrial property," and therefore adopted a zoning ordinance creating an affordable-housing trust fund. The ordinance imposes development fees on all new commercial and non-inclusionary residential development as a condition for site-plan or subdivision approval. The fees for non-inclusionary residential developments are calculated on the basis of the proposed size of the development. The fees for non-residential developments depend on the type of project involved, ranging from twenty-five to fifty cents per square foot. The municipality's stated purpose in creating the fund is to rehabilitate substandard housing and thus provide its fair share of affordable housing.

Middletown Township determined, in light of the need for affordable housing created by employment and growth patterns, that all new development should share "in the cost of that portion of the present and future [*Mt. Laurel*] obligation attributable directly or indirectly to the development." It adopted an ordinance requiring all new major residential-subdivision and site-plan applications to set aside seven percent of the development's total dwelling units for lower-income housing. On residential tracts other than those zoned specifically for inclusionary development, a developer may make a cash contribution to the affordable-housing trust fund in lieu of actually constructing the affordable units. The fee ranges from eighty cents to $1.80 per square foot, depending on the total gross floor area. All non-residential developers are required to pay a development fee into the fund. Density bonuses do not accompany the mandatory set-aside requirement, the fee-in-lieu option, or the mandatory-fee requirement. The trust-fund contributions are to be used to produce affordable housing. . . .

Holmdel Township's zoning ordinance, prior to 1986, permitted a maximum density of .8 dwelling units per acre in the R-40A residential zone. In 1986, an amendment to the ordinance re-zoned a portion of the R-40A zone to create an R-40B zone. The R-40B zone downgraded density from .8 to .4 units per acre. A developer may build .6 units per acre, however, if he or she contributes the equivalent of 2.5% of the purchase price of all units to the municipality's affordable-housing trust fund. The trust fund is used only for "those purposes that produce a direct benefit to the production of either a higher ratio of lower income units in a given project, a reduction in the cost of producing lower income units that shall be passed on to the purchaser or tenant of the unit, or the direct construction of units such as township-sponsored project[s]."

Cherry Hill Township's *Mt. Laurel* obligation is not limited to indigenous need. The Township claims it is approaching "total build out," and therefore adopted a housing impact-fee ordinance. Building permits are issued only for those developments that pay an impact fee into the affordable-housing trust fund. Inclusionary developments and small, inexpensive, single-family detached houses are exempt from the fee requirement. Otherwise, residential developments are assessed a fee based on the proposed size of the project, and commercial development is assessed a fee based on a percentage of the cost of construction. The trust fund is to be used "at the discretion of the Township for the sole purpose of aiding in the provision or rehabilitation of modest income housing."

In sum, the Townships of Chester and South Brunswick have enacted ordinances that impose a mandatory development fee on all new non-inclusionary developments as a condition for development approval. Their ordinances do not give developers a density bonus in exchange for the development fee. Middletown Township's ordinance imposes a mandatory development fee on all new commercial development as a condition for development approval. Non-inclusionary residential developers may choose between constructing the affordable housing or paying an in-lieu fee. Density bonuses do not accompany any of the options. Holmdel Township enacted an ordinance that gives developers a density bonus if they contribute to an affordable-housing trust fund. Cherry Hill Township's ordinance imposes a mandatory development fee on all new commercial developments and non-inclusionary residential developments of a sufficient size.

. . . .

## II.

Any inquiry into the validity of development-fee ordinances must inevitably consider the complex factors that contribute to the persistent and substantial shortage of low- and moderate-income housing (hereafter, lower-income or affordable housing). This inquiry necessarily begins with our seminal decisions in *Mt. Laurel I* and *Mt. Laurel II*.

The core of those decisions is that *every* municipality, not just developing municipalities, must provide a *realistic*, not just a theoretical, opportunity for the construction of lower-income housing. We realized that the solution to the shortage of affordable housing could not "depend on the inclination of developers to help the poor, [but rather must rely] on affirmative inducements to make the opportunity real." . . .

. . . .

The phenomenon of unfettered non-residential development has exacerbated the need for lower-income housing, and has generated widespread efforts to link such needed residential development to non-residential development. Thus, nationwide, municipalities have attempted to shift the externalities of development to non-inclusionary developers.

The broad concept of linkage describes any of a wide range of municipal regulations that condition the grant of development approval on the payment of funds to help finance services and facilities needed as a result of development. In the context of developing affordable housing, linkage refers to any scheme that requires developers to mitigate the adverse effects of non-residential development upon the shortage of housing either indirectly, by contributing to an affordable-housing trust fund, or directly, by actually constructing affordable housing. The idea of linking community housing goals with non-residential real estate development has inspired new governmental efforts to address the lower-income housing crisis.

Affordable-housing linkage ordinances are the most recent phenomenon in this area. Such ordinances link or couple the right to engage in non-residential development to the provision of affordable housing. The ordinances at issue in this appeal are all examples of linkage. Each requires certain developers to help finance the construction of affordable housing either as a condition for receiving permission to build or in order to obtain some type of density bonus. . . .

The linkage trend has gained momentum during the past decade. The fairness and legality of linkage have inspired much debate among legal scholars, the business community, and the judiciary. Proponents . . . forcefully argue that by attracting new residents to an area, commercial developments increase the need for housing in general and thus for affordable housing. To the extent that the additional need for housing is not met with increased supply, housing prices will be pushed upward, exacerbating both the need for, and unattainability of, lower-income housing. Therefore, it is appropriate for municipalities to charge commercial developers with a portion of the responsibility for creating more affordable-housing units. In addition, linkage advocates stress the need to consider the effect of all development on the finite supply of land. Land must be viewed as an essential but exhaustible resource; any land that is developed for any purpose reduces the supply of land capable of being used to build affordable housing.

. . . .

### III.

With that background, we address the issue whether the development-fee ordinances are statutorily authorized. The focal question in this case is whether any statutory grant of power to municipalities can fairly be construed as impliedly authorizing the affordable-housing development fees imposed by these ordinances. We are guided by the principle that municipalities possess "only such rights and powers as have been granted in express terms, or arise by necessary or fair implication, or are incident to the powers expressly conferred, or are essential to the declared objects and purposes of the municipality." We thus approach the issue in light of the statutory authority of the FHA, which deals expressly with affordable housing. That explicit authority, however, must be comprehended in terms of the traditional zoning powers of municipalities, as reflected in the MLUL and the general police powers of municipal government. Hence, although it is the FHA that deals directly with affordable housing, it is instructive to consider initially the zoning and police powers.

## A.

The MLUL, which expresses the zoning powers delegated to local government, seeks generally "[t]o encourage municipal action to guide the appropriate use or development of all lands in this State, in a manner which will promote the public health, safety, morals, and general welfare." "It is plain beyond dispute that proper provision for adequate housing of all categories of people is certainly an absolute essential in promotion of the general welfare required in all local land use regulation."

Affordable housing is a goal that is no longer merely implicit in the notion of the general welfare. It has been expressly recognized as a governmental end and codified under the FHA, which is to be construed *in pari materia* with the MLUL. The FHA specifies that a municipality's zoning power be used to create a housing element "designed to achieve the goal of access to affordable housing to meet present and prospective housing needs, with particular attention to low and moderate income housing." N.J.S.A. 52:27D-310. Also, the municipality must "establish that its land use and other relevant ordinances have been revised to incorporate" provisions for a realistic opportunity for the development of lower-income housing. . . .

. . . .

. . . It has repeatedly been acknowledged that the zoning power is part of the police power. The police power enables a municipality to take such actions "as it may deem necessary and proper for the good government, order and protection of persons and property, and for the preservation of the public health, safety and welfare of the municipality and its inhabitants." A municipality in the exercise of its police power clearly may seek to address housing problems.

In addition to advancing a recognized purpose of zoning, a zoning ordinance must bear a "real and substantial relationship to the regulation of land." . . .

In *Mt. Laurel II*, we held that inclusionary-zoning devices that serve the purpose of providing affordable housing within a region bear a real and substantial relationship to the regulation of land and the zoning power. The fact that defendants seek to accomplish the general-welfare goal of affordable housing by development fees rather than by mandatory set-asides does not negate a "real and substantial relationship" of such development fees to the regulation of land. Although development-fee measures are not site-specific in the same sense as mandatory set-asides, they implicate land-related regulations because they are specifically designed and applied to aid in the creation of affordable residential housing.

. . . .

. . . Plaintiffs argue that linkage fees constitute an impermissible form of exactions because they seek to require developers to provide for off-site public needs that have not been caused by their developments and furnish them no benefits. . . .

In the context of off-site improvements, an exaction generally requires developers to supply or finance public facilities or amenities made necessary by proposed development. We have traditionally required a strong, almost but-for, causal nexus between off-site public facilities and private development in order to justify exactions. That nexus achieves two ends. First, it ensures that a developer pays for improvement that is necessitated by the development itself, or is a "direct consequence" of the development. Second, it protects a developer from paying a disproportionate share of the cost of improvements that also benefit other persons.

. . . [C]ommentators who believe that affordable-housing linkage measures are essentially a type of exaction for off-site improvements generally assume that a similar causal link is required and exists between new commercial space and an increased demand for lower-income housing. We do not believe, however, that the development-fee ordinances before us must be founded on a stringent nexus between commercial construction and the need for affordable housing. We find a sound basis to support a legislative judgment that there is a reasonable relationship between unrestrained nonresidential development and the need for affordable residential development. We do not equate such a reasonable relationship with the strict rational-nexus standard that demands a but-for causal connection or direct consequential relationship between the private activity that gives rise to the exaction and the public activity to which it is applied. Rather, the relationship is to be founded on the actual, albeit indirect and general, impact that such nonresidential development has on both the need for lower-income residential development and on the opportunity and capacity of municipalities to meet that need. . . .

We conclude that the rational-nexus test is not apposite in determining the validity of inclusionary zoning devices generally or of affordable-housing development fees in particular. Inclusionary zoning through the imposition of development fees is permissible because such fees are conducive to the creation of a realistic opportunity for the development of affordable housing; development fees are the functional equivalent of mandatory set-asides; and it is fair and reasonable to impose such fee requirements on private developers when they possess, enjoy, and consume land, which constitutes the primary resource for housing. Such measures do not offend the zoning laws or the police powers.

. . . .

[Part IV is omitted.]

## V.

Plaintiffs' remaining major contention is that the affordable-housing development fees are a form of taxation and, as such, exceed delegated municipal revenue-raising authority in violation of the state constitutional command that all property taxes be levied uniformly. N.J. Const. of 1947 art. VIII, § 1, para. 1.

. . . .

. . . In *Mt. Laurel I*, we concluded that municipalities and developers had engaged in exclusionary practices that effectively precluded the development of low- and moderate-income housing in the suburbs. *Mt. Laurel II* required municipalities to use affirmative inclusionary-zoning measures, including mandatory set-asides, to redress affordable-housing needs. Thus, a residential developer could be required to set aside a percentage of units to be used for low- and moderate-income housing. The Legislature, in effect, has ratified this principle. The FHA, as well as the MLUL, endorses the use of inclusionary-zoning techniques sanctioned in *Mt. Laurel II*.

We cannot overstress the similarities between mandatory set-asides and the development-fee ordinances. . . . In *Mt. Laurel II*, . . . we determined that mandatory set-asides as a form of inclusionary zoning were not analogous to a tax. We viewed them as legitimate regulatory measures suitably addressed to the broad goals of zoning. Development fees, to reiterate, perform an identical function.

. . . .

In sum, because the development fees are a form of inclusionary zoning and similar to other land-use and related exactions, they are regulatory measures, not taxes.

. . . .

The judgment of the Appellate Division is affirmed in part and reversed in part.

For affirmance in part and reversal in part.

## *Questions for Consideration*

1) Based on the various approaches by the communities discussed in the court's opinion, explain: a) a density bonus; b) a mandatory set aside; c) an impact fee; and d) a development fee.

2) What specific requirements were imposed by the various communities in an effort to achieve their inclusionary goals?

3) Do you think there is/should be a difference between linkage programs that require inclusionary measures to be provided on the property owner/developer's property (e.g., set asides and density bonuses), versus measures that provide benefits to other properties (e.g., application of impact and development fee revenue to other properties via an affordable housing trust fund)?

4) Notice in each of the situations discussed in the case, inclusionary requirements are imposed on new development. Do you think that property owners

who are currently living in the community should also have an obligation to contribute to inclusionary housing efforts?

5) Why should developers of commercial real estate projects have to pay for residential housing? What is the connection between an office building or a shopping mall, and affordable residential housing?

### *Takeaway*

- A key concern with respect to providing affordable housing is how to achieve the objective in high-cost communities; such as in the San Francisco Bay area, Boston, and New York City. Should the cost needed to encourage affordable housing come out of general tax revenues and thus fall on everyone in the community; or should it only be assessed against property owners/developers of new construction?

- When costs are assessed in various forms against developers, they will simply seek to pass the costs on to the end buyers and users of the real estate products that they build. Is this a fair and transparent way of providing for affordable housing?

# M. Fair Housing

Related to inclusionary zoning are concerns regarding fair housing and housing discrimination. We have already read cases that cover some of these fair housing and discrimination issues. The following two cases provide additional guidance for legal analysis. In particular, the *Inclusive Communities* case, below, clarifies an important issue under the FHA. Up until this decision, it was not fully clear that discrimination under the FHA could be demonstrated by disparate impact analysis as well as by disparate treatment analysis. And in *Virginia ex rel. Fair Housing Board v. Windsor Plaza Condo. Ass'n*, the Supreme Court of Virginia dealt with fair housing issues in the context of disability law.

## Texas Dep't of Housing and Community Affairs v. Inclusive Communities Project, Inc.

Supreme Court of the United States
135 S. Ct. 2507 (2015)

KENNEDY, Justice. The underlying dispute in this case concerns where housing for low-income persons should be constructed in Dallas, Texas — that is, whether the housing should be built in the inner city or in the suburbs. This dispute comes to the Court on a disparate-impact theory of liability. In contrast to a disparate-treatment case, where a "plaintiff must establish that the defendant had a discriminatory intent or motive," a plaintiff bringing a disparate-impact claim challenges practices that have a "disproportionately adverse effect on minorities" and are otherwise unjustified by a legitimate rationale. *Ricci v. DeStefano*, 557 U.S. 557, 577, 129 S. Ct. 2658, 174 L. Ed. 2d 490 (2009) (internal quotation marks omitted). The question presented for the Court's determination is whether disparate-impact claims are cognizable under the Fair Housing Act (or FHA), 82 Stat. 81, as amended, 42 U.S.C. § 3601 *et seq.*

I

A

Before turning to the question presented, it is necessary to discuss a different federal statute that gives rise to this dispute. The Federal Government provides low-income housing tax credits that are distributed to developers through designated state agencies. 26 U.S.C. § 42. Congress has directed States to develop plans identifying selection criteria for distributing the credits. § 42(m)(1). Those plans must include certain criteria, such as public housing waiting lists, § 42(m)(1)(C), as well as certain preferences, including that low-income housing units "contribut[e] to a concerted community revitalization plan" and be built in census tracts populated predominantly by low-income residents. §§ 42(m)(1)(B)(ii)(III), 42(d)(5)(ii)(I). Federal law thus favors the distribution of these tax credits for the development of housing units in low-income areas.

In the State of Texas these federal credits are distributed by the Texas Department of Housing and Community Affairs (Department). Under Texas law, a developer's application for the tax credits is scored under a point system that gives priority to statutory criteria, such as the financial feasibility of the development project and the income level of tenants. Tex. Govt. Code Ann. §§ 2306.6710(a)-(b) (West 2008). The Texas Attorney General has interpreted state law to permit the consideration of additional criteria, such as whether the housing units will be built in a neighborhood with good schools. Those criteria cannot be awarded more points than statutorily mandated criteria.

The Inclusive Communities Project, Inc. (ICP), is a Texas-based nonprofit corporation that assists low-income families in obtaining affordable housing. In 2008, the ICP brought this suit against the Department and its officers in the United States District Court for the Northern District of Texas. As relevant here, it brought a disparate-impact claim under §§ 804(a) and 805(a) of the FHA. The ICP alleged the Department has caused continued segregated housing patterns by its disproportionate allocation of the tax credits, granting too many credits for housing in predominantly black inner-city areas and too few in predominantly white suburban neighborhoods. The ICP contended that the Department must modify its selection criteria in order to encourage the construction of low-income housing in suburban communities.

The District Court concluded that the ICP had established a prima facie case of disparate impact. It relied on two pieces of statistical evidence. First, it found "from 1999–2008, [the Department] approved tax credits for 49.7% of proposed non-elderly units in 0% to 9.9% Caucasian areas, but only approved 37.4% of proposed non-elderly units in 90% to 100% Caucasian areas." 749 F. Supp. 2d 486, 499 (N.D. Tex. 2010) (footnote omitted). Second, it found "92.29% of [low-income housing tax credit] units in the city of Dallas were located in census tracts with less than 50% Caucasian residents."

The District Court then placed the burden on the Department to rebut the ICP's prima facie showing of disparate impact. 860 F. Supp. 2d 312, 322–323 (2012). After assuming the Department's proffered interests were legitimate, the District Court held that a defendant — here the Department — must prove "that there are no other less discriminatory alternatives to advancing their proffered interests." Because, in its view, the Department "failed to meet [its] burden of proving that there are no less discriminatory alternatives," the District Court ruled for the ICP.

The District Court's remedial order required the addition of new selection criteria for the tax credits. For instance, it awarded points for units built in neighborhoods with good schools and disqualified sites that are located adjacent to or near hazardous conditions, such as high crime areas or landfills. The remedial order contained no explicit racial targets or quotas.

While the Department's appeal was pending, the Secretary of Housing and Urban Development (HUD) issued a regulation interpreting the FHA to encompass disparate-impact liability. See Implementation of the Fair Housing Act's Discriminatory Effects Standard, 78 Fed. Reg. 11460 (2013). The regulation also established a burden-shifting framework for adjudicating disparate-impact claims. Under the regulation, a plaintiff first must make a prima facie showing of disparate impact. That is, the plaintiff "has the burden of proving that a challenged practice caused or predictably will cause a discriminatory effect." 24 C.F.R. § 100.500(c)(1) (2014). If a statistical discrepancy is caused by factors other than the defendant's policy, a plaintiff cannot establish a prima facie case, and there is no liability. After a plaintiff does establish a prima facie showing of disparate impact, the burden shifts to the defendant to "prov[e] that the challenged practice is necessary to achieve one or more substantial, legitimate, nondiscriminatory interests." § 100.500(c)(2). HUD has clarified that this step of the analysis "is analogous to the Title VII requirement that an employer's interest in an employment practice with a disparate impact be job related." 78 Fed. Reg. 11470. Once a defendant has satisfied its burden at step two, a plaintiff may "prevail upon proving that the substantial, legitimate, nondiscriminatory interests supporting the challenged practice could be served by another practice that has a less discriminatory effect." § 100.500(c)(3).

The Court of Appeals for the Fifth Circuit held, consistent with its precedent, that disparate-impact claims are cognizable under the FHA. 747 F.3d 275, 280 (2014). On the merits, however, the Court of Appeals reversed and remanded. Relying on HUD's regulation, the Court of Appeals held that it was improper for the District Court to have placed the burden on the Department to prove there were no less discriminatory alternatives for allocating low-income housing tax credits. Id., at 282–283. In a concurring opinion, Judge Jones stated that on remand the District Court should reexamine whether the ICP had made out a prima facie case of disparate impact. She suggested the District Court incorrectly relied on bare statistical evidence without engaging in any analysis about causation. She further observed that, if the federal law providing for the distribution of low-income housing tax credits ties the Department's hands to such an extent that it lacks a meaningful choice, then there is no disparate-impact liability. See *id.,* at 283–284 (specially concurring opinion).

The Department filed a petition for a writ of certiorari on the question whether disparate-impact claims are cognizable under the FHA. The question was one of first impression, see *Huntington v. Huntington Branch, NAACP,* 488 U.S. 15, 109 S. Ct. 276, 102 L. Ed. 2d 180 (1988) (per curiam), and certiorari followed, 573 U.S. —, 135 S. Ct. 46, 189 L. Ed. 2d 896 (2014). It is now appropriate to provide a brief history of the FHA's enactment and its later amendment.

## B

*De jure* residential segregation by race was declared unconstitutional almost a century ago, *Buchanan v. Warley,* 245 U.S. 60, 38 S. Ct. 16, 62 L. Ed. 149 (1917), but its vestiges remain today, intertwined with the country's economic and social life. Some segregated housing patterns can be traced to conditions that arose in the mid-20th century. Rapid urbanization, concomitant with the rise of suburban developments accessible by car, led many white families to leave the inner cities. This often left minority families concentrated in the center of the Nation's cities. During this time, various practices were followed, sometimes with governmental support, to encourage and maintain the separation of the races: Racially restrictive covenants prevented the conveyance of property to minorities, *see Shelley v. Kraemer,* 334 U.S. 1, 68 S. Ct. 836, 92 L. Ed. 1161 (1948); steering by real-estate agents led potential buyers to consider homes in racially homogenous areas; and discriminatory lending practices, often referred to as redlining, precluded minority families from purchasing homes in affluent areas. By the 1960's, these policies, practices, and prejudices had created many predominantly black inner cities surrounded by mostly white suburbs.

The mid-1960's was a period of considerable social unrest; and, in response, President Lyndon Johnson established the National Advisory Commission on Civil Disorders, commonly known as the Kerner Commission. Exec. Order No. 11365, 3 C.F.R. 674 (1966–1970 Comp.). After extensive fact finding the Commission identified residential segregation and unequal housing and economic conditions in the inner cities as significant, underlying causes of the social unrest. The Commission found that "[n]early two-thirds of all nonwhite families living in the central cities today live in neighborhoods marked by substandard housing and general urban blight." The Commission further found that both open and covert racial discrimination prevented black families from obtaining better housing and moving to integrated communities. The Commission concluded that "[o]ur Nation is moving toward two societies, one black, one white — separate and unequal." To reverse "[t]his deepening racial division," *ibid.,* it recommended enactment of "a comprehensive and enforceable open-occupancy law making it an offense to discriminate in the sale or rental of any housing . . . on the basis of race, creed, color, or national origin."

In April 1968, Dr. Martin Luther King, Jr., was assassinated in Memphis, Tennessee, and the Nation faced a new urgency to resolve the social unrest in the inner cities. Congress responded by adopting the Kerner Commission's recommendation and passing the Fair Housing Act. The statute addressed the denial of housing opportunities on the basis of "race, color, religion, or national origin." Civil Rights Act of 1968, §804, 82 Stat. 83. Then, in 1988, Congress amended the FHA. Among other provisions, it created certain exemptions from liability and added "familial status" as a protected characteristic. See Fair Housing Amendments Act of 1988, 102 Stat. 1619.

## II

The issue here is whether, under a proper interpretation of the FHA, housing decisions with a disparate impact are prohibited. Before turning to the FHA, however, it is necessary to consider two other antidiscrimination statutes that preceded it.

The first relevant statute is §703(a) of Title VII of the Civil Rights Act of 1964, 78 Stat. 255. The Court addressed the concept of disparate impact under this statute in *Griggs v. Duke Power Co.*, 401 U.S. 424, 91 S. Ct. 849, 28 L. Ed. 2d 158 (1971). There, the employer had a policy requiring its manual laborers to possess a high school diploma and to obtain satisfactory scores on two intelligence tests. The Court of Appeals held the employer had not adopted these job requirements for a racially discriminatory purpose, and the plaintiffs did not challenge that holding in this Court. Instead, the plaintiffs argued §703(a)(2) covers the discriminatory effect of a practice as well as the motivation behind the practice. . . .

The second relevant statute that bears on the proper interpretation of the FHA is the Age Discrimination in Employment Act of 1967 (ADEA), 81 Stat. 602 *et seq.*, as amended. . . .

The Court . . . addressed whether this provision allows disparate-impact claims in *Smith v. City of Jackson*, 544 U.S. 228, 125 S. Ct. 1536, 161 L. Ed. 2d 410 (2005). There, a group of older employees challenged their employer's decision to give proportionately greater raises to employees with less than five years of experience.

Explaining that *Griggs* "represented the better reading of [Title VII's] statutory text," 544 U.S., at 235, 125 S. Ct. 1536 a plurality of the Court concluded that the same reasoning pertained to §4(a)(2) of the ADEA. The *Smith* plurality emphasized that both §703(a)(2) of Title VII and §4(a)(2) of the ADEA contain language "prohibit[ing] such actions that 'deprive any individual of employment opportunities or *otherwise adversely affect* his status as an employee, because of such individual's' race or age." 544 U.S., at 235, 125 S. Ct. 1536. As the plurality observed, the text of these provisions "focuses on the *effects* of the action on the employee rather than the motivation for the action of the employer" and therefore compels recognition of disparate-impact liability. . . .

Together, *Griggs* holds and the plurality in *Smith* instructs that antidiscrimination laws must be construed to encompass disparate-impact claims when their text refers to the consequences of actions and not just to the mindset of actors, and where that interpretation is consistent with statutory purpose. . . .

Turning to the FHA, the ICP relies on two provisions. Section 804(a) provides that it shall be unlawful:

> "To refuse to sell or rent after the making of a bona fide offer, or to refuse to negotiate for the sale or rental of, or otherwise make unavailable or deny, a dwelling to any person because of race, color, religion, sex, familial status, or national origin." 42 U.S.C. § 3604(a).

Here, the phrase "otherwise make unavailable" is of central importance to the analysis that follows.

Section 805(a), in turn, provides:

> "It shall be unlawful for any person or other entity whose business includes engaging in real estate-related transactions to discriminate against any person in making available such a transaction, or in the terms or conditions of such a transaction, because of race, color, religion, sex, handicap, familial status, or national origin." § 3605(a).

Applied here, the logic of *Griggs* and *Smith* provides strong support for the conclusion that the FHA encompasses disparate-impact claims. Congress' use of the phrase "otherwise make unavailable" refers to the consequences of an action rather than the actor's intent. . . .

. . . .

In addition, it is of crucial importance that the existence of disparate-impact liability is supported by amendments to the FHA that Congress enacted in 1988. By that time, all nine Courts of Appeals to have addressed the question had concluded the Fair Housing Act encompassed disparate-impact claims.

When it amended the FHA, Congress was aware of this unanimous precedent. And with that understanding, it made a considered judgment to retain the relevant statutory text. . . . Indeed, Congress rejected a proposed amendment that would have eliminated disparate-impact liability for certain zoning decisions.

Against this background understanding in the legal and regulatory system, Congress' decision in 1988 to amend the FHA while still adhering to the operative language in §§ 804(a) and 805(a) is convincing support for the conclusion that Congress accepted and ratified the unanimous holdings of the Courts of Appeals finding disparate-impact liability. . . .

. . . .

The relevant 1988 amendments were as follows. First, Congress added a clarifying provision: "Nothing in [the FHA] prohibits a person engaged in the business of furnishing appraisals of real property to take into consideration factors other than race, color, religion, national origin, sex, handicap, or familial status." 42 U.S.C. § 3605(c). Second, Congress provided: "Nothing in [the FHA] prohibits conduct against a person because such person has been convicted by any court of competent jurisdiction of the illegal manufacture or distribution of a controlled substance." § 3607(b)(4). And finally, Congress specified: "Nothing in [the FHA] limits the applicability of any reasonable . . . restrictions regarding the maximum number of occupants permitted to occupy a dwelling." § 3607(b)(1).

The exemptions embodied in these amendments would be superfluous if Congress had assumed that disparate-impact liability did not exist under the FHA. . . . By adding an exemption from liability for exclusionary practices aimed at individuals with drug convictions, Congress ensured disparate-impact liability would not lie if a landlord excluded tenants with such convictions. The same is true of the provision allowing for reasonable restrictions on occupancy. And the exemption from liability for real-estate appraisers is in the same section as § 805(a)'s prohibition of discriminatory practices in real-estate transactions, thus indicating Congress' recognition that disparate-impact liability arose under § 805(a). In short, the 1988 amendments signal that Congress ratified disparate-impact liability.

. . . .

Recognition of disparate-impact claims is consistent with the FHA's central purpose. . . .

These unlawful practices include zoning laws and other housing restrictions that function unfairly to exclude minorities from certain neighborhoods without any sufficient justification. Suits targeting such practices reside at the heartland of disparate-impact liability. The availability of disparate-impact liability, furthermore, has allowed private developers to vindicate the FHA's objectives and to protect their property rights by stopping municipalities from enforcing arbitrary and, in practice, discriminatory ordinances barring the construction of certain types of housing units. Recognition of disparate-impact liability under the FHA also plays a role in uncovering discriminatory intent: It permits plaintiffs to counteract unconscious prejudices and disguised animus that escape easy classification as disparate treatment. In this way disparate-impact liability may prevent segregated housing patterns that might otherwise result from covert and illicit stereotyping.

But disparate-impact liability has always been properly limited in key respects that avoid the serious constitutional questions that might arise under the FHA, for instance, if such liability were imposed based solely on a showing of a statistical disparity. Disparate-impact liability mandates the "removal of artificial, arbitrary, and unnecessary barriers," not the displacement of valid governmental policies. The FHA is not an instrument to force housing authorities to reorder their priorities. Rather, the FHA aims to ensure that those priorities can be achieved without arbitrarily creating discriminatory effects or perpetuating segregation.

. . . [H]ousing authorities and private developers [are] . . . allowed to maintain a policy if they can prove it is necessary to achieve a valid interest. To be sure, the Title

VII framework may not transfer exactly to the fair-housing context, but the comparison suffices for present purposes.

It would be paradoxical to construe the FHA to impose onerous costs on actors who encourage revitalizing dilapidated housing in our Nation's cities merely because some other priority might seem preferable. Entrepreneurs must be given latitude to consider market factors. Zoning officials, moreover, must often make decisions based on a mix of factors, both objective (such as cost and traffic patterns) and, at least to some extent, subjective (such as preserving historic architecture). These factors contribute to a community's quality of life and are legitimate concerns for housing authorities. The FHA does not decree a particular vision of urban development; and it does not put housing authorities and private developers in a double bind of liability, subject to suit whether they choose to rejuvenate a city core or to promote new low-income housing in suburban communities. As HUD itself recognized in its recent rulemaking, disparate-impact liability "does not mandate that affordable housing be located in neighborhoods with any particular characteristic." 78 Fed. Reg. 11476.

In a similar vein, a disparate-impact claim that relies on a statistical disparity must fail if the plaintiff cannot point to a defendant's policy or policies causing that disparity. A robust causality requirement ensures that "[r]acial imbalance . . . does not, without more, establish a prima facie case of disparate impact" and thus protects defendants from being held liable for racial disparities they did not create. *Wards Cove Packing Co. v. Atonio*, 490 U.S. 642, 653, 109 S. Ct. 2115, 104 L. Ed. 2d 733 (1989), superseded by statute on other grounds, 42 U.S.C. § 2000e-2(k). Without adequate safeguards at the prima facie stage, disparate-impact liability might cause race to be used and considered in a pervasive way and "would almost inexorably lead" governmental or private entities to use "numerical quotas," and serious constitutional questions then could arise. 490 U.S., at 653, 109 S. Ct. 2115.

The litigation at issue here provides an example. From the standpoint of determining advantage or disadvantage to racial minorities, it seems difficult to say as a general matter that a decision to build low-income housing in a blighted inner-city neighborhood instead of a suburb is discriminatory, or vice versa. If those sorts of judgments are subject to challenge without adequate safeguards, then there is a danger that potential defendants may adopt racial quotas — a circumstance that itself raises serious constitutional concerns.

Courts must therefore examine with care whether a plaintiff has made out a prima facie case of disparate impact and prompt resolution of these cases is important. A plaintiff who fails to allege facts at the pleading stage or produce statistical evidence demonstrating a causal connection cannot make out a prima facie case of disparate impact. For instance, a plaintiff challenging the decision of a private developer to construct a new building in one location rather than another will not easily be able to show this is a policy causing a disparate impact because such a one-time decision may not be a policy at all. It may also be difficult to establish causation because of the multiple factors that go into investment decisions about where to construct or renovate housing units. . . .

The FHA imposes a command with respect to disparate-impact liability. Here, that command goes to a state entity. In other cases, the command will go to a private person or entity. Governmental or private policies are not contrary to the disparate-impact requirement unless they are "artificial, arbitrary, and unnecessary barriers." *Griggs*, 401 U.S., at 431, 91 S. Ct. 849. Difficult questions might arise if disparate-impact liability under the FHA caused race to be used and considered in a pervasive and explicit manner to justify governmental or private actions that, in fact, tend to perpetuate race-based considerations rather than move beyond them. Courts should avoid interpreting disparate-impact liability to be so expansive as to inject racial considerations into every housing decision.

The limitations on disparate-impact liability discussed here are also necessary to protect potential defendants against abusive disparate-impact claims. If the specter of disparate-impact litigation causes private developers to no longer construct or renovate housing units for low-income individuals, then the FHA would have undermined its own purpose as well as the free-market system. And as to governmental entities, they must not be prevented from achieving legitimate objectives, such as ensuring compliance with health and safety codes. . . .

Were standards for proceeding with disparate-impact suits not to incorporate at least the safeguards discussed here, then disparate-impact liability might displace valid governmental and private priorities, rather than solely "remov[ing] . . . artificial, arbitrary, and unnecessary barriers." And that, in turn, would set our Nation back in its quest to reduce the salience of race in our social and economic system.

It must be noted further that, even when courts do find liability under a disparate-impact theory, their remedial orders must be consistent with the Constitution. Remedial orders in disparate-impact cases should concentrate on the elimination of the offending practice that "arbitrar[ily] . . . operate[s] invidiously to discriminate on the basis of rac[e]." If additional measures are adopted, courts should strive to design them to eliminate racial disparities through race-neutral means. . . .

While the automatic or pervasive injection of race into public and private transactions covered by the FHA has special dangers, it is also true that race may be considered in certain circumstances and in a proper fashion. . . .

The Court holds that disparate-impact claims are cognizable under the Fair Housing Act. . . .

### III

In light of the longstanding judicial interpretation of the FHA to encompass disparate-impact claims and congressional reaffirmation of that result, residents and policymakers have come to rely on the availability of disparate-impact claims. . . .

. . . [S]ince the passage of the Fair Housing Act in 1968 and against the backdrop of disparate-impact liability in nearly every jurisdiction, many cities have become more diverse. The FHA must play an important part in avoiding the . . . grim prophecy that "[o]ur Nation is moving toward two societies, one black, one white — separate and unequal." The Court acknowledges the Fair Housing Act's continuing role in moving the Nation toward a more integrated society.

The judgment of the Court of Appeals for the Fifth Circuit is affirmed, and the case is remanded for further proceedings consistent with this opinion.

It is so ordered.

## Questions for Consideration

1) What is the disparate impact claim in this case?

2) How does this claim relate to the tax credit program designed to assist low-income families in obtaining affordable housing?

3) What is *de jure* residential segregation?

4) What is "redlining"?

5) What does the HUD interpretation discussed by the Court say about the interpretation of the FHA?

6) What relevance did Title VII of the Civil Rights Act and the Age Discrimination in Employment Act of 1967 have in the Court's discussion of the FHA?

7) Does the FHA apply to zoning?

8) What type of evidence would you develop in preparing for a disparate impact challenge?

## Takeaway

- The *Inclusive Communities* case affirmed the legality of demonstrating discrimination by proof of disparate impact under an FHA challenge. Up until this decision, there was not unanimity among all of the federal circuit courts. This fueled ongoing debate as to the legitimacy of disparate impact analysis. It seems that the Supreme Court has now answered this question by approving disparate impact analysis as a method of demonstrating discrimination in the *Inclusive Communities* case.

- Demonstrating discrimination by disparate impact means that intent is not an element.

- To show disparate impact, one must be able to point to a policy or policies that are causing the alleged disparity in outcome for a protected person or group under the FHA. One must also provide statistical evidence of the asserted disparity. To do this, one must make a comparison among groups.

- Importantly, because the ADA and the RHA have both been consistently interpreted as following the FHA in terms of their anti-discrimination analysis, *Inclusive Communities* seems to mean that disparate impact analysis will also be uniformly applicable to ADA and RHA cases.

# Virginia ex rel. Fair Housing Board v. Windsor Plaza Condo. Ass'n

Supreme Court of Virginia

768 S.E.2d 79 (Va. 2014)

GOODWYN, Justice. In these consolidated appeals, we consider various issues arising under the Virginia Fair Housing Law, Code § 36-96.1 et *seq.* (VFHL), and the Federal Fair Housing Amendments Act of 1988, 42 U.S.C. § 3601 *et seq.* (FHAA).

## Background

On March 4, 2009, Michael Fishel (Fishel) filed complaints with the Virginia Fair Housing Board (FHB) and the United States Department of Housing and Urban Development (HUD), alleging that Windsor Plaza Condominium Association (Windsor Plaza) had discriminated against him in violation of the VFHL and the FHAA. HUD transferred Fishel's complaint to the FHB.

On May 28, 2010, the FHB, after an investigation, determined that reasonable cause existed to believe that Windsor Plaza had engaged in a "discriminatory housing practice . . . in violation of . . . Code § 36-96.3(B)(ii)." Pursuant to Code § 36-96.14, the FHB referred the charge to the Attorney General on June 1, 2010.

On June 30, 2010, the Office of the Attorney General, on behalf of the Commonwealth, filed a complaint against Windsor Plaza in the Circuit Court of Arlington County. The complaint alleged that Windsor Plaza had violated Code § 36-96.3(B)(ii) by failing "to make reasonable accommodations in rules, practices, policies, or services [that were] necessary to afford [Fishel] equal opportunity to use and enjoy [his] dwelling."

. . . .

## Facts

Windsor Plaza Condominium is located in Arlington County and is comprised of two condominium buildings, each with underground parking garages. When the condominium was first built, parking spaces in these garages were general common elements. The site plan for the buildings notes four parking spaces for use by disabled persons. Those parking spaces were designated as "HC" on the site plan.

In 1995, the developer of Windsor Plaza Condominium executed an "Amendment to Condominium Instruments" document. The amendment allowed the developer to assign the previously general common element parking spaces as limited common element parking spaces. Pursuant to the amendment, the developer deeded every parking space in the condominium's underground garages, including the four parking spaces designated for use by disabled persons (hereinafter "disabled parking spaces"), to individual unit owners "as a limited common element for the exclusive use of the unit owner of such condominium unit."

Fishel suffers from "severe osteoarthritis" and must use a wheelchair. In July 2007, the Fishels purchased a condominium unit in the Taylor Street Building of Windsor

Plaza Condominium. The Fishels received a "resale package," which they reviewed carefully for two days before purchasing their unit. In the resale package, a diagram of the parking garages showed four disabled parking spaces. The documents in the resale package also indicated that garage parking spaces at the condominium were limited common elements and that the developer had already assigned all of the parking spaces to individual unit owners.

Before buying their condominium unit, the Fishels visited the site and looked at the unit and underground parking garage. The Fishels saw the parking space that would be purchased with their condominium. They testified at trial that they knew the space was not a disabled parking space and that "[it] wasn't going to meet [their] needs." The Fishels did not inquire about the availability of disabled parking spaces in the garage before purchasing their condominium unit.

Soon after purchasing their condominium unit, the Fishels contacted Joseph Tilton (Tilton), Windsor Plaza's building manager, and informed him that Fishel was unable to park his van in their parking space. Tilton advised the Fishels to park in one of the disabled parking spaces, which they did "a couple times," but the Fishels were soon informed that they could not park in that space because it belonged to another condominium unit owner.

On July 30, 2007, the Fishels emailed Tilton, asking for "a larger parking space" in a better location. Windsor Plaza's Board of Directors (the Board) considered their request at a board meeting, and Tilton relayed the Board's response to the Fishels by email on August 23, 2007:

> The Board of Directors reviewed your request for a larger parking space at last night's meeting. As all existing garage spaces are individually owned by unit owners, assigning a different parking space to your residence is beyond the authority of the Board. This does not preclude you from advertising your interest in trading parking spaces with another owner. If you would like to draft a flyer announcing your need for a larger space, we would be happy to post copies on both bulletin boards. Such a notice may facilitate an exchange of spaces, either as a casual agreement or as a permanent reassignment, based on the preferences of all parties involved.
>
> Please contact us should you have any further concerns.

The Fishels responded to Tilton's August 23, 2007 email and asserted Fishel's "right . . . to park in a handicapped-designated space," but they indicated that they were reluctant to "go this route." The Fishels' email concluded, "Please ask the Board to review this issue again in an expedited manner. We need a parking space that we can actually use."

The next email from Tilton, dated September 12, 2007, related that the Board had met again and that "[a] copy of your request is being sent to the Condominium's counsel so he may instruct us in how to best accommodate your needs."

During the following months, the Fishels inquired periodically about the status of their request. On May 7, 2008, Windsor Plaza's attorney, Raymond Diaz (Diaz), informed the Fishels by letter that Windsor Plaza could not force any of the individual parking space owners to trade with them. Diaz asserted that "it has proven impossible for the Association to persuade the owner of the larger space to conclude an arrangement permitting you the use of the larger garage parking space."

In the same letter, Diaz offered to help the Fishels secure approval from the county to reserve a parking space on the street outside their condominium building. The Fishels rejected this proposal because in order to park on the street, Fishel would have to exit his car into traffic. Moreover, the curb was too steep, and the nearest entrance door was not handicap-accessible.

Diaz wrote another letter dated August 10, 2009, informing the Fishels that the owners of one of the disabled parking spaces were willing to enter into a licensing agreement that would allow the Fishels to use the disabled parking space. The Fishels did not accept this offer because, in the proposed agreement, the parking space owners reserved a right to reclaim the disabled parking space if they sold their condominium or if at some point they had a tenant who needed the disabled parking space.

On March 4, 2009, the Fishels filed complaints with the FHB and HUD. Thereafter, an investigator from the FHB visited the condominium building. Fishel testified that while he was in the garage with the investigator, Tilton walked by, and Fishel raised with Tilton the idea of converting a bicycle storage space, located in the garage, into an accessible parking space. Tilton expressed concern that doing so would be too expensive. Fishel testified that he offered to pay for the "disabled logo and everything." The circuit court found that Fishel did not present any evidence that this option was ever presented to the Board or its counsel.

### Analysis

. . . .

*Modifications and Accommodations under Code §§ 36-96.3(B)(i) and (ii)*

In support of its claim that Windsor Plaza discriminated against Fishel by failing to make reasonable accommodations in rules, practices, policies or services that were necessary to afford him equal opportunity to use and enjoy his dwelling, the Commonwealth presented evidence that the Fishels mentioned to Tilton that there was a common element bicycle storage area in the parking garage that was large enough to be converted into a parking space for Fishel. The circuit court ruled that such request constituted a reasonable modification request rather than a request for a reasonable accommodation.

The Commonwealth asserts that the circuit court erred in ruling that the request for the creation of the disabled parking space was not a request for an accommodation under Code § 36-96.3(B)(ii). According to the Commonwealth, parking is a service, and Fishel sought an accommodation in the "rules, practices, and policies involving the provision of that service." The Commonwealth claims that modifications involve "structural changes" while accommodations involve "cosmetic changes" and that converting the bicycle space into a disabled parking space for Fishel would require only cosmetic changes. The Commonwealth further argues that Windsor Plaza's Policy Resolution No. 7 explicitly authorizes the Board to convert a common elements area, such as the bicycle space, into a limited common element parking space to accommodate the needs of a disabled person. Hence, because the Fishels' request to convert the bicycle space into an accessible parking space required cosmetic changes and an alteration in Windsor Plaza's parking policy, the Commonwealth concludes that its evidence supported a reasonable accommodation claim under Code § 36-96.3(B)(ii).

According to Windsor Plaza, parking is not a service at the condominium because all parking spaces are limited common elements and are assigned to individual unit owners. Windsor Plaza argues that the circuit court correctly determined that the Commonwealth's evidence concerning the possible conversion of the bicycle space supported a cause of action for a reasonable modification because a "modification" is made to "premises," while an "accommodation" is made to "rules, policies, practices, or services."

Whether the Commonwealth's evidence supported a cause of action for failure to provide a reasonable accommodation under Code § 36-96.3(B)(ii) requires statutory interpretation of the VFHL. . . .

The VFHL protects disabled persons from "unlawful discriminatory housing practices." *See* Code § 36-96.3(A) (describing actions that qualify as "discriminatory housing practices"). Code § 36-96.3(A)(9) provides,

> It shall be an unlawful discriminatory housing practice for any person . . . [t]o discriminate against any person in the terms, conditions, or privileges of sale or rental of a dwelling, or in the provision of services or facilities in connection therewith because of a handicap of . . . that person.

"Discrimination" is defined several ways in the VFHL. Relevant to this appeal, Code § 36-96.3(B)(i) states that "discrimination includes . . . a refusal to permit, at the expense of the handicapped person, reasonable modifications of existing premises occupied or to be occupied by any person if such modifications may be necessary to afford such person full enjoyment of the premises." Code § 36-96.3(B)(ii) provides that discrimination also includes "a refusal to make reasonable accommodations in rules, practices, policies, or services when such accommodations may be necessary to afford such person equal opportunity to use and enjoy a dwelling."

The Commonwealth only asserts a violation of Code § 36-96.3(B)(ii). It insists that parking is a service and that the Fishels requested a reasonable accommodation in that service when they requested that Windsor Plaza convert the bicycle space into an accessible parking space for them. However, the plain meaning of the word "service" does not encompass the underground garage parking scheme at Windsor Plaza Condominium.

"Service" is "[l]abor performed in the interest or under the direction of others; specif[ically], the performance of some useful act or series of acts for the benefit of another, usu[ally] for a fee." Black's Law Dictionary 1576 (10th ed.2014). At the condominium, parking spaces have been assigned to individual unit owners as property rights appurtenant to their condominium units. These assigned parking spaces are limited common elements, which are "reserved for the exclusive use" of individual unit owners. Code § 55-79.41. Because parking spaces are forms of real property at the condominium, they are not acts or labor performed to benefit the unit owners, and thus parking is not a service under Code § 36-96.3(B)(ii).

. . . .

We conclude the ruling of the circuit court is faithful to the plain language of Code §§ 36-96.3(B)(i) and (ii). There was no evidence at trial concerning what would be involved in changing the bicycle storage space into a parking space. However, the Commonwealth acknowledges that converting the bicycle space into an accessible parking space for Fishel would require physical alterations, although slight, to the premises. Consequently, the circuit court did not err in determining that the Commonwealth's evidence concerning the conversion of the bicycle space into an accessible parking space supported a cause of action under Code § 36-96.3(B)(i) for a reasonable modification rather than a cause of action under Code § 36-96.3(B)(ii) for a reasonable accommodation.

### Sufficiency of the Evidence: Reasonable Accommodation Claim

The Commonwealth contends that it presented sufficient evidence of a violation of Code § 36-96.3(B)(ii) to survive Windsor Plaza's motion to strike the evidence. The Commonwealth asserts that the parties stipulated at trial that Fishel is disabled and that it is necessary for him to have an accessible parking space. According to the Commonwealth, the evidence showed that Fishel asked for a larger parking space in a different location. The Commonwealth claims that in response Windsor Plaza proposed "two flawed solutions" and "ignored" Fishel's reasonable request to convert the bicycle storage space into an accessible parking space. It adds that even if all four disabled spaces were being used by disabled people, Windsor Plaza would nevertheless be required under the VFHL to consider converting the bicycle space into an accessible parking space for the Fishels. The Commonwealth argues that the Fishels' request for an accessible parking space is reasonable because Windsor Plaza is required by law to provide disabled parking spaces.

By contrast, Windsor Plaza maintains that the evidence showed that it offered the Fishels a reasonable accommodation but that they rejected the offer. According to evidence at trial, Windsor Plaza negotiated a licensing agreement in which the owners of a disabled parking space would allow the Fishels to use their space. Windsor Plaza insists that it is not obligated to provide a permanent accommodation.

To assert a reasonable accommodation claim under the VFHL, the plaintiff bears the burden to prove by a preponderance of the evidence that the requested accommodation is reasonable and necessary to give a disabled person the equal opportunity to use and enjoy housing. *See Scoggins v. Lee's Crossing Homeowners Ass'n*, 718 F.3d 262, 272 (4th Cir.2013) (stating the elements of a reasonable accommodation claim under the FHAA). In the proceedings below, the parties agreed that Fishel is disabled and needs an accessible parking space in order to have an equal opportunity to enjoy his condominium unit, but they disagreed as to whether the Fishels requested a reasonable accommodation.

The Fourth Circuit has recognized several factors a court can use to determine whether an accommodation is reasonable:

> In determining whether the reasonableness requirement has been met, a court may consider as factors the extent to which the accommodation would undermine the legitimate purposes and effects of existing zoning regulations and the benefits that the accommodation would provide to the handicapped. It may also consider whether alternatives exist to accomplish the benefits more efficiently. And in measuring the effects of an accommodation, the court may look not only to its functional and administrative aspects, but also to its costs.

*Bryant Woods Inn, Inc. v. Howard Cnty.*, 124 F.3d 597, 604 (4th Cir.1997) (analyzing whether a request for an exception to zoning regulations was reasonable). An accommodation is not reasonable if it poses "undue financial and administrative burdens or changes, adjustments, or modifications to existing programs that would be substantial, or that would constitute fundamental alterations in the nature of the program." . . .

The Fishels asked for a larger parking space in a different location. However, Virginia's Condominium Act permits the reassignment of limited common elements, such as the parking spaces at issue, only with the consent of all property owners affected by the reassignment. *See* Code § 55.79.57(A). We hold that requesting, as an accommodation, the reassignment of limited common element parking spaces belonging to private individuals is unreasonable because Windsor Plaza has no authority to confiscate property belonging to one unit owner and to reassign that property to another. *See Groner v. Golden Gate Gardens Apartments*, 250 F.3d 1039, 1046 (6th Cir.2001) ("As a matter of law, the [neighbor's] rights did not have to be sacrificed on the altar of reasonable accommodation.").

The Commonwealth also argues that its evidence showed that Windsor Plaza failed to provide the Fishels with a reasonable accommodation by refusing to convert the bicycle storage space into an accessible parking space. However, as stated previously, converting the bicycle space is a modification "of existing premises," not an accommodation "in rules, practices, policies, or services." Therefore, the Commonwealth's evidence concerning the bicycle space did not prove a request for a reasonable accommodation.

The Commonwealth's only evidence of an accommodation request refused by Windsor Plaza was that of reassigning one of the limited common element parking spaces to the Fishels. Because Windsor Plaza does not have the authority to reassign disabled parking spaces that are limited common elements without the consent of the owner of the parking space, this accommodation request was not reasonable, and we hold that the Commonwealth failed to satisfy its burden of proving that Windsor Plaza failed to provide a reasonable accommodation. Consequently, the circuit court did not err in granting Windsor Plaza's motion to strike the Commonwealth's evidence.

. . . .

## Continuing Violations

. . . [T]he Fishels claim that the circuit court erred in determining that Windsor Plaza's alleged violations of Code § 36-96.3(A)(8) and (9) and 42 U.S.C. § 3604(f)(1) and (2) were not continuing violations. They maintain that Windsor Plaza continues to discriminate against them in the sale of their condominium unit as well as continues to make housing unavailable by "operat[ing] a condominium premises that does not provide the accessible garage parking spaces required by [law]." Because Windsor Plaza continues to operate a condominium that lacks handicap-accessible parking while benefitting from the payment of the Fishels' condominium fees, the Fishels argue that "the statute of limitations does not bar [their] claims" because Windsor Plaza's latest discriminatory act falls within the statute of limitations period.

Windsor Plaza responds that the violations alleged by the Fishels are continuing effects, not continuing violations. Windsor Plaza contends that its alleged violations are the continuing effects of the developer's assignment of disabled parking spaces to individual unit owners and cannot extend the statute of limitations.

. . . .

The continuing violation doctrine is one in "which acts occurring outside the statute of limitations may be considered when there is a 'fixed and continuing practice' of unlawful acts both before and during the limitations period." One federal district court has explained the difference in continuing violations and continuing effects of past violations: "[A] continuing violation is occasioned by continual unlawful acts, not continual ill effects from an original violation." *Moseke v. Miller & Smith, Inc.,* 202 F.Supp.2d 492, 495 (E.D.Va.2002).

*In Moseke,* the court concluded that the inaccessible features of three condominium complexes were "more akin to a continuing effect rather than a continuing violation under the FHA[A]." Because the plaintiffs alleged design and construction claims under the FHAA and VFHL, the court reasoned that the last discriminatory act occurred when the defendants completed construction of the complexes. The court was not swayed by the plaintiff's argument that the violation was ongoing because the condominiums continued to operate without disabled parking spaces.

In this case, the circuit court correctly determined that the Fishels did not allege continuing violations of Code §§ 36-96.3(A)(8) and (9) and 42 U.S.C. §§ 3604(f)(1) and (2). The violations alleged by the Fishels — allowing disabled parking spaces to be assigned to residents as limited common elements without reserving a handicap-accessible parking space for the Fishels — occurred at one point in time. The Fishels' not being able to use a disabled parking space is a continuing effect of having assigned all the handicap-accessible parking spaces to other owners before the Fishels bought their condominium. Thus, the circuit court did not err in determining that the alleged discriminatory acts by Windsor Plaza are not continuing in nature but continuing in effect. Therefore, the circuit court did not err in sustaining Windsor Plaza's plea in bar to the Fishels' claims under Code §§ 36-96.3(A)(8) and 9 and 42 U.S.C. §§ 3604(f)(1) and (2).

. . . .

### Conclusion

[The Supreme Court of Virginia affirms the circuit court decision in favor of Windsor Plaza.]

## Questions for Consideration

1)  What is the asserted basis of discrimination in this case?

2)  What was Fishel seeking from the Windsor Plaza Condominium Association (Windsor Plaza)?

3)  Did Fishel know about the parking arrangements prior to the purchase of his condominium unit?

4)  What steps did Windsor Plaza take in its efforts to respond to the request by Fishel?

5)  Was the provision of a parking space considered a service under the Virginia FHA in this case?

6)  What is the nature of the court's discussion concerning the issue of a reasonable modification and a reasonable accommodation in its discussion of the facts of this case?

7)  Did the court determine that Windsor Plaza discriminated against Fishel?

8)  How did the court answer the question of "continuing violations" as raised near the end of the opinion?

## Takeaway

- A condominium is a special form of property ownership. It is generally associated with residential home ownership, but it need not be restricted to housing. In condominium home ownership, as relevant in this case, an individual purchases a unit in a condominium and typically owns the unit in fee simple, *together with an undivided interest in the common elements*. The common elements include everything outside of the defined unit space. Examples of common elements are hallways, stairwells, elevators, green spaces, a clubhouse, and a pool. Such things as parking spaces, patios, and balconies are also typically identified as common elements that are owned in common. Sometimes parking spaces, patios, and balconies are identified as *limited common elements*, meaning that while they are owned in common, they are set aside for the specific use of the owner of a particular condominium unit.

- The condominium ownership form of real property does not exist at common law and is a creature of state statute. Consequently, state condominium law must be consulted. In addition, state condominium statutes require condominium documents to describe the exact meaning of such terms as: unit, common element, and limited common element. Thus, one must read the documents carefully.

- The condominium form of property ownership will also establish a homeowners association with a board to assist in managing the affairs of the condominium. The board is responsible for handling requests such as the one made by Fishel for adjustment in the parking assignments.

- Note that this case does not involve Title II of the ADA because the condominium is a private form of property ownership and the condominium rules and regulations are not actions or regulations of the local planning and zoning officials. Condominiums involve private rules, practices, procedures, and services, and Title II covers public programs, services, and practices.

- An accommodation is not reasonable if it imposes an undue financial or administrative burden or if it will constitute a fundamental alteration in the nature of the program or living arrangement.

- It is important to distinguish between a continuing violation and the continuing effects of an earlier violation. This will be important in such matters as figuring out when the statute of limitations might run.

## Discussion Problem 6.5

The city of Milan has a population of 550,000 people. It is composed of seven distinct neighborhoods and districts. District 3 is a downtown neighborhood. Districts 6 and 7 are upscale and higher income neighborhoods located furthest from the downtown neighborhood and District 3. Districts 1, 2, 4, and 5 are working class communities. Each year, the state provides $1.2 million to assist the city in providing accessible housing to people over age 55 with a particular focus on ensuring that this housing is accessible to people using a wheelchair and with difficulty walking. The state wants to make certain that the housing it is helping to fund will be fully accessible as the residents age in place, so that they will not have to prematurely and involuntarily be moved to another location if their mobility declines. The city partners with private developers in building the housing. The private developers initiate the identification of building locations and then work with the city to construct a housing facility assisted by the state funds. To be eligible for the state-supported funding, the developer and the project must be approved by the city and meet certain accessibility and service guidelines consistent with the Americans with Disabilities Act. Each of the past 10 years, the city of Milan has followed a planning board policy of locating all of the accessible 55 and up housing into clusters within District 3 of the city. This neighborhood now houses 63% of city residents over age 55, living independently outside of nursing homes. Of this population, 57% have some type of disability. This year, Jaxson Housing, Inc., a local property developer, identified a suitable parcel of useable land within District 7, that it proposes to develop for 55 and up accessible housing. Jaxson anticipates that the majority of its residents will have a disability of some type and the project will be highly accessible to meet the needs of anticipated residents. Jaxson's development proposal, as submitted to the city, meets each of the criteria applicable to all of the prior approved housing projects. On submission of his proposal, the city denies his application, stating, "It is the planning policy of the city of Milan to locate all accessible age 55 and up housing in District 3 of the city. As your proposal is to develop land outside of District 3, it is denied." Jaxson Housing sues the city for violating the Fair Housing Act and for discriminating against people over age 55, many of whom have a disability, by forcing them to live within concentrated clusters inside of District 3. Jaxson sues on its own behalf and on behalf of two residents of the city, each age 62 and each using wheelchairs for mobility, who have signed contingent contracts to purchase a home from Jaxson in the event that the city approves his project to be built as proposed and to be located within District 7.

You are a lawyer/journalist working for the Milan Daily Journal and you have been assigned to write a feature story explaining the law applicable to this lawsuit, including an analysis of the merits and demerits of Jaxson's case against the city.

# N. Existing Facilities: Historic Preservation

Under disability law, new construction and alteration to existing facilities and structures must be accessible to the maximum extent possible. The only qualification on this requirement is that of *structural impracticability*. As to existing buildings, there are requirements to upgrade them to remove architectural barriers to accessibility. For public buildings and facilities under Title II, this may be a requirement qualified by raising an *undue financial or administrative burden* defense. As to places of public accommodation, under Title III, this may be qualified by raising a not *readily achievable* defense. Something is not readily achievable if it is difficult to achieve, or if it imposes an undue financial or administrative burden on the defendant. Historic properties, structures and facilities raise additional consideration.

## Molski v. Foley Estates Vineyard and Winery, LLC

United States Court of Appeals for the Ninth Circuit
531 F.3d 1043 (9th Cir. 2008)

D.W. NELSON, Senior Circuit Judge. This case involves a paraplegic who encountered discriminatory barriers to access when he visited a winery with his grandmother. Unwilling to remove barriers to the historic wine-tasting room, Foley Estates Vineyard and Winery ("Foley") began providing services on a gazebo with a "big bell" where individuals barred from the wine-tasting room could ring for service. Jarek Molski and Disability Rights Enforcement, Education, Services ("DREES") sued Foley for injunctive relief and damages to redress physical barriers to wheelchair accessibility. The district court ordered barrier removal within the building, but determined that it would not be readily achievable to make an accessible ramp to the entrance. We affirm the injunction requiring barrier removal within the building and we remand for the district court to apply 28 C.F.R. § 36.405 and the Americans with Disabilities Act Accessibility Guidelines for Buildings and Facilities, 28 C.F.R. § 36 App. A 4.1.7 ("ADAAG § 4.1.7" or "§ 4.1.7") when evaluating whether an accessible ramp would be readily achievable.

### Factual and Procedural Background

On January 18, 2003, Jarek Molski [Jarek Molski is paraplegic and requires a wheelchair for mobility, and he is a member of DREES] visited the Foley Estates Winery with his grandmother. While attending a wine-tasting, Molski encountered multiple physical barriers to entry with his wheelchair. An accessibility expert, Rick Sarantschin, conducted a sub rosa investigation of the property on October 12, 2003. Sarantschin confirmed the existence of barriers to entry including a ramp with a slope that varies between 6% and 20%; a raised threshold measuring 4.5"; a round door knob; a rear door width of only 30"; another door width of 31.25"; and a wine-tasting counter height of 42". Jarek Molski and DREES filed suit against Foley on December 22, 2003.

Prior to the commencement of litigation, Foley undertook $ 23,994 in renovations to provide all services on a wheelchair-accessible gazebo. Renovations included an accessible ramp from the parking lot and a "big bell" to summon for service. Nearly two years into the court proceedings, the Santa Barbara County Historic Landmarks Advisory Commission declared Foley Estates a "Place of Historical Merit"

. . . .

At trial, the court heard expert testimony regarding proposed methods of barrier removal and associated costs. The court also heard testimony from Foley's architectural historian, who opined that an access ramp would have a severe impact on the historical nature of the cottage. The judge determined that it would cost $34,074 to construct an access ramp to the rear of the building, and it would cost $5,130 to remove all physical access barriers inside the building. The judge found that removal of interior barriers would be readily achievable, but removal of exterior barriers would not be readily achievable because it would threaten the architectural significance of the property. In reaching this finding, the judge held that 28 C.F.R. § 36.405 and ADAAG § 4.1.7 do not apply to barrier removal for existing facilities. Thus, the judge allocated the burden of production to the plaintiff to show that the proposed alteration would not threaten the historic significance of the building. The trial judge issued a permanent injunction requiring barrier removal inside the cottage.

DREES timely appeals the district court's findings regarding the applicability of 28 C.F.R. § 36.405 and ADAAG § 4.1.7, and the ready achievability of constructing an accessible ramp. Foley cross-appeals and challenges the permanent injunction requiring removal of interior physical barriers.

. . . .

## Discussion

## I. Exterior Ramp

## A. Applicable Regulations

On appeal, we are asked to decide whether 28 C.F.R. § 36.405 and ADAAG § 4.1.7 apply to barrier removal in existing facilities. By their terms, these regulations apply to "alterations;" however, 28 C.F.R. § 36.304(d)(1) extends their application to readily achievable barrier removal in existing facilities. Despite this regulatory directive, the district court declined to apply § 36.405 and § 4.1.7. We reverse and remand.

Our analysis begins with 28 C.F.R. § 36.304, which regulates barrier removal in existing facilities of public accommodation. That section requires "[a] public accommodation [to] remove architectural barriers in existing facilities . . . where such removal is readily achievable." 28 C.F.R. § 36.304(a). The regulation goes on to specify that, "measures taken to comply with the barrier removal requirements of this section shall comply with the applicable requirements for *alterations* in § 36.402 and §§ 36.404-36.406. . . ." 28 C.F.R. § 36.304(d)(1) (emphasis added). If compliance under those additional regulations would not be readily achievable, "a public accommodation may take other readily achievable measures to remove the barrier that do not fully comply with the specified requirements." 28 C.F.R. § 36.304(d)(2).

In this case, we look to the regulations governing historic buildings because the Santa Barbara County Historic Landmarks Advisory Commission designated the building as a place of local historic merit. Through its plain language, 28 C.F.R. § 36.304(d)(1) directs vendors to comply with 28 C.F.R. § 36.405 when making readily achievable accommodations. Section 36.405 requires qualified historic buildings to "comply to the maximum extent feasible with [ADAAG § 4.1.7]." 28 C.F.R. § 36.405(a). Under § 4.1.7, "if the entity undertaking the alterations believes that compliance with the requirements . . . would threaten or destroy the historic significance of the building . . . the entity should consult with the State Historic Preservation Officer." ADAAG § 4.1.7(2)(b). "If the State Historic Preservation Officer agrees that compliance with the accessibility requirements for accessible routes (exterior and interior), ramps, entrances or toilets would threaten or destroy the historical significance of the building or facility, the alternative requirements in 4.1.7(3) may be used." *Id.* Under our reading, 28 C.F.R. § 36.304(d)(1) requires compliance with § 36.405, which incorporates § 4.1.7(2)(b) and provides a procedure for businesses to seek alternative requirements for historic properties.

Our reading of 28 C.F.R. § 36.304 preserves the leniency allocated to existing facilities under Title III of the Americans with Disabilities Act. The ADA only requires barrier removal in existing facilities "where such removal is readily achievable." 42 U.S.C. § 12182(b)(2)(A)(iv). Section 36.304 integrates the "readily achievable" standard into both § 36.304(a) and § 36.304(d)(2). Section 36.304(a) ensures that only readily achievable barrier removal triggers the incorporation of § 36.405 and § 4.1.7, and § 36.304(d)(2) allows for partial compliance if full compliance with those regulations would not be readily achievable. Thus 28 C.F.R. § 36.304 incorporates § 36.405 and § 4.1.7 into the ready achievability framework, and retains the flexible standard reserved for existing facilities.

Additionally, § 4.1.7 establishes a procedure for determining whether barrier removal in existing facilities will be readily achievable. According to the ADA Title III Technical Assistance Manual ("ADA Manual") § III-4.4200, "[b]arrier removal would not be considered 'readily achievable' if it would threaten or destroy the historic significance of a building or facility that is . . . designated as historic under State or local law." The standard set in § 4.1.7 is identical to the standard of ready achievability proffered by the ADA Manual. This similarity between the language suggests that application of § 4.1.7 is consistent with the standard for existing historic facilities. Therefore, the procedure set forth in § 4.1.7 may be used to determine what is readily achievable in existing historic facilities.

For the foregoing reasons, we find that the district court erred when it refused to apply § 36.405 and § 4.1.7 to readily achievable barrier removal in existing facilities. We acknowledge that three courts have considered historical significance as a factor for determining ready achievability without invoking 28 C.F.R. § 36.405 or ADAAG § 4.1.7. However, we find the explicit regulatory language to be more persuasive than the absence of discussion of these regulations in our sister circuits. Therefore, we remand to the district court to apply § 36.405 and § 4.1.7 when determining whether an exterior ramp would be readily achievable.

### B. Burden of Production

. . . .

We begin by looking to § 36.405 and § 4.1.7 to allocate the burden of production. Under § 4.1.7(2)(b), "if the entity undertaking alterations believes that compliance with the requirements . . . would threaten or destroy the historic significance of the building . . . the entity should consult with the State Historic Preservation Officer." Although this clause uses permissive language, it calls upon the party who believes that compliance would threaten the historical significance of the building to consult the appropriate agency. It does not place that burden on the party advocating for remedial measures. Thus, the language of § 4.1.7(2)(b) counsels in favor of placing the burden of production upon the defendant.

By placing the burden of production on the defendant, we place the burden on the party with the best access to information regarding the historical significance of the building. The defendant sought the historical designation in this case. Thus, the defendant possesses the best understanding of the circumstances under which that designation might be threatened. The defendant is also in the best position to discuss the matter with the Santa Barbara County Historic Landmarks Advisory Commission and to request an opinion on proposed methods of barrier removal. As a result, the defendant is in a better position to introduce, as part of its affirmative defense, detailed evidence and expert testimony concerning whether the historic significance of a structure would be threatened or destroyed by the proposed barrier removal plan.

. . . .

## II. Duty to Remove Interior Barriers

When the district court ordered removal of interior barriers to the building, the court arguably enhanced the probability that persons with disabilities would attempt to traverse the non-compliant ramp to access the building. Foley argues that we should absolve the winery of its responsibility to remove interior barriers because the only existing ramp is non-compliant. We reject this argument and affirm the district court's injunction requiring barrier removal inside the building.

. . . According to [28 C.F.R. § 36.304(d)(2)]:

> If . . . the measures required to remove a barrier would not be readily achievable, a public accommodation may take other readily achievable measures to remove the barrier that do not fully comply with the specified requirements. Such measures include, for example, providing a ramp with a steeper slope. . . . No measure shall be taken, however, that poses a significant risk to the health or safety of individuals with disabilities or others.

. . . .

First, § 36.304(d)(2) expressly contemplates that a venue may provide a ramp with a steeper slope. The provision of such a ramp does not excuse the facility from otherwise making readily achievable accommodations to the maximum extent feasible. Therefore, the fact that there is an existing ramp with a steeper slope also does not excuse the facility from making readily achievable accommodations to the maximum extent feasible. Second, the inaccessibility of entry to one group of individuals does not justify retaining barriers to access inside the building for all others who may safely gain entry. Where readily achievable, the interior of the building must be made accessible for all who may enter.

. . . .

## III. Alternative Gazebo

Foley argues that the provision of all relevant services on the wheelchair-accessible gazebo was legally adequate as a means of barrier removal. We reject this argument and affirm the district court's imposition of readily achievable barrier removal inside the building.

As a threshold matter, a facility may only substitute alternatives to barrier removal where "as a result of compliance with the alterations requirements specified in paragraph (d)(1) of this section, the measures required to remove a barrier would not be readily achievable." 28 C.F.R. § 36.304(d)(2). As noted above, the district court did not abuse its discretion in determining that barrier removal inside the building was readily achievable. In light of this holding, no alternative accommodations can supplant the legally required barrier removal.

Although we find the gazebo inadequate for those who could otherwise access the wine-tasting room, the gazebo provides an important avenue of participation for those who cannot traverse the steps or ramp to the wine-tasting room. We acknowledge Foley's efforts to serve this community; however, these efforts do not change Foley's obligation to make readily available changes to enable the maximum participation possible for those who are able to access the interior of the wine-tasting room. The gazebo places those who could otherwise access the wine-tasting room at a disadvantage that the ADA seeks to remove. Thus, the Gazebo is not an appropriate alternative accommodation.

## Conclusion

We REVERSE and REMAND for the district court to apply § 36.405 and § 4.1.7 and place the burden of production on the defendant. Additionally, we AFFIRM the district court's permanent injunction requiring removal of interior barriers to wheelchair access.

FERNANDEZ, Circuit Judge, concurring and dissenting: I concur in the majority's determination that the district court did not err when it required Foley Estates Vineyard and Winery, LLC, to make changes to the interior of its building pursuant to the Americans with Disabilities Act, 42 U.S.C. § 12181-12189 ("ADA"). However, I dissent from the majority's reversal of the district court's order denying a demand that Foley make the proposed exterior changes.

It is important to note that this is not a case where Foley sought to construct a new facility. See 42 U.S.C. § 12183(a)(1). Nor is it a case where Foley sought to alter an old facility. *See id.* § 12183(a)(2). It is, instead, a case where Foley was not seeking to make any change, but Disability Rights Enforcement Education Services: Helping You Help Others (hereafter "Disability Rights") demanded that changes be made because the failure to do so would be discriminatory. *See id.* § 12182(b)(2)(A)(iv). However, a mere failure to remove an architectural barrier is discriminatory only "where such removal is readily achievable." *Id.* In other words, the mere existence of the barrier does not bespeak wrongdoing; it only becomes wrongful if removal can be readily achieved.

Barrier removal is readily achievable when it is "easily accomplishable and able to be carried out without much difficulty or expense." *Id.* § 12181(9). That definition is extremely important. It imposes a much less stringent standard upon owners of existing properties than that imposed upon owners who undertake new construction and are required to show structural impracticability in order to avoid violating the ADA. *See id.* § 12183(a)(1). It is also less stringent than the "maximum extent feasible" standard imposed upon owners who seek to alter their facilities. *See id.* § 12183(a)(2).

In determining ready achievability, "the nature and cost of the action needed" must be taken into account. *Id.* § 12181(9)(A). Furthermore, because it was never intended that the nation's architectural heritage be destroyed under the banner of readily achievable accessibility, special consideration is given to buildings that "are designated as historic under State or local law." 28 C.F.R. § 36.405(a). As to those, it is important to avoid changes that would "threaten or destroy the historic significance of the building. . . ." *Id.* § 36.405(b). As the Department of Justice puts it: "Barrier removal would not be considered 'readily achievable' if it would threaten or destroy the historic significance of a building or facility that is . . . designated as historic under State or local law." Dep't of Justice, ADA Title III Technical Assistance Manual: Covering Pub. Accommodations & Commercial Facilities, § III-4.4200; *see also* 16 U.S.C. § 470f; Nondiscrimination on the Basis of Disability by Pub. Accommodations & in Commercial Facilities, 56 Fed. Reg. 35,544, 35,568-69 (July 26, 1991). It is through that lens that we must review the district court's decision in this case because the Foley building in question is a Craftsman house which has been designated as a Place of Historic Merit by the Santa Barbara County Historic Landmark Commission. Nobody doubts that.

When that proper method of examining the district court's determination is used, it is apparent that the district court did not clearly err when, based on the record before it, the court determined that the changes suggested by Disability Rights would, in fact, severely impact or destroy the historic significance of Foley's building. In reaching that conclusion, the court relied upon the unrebutted evidence from an expert architectural historian, Dr. Pamela Post, who testified to that effect and added that if the suggested changes had been made previously, they would have made the designation of the house as a Place of Historic Merit problematic. She, by the way, is the person who presented the initial report that supported the designation of the property in the first place.

. . . .

## *Questions for Consideration*

1) How important to the case is the fact that the Santa Barbara County Historical Landmarks Advisory Commission has designated this property as having historical significance? What if people in the community just considered it of historical value and the local newspaper had run a story about its historical qualities?

2) Under what Title of the ADA is this case governed and why?

3) Under the ADA, new construction and alterations must be accessible to the maximum extent feasible. Generally, this means that the primary defense to lack of accessibility is that compliance would be structurally impracticable. There is, however, an exception for alterations to historic structures. In qualified historic buildings, alterations need to be made only to the extent that they are "readily achievable." Explain how to apply the readily achievable standard.

4) In this case, we have three different "components" of the property to evaluate. These include the Gazebo, the interior of the main structure, and the exterior access ramp into the main structure. How does the court deal with

the requirements of the ADA as to each of these three components of the property?

5) Does it make sense as a matter of public policy and of economics to require interior alterations to a building that has an inaccessible ramp for access to the building?

6) How important do you think it is to have an expert on your side when addressing the questions of 1) historical significance of a structure; and 2) the meaning and application of the readily achievable standard?

7) Assume you have a client who owns and operates a bar in the downtown area of a major city. The bar is in an old building and the bathroom is located on the basement level. There is a stairway but no elevator. The bar is not being altered or improved in any way. The bar is located in an old building, but not an historical building. A disability rights group complains that the bar must have an accessible bathroom in order to operate in compliance with the ADA. The group asserts that failure to have an accessible bathroom is discrimination against people with disabilities. How would you advise the bar owner?

## *Takeaway*

- When applying disability law to a property and land use problem, be sure to know if you are proceeding under Title II or Title III of the ADA.

- The ADA does not provide a grandfather provision as might be applicable in a typical zoning situation when zoning law changes. Under the ADA, existing buildings may still have to undertake barrier removal in certain situations. For a place of public accommodation, the barrier must be eliminated to the extent it is reasonably achievable. Moreover, if an existing building adds new construction, the new construction must be accessible to the maximum extent feasible. Likewise, for alterations. Sometimes, difficulty arises in drawing the line between an alteration, and maintenance and upkeep. Being able to advise a client on the amount of work that can be done without crossing the threshold of becoming an alteration may prove important.

- As is often the case in planning and zoning situations, it is important to engage appropriate experts to support your position and to produce evidence that can be submitted on the record in support of your client. It is important to note that under our disability laws, the government has no system of certifying compliance with disability law requirements and regulations. Consequently, one is always open to potential lawsuits asserting non-compliance. This is why it is important to have an architect or other expert opine as to design and building guideline compliance and for you, as the lawyer, to have expertise in the legal issues, definitions, and standards of disability laws applicable to your client's situation.

# O. 1983 Actions

Sometimes a land use and zoning lawyer will confront a "1983 action." This refers to 42 U.S.C. § 1983, which provides for a federal cause of action for the violation of an individual's federal constitutional rights and permits the awarding of damages.

## Bower Associates v. Town of Pleasant Valley

Court of Appeals of New York
814 N.E.2d 410 (N.Y. 2004)

KAYE, Chief Judge. In the two appeals before us, appellants claim they were deprived of civil rights protected by the United States Constitution when the municipal defendants wrongfully refused consent to land-use permit applications. Although the projects ultimately proceeded to completion, appellants seek damages under 42 U.S.C. § 1983 for the delays occasioned by the wrongdoing. We conclude, as did the Appellate Division, that there was no constitutional violation and the complaints should be dismissed.

I.

### Bower Associates v. Town of Pleasant Valley

Bower Associates, a housing developer, owns approximately 91 acres in Dutchess County—88 acres in the Town of Poughkeepsie and three adjacent acres in the Town of Pleasant Valley. In August 1999, Poughkeepsie approved Bower's plan to subdivide the land and construct the Stratford Farms subdivision—134 detached single-family homes and 51 townhouses. The project has two access roads—one wholly within Poughkeepsie, the second partially in Pleasant Valley, through the three-acre Bower Associates subdivision. Poughkeepsie's final approval of Stratford Farms was conditioned on approval by Pleasant Valley of the access road partially within that Town.

In January 1999, Bower applied to the Pleasant Valley Planning Board for permission to subdivide its three acres there to create three residential homes and access roads for use by both Bower subdivisions. In January 2000, the Pleasant Valley Planning Board denied Bower's application, citing numerous environmental concerns relating to the Stratford Farms subdivision.

In Bower's challenge under CPLR article 78, Supreme Court directed approval of the subdivision plan, concluding that the Planning Board's actions were arbitrary in that its determination was not based on environmental concerns unique to the Bower Associates subdivision. Rather, "the determination was driven largely by community pressure because the Stratford Farms subdivision located in the Town of Poughkeepsie would provide no tax benefit to the Town of Pleasant Valley." The Appellate Division affirmed, agreeing that Bower "met all the conditions needed for approval of its subdivision application in both this and the related Stratford [Farms] subdivision."

Its article 78 relief in hand, in March 2001 Bower commenced this civil rights action pursuant to 42 U.S.C. § 1983 against the Town of Pleasant Valley and its Planning Board for $2 million in damages, alleging a denial of procedural and substantive due process, equal protection and just compensation. Supreme Court denied defendants' motion to dismiss, but the Appellate Division reversed, finding no cognizable property interest entitling Bower to substantive due process protection, both because the Board had discretion in granting subdivision approval and because defendants violated no rights protected by the United States Constitution. Further, the Appellate Division dismissed Bower's takings and equal protection claims, concluding that Bower alleged no unlawful taking, and failed to show that the subject property was treated differently from other similarly situated properties. We now affirm.

### Home Depot v. Dunn

In February 1996, Home Depot, U.S.A., Inc., a home improvement retailer, obtained site plan approval from the Village of Port Chester to develop an 8.33 acre site for a retail establishment of approximately 101,467 square feet, with an 18,000 square foot outdoor garden center and 537 parking spaces in Port Chester, at the border between Port Chester and the City of Rye. The facility opened in February 2000, after long wrangling with defendants, the City of Rye, its Mayor and City Council members (collectively Rye).

As an "Interested Agency" in the environmental review process led by Port Chester, Rye demanded that four traffic-mitigating measures be imposed, among them the widening of Midland Avenue in Rye—and Port Chester made that demand a condition for its approval of the project. Because Midland Avenue is a county road within the City of Rye, the plans also required the County's approval, which in turn required the City's approval. Thus, without Rye's go-ahead, Home Depot could not proceed.

... In March 1997, ... after community opposition, the [Rye] City Council ... refused consent to the permit.

In April 1997, Home Depot commenced two suits—an article 78 proceeding to compel Rye to sign (and the County of Westchester to issue) the permit, and a civil rights action pursuant to 42 U.S.C. § 1983 against the Mayor and the City Council members (both personally and officially) seeking $50 million in compensatory damages and unspecified punitive damages, for delaying construction by more than two years. As a July 1997 Home Depot interoffice memorandum reflects, Home Depot saw the "real value" of the section 1983 action "as leverage for settlement."

On January 30, 1998, in Home Depot's article 78 proceeding, Supreme Court—while recognizing that the actions Home Depot sought to compel were "of a discretionary nature"—held that Rye's insistence on additional mitigation measures and its refusal to approve the permit were arbitrary and capricious. The court annulled Rye's denial of the road-widening permit, and the Appellate Division affirmed. At about that time, however, Home Depot's site plan approval from Port Chester expired, which necessitated a third environmental review. Port Chester issued a new site plan approval, which did not require the widening of Midland Avenue or Rye's consent. Construction began almost immediately and the facility opened in February 2000.

Meanwhile, discovery proceeded in the section 1983 action. . . .

## II.

In the land-use context, 42 U.S.C. §1983 protects against municipal actions that violate a property owner's rights to due process, equal protection of the laws and just compensation for the taking of property under the Fifth and Fourteenth Amendments to the United States Constitution. Both cases before us center on alleged deprivation of substantive due process; in this Court, Home Depot also presses a claimed violation of the guarantee of equal protection.

We underscore at the outset of our analysis the Appellate Division's observation that "42 U.S.C. §1983 is not simply an additional vehicle for judicial review of land-use determinations." In the same vein, federal courts dismissing section 1983 land-use claims have repeatedly noted that they do not function as zoning boards of appeal, or substitute for state courts interpreting land-use regulations. The point is simply that denial of a permit — even an *arbitrary* denial redressable by an article 78 or other state law proceeding — is not tantamount to a constitutional violation under 42 U.S.C. §1983; significantly more is required. With that in mind, we turn to consideration of appellants' claims.

### Substantive Due Process

More often litigated in federal courts, the issue of substantive due process in land-use cases has come before this Court once, in *Town of Orangetown v. Magee*, 88 N.Y.2d 41, 643 N.Y.S.2d 21, 665 N.E.2d 1061 [1996]. There, the Magees had acquired 34 acres of land in the Town of Orangetown at an estimated cost of $3 million in order to construct a 184,000 square foot industrial building. Years later, after plans had been approved, a permit issued and more than $4 million spent on the land and building, the Town revoked the permit and amended its Zoning Code to preclude commercial buildings on the land, halting the project. We agreed with the trial court and Appellate Division that the Town's action violated 42 U.S.C. §1983, and affirmed the order reinstating the building permit and awarding the Magees damages of $5,137,126, costs and attorneys' fees.

Drawing on federal precedents, we set out the two-part test for substantive due process violations. First, claimants must establish a cognizable property interest, meaning a vested property interest, or "more than a mere expectation or hope to retain the permit and continue their improvements; they must show that pursuant to State or local law, they had a legitimate claim of entitlement to continue construction." Second, claimants must show that the governmental action was wholly without legal justification.

Key to establishing the Magees' cognizable property interest was that the right to develop their land had vested under state law: they owned the land, a permit and

improvements and "unquestionably would have received the limited future autho-
rizations necessary to complete the project.... [T]he Town had 'engendered a clear
expectation of continued enjoyment' of the permit sufficient to constitute a protect-
able property interest for purposes of a section 1983 claim." The Magees satisfied
the second requirement by establishing that the Town's actions were "without legal
justification and motivated entirely by political concerns."

Federal courts elaborating on the first element of the test have noted that it should
be applied "with considerable rigor." Even if "objective observers would estimate
that the probability of [obtaining the relief sought] was extremely high, the opportunity of the local agency to deny issuance suffices to defeat the existence of a federally protected property interest" (*id.*). Beyond a vested property right arising from
substantial expenditures pursuant to a lawful permit (as in *Magee*), a legitimate
claim of entitlement to a permit can exist only where there is either a "certainty or
a very strong likelihood" that an application for approval would have been granted.
Where an issuing authority has discretion in approving or denying a permit, a clear
entitlement can exist only when that discretion "is so narrowly circumscribed that
approval of a proper application is virtually assured."

As for the second element of the test, "only the most egregious official conduct
can be said to be arbitrary in the constitutional sense."

The two-part test strikes an appropriate balance between the role of local governments in regulatory matters affecting the health, welfare and safety of their citizens,
and the protection of constitutional rights "at the very outer margins of municipal
behavior. It represents an acknowledgment that decisions on matters of local concern should ordinarily be made by those whom local residents select to represent
them in municipal government."

Applying this test, we agree with the Appellate Division that neither appellant
established a cognizable property interest or arbitrary conduct of a constitutional
dimension.

While recognizing the discretion of the Planning Board in the subdivision
approval process, Bower argues that because the Board acted outside its discretion
there was necessarily a deprivation of a protected property right. This claim relies
heavily on the Appellate Division's conclusion in the article 78 proceeding that Bower
had "met all the conditions needed for approval of its subdivision application in both
this and the related Stratford [Farms] subdivision." In effect, Bower argues that vic-
tory in an article 78 proceeding—a finding that conduct was arbitrary, capricious
and without rational basis, or an abuse of discretion, or even action beyond or outside a board's discretion—establishes a constitutionally protected property interest.

The law is otherwise. While the existence of discretion in a municipal actor does
not alone defeat the existence of a property interest in a permit applicant, that discretion must be so narrowly circumscribed that approval is virtually assured....

We reach the same conclusions as to Home Depot, where the actions it sought
to compel were discretionary in nature and that discretion had not been so

circumscribed as to create a clear entitlement to Rye's signature on the County's permit. Moreover, unlike Bower (which owned the subject land), Home Depot at the time of Rye's refusal to consent to the road-widening permit was a contract vendee and, significantly, had only conditional site plan approval for the property it hoped to buy.

In neither case was the challenged conduct constitutionally arbitrary. While the lower courts concluded that the municipalities' actions in both cases were arbitrary, capricious and without rational basis in an article 78 sense, what is lacking is the egregious conduct that implicates federal constitutional law.

Thus, we agree with the Appellate Division in each case that appellant has failed to state a cause of action for a due process violation.

### Equal Protection

Unlike substantive due process, the Equal Protection Clause has generated relatively few federal court decisions in land-use cases, and none in this Court. Because equal protection can no more become another general overseer of local land-use determinations than substantive due process, the standards must be applied with the same "rigor."

The essence of a violation of the constitutional guarantee of equal protection is, of course, that all persons similarly situated must be treated alike. Home Depot's equal protection challenge does not rest on differential treatment as a constitutionally protected suspect class, or denial of a fundamental right. Rather, Home Depot's equal protection claim sounds in selective enforcement.

As such, a violation of equal protection arises where *first,* a person (compared with others similarly situated) is selectively treated and *second,* such treatment is based on impermissible considerations such as race, religion, intent to inhibit or punish the exercise of constitutional rights, or malicious or bad faith intent to injure a person. In that Home Depot does not allege selective treatment based on race, religion or punishment for the exercise of constitutional rights, it must demonstrate that Rye singled out its request for consent to the road-widening permit with malevolent intent.

The "similarly situated" element of the test asks, "whether a prudent person, looking objectively at the incidents, would think them roughly equivalent." But even different treatment of persons similarly situated, without more, does not establish a claim. What matters is impermissible motive: proof of action with intent to injure — that is, proof that the applicant was singled out with an "evil eye and an unequal hand, so as practically to make unjust and illegal discriminations between persons in similar circumstances." . . .

Home Depot argues that it was treated in a manner uniquely different from any other applicant and that Rye withheld its signature from the county permit in order to impede construction, despite having executed other contemporaneous applications within hours or days. There is no proof, however, that other entities were similarly situated to Home Depot — in terms of obtaining Rye's signature on comparable permits — and received more favorable treatment. . . .

While Home Depot makes much of the City Manager's testimony that this was the first permit the City Council reviewed in executive session, the requisite showing of improper motivation is lacking. Home Depot's improper motivation claim more closely addresses the merits of the City's decision than its constitutionality. Even the community's "political" opposition to the high-traffic superstore at the City's border is not the equivalent of the "evil eye and an unequal hand" for constitutional equal protection purposes.

Accordingly, in each case, the order of the Appellate Division should be affirmed, with costs.

Judges G.B. Smith, Ciparick, Rosenblatt, Graffeo and Read concur.

Judge R.S. Smith taking no part. In each case: Order affirmed, with costs.

## Questions for Consideration

1) What is the Bower Associates project?

2) What is the Home Depot project?

3) Bower Associates and Home Depot each brought an Article 78 proceeding under New York law. An Article 78 proceeding is a proceeding to challenge the activities and decisions of any administrative agency in court. Thus, it can be used to challenge a decision by a planning and zoning board. In this appeal to the Court of Appeals of New York, New York's highest court must consider the consequences of the lower court determinations as to an Article 78 review. What were the results of the Article 78 reviews in the lower courts, and what are the claims of the appellants in their appeals to the Court of Appeals?

4) In the land use context, what is the application of 42 U.S.C. § 1983?

5) How did the court resolve the due process claim?

6) How did the court resolve the equal protection claim?

7) Why does the court believe that Bower Associates confused its due process and equal protection claims?

## Takeaway

- A section 1983 action is a federal claim and is usually pursued in a federal court, so this case is a little different in that the New York state court is asked to decide the matter, and to determine if its own lower court judgements substantiated a violation of section 1983.

- As the court points out, equal protection does not mean that the same outcome has to be provided to two different people that are differently situated. In practice, it is always important to position a client's cause as similar to that of others who have obtained the outcome that your client seeks; and to distinguish the client's cause from those who did not obtain the desired outcome.

- State law conclusions based on arbitrary and capricious decision-making by an agency of the state do not necessarily trigger a violation of a federal constitutional right.

# P. Standing and Ripeness

In order to maintain a legal action, one must have standing to sue. This means that a party must be able to demonstrate a connection to and harm from the given action or law being challenged in court. In order for a court to decide a case, it must be ripe for adjudication. This means that the controversy must be real and not speculative or contingent on uncertain future events.

## RHJ Medical Center v. City of DuBois

United States District Court for the Western District of Pennsylvania
754 F. Supp. 2d 723 (W.D. Pa. 2010)

GIBSON, Judge. . . . "This case presents the familiar conflict between the legal principle of non-discrimination and the political principle of not-in-my-backyard." . . .

. . . .

### Facts

RHJ Medical Center, Inc. ("RHJ") is a Pennsylvania corporation in the business of operating methadone treatment facilities. RHJ opened its first methadone treatment center in 2002 in Hunker, Pennsylvania. RHJ has met the standards for federal certification and state licensure in outpatient treatment and methadone maintenance. In February 2006, RHJ began to search for a site on which to open a methadone treatment center in the City of DuBois. The City of DuBois ("the City") is a Third Class City covering 3.1 square miles with a population of less than 10,000. The City's population consists of 55% low to middle income persons. According to RHJ, the methadone treatment center located closest to the City is in the Borough of Clearfield, 20 miles away, and has a significant waiting list. Plaintiff reports that as a result, many of the City's residents make a daily three-hour round trip to the methadone treatment center operated by RHJ in the Borough of Vandergrift. The City asserts that there are private physicians and other healthcare professionals within the City to provide residents with methadone treatment.

RHJ chose a site at 994 Beaver Drive, DuBois, Pennsylvania, 15801 ("the site"), and signed a ten-year lease on March 31, 2006. The site was zoned in the "Transitional District" and was previously occupied by an insurance agency. Adjacent to the rear of the site was a sidewalk known as Beaver Meadow Walkway ("the walkway"), which was dedicated as a public park on June 25, 1979. By law at the time, methadone treatment centers were forbidden to operate within 500 feet of a public park unless the municipal governing body voted to authorize such use following public notice and one or more public hearings.

In late September or early October of 2006, RHJ's plans to open a methadone treatment center became public. RHJ asserts that they were then subjected to a wave of negative press coverage, including a radio interview in which the mayor of DuBois stated that RHJ would likely not receive approval from the City to open such a facility and compared having a methadone treatment center in the City to "other cities dumping their garbage in DuBois."

At a work session on October 19, 2006, the DuBois City Council authorized the City Solicitor to draft a letter to RHJ "to advise them that if they still plan[ed] on opening their Center at 994 Beaver Drive, they need[ed] to follow all procedures, including Public Hearings and to remind them that they [we]re still too close to a recreational park (walkway)." A copy of this letter was distributed at a City Council meeting on October 23, 2006, and also mailed to RHJ on that date. RHJ opened the methadone treatment center as planned two days later, on October 25, 2006.

The City filed suit in the Clearfield County Court of Common Pleas on October 27, 2006, to enjoin RHJ from operating the methadone treatment facility at the site pursuant to Section 621. The court granted the City a preliminary injunction with a continuance hearing scheduled for November 1, 2006. . . . RHJ stipulated that the walkway was a public park within the meaning of Section 621 and that they had not obtained a certificate of use from the City before opening the clinic; and the court granted a permanent injunction until such time as the City approved RHJ's application following a public hearing and granted a certificate of use.

In January of 2007, RHJ submitted to the City an application for a public hearing and a request for certificate of use. The City provided notice to surrounding property owners, and a public hearing was held on April 23, 2007. At a public meeting on May 14, 2007, the City Council voted unanimously to deny RHJ's application and directed the City Solicitor to prepare a document of findings of fact and conclusions of law to support the decision. The Solicitor's document was unanimously adopted at the public City Council meeting on May 29, 2007 and was served on RHJ on June 1, 2007. The finding of the City Council was that RHJ had not presented evidence sufficient to justify deviating from the restrictions of Section 621. The concerns of the Council included the methadone treatment center's lack of on-site security personnel, lack of means to transport patients to the regional medical facility if necessary, and insufficient parking for the expected number of patients and staff. The Council also noted that RHJ had not performed "any need assessment to determine whether its center was needed in the area and had no statistics concerning area drug use."

On June 15, 2007, the Third Circuit Court of Appeals [in a separate case] ruled that § 621 violated the Americans With Disabilities Act ("ADA"), 42 U.S.C. §§ 12101, et seq., and the Rehabilitation Act ("RA"), 42 U.S.C. §§ 12101, et seq., and the Rehabilitation Act ("RA"), 29 U.S.C. §§ 701, et seq. *New Directions Treatment Services v. City of Reading*, 490 F.3d 293 (3d Cir. 2007). . . .

. . . [F]ollowing the Third Circuit decision in *New Directions* . . . the City Council [enacted] Ordinance Number 1720, which amended City zoning in a number of ways, including prohibiting "methadone or drug treatment clinics or centers" in the "Transitional District" and permitting medical facilities "with the exception of methadone treatment facilities and other drug treatment facilities of any kind" in the "Commercial-Highway Zoning District." [This litigation followed.]

### Analysis

### I. Standing

In order to obtain standing, Plaintiff must traverse a jurisdictional labyrinth that would make Daedalus envious. In this case, the Minotaur takes not the form of part-man and part-bull, but rather coalesces from an amalgam of complex jurisdictional questions — determining attenuated third party standing, finding whether an association is imminent under Article III, identifying whether prospective patients suffer from a qualified disability, and answering whether associational standing warrants equitable and compensatory relief. This chimeral conundrum is exacerbated by two decades of precedents that have not fully addressed the constitutional limitations on adjudication for associational standing. This memorandum will address how these issues have swirled together into a jurisprudential maelstrom, and perhaps, to some degree, calm the waters and provide some clarity in a confounding area of the law.

The labyrinth in this case winds as follows. First, in order to avail itself of the protections of the ADA and RA, Plaintiff must establish third party standing by showing an "association" with an individual with a disability. In this case, because no disabled persons were joined in the case or even identified in the complaint, Plaintiff can only receive standing based on a relationship or association with a patient.

Second, because Plaintiff was unable to open up the methadone clinic, it was unable to service any patients. Any patients could only be prospective. Nonetheless, our precedents have construed the ADA and RA as evincing Congress's intent to grant third party standing to entities that have a prospective association with disabled persons.

Third, Plaintiff — which never actually opened the methadone clinic due to the city's zoning decision — must show that the opening of the clinic and admittance of patients was "imminent." Associational standing notwithstanding, this court could not take cognizance of a fledgling clinic that has not taken enough steps towards establishing the requisite association, lest our jurisdiction traverse the boundaries of Article III. In this case, because Plaintiff took sufficient steps towards opening its doors for business, the opening of the clinic is considered imminent, and Article III standing is satisfied.

Fourth, even if the prospective patient suffers from a disability *per se*, Plaintiff must resolve a statutory Gordian knot and show that a curious "carve out" exemption — aimed at allowing employers to discharge employees with drug addictions — is inapplicable in the context of methadone clinics. Congress provided for an exemption for patients, separate from employees, engaging in drug treatment programs — even if those individuals have a current drug addiction.

Fifth, even if the requisite association is established, and the opening of the clinic is imminent, Plaintiff must prove that the prospective patients — none of whom have been ascertained — would be protected by the ADA or RA. Merely having an impairment, such as an opioid addiction is inadequate; rather, the disability must substantially impact a major life activity. The Supreme Court's precedents dictate that inquiries into a person's disabilities must be an individualized *present* examination. This would seem to render generalized *prospective* examinations — the approach several other courts have undertaken — a Sisyphean task. Yet in this case, the Court finds that a serious opioid addiction that warrants admission to a methadone clinic, with the attendant daily disruptions of life activities in order to obtain the treatment, could satisfy this test. This finding would obviate the need for an individualized, fact intensive inquiry.

Sixth, if Plaintiff shows an "association" with an individual with a disability who is protected by the ADA and RA, exemptions notwithstanding, Plaintiff must show that it, RHJ — and not any associated disabled patients — was injured in violation of the ADA and RA. How can an entity be discriminated against by a statute aimed at protecting individuals with disabilities? This counterintuitive standard seems to be in tension with the text of the statute, but comports with subsequent guidance from the DOJ and relevant precedents from some — but not all — Circuits. If Plaintiff shows that it was discriminated against, standing is established in order to bring suit.

Seventh, even if the Plaintiff shows it was injured in violation of the ADA and RA, and can bring suit, the question remains whether standing exists for equitable relief as well for compensatory damages. Associational standing exists to grant third parties the right to sue on behalf of others. The benefit of such litigation should inure to the benefit of those aggrieved. Generally speaking, the third party is not the aggrieved party. Rather, the third party is suing on behalf of wronged individuals. Thus, equitable relief — ordering a city to issue a zoning permit, for example — would seem to be an appropriate remedy. In contrast, compensatory damages — lost profits, for example — would not directly benefit wronged disabled persons. For claims of damages, the Court considers whether the third party *itself* — and not aggrieved individuals — was injured. In such situations, compensatory damages would be appropriate because the benefit would inure to the injured party — the entity — regardless whether any individuals are actually injured.

The Court finds that the Plaintiff meets all of these requirements, and after a journey worthy of Theseus through the heart of the labyrinth, the Minotaur is slain, and the Plaintiff remains in federal court, with standing to proceed on all of its claims.

### ADA and RA Grant Third Party Standing

. . . .

Generally, a "plaintiff . . . must assert his own legal rights and interests, and cannot rest his claim to relief on the legal rights or interests of third parties." However, "Congress may grant an express right of action to persons who otherwise would be barred by prudential standing rules." In certain cases, standing may exist because of statutorily created rights: "[T]he standing question in such cases is whether the constitutional or statutory provision on which the claim rests properly can be understood as granting persons in the plaintiff's position a right to judicial relief." Where Congress grants a right of action to an entity or association, the entity may assert standing either in its own right or on behalf of its members. . . .

The ADA and RA are statutes in which Congress has granted third party standing. The regulation implementing Title II of the ADA provides, "A public entity shall not exclude or otherwise deny equal services, programs, or activities to an individual or entity because of the known disability of an individual with whom the individual or entity is known to *have a relationship or association*." 28 C.F.R. § 35.130(g) (emphasis added). This provision establishes the basis for associational standing. The "prudential limits imposed in pure associational standing cases do not apply to" statutory grants of associational standing. This broad conception of standing does indeed "extend standing to the full limits of Article III." So "long as this requirement [of Article III] is satisfied, persons to whom Congress has granted a right of action, either expressly or by clear implication, may have standing to seek relief on the basis of the legal rights and interests of others, and indeed, may invoke the general public interest in support of their claim."

. . . .

### An "Association" with a Prospective Patient Generates Third Party Standing

A methadone clinic has third party standing if it has an association with disabled patients. The plain text of the statute permits entities to bring suit on behalf of disabled individuals with whom they have an "association." 28 C.F.R. § 35.130(g). This much is clear. What is unclear, however, is whether a methadone clinic that never opened — and thus never treated any actual patients — can claim standing based on a prospective association. The definition of "association," and whether the association can be prospective, presents several wrinkles.

In this case Plaintiff did not join any patients in the suit, and did not name any patients — current or prospective — in the complaint. . . .

. . . .

. . . The Defendant could argue quite convincingly that these patients are still prospective, due to the fact that they have not received any treatment, and have simply signed up on a list. Under this approach an entity will not be protected by the ADA or RA unless they provide treatment to patients in a clinic. But if the entity cannot open — perhaps due to discrimination by a municipality that violates the ADA or RA — and cannot treat any actual plaintiffs, the entity would never possess standing. That is, unless an association with prospective patients is found to satisfy Article III.

. . . .

. . . In order for an entity that seeks associational standing to suffer an injury under the ADA or RA, the entity must have an "association" with a disabled person. 28 C.F.R. § 35.130(g). While Third Circuit precedents have held that an entity itself can suffer an injury — that is experiencing discrimination in violation of the ADA or RA — an injury in the absence of an association still lacks standing. Whether an association is too attenuated to constitute standing is a question that tests the contours of Article III. In order to determine if the association remains within the confines of Article III, the court considers the Supreme Court's standing jurisprudence with a focus on "injury in fact" — more precisely, whether the injury is "actual *or* imminent." *Lujan v. Defenders of Wildlife*, 504 U.S. 555, 560, 112 S. Ct. 2130, 119 L. Ed.2d 351 (1992) citing *Whitmore v. Arkansas*, 495 U.S. 149, 155, 110 S. Ct. 1717, 109 L. Ed.2d 135 (1990) (emphasis added).

The Court's discussion of "injury in fact" in *Lujan v. Defenders of Wildlife* is instructive. *Lujan* involved a challenge to a rule promulgated interpreting the Endangered Species Act of 1973 (ESA), 87 Stat. 892, as amended, 16 U.S.C. § 1536, so as to render it only applicable to actions taken against endangered species within the United States or on the high seas, but not to actions taken against endangered species in foreign nations. Respondent, an organization dedicated to wildlife conservation, filed suit, seeking a declaratory judgment that the new regulation was in error as to the geographical scope. Respondents claimed they were injured by this rule change, as the decrease in funding for endangered species living in foreign nations would "increase the rate of extinction of endangered and threatened species." On appeal, the Supreme Court considered whether respondents had standing to bring this suit.

Writing for the majority, Justice Scalia remarked that "the irreducible constitutional minimum of standing contains three elements":

> First, the plaintiff must have suffered an "injury in fact" — an invasion of a legally protected interest which is (a) concrete and particularized . . . and (b) actual or imminent, not "conjectural" or "hypothetical," Second, there must be a causal connection between the injury and the conduct complained of — the injury has to be "fairly . . . trace[able] to the challenged action of the defendant, and not . . . th[e] result [of] the independent action of some third party not before the court." Third, it must be "likely," as opposed to merely "speculative," that the injury will be "redressed by a favorable decision."

. . . .

RHJ "signed a ten-year lease for the site at 994 Beaver Drive on March 31, 2006, and soon after commenced renovations of the space to meet the standards of the

Pennsylvania Department of Health." RHJ also took the requisite steps towards obtaining the appropriate licenses, as in "September 2006, representatives from the Division of Drugs and Alcohol of the Pennsylvania Department of Health and the DEA conducted an on-site inspection of RHJ's DuBois facility." Further, prior to the scheduled opening date, "RHJ incurred expenses relating to the hiring of staff, setting up utilities, and advertising, in addition to rent and renovations."

. . . .

. . . [W]hile "it may seem trivial" to require an organization to sign a lease or obtain the proper licenses to open a methadone clinic, in the absence of these steps, it is not reasonable to assume that a methadone clinic will in fact open. If a plaintiff takes such concrete steps, the injury should be considered imminent.

Third party standing is an essential tool for methadone clinics to enforce the rights of those with debilitating drug addictions. . . . Allowing treatment facilities, which undoubtedly have better legal resources to bring suit on behalf of patients — to give those with disabilities equal access to the courts and ensure that their disabilities are not used to discriminate against them by improperly restricting their access to drug addiction treatment — vindicates the protections that the ADA and RA champion. While the "broad language of the ADA and RA enforcement provisions evidences a Congressional intent to extend standing to the full limits of Article III," the association with the patients must be imminent to fall within the ambit of Article III. Without this association, Plaintiff cannot recover for an injury under the ADA, even if the Plaintiff itself suffers the injury.

. . . RHJ took certain concrete steps towards opening of the methadone clinic and establishing a relationship with patients. This association was imminent, and not hypothetical or conjectural.

. . . .

### Standing and Remedies

Standing is inextricably linked to the type of relief sought. In this case, RHJ requests both equitable relief and damages. For equitable relief, Plaintiff seeks a declaration that the Defendant's actions and inaction of failing to issue an occupancy permit violates the Constitution, the ADA, and the RA. Plaintiff also seeks an injunction enjoining Defendant from continuing to violate the Constitution, the ADA, and the RA. Finally, Plaintiff seeks an injunction forcing the City to issue Plaintiff a permit to operate a methadone treatment facility. Additionally, Plaintiff seeks "damages for the harm it experienced as a result of Defendant's discriminatory practices," as well as reasonable attorney fees and costs. Before addressing whether plaintiff has standing, the Court first separates the analysis based on the type of relief sought.

The Supreme Court held in *Friends of the Earth, Inc. v. Laidlaw Environmental Services (TOC), Inc.* that "a plaintiff must demonstrate standing separately for each form of relief sought." 528 U.S. 167, 185, 120 S. Ct. 693, 145 L. Ed. 2d 610 (2000). *See also City of Los Angeles v. Lyons*, 461 U.S. 95, 109, 103 S. Ct. 1660, 75 L. Ed. 2d 675 (1983) (notwithstanding the fact that plaintiff had standing to pursue damages, he lacked standing to pursue injunctive relief). These considerations are especially relevant in the context of associational standing. In *Warth v. Seldin*, [422 U.S. 490, 515 (1975),] the Supreme Court commented that

> whether an association has standing to invoke the court's remedial powers on behalf of its members depends in substantial measure on the nature of the relief sought. If in a proper case the association seeks a declaration, injunction, or some other form of prospective relief, it can reasonably be supposed that the *remedy, if granted, will inure to the benefit of those members of the association actually injured*. Indeed, in all cases in which we have expressly recognized standing in associations to represent their members, the relief sought has been of this kind.

. . . .

. . . [The] precedents suggest that courts impose different standing requirements based on the remedy sought. If the remedy sought is injunctive relief, then Article III requires that the injury should be suffered by the third parties as well as the entity itself. In this case, the benefit of the injunctive relief inures to the advantage of both of the injured parties — the patients *and* the entity. In contrast, if the remedy sought is damages, then Article III requires that the injury need only to be suffered by the entity, and not the patients. In this case, the advantage of the damages inures only to the injured party — the entity, and not the patients.

. . . .

Assume a methadone clinic is denied a permit, cannot open, and suffers lost profits. The monetary damages could only possibly inure to the benefit of the methadone clinic itself. Other types of damages — future damages, incidental damages, punitive damages, attorney fees, and filing fees — will similarly only benefit the clinic. It could be argued that a clinic that receives compensatory damages will be better funded, and will be able to provide better services to the patients. However, the inquiry here focuses on the injury at the time of the denial of the permit, and not potential future benefits to the members. . . . The Plaintiff's complaint recognizes this distinction. While praying for damages, the complaint sought "damages for the harm *it* experienced as a result of Defendant's discriminatory practices." That is, the damages *it* experienced, and not any damages to patients.

Assume a methadone clinic is denied a permit, cannot open, and as a result of this denial, disabled patients are unable to receive methadone treatment and drug counseling. The clinic, on behalf of the patients, sues for equitable relief to obtain the permit and stop the discrimination. . . . Equitable relief — such as injunctions, declarations, specific performance, and estoppel — will benefit the patients, as well as the clinic. Unlike compensatory damages, if the court orders the issuance of a permit, the clinic will open, and the injury the patients suffered — discrimination and denial of treatment — will be remedied. Now, the patients can receive treatment at the clinic. Similarly, the injury the entity suffered — the inability to open a clinic — will also be remedied. With a permit, the clinic can open and operate. There is an injury to both parties, a benefit will inure to both parties, and therefore standing exists.

. . . .

In essence, the discrimination against RHJ yielded two separate and cognizable injuries. The first injury — the lost profits by the clinic due to the denial of the permit — was only suffered by the clinic itself, and dictates a remedy of damages. The second injury — the discrimination against the patients who were unable to receive treatment from the unopened clinic — was suffered in part by the patients, and in part by the clinic. This injury dictates an equitable remedy.

Accordingly, the analysis for standing in this case is bifurcated based on the type of remedy.

. . . .

Based on the pleadings, because Plaintiff has shown that any patient who would be admitted to its methadone clinic would by necessity have an impairment that substantially impairs a major life activity, RHJ automatically has an association with an individual known to have a disability. Thus, standing for equitable relief would be proper.

### Standing for Damage Claims

. . . [T]he resolution of the standing inquiry for damages is relatively straightforward. This injury — the lost profits by the clinic due to the denial of the permit — was only suffered by the clinic itself, and dictates a remedy of damages. Plaintiff does not need to rely on any injuries to third parties. While praying for damages, the complaint sought "damages for the harm *it* experienced as a result of Defendant's discriminatory practices." That is, the damages *it* experienced, and not any damages suffered by patients. Because Plaintiff's association with patients afflicted with opioid addicts is "imminent," Article III is satisfied, and the ADA and RA require no further of proof. The injury suffered here creates standing for the claims of damages.

. . . .

### Ripeness

Defendant claims that RHJ's attempt to raise an as-applied challenge to the new ordinance is not ripe. The Third Circuit has held that in as-applied challenges "in cases involving land-use decisions, a property owner does not have a ripe constitutional claim until the zoning authorities have had an opportunity to arrive at a final, definitive position regarding how they will apply the regulations at issue to the particular land in question." Under the "finality rule," a plaintiff property owner must prove that a "final decision has been reached by the agency before it may seek compensatory or injunctive relief in federal court on federal constitutional grounds." It is undisputed that Plaintiff has not applied for a permit or variance under the

New Ordinance. Defendant claims that the failure to seek a final decision from the Council renders this challenge unripe.

However, Plaintiffs do not challenge the constitutionality of the New Ordinance under the 14th Amendment as-applied. Rather, they challenge it on its face. ("A city zoning ordinance that bars the establishment or operation of drug treatment clinic in districts where other medical treatment clinics are permitted to operate is *discriminatory on its face* against persons with disabilities . . .") (emphasis added). The finality rule does not apply "to facial attacks on a zoning ordinance, i.e., a claim that the mere enactment of a regulation either constitutes a taking without just compensation, or a substantive violation of due process or equal protection." "A 'final decision' is not necessary in that context because 'when a landowner makes a facial challenge, he or she argues that any application of the regulation is unconstitutional; for an as-applied challenge, the landowner is only attacking the decision that applied the regulation to his or her property, not the regulation in general.'" Notwithstanding the lack of a "final decision," this matter is ripe for adjudication because, as demonstrated *infra*, Plaintiff states a plausible claim that the mere enactment of this ordinance violates substantive due process and equal protection.

. . . .

Judging by the length and specificity of this memorandum, it seems fairly obvious to the Court that the complaint was sufficiently definite. This claim fails.

And now, this 6th day of December, 2010, the Court denies Defendant's Motion for Judgment on the Pleadings. . . .

## *Questions for Consideration*

1) What is the nature of RHJ's proposed use?

2) In what type of zoning district does RHJ propose to locate its use?

3) What was the problem with this location?

4) What was the decision of the city in response to the application for a public hearing and a request for a certificate of use?

5) How many parties to the lawsuit in this case were protected as persons with disabilities?

6) What is third party standing?

7) In this case, RHJ never actually opened its clinic. How does this affect its standing?

8) At the time of the case, how many clients was RHJ treating at the proposed clinic?

9) Under the ADA and the RHA, does RHJ have standing?

10) The opinion quotes Justice Scalia on standing. What does Scalia say are the minimum elements of standing?

11) How might standing differ depending upon the remedy being sought by a plaintiff?

12) What does the court say about the ripeness of this matter?

## *Takeaway*

- Standing requires an injury in fact that is causally connected to the conduct or law complained of; and, it must be something that the court can remedy.

- In some situations, a third party may have standing to bring and maintain a lawsuit.

- As this case illustrates, it is important to develop clear and specific facts for the record.

- Standing is often an issue that many lawyers forget about when they prepare a case. In practice, standing may seem self-evident in most cases, but it is important to make certain that the plaintiff(s) have standing so that they do not lose on a challenge to it in court.

- A matter is not ripe for judicial review until there has been a final definitive decision on how a rule or matter is to be determined. This means that there must be finality before the matter becomes ripe.

## Rehabilitation Support Services v. City of Albany

United States District Court for the Northern District of New York
2015 U.S. Dist. LEXIS 86081 (N.D.N.Y. July 2, 2015)

KAHN, Judge. Plaintiff Rehabilitation Support Services, Inc. ("RSS" or "Plaintiff") filed this action against Defendant City of Albany (the "City" or "Defendant"), challenging the City's zoning ordinance under the Fair Housing Act ("FHA"), as amended by the Fair Housing Amendments Act of 1988 ("FHAA"), 42 U.S.C. § 3601 et seq., and Title II of the Americans with Disabilities Act ("ADA"), 42 U.S.C. § 12131 et seq. Presently before the Court is Defendant's Motion to dismiss pursuant to Federal Rules of Civil Procedure 12(b)(1) and 12(b)(6). For the following reasons, the Motion is denied.

### Background

Plaintiff is a non-profit organization that operates residential programs for people with disabilities. Currently, "[Plaintiff] is seeking to establish a residence for 24 people who are recovering from alcoholism and substance abuse at a site located at 292 Second Street, Albany, New York." Alcoholism and substance abuse prevents these individuals from living with their families, and "significantly impacts . . . their ability to retain employment and perform other daily living activities." They must live in a residence of this type "because of their disability and in order to further their own recovery." The proposed residence "will be licensed by the New York State Office of Alcoholism and Substance Abuse Services ("OASAS")."

The City of Albany has a zoning ordinance, which regulates the types of buildings and building uses within the City. Plaintiff's proposed residence is located in the R2A zone according to the City's Zoning Ordinance. Under the Zoning Ordinance, "[o]nly single and two family residences and houses of worship are permitted in" an R2A zone, which is a residential zone. Certain multi-unit residences, such as dormitories, nursing homes, and bed and breakfasts, may obtain a special use permit to operate in an R2A district. Other multi-unit dwellings, including Plaintiff's planned residence, must obtain a use variance in order to establish a residence in an R2A zone. The Zoning Ordinance requires residences for people with disabilities to seek a use variance in order to establish a residence in any district in the City. The procedures for obtaining a use variance differ from those required to obtain a special use permit. For example, in order to obtain a use variance, an applicant is required to show "that applicable zoning regulations and restrictions have caused unnecessary hardship." Though individuals seeking a special use permit must also go through an application process, they need not show "unnecessary hardship" in order to obtain a permit. "[O]n or about April 2, 2014, the Albany Board of Zoning Appeals [('BZA')] denied RSS' application for a [use] variance."

On April 30, 2014, Plaintiff filed the present action, alleging that the City's Zoning Ordinance constitutes a facial violation of both the FHA and the ADA. . . .

## Discussion

. . . .

### Article III Standing

Article III of the Constitution grants federal courts limited jurisdiction over only "[c]ases" and "[c]ontroversies." U.S. Const. art. III, § 2, cl. 1. "One element of this case-or-controversy requirement" requires a plaintiff to "establish that [he has] standing to sue." To establish standing under Article III, a plaintiff must demonstrate that: (1) he has suffered "an injury in fact"; (2) there is a "causal connection between the injury and the conduct complained of"; and (3) it is "likely, as opposed to merely speculative, that the injury will be redressed by a favorable decision."

"Both the [FHA] and the ADA prohibit governmental entities from implementing or enforcing housing policies in a discriminatory manner against persons with disabilities." *Tsombanidis* [*v. West Haven Fire Dept.*], 352 F.3d at 573. Under the FHA, it is "unlawful '[t]o discriminate in the sale or rental, or to otherwise make unavailable or deny, a dwelling to any buyer or renter because of a handicap.'" "Similarly, the ADA states 'no qualified individual with a disability shall, by reason of such disability, be excluded from participation in or be denied the benefits of the services, programs, or activities of a public entity, or be subject to discrimination by any such entity.'" Both provisions have been interpreted to include discriminatory zoning restrictions.

The FHA "confers standing to challenge such discriminatory practices on any 'aggrieved person.'" Under the FHA, an "aggrieved person" is one who "(1) claims to have been injured by a discriminatory housing practice; or (2) believes that such person will be injured by a discriminatory housing practice that is about to occur." *Id.* (citing 42 U.S.C. § 3602(i)). "This definition requires only that a private plaintiff allege 'injury in fact' within the meaning of Article III of the Constitution, that is, that he allege 'distinct and palpable injuries that are "fairly traceable" to [defendants'] actions.'"...

An organization may have standing on its own behalf, or "on behalf of its members under the theory of organizational or associational standing." An organization "may file suit on its own behalf 'to seek judicial relief from injury to itself and to vindicate whatever rights and immunities the association itself may enjoy.'" In addition, an organization may bring suit on behalf of its members by demonstrating that: "(a) its members would otherwise have standing to sue in their own right; (b) the interests it seeks to protect are germane to the organization's purpose; and (c) neither the claim asserted nor the relief requested requires the participation of individual members in the lawsuit."

. . . .

Plaintiff alleges the following facts in support of standing under the FHA and ADA: (1) Plaintiff operates residential programs for people with disabilities; (2) Plaintiff's proposed residence would serve individuals suffering from alcohol and substance abuse; (3) Plaintiff's proposed residence is subject to the City's Zoning Ordinance and is located in an R2A district; (4) community residences for individuals with disabilities are "not permitted as of right in any residential or other district within the City;" and (5) Plaintiff must apply for a use variance in order to establish its proposed residence in an R2A zone, while other multi-unit residences such as dormitories and nursing homes need only acquire a special use permit.

Plaintiff argues that as an organization serving individuals with disabilities, it has standing to bring a facial challenge to the Zoning Ordinance under the FHA and ADA. Moreover, Plaintiff argues that the procedures required to obtain a special use permit are "less onerous" than those required to obtain a use variance. Because the City's Zoning Ordinance places a "stricter standard on community residences for people with disabilities than other residences and facilities that appear to be less residential . . . [Plaintiff] is injured by the zoning ordinance." Furthermore, Plaintiff argues that "housing discrimination causes a uniquely immediate injury." Finally, Plaintiff argues that without the Zoning Ordinance, it would be able to establish its proposed residence.

Defendant argues that Plaintiff lacks standing because the only injury alleged is the BZA's denial of its application for a use variance, and Plaintiff fails to allege facts sufficient to claim that the BZA's decision was discriminatory. . . .

Plaintiff's allegation that the Zoning Ordinance requires it to comply with application requirements that are more burdensome than those required of multi-member dwellings serving people without disabilities, and that the ordinance has prevented Plaintiff from opening the proposed residence to serve its members, is sufficient to show an injury in fact that is "fairly traceable" to Defendant's actions. Consequently, Plaintiff has demonstrated that it has standing to bring this action on its own behalf under the FHA and ADA. Furthermore, RSS also has organizational standing to bring this action on behalf of its members, since "(1) it serves a class of individuals with discrimination claims — individuals recovering from substance abuse; (2) the interests of the class are germane to [RSS], which is in the business of developing and operating sober homes; and (3) no individual participation of class members is necessary because the instant litigation involves a facial challenge" to the City's Zoning Ordinance. Accordingly, Plaintiff has demonstrated that it has standing to pursue this action.

. . . .

### Conclusion

Accordingly, it is hereby: Ordered, that Defendant's Motion to dismiss is denied. . . .

### *Questions for Consideration*

1) What services does RHS provide?

2) What is the alleged basis for the discrimination under the zoning code?

3) Is this an as applied or a facial challenge to the zoning ordinance?

4) What criteria for standing are recited in the case?

5) What does the FHA provide with respect to standing?

### *Takeaway*

- In the prior case, we observed that the ADA and the RHA had special standing provisions. Here we see special standing provisions in the FHA. In practice, it is important to check all actions brought pursuant to a statutory right to see if it also includes any special provisions as to standing.

- The case provides a fact pattern that permits us to rethink some of the issues related to the difference between a variance and a special/conditional use permit, as discussed earlier in the materials. It also illustrates the need to review zoning codes to ensure that higher or different standards are not applied to people with disabilities because of their disability. If one is an attorney working with local government, a preventive measure might include a careful review and audit of a local planning and zoning code to make certain that the ordinances are neutral on their face. (Naturally, they must also be applied in a nondiscriminatory manner.)

## Q. Exactions and Unconstitutional Conditions

We have already covered several important takings cases in earlier chapters of the book (*Pennsylvanian Coal, Penn Central, Lucas, Murr,* and *Kelo*). We also examined a claim of a taking from enforcement of the ADA (*Pinnock*). In addition, we noted the *First English* case in appropriate Takeaway notes. In this part of the chapter, we look at a special category of takings cases dealing with exactions and unconstitutional conditions. An *exaction* is involved when the government asks a property owner to give up something in exchange for being granted a permit to make a particular use of property. The giving up of a right as a condition to receiving a benefit may be unconstitutional if it violates certain constitutional guidelines. In this context, we cover three additional U.S. Supreme Court decisions (*Nollan*, *Dolan*, and *Koontz*). This is followed by a state court opinion from California that deals with efforts to provide inclusive and affordable housing opportunities for homebuyers (*California Homebuilders*). The California case analyzes its particular facts with reference to a series of U.S. Supreme Court takings decisions, and it therefore makes for a useful review of key takings law concepts while addressing a new question.

## Nollan v. California Coastal Commission

Supreme Court of the United States
483 U.S. 825 (1987)

SCALIA, Justice. James and Marilyn Nollan appeal from a decision of the California Court of Appeal ruling that the California Coastal Commission could condition its grant of permission to rebuild their house on their transfer to the public of an easement across their beachfront property. 177 Cal. App. 3d 719, 223 Cal. Rptr. 28 (1986). The California court rejected their claim that imposition of that condition violates the Takings Clause of the Fifth Amendment, as incorporated against the States by the Fourteenth Amendment. *Ibid.* We noted probable jurisdiction. 479 U.S. 913, 107 S. Ct. 312, 93 L. Ed. 2d 286 (1986).

### I

The Nollans own a beachfront lot in Ventura County, California. A quarter-mile north of their property is Faria County Park, an oceanside public park with a public beach and recreation area. Another public beach area, known locally as "the Cove," lies 1,800 feet south of their lot. A concrete seawall approximately eight feet high separates the beach portion of the Nollans' property from the rest of the lot. The historic mean high tide line determines the lot's oceanside boundary.

The Nollans originally leased their property with an option to buy. The building on the lot was a small bungalow, totaling 504 square feet, which for a time they rented to summer vacationers. After years of rental use, however, the building had fallen into disrepair, and could no longer be rented out.

The Nollans' option to purchase was conditioned on their promise to demolish the bungalow and replace it. In order to do so, under Cal. Pub. Res. Code Ann. §§ 30106, 30212, and 30600 (West 1986), they were required to obtain a coastal development permit from the California Coastal Commission. On February 25, 1982, they submitted a permit application to the Commission in which they proposed to demolish the existing structure and replace it with a three-bedroom house in keeping with the rest of the neighborhood.

The Nollans were informed that their application had been placed on the administrative calendar, and that the Commission staff had recommended that the permit be granted subject to the condition that they allow the public an easement to pass across a portion of their property bounded by the mean high tide line on one side, and their seawall on the other side. This would make it easier for the public to get to Faria County Park and the Cove. The Nollans protested imposition of the condition, but the Commission overruled their objections and granted the permit subject to their recordation of a deed restriction granting the easement.

On June 3, 1982, the Nollans filed a petition for writ of administrative mandamus asking the Ventura County Superior Court to invalidate the access condition. They argued that the condition could not be imposed absent evidence that their proposed development would have a direct adverse impact on public access to the beach. The court agreed, and remanded the case to the Commission for a full evidentiary hearing on that issue.

On remand, the Commission held a public hearing, after which it made further factual findings and reaffirmed its imposition of the condition. It found that the new house would increase blockage of the view of the ocean, thus contributing to the development of "a 'wall' of residential structures" that would prevent the public "psychologically ... from realizing a stretch of coastline exists nearby that they have every right to visit." The new house would also increase private use of the shorefront. These effects of construction of the house, along with other area development, would cumulatively "burden the public's ability to traverse to and along the shorefront." Therefore, the Commission could properly require the Nollans to offset that burden by providing additional lateral access to the public beaches in the form of an easement across their property. The Commission also noted that it had similarly conditioned 43 out of 60 coastal development permits along the same tract of land, and that of the 17 not so conditioned, 14 had been approved when the Commission did not have administrative regulations in place allowing imposition of the condition, and the remaining 3 had not involved shorefront property.

The Nollans filed a supplemental petition for a writ of administrative mandamus with the Superior Court, in which they argued that imposition of the access condition violated the Takings Clause of the Fifth Amendment, as incorporated against the States by the Fourteenth Amendment. The Superior Court ruled in their favor on statutory grounds, finding, in part to avoid "issues of constitutionality," that the California Coastal Act of 1976, Cal. Pub. Res. Code Ann. § 30000 *et seq.* (West 1986), authorized the Commission to impose public access conditions on coastal development permits for the replacement of an existing single-family home with a new one only where the proposed development would have an adverse impact on public access to the sea. In the court's view, the administrative record did not provide an adequate factual basis for concluding that replacement of the bungalow with the house would create a direct or cumulative burden on public access to the sea. Accordingly, the Superior Court granted the writ of mandamus and directed that the permit condition be struck.

The Commission appealed to the California Court of Appeal. While that appeal was pending, the Nollans satisfied the condition on their option to purchase by tearing down the bungalow and building the new house, and bought the property. They did not notify the Commission that they were taking that action.

The Court of Appeal reversed the Superior Court. 177 Cal. App. 3d 719, 223 Cal. Rptr. 28 (1986). It disagreed with the Superior Court's interpretation of the Coastal Act, finding that it required that a coastal permit for the construction of a new house whose floor area, height or bulk was more than 10% larger than that of the house it was replacing be conditioned on a grant of access. It also ruled that the requirement did not violate the Constitution under the reasoning of an earlier case of the Court of Appeal, *Grupe v. California Coastal Comm'n*, 166 Cal. App. 3d 148, 212 Cal. Rptr. 578 (1985). In that case, the court had found that so long as a project contributed to the need for public access, even if the project standing alone had not created the need for access, and even if there was only an indirect relationship between the access exacted and the need to which the project contributed, imposition of an access condition on a development permit was sufficiently related to burdens created by the project to be constitutional. The Court of Appeal ruled that the record established that that was the situation with respect to the Nollans' house. It ruled that the Nollans' taking claim also failed because, although the condition diminished the value of the Nollans' lot, it did not deprive them of all reasonable use of their property. Since, in the Court of Appeal's view, there was no statutory or constitutional obstacle to imposition of the access condition, the Superior Court erred in granting the writ of mandamus. The Nollans appealed to this Court, raising only the constitutional question.

## II

Had California simply required the Nollans to make an easement across their beachfront available to the public on a permanent basis in order to increase public access to the beach, rather than conditioning their permit to rebuild their house on their agreeing to do so, we have no doubt there would have been a taking. To say that the appropriation of a public easement across a landowner's premises does not constitute the taking of a property interest but rather (as Justice Brennan contends) "a mere restriction on its use," is to use words in a manner that deprives them of all their ordinary meaning. Indeed, one of the principal uses of the eminent domain power is to assure that the government be able to require conveyance of just such interests, so long as it pays for them. Perhaps because the point is so obvious, we have never been confronted with a controversy that required us to rule upon it, but our cases' analysis of the effect of other governmental action leads to the same conclusion. We have repeatedly held that, as to property reserved by its owner for private use, "the right to exclude [others is] 'one of the most essential sticks in the bundle of rights that are commonly characterized as property.'" . . . "[O]ur cases uniformly have found a taking to the extent of the occupation, without regard to whether the action achieves an important public benefit or has only minimal economic impact on the owner," We think a "permanent physical occupation" has occurred, for purposes of that rule, where individuals are given a permanent and continuous right to pass to and from, so that the real property may continuously be traversed, even though no particular individual is permitted to station himself permanently upon the premises.

Justice Brennan argues that while this might ordinarily be the case, the California Constitution's prohibition on any individual's "exclu[ding] the right of way to [any navigable] water whenever it is required for any public purpose," Art. X, § 4, produces a different result here. There are a number of difficulties with that argument. Most obviously, the right of way sought here is not naturally described as one *to* navigable water (from the street to the sea) but *along* it; it is at least highly questionable whether the text of the California Constitution has any prima facie application to the situation before us. Even if it does, however, several California cases suggest that Justice Brennan's interpretation of the effect of the clause is erroneous, and that to obtain easements of access across private property the State must proceed through its eminent domain power. . . .

Given, then, that requiring uncompensated conveyance of the easement outright would violate the Fourteenth Amendment, the question becomes whether requiring it to be conveyed as a condition for issuing a land-use permit alters the outcome. We have long recognized that land-use regulation does not effect a taking if it "substantially advance[s] legitimate state interests" and does not "den[y] an owner economically viable use of his land" . . . . The Commission argues that among these permissible purposes are protecting the public's ability to see the beach, assisting the public in overcoming the "psychological barrier" to using the beach created by a developed shorefront, and preventing congestion on the public beaches. We assume, without deciding, that this is so — in which case the Commission unquestionably would be able to deny the Nollans their permit outright if their new house (alone, or by reason of the cumulative impact produced in conjunction with other construction) would substantially impede these purposes, unless the denial would interfere so drastically with the Nollans' use of their property as to constitute a taking. See *Penn Central Transportation Co. v. New York City, supra.*

The Commission argues that a permit condition that serves the same legitimate police-power purpose as a refusal to issue the permit should not be found to be a taking if the refusal to issue the permit would not constitute a taking. We agree. Thus, if the Commission attached to the permit some condition that would have protected the public's ability to see the beach notwithstanding construction of the new house — for example, a height limitation, a width restriction, or a ban on fences — so long as the Commission could have exercised its police power (as we have assumed it could) to forbid construction of the house altogether, imposition of the condition would also be constitutional. Moreover (and here we come closer to the facts of the present case), the condition would be constitutional even if it consisted of the requirement that the Nollans provide a viewing spot on their property for passersby with whose sighting of the ocean their new house would interfere. Although such a requirement, constituting a permanent grant of continuous access to the property, would have to be considered a taking if it were not attached to a development permit, the Commission's assumed power to forbid construction of the house in order to protect the public's view of the beach must surely include the power to condition construction upon some concession by the owner, even a concession of property rights, that serves the same end. If a prohibition designed to accomplish that purpose would be a legitimate exercise of the police power rather than a taking, it would be strange to conclude that providing the owner an alternative to that prohibition which accomplishes the same purpose is not.

The evident constitutional propriety disappears, however, if the condition substituted for the prohibition utterly fails to further the end advanced as the justification for the prohibition. When that essential nexus is eliminated, the situation becomes the same as if California law forbade shouting fire in a crowded theater, but granted dispensations to those willing to contribute $100 to the state treasury. While a ban on shouting fire can be a core exercise of the State's police power to protect the public safety, and can thus meet even our stringent standards for regulation of speech, adding the unrelated condition alters the purpose to one which, while it may be legitimate, is inadequate to sustain the ban. Therefore, even though, in a sense, requiring a $100 tax contribution in order to shout fire is a lesser restriction on speech than an outright ban, it would not pass constitutional muster. Similarly here, the lack of nexus between the condition and the original purpose of the building restriction converts that purpose to something other than what it was. The purpose then becomes, quite simply, the obtaining of an easement to serve some valid governmental purpose, but without payment of compensation. Whatever may be the outer limits of "legitimate state interests" in the takings and land-use context, this is not one of them. In short, unless the permit condition serves the same governmental purpose as the development ban, the building restriction is not a valid regulation of land use but "an out-and-out plan of extortion."

### III

The Commission claims that it concedes as much, and that we may sustain the condition at issue here by finding that it is reasonably related to the public need or burden that the Nollans' new house creates or to which it contributes. We can accept, for purposes of discussion, the Commission's proposed test as to how close a "fit" between the condition and the burden is required, because we find that this case does not meet even the most untailored standards. The Commission's principal contention to the contrary essentially turns on a play on the word "access." The Nollans' new house, the Commission found, will interfere with "visual access" to the beach. That in turn (along with other shorefront development) will interfere with the desire of people who drive past the Nollans' house to use the beach, thus creating a "psychological barrier" to "access." The Nollans' new house will also, by a process not altogether clear from the Commission's opinion but presumably potent enough to more than offset the effects of the psychological barrier, increase the use of the public beaches, thus creating the need for more "access." These burdens on "access" would be alleviated by a requirement that the Nollans provide "lateral access" to the beach.

Rewriting the argument to eliminate the play on words makes clear that there is nothing to it. It is quite impossible to understand how a requirement that people already on the public beaches be able to walk across the Nollans' property reduces any obstacles to viewing the beach created by the new house. It is also impossible to understand how it lowers any "psychological barrier" to using the public beaches, or how it helps to remedy any additional congestion on them caused by construction of the Nollans' new house. We therefore find that the Commission's imposition of the permit condition cannot be treated as an exercise of its land-use power for any of these purposes. . . .

. . . .

. . . The Commission may well be right that it is a good idea, but that does not establish that the Nollans (and other coastal residents) alone can be compelled to contribute to its realization. Rather, California is free to advance its "comprehensive program," if it wishes, by using its power of eminent domain for this "public purpose," see U.S. Const., Amdt. 5; but if it wants an easement across the Nollans' property, it must pay for it.

Reversed.

Justice BRENNAN, with whom Justice MARSHALL joins, dissenting.

BRENNAN, Justice. (dissenting). Appellants in this case sought to construct a new dwelling on their beach lot that would both diminish visual access to the beach and move private development closer to the public tidelands. The Commission reasonably concluded that such "buildout," both individually and cumulatively, threatens public access to the shore. It sought to offset this encroachment by obtaining assurance that the public may walk along the shoreline in order to gain access to the ocean. The Court finds this an illegitimate exercise of the police power, because it maintains that there is no reasonable relationship between the effect of the development and the condition imposed.

. . . .

## A

There can be no dispute that the police power of the States encompasses the authority to impose conditions on private development. . . .

The Court finds fault with this measure because it regards the condition as insufficiently tailored to address the precise type of reduction in access produced by the new development. The Nollans' development blocks visual access, the Court tells us, while the Commission seeks to preserve lateral access along the coastline. Thus, it concludes, the State acted irrationally. Such a narrow conception of rationality, however, has long since been discredited as a judicial arrogation of legislative authority. "To make scientific precision a criterion of constitutional power would be to subject the State to an intolerable supervision hostile to the basic principles of our Government." . . . ("The Takings Clause has never been read to require the States or the courts to calculate whether a specific individual has suffered burdens . . . in excess of the benefits received").

. . . .

The Court's demand for this precise fit is based on the assumption that private landowners in this case possess a reasonable expectation regarding the use of their land that the public has attempted to disrupt. . . .

## Questions for Consideration

1) What property did the Nollans own?

2) What did the Nollans wish to do with their property?

3) What condition did the government place on the granting of a permit to the Nollans?

4) What was the government's stated rationale for the condition imposed by the government for the granting of the permit?

5) Why is this an exaction case rather than a simple takings case?

6) How does the Court discuss the police power?

7) What if there was a government concern that the public had no access to the beach from nearby properties or roadways, and required the Nollans to provide a narrow five-foot wide easement along the side of their property so that people might walk from the roadway to the beach — would this requirement be constitutional?

## Takeaway

- *Nollan* does not stand for the proposition that all conditions are unconstitutional.

- *Nollan* does stand for the proposition that conditions and exactions must have an *essential nexus* (a close relationship) to the public objective to be achieved by the government requirement.

- An *essential nexus* requirement focuses on finding a "good fit" and not necessarily an exact fit between the public goal to be achieved and the requirement imposed.

## Dolan v. City of Tigard

Supreme Court of the United States
512 U.S. 374 (1994)

REHNQUIST, Justice. Petitioner challenges the decision of the Oregon Supreme Court which held that the city of Tigard could condition the approval of her building permit on the dedication of a portion of her property for flood control and traffic improvements. 317 Ore. 110, 854 P.2d 437 (1993). We granted certiorari to resolve a question left open by our decision in *Nollan v. California Coastal Comm'n*, 483 U.S. 825, 107 S. Ct. 3141, 97 L. Ed. 2d 677 (1987), of what is the required degree of connection between the exactions imposed by the city and the projected impacts of the proposed development.

# I

The State of Oregon enacted a comprehensive land use management program in 1973. Ore. Rev. Stat. §§ 197.005-197.860 (1991). The program required all Oregon cities and counties to adopt new comprehensive land use plans that were consistent with the statewide planning goals. The plans are implemented by land use regulations which are part of an integrated hierarchy of legally binding goals, plans, and regulations. §§ 197.175, 197.175(2)(b). Pursuant to the State's requirements, the city of Tigard, a community of some 30,000 residents on the southwest edge of Portland, developed a comprehensive plan and codified it in its Community Development Code (CDC). The CDC requires property owners in the area zoned Central Business District to comply with a 15% open space and landscaping requirement, which limits total site coverage, including all structures and paved parking, to 85% of the parcel. CDC, ch. 18.66, App. to Pet. for Cert. G-16 to G-17. After the completion of a transportation study that identified congestion in the Central Business District as a particular problem, the city adopted a plan for a pedestrian/bicycle pathway intended to encourage alternatives to automobile transportation for short trips. The CDC requires that new development facilitate this plan by dedicating land for pedestrian pathways where provided for in the pedestrian/bicycle pathway plan.

The city also adopted a Master Drainage Plan (Drainage Plan). The Drainage Plan noted that flooding occurred in several areas along Fanno Creek, including areas near petitioner's property. The Drainage Plan also established that the increase in impervious surfaces associated with continued urbanization would exacerbate these flooding problems. To combat these risks, the Drainage Plan suggested a series of improvements to the Fanno Creek Basin, including channel excavation in the area next to petitioner's property. Other recommendations included ensuring that the floodplain remains free of structures and that it be preserved as greenways to minimize flood damage to structures. The Drainage Plan concluded that the cost of these improvements should be shared based on both direct and indirect benefits, with property owners along the waterways paying more due to the direct benefit that they would receive.

Petitioner Florence Dolan owns a plumbing and electric supply store located on Main Street in the Central Business District of the city. The store covers approximately 9,700 square feet on the eastern side of a 1.67-acre parcel, which includes a gravel parking lot. Fanno Creek flows through the southwestern corner of the lot and along its western boundary. The year-round flow of the creek renders the area within the creek's 100-year floodplain virtually unusable for commercial development. The city's comprehensive plan includes the Fanno Creek floodplain as part of the city's greenway system.

Petitioner applied to the city for a permit to redevelop the site. Her proposed plans called for nearly doubling the size of the store to 17,600 square feet and paving a 39-space parking lot. The existing store, located on the opposite side of the parcel, would be razed in sections as construction progressed on the new building. In the second phase of the project, petitioner proposed to build an additional structure on the northeast side of the site for complementary businesses and to provide more parking. The proposed expansion and intensified use are consistent with the city's zoning scheme in the Central Business District.

The City Planning Commission (Commission) granted petitioner's permit application subject to conditions imposed by the city's CDC. The CDC establishes the following standard for site development review approval:

> "Where landfill and/or development is allowed within and adjacent to the 100-year floodplain, the City shall require the dedication of sufficient open land area for greenway adjoining and within the floodplain. This area shall include portions at a suitable elevation for the construction of a pedestrian/bicycle pathway within the floodplain in accordance with the adopted pedestrian/bicycle plan."

Thus, the Commission required that petitioner dedicate the portion of her property lying within the 100-year floodplain for improvement of a storm drainage system along Fanno Creek and that she dedicate an additional 15-foot strip of land adjacent to the floodplain as a pedestrian/bicycle pathway. The dedication required by that condition encompasses approximately 7,000 square feet, or roughly 10% of the property. In accordance with city practice, petitioner could rely on the dedicated property to meet the 15% open space and landscaping requirement mandated by the city's zoning scheme. The city would bear the cost of maintaining a landscaped buffer between the dedicated area and the new store.

Petitioner requested variances from the CDC standards. Variances are granted only where it can be shown that, owing to special circumstances related to a specific piece of the land, the literal interpretation of the applicable zoning provisions would cause "an undue or unnecessary hardship" unless the variance is granted. Rather than posing alternative mitigating measures to offset the expected impacts of her proposed development, as allowed under the CDC, petitioner simply argued that her proposed development would not conflict with the policies of the comprehensive plan. The Commission denied the request.

The Commission made a series of findings concerning the relationship between the dedicated conditions and the projected impacts of petitioner's project. First, the Commission noted that "[i]t is reasonable to assume that customers and employees of the future uses of this site could utilize a pedestrian/bicycle pathway adjacent to this development for their transportation and recreational needs." The Commission noted that the site plan has provided for bicycle parking in a rack in front of the proposed building and "[i]t is reasonable to expect that some of the users of the bicycle parking provided for by the site plan will use the pathway adjacent to Fanno Creek if it is constructed." In addition, the Commission found that creation of a convenient, safe pedestrian/bicycle pathway system as an alternative means of transportation "could offset some of the traffic demand on [nearby] streets and lessen the increase in traffic congestion."

The Commission went on to note that the required floodplain dedication would be reasonably related to petitioner's request to intensify the use of the site given the increase in the impervious surface. The Commission stated that the "anticipated increased storm water flow from the subject property to an already strained creek and drainage basin can only add to the public need to manage the stream channel and floodplain for drainage purposes." Based on this anticipated increased storm water flow, the Commission concluded that "the requirement of dedication of the flood-plain area on the site is related to the applicant's plan to intensify development on the site." The Tigard City Council approved the Commission's final order, subject to one minor modification; the city council reassigned the responsibility for surveying and marking the floodplain area from petitioner to the city's engineering department.

Petitioner appealed to the Land Use Board of Appeals (LUBA) on the ground that the city's dedication requirements were not related to the proposed development, and, therefore, those requirements constituted an uncompensated taking of her property under the Fifth Amendment. In evaluating the federal taking claim, LUBA assumed that the city's findings about the impacts of the proposed development were supported by substantial evidence. Given the undisputed fact that the proposed larger building and paved parking area would increase the amount of impervious surfaces and the runoff into Fanno Creek, LUBA concluded that "there is a 'reasonable relationship' between the proposed development and the requirement to dedicate land along Fanno Creek for a greenway." With respect to the pedestrian/bicycle pathway, LUBA noted the Commission's finding that a significantly larger retail sales building and parking lot would attract larger numbers of customers and employees and their vehicles. It again found a "reasonable relationship" between alleviating the impacts of increased traffic from the development and facilitating the provision of a pedestrian/bicycle pathway as an alternative means of transportation.

The Oregon Court of Appeals affirmed, rejecting petitioner's contention that in *Nollan v. California Coastal Comm'n*, 483 U.S. 825, 107 S. Ct. 3141, 97 L. Ed. 2d 677 (1987), we had abandoned the "reasonable relationship" test in favor of a stricter "essential nexus" test. The court also disagreed with petitioner's contention that the *Nollan* Court abandoned the "reasonably related" test. Instead, the court read *Nollan* to mean that an "exaction is reasonably related to an impact if the exaction serves the same purpose that a denial of the permit would serve." The court decided that both the pedestrian/bicycle pathway condition and the storm drainage dedica-tion had an essential nexus to the development of the proposed site. Therefore, the court found the conditions to be reasonably related to the impact of the expansion of petitioner's business. We granted certiorari, 510 U.S. 989, 114 S. Ct. 544, 126 L. Ed. 2d 446 (1993), because of an alleged conflict between the Oregon Supreme Court's decision and our decision in *Nollan, supra*.

## II

The Takings Clause of the Fifth Amendment of the United States Constitution, made applicable to the States through the Fourteenth Amendment, provides: "[N] or shall private property be taken for public use, without just compensation." One of the principal purposes of the Takings Clause is "to bar Government from forcing some people alone to bear public burdens which, in all fairness and justice, should be borne by the public as a whole." Without question, had the city simply required petitioner to dedicate a strip of land along Fanno Creek for public use, rather than conditioning the grant of her permit to redevelop her property on such a dedication, a taking would have occurred. *Nollan, supra*, 483 U.S., at 831, 107 S. Ct., at 3145. Such public access would deprive petitioner of the right to exclude others, "one of the most essential sticks in the bundle of rights that are commonly characterized as property."

On the other side of the ledger, the authority of state and local governments to engage in land use planning has been sustained against constitutional challenge as long ago as our decision in *Village of Euclid v. Ambler Realty Co.*, 272 U.S. 365, 47 S. Ct. 114, 71 L. Ed. 303 (1926). "Government hardly could go on if to some extent values incident to property could not be diminished without paying for every such change in the general law." *Pennsylvania Coal Co. v. Mahon*, 260 U.S. 393, 413, 43 S. Ct. 158, 159, 67 L. Ed. 322 (1922). A land use regulation does not effect a taking if it "substantially advance[s] legitimate state interests" and does not "den[y] an owner economically viable use of his land." *Agins v. City of Tiburon*, 447 U.S. 255, 260, 100 S. Ct. 2138, 2141, 65 L. Ed. 2d 106 (1980).

The sort of land use regulations discussed in the cases just cited, however, differ in two relevant particulars from the present case. First, they involved essentially legislative determinations classifying entire areas of the city, whereas here the city made an adjudicative decision to condition petitioner's application for a building permit on an individual parcel. Second, the conditions imposed were not simply a limitation on the use petitioner might make of her own parcel, but a requirement that she deed portions of the property to the city. In *Nollan, supra*, we held that governmental authority to exact such a condition was circumscribed by the Fifth and Fourteenth Amendments. Under the well-settled doctrine of "unconstitutional conditions," the government may not require a person to give up a constitutional right — here the right to receive just compensation when property is taken for a public use — in exchange for a discretionary benefit conferred by the government where the benefit sought has little or no relationship to the property.

Petitioner contends that the city has forced her to choose between the building permit and her right under the Fifth Amendment to just compensation for the public easements. Petitioner does not quarrel with the city's authority to exact some forms of dedication as a condition for the grant of a building permit, but challenges the showing made by the city to justify these exactions. She argues that the city has identified "no special benefits" conferred on her, and has not identified any "special quantifiable burdens" created by her new store that would justify the particular dedications required from her which are not required from the public at large.

## III

In evaluating petitioner's claim, we must first determine whether the "essential nexus" exists between the "legitimate state interest" and the permit condition exacted by the city. *Nollan*, 483 U.S., at 837, 107 S. Ct., at 3148. If we find that a nexus exists, we must then decide the required degree of connection between the exactions and the projected impact of the proposed development. We were not required to reach this question in *Nollan*, because we concluded that the connection did not meet even the loosest standard. *Id.*, at 838, 107 S. Ct., at 3149. Here, however, we must decide this question.

### A

We addressed the essential nexus question in *Nollan*. The California Coastal Commission demanded a lateral public easement across the Nollans' beachfront lot in exchange for a permit to demolish an existing bungalow and replace it with a three-bedroom house. The public easement was designed to connect two public beaches that were separated by the Nollans' property. The Coastal Commission had asserted that the public easement condition was imposed to promote the legitimate state interest of diminishing the "blockage of the view of the ocean" caused by construction of the larger house.

We agreed that the Coastal Commission's concern with protecting visual access to the ocean constituted a legitimate public interest. We also agreed that the permit condition would have been constitutional "even if it consisted of the requirement that the Nollans provide a viewing spot on their property for passersby with whose sighting of the ocean their new house would interfere." We resolved, however, that the Coastal Commission's regulatory authority was set completely adrift from its constitutional moorings when it claimed that a nexus existed between visual access to the ocean and a permit condition requiring lateral public access along the Nollans' beachfront lot. How enhancing the public's ability to "traverse to and along the shorefront" served the same governmental purpose of "visual access to the ocean" from the roadway was beyond our ability to countenance. The absence of a nexus left the Coastal Commission in the position of simply trying to obtain an easement through gimmickry, which converted a valid regulation of land use into "'an out-and-out plan of extortion.'"

No such gimmicks are associated with the permit conditions imposed by the city in this case. Undoubtedly, the prevention of flooding along Fanno Creek and the reduction of traffic congestion in the Central Business District qualify as the type of legitimate public purposes we have upheld. It seems equally obvious that a nexus exists between preventing flooding along Fanno Creek and limiting development within the creek's 100-year floodplain. Petitioner proposes to double the size of her retail store and to pave her now-gravel parking lot, thereby expanding the impervious surface on the property and increasing the amount of storm water runoff into Fanno Creek.

The same may be said for the city's attempt to reduce traffic congestion by providing for alternative means of transportation. In theory, a pedestrian/bicycle pathway provides a useful alternative means of transportation for workers and shoppers: "Pedestrians and bicyclists occupying dedicated spaces for walking and/or bicycling . . . remove potential vehicles from streets, resulting in an overall improvement in total transportation system flow."

## B

The second part of our analysis requires us to determine whether the degree of the exactions demanded by the city's permit conditions bears the required relationship to the projected impact of petitioner's proposed development. *Nollan, supra,* 483 U.S., at 834, 107 S. Ct., at 3147, quoting *Penn Central Transp. Co. v. New York City,* 438 U.S. 104, 127, 98 S. Ct. 2646, 2660, 57 L. Ed. 2d 631 (1978) ("'[A] use restriction may constitute a "taking" if not reasonably necessary to the effectuation of a substantial government purpose'"). Here the Oregon Supreme Court deferred to what it termed the "city's unchallenged factual findings" supporting the dedication conditions and found them to be reasonably related to the impact of the expansion of petitioner's business.

The city required that petitioner dedicate "to the City as Greenway all portions of the site that fall within the existing 100-year floodplain [of Fanno Creek] . . . and all property 15 feet above [the floodplain] boundary." In addition, the city demanded that the retail store be designed so as not to intrude into the greenway area. The city relies on the Commission's rather tentative findings that increased storm water flow from petitioner's property "can only add to the public need to manage the [floodplain] for drainage purposes" to support its conclusion that the "requirement of dedication of the floodplain area on the site is related to the applicant's plan to intensify development on the site."

The city made the following specific findings relevant to the pedestrian/bicycle pathway:

> "In addition, the proposed expanded use of this site is anticipated to generate additional vehicular traffic thereby increasing congestion on nearby collector and arterial streets. Creation of a convenient, safe pedestrian/bicycle pathway system as an alternative means of transportation could offset some of the traffic demand on these nearby streets and lessen the increase in traffic congestion."

The question for us is whether these findings are constitutionally sufficient to justify the conditions imposed by the city on petitioner's building permit. Since state courts have been dealing with this question a good deal longer than we have, we turn to representative decisions made by them.

In some States, very generalized statements as to the necessary connection between the required dedication and the proposed development seem to suffice. We think this standard is too lax to adequately protect petitioner's right to just compensation if her property is taken for a public purpose.

Other state courts require a very exacting correspondence, described as the "specifi[c] and uniquely attributable" test. The Supreme Court of Illinois first developed this test in *Pioneer Trust & Savings Bank v. Mount Prospect*, 22 Ill.2d 375, 380, 176 N.E.2d 799, 802 (1961). Under this standard, if the local government cannot demonstrate that its exaction is directly proportional to the specifically created need, the exaction becomes "a veiled exercise of the power of eminent domain and a confiscation of private property behind the defense of police regulations." We do not think the Federal Constitution requires such exacting scrutiny, given the nature of the interests involved.

A number of state courts have taken an intermediate position, requiring the municipality to show a "reasonable relationship" between the required dedication and the impact of the proposed development. . . .

Some form of the reasonable relationship test has been adopted in many . . . jurisdictions. . . .

We think the "reasonable relationship" test adopted by a majority of the state courts is closer to the federal constitutional norm than either of those previously discussed. But we do not adopt it as such, partly because the term "reasonable relationship" seems confusingly similar to the term "rational basis" which describes the minimal level of scrutiny under the Equal Protection Clause of the Fourteenth Amendment. We think a term such as "rough proportionality" best encapsulates what we hold to be the requirement of the Fifth Amendment. No precise mathematical calculation is required, but the city must make some sort of individualized determination that the required dedication is related both in nature and extent to the impact of the proposed development.

. . . .

It is axiomatic that increasing the amount of impervious surface will increase the quantity and rate of storm water flow from petitioner's property. Therefore, keeping the floodplain open and free from development would likely confine the pressures on Fanno Creek created by petitioner's development. In fact, because petitioner's property lies within the Central Business District, the CDC already required that petitioner leave 15% of it as open space and the undeveloped floodplain would have nearly satisfied that requirement. But the city demanded more — it not only wanted petitioner not to build in the floodplain, but it also wanted petitioner's property along Fanno Creek for its greenway system. The city has never said why a public greenway, as opposed to a private one, was required in the interest of flood control.

The difference to petitioner, of course, is the loss of her ability to exclude others. As we have noted, this right to exclude others is "one of the most essential sticks in the bundle of rights that are commonly characterized as property." It is difficult to see why recreational visitors trampling along petitioner's floodplain easement are sufficiently related to the city's legitimate interest in reducing flooding problems along Fanno Creek, and the city has not attempted to make any individualized determination to support this part of its request.

The city contends that the recreational easement along the greenway is only ancillary to the city's chief purpose in controlling flood hazards. It further asserts that unlike the residential property at issue in *Nollan*, petitioner's property is commercial in character, and therefore, her right to exclude others is compromised. The city maintains that "[t]here is nothing to suggest that preventing [petitioner] from prohibiting [the easements] will unreasonably impair the value of [her] property as a [retail store]."

Admittedly, petitioner wants to build a bigger store to attract members of the public to her property. She also wants, however, to be able to control the time and manner in which they enter. . . . Petitioner would lose all rights to regulate the time in which the public entered onto the greenway, regardless of any interference it might pose with her retail store. Her right to exclude would not be regulated, it would be eviscerated.

If petitioner's proposed development had somehow encroached on existing greenway space in the city, it would have been reasonable to require petitioner to provide some alternative greenway space for the public either on her property or elsewhere. See *Nollan*, 483 U.S., at 836, 107 S. Ct., at 3148 ("Although such a requirement, constituting a permanent grant of continuous access to the property, would have to be considered a taking if it were not attached to a development permit, the Commission's assumed power to forbid construction of the house in order to protect the public's view of the beach must surely include the power to condition construction upon some concession by the owner, even a concession of property rights, that serves the same end"). But that is not the case here. We conclude that the findings upon which the city relies do not show the required reasonable relationship between the floodplain easement and the petitioner's proposed new building.

With respect to the pedestrian/bicycle pathway, we have no doubt that the city was correct in finding that the larger retail sales facility proposed by petitioner will increase traffic on the streets of the Central Business District. The city estimates that the proposed development would generate roughly 435 additional trips per day. Dedications for streets, sidewalks, and other public ways are generally reasonable exactions to avoid excessive congestion from a proposed property use. But on the record before us, the city has not met its burden of demonstrating that the additional number of vehicle and bicycle trips generated by petitioner's development reasonably relate to the city's requirement for a dedication of the pedestrian/bicycle pathway easement. The city simply found that the creation of the pathway "could offset some of the traffic demand . . . and lessen the increase in traffic congestion."

As Justice Peterson of the Supreme Court of Oregon explained in his dissenting opinion, however, "[t]he findings of fact that the bicycle pathway system 'could offset some of the traffic demand' is a far cry from a finding that the bicycle pathway system *will*, or is *likely to*, offset some of the traffic demand." No precise mathematical calculation is required, but the city must make some effort to quantify its findings in support of the dedication for the pedestrian/bicycle pathway beyond the conclusory statement that it could offset some of the traffic demand generated.

## IV

Cities have long engaged in the commendable task of land use planning, made necessary by increasing urbanization, particularly in metropolitan areas such as Portland. The city's goals of reducing flooding hazards and traffic congestion, and providing for public greenways, are laudable, but there are outer limits to how this may be done. "A strong public desire to improve the public condition [will not] warrant achieving the desire by a shorter cut than the constitutional way of paying for the change." *Pennsylvania Coal*, 260 U.S., at 416, 43 S. Ct., at 160.

The judgment of the Supreme Court of Oregon is reversed, and the case is remanded for further proceedings not inconsistent with this opinion.

It is so ordered.

Justice STEVENS, with whom Justice BLACKMUN and Justice GINSBURG join, dissenting.

. . . .

STEVENS, Justice. (dissenting). . . . [A]lthough discussion of the state cases permeates the Court's analysis of the appropriate test to apply in this case, the test on which the Court settles is not naturally derived from those courts' decisions. The Court recognizes as an initial matter that the city's conditions satisfy the "essential nexus" requirement announced in *Nollan v. California Coastal Comm'n*, 483 U.S. 825, 107 S. Ct. 3141, 97 L. Ed. 2d 677 (1987), because they serve the legitimate interests in minimizing floods and traffic congestions. The Court goes on, however, to erect a new constitutional hurdle in the path of these conditions. In addition to showing a rational nexus to a public purpose that would justify an outright denial of the permit, the city must also demonstrate "rough proportionality" between the harm caused by the new land use and the benefit obtained by the condition. The Court also decides for the first time that the city has the burden of establishing the constitutionality of its conditions by making an "individualized determination" that the condition in question satisfies the proportionality requirement. . . .

## *Questions for Consideration*

1) What property did Florence Dolan own, and what did she wish to do with it?

2) What was the focus of the Oregon comprehensive land management program?

3) How did the local regulations of the City of Tigard relate to the Oregon comprehensive land management plan?

4) What did the City of Tigard require of Dolan as a condition to granting permission for her to develop her property in accordance with her plans?

5) How did the Court characterize the nature of the government action in this case with respect to the action being legislative or adjudicative?

6) What does the Court say with respect to the essential nexus test of *Nollan*?

7) What requirement does the *Dolan* court add to the *Nollan* decision?

## *Takeaway*

- As in the *Nollan* decision, the *Dolan* decision does not say all conditions are unconstitutional.

- *Rough proportionality* does not require an exact calculation. It simply requires there be rough proportionality between the cost of the condition imposed on the property owner and the negative externality that the property owner's use imposes on others.

- *Nollan* and *Dolan*, taken together, inform us of a need to find an *essential nexus* and *rough proportionality* in order for a condition to be constitutional.

## Koontz v. St. Johns River Water Management District

Supreme Court of the United States

570 U.S. 595 (2013)

ALITO, Justice. Our decisions in *Nollan v. California Coastal Comm'n*, 483 U.S. 825, 107 S. Ct. 3141, 97 L. Ed. 2d 677 (1987), and *Dolan v. City of Tigard*, 512 U.S. 374, 114 S. Ct. 2309, 129 L. Ed. 2d 304 (1994), provide important protection against the misuse of the power of land-use regulation. In those cases, we held that a unit of government may not condition the approval of a land-use permit on the owner's relinquishment of a portion of his property unless there is a "nexus" and "rough proportionality" between the government's demand and the effects of the proposed land use. In this case, the St. Johns River Water Management District (District) believes that it circumvented *Nollan* and *Dolan* because of the way in which it structured its handling of a permit application submitted by Coy Koontz, Sr., whose estate is represented in this Court by Coy Koontz, Jr. The District did not approve his application on the condition that he surrender an interest in his land. Instead, the District, after suggesting that he could obtain approval by signing over such an interest, denied his application because he refused to yield. The Florida Supreme Court blessed this maneuver and thus effectively interred those important decisions. Because we conclude that *Nollan* and *Dolan* cannot be evaded in this way, the Florida Supreme Court's decision must be reversed.

In 1972, petitioner purchased an undeveloped 14.9-acre tract of land on the south side of Florida State Road 50, a divided four-lane highway east of Orlando. The property is located less than 1,000 feet from that road's intersection with Florida State Road 408, a tolled expressway that is one of Orlando's major thoroughfares.

A drainage ditch runs along the property's western edge, and high-voltage power lines bisect it into northern and southern sections. The combined effect of the ditch, a 100-foot wide area kept clear for the power lines, the highways, and other construction on nearby parcels is to isolate the northern section of petitioner's property from any other undeveloped land. Although largely classified as wetlands by the State, the northern section drains well; the most significant standing water forms in ruts in an unpaved road used to access the power lines. The natural topography of the property's southern section is somewhat more diverse, with a small creek, forested uplands, and wetlands that sometimes have water as much as a foot deep. A wildlife survey found evidence of animals that often frequent developed areas: raccoons, rabbits, several species of bird, and a turtle. The record also indicates that the land may be a suitable habitat for opossums.

The same year that petitioner purchased his property, Florida enacted the Water Resources Act, which divided the State into five water management districts and authorized each district to regulate "construction that connects to, draws water from, drains water into, or is placed in or across the waters in the state." Under the Act, a landowner wishing to undertake such construction must obtain from the relevant district a Management and Storage of Surface Water (MSSW) permit, which may impose "such reasonable conditions" on the permit as are "necessary to assure" that construction will "not be harmful to the water resources of the district."

In 1984, in an effort to protect the State's rapidly diminishing wetlands, the Florida Legislature passed the Warren S. Henderson Wetlands Protection Act, which made it illegal for anyone to "dredge or fill in, on, or over surface waters" without a Wetlands Resource Management (WRM) permit. Under the Henderson Act, permit applicants are required to provide "reasonable assurance" that proposed construction on wetlands is "not contrary to the public interest," as defined by an enumerated list of criteria. See Fla. Stat. § 373.414(1). Consistent with the Henderson Act, the St. Johns River Water Management District, the district with jurisdiction over petitioner's land, requires that permit applicants wishing to build on wetlands offset the resulting environmental damage by creating, enhancing, or preserving wetlands elsewhere.

Petitioner decided to develop the 3.7-acre northern section of his property, and in 1994 he applied to the District for MSSW and WRM permits. Under his proposal, petitioner would have raised the elevation of the northernmost section of his land to make it suitable for a building, graded the land from the southern edge of the building site down to the elevation of the high-voltage electrical lines, and installed a dry-bed pond for retaining and gradually releasing stormwater runoff from the building and its parking lot. To mitigate the environmental effects of his proposal, petitioner offered to foreclose any possible future development of the approximately 11-acre southern section of his land by deeding to the District a conservation easement on that portion of his property.

The District considered the 11-acre conservation easement to be inadequate, and it informed petitioner that it would approve construction only if he agreed to one of two concessions. First, the District proposed that petitioner reduce the size of his development to 1 acre and deed to the District a conservation easement on the remaining 13.9 acres. To reduce the development area, the District suggested that petitioner could eliminate the dry-bed pond from his proposal and instead install a more costly subsurface stormwater management system beneath the building site.

The District also suggested that petitioner install retaining walls rather than gradually sloping the land from the building site down to the elevation of the rest of his property to the south.

In the alternative, the District told petitioner that he could proceed with the development as proposed, building on 3.7 acres and deeding a conservation easement to the government on the remainder of the property, if he also agreed to hire contractors to make improvements to District-owned land several miles away. Specifically, petitioner could pay to replace culverts on one parcel or fill in ditches on another. Either of those projects would have enhanced approximately 50 acres of District-owned wetlands. When the District asks permit applicants to fund offsite mitigation work, its policy is never to require any particular offsite project, and it did not do so here. Instead, the District said that it "would also favorably consider" alternatives to its suggested offsite mitigation projects if petitioner proposed something "equivalent."

Believing the District's demands for mitigation to be excessive in light of the environmental effects that his building proposal would have caused, petitioner filed suit in state court. Among other claims, he argued that he was entitled to relief under Fla. Stat. § 373.617(2), which allows owners to recover "monetary damages" if a state agency's action is "an unreasonable exercise of the state's police power constituting a taking without just compensation."

. . . [T]he trial court found that the property's northern section had already been "seriously degraded" by extensive construction on the surrounding parcels. In light of this finding and petitioner's offer to dedicate nearly three-quarters of his land to the District, the trial court concluded that any further mitigation in the form of payment for offsite improvements to District property lacked both a nexus and rough proportionality to the environmental impact of the proposed construction. It accordingly held the District's actions unlawful under our decisions in *Nollan* and *Dolan*.

The Florida District Court affirmed, 5 So.3d 8 (2009), but the State Supreme Court reversed, 77 So.3d 1220 (2011). . . .

Recognizing that the majority opinion rested on a question of federal constitutional law on which the lower courts are divided, we granted the petition for a writ of certiorari, 568 U.S. —, 133 S. Ct. 420, 184 L. Ed. 2d 251 (2012), and now reverse.

We have said in a variety of contexts that "the government may not deny a benefit to a person because he exercises a constitutional right." . . .

*Nollan* and *Dolan* "involve a special application" of [the doctrine of unconstitutional conditions] that protects the Fifth Amendment right to just compensation for property the government takes when owners apply for land-use permits. Our decisions in those cases reflect two realities of the permitting process. The first is that land-use permit applicants are especially vulnerable to the type of coercion that the unconstitutional conditions doctrine prohibits because the government often has broad discretion to deny a permit that is worth far more than property it would like to take. By conditioning a building permit on the owner's deeding over a public right-of-way, for example, the government can pressure an owner into voluntarily giving up property for which the Fifth Amendment would otherwise require just compensation. So long as the building permit is more valuable than any just compensation the owner could hope to receive for the right-of-way, the owner is likely to accede to the government's demand, no matter how unreasonable. Extortionate demands of this sort frustrate the Fifth Amendment right to just compensation, and the unconstitutional conditions doctrine prohibits them.

A second reality of the permitting process is that many proposed land uses threaten to impose costs on the public that dedications of property can offset. Where a building proposal would substantially increase traffic congestion, for example, officials might condition permit approval on the owner's agreement to deed over the land needed to widen a public road. Respondent argues that a similar rationale justifies the exaction at issue here: petitioner's proposed construction project, it submits, would destroy wetlands on his property, and in order to compensate for this loss, respondent demands that he enhance wetlands elsewhere. Insisting that landowners internalize the negative externalities of their conduct is a hallmark of responsible land-use policy, and we have long sustained such regulations against constitutional attack. See *Village of Euclid v. Ambler Realty Co.*, 272 U.S. 365, 47 S. Ct. 114, 71 L. Ed. 303 (1926).

*Nollan* and *Dolan* accommodate both realities by allowing the government to condition approval of a permit on the dedication of property to the public so long as there is a "nexus" and "rough proportionality" between the property that the government demands and the social costs of the applicant's proposal. Our precedents thus enable permitting authorities to insist that applicants bear the full costs of their proposals while still forbidding the government from engaging in "out-and-out . . . extortion" that would thwart the Fifth Amendment right to just compensation. *Ibid.* (internal quotation marks omitted). Under *Nollan* and *Dolan* the government may choose whether and how a permit applicant is required to mitigate the impacts of a proposed development, but it may not leverage its legitimate interest in mitigation to pursue governmental ends that lack an essential nexus and rough proportionality to those impacts.

The principles that undergird our decisions in *Nollan* and *Dolan* do not change depending on whether the government *approves* a permit on the condition that the applicant turn over property or *denies* a permit because the applicant refuses to do so. We have often concluded that denials of governmental benefits were impermissible under the unconstitutional conditions doctrine. In so holding, we have recognized that regardless of whether the government ultimately succeeds in pressuring someone into forfeiting a constitutional right, the unconstitutional conditions doctrine forbids burdening the Constitution's enumerated rights by coercively withholding benefits from those who exercise them.

. . . .

Respondent and the dissent argue that if monetary exactions are made subject to scrutiny under *Nollan* and *Dolan*, then there will be no principled way of distinguishing impermissible land-use exactions from property taxes. See *post*, at 2607–2608. We think they exaggerate both the extent to which that problem is unique to the land-use permitting context and the practical difficulty of distinguishing between the power to tax and the power to take by eminent domain.

It is beyond dispute that "[t]axes and user fees . . . are not 'takings.'" This case therefore does not affect the ability of governments to impose property taxes, user fees, and similar laws and regulations that may impose financial burdens on property owners.

. . . .

We hold that the government's demand for property from a land-use permit applicant must satisfy the requirements of *Nollan* and *Dolan* even when the government denies the permit and even when its demand is for money. The Court expresses no view on the merits of petitioner's claim that respondent's actions here failed to comply with the principles set forth in this opinion and those two cases. The Florida Supreme Court's judgment is reversed, and this case is remanded for further proceedings not inconsistent with this opinion.

It is so ordered.

Justice KAGAN, with whom Justice GINSBURG, Justice BREYER, and Justice SOTO-MAYOR join, dissenting.

KAGAN, Justice. (dissenting). In the paradigmatic case triggering review under *Nollan v. California Coastal Comm'n*, 483 U.S. 825, 107 S. Ct. 3141, 97 L. Ed. 2d 677 (1987), and *Dolan v. City of Tigard*, 512 U.S. 374, 114 S. Ct. 2309, 129 L. Ed. 2d 304 (1994), the government approves a building permit on the condition that the landowner relinquish an interest in real property, like an easement. The significant legal questions that the Court resolves today are whether *Nollan* and *Dolan* also apply when that case is varied in two ways. First, what if the government does not approve the permit, but instead demands that the condition be fulfilled before it will do so? Second, what if the condition entails not transferring real property, but simply paying money? . . .

I think the Court gets the first question it addresses right. The *Nollan-Dolan* standard applies not only when the government approves a development permit conditioned on the owner's conveyance of a property interest (*i.e.*, imposes a condition subsequent), but also when the government denies a permit until the owner meets the condition (*i.e.*, imposes a condition precedent). That means an owner may challenge the denial of a permit on the ground that the government's condition lacks the "nexus" and "rough proportionality" to the development's social costs that *Nollan* and *Dolan* require. Still, the condition-subsequent and condition-precedent situations differ in an important way. When the government grants a permit subject to the relinquishment of real property, and that condition does not satisfy *Nollan* and *Dolan*, then the government has taken the property and must pay just compensation under the Fifth Amendment. But when the government denies a permit because an owner has refused to accede to that same demand, nothing has actually been taken. The owner is entitled to have the improper condition removed; and he may be entitled to a monetary remedy created by state law for imposing such a condition; but he cannot be entitled to constitutional compensation for a taking of property. So far, we all agree.

Our core disagreement concerns the second question the Court addresses. The majority extends *Nollan* and *Dolan* to cases in which the government conditions a permit not on the transfer of real property, but instead on the payment or expenditure of money.... The boundaries of the majority's new rule are uncertain. But it threatens to subject a vast array of land-use regulations, applied daily in States and localities throughout the country, to heightened constitutional scrutiny. I would not embark on so unwise an adventure, and would affirm the Florida Supreme Court's decision.

## *Questions for Consideration*

1)  When did Koontz purchase the property and when did the State of Florida enact the Water Resource Act and the Henderson Wetlands Protection Act?

2)  What was the nature of Koontz's property? How would you describe the surrounding environment, its suitability for development, natural topography, and potential as a wildlife habitat?

3)  Koontz owned 14.9 acres and wanted to develop 3.7 acres. When he applied for a permit, what was his original proposal to the St. Johns River Water Management District?

4)  In response to Koontz's application, what did the Water Management District require?

5)  How does the Court apply the reasoning of *Nollan* and *Dolan* to this case?

6)  What does the Court say about the exercise of the police power and the problem of negative externalities (negative spillover effects)?

7)  Explain the meaning of a *monetary exaction*.

8)  What do you make of Justice Kagan's argument in the dissent with respect to identifying a difference between a condition subsequent and a condition precedent with respect to the implications for takings law?

## *Takeaway*

• *Koontz* establishes a standard for evaluating monetary exactions in terms of the jurisprudence related to takings law and unconstitutional conditions. Monetary exactions are held to the *Nollan* and *Dolan* requirements of having to establish an essential nexus, and rough proportionality.

# California Building Industry Ass'n v. City of San Jose

Supreme Court of California
351 P.3d 974 (Cal. 2015)

CANTIL-SAKAUYE, Judge. Health and Safety Code section 50003, subdivision (a), currently provides: "The Legislature finds and declares that . . . there exists within the urban and rural areas of the state a serious shortage of decent, safe, and sanitary housing which persons and families of low or moderate income . . . can afford. This situation creates an absolute present and future shortage of supply in relation to demand . . . and also creates inflation in the cost of housing, by reason of its scarcity, which tends to decrease the relative affordability of the state's housing supply for all its residents."

This statutory language was first enacted by the Legislature *over 35 years ago,* in the late 1970s. It will come as no surprise to anyone familiar with California's current housing market that the significant problems arising from a scarcity of affordable housing have not been solved over the past three decades. Rather, these problems have become more severe and have reached what might be described as epic proportions in many of the state's localities. All parties in this proceeding agree that the lack of affordable housing is a very significant problem in this state.

As one means of addressing the lack of a sufficient number of housing units that are affordable to low and moderate income households, more than 170 California municipalities have adopted what are commonly referred to as "inclusionary zoning" or "inclusionary housing" programs. As a 2013 publication of the United States Department of Housing and Urban Development (HUD) explains, inclusionary zoning or housing programs "require or encourage developers to set aside a certain percentage of housing units in new or rehabilitated projects for low- and moderate-income residents. This integration of affordable units into market-rate projects creates opportunities for households with diverse socioeconomic backgrounds to live in the same developments and have access to [the] same types of community services and amenities. . . ." (U.S. Dept. of Housing and Urban Development, *Inclusionary Zoning and Mixed-Income Communities* (Spring 2013).

In 2010, after considerable study and outreach to all segments of the community, the City of San Jose (hereafter sometimes referred to as the city or San Jose) enacted an inclusionary housing ordinance that, among other features, requires all new residential development projects of 20 or more units to sell at least 15 percent of the for-sale units at a price that is affordable to low or moderate income households.

Very shortly after the ordinance was enacted and before it took effect, plaintiff California Building Industry Association (CBIA) filed this lawsuit in superior court, maintaining that the ordinance was invalid on its face on the ground that the city, in enacting the ordinance, failed to provide a sufficient evidentiary basis "to demonstrate a reasonable relationship between any adverse public impacts or needs for additional subsidized housing units in the City ostensibly caused by or reasonably attributed to the development of new residential developments of 20 units or more and the new affordable housing exactions and conditions imposed on residential development by the Ordinance." . . . CBIA's challenge is based on the premise that the conditions imposed by the San Jose ordinance constitute "exactions" for purposes of that doctrine. The superior court agreed with CBIA's contention and issued a judgment enjoining the city from enforcing the challenged ordinance.

The Court of Appeal reversed the superior court judgment, concluding that the superior court had erred (1) in finding that the San Jose ordinance requires a developer to dedicate property to the public within the meaning of the takings clause, and (2) in interpreting the controlling constitutional principles . . . as limiting the conditions that may be imposed by such an ordinance to only those conditions that are reasonably related to the adverse impact the development projects that are subject to the ordinance themselves impose on the city's affordable housing problem. . . . The Court of Appeal concluded that the matter should be remanded to the trial court for application of this traditional standard.

CBIA sought review of the Court of Appeal decision in this court. . . . We granted review to determine the soundness of the Court of Appeal's ruling in this case.

For the reasons discussed below, we conclude that the Court of Appeal decision in the present case should be upheld. As explained hereafter, contrary to CBIA's contention, the conditions that the San Jose ordinance imposes upon future developments do not impose "exactions" upon the developers' property so as to bring into play the unconstitutional conditions doctrine under the takings clause of the federal or state Constitution. Furthermore, . . . the conditions imposed by the San Jose ordinance at issue here do not require a developer to pay a monetary fee but rather place a limit on the way a developer may use its property. In addition, the conditions are intended not only to mitigate the effect that the covered development projects will have on the city's affordable housing problem but also to serve the distinct, but nonetheless constitutionally legitimate, purposes of (1) *increasing the number of affordable housing units in the city* in recognition of the insufficient number of existing affordable housing units in relation to the city's current and future needs, and (2) assuring that new affordable housing units that are constructed *are distributed throughout the city as part of mixed-income developments* in order to obtain the benefits that flow from economically diverse communities and avoid the problems that have historically been associated with isolated low income housing.

Accordingly, we conclude that the judgment of the Court of Appeal in this case should be affirmed.

## I. Statutory background

We begin with a brief summary of the California statutes that form the background to the San Jose ordinance challenged in this case.

Nearly 50 years ago, the California Legislature enacted a broad measure requiring all counties and cities in California to "adopt a comprehensive, long-term general plan for the physical development of the county or city." Each municipality's general plan is to contain a variety of mandatory and optional elements, including a mandatory housing element consisting of standards and plans for housing sites in the municipality that "shall endeavor to make adequate provision for the housing needs of all economic segments of the community."

A little more than a decade later, . . . the Legislature enacted a separate, comprehensive statutory scheme that substantially strengthened the requirements of the housing element component of local general plans. The 1980 legislation — commonly referred to as the "Housing Element Law" sets forth in considerable detail a municipality's obligations to analyze and quantify the locality's existing and projected housing needs for all income levels, including the locality's share of the regional housing need as determined by the applicable regional "'[c]ouncil of governments'" (Gov.Code, § 65582, subd. (b)), and to adopt and to submit to the California Department of Housing and Community Development a multiyear schedule of actions the local government is undertaking to meet these needs. . . .

In addition to adopting the Housing Element Law, the Legislature has enacted a variety of other statutes to facilitate and encourage the provision of affordable housing, for example, prohibiting local zoning and other restrictions that preclude the construction of affordable housing units, and requiring local governments to provide incentives, such as density bonuses, to developers who voluntarily include affordable housing in their proposed development projects. . . .

### II. Background and description of challenged San Jose inclusionary housing ordinance

It is within the context of the foregoing statutory framework that San Jose began considering the need and desirability of adopting an inclusionary housing ordinance. As noted, the statewide Housing Element Law places responsibility upon a city to use its powers to facilitate the development of housing that makes adequate provision for all economic segments of the community, in particular extremely low, very low, lower and moderate income households, including the city's allocation of the regional housing need as determined by the applicable regional council of governments.

In December 2008, the Association of Bay Area Governments (ABAG), the regional council of governments within whose jurisdiction the City of San Jose falls (see Gov.Code, § 65588, subd. (e)(1)(B)), calculated San Jose's share of the regional need for new housing over the 2007–2014 planning period as approximately 34,700 units, of which approximately 19,300 units — *or about 60 percent of the new housing units in San Jose* — would be needed to house moderate, low, very low, and extremely low income households. . . .

. . . Between 1999 and 2009, more than 10,000 affordable housing units had been built in the redevelopment areas of San Jose under the city's redevelopment inclusionary housing policy.

In part as a result of this experience with a mandatory inclusionary housing requirement in its redevelopment areas, the city began considering the feasibility of adopting a *citywide* inclusionary housing policy. . . . [T]he city retained a private consulting firm to conduct an economic feasibility study of a citywide inclusionary housing policy. The very extensive 300-page study, prepared by the consulting firm with input from developers, affordable housing advocates, community organizations and others, concluded that inclusionary housing could be economically feasible with certain developer incentives and under improved economic conditions.

After reviewing the study, the city council directed city staff to obtain further input from affected stakeholders and the community generally and then to bring a draft policy to the council for its consideration. Between June and December 2008, officials at the city housing department held more than 50 meetings with community members, developer and labor associations, affordable housing advocates and community organizations, and presented a draft policy to the council. In December 2008, after discussion, the city council directed staff to draft an inclusionary housing ordinance that would meet specified requirements agreed upon by the council. A draft ordinance was written and released for public review in July 2009, and between July and October 2009 nine public meetings were held throughout the city to discuss the draft ordinance. On January 26, 2010, the city council adopted the citywide inclusionary housing ordinance at issue in this case.

. . . .

The ordinance begins with a list of findings and declarations, detailing the steady increase in the cost of housing in San Jose generally and the substantial need for affordable housing for extremely low, very low, lower, and moderate income households to meet the city's regional housing needs allocation as determined by ABAG. The findings note that "[r]equiring affordable units within each development is consistent with the community's housing element goals of protecting the public welfare by fostering an adequate supply of housing for persons at all economic levels and maintaining both economic diversity and geographically dispersed affordable housing." The findings further observe that requiring builders of new market rate housing to provide some housing affordable to low and moderate income families "is also reasonably related to the impacts of their projects, because: 1. Rising land prices have been a key factor in preventing development of new affordable housing. New market-rate housing uses available land and drives up the price of remaining land. New development without affordable units reduces the amount of land development opportunities available for the construction of affordable housing. 2. New residents of market-rate housing place demands on services provided by both public and private sectors, creating a demand for new employees. Some of these public and private sector employees needed to meet the needs of the new residents earn incomes only adequate to pay for affordable housing. Because affordable housing is in short supply in the city, such employees may be forced to live in less than adequate housing within the city, pay a disproportionate share of their incomes to live in adequate housing in the city, or commute ever increasing distances to their jobs from housing located outside the city. These circumstances harm the city's ability to attain employment and housing goals articulated in the city's general plan and place strains on the city's ability to accept and service new market-rate housing development."

. . . .

. . . The requirements contained in the ordinance apply to all residential developments within the city that create 20 or more new, additional, or modified dwelling units. With regard to such developments, the ordinance's basic inclusionary housing requirement specifies that 15 percent of the proposed on-site for-sale units in the development shall be made available at an "affordable housing cost" to households earning no more than 120 percent of the area median income for Santa Clara County adjusted for household size. The ordinance generally defines affordable housing cost . . . as 30 percent of the area median income of the relevant income group (i.e. extremely low, very low, lower and moderate income).

As an alternative to providing the required number of for-sale inclusionary units on the same site as the market rate units, the ordinance affords a developer a number of compliance options. At the same time, as an apparent incentive to encourage developers to choose to provide on-site inclusionary units, the ordinance provides that when a developer chooses one of the alternative compliance options, the inclusionary housing requirement increases to no less than 20 percent of the total units in the residential development, as contrasted with the no less than 15 percent requirement that applies to on-site inclusionary units. The alternative compliance options include: (1) constructing off-site affordable for-sale units, (2) paying an in lieu fee based on the median sales price of a housing unit affordable to a moderate income family, (3) dedicating land equal in value to the applicable in lieu fee, or (4) acquiring and rehabilitating a comparable number of inclusionary units that are affordable to low or very low income households.

As additional incentives to encourage developers to comply with the ordinance by providing affordable units on site, the ordinance permits a developer who provides all of the required affordable units on the same site as the market rate units to apply for and obtain a variety of economically beneficial incentives, including (1) a density bonus . . . (2) a reduction in the number of parking spaces otherwise required by the San Jose Municipal Code, (3) a reduction in minimum set-back requirements, and (4) financial subsidies and assistance from the city in the sale of the affordable units.

The ordinance also addresses the characteristics of the affordable units to be constructed on site. The ordinance requires that such units have the same quality of exterior design and comparable square footage and bedroom count as market rate units, but permits some different "unit types" of affordable units, and also allows the affordable units to have different, but functionally equivalent, interior finishes, features, and amenities, compared with the market rate units.

The ordinance additionally contains a number of provisions intended to ensure that the number of affordable housing units required by the ordinance is not lost upon resale of an affordable unit. . . .

The ordinance further contains a waiver provision, declaring that the ordinance's requirements may be "waived, adjusted, or reduced" by the city "if an applicant shows, based on substantial evidence, that there is no reasonable relationship between the impact of a proposed residential development and the requirements of this chapter, or that applying the requirements of this chapter would take property in violation of the United States or California Constitutions." . . .

. . . .

### III. Lower court proceedings

. . . .

### IV. Does the San Jose inclusionary housing ordinance, in requiring new residential developments to sell some of the proposed new units at an affordable housing price, impose an "exaction" on developers' property under the takings clauses of the federal and California Constitutions, so as to bring into play the unconstitutional conditions doctrine?

We begin with the well-established principle that under the California Constitution a municipality has broad authority, under its general police power, to regulate the development and use of real property within its jurisdiction to promote the public welfare. . . . As a general matter, so long as a land use restriction or regulation bears a reasonable relationship to the public welfare, the restriction or regulation is constitutionally permissible.

We review challenges to the exercise of such power deferentially. "In deciding whether a challenged [land use] ordinance reasonably relates to the public welfare, the courts recognize that such ordinances are presumed to be constitutional, and come before the court with every intendment in their favor." Accordingly, a party challenging the facial validity of a legislative land use measure ordinarily bears the burden of demonstrating that the measure lacks a reasonable relationship to the public welfare. Nonetheless, although land use regulations are generally entitled to deference, "judicial deference is not judicial abdication. The ordinance must have a *real and substantial* relation to the public welfare. There must be a reasonable basis in fact, not in fancy, to support the legislative determination. Although in many cases it will be 'fairly debatable' [citation] that the ordinance reasonably relates to the regional welfare, it cannot be assumed that a land use ordinance can *never* be invalidated as an enactment in excess of the police power."

In the present case, however, CBIA contends that this traditional standard of judicial review is not applicable and that the conditions that the ordinance imposes upon a proposed new development are valid only if those conditions bear a reasonable relationship to the amount of the city's need for affordable housing that is attributable to the proposed development itself, rather than that the ordinance's conditions bear a reasonable relationship to the public welfare of the city and region as a whole. It also contends that the city, rather than the party challenging the ordinance, bears the burden of proof regarding the validity of the ordinance.

... CBIA's constitutional claim ... rests upon the takings clauses of the United States and California Constitutions (U.S. Const., 5th and 14th Amends.; Cal. Const., art. I, §19), and, more specifically, on the claim "that the Ordinance violates the unconstitutional conditions doctrine, as applied to development exactions." As we shall explain, however, there can be no valid unconstitutional-conditions takings claim without a government exaction of property, and the ordinance in the present case does not effect an exaction. Rather, the ordinance is an example of a municipality's permissible regulation of the use of land under its broad police power.

As a general matter, the unconstitutional conditions doctrine imposes special restrictions upon the government's otherwise broad authority to condition the grant of a privilege or benefit when a proposed condition requires the individual to give up or refrain from exercising a constitutional right. In the takings context, the special limitations imposed by the unconstitutional conditions doctrine upon which CBIA relies derive from the United States Supreme Court's decisions in *Nollan v. California Coastal Commission* (1987) 483 U.S. 825, 107 S. Ct. 3141, 97 L. Ed. 2d 677 (*Nollan*) and *Dolan v. City of Tigard* (1994) 512 U.S. 374, 114 S. Ct. 2309, 129 L. Ed. 2d 304 (*Dolan*).

In both *Nollan, supra,* 483 U.S. 825, 107 S. Ct. 3141, and *Dolan, supra,* 512 U.S. 374, 114 S. Ct. 2309, the high court considered the validity of ad hoc administrative decisions regarding individual land-use permit applications that required a property owner, as a condition of obtaining a sought-after permit, *to dedicate a portion of the property to public use.* In *Nollan,* the California Coastal Commission had conditioned its grant of a permit to allow the property owner to demolish a small beachfront bungalow and construct a three-bedroom residence upon the owner's agreement to grant an easement to the public to enter and cross the owner's beachfront property near the water's edge. In *Dolan,* the city had conditioned its grant of a permit to allow the property owner to substantially increase the size of its existing retail business upon the owner's agreement to give a strip of the property to the city for use as part of a public flood-control greenway and bike path.

In *Nollan, supra,* 483 U.S. 825, 107 S. Ct. 3141, in explaining why the takings clause justified special scrutiny of the coastal commission's imposition of the challenged permit condition at issue in that case, the high court began its analysis by observing: "Had California simply required the Nollans to make an easement across their beachfront available to the public on a permanent basis in order to increase public access to the beach, rather than conditioning their permit to rebuild their house on their agreeing to do so, we have no doubt there would have been a taking." (*Id.* at p. 831, 107 S. Ct. 3141.) Similarly, in *Dolan,* the high court noted that "had the city simply required petitioner to dedicate a strip of land . . . for public use, rather than conditioning the grant of her permit to redevelop her property on such a dedication, a taking would have occurred." (*Dolan, supra,* 512 U.S. at p. 384, 114 S. Ct. 2309.) Because under the takings clause a property owner has the right to be paid just compensation when the government takes his or her property for public use, the court in *Nollan* declared that special scrutiny of a governmental action is warranted "*where the actual conveyance of property* is made a condition for the lifting of a land-use restriction, since in that context there is heightened risk that the [government's] purpose is avoidance of the compensation requirement, rather than the stated police-power objective" upon which the condition is ostensibly based. (*Nollan,* at p. 841, 107 S. Ct. 3141, italics added.) Thereafter, the *Nollan* and *Dolan* decisions proceeded to explain and describe the nature and extent of the special scrutiny that is called for under the takings clause when the government conditions the grant of a land use permit on the property owner's agreement to dedicate a portion of its property for public use without the payment of just compensation. Under *Nollan* and *Dolan,* the government may impose such a condition only when the government demonstrates that there is an "essential nexus" and "rough proportionality" between the required dedication and the projected impact of the proposed land use. (See *Nollan, supra,* at pp. 837–840, 107 S. Ct. 3141; *Dolan, supra,* at pp. 388–395, 114 S. Ct. 2309.)

More recently, in *Koontz v. St. Johns River Water Mgmt. Dist.* (2013) 570 U.S. — , 133 S. Ct. 2586, 186 L. Ed. 2d 697 (*Koontz*), the high court held that the *Nollan/Dolan* test applies not only when the government conditions approval of a land use permit on the property owner's dedication of a portion of the property for public use but also when it conditions approval of such a permit upon the owner's payment of money. In *Koontz,* the property owner applied for a permit to develop a portion of an undeveloped parcel of land, most of which was classified as wetlands by the state. In his application, the owner agreed to dedicate a portion of the property to the local public water management district as a conservation easement, but the district considered the size of the property owner's proposed conservation easement to be inadequate and instead proposed that the property owner either dedicate a larger portion of the property as a conservation easement or, alternatively, pay for the improvement of other district-owned wetlands within several miles of the owner's property. The property owner refused to accede to the district's proposal, and brought an action in Florida state court against the district, contending among other matters that the district's proposal that he pay a sum of money as an alternative to dedicating an additional portion of his property was itself subject to the *Nollan/Dolan* test and thus that the district was required to show that the amount of money in question satisfied the "essential nexus" and "rough proportionality" requirements set forth in those decisions. The Florida Supreme Court rejected the property owner's contention on the ground that a permit condition that requires a property owner to pay or spend money, as contrasted with a condition that requires the owner to give the public a tangible interest in real property, does not provide a basis for a takings claim, and thus was not subject to the *Nollan/Dolan* test.

In *Koontz, supra,* 570 U.S. at pages —, 133 S. Ct. at pp. 2598–2603, 186 L. Ed. 2d at pp. 712–717, a majority of the United States Supreme Court disagreed with the Florida Supreme Court's conclusion on this point. The majority began its analysis of this issue by noting "as an initial matter that if we accepted this argument [that the *Nollan/Dolan* test does not apply to a permit condition that requires the property owner to pay money] it would be very easy for land-use permitting officials to evade the limitations of *Nollan* and *Dolan.* Because the government need only provide a permit applicant with one alternative that satisfies the nexus and rough proportionality standards, a permitting authority wishing to exact an easement could simply give the owner a choice of either surrendering an easement or making a payment equal to the easement's value. . . . For that reason and those that follow, we reject respondent's argument and hold that so-called 'monetary exactions' must satisfy the nexus and rough proportionality requirements of *Nollan* and *Dolan.*" (*Id.* at p. —, 133 S. Ct. at p. 2599, 186 L. Ed. 2d at p. 713.)

It is clear from the decision in *Koontz, supra,* 570 U.S. —, 133 S. Ct. 2586, 186 L. Ed. 2d 697, that the *Nollan/Dolan* standard applies to the type of "so-called 'monetary exactions'" (*Koontz,* at p. —, 133 S. Ct. at p. 2599, 186 L. Ed. 2d at p. 713) involved in *Koontz* itself — that is, a monetary payment that is a substitute for the property owner's dedication of property to the public and that is intended to mitigate the environmental impact of the proposed project. However, the full range of monetary land-use permit conditions to which the *Nollan/Dolan* test applies under the *Koontz* decision remains at least somewhat ambiguous. Nonetheless, the *Koontz* decision explicitly acknowledges that "[a] predicate for any unconstitutional conditions claim is that the government could not have constitutionally ordered the person asserting the claim to do what it attempted to pressure that person into doing." (*Koontz, supra,* at p. —, 133 S. Ct. at p. 2598, 186 L. Ed. 2d at p. 712.) Or, in other words, the condition is one that would have constituted a taking of property without just compensation if it were imposed by the government on a property owner outside of the permit process. (*Id.* at pp. —, 133 S. Ct. at pp. 2598–2599, 2600, 186 L. Ed. 2d at pp. 712–713, 714; see *Lingle v. Chevron U.S.A. Inc.* (2005) 544 U.S. 528, 547, 125 S. Ct. 2074, 161 L. Ed. 2d 876 (*Lingle*) [*Nollan* and *Dolan* both involved "dedications of property so onerous that, outside the exactions context, they would be deemed *per se* physical takings"].) Nothing in *Koontz* suggests that the unconstitutional conditions doctrine under *Nollan* and *Dolan* would apply where the government simply restricts the use of property without demanding the conveyance of some identifiable protected property interest (a dedication of property or the payment of money) as a condition of approval. It is the governmental requirement that the property owner convey some identifiable property interest that constitutes a so-called "exaction" under the takings clause and that brings the unconstitutional conditions doctrine into play. (See *Lingle, supra,* at pp. 546–547, 125 S. Ct. 2074; *Monterey v. Del Monte Dunes at*

*Monterey, Ltd.* (1999) 526 U.S. 687, 702, 119 S. Ct. 1624, 143 L. Ed. 2d 882 ["[W]e have not extended the rough-proportionality test of *Dolan* beyond the special context of exactions — land-use decisions conditioning approval of development on the dedication of property to public use."].)

In the present case, contrary to CBIA's contention, the San Jose inclusionary housing ordinance does not violate the unconstitutional conditions doctrine because there is no exaction — the ordinance does not require a developer to give up a property interest for which the government would have been required to pay just compensation under the takings clause outside of the permit process. As summarized above, the principal requirement that the challenged ordinance imposes upon a developer is that the developer sell 15 percent of its on-site for-sale units at an affordable housing price. This condition does not require the developer to dedicate any portion of its property to the public or to pay any money to the public. Instead, like many other land use regulations, this condition simply places a restriction on the way the developer may use its property by limiting the price for which the developer may offer some of its units for sale. Contrary to CBIA's contention, such a requirement does not constitute an exaction for purposes of the *Nollan/Dolan* line of decisions and does not trigger application of the unconstitutional conditions doctrine.

Rather than being an exaction, the ordinance falls within what we have already described as municipalities' general broad discretion to regulate the use of real property to serve the legitimate interests of the general public and the community at large. . . .

As a general matter, so long as a land use regulation does not constitute a physical taking or deprive a property owner of all viable economic use of the property, such a restriction does not violate the takings clause insofar as it governs a property owner's future use of his or her property, except in the unusual circumstance in which the use restriction is properly found to go "too far" and to constitute a "regulatory taking" under the ad hoc, multifactored test discussed by the United States Supreme Court in *Penn Central Transp. Co. v. New York City* (1978) 438 U.S. 104, 98 S. Ct. 2646, 57 L. Ed. 2d 631 (*Penn Central*). (See *Lingle, supra,* 544 U.S. at pp. 538–539, 125 S. Ct. 2074.) Where a restriction on the use of property would not constitute a taking of property without just compensation if imposed outside of the permit process, a permit condition imposing such a use restriction does not require a permit applicant to give up the constitutional right to just compensation in order to obtain the permit and thus does not constitute "an exaction" so as to bring into play the unconstitutional conditions doctrine. (See, e.g., *Powell v. County of Humboldt* (2014) 222 Cal. App. 4th 1424, 1435–1441, 166 Cal. Rptr. 3d 747.)

As noted, the legislative history of the ordinance in question establishes that the City of San Jose found there was a significant and increasing need for affordable housing in the city to meet the city's regional share of housing needs under the California Housing Element Law and that the public interest would best be served if new affordable housing were integrated into economically diverse development projects, and that it enacted the challenged ordinance in order to further these objectives. The objectives of increasing the amount of affordable housing in the city to comply with the Housing Element Law and of locating such housing in economically diverse developments are unquestionably constitutionally permissible purposes. (See, e.g., *Santa Monica Beach, supra,* 19 Cal. 4th at p. 970, 81 Cal. Rptr. 2d 93, 968 P.2d 993; *Home Builders Assn. v. City of Napa* (2001) 90 Cal. App. 4th 188, 195, 108 Cal. Rptr. 2d 60 (*City of Napa*).) CBIA does not argue otherwise.

There are a variety of conditions or restrictions that a municipality could impose on new residential development in an effort to increase the community's stock of affordable housing and promote economically diverse residential developments. For example, a municipality might attempt to achieve these objectives by requiring all new residential developments to include a specified percentage of studio, one-bedroom, or small-square-footage units, on the theory that smaller units are more likely to be affordable to low or moderate income households than larger units. Although such use restrictions might well reduce the value of undeveloped property or lessen the profits a developer could obtain in the absence of such requirements, CBIA cites no authority, and we are aware of none, suggesting that such use restrictions would constitute a taking of property outside the permit process or that a permit condition that imposes such use restrictions on a proposed development would constitute an exaction under the takings clause that would be subject to the *Nollan/Dolan* test.

Here, the challenged ordinance seeks to increase the city's stock of affordable housing and promote economically diverse residential projects by placing controls on the sales price of a portion of a developer's on-site for-sale units rather than by placing restrictions on the size or other features of a portion of the for-sale units. But the fact that the ordinance imposes price controls rather than other use restrictions in order to accomplish its legitimate purposes does not render such price controls an exaction or support application of a constitutionally based judicial standard of review that is more demanding than that applied to other land use regulations. The governing federal and state authorities plainly establish that price controls, like other forms of regulation, are, as a general matter, a constitutionally permissible means to achieve a municipality's legitimate public purposes. . . .

. . . .

. . . [A]n ordinance that places nonconfiscatory price controls on the sale of residential units and does not amount to a regulatory taking would not constitute a taking of property without just compensation even if the price controls were applied to a property owner who had not sought a land use permit. Accordingly, the inclusionary housing ordinance's imposition of such price controls as a condition of a development permit does not constitute the imposition of an exaction for purposes of the unconstitutional conditions doctrine under the takings clause.

. . . [T]he judgment of the Court of Appeals is affirmed.]

## *Questions for Consideration*

1) Who is bringing the lawsuit? Does an association have standing to bring such a suit?

2) Looking at the statutory background of the case, what steps were taken to develop the policy and the requirements currently being objected to by the plaintiff?

3) The case opinion indicates that the ordinance in question begins with a list of findings. What findings are identified in support of the ordinance?

4) The ordinance has certain on-site requirements that a developer must meet and provides off-site alternatives. What are the on-site requirements and the off-site alternatives?

5) What additional incentives were available to developers that provide affordable units on-site?

6) Did the ordinance provide for a variance or waiver to strict compliance with its requirements?

7) What was the basis of the plaintiff's constitutional challenge to the ordinance?

8) How does the court address each of the following cases: *Nollan, Dolan*, and *Koontz*?

9) Does the court decide that this is an exaction subject to the requirements set out in *Nollan, Dolan*, and *Koontz*? If not, how does the court describe and characterize the requirements imposed under the ordinance?

## *Takeaway*

- The infrastructure and affordable housing needs of many communities are expensive and difficult to get taxpayers to voluntarily fund. This is true even when there are many good reasons for supporting investment in order to protect and advance the public health, safety, welfare, and morals. This often drives public officials to be creative in finding ways of making property owners and developers share the cost of infrastructure and housing needs. The takings cases seek to identify a framework for analyzing when such efforts "go too far" (paraphrasing from *Pennsylvania Coal* and *Penn Central*).

- The takings cases provide "touch points" for analysis and not easy answers. We have factors to consider in our analysis, but takings cases are fact specific.

- In the situation of an exaction, we must apply *Nollan, Dolan*, and *Koontz*. In the standard takings case, not involving an exaction, we basically still follow the balancing test of *Penn Central*, or the per se rules of *Lucas*.

# R. Right to Exclude

The *Cedar Point* case that follows raises an interesting question about whether the *Penn Central* balancing test applies to an access regulation that grants labor organizations a right to invade a landowner's property, or whether such a regulation constitutes a *per se* physical taking.

## Cedar Point Nursery v. Hassid

Supreme Court of the United States
141 S. Ct. 2063 (2021)

ROBERTS, Chief Justice. A California regulation grants labor organizations a "right to take access" to an agricultural employer's property in order to solicit support for unionization. Cal. Code Regs., tit. 8, § 20900(e)(1)(C) (2020). Agricultural employers must allow union organizers onto their property for up to three hours per day, 120 days per year. The question presented is whether the access regulation constitutes a *per se* physical taking under the Fifth and Fourteenth Amendments.

### I

The California Agricultural Labor Relations Act of 1975 gives agricultural employees a right to self-organization and makes it an unfair labor practice for employers to interfere with that right. Cal. Lab. Code Ann. §§ 1152, 1153(a) (West 2020). The state Agricultural Labor Relations Board [(the "Board")] has promulgated a regulation providing, in its current form, that the self-organization rights of employees include "the right of access by union organizers to the premises of an agricultural employer for the purpose of meeting and talking with employees and soliciting their support." Under the regulation, a labor organization may "take access" to an agricultural employer's property for up to four 30-day periods in one calendar year. §§ 20900(e)(1)(A). . . . Two organizers per work crew . . . may enter the employer's property for up to one hour before work, one hour during the lunch break, and one hour after work. . . . Interference with organizers' right of access may constitute an unfair labor practice, which can result in sanctions against the employer.

Cedar Point Nursery is a strawberry grower in northern California. It employs over 400 seasonal workers and around 100 full-time workers, none of whom live on the property. [M]embers of the United Farm Workers entered Cedar Point's property without prior notice. . . . Calling through bullhorns, the organizers disturbed operations, causing some workers to join the organizers in a protest and others to leave the worksite altogether. . . .

Fowler Packing Company is a Fresno-based grower and shipper of table grapes and citrus. It has 1,800 to 2,500 employees in its field operations and around 500 in its packing facility. As with Cedar Point, none of Fowler's workers live on the premises. In July 2015, organizers from the United Farm Workers attempted to take access to Fowler's property, but the company blocked them from entering. . . .

Believing that the union would likely attempt to enter their property again in the near future, the growers filed suit in Federal District Court. . . . The growers argued that the access regulation effected an unconstitutional *per se* physical taking under the Fifth and Fourteenth Amendments by appropriating without compensation an easement for union organizers to enter their property. . . .

The District Court denied the growers' motion for a preliminary injunction. . . . The court rejected the growers' argument that the access regulation constituted a *per se* physical taking, reasoning that it did not "allow the public to access their property in a permanent and continuous manner for whatever reason."

. . . In the court's view, the regulation was instead subject to evaluation under the multifactor balancing test of *Penn Central Transportation Co. v. New York City*, 438 U.S. 104 (1978), which the growers had made no attempt to satisfy.

A divided panel of the Court of Appeals for the Ninth Circuit affirmed. The court identified three categories of regulatory actions in takings jurisprudence: regulations that impose permanent physical invasions, regulations that deprive an owner of all economically beneficial use of his property, and the remainder of regulatory actions. On the court's understanding, while regulations in the first two categories constitute *per se* takings, those in the third must be evaluated under *Penn Central*. 923 F.3d, at 531.

. . . .

The Ninth Circuit denied rehearing en banc. Judge Ikuta dissented, joined by seven other judges. She reasoned that the access regulation appropriated from the growers a traditional form of private property — an easement in gross — and transferred that property to union organizers. The appropriation of such an easement, she concluded, constituted a *per se* physical taking under the precedents of this Court. *Id.*, at 1168.

We granted certiorari. 592 U.S. __ (2020).

## II

### A

The Takings Clause of the Fifth Amendment, applicable to the States through the Fourteenth Amendment, provides: "[N]or shall private property be taken for public use, without just compensation." The Founders recognized that the protection of private property is indispensable to the promotion of individual freedom. As John Adams tersely put it, "[p]roperty must be secured, or liberty cannot exist." Discourses on Davila, in 6 Works of John Adams 280 (C. Adams ed. 1851). This Court agrees, having noted that protection of property rights is "necessary to preserve freedom" and "empowers persons to shape and to plan their own destiny in a world where governments are always eager to do so for them." *Murr v. Wisconsin*, 582 U.S.__, __ (2017) (slip op., at 8).

When the government physically acquires private property for a public use, the Takings Clause imposes a clear and categorical obligation to provide the owner with just compensation. *Tahoe-Sierra Preservation Council, Inc. v. Tahoe Regional Planning Agency*, 535 U.S. 302, 321 (2002). The Court's physical takings jurisprudence is "as old as the Republic." *Id.*, at 322. The government commits a physical taking when it uses its power of eminent domain to formally condemn property. See *United States v. General Motors Corp.*, 323 U.S. 373, 374–375 (1945); *United States ex rel. TVA v. Powelson*, 319 U.S. 266, 270–271 (1943). The same is true when the government physically takes possession of property without acquiring title to it. See *United States v. Pewee Coal Co.*, 341 U.S. 114, 115–117 (1951) (plurality opinion). And the government likewise effects a physical taking when it occupies property — say, by recurring flooding as a result of building a dam. See *United States v. Cress*, 243 U.S. 316, 327–328 (1917). These sorts of physical appropriations constitute the "clearest sort of taking," *Palazzolo v. Rhode Island*, 533 U.S. 606, 617 (2001), and we assess them using a simple, *per se* rule: The government must pay for what it takes. See *Tahoe-Sierra*, 535 U.S., at 322.

When the government, rather than appropriating private property for itself or a third party, instead imposes regulations that restrict an owner's ability to use his own property, a different standard applies. *Id.*, at 321–322. Our jurisprudence governing such use restrictions has developed more recently. Before the 20th century, the Takings Clause was understood to be limited to physical appropriations of property. See *Horne v. Department of Agriculture*, 576 U.S. 351, 360 (2015) .... In *Pennsylvania Coal Co. v. Mahon*, 260 U.S. 393 (1922), however, the Court established the proposition that "while property may be regulated to a certain extent, if regulation goes too far it will be recognized as a taking." *Id.*, at 415. This framework now applies to use restrictions as varied as zoning ordinances, *Village of Euclid v. Ambler Realty Co.*, 272 U.S. 365, 387–388 (1926), orders barring the mining of gold, *United States v. Central Eureka Mining Co.*, 357 U.S. 155, 168 (1958), and regulations prohibiting the sale of eagle feathers, *Andrus v. Allard*, 444 U.S. 51, 65–66 (1979). To determine whether a use restriction effects a taking, this Court has generally applied the flexible test developed in *Penn Central*, balancing factors such as the economic impact of the regulation, its interference with reasonable investment-backed expectations, and the character of the government action. 438 U.S., at 124.

Our cases have often described use restrictions that go "too far" as "regulatory takings." But that label can mislead. Government action that physically appropriates property is no less a physical taking because it arises from a regulation. That explains why we held that an administrative reserve requirement compelling raisin growers to physically set aside a percentage of their crop for the government constituted a physical rather than a regulatory taking. *Horne*, 576 U.S., at 361. The essential question is not, as the Ninth Circuit seemed to think, whether the government action at issue comes garbed as a regulation (or statute, or ordinance, or miscellaneous decree). It is whether the government has physically taken property for itself or someone else — by whatever means — or has instead restricted a property owner's ability to use his own property. See *Tahoe-Sierra*, 535 U.S., at 321–323.

Whenever a regulation results in a physical appropriation of property, a *per se* taking has occurred, and *Penn Central* has no place.

## B

The access regulation appropriates a right to invade the growers' property and therefore constitutes a *per se* physical taking. The regulation grants union organizers a right to physically enter and occupy the growers' land for three hours per day, 120 days per year. Rather than restraining the growers' use of their own property, the regulation appropriates for the enjoyment of third parties the owners' right to exclude.

The right to exclude is "one of the most treasured" rights of property ownership. *Loretto v. Teleprompter Manhattan CATV Corp.*, 458 U.S. 419, 435 (1982). According to Blackstone, the very idea of property entails "that sole and despotic dominion which one man claims and exercises over the external things of the world, in total exclusion of the right of any other individual in the universe." 2 W. Blackstone, Commentaries on the Laws of England 2 (1766). In less exuberant terms, we have stated that the right to exclude is "universally held to be a fundamental element of the property right," and is "one of the most essential sticks in the bundle of rights that are commonly characterized as property."

Given the central importance to property ownership of the right to exclude, it comes as little surprise that the Court has long treated government-authorized physical invasions as takings requiring just compensation. The Court has often described the property interest taken as a servitude or an easement....

In *Loretto v. Teleprompter Manhattan CATV Corp.*, we made clear that a permanent physical occupation constitutes a *per se* taking regardless of whether it results in only a trivial economic loss....

We reiterated that the appropriation of an easement constitutes a physical taking in *Nollan v. California Coastal Commission*. The Nollans sought a permit to build a larger home on their beachfront lot. 483 U.S., at 828. The California Coastal Commission issued the permit subject to the condition that the Nollans grant the public an easement to pass through their property along the beach. *Ibid.* As a starting point to our analysis, we explained that, had the Commission simply required the Nollans to grant the public an easement across their property, "we have no doubt there would have been a taking." *Id.*, at 831; see also *Dolan*, 512 U.S., at 384 (holding that compelled dedication of an easement for public use would constitute a taking)....

The upshot of this line of precedent is that government-authorized invasions of property — whether by plane, boat, cable, or beachcomber — are physical takings requiring just compensation. As in those cases, the government here has appropriated a right of access to the growers' property, allowing union organizers to traverse it at will for three hours a day, 120 days a year. The regulation appropriates a right to physically invade the growers' property — to literally "take access," as the regulation provides. It is therefore a *per se* physical taking under our precedents. Accordingly, the growers' complaint states a claim for an uncompensated taking in violation of the Fifth and Fourteenth Amendments. . . .

There is no reason the law should analyze an abrogation of the right to exclude in one manner if it extends for 365 days, but in an entirely different manner if it lasts for 364. . . . The duration of an appropriation — just like the size of an appropriation, bears only on the amount of compensation. . . . .

Next, we have recognized that physical invasions constitute takings even if they are intermittent as opposed to continuous. And while *Nollan* happened to involve a legally continuous right of access, we have no doubt that the Court would have reached the same conclusion if the easement demanded by the Commission had lasted for only 364 days per year. After all, the easement was hardly continuous as a practical matter. As Justice Brennan observed in dissent, given the shifting tides, "public passage for a portion of the year would either be impossible or would not occur on [the Nollans'] property." 483 U.S., at 854. What matters is not that the easement notionally ran round the clock, but that the government had taken a right to physically invade the Nollans' land. And when the government physically takes an interest in property, it must pay for the right to do so. The fact that a right to take access is exercised only from time to time does not make it any less a physical taking. . . .

The Board also takes issue with the growers' premise that the access regulation appropriates an easement. In the Board's estimation, the regulation does not exact a true easement in gross under California law because the access right may not be transferred, does not burden any particular parcel of property, and may not be recorded. This, the Board says, reinforces its conclusion that the regulation does not take a constitutionally protected property interest from the growers. The dissent agrees, suggesting that the access right cannot affect a *per se* taking because it does not require the growers to grant the union organizers an easement as defined by state property law.

These arguments misconstrue our physical takings doctrine. As a general matter, it is true that the property rights protected by the Takings Clause are creatures of state law. But no one disputes that, without the access regulation, the growers would have had the right under California law to exclude union organizers from their property. And no one disputes that the access regulation took that right from them. The Board cannot absolve itself of takings liability by appropriating the growers' right to exclude in a form that is a slight mismatch from state easement law. Under the Constitution, property rights "cannot be so easily manipulated."

Our decisions consistently reflect this intuitive approach. We have recognized that the government can commit a physical taking either by appropriating property through a condemnation proceeding or by simply "enter[ing] into physical possession of property without authority of a court order."

. . . .

Restrictions on how a business generally open to the public may treat individuals on the premises are readily distinguishable from regulations granting a right to invade property closed to the public.

. . . .

In "ordinary English" "appropriation" means "*taking* as one's own," 1 Oxford English Dictionary 587 (2d ed. 1989) (emphasis added), and the regulation expressly grants to labor organizers the "right to *take* access," Cal. Code Regs., tit. 8, § 20900(e)(1)(C) (emphasis added). We cannot agree that the right to exclude is an empty formality, subject to modification at the government's pleasure. On the contrary, it is a "fundamental element of the property right," *Kaiser Aetna* [*v. United States*], 444 U.S., at 179–180, that cannot be balanced away. Our cases establish that appropriations of a right to invade are *per se* physical takings, not use restrictions subject to *Penn Central*: . . . With regard to the complexities of modern society, we think they only reinforce the importance of safeguarding the basic property rights that help preserve individual liberty. . . .

. . . .

. . . [T]he government may require property owners to cede a right of access as a condition of receiving certain benefits, without causing a taking. In *Nollan*, we held that "a permit condition that serves the same legitimate police- power purpose as a refusal to issue the permit should not be found to be a taking if the refusal to issue the permit would not constitute a taking." 483 U.S., at 836. The inquiry, we later explained, is whether the permit condition bears an "essential nexus" and "rough proportionality" to the impact of the proposed use of the property. *Dolan*, 512 U.S., at 386, 391; see also *Koontz v. St. Johns River Water Management Dist.*, 570 U.S. 595, 599 (2013).

Under this framework, government health and safety inspection regimes will generally not constitute takings. See, *e.g.*, *Ruckelshaus v. Monsanto Co.*, 467 U.S. 986, 1007 (1984). When the government conditions the grant of a benefit such as a permit, license, or registration on allowing access for reasonable health and safety inspections, both the nexus and rough proportionality requirements of the constitutional conditions framework should not be difficult to satisfy.

. . . .

None of these considerations undermine our determination that the access regulation here gives rise to a *per se* physical taking. Unlike a mere trespass, the regulation grants a formal entitlement to physically invade the growers' land. Unlike a law enforcement search, no traditional background principle of property law requires the growers to admit union organizers onto their premises. And unlike standard health and safety inspections, the access regulation is not germane to any benefit provided to agricultural employers or any risk posed to the public. . . .

The access regulation grants labor organizations a right to invade the growers' property. It therefore constitutes a *per se* physical taking.

The judgment of the United States Court of Appeals for the Ninth Circuit is reversed, and the case is remanded for further proceedings consistent with this opinion.

*It is so ordered.*

KAVANAUGH, J. (concurring). I join the Court's opinion, which carefully adheres to constitutional text, history, and precedent. . . .

BREYER, J. (dissenting). A California regulation provides that representatives of a labor organization may enter an agricultural employer's property for purposes of union organizing. They may do so during four months of the year, one hour before the start of work, one hour during an employee lunch break, and one hour after work. The question before us is how to characterize this regulation for purposes of the Constitution's Takings Clause.

Does the regulation *physically appropriate* the employers' property? If so, there is no need to look further; the Government must pay the employers "just compensation." . . . Or does the regulation simply *regulate* the employers' property rights? If so, then there is every need to look further; the government need pay the employers "just compensation" only if the regulation "goes too far." *Pennsylvania Coal Co. v. Mahon*, 260 U.S. 393, 415 (1922) (Holmes, J., for the Court); see also *Penn Central Transp. Co. v. New York City*, 438 U.S. 104, 124 (1978) (determining whether a regulation is a taking by examining the regulation's "economic impact," the extent of interference with "investment-backed expectations," and the "character of the governmental action"); . . .

The Court holds that the provision's "access to organizers" requirement amounts to a physical appropriation of property. . . . But this regulation does not "appropriate" anything; it regulates the employers' right to exclude others. . . . In my view, the majority's conclusion threatens to make many ordinary forms of regulation unusually complex or impractical. . . . With respect, I dissent from the majority's conclusion that the regulation is a *per se* taking. . . .

## *Questions for Consideration*

1) The dissent in this case argues that the law in question is a *regulation* respecting how property owners use their property. The regulation permits farm workers to learn about their rights to be unionized by giving access to union organizers. The workers do not live at the location, so presumably, the best and easiest way to reach them with information about the union is at the job location. If the union has no access to the land, how will workers learn of their rights to organize?

2) Should the right of the farm workers to learn about the union in an easy and convenient way trump the rights of the property owners?

3) Are property owners excluding *people* from their property or excluding the *information* that farm workers need to exercise their right to join a union?

4) The dissent says that this case involves a land regulation. As a regulation on the use of land, the *Penn Central* balancing test for determining a taking is applicable. What arguments are used by the majority to frame the case as something other than a land use regulation?

5) We know what the majority held in this case, but are you persuaded that they got the correct result? Why or why not?

6) If the regulation provided that only on one day each year, union organizers were to have access to the land of the growers for the purpose of speaking to farm workers about joining the union, would this be a taking? Under what analysis would it be a taking?

7) Would it make a difference to your analysis if you learned that the growers (property owners) were receiving federal agricultural subsidies to grow and harvest their crops? Should this make a difference to the rights of property ownership?

8) What if in Question 7, above, the receiving of federal agricultural subsidies was conditioned on granting access to the property? That is, property owners/ growers that do not take a subsidy do not have to permit access, but if they take a subsidy, then they have to grant access to union organizers.

9) If the Court had been persuaded to use the *Penn Central* balancing test to determine a taking in this case, what outcome do you predict from such an approach?

## *Takeaway*

- The Constitution protects property rights, but property rights are defined by state law. This is important to keep in mind. This is why the Court in *Cedar Point* has to make a determination with respect to the state law definition of an easement. Although the federal courts may bring an interpretive perspective to reading state law, they should, nonetheless, follow state law with respect to the legal definition of property.

- Property ownership generally involves several characteristics. Ownership includes 1) the rights of use and possession, 2) the right to exclude others, 3) the right to transfer the property, and 4) the right to the profits of ownership. When we analyze a takings claim, we should be thinking about these various aspects of the protected right to property. In this case, the Court is focused on the right to exclude. The Court reiterates a long-standing position of the common law that the most important of these rights of ownership is the right to exclude others.

- Note one of the difficulties with this case; the taking is based on a regulation. This is not the case of the government needing to acquire property for a school, a road, a water project, or such. This case involves a government regulation that affects the property owner's use and control of its land. Regulations regarding use are typically addressed using the *Penn Central* balancing test. This is the way that the dissent frames the case. The majority looks more closely at what it sees as the practical effects of the regulation and frames the case as one that eliminates the fundamental right of an owner to exclude others from one's property. As lawyers, it is important to think carefully about how to frame a case. Here, three Justices were persuaded by framing this as a regulation on use governed by *Penn Central*, thus the case was not an easy one even though the majority framed the case differently. As a practice skill, we must learn to frame and reframe a case in ways that best implicate legal rules and outcomes that will favor our clients.

- In a takings case, it is important to keep in mind that the degree of injury and the duration of the injury may go to the determination of just compensation, but they are not per se determinative as to the finding of a taking.

## Discussion Problem 6.6

Frankie owns a small pizza shop in East City. East City is located in a region of the country that experiences all four seasons in terms of dramatically different outdoor temperatures at different times of the year. The pizza shop is located in an old and somewhat run-down neighborhood, but it is located along the waterfront of a nice freshwater lake. The lake is popular with residents and the few tourists that come through town each year. East City is hoping to improve the image of the city as a nice place to live and to visit by expanding access points to the lake and improving the beaches. Frankie's Pizza is on the water and near a location where the city wishes to build up a new beach for swimming and recreational use. The city hopes to acquire easements for people to access the water and the beach by having waterfront property owners grant the city easements for pedestrian access from the nearby road to the water. The problem is that it will be very expensive for the city to acquire these easement rights if they have to purchase them from property owners at a fair market price. Frankie's location, and that of several other local restaurants, are in ideal locations for the placement of pedestrian access easements to the water.

The pizza shop has been in its current location for 20 years. As part of the city plan to improve the beaches and waterfront access, it passes a new zoning code changing the zoning in the neighborhood from one that permits restaurants and small businesses to one restricted to residential uses. No commercial uses are allowed under the new code. Frankie is allowed to operate for a limited time period under a "grandfather" provision in the local code. The code, consistent with state law, provides for the amortization of non-conforming uses. This means that non-conforming uses such as Frankie's pizza shop can be eliminated under the code over a period of time. East City set its amortization provision at 5 years. This time period applies to all uses on all properties abutting the waterfront in the entire city. Every property owner faced with a zoning change that makes the current use non-conforming is given a 5-year amortization schedule. At the end of five years, the non-conforming use must cease and the use of the property repurposed consistent with the current code. In actuality, even though this new code applies to every property on the waterfront, in fact, it actually only affects Frankie and two other property owners. There is a condition in the new zoning code that provides for a variance from the amortization provisions for a property owner who executes a "right of access agreement" in favor of the city for purposes of permitting pedestrian access to the waterfront by passing over the owner's property. This right of access would permit pedestrians to walk from the road to the waterfront and the beach. The exact location of the right of access would be determined in a process of site plan review, and would be placed along a lot line in a way that seeks to minimize interference with a property owner's lawful use of the property. The right of access provision does not require the property owner to formally grant an easement to the city.

The city explains that given the climate of East City, actual use of the beaches and the right of access will likely be limited to a three-month period during the year. This is when temperatures are high enough and the water warm enough to make swimming and water recreation appealing to most potential users. The city also points out that people will just be walking along the right of access to get to the water; the right of access is for temporary passage to the waterfront and back, it is not for purposes of permanently occupying the land.

Frankie's wife has recently been diagnosed with cancer, and Frankie needs money. He needs to keep operating his business, which remains popular with people in the neighborhood. He discusses the situation with city planners and zoning officials. They tell Frankie that it is up to him. Frankie can simply grant the city the easement it seeks, and keep operating his pizza business, or Frankie can conclude his business operations at the end of the 5-year amortization period. Under stress from dealing with his business and his wife's health issues, Frankie feels he has to grant the city the requested easement.

In this case, explain how an amortization provision works and opine as to the fairness of the way this amortization provision is applied here and across the city. Is there a potential claim for a taking in violation of the Fifth Amendment to the U.S. Constitution? Is the amortization unconstitutional? Is the condition for a variance unconstitutional?

# S. Dillon Rule, Home Rule, and the Police Power

As discussed in this book, the police power to regulate land use is generally vested in the 50 state governments. The states in turn may delegate some of their police power to local municipalities. This is either done in the state constitution or in state statutes. One approach to delegation is illustrated by the *Dillon Rule*. The Dillon Rule is named after Justice John F. Dillon of the Iowa Supreme Court. In the 1868 case of *City of Clinton v. The Cedar Rapids & Missouri River Railroad Co.*, 24 Iowa 455, Justice Dillon explained that as the police power is vested in the states, the subsequent delegation of state police power to local governments should be narrowly construed. In essence, the delegation should only include powers expressly delegated to the local government, powers necessarily implied by the express delegation, and those essential for the local government to carry out the goals and objectives of the delegation. The Dillon Rule was approved in a decision by the U.S. Supreme Court in *Hunter v. City of Pittsburg*, 207 U.S. 161 (1907) and has been debated in multiple cases since.

In contrast to the Dillon Rule, many states have a broader and more permissive view of delegation. In the permissive view, local governments are presumed to be acting within their delegated authority unless the language of the delegation limits or prohibits the local government's actions. The permissive view of delegation is often related to the concept of *home rule*. The idea of home rule is that local governments are presumed to have the authority to properly exercise the delegated police power from the state with minimal or no interference. Some states grant home rule power to all municipalities in the state while others expressly limit it to designated cities of a certain size and population. Home rule authority will usually be expressed in a state constitution or in state statutes.

# T. Alternatives to Euclidean Planning and Zoning

A baseline for understanding planning and zoning is our traditional reference to Euclidean zoning. You can refer back to the case of *Village of Euclid v. Ambler Realty Co*, in Chapter 3, *supra* to refresh yourself on the case and the notes that follow it. In the notes we identify the traditional characteristics of Euclidean zoning. Most importantly, this method of planning and zoning is based on dividing a jurisdiction into zones. These zones identify permitted and prohibited uses. The goal is to separate and mange uses so as to advance the public health, safety, welfare, and morals. Over the years, people have complained that strict Euclidean zoning lacks flexibility and as a result modifications have been introduced in many zoning codes. For example, we explain that such things as conditional zoning, floating zones, and mixed-use zones, are zoning approaches that modify traditional Euclidean zoning. Referencing back to the standard characteristics of Euclidean zoning discussed in Chapter 3, is useful for understanding contemporary zoning and the ways in which zoning has evolved since the *Euclid* decision in 1926.

In addition to changes in zoning codes over time, there have been changes in the way land planners approach their work. As zoning lawyers, we focus on the language and requirements of the zoning code no matter what approach is taken by our local planning office. Nonetheless, different approaches to planning may influence what we do in zoning. Therefore, it is helpful to have some familiarity with a few new zoning terms and with the basics of a few contemporary planning alternatives.

- *Performance zoning.* This type of zoning focuses on specifically defined performance standards as a more flexible way of regulating uses. For example, instead of describing the various types of uses that can be made in a given industrial zone, the code might describe the permitted noise levels of operation, intensity of use, impact of lighting on nearby properties, and requirements for containment of water run-off in the zone. A use that meets the performance standard would be allowed in the zone. Thus, instead of developing a list of specific permitted uses, the code would develop a list of performance standards for uses in the zone. Uses typically must also be consistent with the character of the neighborhood or surrounding properties.

- *Concurrency.* This concept requires development of land uses to match the ability of local governments to service the uses. Thus, development of single-family residential subdivisions should occur at a rate that is consistent with development of expanding roads, water and sewer lines, schools, and other public services such as police and fire protection. Concurrency is a way to manage growth. Local governments, however, may not prevent development by simply refusing to approve needed and related infrastructure.

- *New Urbanism.* In general, new urbanism focuses on promoting walkable communities with mixed uses including housing and retail, transportation alternatives to the automobile, increased density, green spaces, and the bringing of structures closer to the streetscape while placing parking lots behind buildings to create a greater sense of a neighborhood.

- *Form-Based Zoning.* Instead of focusing on uses, as in Euclidean zoning, form-based zoning centers on the importance of buildings and streetscapes in determining the character and livability of a community. Thus, planning considers the public facades of buildings, the bulk, mass and placement of buildings in connection to other buildings, the streetscape, and open space among and between buildings. In general, controlling the style, features, and placements of structures becomes more important than regulating the particular uses within these structures.

- *Transect Zoning.* This is generally used with form-based zoning. Basically, it involves looking at the jurisdictional landscape of a community and dividing it into transitional zones where a form-based zoning approach can be used to create a hierarchy of uses going from the most natural or rural uses to the more dense and intense uses of an urban center. Transect zones might include zones identified in a hierarchical form ranging from natural habitat, rural, suburban, general urban, urban center, to urban core. In each transect zone, form-based zoning would address the intensity and density of structures, and shape a landscape designed to facilitate a sense of community, neighborhood, and connectivity.

In practice, a given jurisdiction may have elements of several approaches to planning and these may all be reflected in elements of their zoning code.

# U. Preemption

In a legal system such as that of the United States, there are at times questions about controlling law as to a legal question or dispute when there are inconsistencies among laws enacted by different levels of government. For example, if a state law conflicts with a local zoning ordinance, or if a federal law conflicts with a state or local ordinance. The issue is one of legal hierarchy. State law can be supreme within the jurisdiction of the state, and federal law is the supreme law of the country. When there is a conflict among these different levels of the legal hierarchy, which controls? In terms of preemption, the question to be asked is—does a law enacted by the higher legal authority control in the situation of an apparent conflict? It does if there actually is preemption by that higher authority, but not if the law in question leaves room for the other law to operate. In other words, one must determine if the higher legal authority intended to take over regulatory control of the subject matter and eliminate the prerogative of inferior law-making bodies to regulate.

For example, a state may pass legislation governing the regulation of land uses with respect to the cultivation and retail sale of marijuana. At the same time a local municipality may have a zoning regulation prohibiting all cultivation and retail sales of marijuana within its jurisdiction. A property owner seeking to use its property for the cultivation or retail sale of marijuana may challenge the local zoning ordinance preventing this use based on the state regulation that seems to permit it. The local municipality may assert that the state regulation applies to regulate the subject matter where the activity is permitted, but the local community has the authority under its police power to simply exclude the uses from its jurisdiction. The preemption question is one of determining if the state regulation occupies the field, that is, covers the entire legal domain as to these identified uses, or does it leave room for local regulation.

A similar issue arises with respect to federal regulation. When the federal government has statutory authority to protect wetlands, clean air, and clean water, do local governments retain any authority to regulate in these areas? If the field is preempted, it means that the federal government has eliminated the authority of local governments to regulate. This is sometimes the case. Often, however, the preemption will be limited. For example, the federal government may pass regulations that require every community to include cell towers for cell phone use, while permitting local authorities to have some input on the exact location of the towers within certain guidelines established by the federal regulations.

Preemption is an issue that sometimes comes up in a local zoning practice. In general, however, preemption is a legal issue arising when there are conflicts with federal regulation rather than when dealing with the legal problems that arise under local planning and zoning laws.

# V. Practice Problems

6.1 Attend a day of hearings at your local zoning board of appeal (ZBA). A ZBA hearing is functionally a local administrative "court" proceeding. In the standard situation, a property owner petitions the ZBA when she has been denied the right to use her property in a way that she desires. Typically, a property owner petitions the ZBA seeking an exception to the local land regulations (the exception is a *variance*). In this proceeding, the property owner is entitled to *due process* rights that include presenting evidence, bringing in witnesses, challenging counter evidence or witnesses, and being able to review a record of the proceeding. The ZBA listens to the oral presentations, and reviews the evidence on the record against legal criteria, and the provisions of the land regulations contained in the zoning code. The ZBA members discuss the evidence and the criteria, and then they vote on granting or denying the petition. A decision is rendered by the ZBA, and a written version of the decision is made available to the petitioner and to the public. If a property owner or a person with standing is not satisfied with the decision, she can appeal the decision to a court.

As a student of land use and zoning law, your assignment is to attend a local ZBA meeting and prepare a 2–4 page report on your experience. In your report, you must address the items listed below.

a) The meeting I attended was in the Town of/City of: _____. Date, Time, and Place of the meeting: _____.

b) The name of the Chairperson of the ZBA is: _____. The number of ZBA members is: _____. The ZBA was represented by an attorney (Yes/No), name: _____.

c) The property owner petitioning the ZBA was seeking what kind of an action/outcome? (Identify for each petition in front of the ZBA.)

d) The property owner petitioning the ZBA was self-represented (Yes/No) or was represented by what kind of person? (Attorney, architect, landscaper, sign company representative, engineer, other (identify). (Identify for each petition in front of the ZBA.)

e) What kind of evidence was presented to and examined by the ZBA at the meeting? (Oral testimony, written testimony, maps, survey, drawings, Google maps, photos, letters, etc.) (Identify for each petition in front of the ZBA.)

f) Did anyone speak in support of the property owner/petitioner? (Identify for each petition in front of the ZBA.)

g) Did anyone speak against the property owner/petitioner? (Identify for each petition in front of the ZBA.)

h) What was the ZBA decision in each case that was presented? (Grant, deny, condition, continuance, dismiss?)

i) In a paragraph, provide your personal reflection on what you observed.

6.2 Assume you have a solo law practice, and you are contacted by Paul and Ann. Paul and Ann own a single-family residential home in the nearby city of Sunnyville. They seek your legal assistance in fighting a zoning enforcement action by the local city attorney. Paul and Ann both enjoy cooking and sharing their cooking with others. As background, they inform you that their home is located in an R-1 zoning district. The R-1 district only permits one and two-story single-family residences on half-acre lots. Paul and Ann usually spend their weekend evenings preparing classic Italian dishes and enjoying fine Italian wines. About six months ago, they signed up with a new venture called "Dine-In." This company is internet-based and facilitates the matching of people willing to serve specialty dinners with small groups of people looking for a new dining experience. Under the arrangement, Paul and Ann prepare and serve meals at their home for four to six guests on Friday and Saturday nights three weeks out of each month. Guests make reservations via Dine-In. Guests must register with Dine-In to use its app and to book and pay for any meals. Consequently, guests cannot simply be anyone who walks in off the street. The meals offered by Paul and Ann include wine, a pre-set menu, and are priced at a flat fee of $60 per guest, with Dine-In receiving 10% for its services. One sitting is offered each evening, and guests enjoy drinks and appetizers while food is prepared fresh as part of the dining experience. The meal runs between the hours of 8–11:00 PM. Paul and Ann have been doing this successfully in their home for five months.

Recently, a neighbor of Paul and Ann made a complaint to the Sunnyville Zoning Code Enforcement Office. The complaint stated that Paul and Ann are illegally operating a restaurant in a single-family residential zone. The complaint demanded that the City enforce the zoning code and prevent Paul and Ann from continuing this activity. After looking into this issue on-line, the city attorney observed that this type of activity is occurring in a number of cities across the country. This is the first complaint of this type filed in Sunnyville. Paul and Ann argue that cooking and serving dinner to guests is a customary and permitted use of a single-family home.

a) Using your knowledge of zoning law, address the issues raised by Dine-In and address the legal arguments likely to be raised in pursuing the complaint against Paul and Ann.

b) Considering the way that Dine-In operates, do you think that Paul and Ann may be using their home as a place of public accommodation as defined under Title III of the ADA? If so, does their home have to be ADA compliant with respect to accessibility (at a minimum having an accessible front door entrance, bathroom, and dining area)?

6.3 Carlos owns a one-quarter acre lot on the south shore of Lake Ontario in the town of Lakeview in the central region of New York State. The lot currently has a small 800 square foot home on it that was built in the 1950s. The current zoning code permits homes of up to 1,800 square feet to be constructed on all lots of at least a one-quarter acre. Under an ordinance enacted a year earlier, any permits issued for new or expanded construction are conditioned on paying a Lakeview Restoration fee equal to 5% of the cost of the new construction. The fee is set at 5% of the cost of new construction because the Lakeview Town Board determined that larger construction projects have a greater impact on the lakeshore than smaller ones. Thus, larger projects pay the same rate but contribute more to the Restoration fund. The Restoration fund actually uses the fees collected in two different ways. First, pursuant to an approved plan to protect and restore the shoreline of this part of Lake Ontario, three percent of the fee is used for shoreline restoration, control of water run-off, and protection of ecosystem habitat. The other two percent of the fee is used for restoration of a historic hotel in downtown Lakeview. The hotel restoration project is designed to improve tourism to Lakeview by providing a beautiful and comfortable place for people to stay when visiting Lakeview and the south shore of Lake Ontario. Town officials believe that increased tourism will benefit everyone in the community.

Currently, the shoreline of Lakeview consists of properties similar to that owned by Carlos. Lots in the area range from one-quarter acre to a full one acre in size, and the homes on them date from the 1950s and early 1960s. All are small camp style homes. In recent years, new owners have undertaken home improvements and have been expanding the size of the homes or constructing new and bigger homes on the lots. In response to the desire for bigger homes, Lakeview adopted a comprehensive plan designed to protect the lakeshore and to control construction.

Carlos has designed a new housing structure of 1,700 square feet for his property, and he seeks a permit to take down the existing structure and replace it with a new home on the lot. He estimates the cost of his construction project at $400,000. As part of his project, Carlos is also requesting three variances. (Assume you are applying the multi-factor variance criteria of New York as set out earlier in part 'c' of this chapter.) The first variance is for a 5-foot exception to the front yard setback. In order to maximize the use of his overall lot, Carlos seeks to have the front of his house built at a point five feet closer to the edge of the road than the required setback line of 25 feet. This positioning will give him extra space on the waterfront side of his house (the back), and this will enable him to install an extra big deck in this location. The plan for the front of the house calls for a ramped entranceway to the home to accommodate his mother's use of a wheelchair. His mother will live with him at the home. The ramped entranceway will be part of the structure, and it will extend out into the setback by five feet. This is the reason for the front yard variance request of five feet. As Carlos points out, the ramp is needed because local regulations require all homes along the waterfront to be elevated by at least two feet, as a precaution against flooding. Given the two-foot elevation requirement, a ramp is needed, since it will be impossible for Carlos to construct a "zero-step" entrance way that is simply level with the ground. Carlos submits that there is no easy alternative design of the house that maximizes use of the entire lot, unless Carlos builds a smaller house of 1,300 square feet, or reduces his plans for the waterfront deck at the back of his house. Carlos proposes building a wooden ramp made of 2 × 4 lumber that will be attached to the front of his home. This is estimated to cost about $1,000. The second variance request is for an enlarged deck at the back of the house (facing the water). The purpose of the enlarged deck is to accommodate his mother's wheelchair. The zoning code permits a 300 square foot deck but Carlos is requesting 500 square feet so that his mother has more room to safely navigate the deck. The third variance is for a wooden walkway leading from the deck to the beach. Without the wooden walkway, Carlos's mother will be unable to enjoy the beach area to an extent similar to others who reside in houses along the shoreline. The wooden walkway will allow his mother to use her wheelchair to get close to the waterline and to fully experience the beauty of Lake Ontario. The zoning code does not permit a wooden walkway to the beach. This is not permitted because Lakeview seeks to keep the space between the back of a house and the beach open to facilitate natural vegetation and wildlife along the shoreline.

At the meeting of the zoning board of appeal, Carlos's variance requests are being considered. During the discussion of the merits of the petition, zoning board members decide that, if a variance for the ramp is granted, they will require the ramp to be physically attached to the home and built of high quality materials that match the color and materials currently existing on the house. Constructing such a ramp would cost about $4,000. In addition, the members of the zoning board discuss other issues related to the ramp, deck, and the wooden walkway. Assume you are the Lakeview town attorney.

a) As part of the zoning board's deliberation, the chair of the zoning board asks you, the Lakeview town attorney, to explain the legal requirements that guide their decision on each of the variance requests, using the New York criteria for evaluating such petitions. Opine as to the merits of each requested variance under the criteria.

b) In the alternative, the zoning board would like to know if they deny the variances in Carlos's petition, would they nonetheless need to permit any or all of his requests as a reasonable accommodation (modification) given that his mother resides with him at his home? Furthermore, they want to know if they approve the front entrance ramp as a reasonable accommodation, can they require Carlos to spend more than he wants to by imposing certain design criteria that will raise the cost of building the ramp from $1,000 to $4,000; and, can they require him to remove the ramp when his mother no longer resides at the property?

c) During his oral presentation at the zoning board hearing, Carlos asserted that the 5% restoration fee being assessed as a condition to issuance of a building permit amounted to an unlawful taking of property. Members of the zoning board of appeal express some doubt that this claim is valid but ask for your opinion regarding the potential merits of his claim should he or any other property owner decide to pursue the matter in court.

# Appendix

## Part I

### Primer on Disability Law*

This Primer will guide the reader through the key provisions of the Americans with Disabilities Act (ADA), the Rehabilitation Act (RHA), and the Fair Housing Act (FHA). The basic considerations for zoning are that our disability laws seek to prohibit discrimination against people with disabilities. In general, our laws do not create positive rights. In addition, most of the claims made by and on behalf of people with disabilities are made under the primary sources of federal regulation and not directly on constitutional grounds. Finally, many of our disability laws are not absolute and many require a cost-conscious approach to application. For example, <u>new construction and alterations</u> to existing structures and facilities must be fully accessible, <u>unless</u> doing so is *structurally impracticable*. A request for a <u>reasonable accommodation or a reasonable modification</u> requires a *cost-benefit analysis* as part of determining reasonableness. In <u>making programs, services, and activities</u> of local government accessible to people with disabilities, a defense is available to the extent that greater accessibility imposes an *undue financial or administrative burden*. Likewise, consider the requirement to update older buildings and structures. In seeking to remove barriers to accessibility, a party may defend against <u>removal of a pre-existing barrier</u> if removal is not *readily achievable*.

**Primary Sources of Federal Regulation:** The primary sources of federal regulation with respect to disability law are identified below.

- *Architectural Barriers Act of 1968.*[1] The Architectural Barriers Act (ABA) requires that buildings and facilities designed, constructed, altered, or leased with certain federal funds, after September 1969, must be accessible to and useable by people with disabilities. It addresses construction-based standards of accessibility for new and renovated buildings, rather than the services or programs

---

* This Primer is taken from Robin Paul Malloy, *A Primer on Disability for Land Use and Zoning Law*, 4 JOURNAL OF LAW, PROPERTY, AND SOCIETY 1-43 (2018). For additional references supporting this Primer, see ROBIN PAUL MALLOY, DISABILITY LAW FOR PROPERTY, LAND USE, AND ZONING LAWYERS (ABA, 2020); ROBIN PAUL MALLOY, LAND USE LAW & DISABILITY: PLANNING AND ZONING FOR ACCESSIBLE COMMUNITIES (Cambridge University Press, 2015) (both books include materials from the original law review article).

1. Architectural Barriers Act of 1968, Pub. L. No. 90-480, 82 Stat. 718 (codified as amended at 42 U.S.C. §§ 4151-4157 (2016)).

being provided in such buildings. Private market construction of single-family housing is not covered by the ABA.

- *Section 504 of the Rehabilitation Act of 1973, codified in Section 794 of the United States Code as amended by the Rehabilitation Act of 1978 (RHA).*[2] Section 504 prohibits discrimination based on disability in any *program* or *activity* receiving federal financial assistance. Reasonable accommodations must be made for employees, and this includes the physical environment. New construction and alterations must be accessible. To the extent that Section 504 applies to housing, it covers housing programs receiving federal funding and not privately funded single-family residential housing. As to planning and zoning, the reasonable accommodation requirement under Section 504 is similar to that of the FHA, but Section 504 applies only to programs and activities receiving federal funds, while the FHA has a broader application.

- *Fair Housing Amendments Act of 1988.*[3] The FHA prohibits discrimination in housing on the basis of race, color, religion, sex, national origin, familial status, and disability, and it applies to private housing, as well as publicly supported housing.[4] Activities covered include selling, advertising, leasing, and financing of housing. Zoning can also be covered. The FHA requires owners and zoning officials to make reasonable exceptions to policies and practices to afford people with disabilities an equal opportunity to obtain housing. The focus is on providing an equal opportunity to obtain housing. This may require zoning officials to grant a variance or exception to a zoning requirement, if the person with a disability can show that doing so is a reasonable accommodation and that it is necessary for the person to be afforded an equal opportunity to obtain housing. A "but for" test is used, which requires the person seeking the accommodation to demonstrate that, without the variance or exception ("but for the variance or exception"), he or she will not have an equal opportunity to obtain housing. The FHA may also require landlords to make reasonable accommodations, such as permitting a pet guide dog in an apartment when the apartment has a no pet policy. The FHA may also require a landlord to permit a tenant to make modifications to a structure in order for it to be reasonably accessible, even if the landlord's lease otherwise prohibits structural modifications. It also provides mandates for all new multi-family housing to meet specific inclusive design standards, including guidelines for common areas, entranceways, hallways, light switches, grab bars, spacing to accommodate use of a wheelchair, and other design elements.

---

2. 29 U.S.C. § 794 (2016).

3. Fair Housing Amendments Act of 1988, Pub. L. No. 100-430, 102 Stat. 1619 (codified as amended at 42 U.S.C. § 3601 (2016)) (amending Civil Rights Act of 1968, Pub. L. No. 90-284, Title VIII, 82 Stat. 81 (codified as amended at 42 U.S.C. § 3601 (2016))). (*See generally* BLOOMBERG LAW, DISABILITIES LAW MANUAL, Title III, Adam 30:3.)

4. 42 U.S.C. § 3601.

- *The Americans with Disabilities Act of 1990 (ADA).*[5] The ADA prohibits discrimination against people with disabilities in employment, state and local government services, public accommodation, and telecommunications.[6] The ADA was enacted in 1990 and signed into law by President George H.W. Bush,[7] and in 2008, President George W. Bush signed the ADA Amendment Act.[8] The ADA requires accessibility, and accessibility guidelines are published by the United States Access Board (USAB) as the AMERICANS WITH DISABILITIES ACT ACCESSIBILITY GUIDELINES (ADAAG).[9] The DOJ also has a detailed publication in relation to the 2010 ADA Standards for Accessible Design.[10]

  i) *Title I of the Americans with Disabilities Act of 1990.*[11] Under Title I, employers must provide "reasonable" accommodations to qualified employees with a disability.[12]

  ii) *Title II of the Americans with Disabilities Act of 1990.*[13] Title II prohibits discrimination based on disability in programs, services, and activities provided or made available by public entities.[14] It is designed to ensure that qualified individuals with disabilities have access to programs, services, and activities of state and local governments on a basis that is equal to that of people without disabilities. Activities of planning and zoning boards are covered under this Title. Part A of Title II covers a general range of programs, services, and activities, while Part B focuses on public transportation.

  iii) *Title III of the Americans with Disabilities Act of 1990.*[15] Title III prohibits discrimination based on disability in the provision of goods, services, facilities, privileges, advantages, or accommodations of any place of public accommodation by any person owning, leasing, or operating a place of

---

5. Americans with Disabilities Act of 1990, Pub. L. No. 101-336, 104 Stat. 327 (codified as amended at 42 U.S.C. § 12101-12213 (2016)). (*See generally*, BLOOMBERG LAW, DISABILITIES LAW MANUAL, *supra* note 3).

6. *Id.* 42 U.S.C. § 12101.

7. 136 Cong. Rec. S16,826-04 (daily ed. Oct. 23, 1990) (Presidential Approvals).

8. ADA Amendments Act of 2008, Pub. L. No. 110-325, 122 Stat. 3554 (codified as amended at 42 U.S.C. § 12101 et seq. (2016)).

9. U.S. ACCESS BD., AMERICANS WITH DISABILITIES ACT ACCESSIBILITY GUIDELINES (2002), *available at* http://www.access-board.gov/guidelines-and-standards/buildings-and-sites/about-the-ada-standards/background/adaag#2.

10. U.S. DEP'T OF JUSTICE, 2010 ADA STANDARDS FOR ACCESSIBLE DESIGN (2010), *available at* https://www.ada.gov/regs2010/2010ADAStandards/2010ADAstandards.htm.

11. Americans with Disabilities Act of 1990, Pub. L. No. 101-336, 104 Stat. 327 (codified as amended at 42 U.S.C. §§ 12111-12117 (2016)).

12. *Id.*

13. Americans with Disabilities Act of 1990, Pub. L. No. 101-336, 104 Stat. 327, 337-53 (codified as amended at 42 U.S.C. §§ 12131-12161 (2016)).

14. *Id.*

15. Americans with Disabilities Act of 1990, Pub. L. No. 101-336, 104 Stat. 327, 353-365 (codified as amended at 42 U.S.C. §§ 12181-12189 (2016)).

public accommodation.[16] Title III defines public accommodation and provides a list of examples. Private entities and property owners are considered to be operating places of public accommodation when they are open to the public.[17] Places of public accommodation are not government owned or operated, as publicly operated facilities and services are covered under Title II. A partial list of examples of places of public accommodation, for illustrative purposes, includes the following: hotels, restaurants, auditoriums, shopping malls, concert halls, retail centers, and banks. Various commercial facilities are also covered under Title III. Commercial facilities are slightly different from places of public accommodation, and while they must comply with the new construction and alteration requirements, commercial facilities do not come within the barrier removal requirements. A commercial facility might be a factory or an office building where the employees are the only people allowed in the facility, but if the facility offers tours to the public or to the extent it has areas open to accommodate a range of people, it will then be subject to the full requirements of a place of public accommodation. Private clubs are not covered by Title III, unless the club makes its facilities available to nonmembers.[18] A single-family residential house is not considered a place of public accommodation, but if there is a business operating out of part of the house, that part of the building is covered by Title III.[19] A mixed-use hotel development project with an area devoted to residential housing and an area with rooms let out as hotel rooms is subject to Title III with respect to the hotel rooms but subject to the FHA with respect to the residences.[20] A day care center or senior facility run by a church is covered by Title III, but the actual church itself has a religious exemption.[21] Title III requires facilities to be accessible following ADA Guidelines. This means that buildings and facilities need such things as ramps, lifts, accessible bathrooms, automatic doors, and readily accessible entranceways. For facilities and structures that predate 1992, barriers to accessibility need to be removed to the extent that doing so is readily achievable. When older buildings are altered, they must then be accessible to the maximum extent possible.

iv) *Title IV of The Americans with Disabilities Act.*[22] Title IV covers equal access to telecommunications systems.[23]

---

16. *Id.*

17. *Id.* §12181(7) (defining public accommodations).

18. 28 C.F.R. §36.102(e).

19. *Id.* §36.207; BLOOMBERG LAW, DISABILITIES LAW MANUAL, *supra* note 3.

20. 28 C.F.R. §36 app. C; BLOOMBERG LAW, DISABILITIES LAW MANUAL, *supra* note 3.

21. *Id.*; BLOOMBERG LAW, DISABILITIES LAW MANUAL, *supra* note 3.

22. Americans with Disabilities Act of 1990, Pub. L. No. 101-336, 104 Stat. 327, 365 (codified as amended at 42 U.S.C. §§12181-12189 (2016)).

23. *Id.*

- *Executive Order 13217.*[24] Executive Order 13217 requires federal agencies to evaluate their policies and programs to determine if any can be revised or modified to improve the availability of community-based living arrangements for persons with disabilities. Community-based living might include senior housing, group homes, provisions of clinical or health services, and other types of arrangements that facilitate integrating people with disabilities into the broader community rather than isolating them in institutions.

**People Protected by our Disability Laws.** Who is protected under our disability laws?

*Americans with Disabilities Act (ADA):* The enactment of the ADA was intended to protect people with disabilities from discrimination. The broad definition of disability employed by the ADA is applicable to all Titles of the ADA. The term "disability" means, with respect to an individual — (A) a physical or mental impairment that substantially limits one or more major life activities of such individual; (B) a record of such an impairment; or (C) being regarded as having such an impairment.[25]

Thus, there are three categories of being a person with a disability under the ADA. People can be "actually impaired" under section (A), have a "record of" impairment under section (B), and "regarded as" impaired under section (C). For a person to be considered actually impaired, she must show that she actually has an impairment. Second, she needs to demonstrate that the impairment affects at least one major life activity. Third, she needs to demonstrate that the impairment substantially limits the named major life activity.

The ADA identifies a non-exhaustive list of major life activities including: "caring for oneself, performing manual tasks, seeing, hearing, eating, sleeping, walking, standing, lifting, bending, speaking, breathing, learning, reading, concentrating, thinking, communicating, and working." These activities are considered as essential to daily life.

An individual is "regarded as" having an impairment for purposes of 42 U.S.C. §12102(1)(C) when "the individual establishes that he or she has been subjected to an action prohibited under this chapter because of an actual or perceived physical or mental impairment whether or not the impairment limits or is perceived to limit a major life activity."[26] Thus, someone who is perceived by others as being a person with a disability, but in fact does not have a disability, is still protected from discrimination under the ADA.

The following conditions are not considered an impairment: homosexuality, bisexuality, transvestism, gender identity disorders, sexual behavior disorders,

---

24. Exec. Order No. 13,217, 3 C.F.R. §774 (2002), reprinted in 42 U.S.C. §12131 (2016).
25. 42 U.S.C. §12102(1).
26. 42 U.S.C. §12102(3)(A).

compulsive gambling, kleptomania, pyromania, and psychoactive substance abuse disorders.[27]

Alcoholism is a condition protected under the ADA.[28]

The ADA, RHA, and FHA deny protection to individuals who are currently engaged in the illegal use of drugs.[29] However, the ADA and RHA protect individuals who have successfully completed a supervised drug rehabilitation program and are no longer engaged in the use of illegal drugs.

*Section 504 of the Rehabilitation Act (RHA):* Similar to the ADA, the RHA only protects individuals who have a qualifying disability.

*The Fair Housing Act (FHA):* The FHA prohibits housing discrimination in both public and private real estate transactions on the basis of race, color, religion, sex, disability, familial status, and national origin. The FHA specifically uses the outdated term "handicap" rather than disability (the addition of language to the FHA to protect people with a handicap was added by the FHAA). The FHA defines handicap in the same manner as the ADA and RHA define disability. Therefore, case law on the issue of disability concerning the ADA and RHA will impact cases arising under the FHA.

## Coverage of the ADA, RHA, and FHA

*ADA:* Title II of the ADA covers "services, programs and activities provided or made available by public entities."[30] A public entity is defined as "(A) any state or local government; (B) any department, agency, special purpose district, or other instrumentality of a state or states or local government; and (C) the National Railroad Passenger Corporation, and any commuter authority (as defined by section 24102(4) of Title 49)." By this definition, Title II is meant to apply to all state and local governments but does not apply to the federal government. Courts have held that municipal planning and zoning are covered programs, services, or activities under Title II of the ADA.[31]

---

27. 42 U.S.C. § 12211 (2009); 29 U.S.C. § 705(20)(E)–(F) (2014) (applying to Section 504 of the Rehabilitation Act).

    § 12211. Definitions: . . . (a) Homosexuality and bisexuality . . . For purposes of the definition of "disability" . . . homosexuality and bisexuality are not impairments and as such are not disabilities under this chapter. . . . (b) Certain conditions . . . Under this chapter, the term "disability" shall not include — (1) transvestism, transsexualism, pedophilia, exhibitionism, voyeurism, gender identity disorders not resulting from physical impairments, or other sexual behavior disorders; (2) compulsive gambling, kleptomania, or pyromania; or (3) psychoactive substance use disorders resulting from current illegal use of drugs.

28. Mararri v. WCI Steel, 130 F.3d 1180, 1180 (6th Cir. 1997).

29. 42 U.S.C. § 12210(a) (2009); 29 U.S.C. § 705(20)(C)(i).

30. 42 U.S.C. § 12132; 28 C.F.R. § 35.102(a).

31. Wis. Cmty. Servs., Inc. v. Milwaukee, 465 F.3d 737, 750 (7th Cir. 2006).

*RHA:* The RHA precludes discrimination against people with disabilities in "programs or activities" that receive "federal financial assistance" from a federal agency.[32]

*FHA:* The FHA covers private housing, housing that receives federal financial assistance, state and local government housing, lending, planning, and zoning practices, new construction design, advertising, and private land regulations such as those contained in covenants and restrictions and in a declaration of condominium.

## Anti-Discrimination Provisions

The vast majority of land use and zoning issues covered under the ADA, RHA, and FHA will relate to a claim of discrimination, including the claim that an individual has been denied a reasonable accommodation or a request for a reasonable modification.

*ADA.* [N]o qualified individual with a disability shall, by reason of such disability, be excluded from participation in or be denied the benefits of services, programs, or activities of a public entity, or be subjected to discrimination by any such entity.

*RHA.* No otherwise qualified individual with a disability in the United States, shall solely by reason of her or his disability, be excluded from the participation in, be denied the benefits of, or be subjected to discrimination under any program or activity receiving federal financial assistance or under any program or activity conducted by any Executive agency or the United States Postal Service.

*FHA.* It shall be unlawful for any person or other entity whose business includes engaging in residential real estate-related transactions to discriminate against any person in making available such a transaction, or in the terms or conditions of such a transaction, because of race, color, religion, sex, handicap, familial status, or national origin.

## Methods of Demonstrating Discrimination

There are three methods of demonstrating discrimination under the ADA, RHA and FHA: (a) disparate treatment; (b) disparate impact; and (c) the denial of a legitimate request for a reasonable accommodation or a reasonable modification. The ADA and RHA prohibit discrimination in the programs, services, or activities of public entities (this includes planning and zoning). Both Title II of the ADA and section 504 of the RHA prohibit discrimination based on a disability by a public entity. In applying our disability laws to planning and zoning, there are three ways of demonstrating discrimination in violation of the laws protecting people with disabilities; disparate treatment, disparate impact, and failure to provide a reasonable accommodation / modification.

---

32. 29 U.S.C. §794(a).

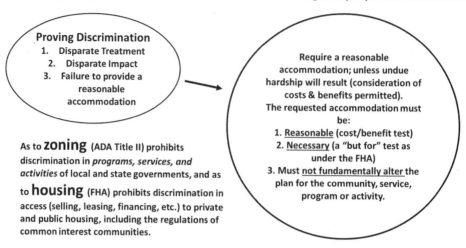

**Disability laws prohibit direct and indirect discrimination against people with disabilities.**

## A. *Disparate Treatment (Intentional Discrimination)*

Quoting from the opinion in *Candlehouse, Inc. v. Town of Vestal, NY.*[33]

Claims of intentional discrimination are properly analyzed utilizing the familiar, burden shifting model developed by the courts for use in employment discrimination settings.... Under that analysis, a plaintiff must first establish a prima facie case of intentional discrimination ... by "present[ing] evidence that animus against the protected group was a significant factor in the position taken by the municipal decision-makers themselves or by those to whom the decision makers were knowingly responsive." ...

The key inquiry in the intentional discrimination analysis is whether discriminatory animus was a motivating factor behind the decision at issue. The Second Circuit has identified the following five factors a fact-finder may consider in evaluating a claim of intentional discrimination: (1) the discriminatory impact of the governmental decision; (2) the decision's historical background; (3) the specific sequence of events leading up to the challenged decision; (4) departures from the normal procedural sequences; and (5) departures from normal substantive criteria.[34]

---

33. Candlehouse, Inc. v. Town of Vestal, NY, 2013 WL 1867114 (N.D.N.Y. May 3, 2013); *See also* Cinnamon Hills Youth Crisis Centers, Inc. v. Saint George City, 685 F.3d 917 (10th Cir. 2012); Robin Paul Malloy, Land Use Law and Disability: Planning and Zoning for Accessible Communities 5 (2015).

34. *Candlehouse, Inc.*, 2013 WL 1867114.

## B. Disparate Impact

A starting place for the discussion of disparate impact discrimination is the U.S. Supreme Court decision of *Texas Department of Housing and Community Affairs v. Inclusive Communities Project, Inc.*[35]

Disparate impact analysis involves an outwardly neutral policy alleged to have a significantly different impact on a protected class of people. Disparate impact analysis requires a comparison between groups with statistical evidence indicating that the disparate outcome between the groups has a causal connection to a land use or housing policy.[36] The causal connection must be more than casual.[37] Disparate impact analysis is designed to address zoning laws and housing practices that result in exclusion of minorities from certain neighborhoods without a sufficient non-discriminatory justification. In defending against a disparate impact claim, local officials and developers have leeway to provide explanations for policies and practices. Appropriate explanations and justifications might make the policies and practices acceptable even if there is a statistical difference in outcome as between identifiable comparison groups.

## C. Failure to Provide a Reasonable Accommodation or Reasonable Modification

### Reasonable Accommodation

Quoting from the opinion in *Cinnamon Hills Youth Crisis Centers, Inc. v. Saint George City.*[38]

> A claim for reasonable accommodation ... does not require the plaintiff to prove that the challenged policy intended to discriminate or that in effect it works systematically to exclude the disabled. Instead, in the words of the FHA, a reasonable accommodation is required whenever it "may be necessary to afford [a disabled] person equal opportunity to use and enjoy a dwelling." 42 U.S.C. § 3604(f)(3)(B).
>
> What does it mean to be "necessary"? The word implies more than something merely helpful or conducive. It suggests instead something "indispensable," "essential," something that "cannot be done without." ... What's more, the FHA's necessity requirement doesn't appear in a statutory vacuum, but is expressly linked to the goal of "afford[ing] ... equal opportunity to use and enjoy a dwelling." 42 U.S.C. § 3604(f)(3)(B). And this makes clear that the object of the statute's necessity requirement is a level playing field in housing for the disabled. Put simply, the statute requires accommodations that are

---

35.  *See* 135 S. Ct. 2507 (2015).

36.  *Id.* at 2522.

37.  *Id.* at 2523–24.

38.  685 F.3d 917 (10th Cir. 2012).

necessary (or indispensable or essential) to achieving the objective of equal housing opportunities between those with disabilities and those without.

Of course, in some sense all reasonable accommodations treat the disabled not just equally but preferentially. Think of the blind woman who obtains an exemption from a "no pets" policy for her seeing eye dog, or the paraplegic granted special permission to live on a first floor apartment because he cannot climb the stairs. But without an accommodation, those individuals cannot take advantage of the opportunity (available to those without disabilities) to live in those housing facilities. And they cannot because of conditions created by their disabilities. . . .

But while the FHA requires accommodations necessary to ensure the disabled receive the same housing opportunities as everybody else, it does not require more or better opportunities. The law requires accommodations overcoming barriers, imposed by the disability, that prevent the disabled from obtaining a housing opportunity others can access. But when there is no comparable housing opportunity for non-disabled people, the failure to create an opportunity for disabled people cannot be called necessary to achieve equality of opportunity in any sense. So, for example, a city need not allow the construction of a group home for the disabled in a commercial area where nobody, disabled or otherwise, is allowed to live.

Requesting a reasonable accommodation for financial feasibility reasons does not qualify as a necessary accommodation. The fact that a person with a disability may prefer to conduct a use of property in a less costly way, or that a given project would be more economically feasible if done on a larger scale, does not make the use necessary for FHA purposes.

When a planning board or a zoning board of appeal is presented with a claim for a reasonable accommodation, it must make specific findings. First, it should make an assessment as to the application of the various disability laws to the applicant raising the claim. (That is, whether the applicant is a person protected by the various federal laws addressed herein.) Second, it should proceed to evaluate the criteria for an accommodation determining: 1) is it reasonable; 2) is it necessary; and 3) does it fundamentally alter the planning and zoning scheme. There is no one factor that seems to trump the evaluation of the rest. Findings should be made on each of the criteria and then a balancing test should be applied. Based on this, a rational decision should be made that is supported by substantial competent evidence on the record. Reasons and justification for the decision should be included.

There is a similar duty to make a reasonable accommodation under both Section 504 of the RHA and the FHA.[39] There is no express language of reasonable accommodation requirement stated in Title II of the ADA, but "The Supreme Court

---

39. *Wis. Cmty. Serv. Inc.*, 465 F.3d at 746–46.

has located a duty to accommodate in the statute generally."[40] Thus, all Titles of the ADA require a reasonable accommodation or reasonable modification when appropriate.

## *Reasonable Modification*

A reasonable modification is treated in a similar way as a reasonable accommodation. In practice, courts have treated modifications as changes to the physical environment,[41] such as modifying an entranceway by making it wider or by eliminating a step-up at an entranceway. In contrast, an adjustment in a rule or a practice is often treated as a reasonable accommodation. Requesting a reasonable accommodation or modification for financial feasibility reasons does not qualify as a necessary accommodation.[42]

## Additional Matters to Consider: ADA Title III

Title III applies to private entities and precludes discrimination based on disability in the provision of goods, services, facilities, privileges, advantages, or accommodations by any place owning, leasing, or operating a place of public accommodation.[43] Places of public accommodation are places that are not government owned or operated as publicly operated facilities.[44] "A partial list of examples of places of public accommodation, for illustrative purposes, includes hotels, restaurants, auditoriums, shopping malls, concert halls, retail centers, and banks."[45] Private clubs are not covered under Title III of the ADA unless the private club opens itself up to nonmembers.

Under limited circumstances, single-family homes are covered under Title III of the ADA, even though they are not covered under Title II of the ADA; for example, if a business is operated out of part of the house.[46] In the case of a home office or a home-based business, the home should be ADA compliant with respect to an entrance and as to those parts of the home where the public is welcome.

While Title III applies to private places of public accommodation, there is an exception for religious organizations and entities controlled by religious organizations.[47] But note, if a religious entity receives federal funds, it is subject to Section 504 of the RHA.[48]

---

40. *Id.*
41. Fair Housing Board v. Windsor Plaza Condominium, 768 S.E.2d 79, 87 (2014).
42. MALLOY, LAND USE LAW AND DISABILITY, *supra* note 33, at 146.
43. 42 U.S.C. § 12181(7).
44. 42 U.S.C. § 12181(7).
45. MALLOY, LAND USE LAW AND DISABILITY, *supra* note 33, at 117.
46. 28 C.F.R. § 36.207.
47. 42 U.S.C. § 12187.
48. 29 U.S.C. § 794.

## Some Additional Provisions for Housing

*Single-Family.* Privately owned single-family detached homes have the least amount of regulation in terms of the ADA, Section 504 of the RHA, and the FHA.[49] In terms of design, there are two common reference points. First, is *universal design.* Universal design seeks to make a building universally accessible to the fullest extent possible. This includes entranceways, hallways, access to cabinets, light switches, sinks, showers/bathtubs, etc. Second, is *visitability.* The idea of visitability is that a building or a home may not meet all of the requirements of universal design throughout the entire structure but that it is generally accessible enough to be easily and safely visited by a person with a disability, perhaps a person using a wheelchair. This means that the entranceway and the primary social area of the structure should be accessible, and there should be at least a half-bath that is accessible to visitors.

*Multi-Family.* The FHA requires "all new multi-family housing to meet specific inclusive design standards, including guidelines for common areas, entranceways, hallways, light switches, grab bars, space to accommodate use of a wheelchair, and other design elements."[50] Design and construction requirements are issued by both HUD and DOJ. Any failure to make multi-family housing compliant with these standards is a violation of the FHA. A multi-family dwelling is defined as "(A) buildings consisting of four or more units if such buildings have one or more elevators; and (B) ground floor units in other buildings consisting of four or more units."[51]

*Private v. Public Housing.* HUD enforces Title II of the ADA when it relates to state and local public housing, housing assistance, and housing referrals.[52] Under HUD regulations, "five percent of qualifying public housing units must be fully accessible in terms of universal design."[53]

*Condominiums, Subdivisions, and Cooperative Housing.* A "covered multi-family dwelling" under the FHA has design and construction requirements, and this may include "condominiums, cooperatives, apartment buildings, vacation and time share units, assisted living facilities, continuing care facilities, nursing homes, public housing developments, housing projects funded with federal funds, transitional

---

49. Malloy, Land Use Law and Disability, *supra* note 33, at 113; 42 U.S.C. § 3603.

50. Malloy, Land Use Law and Disability, *supra* note 33, at 114; U.S. Dep't of Housing & Urban Dev. & U.S. Dep't of Justice, Accessibility (Design and Constriction) Requirements for Covered Multifamily Dwellings under the Fair Housing Act (2013).

51. 42 U.S.C. § 3604(f)(7).

52. Malloy, Land Use Law and Disability, *supra* note 33, at 116.

53. Malloy, Land Use Law and Disability, *supra* note 33, at 118.

housing, single room occupancy units, shelters designed as residence for homeless persons, dormitories, hospices, extended stay or residential hotels," etc.[54]

**Additional Requirements for New Construction and Alterations.** New *construction* of, and *alterations* to *facilities* and structures must be accessible to the maximum possible extent. The only defense to lack of accessibility is *structural impracticability*. Evidence of structural impracticability will include reports and opinions of engineers and others who are qualified to address the matter. A demonstration of high cost is not sufficient on its own. The problem arises in determining when something is merely a form of maintenance, upkeep, repair, remodeling, or an alteration, as opposed to new construction.

**Requirements as to State and Local Programs, Services, and Activities.** *Programs, services, and activities* include planning and zoning activities. They must be accessible to people with disabilities to the *maximum extent possible*. A defense to a claim of noncompliance includes demonstrating that compliance imposes an *undue administrative or financial burden* on the defendant. Costs are considered in the determination of an undue financial or administrative burden.

**Requirements for Rehabilitation, Updating, and Historic Preservation.** Based on the year of construction, older buildings, facilities, and structures are subject to disability laws. A person may be required to update to current accessibility standards, and to *eliminate barriers* to full accessibility. For public buildings and facilities under Title II, this may be a requirement qualified by raising an *undue financial or administrative burden* defense. As to places of public accommodation, under Title III, this may be qualified by raising a not *readily achievable* defense. Something is not readily achievable if it is difficult to achieve, or imposes an undue financial or administrative burden on the defendant.

As to historic preservation, the prerequisite to non-compliance is that the building, facility, or district must actually be declared historic by a public entity. If it is historic, elimination of barriers is required unless not *readily achievable*, and any · new construction or alterations must be accessible to the fullest extent possible (subject to structural impracticability). An additional consideration involves evaluation of the impact accessible design has on the elements that make the structure worthy of protecting for historical and cultural purposes in the first instance.

**Animals.** *Service animals* are different from *emotional support animals* (ESA). Under the ADA, only dogs and, under special criteria, miniature horses are service animals. A service animal must be trained to do work or perform tasks that assist the owner with a disability. The service animal is permitted to go wherever the person with a disability can go. Under the FHA and the RHA, the language is

---

54. U.S. Dep't of Housing and Urban Development & DOJ, Accessibility (Design and Construction) Requirements for Covered Multifamily Dwellings under the Fair Housing Act, Joint Statement (Apr. 30, 2013), https://www.treasurer.ca.gov/ctcac/2013/hud_doj.pdf.

confusing, because an ESA is also called a service animal. For an ESA, one can take it wherever the owner goes subject to a reasonable accommodation analysis.

## Standing

*ADA.* To establish standing to bring a case in court, a plaintiff must show an injury in fact that meets the following three requirements: (1) concrete and particularized or an actual and imminent injury that is not hypothetical; (2) the injury is fairly traceable to a challenged action of the defendant; and (3) the injury is likely to be redressed by a favorable decision.[55]

*Statute of Limitations.* There is no specific statute of limitations under the ADA. Typically, the state statute of limitations that is most analogous to the plaintiff's claim will govern.

*Section 504 of the RHA.* The general rule is that an individual who is not disabled within the terms of the RHA lacks standing to sue under Section 504. However, a group of disabled persons that form an organization will traditionally have standing to sue if the group can establish a sufficient nexus between the organization and the injury claimed.

*Third Party Standing.* The ADA and RHA are statutes in which Congress has expressly granted third party standing.

*FHA.* Standing under FHA is satisfied by the minimum constitutional case or controversy requirements of Article III.[56] This requires: (1) actual or threatened injury; (2) injury that is caused by defendant's challenged action; and (3) injury that is likely to be redressed by a favorable court decision.[57]

## Remedies

It is not necessary for a plaintiff to exhaust administrative remedies before filing a cause of action against a public entity with a federal court.[58]

---

55. Transport Workers Union of America v. New York City Transit Authority, 342 F. Supp. 2d 160, 165–67 (S.D.N.Y. 2004); Ross v. City of Gatlinburg, Tenn., 327 F. Supp. 2d 834, 841–43 (E.D. Tenn. 2003).

56. *See* 42 U.S.C. § 3610(1)(A)(i); 42 U.S.C. § 3602(i); Trafficante v. Metropolitan Life Ins. Co., 409 U.S. 205, 209 (1972); Hallmark Developers, Inc. v. Fulton County, Georgia, 386 F. Supp. 2d 1369, 1381 (N.D. Ga. 2005).

57. *Hallmark Developers*, 386 F. Supp. 2d at 1381.

58. Bledsoe v. Palm Beach Cty. Soil & Water Conserv. Dist., 133 F.3d 816, 824 (11th Cir. 1998); *see, e.g.*, Bogovich v. Sandoval, 189 F.3d 999 (9th Cir. 1999).

# Part II

### Form for a Zoning Code Interpretation when Applying a Reasonable Accommodation

This interpretation of the zoning code is a response to a request for a reasonable accommodation. It shall not be considered an application for a variance. If granted, the accommodation is personal and shall not run with the land.

### Determination:

**Applicability:** Does the applicant have or does the Zoning Board of Appeal accept that the applicant has a disability protected by the ADA, RHA, or FHA pursuant to the following definition.

> Disability means having a) a physical or mental impairment that substantially limits one or more major life activities; b) a record of such an impairment; or c) being regarded as having such an impairment.

Yes ____

No ____If no, explain: _____

_____.

On what evidence or lack thereof is the decision based. _____

_____.

### Factors for consideration:

1. Has the applicant requested a reasonable accommodation?

Yes ____ / No ____

The accommodation requested is for a: _____

_____

_____

2. Are there alternatives to the specific accommodation requested that can also provide the applicant with a reasonable accommodation? (If there are reasonable alternatives, an alternative remedy can be granted in place of the specific preference requested by the applicant.) _____

_____

_____

_____

3. Is the request reasonable? Apply a cost and benefit analysis to this determination. What are the benefits to the applicant in comparison to the costs to the community from the requested exception to the rule requirements? Does it impose an undue financial or administrative burden? Does it impact the nature of the neighborhood? Is the design and construction inconsistent with the structure or with that of nearby

properties? (Even when a request is reasonable, reasonable design and construction standards can be placed on the applicant.)

_____

_____

_____

4. Is the request necessary? In "but for" terms, ask (a) whether, "but for" the granting of the requested accommodation, the applicant will be unable to enjoy an equal opportunity to use and enjoy the property in the same way as others without a disability; and (b) whether the requested accommodation has a nexus to addressing the disability of the applicant.

_____

_____

_____

5. Will the requested accommodation fundamentally alter the plan of the zoning code or the comprehensive plan applicable to the property and the surrounding neighborhood?

_____

_____

_____

_____

6. Can the impact of the requested accommodation on the property and neighboring properties be mitigated by imposing reasonable restoration requirements on the applicant? (Example: requiring the removal of a ramp once the person with a disability is no longer on the property or in need of the accommodation.)

_____

_____

_____

### Determination of the Zoning Board of Appeals Based on the Above Factors

The Zoning Board of Appeal, after taking into consideration the above factors and balancing the various considerations with respect to the benefits to the applicant and the detriment to the community, holds:

The request for a reasonable accommodation is ___ / is not ___ granted to the applicant.

If granted, the following conditions, if any, apply. _____

_____

_____

The record vote of ZBA Members is as follows:

| Member Name | Yes | No |
|---|---|---|
| | | |
| | | |
| | | |
| | | |
| | | |
| | | |
| | | |

# Part III

## ZONING BOARD OF APPEALS

### Area Variance Petition (NY Criteria)

Name of Applicant: _____

Property Tax Map# _____ Zoning District: _____

Existing Land Use: _____

Proposed Land Use: _____

Relief sought: _____

The ZBA may not grant an area variance without a showing by the applicant that the applicable zoning regulations have caused "practical difficulties." In order to prove this, the applicant shall respond in writing to each of the following five criteria set out below. (Add additional sheets if necessary.) The Applicant may submit additional supporting documentation for the record. The ZBA in deciding to grant a variance will apply a <u>balancing test</u> of the following five (5) criteria:

(a) whether an undesirable change will be produced in the character of the neighborhood or a detriment to nearby properties will be created by the granting of the area variance Yes/No and state why; **Applicant response:**

_____

_____

(b) whether the benefit sought by the applicant can be achieved by some method, feasible for the applicant to pursue, other than an area variance Yes/No and state why; **Applicant response:**

_____

_____

(c) whether the requested area variance is substantial Yes/No and state why; **Applicant response:**

_____

_____

(d) whether the proposed variance will have an adverse effect or impact on the physical or environmental conditions in the neighborhood or district Yes/No and state why; **Applicant response:**

_____

_____

(e) and whether the alleged difficulty was self-created, which consideration shall be relevant to the ZBA decision, but shall not necessarily preclude the granting of the area variance Yes/No and state why. **Applicant response:**

_____

_____

The Board shall vote by member name on the granting or denial of the variance and shall issue a written memorandum in support of its decision. The memorandum shall address the Board's thinking as to each of the five criteria, balancing of the criteria, and its rationale for its ultimate decision on the Petition.

# Part IV

## ZONING BOARD OF APPEALS

### Use Variance Petition (NY Criteria)

Name of Applicant: _____

Property Tax Map#_____ Zoning District:_____

Existing Land Use: _____

Proposed Land Use:_____

Other land uses allowed in zoning district:_____

The ZBA may not grant a use variance without a showing by the applicant that the applicable zoning regulations have caused "unnecessary hardship." In order to prove unnecessary hardship, the applicant shall respond in writing to each of the four criteria set out below. (Add additional sheets if necessary) The Applicant may submit additional supporting documentation for the record.

That for each and every permitted use under the Zoning Ordinance for the district in which the property is located:

1. the applicant cannot realize a reasonable return, provided that lack of return is substantial as demonstrated by competent financial evidence; **Applicant response:**

_____

_____

_____

2. that the alleged hardship relating to the property in question is unique, and does not apply to a substantial portion of the district or neighborhood; **Applicant response:**

_____

_____

_____

3. that the requested use variance, if granted, will not alter the essential character of the neighborhood; **Applicant Response:**

_____

_____

_____

4. that the alleged hardship has not been self-created. **Applicant response:**

_____

_____

_____

The ZBA may grant a use variance only if **each of the four criteria** above have been met; failure to satisfy one or more of the statutory requirements means that the variance must be denied. Conversely, where the applicant meets all the criteria, the use variance must be granted. The Board shall vote on the petition by member name. The Board shall issue a written memorandum of its decision explaining its thinking as to each of the four criteria and as to its ultimate decision on the Petition.

# Index